J.D. Reuss

Alphabetical register of all the authors actually living in Great Britain, Ireland and in the United Provinces of America

From the year 1770 to the year 1790

J.D. Reuss

Alphabetical register of all the authors actually living in Great Britain, Ireland and in the United Provinces of America

From the year 1770 to the year 1790

ISBN/EAN: 9783742886453

Manufactured in Europe, USA, Canada, Australia, Japa

Cover: Foto ©Andreas Hilbeck / pixelio.de

Manufactured and distributed by brebook publishing software (www.brebook.com)

J.D. Reuss

Alphabetical register of all the authors actually living in Great Britain, Ireland and in the United Provinces of America

ALPHABETICAL
REGISTER
OF
ALL THE AUTHORS

ACTUALLY LIVING

IN

GREAT-BRITAIN, IRELAND AND IN THE UNITED PROVINCES OF NORTH-AMERICA,

WITH

A CATALOGUE OF THEIR PUBLICATIONS.

FROM THE YEAR 1770 TO THE YEAR 1790.

BY

JEREM. DAV. REUSS,

PROFESSOR OF PHILOSOPHY AND UNDER-LIBRARIAN AT THE PUBLIC LIBRARY OF THE UNIVERSITY OF GOTTINGEN.

BERLIN AND STETTIN,

printed for FREDERIC NICOLAI

1791.

DAS GELEHRTE ENGLAND

ODER

LEXIKON

DER JEZTLEBENDEN

SCHRIFTSTELLER

IN

GROSBRITANNIEN, IRLAND UND NORD-AMERIKA

NEBST EINEM

VERZEICHNIS IHRER SCHRIFTEN.

VOM JAHR 1770 BIS 1790.

VON

JEREMIAS DAVID REUSS,

ORDENTLICHEN PROFESSOR DER PHILOSOPHIE UND UNTER-BIBLIOTHEKAR BEY DER UNIVERSITÄTS-BIBLIOTHEK ZU GÖTTINGEN.

BERLIN UND STETTIN,

BEY FRIED. NICOLAI

1791.

To the English Reader.

Whenever a new publication is offered to the publick, the author should have it in his power to point out the use and neceſſity of increaſing, by his performance, that immenſe litterary ſtore, which, however it may forward the profeſſedly learned in their researches, ſeems likely enough to puzzle the ſtudent, who treads the mazes of ſcience without a clue to conduct him. Indeed, ſince the revival of letters in Europe and the invention of the art of printing, the number of printed books has increased in ſuch a rapid proportion, as to baffle the efforts of the moſt aſſiduous collectors and bibliographers, who have attempted, either to accumulate general libraries, or to compile what may be termed an hiſtory of universal litterature. It is a well known fact among the lovers of bibliographical knowledge, that many an eminent litterator, after having ſpent his life in the tedious occupation of collecting the titles of books, has left his ſucceſſors in that branch of ſcience to lament the unfinished ſtate of his labours. And, when it is conſidered, that the annual harveſt of new publications in Germany alone, upon an average amounts to near three thousand works, we shall not ſurely overrate the litterary produce of all Europe, by fixing it at ten thousand volumes in the course of every year. Agreably to this computation, a ſingle cen-

century bids fair to be productive of a million of books and *Leibnitz* seems not to have conjectured amiss, when he facetiously maintained the increase of litterature to be such, that future generations would find whole cities insufficient to contain their libraries. It was undoubtedly from the same comprehensive view of this great object, that one of the first philosophick characters in England (the present illustrious President of the Royal Society) has been heard to urge the necessity of rejecting hence forward the idea of *general* collections of book in the capital and recommending in its place, as the proper object of *private collectors*, to confine their libraries to one *individual branch* of human knowledge, by which means a great number of particular collections, each compleat in its kind, would quickly be brought forward and the purposes of instruction be more easily attained, than whilst the rage of indiscriminate collection subsisted and the number of competitors for the same book precluded the possibility of completion.

The ſame difficulty, which attends the methodical arrangement and compleat enumeration of all the books now extant in print, will likewise apply to that part of litterature, by which we are taught to conſider the authors themselves exerting their talents, under various points of view, either, as they happened to be contemporaries, or according to the different ages and countries in which they flourished, or with a view to the diſtinct branches of knowledge, which they cultivated and the proportion, in which they contributed to the common ſtock of improvement. To the works, which have appeared upon this ſubject, inconſiderable as their number and defective as their contents may have been, we are indebted for ſome general ideas concerning the comparative quantity of litterary exertion, which different nations have ſhewn within certain periods of time, the ſciences which they have cultivated in preference to others and the differences and ſingularities of national taſte.

Germany has hitherto been moſt ſucceſſfull in the laborious endeavours to illuſtrate the hiſtory of its own litterati. The indefatigable application of *Hamberger* and of his ſucceſſor *Meusel* has furniſhed a catalogue of the authors now living in that country, in which their names and works are collected with ſurprizing accuracy. Their example has encouraged a number of aſſiduous bibliographers to illuſtrate the litterary hiſtory of their ſeveral provinces. In other countries this useful and neceſſary branch of compilation has been to much neglected. *La France litteraire*, that meagre and defective performance, has not been continued since the Year 1784. The liſt of Spanish authors during the reign of Carlos III., by *Juan Sempere* y *Guarinos*, only extends to writers of ſome eminence, whilſt Italy and all the Northern countries have not so much as attempted any thing of the kind.

Ayscough's index to the ſeventy volumes of the Monthly Review, though a work of great merit, was not however calculated to ſupply this deficiency with regard to English litterature, as its plan excluded all the books which had not been reviewed in those volumes. As to the catalogue of five hundred celebrated authors of Great-Britain now living, (London 1788. 8vo) it does not require great penetration to observe that those names only have been ſelected from the bulk of English writers, on whom the anonymous critick has thought proper to paſs either censure or commendation. When these circumſtances are impartially weighed, the propriety of the present publication may perhaps be the more easily admitted. Indeed the prevailing taſte for English books in Germany ſeemed more particularly to demand an enumeration, which has not hitherto been attempted in England.

The author has confined himself intirely to the moſt recent litterary productions of Great-Britain, Ireland and the United ſtates of America. A period of twenty years, from 1770 to 1790 ſeemed to him to be moſt adequate to the term of modern litterature. He has ſubjoined to the

the names of the living authors the titles of their works together with their prices; always taking care to notice the german translation, where it was known, to exiſt. Translations into other languages as well as biographical notes concerning the authors themselves, would have ſwelled, what was intended for a compendious eſſay, to the extent of ſeveral volumes. For the ſame reason, though the names of authors deceased within these laſt twenty years have been inserted, yet it has not been thought proper to recount their publications. In this part of his performance however, the author has met with the greateſt difficulty and thinks it very probable, from the imperfection of the intelligence which he has been able to procure, that he may have placed ſeveral persons among the living, who have already paid the debt of nature. English books, written by foreigners, will naturally find a place in the litterary catalogues of these nations, to whom they respectively belong, and are of course omitted here; but anonymous works have generally been referred to their proper

per authors and inserted in the present collection with an asterisk (*) prefixed to them.

In an undertaking of this arduous nature, it is next to impossible, to avoid mistakes and omissions. These can only be corrected or supplied by the candid communications of the reader and will be received with grateful acknowledgment by the author, who takes this opportunity of returning his sincere thanks to several friends, from whom he has experienced the most valuable assistance. The author's situation having furnished him with all the printed subsidies relative to his undertaking, it will perhaps apologize for the seeming presumption of a foreigner in venturing to furnish his own countrymen with a list of British authors.

But the writer of this preface fears to have trespassed upon the indulgence of his readers, having lost the habit of writing in a language which was once familiar to him, he is aware that the eagerness to obey the summons of a friend, may prove a very unsatistisfactory excuse for thus attempting to give the publick ſome account of the motives and the plan of the present publication.

Mayence. Sept. 15th
1791.

George Forster.

ABERCROMBIE [John] *Gardener at Tottenham-Court.*

J. Abercrombie and *Th. Mave's* univerſal gardener and botaniſt: or, a general dictionary of gardening and botany. 1778. 4. (1 L. 7. Sh.) The garden muſhroom; its nature and cultivation 1779. 8. (1 Sh. 6. d.) The britiſh fruit Gardener; and art of pruning 1779. 8. (4 Sh.) überſ. von *G. H. H. Lüder.* Lübek 1781. 8. Every man his own gardener by *Mawe* and *Abercrombie.* 1767. 8. (4 Sh.) Ed. VIII. 1779. 8. überſ. Leipzig. 1776. 8. The complete forcing gardener; or the practice of forcing fruits, flowers and vegetables to early maturity and perfection by the aid of artificial heat. 1781. 8. (2 Sh. 6. d.) The complete wall -- tree pruner. 1783. 8. (3. Sh.) The propagation and botanical arrangements of plants and trees. 1783. 8. Vol. 1. 2. (6Sh.) The Gardener's pocket dictionary. 1786. 8. (10 Sh. 6. d.) The Gardener's daily aſſiſtant. 1787. 8. (3 Sh.) The univerſal gardener's kalendar, and ſyſtem of practical gardening. 1789. 8. (5 Sh.) The complete kitchen gardener and hot bed forcer. 1789. 8. (5 Sh) The garden vade mecum or compendium of general gardening. 1789. 8. (4 Sh.) The Hot-houſe gardener. 1789. 8. (8 Sh. 6 d.)

ABINGDON, Earl of, ſee *Willoughby Bertie.*

ACHERLEY, [Roger] *Esq. of the Inner Temple.*
Reaſons for uniformity in the ſtate. 1780. 8. (1 Sh.)

ACLAND, [John] *Rector of Broad-cliſt and one of his Majeſty's juſtices of peace for the county of Devon.*
Plan for rendering the poor independent on public contribution. 1786. 8. (1 Sh.)

ADAIR, [James] *M. D. Phyſician in Wincheſter.*
Some remarks on certain articles of the materia medica. (*Duncan's* M. C. Vol. 10. p. 233.)

A ADAIR,

ADAIR, [James] *Esq. Trader with the Indians and Resident in their country 40 Years.* The history of the american indians. 1775. 4. (15 Sh.) überf. (von *S. H. Ewald.*) Breslau 1782. 8.

ADAIR, [James Makittrick] *M. D. one of the judges of the courts of King's Bench and Common Pleas in the Island of Antigua; Physician to the Commander in Chief and the colonial troops of Antigua.* Observations on regimen and preparation under inoculalation and on the treatment of the natural small pox in the West-Indies. (*Duncan's* M. C. Vol. 8. p. 211.) A few hints on particular articles of the Materia Medica. (*Duncan's* M. C. Vol. 9. p. 206. überf. Saml. f. A. Th. XI. S. 275. Medical cautions for the consideration of invalids, those especially who resort tho Bath —. 1786. 8. (3 sh. 6 d.) Ed. 2. 1787. 8. (6 sh.) Sketch of the natural history of the human body and mind —. 1787. 8. (4 sh.) übers. von C. F. *Michaelis.* Zittau u. Leipz. 1788. 8. Case of inflammatory constipation of the bowels successfully treated. (Mem. of M. S. of L. Vol. 2.) Unanswerable objections against the abolition of the Slave trade. 1789. 8. (5 sh.)

— [Robert] *Surgeon general to the Army.* born... died d. Mart. 1790.

ADAM, [Alexander] *LL. D. Rector of the high school at Edinburgh.* The principles of latin and english grammar 1772. 8. (3 sh. 6 d.) A summary of geography and history. 17 . . 8.

— [James] *Esq.* Practical essays on agriculture. 1789. 8. Vol. 1. 2. (12 sh.)

— [James] and his brother.

— [Robert] *F. R. S: F. A. S: Architect to the King and to the Queen.* Ruins of the palace of the emperor Diocletian at Spalatro in Dalmatia. 1764. fol. (3 L. 10 sh.) Works in Architecture. *Numb.* 1. Designs of Sion House, seat of the Duke of Northumberland in the county of Middlesex. 1773. *Numb.* 2. Designs of Lord Mansfield's Villa at Kenwood. 1774. *Numb.* 3. Designs of Luton Park-house in Bedfordshire. 1775. *Numb.* 4. Designs of public buildings. 1776. fol. (4 L. 7 sh.)

ADAM, [Thomas] *Rector of Wintringham, Lincolnshire.* born . . . . died 17 . .

ADAMS, [George] *Mathematical Instrumentmaker to his Majesty.* born . . . . died 1772.

— [George] *Mathematical Instrumentmaker to his Majesty.* On electricity — with an essay on Magnetism. 1784. 8. (5 sh.) Essay on the Microscope. 1787. 4. (1 L. 6 sh.) History on vision, explaining the fabric of the eye and nature of vision. 1789. 8. (3 sh.) Astronomical and geographical essays. 1789. 8. (10 sh. 6 d.)

— [John] *LL. D. Member of the Academy of arts and sciences at Boston. Ambassador for the congress of the united states of America to the court of London.* Collection of State papers, relative to the first acknowledgment of the sovereignity of the united states of America. 1782. 8. (2 sh.) History of the disputes with America, from their origin —. 1784. (2 sh. 6 d.) Defence of the constitution of government of the united states of America. Vol. 1. 2. 3. 1787. 1788. 8. (17 sh.)

— [John] *A. M.* Lectiones selectae: or select latin lessons in morality, history and biography. 1784. 8. (8 d.) Ed. 2. 1789. 8. (1 sh.) The flowers of ancient history, comprehending the most remarkable and interesting events, as well as characters of antiquity. 1787. 8. (3 sh.) The flowers of modern history — 1788. 8. (3 sh.) The flowers of modern travels. 1788. 8. Vol. 1. 2. (6 sh.) Exercises in latin composition. 1788. 8. (1 sh. 6 d.) Anecdotes, bons mots, and characteristic tracts of the greatest princes, politicians, philosophers, orators and wits of modern times. 1789. 8. (3 sh.)

— [John] *A. B.* The english Parnassus — extracted from the works of the latest and most celebrated poets. 1789. 8. (3 sh.)

— [John] The young Sea-Officers assistant. 1773. 4. (3 sh.)

— [Samuel] *Member of the General Congress of America.* Oration at the Statehouse in Philadelphia. 1776. 8. (1 sh.)

— [Thomas Maxwell] *Esq.* On the slave trade. 1788. 8. (1 sh. 6 d.)

ADAMS, [William] D. D. *Prebendary of the cathedral at Gloucester and Master of Pembroke College*, Oxford. born . . . . died d. 14. Jan. 1789.

—— [William] *Surgeon.* Disquisition on the stone and gravel and other diseases of the bladder. 1773. 8. (2 sh.)

ADDINGTON, [Anthony] *M. D.* born . . . . . died d. 21. March. 1790.

—— [Stephen] *D. D:* *On religious knowledge of the antient jews and patriarchs — 1757. 4. (1 sh. 6 d.) The rudiments of greek tongue. 1761. 8. (2 sh.) Eusebes to Philetus: or a letter to a son on a devout temper and life. 1767. 8. (2 sh.) The Youth's geographical grammar. 1770. 8. (4 sh.) The christian Minister's reasons for baptizing infants. 1771. 8. (2 sh.) Summary of the christian ministers reasons for baptizing infants. 1777. 8. (6 d.) On afflictions, with a discourse on visiting the Sick. 1778. 8. (2 sh.) Sermon on the death of *W. Ford.* 1783. 8. (6 d.) The life of Paul the Apostle with remarks on his discourses and writings 1784. 8. (5 sh.) Sermon on the death of *John Olding*, Pastor at Butt-Lane Deptford. 1785. 8. (6 d.)

—— [William] *Esq. One of the Magistrates presiding at the public office at London.* Abridgment of penal statutes. 1775. (8 sh.) Ed. 3. 1786. 4. (1 L. 6 sh.)

ADEE, [Swithin] *M. D: F. R. S: F. A. S.* born . . . died d. 12 Aug. 1786.

AERY, [Lancelot] *M. D: Physician at Whitehaven.* Diss. De Gonorrhoea virulenta. Lugd. Bat. 1772. 4. The symptoms, nature, causes and cure of the essera or nettle rash; with observations on the causes and cure of cutaneous diseases. 1774. 8.

—— [Thomas] *M. D. Physician at Whitehaven.* On the cure of a wound in the cornea of the eye and of a laceration of the uvea. (Phil. Transact. 1755. p. 411.) History of a case of hydrocephalus successfully treated by Mercury. (*Duncan's* M. C. Vol. VIII. p. 332.) A case of hydrocephalus internus cured by Mercury. (London M. J. 1781. p. 424. übers. Samml. f. A. Th. 7. S. 195.) Aphtha, method of curing

curing in infants. (Médical Museum. Vol. 2.) Letter concerning Mrs. *Folke's* case. 1773. 8.

AIKIN (. . . .) England delineated; or, a geographical description of every county in England and Wales with an account of its most important products, natural and artificial. 1788. 8. (4 sh. 6 d.)

— [John] *D. D:* born . . . . died 1781.

— [John] *M. D: Physician at Great-Yarmouth in the county of Norfolk.* Essay on the ligature of arteries. (vid. *White's* cases in surgery. P. I. übers. Samml. f. W. A. St. 7. S. 81.) Miscellaneous pieces in prose. 1773. 8. (3 sh.) nachgedr. Altenburgh 1775. 8. (Diese Samml. gab er gemeinschaftlich mit seiner Schwester Mistress *Barbauld* heraus.) Essays on song writing, with a collection of english songs. Ed. 2. 1774. 8. (4 sh.) (Einige Stücke übersezt in *Ursinus* Balladen und Lieder altengl. Diehter. 1777. 8.) On the application of natural history to poetry. 1777. 8. (2 sh. 6 d.) übers. von *C. H. Schmid.* Leipz. 1779. 8. On the situation, manners and inhabitants of Germany and the life of Agricola by *C. C. Tacitus*; translated with notes. 1778. 8. (4 sh.) *Thomson's* seasons, with an essay on the plan and the character of the poem 1778. 8. (4 sh.) nachgedr. Leipzig 1781. 8. The Calendar of nature — for the instruction of young persons. 1784. 8. übers. Leipzig 1787. 8. *Lewis's* Materia medica. Ed. 3. 1784. 4. Manual of materia medica. 1785. 8. (2 sh. 6 d.)

— [*Aitken*] John, *M. D. fellow of the royal College of Surgeon's and lecturer on the practice of physik, Anatomy, Surgery and Chemistry in Edinburgh.* born . . . . died d. 22 Sept. 1790.

AINSLIE, [J. . . .] *M. D.* On the nature and properties of Marle. (*Hunter's* G. E. Vol. 3. p. 25.)

AITON, [William] *Gardener to his Majesty at Kew.* Hortus Kewensis, or a catalogue of the plants cultivated in the royal botanic garden at Kew. Vol. 1. 2. 3. 1789. 8. (1 L. 1 sh.)

AKENSIDE, [Mark] *M. D: F. R. S. and Physician to her Majesty.* born at Newcastle-upon-Tyne. d. 9 Nov. 1721. died d. 23 June 1770.

ALANSON (Edward) *Surgeon at Liverpool*, Account of a ſimple fracture of the tibia in a pregnant woman; in which caſe the callus was not formed till after delivery. (Med. Obſ. Vol. 4. p. 410.) Practical obſervations upon amputation and the after treatment. 1779. 8. (1 ſh. 6 d.) Ed. 2. 1783. 8. überſ. Samml. f. W. A. St. 7. S. 131. überſ. Gotha 1785. 8. Th. 1. 2.

ALCHORNE, [Stanesby] *Of his Majeſty's Mint and Member of the ſociety of Apothecaries.* Catalogue of 50 plants from Chelſea. 1770. (Phil. Tranſact. 1771. p. 390.) Catalogue of 50 plants from Chelſea. 1771. (Ibid. 1773. p. 30.) Examination of the ores in the muſeum of Dr. *Hunter.* (Ibid. 1779. p. 529.) Experiments on mixing gold with tin. (Ibid. 1784. p. 463.)

ALCOCK, [Nathan] *M. D. F. R. S.* born at Runcorn in Cheſhire. 1707. died d. 6 Dec. 1779.

ALDBOROUGH, Earl of; ſee *Stratford.*

ALDERSON, [J. . . .) *M. D.* On the nature and origin of the contagion of fevers. 1788. 8. (2 ſh.) überſ. von *W. F. S. Bucholtz.* Jena 1790. 8.

ALEXANDER, [Caleb] Account of eruptions and the preſent appearances in Weſtriver-mountain. (Mem. of B. A. Vol. 1. p. 316.)

—— [John] *Phyſician in Halifax, Yorkſhire.* The hiſtory of an exceſſive diſcharge of water from the uterus during pregnancy. (Med. Comm. of Ed. Vol. 3. p. 187.)

—— [John] *Surgeon in the ſervice of the Eaſt-India Company.* Account of the goods effects derived from the eau de Luce, taken internally, againſt the bite of the viper. (*Duncan's* M. C. Dec. 2. Vol. 4. p. 297.)

—— [*William*] *M. D. at Edinburgh.* Experimental eſſays — on the external application of antiſeptics in putrid diſeaſes; on the doſes and effects of Medicines; on diuretics and ſudorifics. 1768. 8. (3 ſh. 6 d.) On the cauſes of putrid diſeaſes. 1773. 8. (4 ſh. 6 d.) (Dieſes und das vorhergehende Buch überſezt unter dem Titel: Mediziniſche Verſuche und Erfahrungen. Leipzig 1773. 8.) The caſe of a perſon who was ſeemingly killed by a blow on the breaſt, recovered by bleeding and the warm bath.

bath. (Eſſ. and Obſerv. Edinb. Vol. 3. p. 512.) The hiſtory of women, from the earlieſt antiquity to the preſent time. 1779. 4. Vol. 1. 2. (1 L. 10 ſh.) überſ. Leipzig. Th. 1. 2. 1781. 8.

ALISON, [Archibald] *LL. B: F. R. S.* On the nature and principles of taſte. 1789. 4. (16 ſh.)

ALLEYNE, [John] *Esq. Barriſter at Law.* The legal degrees of marriage ſtated and conſidered in a ſeries of letters. 1774. 8. (1 ſh.)

ALVES, [Robert] *A. M.* Odes on ſeveral ſubjects. 1778. 8. (1 ſh.) Ode to Britannia. 1780. 4. (6 d.) Poems. 1784. 8. (4 ſh.) Edinburgh, a poem. 1790. 8. (2 ſh.)

AMBROSS [. . . . . .] *Miſſ.* The life and memoirs of the late Miſſ *Ann Catley* the celebrated actreſſ: with biographical ſketches of Sir *Franc. Blake* Delaval and *Iſab. Pawlet*, daughter of the Earl of Thanet. 1789. 8. (1 ſh. 6 d.)

AMNER, [Richard] On the inſtitution of chriſtianity. 1774. 8. (2 ſh.) On an interpretation of the prophecies of Daniel. 1776. 8. (3 ſh.)

AMORY, [Thomas] *D. D.* born d. 28 Jan. 1700. died d. 24 Jun. 1774.

— [Thomas] *Esq.* born 1691. died d. 25 Nov. 1788.

AMSTER, [. . . . .] Speculation; or a defence of mankind: a poem. 1780. 4.

ANBUREY, [Thomas] *Officer.* *Travels through the interior parts of America, in a ſeries of letters, by an Officer. Vol. 1. 2. 1789. 8. (14 ſh.)

ANCEL, [Samuel] *Clerk tho the 58 Regiment.* Journal of the late and important blockade and ſiege of Gibraltar from 1779 to 1783. 1786. 8. (5 ſh.)

ANDERSON, [. . . . .] Account of a large ſtone near Cape Town. (Phil. Transact. 1778. p. 102.)

— [Adam] born . . . . died 17 . .

— [Alexander] Account of a bituminous lake or plain in the iſland of Trinidad. (Phil. Transact. 1789. p. 65. überſ. *Sprengel* u. *Forſter*'s N. Beytr. zur Völker u. Länderk. Th. 3. S. 259. und in *Gren* Journ. der Phyſ. T. 2. S. 81.

— [G . . . .] * The Arenarius of *Archimedes* translated —. 1784. 8. (2 ſh. 6 d.)

— [James] *LL. D: F. R. S: F. A. S: Farmer at Monkshill, Aberdeenſhire.* born in Scotland. * Eſſays

 rela-

relating to Agriculture and rural affairs. 1775. 8. (6 sh.) Ed. 2. 1777. 8. Vol. 1. 2. (12 sh.) Ed. 3. mit des Verf. Nahmen, 1784. 8. Vol. 1. 2. Observations on the means of exciting a spirit of national industry — and manufactures of Scotland. 1777. 4. (18 sh.) On the corn laws with a view to the new corn bill proposed for Scotland. 1777. 8. (1 sh. 6 d.) Inquiry into the causes that have hitherto retarded the advancement of agriculture in Europe. 1779. 4. (3 sh.) Account of ancient monuments and fortifications in the highlands of Scotland. (Arch. Vol. 5. p. 241. Vol. 6. p. 87.) Interest of Great Britain, with regard to her American colonies. 1782. 8. (2 sh. 6 d.) On the present state of the hebrides and western coasts of Scotland. 1785. 8. (7 sh. 6 d.) übers. Berlin. 1789. 8. —. and Sir *John Sinclair's* Report of the committee of the Highland society of Scotland, to whom the subject of Shetland wool was referred — 1790. 8.

ANDERSON, [James] *M. D. Physician General at ..adras in the East-Indies.* Letters on the subject of cochineal insects discovered at Madras. Madras, 1788. 8.

—— [James] *Surgeon.* Account of Morne Garou, a mountain in the Island of St. Vincent, with a description of the Volcano on its summit. (Phil. Transact. 1785. p. 16.) Account of a monster of the human species. (Ibid. 1789. p. 157.)

—— [John] *M. D.* Medical remarks on natural, spontaneous and artificial evacuation. 1787. 8. (2 sh. 6 d.) Ed. 2. 1788. 8. (3 sh.) übers. von C. F. *Michaelis.* Breslau, 1789. 8.

—— [John] The tariff or book of rates and duties on goods passing through the Sound at Elsinoor — 1771. 8. (1 sh. 6 d.)

—— [Thomas] *Surgeon in Leith. F. R. S. Edinb.* Account of a very extraordinary enlargement of the Stomach, discovered upon dissection. (Med. Com. of Ed. Vol. 2. p. 294.) History of a case, in which pus into scrotum gave the appearance of a hernia. (Ibid. Vol. 2. p. 423.) Two cases of dislocation of the femur, with an account of the method of reduction. (Ibid. Vol. 3. p. 424.) Pathological observations on the brain. (London M. J. *Vol. XI. P. 2.*)

ANDER-

ANDERSON, [Walter] *D. D.* born in Scotland. History of France. 1769 – 1782. 4. Vol. 1 – 5. (4 L. 4 sh.)

— [William] *Surgeon in Edinburgh.* Observations on the use of the cabbage-tree-bark, as an anthelmintic. (Med. Com. of Ed. Vol. 4. p. 84.) Account of some poisonous fish in the south seas. (Phil. Transact. 1776. p. 544.) Account of a large stone near Cape-Town with a letter from sir *Will. Hamilton* on having seen some pieces of the said stone. (Ibid. 1778. p. 102.)

ANDRE', [William] *Surgeon.* A microscopic description of the eyes of the Monoculus Polyphemus Linnaei. (Phil. Transact. 1782. p. 440.) Description of the teeth of the Anarrhichas Lupus *Linnaei* and of those of the chaetodon nigricans of the same author; with an attempt to prove that the teeth of cartilagineous fishes are perpetually renewed. (Ibid. 1784. p. 274.)

ANDRE'E [John] *Surgeon to the Magdalen-Hospital and Teacher of Anatomy.* Observations upon Dr. *Störk's* treatise on the virtues of hemlock in the cure of cancers. 1761. 8. (1 sh.) Inoculation impartially considered. 1765. 8. (1 sh.) A suppression of urine, from a slough in the urethra. (Med. Obs. & Inq. Vol. 5. p. 342.) On the Theory and cure of the venereal gonorrhoea. 1777. 8. (1 sh.) Ed. 2. 1781. 8. übers. Leipz. 1779. 8. u. 1781. 8. On the theory and cure of the venereal disease. 1779. 8. (3 sh.) übers. Leipz. 1781. 8. Account on an elastic trochar. 1781. 8. (1 sh.)

— [John] *M. D. at Hertford.* Considerations on bilious diseases, and some particular affections of the liver and the gall bladder. 1788. 8. (1 sh. 6 d.)

ANDREWS [. . . . .] *Advice humbly offered to the prince of Wales, by a well-meaning Briton. 1789. 8. (6 d.)

— [John] *LL. D.* The scripture doctrine of grace. 1769. 8. (3 sh.) History of the revolutions of Denmark &c. 8. Vol. 1. 2. 1774. (12 sh.) übers. Kopenh. u. Flensb. Th. 1. 1786. 8. Letters to the Count de Welderen on the present situation of affairs between great Britain and the united provinces. 1781. 8. (1 sh. 6 d.) Two additional letters.

 1781.

1781. 8. (2 ſh.) On the manners taſte and amuſements of the two laſt centuries in England. 1782. 8. (2 ſh. 6 d.) On republican principles and on the inconveniences of a commonwealth in a large country and nation. 1783. 8. (1 ſh. 6 d.) On the principal duties of ſocial life. 1783. 8. (3 ſh.) Remarks on the french and engliſh ladies. 1783. 8. (5 ſh.) Letters to a young gentleman on his ſetting out for france, containing a ſurvey of Paris and review of french litterature. 1784. 8. (6 ſh.) Hiſtory of the war with America, France, Spain and Holland. 1775–1783. Vol. 1–4. 1786. 8. (1 L. 10 ſh.) Defence of the ſtadholderſhip, wherein the neceſſity of that office in the united provinces is demonſtrated. 1787. 8. (2 ſh.)

ANDREWS [James Petit] F. A. S. Appeal to the humane, on behalf of the moſt deplorable claſſ of ſociety, the climbing boys employed by the chimney-ſweepers. 1788. 12. (1 ſh.) Anecdotes ancient and modern. 1789. 8. (6 ſh.)

—— [Miles Peter] *Esq. Dealer in Gunpowder* The Election. 1774. 8. Summer amuſements or an adventure at Margate; a Comic Opera. 1779. Fire and water, a comic Opera. 1780. 1. (1 ſh.) Diſſipation, a Comedy. 1781. 8. (1 ſh. 6 d.) The Baron Kinkvervankotsdorſtrakingatchdern, a new muſical comedy. 1781. 8. (1 ſh. 6 d.) The beſt biddler, a farce. 1782. The reparation, a Comedy. 1784. 8. (1 ſh. 6 d.) The enchanted caſtle. 1786.

—— [William] *Attorney at Law.* Addreſſ on the behaviour of the mayor and corporation of Southampton. 1774. 4. (6 d.)

ANSTY [Charles] *The new. bath guide, or, memoirs of the B– R– D– family in a ſeries of poetical epiſtles. 1766. 4. (5 ſh.) Ed. 3. 1766. (3 ſh. 6 d.) *An Election Ball ––. 17.. 4. (2 ſh. 6 d.) *The prieſt diſſected; a poem. 1774. 4. (2 ſh. 6 d.) Ad C. W. Bampfylde epiſtola poetica familiaris ––. 1776. 4. (5 ſh.) Familiar epiſtle to C. W. Bampfylde –– translated. 4. 1777. (1 ſh.) *Speculation: or, a defence of mankind; a poem. 1780. 4. (2 ſh. 6 d.)

ANSTICE,

ANSTICE, [Robert] Remarks on the comparative advantages of wheel, carriages of different ſtructure and draught. 1790. 8. (2 ſh. 6 d.)

ANSTIE, [John] General view of the bill preſented to parliament — for preventing the illicit exportation of wool and live ſheep —. 1787. 8. (2 ſh.) *Letter to Edw. Philips — on the advantages of manufacturing the combing wool of England -- by the chairman of the wool meeting. 1788. 4. (1 ſh. 6 d.)

ANTILL, [Edward] *Eſq. One of his Majeſty's Council for the province of New-Jerſey.* born 17.. died. 1770.

APPLEGARTH, [Robert] Theological ſurvey of the human underſtandig. 1779. 8. (5 ſh.) Apology for the two ordinances of Jeſus Chriſt, the holy communion and baptiſm. 1789. 8. A plea for the poor; or, remarks on the price of proviſions, and the peaſant's labour -- 1789. 8. (6 d.)

APTHORP, [Eaſt] *DD. Rector of St. Mary-le-Bow, Cheapſide.* Review of Dr. *Mayhew's* remarks on the anſwer to his obſervations on the charter and conduct of the Society for the propagation of the goſpel in foreign parts. 1765. 8. (1 ſh.) Letters on the prevalence of Chriſtianity, before its civil eſtabliſhment; with obſervations on *(Gibbon's)* Hiſtory of the decline of the roman empire. 1778. 8. (5 ſh.) Two ſermons. 1780. 4. (1 ſh.) *Select devotions for families, particular perſons and for the celebration of the holy euchariſt. 1785. 12. (1 ſh.) Diſcourſes on prophecy. 1786. 8. Vol. 1. 2. (10 ſh.)

ARCHDALE, [Meruyn] *A. M. Member of the R. Iriſh Acad. Rector of Slane.* Monaſticum hibernicum, or hiſtory of the abbies, priories and other religious houſes in Ireland. 1786. 4. (1 L. 5 ſh.) *John Lodge's* peerage of Ireland; or, a general hiſtory of the preſent nobility of that kingdom — reviſed, enlarged and continued to the preſent time. *Vol.* 1-7. 1789.

ARCHER, [Anne] *Mrs.* (her maiden name *Sheldon*) Authentic and intereſting memoirs. 1787. 8. Vol. 1-4. (10 ſh.)

ARCHER, [Edward] *M. D. Physician of the united hospitals for the small pox and Inoculation.* born 1717. died. d. 28. Apr. 1789.

ARMSTRONG, [Charles] *Surgeon and Man-midwife.* On the symptoms and cure of the virulent gonorrhoea in females. 1783. 8. (1 sh.)

— [Francis] *M. D. at Uppingham, Rutland.* On the use of Matlock waters. (*Duncan's* M. C. Vol. 7. p. 242.) Account of a new invented green paint --. 1783. 4. (1 sh.) Account of a singular convulsive fits in 3 children of one family. (*Duncan's* M. C. Vol. 9. p. 317.)

— [George] *M. D. Physician to the Dispensary.* *Essay on the diseases most fatal to infants. 1768. 8. (2 sh. 6 d.) Ed. 2. 1771. 8. übers. Zelle. 1769. 8. Account of the diseases most incident to children. 1777. 8. (3 sh.) Ed. 2. 1783. 8. übers. von *J. C. B. Schaeffer.* Regensb. 1786. 8. und in Samml. f. A. Th. 4. S. 52-144.

— [John] *M. D. Physician to his Majesty's Army.* born at Castleton, Roxburgshire. 17.. died d. 7. Sept. 1779.

— [John] Juvenile poems, with remarks on poetry and a dissertation on the best method of punishing and preventing crimes. 1789. 8. (2 sh. 6 d.)

— [Mostyn John] *Geographer and County Surveyor.* Actual Survey of the great-post-roads between London and Edinburgh. 1776. 8. (7 sh. 6 d.) Actual survey of the great-post-roads between London and Dover. 1777. 8. (3 sh.)

ARNE [Thomas Augustine] *Doctor of Music.* born d. 28 May. 1710. died d. 5 March. 1778.

ARNOLD, [Charles Henry] History of South and North America. 1782. 8. (3 sh.)

— [John] Account of his pocket chronometer --. 1780. 4. (1 sh.) On the longitude. --. 1781. 4. (2 sh. 6 d.) Answer to an anonymous letter on the longitude. 1782. 4. (1 sh.)

— [Thomas] *M. D. Physician at Leicester,* Diss. De Pleuritide. Edinb. 1766. 8. Observations on the nature, kinds, causes and prevention on insanity, lunacy, and madness. Vol. 1. 1782. Vol. 2. 1786. 8. (7 sh.) übers. von *J. C. B.* Ackermann. Th. 1. 2. Leipz. 1788. 8.

ARNOT,

ARNOT, [Hugo] *Advocate.* Hiſtory of Edinburgh. 1779. 4. (1 L. 5 ſh.) Collection and abridgment of celebrated criminal trials in Scotland from 1536 to 1784. 4. 1786. (18 ſh.)

— [W.....] *Miniſter of Kennoway.* Harmony of law and goſpel, in the method of grace, demonſtrated, 1786. 8.

ARTHUR, [Edward] *Miniſter at Baremore, Etal.* Sermons on various ſubjects. 1783. 8. (4 ſh.)

— [J....] *Manager of the playhouſe at Bath.* born.... died d. 8 Apr. 1772.

— [Michael] Expoſition — of the Aſſembly's ſhorter catechiſm delivered in a ſeries of Sabbath evening lectures. Vol. 1. 1789. 8. (4 ſh.)

ASCOUGH, [Charles Edward] born.... died d. 14. Oct. 1779.

ASH [Edward] M. D. * The Speculator, publiſhed in weekly Numbers. 1790. 8.

— [John] *LL. D. Diſſenting Miniſter of Perſhore, Worceſterſhire.* born 1724. died d. 10 Apr. 1779.

— [John] *M. D: F. R. S: F. A. S.* Experiments and obſervations to inveſtigate the medicinal properties of the mineral waters of Spa and Aix la Chapelle in Germany and of the Waters — in french Flanders. 1788. 12. (5 ſh.)

ASHBY [.....] *B. D. Preſident of St. John's College, Cambridge.* On a ſingular coin of Nerva. (Arch. Vol. 3. p. 165.)

ASHDOWNE, [William] Eſſay explaining Jeſus true meaning in his parables. 1780. 8. (1 ſh. 6 d.) The unitarian, Arian and Trinitarian opinion reſpecting Chriſt, examined and tried by ſcripture evidence alone. 1789. 8. (1 ſh.)

ASHE, [Robert] *Curate of Crewkerne and Maſter of the free grammar ſchool.* publiſhed *John Browne* of Crewkerne, Somerſet; (a boy of 11 Years old) poetical translations from various authors. 1787. 4. (2 ſh. 6 d.)

ASHMORE, [T.....] Analyſis of the ſeveral bank annuities. 1774. 4. (1 Sh.)

ASHTON, [James] The chriſtian expoſitor. 1774. 8. (5 Sh.) The new expoſitor; containing tables of words from two to ſeven ſyllables, accented, explaind

plaind and divided according to the most approued method of pronunciation. 1788. 8. (1 Sh.)

ASHTON, [Thomas] *DD. Rector of St. Botolph, Bishopsgate.* born 1716. died d. 19. March. 1775.

ASHWORTH, [Caleb] *Tutor of the dissenting Academy at Daventry in Northamptonshire.*
born.... died 1775.

ASKEW, [Anthony] *M. D.*
born .... died d. 27 Febr. 1773.

ASTELL, [....] *Mrs.* * The unfashionable wife: a Novel. *Vol.* 1. 2. 1771. 8. (5 Sh.)

ASTLE, [Thomas] *F. R. S: F. A. S: Keeper of the records in the tower of London.* On the events produced in England by the grant of Sicily to prince Edmund. (Arch. Vol. 4. p. 195.) Origin and progress of writing, as well hieroglyphic as elementary. 1784. 4. (1 L. 11 Sh. 6 d.) On the radical letters of the pelasgians and their derivation. (Arch. Vol. 7. p. 348.) * The will of King Alfred. 1788. 4. (3 Sh.) * The will of King Henry the VII. 1789. 4. (3 Sh. 6 d.)

ATCHISON, [Robert] *Surgeon.* Observations on the dysentery, as it appears among the negroes on the coast of Guinea. (Duncan's M. C. Vol. 9. p. 268.)

ATKINS, [James] *M. A.* The ascension, a poem. 1780. 4. (6 d.)

—— [John] A meteorological journal for the Year 1782. (Phil. Transact. 1784. p. 58.)

ATKINSON, [Christopher] *Rector of Yelden, Bedfordshire.* Poetical sermon on the benefit of affliction. 1766. 4. (1 Sh. 6 d.) Sermons on the most interesting and important subjects. 1775. 8. (6 Sh.)

—— [William] *M. A. fellow of Jesus College, Cambridge.* Poetical essays. 1786. 4. (1 Sh.)

ATWOOD, [George] *M. A: F. R. S.* A general theory for the mensuration of the angle subtended by two objects, of which one is observed by rays after two reflections from plane surfaces and the other by rays coming directly to the spectator's eye. (Phil. Transact. 1781. p. 395.) On the rectilinear motion and rotation of bodies. 1784. 8. (10 Sh. 6 d.) On the principles of natural philosophy. 1784. 8. (5 Sh.)

ATWOOD,

ATWOOD, [Thomas] Observations on the true methods of treatment and usage of the Negroslaves in the british West-India Islands. 1789. 8. (1 sh.)

AUFRERE, [Anthony] *Esq.* Tribute to the memory of *Ulric* of *Hutten* — translated from the german of *Goethe*, 1789. 8. (3 sh.)

AUSTIN, [....] *Mrs.* The noble family; in a series of letters. Vol. 1. 2. 3. 1771. 8. (9 sh.)

— [William] *M. D.* Examination of the first six books of *Euclids* elements. 1781. 8. (2 sh. 6 d.) Experiments on the formation of volatile alkali and on the affinities of the phlogisticated and light inflammable airs. (Phil. Transact. 1788. p. 379. übers. *Gren* J. d. Ph. T. 1. S. 418.) Experiments on the analysis of the heavy inflammable air. (Phil. Transact. 1790 p. 51.)

AYLOFFE, [Joseph] *Baronet*, *Vicepresident of the Antiq. Soc. and F. R. S.*
born 1709. died. d. 19. Apr. 1781.

AYRES, [William Thomas] *Esq.* Comparative view of the differences between the english and irish statute and common law -- *Vol.* 1. 2. 1781. 8. (12 sh.)

AYSCOUGH, [Georg Edward Lyttelton] *Captain.* (Schwager *George* Lord *Lyttelton's*)
born .... died d. 19 Oct. 1779.

— [Samuel] *Clerk*, *Assistant Librarian of the british Museum in the department of natural history.* Catalogue of the Manuscrits preserved in the british Museum hitherto undescribed. 1782. 4. Vol. 1. 2. (2 L. 2 sh.) *Remarks on the letters from an American farmer: or a detection of the errors of Mr. *J. Hector St. John*. 1783. 8. (6 d.) General Index to the Monthly Review from its commencement to the 70 Volume. 1786. 8. Vol. 1. 2. (15 sh.) General Index to the 56 Volumes of the Gentleman's Magazine --. Vol. 1. 2. 1789. 8.

BABINGTON, [William] *Apothecary to Guy's Hospital.* A case of hydrophobia. (M. C. Vol. 1. p. 215.)

BACHMAIR, [John James] *M. A.* The revelation of St. John historically explained -- 1778. 8. (5 sh.)

BACKHOUSE, [William] *D. D. Rector of Deal and Archdeacon of Canterbury.*
born.... died d. 29 Aug. 1788.

BACON,

BACON, [John] *Apothecary in York.* Hiſtory of a carcinomatous ulcer in the mouth cured by the application of leeches. (Med. Com. of Ed. Vol. 2. p. 296.)

—— [Manuel] *DD. Rector at Balden and Vicar of Bramber, Suſſex.* born .... died d. 2 Jan. 1783.

BADCOCK, [Samuel] *Diſſenting miniſter of South-Moulton, Devonſhire.* born 1750. died d. 19 May 1788.

BADENACH [James] *M. D.* Obſervations on the bilious fever uſual in voyages to the Eaſt-Indies. (Med. Obſ. Vol. 4. p. 156.) Obſervations on the uſe of wort in the cure of the ſcuruy at ſea. (Ibid. Vol. 5. p. 61.) Technical deſcription of an uncommon bird from Malacca. (Phil. Tranſact. 1772. p. 1.)

BAGGS [S....] *M. A. Pinto,* on circulation and credit, translated. 1774. 4. (10 ſh. 6 d.)

BAGOT, [Lewis] *D. D. Biſhop of Norwich.* (brother of Lord *William Bagot.*) Twelve diſcourſes on the prophecies concerning chriſtianity. 1780. 8. (5 ſh.) (Several ſingle ſermons.)

BAILEY, [Alexander Mabyn] born .... died 17..

—— [William] *Regiſter to the ſociety for the encouragement of arts, manufactures and commerce.* born .... died 17..

BAILLIE [....] *Captain, late Lieut. Governor of the Royal Hoſpital for ſeamen at Greenwich.* Solemn appeal to the public —. 1779. fol. (2 L. 2 ſh.)

—— [Hugh] *LL. D. late Judge of the court of Admiralty in Ireland.* Letter to Dr. *Shebbeare*, containing a confutation of his arguments concerning the Boſton and Quebec acts of parliament. 1775. 8. (2 ſh.)

—— [Matthew] *M. D. Truſtee of the Muſeum of the late Dr. Hunter.* Account of a remarkable transpoſition of the viſcera. (Phil. Tranſact. 1788. p. 350. London M. J. Vol. X. P. 2.) Account of a particular change of Structure in the human ovarium. (Ibid. 1789. p. 71. London M. J. Vol. X. P. 3. überſ. Samml: f. A. Th. 13. S. 354.)

BAKER, [....] * Remarks on the engliſh language —. 1771. 8. (2 ſh.)

—— [David Erskine] *Eſq.* The Muſe of Oſſian, a dramatic poem. 1763. 12. Biographia Dramatica, or a companion to the playhouſe. 1782. 8. Vol. 1. 2.

BAKER,

BAKER, [George] *M. D: F. R. S. Baronet, Prefident of the College of Phyficians and Phyfician to her Majefty's Houshold.*

Opufcula medica. Innhalt: De Catarrho et De Dyfenteria Londinenli epidemica. De affectibus animi et morbis inde oriundis. Oratio Harvejana. De *Joh. Cajo* Anatomiae conditore apud noftrates. *Ed.* 2. 1771. 8. (5 fh.) On the merits of inoculating the fmallpox. 1766. 8. (1 fh. 6 d.) überf. von *C. F. T.* Leipz. 1767. 8. Inquiry concerning the caufe of the endemial colic of Devonfhire. (Med. Transact. Vol. 1. p. 175. p. 460) Examination of feveral means by which the poifon of lead may be fuppofed frequently to gain admittance into the human body unobferved and unfufpected. (Ibid. Vol. 1. p. 257. Vol. 2. p. 419.) Attempt towards an hiftorical account of the colic of Poitou. (Ibid. Vol. 1. p. 319.) Examination of the feveral caufes, to which the colic of Poitou has been attributed. (Ibid. Vol. 1. p. 364. Vol. 3. p. 407.) Flos Cardamines recommended to the tryal of phyficians as an antifpafmodic remedy. (Ibid. Vol. 1. p. 442.) Account of a fingular difeafe, which prevailed among fome poor children, maintained by the parifh of St. James in Weftminfter. (Ibid. Vol. 3. p. 113.) Obfervations on the late intermittent fevers; with a hiftory of the Peruvian bark. (Ibid. Vol. 3. p. 141.) Obfervations on *Erafm. Darwin's* account of the ufe of foxglove in fome dropfies and in the pulmonary confumption. (Ibid. Vol. 3. p. 287.) A Sequel to the cafe of *Thom. Wood* of Billericay in the county of Effex. (Ibid. Vol. 3. p. 309.) Several extraordinaries inftances of the cure of the dropfy. (Ibid. Vol. 2. p. 235.) Obfervations on the modern method of inoculating the fmall-pox. (Ibid. Vol. 2. p. 275.)

— [Henry] *F. R. S: F. A. S.*

born .... died at London d. 25 Nov. 1774.

— [Richard] *A. M. Rector of Cawfton in Norfolk.*

Sermon on falvation. 1782. 4. (1 fh.) Harmony of IV Evangelifts. P. 1-4. 1787. 8. (10 fh. 3 d.)

— [Robert] *B. D.*

Account of a ftag's head and horns, found at Al-

 port,

port, in the pariſh of *Youlgreave* in the county of *Derby*. (Phil. Transact. 1785. p. 353.)

BALDWIN, [Loammi] *Esq. F. A. Acad.*
Account of a very curious appearance of the electrical fluid, produced by raiſing an electrical kite in the time of a thunder ſhower. (Mem. of B. A. T. I. p. 257.)

—— [Samuel] *of the Cuſtomhouſe.*
Survey of the britiſh cuſtoms, containing the rates of merchandizes — and other ſtatutes. 1775. 4. (18 ſh.)

—— [Thomas] *Esq. A. M.*
Airopaedia: or narrative of a balloon excurſion from Cheſter 1785. —. 1786. 8. (7 ſh. 6 d.)

BALDWYN, [Edward]
*Critique on the poetical eſſays of *Will. Atkinſon.* — 1787. 8. (2 ſh. 6 d.)

BALFOVR, [Francis] *M. D. Phyſician at Calcutta.*
Diſſertatio de Gonorrhoea virulenta. Edinb. 1767. 4. On the influence of the moon in fevres. Calcutta. 1784. London 1785. 8. (1 ſh. 6 d.) überſ. von A. T. W. Straſsb. 1786. 8. The forms of Herkern; — translated into engliſh with an index of arabic words. 1787. 4. (1 L. 1 ſh.)

—— [James] *Esq.*
Philoſophical diſſertations. 1782. 8. (2 ſh. 6 d.)

BALGUY, [Thomas] *D. D. Arch-Deacon and Prebendary of Wincheſter.*
W. S. Powell's Diſcourſes on various ſubjects publiſhed. 1776. 8. (5 ſh.) Diſcourſes on various ſubjects. 1785. 8. (5 ſh.) (ſeveral ſingle ſermons.)

BALL, [John] *M. D.*
born .... died d. 15 Oct. 1779.

BALLIN, [....] *Miſſ.*
The ſtatue room, an hiſtorical tale. 1790. 8. Vol. 1. 2. (5 ſh.)

BALTIMORE, [Frederic] *Lord.*
born 1731. died at Neapel d. 8 Sept. 1771.

BANCROFT, [Edward] *M. D.*
*Natural Hiſtory of Guiana in South-America. 1769. 8. (6 ſh.) überſ. Frankf. u. Leipz. 1769. 8. *Hiſtory of Charles Wentworth, Esq. Vol. 1. 2. 3. 1769. 8. (7 ſh. 6 d.)

BAN-

BANCROFT, [T....]

Prolusiones poeticae; or, a selection of poetical exercises in greek, latin and english. 1788. 8. (3 sh.)

BANDINELL, [James] *D. D.*

Eight sermons. 1780. 8. (4 sh.)

BANNISTER, [James]

*Select Tragedies of *Euripides*, translated from the greek. 1780. 8. (7 sh.) View of the arts and sciences, from the earliest times to the age of Alexander the great. 1785. 8. (3 sh.)

BARBAULD, [Anna Laetitia] (Sister of Dr. *John Aikin, at Hampstead near London.)*

Poems. 1773. 4. (6 sh.) Miscellaneous pieces in prose. 1773. 8. (3 sh.) Devotional pieces, compiled from the Psalms and the book of Job — thoughts on the devotional taste, on sects and on establishments. 1775. 8. (2 sh. 6 d.) Lessons for children from two to three Years old. 1778. 4. (6 d.) *Hymns in prose for children. 1781. 8. (1 sh.) *An Address to the opposers of the repeal of the corporation and Test-Acts. 1790. 8. (1 sh.)

BARBUT, [James]

The genera insectorum of Linnaeus, exemplified by various specimens of english insects drawn from nature. 1781. 4. (2 L. 12 sh. 6 d.) The genera vermium —. P. 1. 2. 1788. 4. (3 L. 9 sh.)

BARCLAY, [James] *Curate of Edmonton in Middlesex.*

*The greek rudiments. 1754. 8. (4 sh.) The rudiments of the latin tongue. 1758. 8. (2 sh.) Complete and universal english dictionary on a new plan —. 1774. 8. (6 sh.)

(several single sermons.)

BARD, [Samuel] *M. D. Professor of the practice of Physic, Kings-College, New-York.*

Enquiry into the nature cause and cure of the Angina suffocativa, or sore throat distemper. (Tr. of A. S. Vol. 1. p. 322.)

BARFOOT, [P....] *Esq.*

Two letters — for obtaining an equal system of taxation and for reducing the national debt. 1786. 8. (1 sh.)

BARING, [Francis] *Memb. of Parl. Director of the East-India Company.*

 The

The principle of the commutation Act eſtabliſhed by facts. 1786. 8. (1 ſh.)

BARKER, [John]

On Cheltenham water, and its great uſe in the preſent peſtilential conſtitution. 1786. 8. (1 ſh. 6 d.) Obſervations on the publication on Cheltenham water. 1787. 8.

— [Robert] *Sir, Knight. Commander in chief of the Eaſt-India Company's forces in Bengal.*

born .... died d. 14 Sept. 1789.

— [Thomas] *Esq. of Lyndon in Rutlandſhire.*

Account of a meteor ſeen in the county of Rutland which reſembled a water ſpout. (Phil. Transact. 1756. p. 248.) On the return of the comet expected in 1757 or 1758. (Ibid. 1759. p. 347.) On the mutations of the ſtars. (Ibid. 1761. p. 498.) Account of a remarkable Halo, May 20. 1737. (Ibid, 1762. p. 3.) Obſervations on the quantities of rain fallen at Lyndon, in Rutland, for ſeveral Years. (Ibid. 1771. p. 221.) On the ſame ſubject, with obſervations for determining the latitude of Stamford in Lincolnſhire. (Ibid. 1771. p. 227.) The duty, circumſtances and benefits of baptiſm. 1771. 8. (3 ſh. 6 d.) Regiſter of the Barometer, Thermometer and rain at Lyndon in Y. 1771. (Phil. Transact. 1772. p. 42.)
— 1772. (ibid. 1773. p. 221.)
— 1773. (ibid. 1774. p. 202.)
— 1774. (ibid. 1775. p. 199.)
— 1775. (ibid. 1776. p. 370.)
— 1776. (ibid. 1777. p. 350.)
— 1777. (ibid. 1778. p. 554.)
— 1778. (ibid. 1779. p. 547.)
— 1779. (ibid. 1780. p. 474.)
— 1780. (ibid. 1781. p. 351.)
— 1781. (ibid. 1782. p. 281.)
— 1782. (ibid. 1783. p. 242.)
— 1783. (ibid. 1784. p. 283.)
— 1784. (ibid. 1785. p. 481.)
— 1785. (ibid. 1786. p 236.)
— 1786. (ibid. 1787. p. 368.)
— 1787. (ibib. 1788. p. 408.)
— 1788. (ibid. 1789. p. 162.) Meſſiah. 1780. 8. (2 ſh. 6 d.) The nature and circumſtances of the demo-

demoniacs in the Gofpel ftated, methodized and confidered in the feveral particulars. 1783. 8. (1 fh. 6 d.)

BARKER, [William] *Hair-Dreffer.*

On the principles of hair dreffing —. 1784. 8. (1 fh. 6 d.)

— [W.... H....] *A. B. Mafter of the grammar fchool, Carmarthen.*

Grammar of the hebrew language. — 1774. 8. (1 fh. 6 d.)

BARLOW, [Frederic] *M. A.*

Complete englifh Dictionary. 17.. The complete englifh peerage; or, a genealogical and hiftorical account of the peers and peereffes of this realm. Vol. 1. 2. 1773. 8. (12 fh. 6 d.) Ed. 2. Vol. 1. 2. 1775. 8. (12 fh.)

— [Joel]

The vifion of Columbus, a poem. 1787. 8. (2 fh. 6 d.)

BARNARD, [....] *D. D. Bifhop of Killaloe. M. R. Irifh Acad. and F. R. S.*

Enquiry concerning the original of the Scots in Britain. (Tr. of J. A. 1787. p. 25.)

— [James]

The divinity of our Lord Jefus Chrift demonftrated from the holy fcriptures and from the doctrine of the primitive church; —. 1789. 8. (3 fh.)

— [William] *Ship-Builder.*

Of an explofion in a coal-pit. (Phil. Transact. 1773. p. 217.) Method for the removal of Ships that have been driven on fhore and damaged in their bottoms. (Ibid. 1780. p. 100.)

BARNES, [Thomas] *D. D. Member of the litterary and philofophical fociety of Manchefter.*

On the nature and effential character of poetry as diftinguifhed from profe. (Mem. of M. Vol. 1. p. 54.) On the affinity, fubfifting between the arts, with a plan for promoting and extending manufactures by encouraging thofe arts, on which manufactures principally depend. (Ibid. Vol. 1. p. 72.) On the pleafure which the mind in many cafes receives from contemplating fcenes of diftrefs. (Ibid. Vol. 1. p. 144.) On the influence of the imagination and the paffions upon the underftanding.

 (Mem.

(Mem. of M. Vol. 1. p. 375.) On public and private education. (Ibid. Vol. 2. p. 1.) Plan for the improvement and extenſion of liberal education in Mancheſter. (Ibid. Vol. 2. p. 16.) Propoſals for eſtabliſhing a plan of liberal education in Mancheſter. (Ibid. Vol. 2. p. 30.) On the voluntary power which the mind is able to exerciſe over bodily ſenſation. (Ibid. Vol. 2. p. 451.)
(ſeveral ſingle ſermons.)

BARR, [.....]
Journal of the weather at Montreal from Dec. 1776 to March 1777. (Phil. Transact. 1778. p. 557.)
—— from Dec. 1778 to April 1779. (Ibid. 1780. p. 272.)

BARRET, [John] *B. D. fellow of Trinity College, Dublin.*
Account of a greek Manuſcript of St. Matthew's goſpel in the library of Trinity College, Dublin. (Tr. of J. A. 1787. p. 121. überſ. *Eichhorn's* Biblioth. der bibl. Litterat. Th. 2. S. 584.)

—— [Onſlow] *M. D.*
On the gout. 1785. 8. (1 ſh. 6 d.)

—— [Phineas] *Merchant at Lisbon.*
Tables of the ſeveral european exchanges —. 1771. 4. (2 L. 2 ſh.)

—— [William] *F. A. S. Surgeon at Briſtol.*
born .... died d. 15 Sept. 1789.

BARRINGTON, [Daines] *F. R. and A. S. Vice-Preſident of the Royal ſociety at London.*
Letter on ſome particular fiſh, found in Wales. (Phil. Transact. 1767. p. 204.) Inveſtigation of the difference between the preſent temperature of the air in Italy and ſome other countries, to what it was 17 centuries ago. (Ibid. 1768. p. 58.) On the trees, which are ſuppoſed to be indigenous in Great-Britain. (Ibid. 1769. p. 23.) Account of a very remarkable young muſician. (Ibid. 1770. p. 54.) Letter concerning Chesnut trees. (Ibid. 1771. p. 167.) Account of a mole from North-America. (Ibid. 1771. p. 292.) Account of ſome experiments made in North-Wales, to aſcertain the different quantities of rain, which fell in the ſame time at different heights. (Ibid. 1771. p. 294.) Inveſtigation of the ſpecific characters, which diſtinguiſh the rabbit from the hare. (Ibid. 1772. p. 4.)

On

On the periodical appearing and disappearing of certain birds at different times of the Year. (Phil. Transact. 1772. p. 265.) Account of a fossil lately found near Christ-church in Hampshire. (Ibid. 1773. p. 171.) Observations on the lagopus or ptarmigan. (Ibid. 1773. p. 224.) Experiments and observations on the singing of birds. (Ibid. p. 249.) Of the Gillaroo trout. (Ibid. 1774. p. 116.) Observations on the welsh castles. (Arch. Vol. 1. p. 278.) Account of two musical instruments used in Wales. (Ibid. Vol. 3. p. 30.) Answer to Mr. *Pegge*, on the growth of the vine in England. (Ibid. Vol. 3. p. 67.) On the expiration of the cornish language. (Ibid. Vol. 3. p. 278.) Observations on the Corbridge Altars. (Ibid. Vol. 3. p. 324.) On the term Levant. (Ibid. Vol. 4. p. 27.) On the Apamean medal. (Ibid. Vol. 4. p. 315.) Observations on *Caesar's* invasion of Britain and — his passage across the thames. (Ibid. Vol. 2. p. 134.) On the cornish language. (Ibid. Vol. 5. p. 81.) Observations on patriarchal customs and manners. (Ibid. Vol. 5. p. 119.) * The probability of reaching the Northpole discussed. 1775. 4. (2 sh. 6 d.) übers. von *S. Engel.* Bern 1777. 4. Miscellanies. 1781. 4. (18 sh.) Observations on St. *Justin's* tomb. (Arch. Vol. 5. p. 143.) Observations on the earliest introduction of cloks. (Ibid. Vol. 5. p. 416. übers. von *Joh. Beckmann*, Beytr. zur Gesch. der Erfind. Th. 1. S. 301.) Observations on the vitrified walls in Scotland. (Ibid. Vol. 6. p. 100.) Observations on the practice of Archery in England. (Ibid. Vol. 7. p. 46.) On the progress of gardening. (Ibid. Vol. 7. p. 113.) Account of pits or caverns in the earth in the county of Berks. (Ibid. Vol. 7. p. 236.) Observations on a picture by Zuccaro — supposed to represent the game of Primero. (Ibid. Vol. 8. p. 133.) Observations on the antiquity of card-playing in England. (Ibid. Vol. 8. p. 134.) Observations on the grey weathers in Berkshire and the crypts in Canterbury cathedral. (Ibid. Vol. 8. p. 442.) Historical disquisition on the game of chess. (Ibid. Vol. 9. p. 16.) On the origin of the arms — the Pegasus and the holy lamb. (Ibid. Vol. 9. p. 187.

BARRY, [Edward] *Sir: Baronet, M. D: F. R. S: Physician in general to his Majesty's forces in Ireland.* born .... died d. 29 March. 1776.

—— [Edward] *A. M. et M. D. Chaplain to the Lord Bishop of Kildare.*
Twelve ſermons on particular occaſions. 1789. 8. (5 ſh.) Letter on the practice of boxing. 1790. 8. (1 ſh.)
(ſeveral ſingle ſermons.)

—— [James] *Profeſſor of painting to the Royal Academy.* born at Cork in Ireland.
Enquiry into the real and imaginary obſtructions to the acquiſition of the arts in England. 1775. 8. (4 ſh.) Account of a ſeries of pictures in the great room of the ſociety of arts, manufactures and commerce at the Adelphi. 1783. 8. (3 ſh. 6 d.)

BARTLET, [Benjamin] *F. A. S. Quacker.* (formerly Apothecary at Bradford.)
born .... died d. 3 March. 1787.

BARTON, [Benjamin Smith] *Member of the Royal Society of Edinburgh.*
Obſervations on ſome parts of natural hiſtory —. P. 1. 1787. 8. (2 ſh.)

BARTRAM. [Iſaac]
Memoir on the deſtillation of perſimons. (Tr. of A. S. Vol. 1. p. 231.)

—— [Moſes]
Obſervations on the native ſilk worms of North-America. (Tr. of A. S. Vol. 1. p. 224.)

BARUH, [Raphael]
Critica ſacra examined —. 1775. 8. (5 ſh.)

BASTARD, [William] *Esq. of Kitley in Devonſhire.*
On the culture of pine-apples. (Phil. Transact. 1777. p. 649.)

BATE, [Henry] ſee *Dudley.*

—— [Julius] *M. A. Rector of Sutton, Suſſex.*
born .... died 1771.

BATEMAN, [Thomas] *A. M. Chaplain to his Grace the Duke of Gordon, Vicar of Whaplode, Lincolnſhire.*
On agiſtment tithe —. 1778. 8. Appendix 1779. (5 ſh. 6 d.) Two ſermons on the reſurrection of the body —. 1780. 4. (1 ſh.) The royal eccleſiaſtical gazetteer; or, Clergyman's pocket kalendar —.

der —. 1781. 8. (3 ſh.) The eccleſiaſtical patronage of the church of England. 1783. 8. (3 ſh. 6 d.)

BATH, [Robert] *Surgeon.*

Addreſſ on the ſubject of inoculation —. 1778. 8. (6 d.) On the nature and quality of diſeaſes of the liver and biliary ducts —. 1777. 8. (2 ſh.) On the medical character, with a view to define it. 1785. 8. (2 ſh. 6 d.) Ed. 3. 1789.

BATLEY, [Jeremiah] *Esq.*

Two letters on parliamentary repreſentation. 1783. 8. (1 ſh. 6 d.)

BATT, [Charles William] *M. A. Chaplain to Lord Malmesbury.*

*Diſſertation on the meſſage from John the Baptiſt to our ſaviour Luk. VII. 9. Ed. 2. 1789. 8. (2 ſh. 6 d.)

BATTIE, [William] *M. D.*

born at Devon 1704. died d. 13 Jun. 1776.

BAVERSTOCK [....] *Brewer at Alton, Hampſhire.*

*Hydrometical obſervations and experiments in the brewery. 1785. 6. (2 ſh.)

BAXTER, [Alexander] *Eſq.*

Deſcription of a ſet of Halo's and parhelia, ſeen in the Year 1771. in North-America. (Phil. Transact. 1787. p. 44.)

BAYFORD, [David] *of Lewes. M. D: F. R. S.*

born 1739. died d. 16 Apr. 1790.

— [Thomas] *Surgeon at London.*

The effects of injections into the urethra and the uſe and abuſe — in the cure — of the virulent gonorrhoea. 1773. 8. (1 ſh. 6 d.) überſ. Altenb. 1777. 8.

BAYLEY, [Anſelm] *LL. D. Sub-Dean of his Majeſty's Chapels Royal.*

The antiquity, evidence and certainty of chriſtianity canvaſſed, on *Middleton's* examination of the biſhop of London's diſcourſes on prophecy. 1750. (1 ſh. 6 d.) On ſinging and playing with juſt expreſſing and real elegance —. 1771. 8. (2 ſh.) Grammar of the engliſh language. 1772. 8. (2 ſh.) The old teſtament, engliſh and hebrew with remarks critical and grammatical on the hebrew and corrections of the engliſh. Vol. 1-4. 1774. 8. (2 L. 2 ſh.) Grammar of the hebrew language. 1774. 8. (2 ſh.) Two ſermons, the commandmandments of God, in nature, inftitution and religious ftatutes in the jewifh and chriftian churches. 1778. 8. (1 fh.) *Remarks on *David Levi's* fecond letter to Dr. *Prieftley* — by Anti-focinus. 1787. 8. (1 fh.) The alliance of Mufic, Poetry and Oratory. 1789. 8. (6 fh.)

BAYLEY, [C.....]
Entrance into the facred language containing the neceffary rules of hebrew grammar. 1782. 8. (5 fh.) Sermon on Galatians IV. 6. Ed. 2. 1786. 8. (1 fh.)

—— [E....]
Addreff to perfons, afflicted with the gout. 1783. 8. (6 d.)

—— [John] *Student of Gray's Inn.*
On the law of bills of exchange, cafh bills and promiffory notes. 1789. 8. (2 fh.)

—— [Richard] *Surgeon.*
Cafes of the angina trachealis with the mode of cure —. New-York. 1781. 8.

—— [T... B...] *Esq. of Hope near Manchefter: F. R. S.*
On a cheap and expeditious method of draining land. (*Hunter's* G. E. Vol. 4. p. 143.) On the culture of cabbages. (Ibid. Vol. 5. p. 167.) On fecuring apple trees from cattle. (Ibid. Vol. 5. p. 268.)

BAYLIE, [William] *Königl. Preuffifcher Geheimer Rath und Leibarzt.* born 1718. died at Berlin d. 2 Merz. 1787.

BAYLY, [William] *Affiftant at the Royal obfervatory at Greenwich.*
born.... died 17..

BEARDSLEY, [Ebenezer] *Surgeon of the 22d Regiment of the American Army in the campaign of* 1776.
Remarks on the effects of ftagnant air. (Mem. of B. A. Vol. 1. p. 542.)

BEATSON, [Robert] *Esq.*
Political index to the hiftories of great Britain and Ireland, or, a complete regifter of the hereditary honours, public offices and perfons in office from the earlieft periods to the prefent time. 1786. 8. (9 fh.) Ed. 2. Vol. 1. 2. 1788. 8. (15 fh.)

BEATTIE, [James] *LL. D: F. R. S. Edin: Profeffor of moral philofophy and Logic in the Univerfity of Aberdeen.*

Origi-

Original poems and translations. 1760. 8. (3 ſh.) The judgment of Paris. 1764. 4. (1 ſh. 6 d.) On the nature and immutability of truth. 1770. 8. (6 ſh.) Ed. 2. 1777. 4. (1 L. 1 ſh.) überſ. von *H. W. Gerſtenberg*. Kopenh. u. Leipz. 1772. 8. The Minſtrel, or, the proceſſ of Genius, a poem. Book 1. 2. 1774. 4. (3 ſh.) nachgedrukt in *Benzler's* poetical library. Leipzig. Vol. 1. Poems on ſeveral occaſions. 1780. Diſſertations moral and critical. 1783. 4. überſ. von *K. Groſſe* Th. 1–3. Göttingen 1789. 8. On the evidences of the chriſtian religion. 1787. 8. Vol. 1. 2. The Theory of language. 1788. 8. (5 ſh.) Elements of Moral ſcience. Vol. 1. 1790. 8. (6 ſh.) überſ. von *K. P. Moritz* Th. 1. Berlin 1790. 8.

BEATY, [M....] *Teacher of the claſſics.*

The Monitor, or an addreſſ — on the preſent ſituation of affairs. 1786. 8. (3 ſh.)

BEAUCHAMP, [....] *Lord.*

Account of a fire ball ſeen in the air and of an exploſion heard Dec. 11. 1741. near London. (Phil. Transact. 1751. p. 870.) *Letter to the firſt belfaſt company of volunteers by a member of the britiſh parliament. 1782. 8. (1 ſh. 6 d.)

BEAUFORD, [William] *A. M.*

Account of antient coins, found at Ballylinam in the Queen's County, Ireland. (Tr. of J. A. 1787. p. 139.) Account of an antient ſepulchre, diſcovered in the county of Kildare at Golverſton, near Kilcullen. 1788. (Tr. of J. A. 1788.)

BEAUFOY, [Henry] *Member of Parliament, F. R. S.*

Life of Lord *Robert Clive's*. (vid. *Kippis* Biographia Britannica. Vol. 3. p. 645.) Speech on his motion for the repeal of the teſt and corporation acts —. 1786. 8. (1 ſh.) Speech — for extending the fiſheries. 1787. 8. (1 ſh. 6 d.)

BECKET, [J... B....] *Bookſeller in Briſtol.*

The uſe of the hydroſtatic balance made eaſy and applied particularly to the purpoſe of detecting counterfeit gold coin 1775. 8. (1 ſh.) On the air extracted from the water of the hotwell and on the air of that city and the neighbourhood. (*Prieſtley's* Experiments on Natur. Philoſ. Vol. 1. p. 466.) On the ſubject of air from ſeawater. (Ibid. p. 468.)

BECK-

BECKFORD, [Peter] *Esq.*
Thoughts on hunting. 1782. 4. (7 ſh. 6 d.)

—— [W....] *Jun.*
Remarks upon the ſituation of Negroes in Jamaica. 1788. 8. (2 ſh.) Deſcription of Jamaica. Vol. 1. 2. 1790. 8. (14 ſh.)

BECKWITH, [Joſiah] *F. A. S.*
Thom. Blount's fragmenta antiquitatis; or ancient tenures of land and jocular cuſtoms of ſome manors. 1784. 8. (6 ſh.)

BEDDOES, [Thomas] *at Edinburgh. M. D.*
*The chemical eſſays of *C. W. Scheele* translated 1785. 8. (6 ſh.) Account of ſome new experiments on the production of artificial cold. (Phil. Transact. 1787. p. 282. überſ. Samml. zur P. u. N. G Th. 4. S. 225.) (*John Mayow's*) chemical experiments and opinions; extracted from a work publiſhed in the laſt century. 1790. 8. (2 ſh. 6 d.)

BELCHIER, [William] *Esq. Kent.*
Eſſays on various ſubjects, critical and moral —. 1786. 8. Vol 1. 2. (5 ſh.)

BELFOUR, [John]
New hiſtory of Scotland from the earlieſt accounts to the preſent time. 1770. 8. (3 ſh. 6 d.)

BELKNAP, [Jeremy] *A. M. Member of the American philoſophical Society at Philadelphia. F. A. A.*
Hiſtory of New-Hampſhire. Vol. 1. 1784. 8. (5 ſh. 3 d.) Deſcription of the white mountains in New-Hampſhire. (Tr. of A. S. Vol. 2. p. 42.) Obſervations on aurora borealis. (Ibid. Vol. 2. p. 196.) On the preſerving of parsnips by drying. (Ibid. Vol. 2. p. 199.) Account of large quantities of a foſſil ſubſtance containing vitriol and ſulphur, found at Lebanon, in the ſtate of New-Hampſhire. (Mem. of B. A. Vol. 1. p. 377.)

BELL, [Andrew] *F. A. S.*
Proſpectus of a ſyſtem of anatomy illuſtrated with 240 copper plates. 1787. fol.

—— [Archibald]
The church members directory; or, a goſpel church deſcribed —. 1776. 8. (2 ſh.)

—— [Beaupré] *Esq.*
On the horologia of the antients. (Arch. Vol. 6. p. 133.)

BELL, [Benjamin] *Surgeon at Edinburgh.*
On the theory and management of Ulcers, and Dissertation on white swellings of the joints with an essay on the chirurgical treatment of inflammation and its consequences. 1778. 8. (5 sh.) übers. Leipz. 1779. 8. System of Surgery. Vol. 1-6. 1788. 8. (1 L. 16 sh.) übers. Leipz. Th. 1-5. 1791. 8. The case of a man affected with an obstinate epilepsy considerably relieved by the use of the flowers of zink. (Med. Com. of Ed. Vol. 1. p. 204.) The history of a case, in which some of the vertebrae were found dissolved. (Ibid. Vol. 3. p. 82.)

— [Benjamin] *Surgeon at Wigton in Cumberland.*
History of a case of obstinate cough, returning at intervals, removed by the vse of the cuprum ammoniacum. (*Duncan's* M. C. Dec. 2, Vol. 4. p. 307.)

— [George] *M. D. Physician at Manchester.*
born in the county of Dumfries. died d. 2 Febr. 1784.

— [George] *Surgeon, at Redditch.*
Thoughts on the cancer of the breast. 1788. 8. (1 sh.)

— [John] *M. D.* born... died at his country-house, at Antermonie d. 28 Aug. 1780.

— [Robert] *Surgeon in Cork.*
Account of a case, in which a very large portion of the lungs was protruded and strangulated, occasioned by a wound in the thorax. (*Duncan's* M. C. Dec. 2. Vol. 1. p. 349.)

— [Thomas] *Sir, Knight. M. D. of the city of Dublin,*
The history of a case, in which two faetuses, that had been carried near 21 months, were successfully extracted from the abdomen by incision. (Med. Com. of Ed. Vol. 1. p. 72.)

— [Thomas] *Major.*
On military first principles. 1770. 8. (4 sh.)

— [William] *D. D. Prebendary of Westminster, Treasurer of St. Paul's and Chaplain to the Princess Amelia.*
Dissertation — what causes principally contribute to render a nation populous? and what effect has the populousness of a nation on its trade? 1756. 4. (1 sh.) übers. Wien 1768. 8. Enquiry into the divine

divine missions of John the Baptist and Jesus Christ —. 1761. 8. (5 sh.) übers. von *H. P. C. Henke.* Braunschw. 1779. 8. Attempt to illustrate the nature and effects of the Lord's supper. 1780. 8. Supplem. 1790. 8. (4 sh.) *P. F. le Courayer* sentiments on the different doctrines of religion — with his life. 1787. 8. (2 sh. 6 d.)

(several single sermons.)

BELL, [William] *A. B. private Teacher of the latin and greek languages*

Grammar of the latin tongue. 1772. 8. (1 sh. 6 d.) 1775. 8. (1 sh. 6 d.) Grammar of the greek tongue. 1775. 8. (1 sh. 6 d.)

BELLAMY, [Daniel] *Vicar at Kew and Petersham.*

born.... died d. 15 Febr. 1788.

—— [George Anne] *Actress.*

died d. 16 Febr. 1788.

—— [Thomas]

The benevolent planter; a dramatic piece. 1789. 8. (1 sh.)

BELOE, [William] *of Norwich.*

Ode to Miss Boscawen. 1783. 4. (1 sh.) *The rape of Helen, from the greek of Coluthus, with notes. 1786. 4. (2 sh. 6 d.) Poems and translations. 1788. 8. (5 sh.)

BENNET, [....] *Mrs.*

The welch heiress and juvenile indiscretions. 17.. Agnes de Courci, a domestic tale. Vol. 1–4. 1789. 8. (12 sh.)

—— [Abraham] *M. A.*

Description of a new electrometer. (Phil. Transact. 1787. p. 26. übers. Samml. zur P. u. N. G. Th. 4. S. 419.) Account of a doubler of electricity, or a machine by which the least conceivable quantity of positive or negative electricity may be continually doubled, till it becomes perceptible by common electrometers, or visible in sparks. (Phil. Transact. 1787. p. 288.)

—— [H....] *M. A.*

The treasury of wit. Vol. 1. 2. 1786. 8. (5 sh.)

—— [James] *M. D. Physician in Cork.*

History of a singular affection of the action of the heart, terminating favourably. (*Duncan's* M. C. Dec. 2. Vol. 2. p. 316.)

BENNET, [John] *Curate of St. Mary's, Manchester.*
Divine revelation, impartial and univerſal, or, an attempt to defend Chriſtianity —. 1783. 8. (3 ſh.) Letters to a young lady. Vol. 1. 2. 1789. 8. (5 ſh. 6 d.)
(ſeveral ſingle ſermons.)

— [John] *a journeyman Shoemaker.*
Poems on ſeveral occaſions. 1774. 8. (2 ſh. 6 d.)

— [Thomas] *M. A.*
Lectures on — the Apoſtle's creed. 1776. 8. (5 ſh.)

— [William] *Surgeon.*
On the teeth and gums and the ſeveral diſorders to which they are liable. 1779. 8. (1 ſh.)

BENSON, [....] of Stainley.
A new and profitable method of raiſing a crop of turnips in Drill. (*Hunter's* G. E. Vol. 5. p. 210.)

BENT, [James] *Surgeon at Newcaſtle under Line, Staffordſhire.*
Account of a woman enjoying the uſe of her right arm after the head of the os humeri was cut away. (Phil. Transact. 1774. p. 553.)

— [William]
A meteorological journal of the Year 1787. kept in Paternoſter-Row, London. 17.. 4.

BENTHAM, [Edward] *D.D. Prof of Divinity at Oxford.* born at Ely d. 23 Jul. 1707. died d. 1 Aug. 1776.

— [James] *M. A. F. A. S. Rector of Felrwell St. Nicholas*, Norfolk.
Hiſtory and antiquities of the conventual and cathedral church of Ely from the foundation of the monaſtery A. D. 673. to the Y. 1771. 1771. 4. (1 L. 11 ſh. 6 d.) Account of certain diſcoveries in Ely Minſter. (Arch. Vol. 2. p. 364.)

— [Jeremy] of Lincoln's-Inn: at preſent at *Cherſon* in the *Crimea.*
View of the hard labour bill —. 1778. 8. (2 ſh. 6 d.) Defence of uſury, ſhewing the impolicy of the preſent legal reſtraints on the term of pecuniary bargains; with a letter on the diſcouragement oppoſed — to the progreſſ of inventive induſtry. 1787. 8. (3 ſh. 6 d.) Introduction to the principles of morals and legiſlation. 1789. 8. (19 ſh.)

BENTLEY, [....] *Surgeon at Patrington near Hull.*
Caſe of ſuppreſſion of urine, ſucceſsfully treated, in

in which the bladder was punctured through the rectum. (M. C. Vol. 1. p. 256.)

BENTLEY, [Richard] Sohn des Philologen *Rich. Bentley.* born .... died d. 23 Oct. 1782.

—— [Samuel]
The river dove; a lyric pastoral. 1768. 4. (1 sh.) Poems on various occasions. 1776. 8. (6 sh.)

—— [Thomas] *LL. D. Rector at Narlston, Leicestershire.* born 1704. died d. 4 March. 1786.

BERDMORE, [Thomas] *Surgeon - Dentist to the King.* On the disorders and deformities of the teeth and gums. 1770. 8. (3 sh.)

BERDOE, [Marmaduke] *M. D.*
Enquiry into the influence of the electric fluid in the structure and formation of animal beings. 1771. 8. (4 sh) On the pudendagra. 1771. 8. (1 sh.) On the gout. 1772. 8. (1 sh. 6 d.) Doubts concerning the inversion of objects on the retina. 1772. 8. (1 sh. 6 d.) On the nature and circulation of the blood. P. 1. 2. 1772. 8. (1 sh. 6 d.) Theory of the human sensations. 1773. 8. (1 sh.)

BERENGER, [Richard] *Gentleman of the horse to his Majesty.*
Translation of *Bourgelat's* new system of Horsemanship. 1754. 4. (10 sh. 6 d.) The history of the art of Horsemanship. Vol. 1. 2. 1771. 4. (2 L. 2 sh.)

BERINGTON, [Joseph] *a Roman Catholic Clergyman.*
* Letter on materialism and *Hartley's* Theory of the human mind. 1776. 8. (3 Sh.) Immaterialism delineated; or, a view of the first principles of things. 1779. 8. (5 Sh.) Addreſſ to the protestant dissenters who have lately petitioned for a repeal of the corporation and test acts. 1786. 8. (1 Sh.) Reflexions — with an exposition of roman catholic principles in reference to god and the country —. 1787. (1 Sh. 6 d.) History of the lives of Abeillard and Heloisa —. 1784. Ed. 2. 1787. 4. (1 L. 1 Sh.) Account of the present state of the Roman Catholics in Great - Britain. 1787. On the depravity of the nation, with a view to the promotion of Sunday schools —. 1788. 8. (1 Sh.) The rights of dissenters from the established church, in relation, principally, to english catholics. 1789. 8. (1 Sh.)

(1 Sh.) The hiſtory of the reign of Henry II. and of Richard and John, his ſons —. 1790. 4. (1 L. 1 ſh.)

BERKELEY; [George-Monck] *Esq. LL. B: F. A. S. and of the Inner temple London.*

Literary relics: containing original letters from King Charles II. King James II. the Queen of Bohemia, Swift —. with an inquiry into the life of *Swift*. 1789. 8. (6 ſh.)

BERKENHOUT, [John] *M. D.*

Account of the laſt attempt on the coaſt of france. 17.. 8. (1 ſh.) * Count *Teſſin's* letters from an old man to a young prince with the anſwers, translat: from the Swediſh. Vol. 1-3. 1759. 8. (9 ſh.) * Clavis Anglica linguae botanicae; or a botanical lexicon. 1763. 8. (3 ſh. 6 d.) Pharmacopoea medica. 1766. 8. (2 ſh. 6 d.) Outlines of the natural hiſtory of great Britain and Ireland. Vol. 1-3. 1771. 8. (11 ſh. 6 d.) *Ed.* 2. 1789. 8. Vol. 1. 2. (10 ſh.) Dr. *Cadogan's* diſſertation on the gout and all other diſeaſes examined and refuted. 1772. 8. (1 ſh.) *Pomme* on hyſterical and hypochondriacal diſeaſes, translated. 1777. 8. (5 ſh.) Biographia litteraria. Vol. 1. 1777. 4. (18 ſh.) Lucubrations on ways and means. 1780. 8. (2 ſh.) On the bite of a mad-dog. 1783. 8. (1 ſh. 6 d.) Symptomatology. 1784. 8. (3 ſh.) Firſt lines of the theory and practice of philoſophical chemiſtry. 1788. 8. (6 ſh. 6 d.)

BERKLEY, [....]

* Maria, or the generous ruſtic. 1784. 8. (2 ſh. 6 d.) * Heloiſe; or, the ſiege of Rhodes, a legendary tale. Vol. 1. 2. 1788. 8. (3 ſh. 6 d.)

BERNARD, [Francis] *Sir. Baronet.*

born .... died d. 16 June 1779.

— [....] *Governor at Boſton.*

Letters on the trade and government of America and the principles of law and polity applied to the american colonies. 1774. 8. (2 ſh.)

— [Giffard]

Translation of *Bemetzrieder's* muſic made eaſy to every capacity —. 1778. 4. (3 ſh. 6 d.)

— [William] *Ship-Builder, Grove-ſtreet, Deptford.*

Account of an exploſion of air in a coal-pit at

 Middle-

Middleton, near Leeds in Yorkshire. (Phil. Transact. 1773. p. 217.) Method for the removal of ships that have been driven on shore and damaged in their bottoms. (Ibid. 1780. p. 100.)

BERROW, [Capel] *A. M. Rector of Finningley, Nottinghamshire.*

A pre-existent lapse of human souls demonstrated from reason —. 1762. 8. (2 sh. 6 d.) A lapse of human souls in a state of pre-existence —. 1766. 8. (3 sh.) Deism not consistent with the religion of reason and nature. 1780. 4. (4 sh.)

BERTEZEN, [S....]

Thoughts on the different kinds of food given to young silk worms and the possibility of their being brought to perfection in the climate of England —. 1789. 8. (1 sh)

BERTIE, [Willoughby] *Earl of Abingdon.*

Thoughts on the letter of — Edm. Burke — on the affairs of America. 1777. 8. (1 sh.) Dedication to the collective body of the people of England on the present political distractions. 1780. 8. (1 sh. 6 d.)

BEST, [....]

Matilda an original poem. 1789. 4. (2 sh. 6 d.)

—— [Thomas] *Gentl. late of his Majesty's Drawing room in the tower.*

On the art of angling — with the complete flyfisher. 1787. 12. (2 sh.)

BETTESWORTH, [John] *Master of the naval Academy at Chelsea.*

The universal reckoner; or, every trader's infallible guide —. 1778. 8. (1 sh.) Arithmetic in the first four fundamental rules. 1779. 8. (3 d.) System of naval mathematics; or, practical rules of the art of navigation. 1787. 12. (5 sh.)

BEVER, [Thomas] *LL. D.*

On the study of Jurisprudence and the civil law —. 1766. 8. (1 sh. 6 d.) History of the legal polity of the roman states and of the rise, progress and extent of the roman laws. 1781. 4. (18 sh.) übers. von C. *Völkel.* Leipz. 1787. 8.

BEVERLEY, [John] *M. A.*

The poll for the election of two representations in parlia-

parliament for the univerſity of Cambridge. 3 Apr. 1784 —. 1784. 8.

BEVIS, [John] *M. D. F. R. S.*
born .... died d. 6 Nov. 1771.

BEW, [George] *M. D. Phyſician at Mancheſter.*
Obſervations on blindneſſ and on the employment and of the other ſenſes to ſupply the loſſ of ſight. (Mem. of M. Vol. I. p. 159.) Of the epidemic catarrh of the Year 1788. (Lond. M. J. Vol. IX. Part. 10.) Caſe of a ſtudent who ſwallowed a golden breaſtpin four inches in length, and voided it by ſtool, without any ill conſequence. (Ibid. Vol. 4. p. 77.)

BEWLEY, [William] *Surgeon and Apothecary at Great-Maſſingham in Norfolk.*
born 1725. died d. 5 Sept. 1783.

BICKERSTAFF, [Iſaac] *Marine-Officer.* born in Ireland.
Leucothoe. 1756. 8. Thomas and Saily; or the ſailor's return. 1760. 8. Judith. 1761. 4. Love in avillage 1762. 8. (1 ſh. 6 d.) The maid of the mill. 1765. 8. (1 ſh. 6 d.) Daphne and Amintor. 1765. 8. (1 ſh.) The plain dealer. 1766. 8. Love in the city. 1767. 8. (1 ſh. 6 d.) The Royal Garland. 1768. 8. Lionel and Clariſſa. 1768. 8. Ed. 2. 1770. 8. The abſent man. 1768. 8. The Padlock. 1768. 8. The Hypocrite. 1768. 8. The epheſian matron. 1769. 8. Dr. *Laſt* in his chariot. 1769. 8. The captive. 1769. 8. 'Tis well it's no worſe. 1770. 8. The recruiting ſerjeant. 1770. 8. He would if he could; or, an old fool worſe than any. 1771. 8. The ſultan; a farce. 1787. 8. (6 d.)

BICKNELL, [Alexander] *Esq.*
Hiſtory of Lady Anne Neville; 17.. Hiſtory of Iſabelle, or the reward of good nature. 17.. *Philoſophical diſquiſitions on the chriſtian religion —. 1777. 12. (2 ſh. 6 d.) *The hiſtory of Edward Prince of Wales commonly termed the black prince —. 1777. 8. (5 ſh.) The life of Alfred the great King of the Angloſaxons. 1777. 8. (6 ſh.) The putrid Soul: a poetical epiſtle —. 1780. 4. (1 ſh. 6 d.) The patriot king; or, Alfred and Elvida, a Tragedy. 1788. 8. (2 ſh. 6 d.) Doncaſter races; or the hiſtory of Miſſ Maitland, a

 tale

tale of truth: — Vol. 1. 2. 1789. 8. (5 ſh.) Painting perſonified, or, the caricature and ſentimental pictures of the principal artiſts of the preſent times fancifully explained. Vol. 1. 2. 1790. 8. (6 ſh.) The grammatical wreath; or, a complete ſyſtem of engliſh grammar —. 1790. 8. (3 ſh.)

BIDDLE, [Owen]

Obſervations on the tranſit of venus, June 3. 1769 made at Leweſtown in Penſylvania. (Phil. Transact. 1769. p. 414.) Account of the tranſit of venus over the ſun's diſc, as obſerved near Cape-Henlopen on Delaware-Bay June 3. 1769. (Tr. of A. S. Vol. 1. p. 89.)

BINGHAM, [George] *B. D. Rector of Pimperne and of Moo-Critchell in the county of Dorſet and Dioceſe of Briſtol.*

Vindication of the doctrine and liturgy of the church of England —. 1774. 8. (1 ſh. 6 d.)

BINGLEY, [W....]

* The riddle by the late unhappy *George Rob. Fitzgerald* with notes. 1787. 4. (1 ſh.)

BINNEY, [Barnabas] *Hoſpital-Phyſician and Surgeon in the American Army* 1782.

A remarkable caſe of gunſhot wound. (Mem. of B. A. Vol. 1. p. 544. London M. J. Vol. VII. P. 3.)

BIRCH, [John] *Army-Surgeon.*

On the efficacy of electricity in removing female obſtructions. 1779. 8. (1 ſh. 6 d.) *Ed.* 2. 1780. 8. (1 ſh. 6 d.) überſ. Samml. f. A. Th. 5. S. 575.

—— [Samuel] *Paſtry-Cook.*

Conſilia, or thoughts on ſeveral ſubjects. 1785. 8. (2 ſh. 6 d.) Ed. 2. (with the author's name) 1786. 8. (2 ſh. 6 d.) The Abbey of Ambresbury, a poem. P. 1. 2. 1789. 4. (4 ſh.)

BIRD, [John] *Mathematical Inſtrumentmaker at London.* born 1709. died d. 31 March. 1776.

—— [Robert] *Eſq.*

Propoſals for paying great part of the national debt and reducing taxes —. 1780. 8. (1 ſh.)

—— [William] *Surgeon and Man-midwife at Chelmsford, Eſſex.*

Account of a retroverſio uteri. (Med. Obſ. Vol. 5. p. 110.)

BISSET, [....]
Three discourses — on the character and office of a clergyman of the excellency of the british constitution — of liberty, public spirit and the power of the british legislature. 1775. 8. (1 sh.)

— [Charles] *M. D. Physician at Knayton Yorkshire.* On the scuruy, designed chiefly for the use of the British nauy. 1756. 8. (2 sh. 6 d.) *Essay on the medical constitution of Great-Britain —. 1762. 8. (5 sh.) übers. von *J. W. Müller.* Warschau 1779. Medical essays and observations — 1766. 8. (5 sh.) übers. von *P. W. Möller.* Breslau 1781. 8. Observations on lymphatic encysted tumours. (*Duncan's* M. C. Vol. 8. p. 244.)

— [Thomas] *D. D. Minister of Logierait.* Sermons. 1789. 8. (6 sh.)

BLACK, [J....]
The vale of innocence; a vision; verses and sonnets. 1785. 4. (1 sh.)

— [James] *of Morden in Surry.* Observation on the tillage of the earth and on the theory of instruments adapted to his end. 1778. 4. (5 sh.)

— [Joseph] *M. D. Professor of Medicine and Chemistry in the University of Edinburgh.* Diss. De humore acido a cibis orto et magnesia alba. Edinb. 1754. Experiments upon Magnesia alba, Quic-lime and some other alkaline-substances. (Ess. and Observ. Edinb. Vol. 2. p. 157.) The supposed effect of boiling upon water, in disposing it to freeze more readily, ascertained by experiments. (Phil. Transact. 1775. p. 124.)

— [William] *M. D. Of the Royal college of Physicians.* Observations on the small-pox and inoculation. 1781. 8. (2 sh. 6 d.) Historical sketch of Medicine and surgery from their origine to the present time. 1782. 8. (5 sh.) übers. von *J. C. F. Scherf.* 1789. 8. Comparative view of the mortality of the human species at all ages and of the diseases and casualities by which they are destroyed or annoyed. 1788. 8. (6 sh.) übers. Leipz. 1789. 8.

BLACKBURNE, [Francis] *M. A. Archdeacon of Cleveland.*

Enquiry into the uſe and importance of external religion. 1752. (and in the Pillars of Prieſter Vol. 4.) * The confeſſional; or, enquiry into the right, utility, edification and ſucceſſ of eſtabliſhing ſyſtematical confeſſions of faith and doctrine in proteſtant churches. 1766. 8. (5 ſh.) Ed. 2. 17.. Ed. 3. 1770. 8. (7 ſh.) Conſiderations on the preſent ſtate of the controverſy between the proteſtant and papiſts of Great-Britain and Ireland. 1768. 8. (5 ſh.) Four diſcourſes. 1775. 8. (3 ſh.) (ſeveral ſingle ſermons.)

BLACKBURNE, [Thomas] *M.D: Phyſician at Durham: F.R.S.*

born 1749. died d. 23 June 1782.

—— [William] *M. D: F. R. S.*

Diſſert. De ſale communi. Edinb. 1781. Caſe in which the ſubſtance of the uterus was in a great meaſure deſtroyed during pregnancy. (London M. J. Vol. VIII. P. 1.) On the effects of a large doſe of emetic tartar. (Ibid. Vol. IX. p. 61. überſ. Samml. f. A. Th. 12. S. 737.)

BLACKETT, [Mary Dawes]

Suicide, a poem. 1789. 4. (1 ſh. 6 d.)

BLACKLOCK, [Thomas] *LL. D. at Edinburgh.*

born at Anan in Scotland 1721. (deprived of his eye-ſight by the ſmall-pox in the ſixth month of his life.)

Joſeph *Spence's* account of the life, characters and poems of Mr. *Blacklock.* 1754. 8. (1 ſh.) Collection of originals poem. 1761. 8. (2 ſh. 6 d.) Paraclaeſis; or, conſolations deduced from natural and revealed religion: in two diſſertations. 1767. (5 ſh.) Translation of *Armand's* two diſcourſes on the ſpirit and evidences of chriſtianity. 1768. 8. (2 ſh.) The Graham, an heroic ballad. 1774. 4. (2 ſh. 6 d.)

BLACKRIE, [Alexander] *Apothecary at Bromfield.*

born.... died d. 29 May 1772.

BLACKSTONE, [Henry] *Esq. of the Middle-Temple.*

Reports of caſes argued and determined in the court of common pleas — in the 28 Year of Georg III. Part. 1–3. fol. 1789. (15 ſh.)

—— [William] *Profeſſor of law at Oxford.*

born

born at Cheapside d. 10 July 1723. died d. 14 Febr. 1780.

BLAGDEN, [Charles] *M. D: F. R. S: F. A. S: Physician to the army.*

Diss. De causa apoplexiae. Edinb. 1768. 8. Experiments and observations in an heated room. (Phil. Transact. 1775. p. 111. and p. 484.) On the heat of the water in the gulf-stream. (Ibid. 1781. p. 334.) Account of some late fiery meteors; with observations. (Ibid. 1784. p. 201.) Observations on ancient inks, with the proposal of a new method of recovering the legibility of decayed writings. (Ibid. 1787. p. 451.) Experiments on the cooling of water below its freezing point. (Ibid. 1788. p. 125. übers. *Gren* J. d. P. Th. 1. S, 87.) Experiments on the effect of various substances in lowering the point of congelation in water. (Ibid. 1788. p. 277. übers. *Gren* J. d. P. Th. 1. S. 389.) History of the congelation of Quicksilver. (Ibid. 1783. p. 329. übers. Samml. zur P. u. N. G. Th. 3. S. 347. u. S. 515.)

BLAGRAVE, [J....] *Notary public.*

Laws for regulating bills of Exchange, inland and foreign —. 1783. 12. (1 sh.) *Ed.* 2. 1788. 12. (1 sh.)

BLAIR, [Hugh] *D. D. Emeritus Professor of Rhetorik in the University of Edinburgh.*

*Critical Dissertation on the poems of Ossian, the Son of Fingal. 1762. 4. (2 sh. 6 d.) übers. von *O. A. H. Oelrichs.* Hannover 1785. 8. Sermons. Vol. 1-3. 1777-1790. 8. (18 sh.) übers. (von *F. S. G. Sack*) Th. 1. 2. Leipz. 1781. 8. Lectures on Rhetoric and belles lettres. Vol. 1. 2. 1783. 4. (1 L. 16 sh.) nachgedr. Basil. T. 1. 2. 3. 1788. 8. übers. von *K. G. Schreiter.* Th. 1-3. Liegniz. 1788. 8.

BLAIR, [John] *D. D. Rector of St. John, Westminster, and Prebendary of Westminster-Abbey. F. R. S: F. A. S.*

born .... died d. 24 June 1782.

— [Robert]

Description of an accurate and simple method of adjusting *Hadley's* Quadrant for the back observation. (Nautical Almanac 1788.)

BLAKE,

BLAKE, [Francis] *Sir, Baronet.*
On the beſt proportion for ſteam engine cylinders of a given content. (Phil. Transact. 1757. p. 379.) Spherical Trigonometry reduced to plain. (Ibid. 1757. p. 441.) On the greateſt effects of engines, with uniformley accelerated motions. (Ibid. 1757. p. 1.) The lunar eclipſe Oct. 11. 1772. obſerved at Canton. (Ibid. 1774. p. 46.) The efficacy of a ſinking fund of one million per annum conſidered. 1785. 8. (1 ſh.) The propriety of an actual payment of the public debt conſidered. 1786. 8. (1 ſh) The true policy of great Britain conſidered. 1787. 8. (1 ſh.) Political tracts. 1790. 8. (5 ſh.)

—— [John] *Surgeon at Briſtol.*
On Inoculation. 1771. 8. (1 ſh. 6 d.)

—— [W....]
King Edward the third. Drama. 1783. 8.

BLAND, [Robert] *M. D. Phyſician Man-Midwife to the Weſtminſter General diſpenſary.*
Some calculations of the number of accidents or deaths which happen in conſequence of parturition and of the proportion of male to female children as well as of twins, monſtrous productions, and children that are dead — born; taken from the midwifery reports of the Weſtminſter General diſpenſary —. (Phil. Transact. 1781. p. 355. überſ. Journal für Geburtshelfer. St. 1.) On the treatment of convulſions during parturition. (London M. J. Vol. 2. p. 328. überſ. Samml. f. A. Th. 7. S. 498.) Account of a woman who had the ſmall pox during pregnancy and who communicated the ſame diſeaſe to her foetus. (Ibid. Vol. 2. p. 204.) Account of two caſes of haematuria. (Ibid. Vol. 4. p. 282.)

BLAND, [T....] *M. D. of Blandford in Virginia.*
Account of a extra uterine conception. (*Duncan's* M. C. Dec. 2. Vol. 1. p. 334.)

—— [Thomas] *Surgeon at Newark.*
Account of the effects of the cuprum ammoniacum in the cure of epilepſy. (*Duncan's* M. C. 1780. p. 240. überſ. Samml. f. A. Th. XI. S. 176.)

BLANE, [Gilbert] *M. D: F. R. S: Phyſician extraord. to the Prince of Wales, Phyſician to St. Thoma's Hoſpital.*

Obſer-

Obſervations on the diſeaſes incident to ſeamen. 1785. 8. (6 ſh.) überſ. Marburg 1788. 8.

BLANE, [William] *Esq.*

Eſſays on hunting — with an account of the *Vizier's* manner of hunting in the mogul empire. 1788. 8. (4 ſh.) Ed. 2. 1788. 8. (6 ſh.)

Some particulars relative to the production of borax. (Phil. Transact. 1787. p. 297. überſ. Samml. zur P. u. N. G. Th. 4. S. 285.)

BLAYMIRES, [J....]

The chriſtian's ſpelling-book, for the uſe of ſchools and private families. 1790. 8. (1 ſh.)

BLAYNEY, [Benjamin] *D. D. Profeſſor of Hebrew in the Univerſity of Oxford.*

Diſſertation on — Daniel's prophecy of 70 weeks — with remarks on J. D. *Michaelis* letters. 1775. 4. (2 ſh. 6 d.) überſ. (von *J. C. F. Schulz*) Halle 1777. Anhang 1780. 8. Jeremiah and lamentations, a new translation with notes. 1784. 4. (1 L. 1 ſh.) (ſeveral ſingle ſermons.)

BLICKE, [Charles]

On the bilious or yellow fever of Jamaica. 1772. 8. (1 ſh. 6 d.)

BLIGH, [William] *Lieutenant in the navy.*

Narrative of the mutiny on board his Majeſty's ſhip Bounty and the ſubſequent voyage of part of the crew in the ſhip's boat from Tofoa, one of the friendly Islands, to Timor, a dutch ſettlement in the eaſtindies — with charts. 1790. 4. (7 ſh.)

BLIZARD, [William] *F. A. S. Surgeon to the London Hoſpital and Lecturer in Anatomy. F. R. S. of Gottingen.*

Experiments and obſervations on the danger of copper and bell-metal in pharmaceutical and chemical preparations. 1786. 8. (1 ſh.) Deſcription of the ſituation of the large blood-veſſels of the extremities, the inſtrument Tourniquet and the methods of making effectual preſſure on the arteries in caſes of dangerous effuſions of blood from wounds. 1786. 8. (1 ſh. 6 d.) Deſultory reflections on police with an eſſay on the means of preventing crimes and amending criminals. 1786. 8. (2 ſh.) A new method of treating the fiſtula lachrymalis. (Phil. Transact. 1780. p. 239. London

M. J. Vol. 1. p. 62.) übers. Leipz. 1784. 8. On the external use of emetic tartar. (Ibid. Vol. VIII. P. 1. übers. Samml. f. A. Th. XI. S. 726.) On the use of electricity in deafness. (Ibid. Vol. XI. P. 1.)

BLOWER, [Eliza] *Miss.*

*Maria: the genuine memoirs of an admired lady of rank and of some of her friends. Vol. 1. 2. 1763. 8. (4 Sh.) *George Bateman. Vol. 1–3. 1782. 8. (7 Sh. 6 d.) Features from life; or a summer visit. Vol. 1. 2. 1788. 8. (6 Sh.)

BLUNT, [John] *Surgeon at Leominster, Herefordshire.*

Practical farriery —. 1773. 8. (3 Sh. 6 d.)

—— [Robert] *Surgeon at Odiham, in Hampshire.*

Case of a painful affection of the face cured by electricity. (London M. J. Vol. VII. P. 2.) übers. Samml. f. A. Th. XII. S. 8.

BODDINGTON, [John] *Esq.*

Account of some bones found in the rock of Gibraltar with remarks by Dr. *Hunter.* (Phil. Transact. 1770. p. 414.)

BOLTON, [James] *Member of the Natural Hist. Society at Edinburgh.*

History of funguses growing about Halifax (Yorkshire) —. Vol. 1. 2. 1788. 4. (2 L. 2 Sh.) Filices Britannicae; an history of the british proper ferns. 1785. 4. (13 Sh.) (coloured 1 L. 1 sh.)

BOLTS, [William] *Merchant, and Alderman or Judge of the Mayor's Court of Calcutta.*

Considerations on india affairs; particularly respecting the present state of Bengal and its dependencies —. Vol. 1. 2. 1772. 4. (1 L. 10 sh.) übers. von *J. C. F. Schulz.* Leipz. 1780. 8.

BONHOTE, [Elizabeth] *Mrs.*

The parental monitor. Vol. 1. 2. 1788. 8. (5 Sh.) Darnley vale; or Emilia Fitzroy, a novel. Vol. 1-3. 1789. 8. (9 Sh.) Olivia. 17.. Ellen woodley, a novel. Vol. 1. 2. 1790. 8. (5 Sh.)

BONNYCASTLE, [John] *of the royal military academy, Woolwich.*

The scholar's guide to arithmetic —. 1780. 12. (2 Sh.) Introduction to mensuration and practical geometry —. 1782. 12. (3 Sh.) Introduction to Algebra. 1782. 12. (3 Sh.) Introduction to astronomy.

nomy. 1786. 8. (7 Sh.) Ed. 2. 1787. 8. *Euclid's* Elements of geometry. 1789. 8. (5 ſh.)

BOOKER, [Luke]

Poems on ſubjects ſacred, moral and entertaining. Vol. 1. 2. 1785. 8. (5 ſh.) The Highlanders, a poem. 1787. 4. (2 ſh. 6 d.) Miſcellaneous poems. 1790. 8. (6 Sh.)

BOOTE, [Richard] *Attorney at Law, at Abingdon, Berks.*

born .... died d. Febr. 1782.

BOOTH, [....] *Mrs.*

The little french lawyer. a Comedy. 1778. 8.

— [Abraham] *Methodiſtical Preacher.*

Apology for the baptiſts. 1778. 8. (1 ſh.) Paedobaptiſm examined. 1784. 8. (4 ſh.) Ed. 2. Vol. 1. 2. 1787. 8. (8 ſh.)

(ſeveral ſingle ſermons.)

— [Joſeph] *Portrait - Painter.*

Addreſſ to the public on the polygraphic art, or the copying or multiplying pictures in oil colours, by a chemical and mechanical proceſſ —. 1788. 8. (1 ſh.)

BORLASE, [William] *D. D: F. R. S.*

born at Pendeen Cornwallis 1695. died d. 24 Aug. 1772.

BORTHWICK, [George] *Surgeon of the XIV. Regiment of Dragoons.*

A Cataract in the eye, with a preternatural membrance attacted to the iris, extracted. (Med. Com. of Ed. Vol. 2. p. 84.) Treatiſe upon the extraction of the chryſtalline lens. 1775. 8. (1 ſh.) The hiſtory of a fractured ſternum. (Med. Com. of Ed. Vol. 5. p. 185.) The hiſtory of a ſingular caſe of delirium from a wound of the head. (*Duncan's* M. C. 1780. p. 439.) Account of the ſucceſſfull operation of the trepan on the left temple, with the extraction of a ſplinter of ſtone, penetrating the dura mater. (*Duncan's* M. C. Vol. 8. p. 322.)

— [William] *Esq.*

Inquiry into the origin and limitations of the feudal dignities of Scotland. 1775. 8. (1 ſh. 6 d.) Remarks on britiſh antiquities —. 1776. 8. (2 ſh. 6 d.)

BOSWELL, [....]

*Treatiſe on watering meadows. 1780. 8. (2 ſh. 6 d.)

BOSWELL,

BOSWELL, [James] *Esq.* (Son to Lord *Auchinleck.*)
°Account of Corſica, the journal of a tour to that island and memoirs of *Paſcal Paoli.* 1768. 8. (6 ſh.) überſ. von *A. E. K.* (Klauſing) Leipz. 1768. 8. Ausg. 2. Leipz. 1769. 8. überſ. im Auszug (von *H. A. Mertens*) Augsb. 1769. 8. Britiſh eſſays in favour of the brave Corſicans by ſeveral hands. 1769. 8. (2 ſh.) Letter to the people of Scotland, on the preſent ſtate of the nation. 1784. 8. (1 ſh.) Letter to the people of Scotland on the alarming attempt to infringe the articles of the union. 1785. 8. (2 ſh. 6 d.). Journal of a tour to the hebrides with *Sam Johnſon* —. 1774. Ed. 2. 1785. überſ. 1775. überſ. (von *A. Wittenberg*) Lübek 1787.

BOTT, [Edmund] *Esq. Barriſter: F. A. S.*
Collection of deciſions of the court of King's bench upon the poor's laws, down to the preſent time. 1773. 8. (7 ſh.)

BOURN, [Daniel]
On Wheel-Carriages —. P. 1–3. 1769. 8. (3 ſh.) Remarks on Mr. *Jacob's* treatiſe on wheel-carriages. 1773. 8. (1 ſh.)

BOURNE, [Vincent] *M. A: Uſher of Weſtminſter ſchool.*
Miſcellaneous poems. 1772. 4. (11 ſh.)

BOUTCHER, [William] *Nurſeryman, at Comely Garden.*
On foreſt trees —. 1775. 4. (15 ſh.)

BOWDLER, [....] *Miſſ. of Bath.*
born.... died 17..

—— [Thomas] *F. R. S: F. A. S.*
Letters written in Holland in the months of Sept. and Oct. 1787. 1788. 8. (5 ſh.)

BOWDOIN, [James] *Esq. L. L. D. Governour of the Commonwealth: Preſident of the American Academy at Boſton.*
Philoſophical diſcourſe – when he was inducted into office as preſident. (Mem. of B. A. Vol. 1. p. 1.) Obſervations upon an hypotheſis for ſolving the phenomena of light —. (Ibid. Vol. 1. p. 187.) Obſervations on light and the waſte of matter in the ſun and fixt ſtars, occaſioned by the conſtant efflux of light from them —. (Ibid. Vol. 1. p. 195.) Obſervations tending to prove — the exiſtence of an orb which ſurrounds the whole viſible material ſyſtem —. (Ibid. Vol. 1. p. 208.)

BOWEN,

BOWEN, [James] *Surgeon to the 30th Regiment.*
Account of a ſingular tumour in the groin, removed by extirpation. (*Duncan's* M. C. Vol. 9. p. 233.)

— [....]
Hiſtorical account of the origin progreſſ and preſent ſtate of Bethlehem hoſpital —. 1783. 4. (—)

BOWLE, [John] *M. A: F. A. S. Vicar of Idmiſton, near Salisbury.*
born.... died d. 26 Oct. 1788.

BOWLES, [W.... Lisle] *A. B. of Trinity College.*
* Fourteen Sonnets: 1789. 4. (1 ſh.) Ed. 2. (with the author's name) 1789. 4. (2 ſh.) Verſes on the benevolent inſtitution of the philantropic ſociety. 1789. 4. (2 ſh.) Verſes to *John Howard* on his ſtate of priſons and lazarettos. 1789. 4. (1 ſh. 6 d.) The grave of *Howard*, a poem. 1790. 4. (2 ſh.)

BOWYER, [William] *F. A. S: Printer.*
born at London d. 17 Dec. 1699. died d. 18 Nov. 1777.

BOX, [George] *of Abingdon ſtreet, Weſtminſter.*
Plans for reducing the extraordinary expences of the nation, and gradually paying of the national debt —. 1784. 8. (1 ſh.)

BOYCE, [....] *A. M. Rector of Worlingham in Suffolk and Chaplain to the Earl of Suffolk.*
Harold; a Tragedy. 1786. 4. (3 ſh.)

— [Gilbert]
Reply to *Dan. Taylor's* diſſertation on ſinging in the Worſhip of God. 1787. 8. (1 ſh.)

— [Samuel]
born.... died d. 16 March. 1775.

— [Thomas]
* Specimen of elegiac poetry. 1773. 4. (1 ſh.)

BOYD, [Henry] *A. M.*
Translation of the inferno of *Dante Alighieri*, in engliſh verſe — with a ſpecimen of a translation of the Orlando furioſo of *Arioſto*. Vol. 1. 2. 1785. 8. (10 ſh. 6 d.)

— [Robert] *LL. D.*
Office, powers and jurisdiction of his Majeſty's juſtices of the peace and commiſſioners of ſupply. Vol. 1. 2. 1787. 4. (1 L. 11 ſh. 6 d.)

BOYDELL, [James] *Wine Merchant.*
The Ullage caſk gauger —. 1784. 8. (12 ſh. 6 d.)

BOYDELL, [John]
Collection of prints, engraved after the moſt capital paintings in England. Vol. 1. 2. 1772. fol. (12 Guin.)

BOYER, [Iſaac]
Propoſal for determining the longitude at ſea by obſervation, independent of any time-keeper or of the truth of the magnetic compaſſ —. 1774. 8. (6 d.)

BOYS, [....] *Mrs.*
The coalition: or family anecdotes. Vol. 1. 2. 1785. (6 ſh.)

—— [....]
Collection for a hiſtory of Sandwich. P. 1. 1788. 4.

—— [William] *F. A. S. Surgeon at Sandwich, Kent.*
Caſe of a child who ſwallowed a pin. (London M. J. Vol. 6. p. 401.)

BRADBERRY, [David]
Letter to *Edw. Jefferies* — for applying to Parliament for a repeal of the corporation and teſt acts, ſo far as they concern proteſtant diſſenters. 1789. 4. (1 ſh.)

BRADLEY, [John]
born.... died 17..

BRAND, [....] *Secretary.*
Explanation of the inſcriptions on a roman Altar and tablet found at Tinmouth Caſtle in Northumberland. 1783. (Arch. Vol. 8. p. 326.)

—— [....] *M. A.*
Obſervations on Mr. *Gilbert's* bill. 1776. 8. (2 ſh.)

—— [Charles]
On aſſurances and annuities on lives —. 1775. 8. (3 ſh. 6 d.) Letter in defence of his treatiſe on aſſurances — with notes. (Critical Review Vol. XLI. p. 160.)

—— [F.... J....] *M. A.*
Select diſſertations from the amoenitates academicae, a ſupplement to *Stillingfleet's* tracts relating to natural hiſtory — tranſlated. Vol. 1. 2. 1781. 8. (5 ſh. 3 d.)

—— [John] *M. A: Fellow and Secretary of the Society of Antiquaries at London.*
Conſcience, an ethical eſſay. 1772. 4. (2 ſh.) On illicit love, a poem. 1776. 4. (1 ſh. 6 d.) Obſervations

vations on popular antiquities, including the whole of Mr. *Bourne's* Antiquitates vulgares —. 1777. 8. (5 ſh.) Hiſtory and Antiquities of Newcaſtle upon Tyne. Vol. I. 2. 1789. 4. (3 L. 3 ſh.)

BRAND, [Robert]

The true method of reducing ruptures and retaining them in the abdomen and in the navel. 1771. 8. (1 ſh.)

— [Thomas] *Surgeon.*

Translation of M. *Sage's* treatiſe on the fluor alcali. 1778. 8. (1 ſh.) Chirurgical eſſays on the cauſes and ſymptoms of ruptures. 1783. 8. (2 ſh.) Strictures in vindication of ſome of the doctrines miſrepreſented by Mr. *Foot* in his obſervations upon the new opinions of *John Hunter*, in his late treatiſe —. 1787. 4. (2 ſh. 6 d.) The caſe of a boy who had been miſtaken for a girl —. 1787. 4. (2 ſh.)

BRANDER, [Guſtavus] *Esq. F. R. S: F. A. S: Curator of the Britiſh Muſeum.*

born 1717. died d. 21 Jan. 1787.

BRANDISH, [Joſeph] *Surgeon at Alceſter in Warwickſhire.*

Account of a caſe in which the head of the os femoris, ſhattered by a gun ſhot, is ſuppoſed to have been regenerated. (London M. J. Vol. VII. P. 2) Caſe of mortification of the leg. (Ibid. Vol. VIII. P. 2.) Account of a caſe; in which a conſiderable portion of the lower jaw bone was removed —. (Ibid. Vol. VIII. P. 3.)

BRAY, [William] *F. A. S.*

* Sketch of a tour into Derbyſhire and Yorkſhire —. 1778. 8. (2 ſh. 6 d.) Ed. II. (with the author's name) 1783. 8. (6 ſh.) Obſervations on the indian method of picture-writing. (Arch. Vol. 6. p. 159.) On the Leiceſter roman miliary ſtone. (Ibid. Vol. 7. p. 84.) Remark on *Mooke's* account of ſome druidical remains in Derbyſhire. (Ibid. Vol. 7. p. 178.) Account of the obſolete office of purveyor to the King's houſehold. (Ibid. Vol. 8. p. 329.) Account of a roman road leading from Southampton by Chiceſter and Arundell through Suſſex and Surrey to London —. (Ibid. Vol. 9. p. 96.)

BREAKS, [Thomas]
Complete ſyſtem of Land - Surveying, both in theory and practice. 1771. 8. (7 ſh. 6 d.)

BRERETON, (Owen Salisbury) *Esq. F. R. S: F. A. S.*
Obſervations on *Pet. Collinſon's* paper on the round towers in Ireland. (Arch. Vol. 2. p. 80.) Obſervations in a tour through South - Wales Shropſhire. (Ibid. Vol. 3. p. 111.) Extracts from a Mſ. dated apud Eltham Jan. 22. Hen. VIII. (Ibid. Vol. 3. p. 154.) Deſcription of a third unpubliſhed royal ſeal. (Ibid. Vol. 5. p. 280.) Account of the violent ſturm of lightning at Eaſtbourn in Suſſex. Sept. 17. 1780. (Phil. Transact. 1781. p. 42.)

BRETT, [John] *Captain:*
born .... died 1785.

BREWSTER, [John] *M. A.*
Sermons for priſons with prayers for the uſe of priſoners in ſolitary confinement. 1790. 8. (2 ſh. 6 d.)

BRICE, [Andrew] *Printer.*
born at Exeter. 1690. died d. 14 Nov. 1773.

—— [Thomas] *Printer.*
The ſtate coach in the mire, a tale. 1783. 4 (1 ſh.)

BRICKNELL, [A.....]
The life of Alfred the great king of the Anglo-ſaxons. 1777. (6 ſh.)

BRIDGES, [George] *Sir.* ſee Lord *Rodney.*

—— [Thomas] *Wine Merchant at Hull.*
born at Yorkſhire.
Under the ſuppoſed name *Cauſtic Barebones* he publiſhed: New translation of *Homer's* Iliad adapted to the capacity of honeſt engliſh roaſt beef and pudding eaters. Vol. 1. 2. 1764. 12. (5 ſh. 6 d.) Dido. a comic opera. 1771. 8. The dutchman; a muſical entertainment. 1775. 8. (1 ſh.)

BRIGGS, [Richard] *Cook at the Temple Coffeehouſe.*
The engliſh art of cookery —. 1788. 8. (7 ſh.)

BRIGHT, [Henry] *M. A. Maſter of New College ſchool, Oxford.*
The praxis; or a courſe of engliſh and latin exerciſes —. 1784. 8. (5 ſh.)

BRISBAINE, [John] *M. D. Phyſician to the Middleſex hoſpital at London.*

The

The anatomy of painting —. 1769. fol. (1 L. 8 ſh.) Select cases in the practice of medicine. 1772. 8. (1 ſh. 6 d.)

BRISTOW, [W.....] *Esq.*

On the policy, juſtice and expediency of repealing the teſt and corporation acts. 1789. 8. (1 ſh. 6 d.)

BROCKLESBY, [Richard] *M. D: F. R. S: Phyſician to the Army.*

Diſſert. De ſaliva ſana et morboſa. Lugd. Bat. 1745. 4. Eſſay concerning the mortality of horned cattle. 1746. 8. On the Indian poiſon. (Phil. Transact. 1754. p. 408.) On the ſounds and hearing of fiſh. (Ibid. 1755. p. 233.) On a poiſonous root lately found among gentian. (Ibid. 1755. p. 240.) Experiments on the ſenſibility and irritability of the ſeveral parts of animals. (Ibid. 1759. p. 240.) Eulogium medicum, ſ. Oratio anniverſarii *Harvejana.* 1760. 4. (1 ſh.) Oeconomical and medical obſervations — tending to the improvement of military hoſpitals and to the cure of camp diſeaſes —. 1764. 8. (5 ſh.) überſ. von *Chr. Gottl. Selle.* Berlin. 1772. 8. The caſe of a lady labouring under a diabetes, attended with uncommon irregularities of the pulſe and palpitations of the heart. (Med. Obſ. Vol. 3. p. 274.) Experiments relative to the analyſis and virtues of Selzer water. (Ibid. Vol. 4. p. 7.)

BROCKWELL, [Joſeph] *M. A. Rector of Weſt-Merſea, Eſſex.*

Practical expoſition on the Lord's prayer. 1783. 8. (1 ſh.)

LE BROCQ, [Philipp] *M. A: Curate of Eling.*

Project for the payment of the national debt. 17.. Hints relative to the management of the poor. 1784. 8. (1 ſh. 6 d.) Deſcription of certain methods of planting, training and managing all kinds of fruit trees, vines —. 1785. 8. (1 ſh. 6 d.) (ſeveral ſingle ſermons.)

BROMEHEAD, [Joſeph] *M. A.*

The melancholy ſtudent, an elegiac poem. 1769. 4. (1 ſh.) *Ed.* 2. 1776. Oration on the utility of public infirmaries. 1772. 4. (1 ſh.)

BROMFIELD, [William] *Surgeon to the Queen's Houshold, and to St. George's and the Lock's - Hoſpitals.*

Cafe of a woman who had a foetus in her abdomen for 9 years. (Phil. Transact. 1751. p. 697.) Account of the englifh nightfhades, and their effects —. 1757. 12. (2 fh.) Narrative of a phyfical transaction with Mr. *Aylett*, Surgeon and Apothecary at Windfor. 1759. 8. (1 fh.) Thoughts concerning the prefent peculiar method of treating perfons inoculated for the Small-Pox —. 1767. 8. (2 fh. 6 d.) Chirurgical obfervations and cafes. Vol. 1. 2. 1773. 8. (14 fh.) überf. Leipz. 1774. 8.

BROMLEY, [George] *Sir, Baronet.*

Collection of original royal letters, written by King Charles 1. and 2, King James II. and the King and Queen of Bohemia — from 1619 to 1665. 1787. 8. (10 fh. 6 d.)

—— [Robert Anthony] *Rector of St. Mildred's in the Poultry. Lecturer of St. John's Hackney and Minifter of Fitzroy Chapel.*

Inquiry into the neceffity of preparation for the Lord's fupper. 1770. 8. (3 fh.) Difcourfe on the confideration of our letter end. 1772. 8. (5 fh.) (feveral fingle fermons.)

BROMWICH, [Bryan J'Anfon]

* The experienced bee-keeper; containing an effay on the management of bees —. 1783. 8. (2 fh.) überf. von C. F. *Michaelis.* Leipz. 1785. 8.

BROOKE, [....] *Mifs.*

Reliques of irifh poetry — with notes. 1790. 4. (16 fh.)

BROOK, [Abraham].

Mifcellaneous experiments and remarks on electricity, the air pump, and the barometer; with the defcription of an electrometer of a new conftruction. 1789. 4. (1 fh.) Account of a new electrometer. (Phil. Transact. 1782. p. 384.)

BROOKE, [Francis] *Mrs.* (late Mifs *Moore*, her husband *Brooke*, *Rector of Colney in Norfolk.*)

born.... died d. 23. Jan. 1789.

—— [Edward]

Table or chronological index to the books of reports of the determinations in the feveral courts of judicature in England. 1780 (10 fh. 6 d.) Bibliotheca legum Angliae —. Vol. 1. 2. 1788. 12. (5 fh.)

BROOKE, [Henry] *Barrak-Master of Mellingar in Ireland.* born .... died 1783.

— [John Charles] *Esq. of the Herald's College. F. A. S.* Conjecture on Sir *Rich. Worsley's* Seal. (Arch. Vol. 4. p. 182.) The ceremonial of making the King's bed. (Ibid. Vol. 4. p. 311.) Illustration of a Saxon inscription on the church of Kirkdale in Rydale in the North-Riding of the county of York. (Ibid. Vol. 5. p. 188.) Account of an ancient seal of Robert, Bar. *Fitzwalter.* (Ibid. Vol. 5. p. 211.) Description of the great Seal of Queen *Catherine* Parr the 6 Wife of Henry VIII. (Ibid. Vol. 5. p. 232.) Description of the great Seal of Mary d'Esté, the second wife of King James II. (Ibid. Vol. 5. p. 367.) Account of a saxon inscription in Aldbrough church, in Holdernesse in the east riding of the County of York. (Ibid. Vol. 6. p. 39.)

— [Thomas Digby]
Short and easy method of prayer translated from the french of Mad. *Guion.* 1775. 12. (1 sh.)

— [W.....] *Major.*
*Plans of the sunday-schools and school of industry, established in the city of Bath —. 1789. 8. (6 d.)

BROMHEAD, [Joseph] *M. A.*
Oration on the utility of public infirmaries. 1772. 4. (1 sh.)

BROUGH, [Anthony] *Esq.*
On the necessity of lowering the exorbitant freight of ships employed in the service of the east india Company. 1786. 8. (1 sh.) View of the importance of the trade between great Britain and Russia. 1789. 8. (1 sh.)

BROUGHTON, [Arthur] *M. D. Physician to the hospital at Bristol.*
Observations on the influenza or epidemic cattarrh — during the Months of May and June 1782. 1782. 8. (1 sh.) Enchiridion botanicum —. 1782. 8. (4 sh.) The history of two cases of dropsy. (*Duncan's* M. C. Vol. 9. p. 368.)

— [Thomas] *Rector of Alhallows, Lombard-Street and of Wotton in Surry: Secretary to the society for promoting christian knowledge.*
born.... died d. 14 Dec. 1777.

BROUGHTON, [Thomas] *Vicar of Bedminſter, near Briſtol.*
born d. 5 Jul. 1704. died d. 21 Dec. 1774.

BROWN, [Hugh]
The true principles of gunnery inveſtigated and explained, comprehending translations of *Euler's* obſervations upon the new principles of gunnery by *Benj. Robins* —. with additions. 1777. 4. (15 ſh.)

—— [John] *Painter.*
born .... died 17..

—— [John] *M. D.*
born .... died d. 7 Oct. 1788.

—— [Joſeph] *Esq.*
Obſervation of a ſolar eclipſe Oct. 27. 1780. at Providence. (Mem. of B. A. Vol. 1. p. 149.)

—— [Joſiah] *Esq. Barriſter at law.*
Reports of caſes upon appeals and writs of error in the high court of parliament from the Year 1701-1779. Vol. 1-7. fol. 1779-1783. (10½ Guin.)

—— [Peter].
Illuſtrations of zoology —. 1776. 4. (3 L. 3 ſh.)

—— [Richard] *Profeſſor of Hebrew and Arabic in the Univerſity of Oxford.*
born .... died d. 20 March 1780.

—— [Thomas]
The evangelical hiſtory of our lord and ſaviour Jeſus Chriſt —. Vol. 1. 2. 1777. 8. (6 ſh.)

—— [Thomas] *Surgeon, near Glasgow.*
Deſcription of the exocoetus volitans, or flying fiſh. (Phil. Transact. 1778. p 791.)

—— [William] *Phyſician at Kolyvan in Siberia.*
On the ſcurvy, which prevailed in Ruſſia. 1785. (*Duncan's* M. C. Dec. 2. Vol 2. p. 339.)

—— [William] *Esq. Of the Inner-Temple; Barriſter at Law.*
Reports of caſes argued and determined in the high court of chancery — from 1778-1787. fol. 1788. (2 Guin.)

—— [W.... L....] *D. D. Miniſter of the engliſh church at Utrecht.*
Eſſay on the folly of ſcepticiſm; the abſurdity of dogmatizing on religious ſubjects —. 1788. 8. (2 ſh. 6 d.)

BROWNE,

BROWNE, [Arthur] *Esq. Repreſentative in Parliament for the Univerſity of Dublin.*

Review of the queſtion, whether the articles of Limerick have been violated? 1788. 8.

— [Moſes] *Chaplain of Morden College, Vicar of Olney and of Sutton, Lincolnſhire.*

born 1703. died d. 13 Sept. 1787.

— [Robert] *Gardener at Gunton in Norfolk.*

Method to preſerve peach and nectarine trees from the effects of the mildew. 1786. 12. (5 ſh.)

— [Thomas] *Esq* . .

The times. a ſatire —. 1783. 4. (2 ſh.)

— [William] *Sir: M D: Phyſician at Lynn, Norfolk.*

born 1692. died at London 1774.

BROWNRIGG, [John]

Account of the fort of Ardnorcher or Horſeleap near Kilbegan, in the county of Weſtmeath. (Tr. of J. A. 1788.)

— [William] *M. D: F. R. S: Phyſician at Keswick, Cumberland.*

Diſſ. De praxi medica ineunda. Lugd. Bat. 1737. 4. The art of making common ſalt. 1748. 8. überſ. von *F. W. Heun*. Leipz. 1776. 8. Thoughts on Dr. *Hale's* method of deſtillation. (Phil. Transact. 1759. p. 534.) Enquiries on the nature of the mineral elaſtic ſpirit, or air, contained in the Spa water. (Ibid. 1765. p. 218. 1774. p. 357.) Extract of an eſſay, intituled, „on the uſes of a knowledge of mineral exhalations when applied to diſcover the principles and properties of mineral waters, the nature of burning fountains and of thoſe poiſonous lakes, which the ancients called Averni. (Ibid. 1765. p. 236.) Conſiderations on the means of preventing the communication of peſtilential contagion. 1771. 4. (1 ſh 6 d.) Of the ſtilling of waves by means of oil. (Phil. Transact. 1774. p. 445.) On ſome ſpecimens of native ſalts. (Ibid. 1774. p. 480.)

BRUCE, [James] *of Kinnaird, Esq. F. R. S.*

Some obſervations upon Myrrh, made in Abyſſinia in the Year 1771. (Phil. Transact. 1775. p. 408.) Travels to diſcover the ſource of the nile in the Year 1768 - 1773. containing a yourney through Egypt, the three Arabias and Ethiopia —. Vol. 1 - 5.

 1790.

1790. 4. (5 L. 5 ſh.) überſ. von *J. J. Volkmann*, mit Zuſ. u. Anmerk. von *J. F. Blumenbach*. Th. 1. 2. 1790. 8.

BRUCE, [John] *A. M: F. R. S. of Edinb. Profeſſor of Logic in the Univerſity of Edinburgh.*

First principles of philoſophy. 1780. 8. (2 ſh. 6 d.) *Ed.* 2. 1782. 8. (3 ſh.) *Ed.* 3. 1785. 8. (3 ſh) überſ. von *K. G. Schreiter* 1788. 8. Elements of ſcience of Ethics. 1786. 8. (5 Sh.]

BRUCE. [Robert] *M. D.*

Account of the ſenſitive quality of the tree Averrhoa Carambola. (Phil. Transact. 1785. p. 356. überſ. Samml. zur P. u. N. G. Th. 3. S. 659.)

BRUCKSHAW, [....]

One more proof of the iniquities of private madhouſes. 1774. 8. (1 Sh. 6 d.)

BRUEN, [Lewis]

A Book of truly chriſtian pſalms, anthems and a chant —. 1788. 12. (1 Sh.)

BRUMWELL, *Surgeon in the Suſſex militia.*

Dangerous effects from eating a quantity of ripe berries of Belladonna. (Med. Obſ. Vol. 6. p. 222.)

BRYANT, [Charles] *Norwich.*

Account of two ſpecies of Lycoperdon —. 1782. 8. (2 Sh.) Flora Diaetetica: or, hiſtory of eſculent plants, both domeſtic and foreign. 1783. 8. (6 Sh) überſ. Th. 1. 2. Leipz. 1786. 8.

—— [Henry] *A. M: Rector of Colby and Vicar of Langham, Norfolk.*

Enquiry — of the diſeaſe in wheat called brand —. 1783. 8. (1 ſh.)

—— [James] *Esq.*

Obſervations on ancient hiſtory. 1767. 4. (15 Sh.) aus dieſer überſ. von den Menſchenopfern der Alten (von *C. F. Michaelis*). Gött. u. Gotha. 1774. 8. *Vindication of the Apamean medal. 1775. 4. (1 Sh.) New ſyſtem or an Analyſis of ancient mythology. Vol. 1-3. 1776. (3 L. 6 Sh.) Vindiciae Flavianae; or a vindication of the teſtimony given by Joſephus concerning our Saviour Jeſus Chriſt. 1780. (1 ſh. 6 d.) *Addreſſ to *Prieſtley* upon his doctrine of philoſophical neceſſity illuſtrated. 1780. 8. (2 Sh.) Obſervations on the poems of Thomas *Rowley*. Vol. 1. 2. 1781. 8. (8 Sh. 6 d.)

Colle-

Collections on the Zingara or Gypfey language. (Arch. Vol. 7. p. 387.) *Gemmarum antiquarum delectus ex praeftantioribus defumtus in dactyliotheca Ducis Marlburienfis. Vol. 1. fol. 1783.

BRYANT, [William] *Esq.*

Account of an electrical eel, or the torpedo of Surinam. (Tr. of A. S. Vol. 2. p. 166.)

BRYDGES, [S Egerton] *Esq.*

Sonnets and other poems. 1785. 8. (2 fh. 6 d.)

BRYDONE, [Patrick] *Esq. F. R. S: F. A. S.*

Inftance of a palfy cured by electricity. (Phil. Transact. 1760. p. 392.) Effects of electricity in the cure of fome difeafes. (Ibid. 1760. p. 695.) Tour through Sicily and Malta. Vol. 1. 2. 1773. (12 fh.) überf. Th. 1. 2. Leipz. 1774. Aufl. 2. Th. 1. 2. Leipz. 1777. 8. Account of a fiery Meteor, feen on the 10th of Febr. 1772. and alfo of fome new electrical experiments. (Phil. Transact. 1773. p. 163.) Account of a thunder-ftorm in Scotland; with fome meteorological obfervations. (Ibid. 1787. p. 61.)

BRYMMER, [Alexander] *Surgeon at Stirling.*

Account of the happy effects of a feton in the fide (Med. Com. of Ed. Vol. 3. p. 422.)

BRYSON, [James] *A. M.*

Sermons on feveral important fubjects. 1778.

BUCHAN, [William] *M. D. at London.*

Diff. de infantum vita confervanda. Edinb. 8. 17.. Domeftic medicine; or, on the prevention and cure of difeafes by regimen and fimple medicines. Ed. 2. 1772. 8. (7 fh.) überf. Altenb. 1774. 8. Ed. 9. 17.. Caution concerning cold bathing, and drinking the mineral waters. 1786. 8. (6 d.)

— Earl of, fee *David Erskine.*

BUCHANAN, [George] *M. D. Prefident of the Roy. Phyf. Soc. of Edinb. and Member of the Amer. Philof. Soc.*

On the typhus fever. 1789. 8. (1 fh.)

BUKINGTON, [Nathaniel] *Esq. Barrifter at Law.*

Confiderations on the political conduct of Lord *North* —. 1783. 8. (2 fh.)

BULKELEY, [Charles] *Methodiftical Preacher.*

Difcourfes —. 1752. 8. (5 fh.) Vindication of Lord *Shaftsbury*, on the fubjects of morality and religion.

gion. 1752. 8. (1 ſh. 6 d.) Two diſcourſes on catholic communion. 1755. 8. (1 ſh.) Notes on the philoſophical writing of Lord *Bolingbroke*. 1755. 8. (2 ſh. 6 d.) Obſervations upon natural religion and chriſtianity. 1757. 8. (1 ſh 6 d.) Sermons on public occaſions. 1760. 8. (5 ſh.) The oeconomy of the goſpel in 4 books. 1765. 4. (10 ſh. 6 d.) Diſcourſes on the parables of our bleſſed ſaviour and the miracles of his holy goſpel. Vol. 1-4. 1771. 8. (1 L.) Catechetical exerciſes. 1774. 8. (3 ſh.) (ſeveral ſingle ſermons.)

BULLER, [Francis] *Esq. Judge of the Court of King's Bench.*

Introduction to the law relative to trials at niſi prius. 1772. 4. (18 ſh.)

BULLIVANT, [Daniel] *Surgeon at Oakham, Rutlandſhire.*

Caſe of violent ſpaſms which ſucceded the amputation of an arm. (Med. Com. of Ed. Vol. 4. p. 447.)

BURDER, [George]

Evangelical truth defended —. 1788. 8. (6 d.) Pilgrim's progreſſ by *John Bunyan*, a new edition with notes. 1786. 12. (3 ſh. 6 d.)

BUREAU, [James] *Surgeon at Aldermanbury.*

On the eryſipelas, or that diſorder commonly called St. Anthony's fire. 1777. 8. (1 ſh.) Caſe of an ileus, with obſervations on an hydraulic machine. (Mem. of M. S. of L. Vol. 2.)

BURGES, [James Bland] *Barriſter at Law and Member of Parliament.*

(He aſſiſt in the Houſe of Commons the cauſe of Mr. Haſtings.)

Conſiderations on the law of inſolvency. 1783. 8. (5 ſh.) Letter to the Earl of Effingham on his lately propoſed act of inſolvency. 1783. 8. (2 ſh.) Addreſſ to the country Gentlemen of England and Wales. 1780. 8. (1 ſh. 6 d.)

BURGESS, [....] *Mrs.*

The oaks, or the beauties of Canterbury. a Comedy. 1780. 8.

—— [Thomas] *of Corpus Chriſti College, Oxford. Domeſtic Chaplain to the Lord Biſhop of Salisbury.*

John Burton's pentalogia ſ. tragoediarum graecarum delectus —. Vol. 1. 2. 1780. 8. (10 ſh. 6 d.)

Mich.

Mich. Dawes Miſcellanea critica, iterum edita —. 1781. 8. (7 ſh) *Eſſay on the ſtudy of antiquities. Ed. II. 1783. 8. (2 ſh. 6 d.) Conſpectus criticarum obſervationum in ſcriptores graecos et latinos ac locos antiquae eruditionis edendarum una cum enarrationibus, collationibusque veterum codicum Mſtorum et ſylloge anecdotorum graecorum. 1788. 8. Initia Homerica ſ. excerpta ex Iliade *Homeri* cum locorum omnium graeca metaphraſi, ex codicibus Bodlejanis et Novi Collegii Mſſ. majorem in partem nunc primum edita. 1788. 8. (2 ſh. 6 d.) Remarks on *Joſephus's* account of Herod's rebuilding of the temple at Jeruſalem. 1788. 8. (2 ſh. 6 d.) *Tractatus varii latini a *Crevier*, *Brotier*, *Auger* aliisque — conſcripti et ad rem, cum criticam tum antiquariam, pertinentes —. 1788. 8. *Conſiderations on the abolition of ſlavery and the ſlave trade upon grounds of natural, religious and political duty. 1789. 8. (2 ſh. 6 d.)

BURGH, [James] *Maſter of an Academy at Newington Green.*

born at *Madderty in Pertſhire* 1714. died d. 26. Aug. 1775.

— [William]

Inquiry into the belief of the chriſtians of the firſt three centuries reſpecting the godhead —. 1778. 8. (6 ſh. 6 d) Scriptural confutation of the arguments againſt the one godhead of the father, ſon and holy ghoſt —. 1774. 8. (3 ſh.)

BURGOYNE, [Bourgoyne] John; *Member of Parliament: Lieutenant General and privy Counſellor of Ireland.*

*The maid of the oaks: a dramatic entertainment. 1774. 8. (1 ſh. 6 d.) The ſubſtance of his ſpeeches —. 1778. 8. (1 ſh.) Letter to his conſtituents on his late reſignation with the correſpondences between the ſecretaries of war and him —. 1779. 8. (1 ſh.) State of the expedition from Canada; with ſupplement, containing orders, reſpecting the principal movements and operations of the army, to the raiſing of the ſiege of Ticonderoga. 1780. 4. (14 ſh.) Ed. 2. 17.. *The Lord of the Manor, a comic opera. 1781. 8. (1 ſh. 6 d.) The Heireſſ a

Comedy. 1785. 8. Richard coeur de Lion; an Opera. translated from the French. 1786. 8.

BURKE, [Edmund] *LL. D. Member of Parliament*. born in Ireland.

*Vindication of natural ſociety. 1756. 8. (1 ſh. 6 d.) *Account of the European Settlements in America. 1757. 8. Vol. 1. 2. (8 ſh.) Ed. 3. 1760. 8. überſ. (von *Sam. Wilh. Turner*) Th. 1–4. Danzig 1781. *Enquiry into the origin of our ideas of the ſublime and beautiful: 1757. 8. (3 ſh.) Ed. 5. 17.. überſ. von *Ch. Garve*, Riga 1773. 8. Thoughts on the cauſe of the preſent diſcontents. 1770. 8. (2 ſh. 6 d.) Speech on american taxation. 1774. 4. (2 ſh. 6 d.) 8. (2 ſh.) Speeches at his arrival at Briſtol and at the concluſion of the poll. 1774. 4. (6 d.) Speech on moving his reſolutions for conciliation with the colonies. 1775. 4. (2 ſh. 6 d.) De Tumultibus Americanis, deque eorum concitatoribus. 1776. 8. (1 ſh.) Letters on the affairs of America. 1777. 8. (1 ſh. 6 d.) Two letters relative to the trade of Ireland. 1778. 8. (1 ſh.) Speech on the independency of Parliament and the oeconomical reformation of the civil and other eſtabliſhments. 1780. 8. (2 ſh.) Speech in the houſe of commons on his motion for a plan of public oeconomy. 1780. 8. (1 ſh. 6 d.) *Letter from a gentleman in the engliſh houſe of commons in vindication of his conduct, with regard to the affairs of Ireland. 1780. 8. (1 ſh. 6 d.) Speech upon certain points relative to his parliamentary conduct. 1780. 8. (1 ſh 6 d.) Speech — on *Fox's* eaſt India bill. 1783. 8. (2 ſh.) überſ. (von *J. M. Sprengel*) Hiſtor. Portefeuille. 1784. S. 75. A repreſentation to his majeſty. 1784. 4. (1 ſh 6 d.) Speech on the Nabob of Arcot's debts to Europeans, on the revenues of the Carnatic. 1785. 8. (3 ſh. Charges againſt *Haſtings*. P. 1 - 4. 1786. 8. (8 ſh.) Letter to *Philip Francis*. 1788. 8. (1 ſh.) Subſtance of his ſpeech, in the Debate on the Army eſtimates in the Houſe of Commons the 9 Febr. 1790. comprehending a diſcuſſion of the preſent ſituation of affairs in France. 1790. 8. Reflections on the revolution in France and on the proceedings in certain ſocieties in London relative to that event, in in a letter intended to have been ſent to a gentleman in Paris. 1790. 8.

BURKE, [John] *M. D.*

Translation of *Tiſſot's* letter to *Zimmermann* on the morbus niger. 1776. 8. (1 ſh. 6 d.)

BURMAN, [Charles]

The lives of thoſe eminent antiquaries, *Elias Aſhmole*, and *William Lilly* — with *Lilly's* life and death of Charles I. 1774. 8. (6 ſh.)

BURN, [....]

* Miſcellany ſermons, extracted chiefly from the works of divines of the laſt century. Vol. 1-4. 1773. 8. (1 L.) überſ. Th. 1-3. Halle 1778. 8.

— [A....] *Teacher of the mathematics in Tarporley, Cheſhire.*

Geodoeſia improved. 1771. Ed. 2. P. 1. 2. 1775. 8. (6 ſh.)

— [Edward] *A. B.*

Letters to Dr. *Prieſtley* on the infallibility of the apoſtolic teſtimony concerning the perſon of Chriſt. 1790. 8. (1 ſh.)

— [Richard] *LL. D: Vicar of Orton, in the county of Weſtmoreland.*

born at Winton in Weſtmoreland 17.. died d. 20 Nov. 1785.

BURNABY, [Andrew] *D. D. Vicar of Eaſt Greenwich, Kent and Archdeacon of Leiceſter.*

Travels through the middle ſettlements in North-America in the Years 1759 and 1760. with obſervations upon the ſtate of the Colonies —. 1775. 4. (3 ſh. 6 d.) überſ. (von C. D. *Ebeling*). Hamb. u. Kiel 1776. 8. (ſeveral ſingle ſermons.)

BURNBY, [John]

Hiſtorical deſcription of Canterbury Cathedral. 17.. Addreſſ to the people of England on the increaſe of their poor rates. 1780. 8. (1 ſh.) Summer amuſement; or, miſcellaneous poems. 1783. 8. (2 ſh. 6 d.) Thoughts on the freedom of election. 1784. 8. (6 d.)

BURNE, [James]

The man of nature. translated from the french. Vol. 1. 2. 1773. 12. (5 ſh.)

BURNET, [....] *Judge.* (Son of the Biſhop *Burnet.*)

Verſes

Verses written on several occasions between the Years 1712 and 1721. 1777. 4. (2 sh. 6 d.)

BURNET, [George]

A short catechism — on some of the main points of the christian religion. 1773. 12. (6 d.)

—— [James] Lord *Monboddo. One of the Lord of Session for the Kingdom of Scotland.*

* On the origin and progress of language. Vol. 1-4. 1773-1787. (1 L. 4 sh.) übers. von *F. A. Schmidt* Th. 1. 2. Riga 1785. 8. * Ancient metaphysics; or the science of Universals. Vol. 1-3. 1779-1784. 4. (1 L. 11 sh.)

BURNEY, [Charles] *D. Mus. F. R. S.*

The cunning man, a musical entertainment. 1766. 8. Present state of Music in France and Italy; or the journal of a tour through those countries. 1771. 8 (5 sh.) Ed. 2. 1773. 8. (6 sh.) * Translation of Sign. *Tartini's* letter to Sign. *Lombardini* published as an important lesson to performers on the violin. 1771. 4. (1 sh.) Present state of Music in Germany, the Netherlands and united provinces, or the journal of a tour through those countries. Vol. 1. 2. 1773. 8. (10 sh.) übers. Tagebuch seiner musikalischen Reisen von *C. D. Ebeling* u. *Bode.* Hamb. 1773. 8. Th. 1-3. General History of Music, from the earliest ages to the present period with a dissertation on the music of the antients. Vol. 1-4. 1776-1789. 4. (5 L. 5 sh.) übers. Ueber die Musik der Alten, von *J. J. Eschenburg.* 1781. Leipz. 4. Account of the musical performances in Westminster Abbey in Commemoration of *Handel.* 1785. 4. (1 L. 1 sh.) übers. von *J. J. Eschenburg.* Berlin u. Stettin 1785. 8. Account of an infant musician. (Phil. Transact. 1779. p. 183.)

—— [Frances] *Miss.* (Daughter of *Charles Burney* D. Mus.) *Keeper of the Robes to her Majesty.*

* Evelina; or a young lady's entrance into the world. 1778. 8. Vol. 1-3. (9 sh.) übers. Leipz. 1783. 8. neu bearbeitet u. abgekürzt von *Brömel.* Berlin. 1789. 8. * Cecilia, or memoirs of an heiress. 1785. 8. Vol. 1-5. (15 sh.) * *Georgina.* 17.. übers. Tübingen. 1790. 8.

BURNS, [Robert] *A Ploughman in the county of Ayr at Scotland.*

Poems,

Poems, chiefly in the ſcottiſh dialect. 1786. 8. Ed. 2. 1787. 8. (6 ſh.)

BURROW, [James] *Sir. Knight, Maſter of the Crown-Office*: *F. R. S*: *F. A. S*:
born .... died d. 5 Nov. 1782.

— [Reuben] *Esq.*
Reſtitution of the geometrical treatiſe of *Apollonius Pergaeus* on inclinations; alſo the theory of gunnery —. 1779. 4. (2 ſh.) Hints relative to friction in Mechanics. (Aſiat. Reſ. Vol. 1. p 171.) Method of calculating the moon's parallaxes, in latitude and longitude. (Ibid. p. 320.) Remarks on the artificial horizons —. (Ibid p. 327.) Demonſtration of a theorem concerning the interſections of curves. (Ibid. p. 330.) Corrections of the lunar method of finding the longitude. (Ibid. p. 433.)

BURROWES, [Robert] *A. M. and M. R. J. A.*
On the ſtile of *Sam. Johnſon*. (Tr. of J. A. 1787. p. 27.)

BURT, [Adam] *Surgeon.*
A tract on the biliary complaints of europeans in hot climates, founded on obſervations in Bengal and conſequently deſigned to be particularly uſeful to thoſe in that country. Calcutta. 1785. 8.

BURTENSHAW, [....]
Letter to — the Earl of *Mansfield*. 1781. 4. (10 ſh. 6 d.) Specimens of juſtice, humility and uniformity —. 1782. 4. (3 ſh.)

BURTON, [Edmund] *A. M.*
The ſatyrs of *Perſius*, translated into Engliſh. 1752. 4. (3 ſh.) Antient characters deduced from claſſical remains. 1764. 8. (4 ſh.) Manilii aſtronomicon Lib. V. 1783. 8. (5 ſh.)

— [George] *M. A. Rector of Eldon in Suffolk.*
Analyſis of two chronological tables — the one being a table to aſſociate ſcripturally the different chronologies of all ages and nations, the other, to ſettle the paſcha feaſt from the beginning to the end of time. 1787. 4. (2 ſh 6 d,)

— [John] *D. D: of Eton.*
born at Wembworth in Devonſhire 1696. died d. 10 Febr. 1771.

— [John] *M. D*: *F. A. S.*
Caſe of the extirpation of an excreſcence from the womb.

womb. (Phil. Transact. 1756. p. 520.) Account of a roman sepulchre, found near York 1768. (Arch. Vol. 2. p. 177.) Extract of two letters concerning the roman antiquities discovered in Yorkshire. (Ibid. p. 181.)

BURTON, [Philip] *Secondary and first Attorney in the court of Exchequer.*

Nature and extent of the businesſ in the exchequer office of pleas —. Vol. 1. 1770. 8. (7 ſh. 6 d.)

—— [Philippina]

Faſhion diſplayed. a Comedy. 1770.

—— [William]

Superſtition, fanaticiſm and faction; a poem. 1781. 4. (1 ſh.)

BUSBY, [Thomas]

The age of genius! a ſatire on the times. 1786. 4. (3 ſh.)

BUTLER, [Charles] *Esq.*

Sir *Edw. Coke's* commentary upon *Littleton* Ed. 13. with additions by *Franc. Hargrave* and *Charles Butler* —. 1788. fol. (3 L. 3 ſh.)

—— [James]

Juſtification of the tenets of the roman catholic religion —. 1787. 8. (2 ſh. 6 d.)

—— [Rachael]

The new London and country cook. 1779.

—— [William]

Introduction to Arithmetic —. 1785. 8. (2 ſh.)

BUTT, [George] *A. M: Rector of Stanford, Vicar of Clifton upon Teme and Chaplain to the Earl of Finlater.*

Sermon on Biſhop of Worceſter, *Johnſon's* death. 1775. 4. (1 ſh.) Iſaiah verſified. 1785. 8. (5 ſh.)

BUTTER, [William] *M. D: Phyſician at Derby.*

A method of cure for the ſtone, chiefly by injections. 1754. 8. (1 ſh. Diſſ. De frigore quatenus morborum cauſſa. Edinb. 1757. 8. Diſſ. De Arteriotomia. Edinb. 1761. 8. On the kinkcough with an appendix of Hemlot and its preparations. 1773. 8. (3 ſh.) überſ. von *J. C. F. Scherf.* Stendal. 1782. 8. Account of puerperal fevers in Derbyſhire. 1775. 8. (2 ſh. 6 d.) On the infantile remittent fever. 1782. 8. (1 ſh.) überſ. Samml. f. A. Th. 8. S. 347. * On opening the temporal artery

artery and new method for extracting the cataract. 1783. 8. (4 sh.)

BUTTERWORTH, [John] *Minister of the Gospel.*
A new concordance to the holy scriptures of the old and new testament —. 1767. 8. (6 sh.) Ed. II. 1785 8. (8 sh.)

— [Laur.]
The superexcellency of the christian religion displayed, or, on natural and revealed religion; with an answer to *Lindseys* argument against the divinity of the Lord Jesus Christ. 1784. 8. (2 sh.)

BUTTON, [William]
Remarks on *Andr Fuller's* treatise „The gospel of christ worthy of all acceptation. 1785. 12. (1 sh.)

BUXTON, [....] *Norfolk.*
On the most profitable method of managing light arable lands. (*Hunter's* G. E. Vol. 5. p. 199.) On claying land. (Ibid. Vol. 5. p. 260.)

BYROM, [John] *M. D. F. R. S.*
Remarks on Mr. *Jeake's* plan for short-hand. (Phil. Transact. 1755. p. 388.) Remarks on Mr. *Lodwick's* Alphabet. (Ibid. 1755. p. 401.) Miscellaneous poems. Vol. 1. 2. 1773. 8. (10 sh.)

BYRON, [John] *Admiral.*
born d. 8 Nov. 1732. died 1786.

CADE, [John] *Esq of Durham.*
On the roman roads and other antiquities in the county of Durham. (Arch. Vol. 7. p. 74.) Conjectures on the name of the roman station Vinovium or Binchester. (Ibid. Vol 7. p. 160.) Observations on the roman station Cataractonium with an account of antiquities in the neighbourhood of Piersbridge and Gainford. (Ibid. Vol. 9. p. 276.)

CADOGAN, [William] *M. D. at London.*
Oratio anniversaria Harvejana. 1764. 4. (1 sh. 6 d.) On the nursing and management of children. 17.. übers. 1782. 8. Dissertation on the gout and all chronic diseases. 1772. 8. (1 sh. 6 d.) übers. Frankf. u. Leipz. 1772. 1790. 8. ° Sermon on temperance and exercise by a physician. 1772. 8. (1 sh)

CAIRNCROSS, [Andrew] *Surgeon to the 73d regiment.*
A curious case of a — recovery — attended with a fracture of the cranium requiring the trephine, —

a coma compound fracture of the lover extremity, requiring amputation, and several other wounds. (*Duncan's* M. C. Vol. 8. p. 296.)

CALDECOTT. [Thomas] *of the Middle temple. Esq.* Reports of cases relative to the duty and office of a justice of the peace from 1776-1785. Vol. I. 2. 1789. 4. (19 Sh.)

CALDERWOOD, [Robert] *Surgeon, Dalkeith.* Account of the discharge of animals by the anus, much resembling the common caterpillar, and which were found to be the larva of an insect. (*Duncan's* M. C. Vol. 9. p. 223.)

CALDWELL. [James] *Sir. F. R. S.* Examination of the question whether papishs should take securities for money. 1764. (1 Sh.) Inquiry into the restrictions on the trade of Ireland. —. 1779. 8. (1 Sh. 6 d.)

CALEF, [John] *Agent for the inhabitants of Penobscot.* *The siege of Penobscot by the rebels in the July 1779 —. 1781. 8. (2 Sh. 6 d.)

CALEY, [John] *F. A. S.* On the origin of the jews in England. (Arch. Vol. 8. p. 389.) Extract from a Mscpt (*Wardrobe's* account of Henry VIII) in the augmentation office. (Ibid. Vol. 9. p. 243.)

CALL, [John] *Esq.* Sketch of the signs of the Zodiac, found in a pagoda, near Cape *Comorin* in India. (Philos. Transact. 1772. p. 353.)

CALLAM, [James] *Surgeon of his Majesty's ship Supply.* Letter containing an account of a voyage from the cape of good Cape to Botany-Bay with a description of the inhabitants and settlement of the Colony. 1789. 8. (6 d.)

CALLANDER, [James] *Colonel.* Military maxims —. 1782. 12. (2 Sh. 6 d.)

—— [John] *Esq. of Craighforth.* Two ancient scottish poems; the Gaberlunzie-Man and Christ's kirk on the green; with notes — 1785. 8. (2 Sh. 6 d.)

CAMBRIDGE, [Richard Owen] *Esq.* The scribleriad: an heroic poem. 1751. 4. (6 Sh.) Dialogue between a member of parliament and his servant. 1752. 4. (1 Sh.) The intruder, a poem. 1753.

1753. 4. (1 ſh.) *The Fakeer, a tale. 1756. 4. (6 ſh.) Account of the war in India, between the engliſh and french on the coaſt of Coromandel from the Year 1750–1760. 1760. 4. (1 L. 1 ſh.) (One of the original contributors to the World, a periodical paper by *Edw Moore*. Miſcellaneous poems in *Dodsley's* collection of poems.)

CAMERON, [Charles] *Architect.*
The baths of the romans explained and illuſtrated. 1772. fol. (4 L. 4 ſh.)

—— [Ewen]
The fingal of Oſſian, an ancient epic poem — now rendered into heroic verſe. 1777. 4. (15 ſh)

—— [John]
The Meſſiah. 1770. 8. (4 ſh.)

CAMMEL, [....] *Surgeon at Bungay in Suffolk.*
Caſe of an extrauterine foetus. (Lond. M. J. Vol. 5. p. 396.)

CAMPBELL, [A....] *M. D. Phyſician, Hereford.*
Account of the ſucceſſful treatment of a caſe of hydrocephalus, by Mercurials. (*Duncan's* M. C. Vol. 9. p. 240.)

—— [Alexander]
*The Hiſtory of Dover Caſtle, by *Will. Darell*, Chaplain to Queen Elizabeth —. 1780. fol. (1 ſh. 6 d.)

—— [David] *M. D.*
Obſervations on the typhus —. 1785. 8. (2 ſh.) überſ. von *A. F. A. Diel.* Altenb. 1788. 8.

—— [George] *D. D. Principal of the Mariſhall College at Aberdeen. F. R. S.*
Diſſertation on miracles, containing an examination of the principles advanced by *Dav. Hume.* 1762. 8. (4 ſh.) The philoſophy of rhetorik. Vol. 1. 2. 1776. 8. (12 ſh.) *John Farquhar's* ſermons on various ſubjects — corrected from the Author's Manuſcripts by *G. Campbell* and *Alex. Gerard* D. D. Prof. of Divinity in King's College Aberdeen. Vol. 1. 2. 1772. 8. (7 ſh.) Addreſſ to the people of Scotland upon the alarms that have been raiſed in regard to popery. 1779. 8. (1 ſh.) The IV Goſpels, translated — with diſſertations and notes. Vol. 1. 2. 1789. 4. (2 L. 2 ſh.) (ſeveral ſingle ſermons.)

CAMPBELL, [John] *LL. D.*
born at Edinburgh, 1708. died d. 28 Dec. 1775.

—— [Ivie] *near Inverary.*
Account of a ſewing needle lodged in the breaſt of a woman being removed by incision. (*Duncan's* M. C. Vol. 9. p. 275.)

—— [Thomas] *LL. D. Chancellor of St. Macartins Clogher.*
Sermon, for the ſupport of 12 boys and 8 Girls —. 1780. 4. (1 ſh.) Strictures on the eccleſiaſtical and literary hiſtory of Ireland —. 1790. 8.

—— [William] *D. D. diſſenting Miniſter of Armagh in Ireland.*
Vindication of the principles and character of the presbyterian of Ireland. Ed. 3. 1787. 8. (1 ſh. 6 d.) Examination of the Biſhop of *Cloyne's* defence of his principles. 1788. 8. (ſeveral ſingle ſermons.)

CANNING, [George] *Esq. of the Middle Temple.*
born in Ireland 17.. died d. 11 Apr. 1771.

CANTON, [John]
born at Strout, Glouceſterſhire 1718. died d. 22 March. 1772.

—— [John] *late private ſecretary to the Marquis of Rockingham.*
The adventures of Telemachus the ſon of Ulyſſes; translated into blank verſe. 1788. 4. (2 ſh.)

CAPEL, [Edward] *Esq. Deputy Inſpector of Plays.*
born.... died d. 24 Febr. 1781.

CAPPER, [James] *Colonel in the ſervice of the Eaſt-India Company.*
Obſervations on the paſſage to India through Egypt and acroſſ the great deſert. 1784. 4. (7 ſh. 6 d.) überſ. *Sprengel's* Beytr. zur Völker und Länderk. Th 4 S. 183.

CARDALE, [Paul] *Diſſenting Clergyman at Evesham Worceſterſhire.*
born 1705. died d. 1 March. 1775.

CARDONNEL, [Adam de] *Member of the Antiquarian Society of Edinburgh.*
Numismata Scotiae; or a ſeries of the ſcottiſh coinage, from the reign of William the Lion, to the union. 1786. 4. (1 L. 1 ſh.) Picturesque antiquities of Scotland. Vol. 1. 2. 1788. 8. (18 ſh.)

CAREY, [George Savile] *Printer.*
The inoculator, a Comedy. 1766. 8. The cottagers,

tagers, an Opera. 1766. 8. Liberty chaſtiſed, or, patriotiſm in chains. 1768. 8. *Shakeſpeare's* jubilee. 1769. 8. The three old women weather wiſe. 1770. 8. The magic girdle. 1770. 4. The nut brown maid, a comic opera. 1770. 8. *Poems, written in the time of Oliver Cromwell. 1771. 4. (1 Sh. 6 d.) *Analects, in verſe and proſe. 1771. 8. (2 Sh.) Lecture on mimickry. 1776. 12. (1 Sh.) A rural ramble: with a poetical tagg; or Brighthelmſtone guide. 1777. 8. (2 Sh.) Poetical efforts. 1787. 8. (2 Sh.)

CARLISLE, Earl of, ſee HOWARD.

CARMICHAEL. [James] *Surgeon at Port-Glaſgow.* Hiſtory of a puerperal affection terminating in a diſcharge of pus from the umbilicus. (Med. Com. of Ed. Vol. 4. p. 445.) Hiſtory of a caſe, in which the left arm of a child was torn off by a milt, without any ſucceeding haemorrhage. (Ibid. Vol. 5. p. 79.)

CARPENTER, [B....]
Four ſermons on conformity to the world. 1790. 8. (1 Sh. 6 d.)

CARR, [John] *Maſter of the ſchool at Hertford.*
Epponina, a dramatic entertainment. 1765. 8. Translation of the dialogues of Lucian. Vol. 1-3. 1786. 8. (9 Sh.)

— [Samuel]
Eugenia, a Tragedy. 1770. 8.

CARROL, [....] *D. D.*
Addreſſ to the roman catholics of the united ſtates of North-America —. 1787. 8. (1 Sh. 6 d.)

CARTER, [Francis] *Esq. F. A. S.*
born .... died at Woodbridge, Suffolk. d. 1 Aug. 1783.

— [Francis] *M. D.*
Account of the various ſyſtems of medicine, from the days of *Hippocrates*, to the preſent time collected from the beſt latin, french and engliſh authors, particularly from the works of *John Browne*, M. D. Vol. 1. 2. 1788. 8. (10 Sh. 6 d.)

— [John]
Short ſtrictures on infant baptiſm —. 1780. The reviewer reviewed; or a reply to Mr. *Will. Richard's* review on infant baptiſm —. 1781. 8. (1 Sh.)

(1 Sh.) Remarks on *Will. Richard's* „observations on infant ſprinkling. 1782. 8. (1 Sh.)

CARTER, [Laudon] *of Sabine-Hall, Virginia.*
Obſervations concerning the fly-weevil, that deſtroys the wheat, with ſome uſeful diſcoveries and concluſions, concerning the propagation and progreſſ of that inſect and the methods to be uſed to prevent the deſtruction of the grain by it. (Tr. of A. S. Vol. 1. p. 205.)

—— [William] *Lieutenant of the 40th regiment of foot.*
Detail of the ſeveral engagements, poſitions — of the royal american armies during the Years 1775 and 1776 —. 1784. 4. (2 Sh. 6 d.)

—— [William] *Med. D. at Canterbury.*
Examination of *Cadogan's* diſſertation on the gout and chronic diſeaſes 1771. 8. (1 Sh.) Caſe of a locked jaw. (Med. Transact. Vol. 2. p. 39.)

CARTERET, [Philip] *Captain of the Swallowſloop.*
Letter on the inhabitants of the coaſt of Patagonia. (Phil. Transact. 1770. p. 20.) Letter on a Camelopardalis found about the cape of good hope. (Ibid. 1770. p. 27.)

CARTWRIGHT, [....] *Mrs.*
*Armine and Elvira; a legendary tale. 1771. 4. (2 Sh.) Letters on female education —. 1777. 12. (2 Sh.) Memoirs of Lady *Eliza Audley*. Vol. 1. 2. 1779. 12. (5 Sh.) The generous ſiſter. Vol. 1. 2. 1779. 12. (5 Sh.) *The Prince of peace and other poems. 1779. 4. (2 Sh. 6 d.) Letters moral and entertaining. 1781. 8. (3 Sh.) The duped guardian: or the amant malade. Vol. 1. 2. 1785. 12. (5 Sh.) The platonic marriage, a novel. Vol. 1-3. 1786. 12. (9 Sh.) Retaliation; or the hiſtory of Sir Edward Oſwald and Lady Frances Seymour; a novel. Vol. 1-4. 1787. 12. (10 Sh.)

—— [Charles] *Deputy Accomptant to the Eaſt-India Company.*
Abſtract of the orders and regulations of the court of directors of the Eaſt-India Company — to the pains and penalties the commanders and officers of ſhips in the Company's ſervice are liable to, for breach of Orders, illicit trade — 1788. 8. (5 Sh.)

—— [John] *Major of the Northamptonſhire Militia.*
*American independence the intereſt and glory of great

Great Britain. 1774. 8. (1 Sh. 6 d.) Ed. II. 1775. 8. (2 Sh. 6 d.) *Take your choice. 1776. 8. (1 Sh. 6 d.) Ed. 2. (with the author name and with the title) The legislative rights of the commonalty vindicated; or take your choice. 1777. 8. (3 Sh. 6 d.) The legislative rights of the commonalty vindicated. 1778. (3 Sh. 6 d.) Letter to the *Earl* of *Abingdon*, difcuffing a pofition relative to a fundamental right of the conftitution, contained in his lordfhips thoughts on the letter of *Edmund Burke*. 1778. 8. (1 Sh.) The people's barrier againft undue influence and corruption —. 1780. 8. (2 Sh. 6 d.) Give us our rights or a letter to the electors of Middlefex —. 1782. 8. (1 Sh.) Internal evidence; or an inquiry how far truth and the chriftian religion have been confulted by the author of „Thoughts on a parliamentary reform„ 1784. 8. (1 Sh. 6 d.)

CARVER, [John] *Captain of a Company of provincial troops during the late War with France.*
born at Stittwater in New-England 1732. died 1780.

CARWITHIN, [William] *A. B.*
The feafons of life, a poem. 1786. 8. (5 Sh.)

CARY, [Henry Francis] (born 1772.)
Ode to General Elliot 1787. 4. Sonnets and odes. 1788. 4. (1 Sh. 6 d.)

CARYSFORT, Lord, fee *Proby*.

CASE, [Charles] *M. A.*
Sermons on primitive chriftianity —. 1774. 12. (3 Sh. 6 d.)

CATLOW, [Samuel] *of Mansfield.*
Addreff to the diffenters on the fubject ef their political and civil liberty, as fubjects of Great Britain. 1788. 8. A proteftant catechifin for the ufe of young perfons translated from french. 1789. 8. (6 d.)

CAVENDISH, [Henry] *F. R. S: F. A. S.*
Experiments on factitious air. (Phil. Transact. 1766. p. 141.) Experiments on Rathbone — place water. (Ibid. 1767. p. 92.) Attempt to explain fome of the principal phaenomena of electricity, by means of an elaftic fluid. (Ibid. 1771. p. 584.) On pointed conductors. (Ibid. 1773. p. 66.) Account

count of ſome attempts to imitate the effects of the torpedo by electricity. (Ibid. 1776. p. 196.) Account of the meteorological inſtruments uſed at the royal ſociety's houſe. (Ibid. 1776. p. 375.) Experiments on air. (Ibid. 1784. p. 119. p. 170. 1785. p. 372.) Experiments on *Hutchins's* experiments for determining the degree of cold at which Quickſilver freezes. (Ibid. 1783. P. 2.) Account of a new eudiometer. (Ibid. 1783. p. 106.) Account of experiments, relating to freezing mixtures. (Ibid. 1786. p. 241.) Account of experiments made by Mr. *John M' Nab* at *Albanyfort*, *Hudſonsbay*, relative to the freezing of nitrous and vitriolic acids. (Ibid. 1788. p. 166. überſ. *Gren* J. d. P. Th. 1. S. 113.) On the converſion of a mixture of dephlogiſticated and phlogiſticated air into nitrous acid, by the electric ſpark. (Ibid. 1788. p. 261. überſ. *Gren* J. d. P. Th. 1. S. 282.) On the height of the luminous arch which was ſeen on Febr. 23. 1784. (Ibid. 1790. p. 101.)

CAVERHILL, [John] *M. D: F. R. S.*

born .... died at Old-Melroſe, Roxburgſhire, d. 1 Sept. 1781.

CAUL, [Goverdhan]

On the litterature of the Hindus from the ſanſcrit with a ſhort commentary. (Aſiat. Reſ. Vol. 1. p. 340.)

CAULDWELL, [Ralph] *at Goodwickhall near Swaffham in Norfolk.*

On the deſcent of titles of honour, particularly baronies, through the female line: transſcribed from a Mſ. of *Sayntlowe Kniveton*, (Arch. Vol. 3. p. 285.)

CAULFIELD, [J....] *Esq. late Cornet of the Queen's Regiment of Dragoon guards*

The manners of paphos; or triumph of love. 1777. 4. (3 Sh.)

CAUSER, [John] *Surgeon at Stourbridge, in Worceſterſhire.*

Caſe of a fracture of the ſcull ſucceſsfully treated (Lond. M. J. Vol. VII. P. 2.)

CAUTY, [William] *Cabinetmaker.*

Natura, philoſophia et ars in concordia; or nature, philoſophy and art in friendſhip. 1772. 8. (2 Sh.)

CAWDLE, [Amy]

Legal attempt to enforce the practice of infant baptism being a copy of a petition to parliament — against the Anabaptists. 1786. 12. (6 d.)

CAWLEY, [Thomas] *M. D. late chief Surgeon to the forces in Jamaica.*

A case of inverted uterus successfully treated; two cases of the spontaneous evolution of the foetus; and an instance of the caesorean operation performed by a woman on herself. (London M. J. Vol. 6. p. 366.) Account of the dysentery, as it appeared amongst his Majesty's troops in Jamaica during the last war —. (Ibid. Vol. 7. P. 4. übers. Samml. f. A. Th. 12. S. 113.) A singular case of Diabetes, consisting entirely in the quality of the urine —. (Ibid. Vol. IX. P. 3. übers. Samml. f. A. Th. 13. S. 112.)

CAWTE, [R....] *of Croydon, in Surry.*

Academic lessons; comprizing a system of education particularly adapted to female Seminaries. 1786. 8. (2 Sh. 6 d.)

CELESIA, [....] *Mrs.* (daughter of *Dav. Mallet* Esq.)

* Almeida: a tragedy. 1771. 8. (1 Sh. 6 d.) * Indolence, a Poem. 1772. 4. (1 Sh.)

CHALMERS, [George]

Political annals of the present united colonies from their settlement to the peace of 1763. Vol. 1. 1779. 4. (1 L. 1 Sh.) Estimate of the comparative strength of Britain during the present and four preceding reigns — with *Justice Hale's* essay on population. 1782. 4. (5 Sh.) Ed. 2. 1786. 8. (3 Sh. 6 d.) Opinions on interesting subjects of public law and commercial policy arising from American independence —. 1784. 8. (3 Sh.) The life of *Daniel De Foe.* 1790. 8. (3 Sh.)

— [Lionel] *M. D: of Charlestown, South-Carolina.*

Observations on Opisthotonos and Tetanos. (Med. Obs. Vol. 1. p...) Essay on fevers —. 1768. 8. (2 Sh.) übers. Riga. 1773. 8. On the weather and diseases of South-Carolina. 1776. 8. Vol. 1. 2. (6 Sh.) übers. Th. 1. Stendal. 1788. 8.

CHALMERS, [William] *Surgeon in Edinburgh.*
A caſe of incarcerated hernia cured. (Med. Com. of Ed. Vol. 1. p. 413.)

CHALONER, [Charles]
The method of making whale-compoſt. (*Hunter's* G. E. Vol. 5. p. 225.) On feeding hogs with potatoes. (Ibid Vol. 5. p. 243.)

CHAMBERLAINE, [William] *Surgeon.*
On the efficacy of Stizolabium or cowhage in diſeaſes occaſioned by worms with obſervations on other anthelmintic medicines of the Weſtindies. 1784. 8. (1 ſh. 6 d) überſ. Altenburg. 1786. 8. Remarks on the ſolvent powers of Camphor. (Mem. of M. S. of L. Vol. 2.)

CHAMBERS, [Amelia] *Mrs.*
The ladies beſt companion, or a golden treaſure for the fair ſex; containing the whole arts of cookery, paſtry, confectionary, potting, pickling, preſerving — to which are added, every lady her own and family's phyſician. 1772. 8. (2 ſh.)

—— [William] *Sir. Knight. Knight of the Polar ſtar, Surveyor general of the board of Works and Treaſurer of the Royal Academy.*
Plans elevations, ſections and perſpective views of the gardens and buildings at Kew. 1762. fol. (2 L 2 ſh.) On oriental gardening. 1772. 4. (5 ſh.) überſ. (von *S. H. Ewald*) Gotha. 1775. 8. *W. Chamber's*, *W. Jones's* and other literary gentleman's aſiatic miſcellany, conſiſting of translations, imitations, fugitives pieces, original productions and extracts from curious publications. 1785. 8. (3 ſh.) Account of the ſculptures and ruins of Mavalipuram, a place, a few miles North of Sadras, and known to ſeamen by the name of the ſeven Pagodas. (Aſiat. Reſ. Vol. 1. p. 145.) Account of the Marratta ſtate; written in Perſian by a Munſhy, translated by *W. Chambers* — with M. *Caeſar Frederike's* voyages and travels into the Eaſt-Indies and beyond the Indies, Calcutta, 1787. 8. (2 ſh)

CHAMIER, [John] *Secretary to the military and political department of the Government at Madras.*
*Meteorological account of the weather at Madras from 1 June 1787 to 31 May 1788.

CHAM-

CHAMPION, [Joseph] *Esq.*
The progress of freedom, a poem. 1776. 4. (1 sh.) Poems; imitated from the Persian. 1787. 4. (2 sh. 6 d.) The poems of *Ferdosi*, translated from the Persian. Vol. 1. 1788. 4. (12 sh.)

— [Richard] *Esq.*
On the present situation of Great-Britain and the united states of America. 1784. 8. Comparative reflections on the past and present political, commercial and civil state of Great Britain. 1787. 8. (5 sh.)

CHANDLER, [Benjamin] *Surgeon.*
Case of a stone in the bladder. (London M. J. Vol. 5. p. 387.)

— [Bernhard] *M. D. Surgeon at Canterbury.*
On the present successfull and most general method of inoculation. 1767. 8. (1 sh.) On the various theories and methods of cure in apoplexies and palsies. 1785. 8. (3 sh.) übers. Leipzig. 1787. 8. Stendal. 1787. 8.

— [George] *Surgeon at London.*
On cataract, its nature, species, causes and symptoms —. 1775. 8. (2 sh. 6 d.) On the diseases of the eye and their remedies. 1780. 8. (3 sh.) übers. Leipz. 1782. 8.

— [John] *F. R. S. Apothecary at London.*
born 1700. died d. 12 Dec. 1780.

— [Richard] *D. D. Fellow of Magdalen College, Oxford. F. A. S.*
*Marmora Oxoniensia. 1764. fol. Jonian antiquities. 1769. fol. (1 L. 11 sh. 6 d.) Inscriptiones antiquae — in Asia minori et Graecia praesertim Athenis collectae. 1774. fol. (1 L. 5 sh.) Travels in Asia minor. 1775. 4. (15 sh.) übers. (von *H. C. Boje*) Leipz. 1776. 8. Travels in Greece —. 1776. 4. (16 sh.) übers. (von *H. C. Boje*) Leipz. 1777. 8.

CHAPMAN, [George] *A. M: Master of the grammar school of Dumfries.*
On education. 1773. 12. (3 sh.)

— [John] *D. D. Rector of Mersham and of Aldington.*
born 1704. died 1784.

— [Samuel] *M. D. of Sudbury in Suffolk.*
Pulmonary and other complaints, apparently suppor-

ported by fever, of the intermittent or remittent kind and cured by the bark, (M. C. Vol. 1. p. 260.)

CHAPMAN, [William] *A. M.*

The parriad addreſſ to the editor of Bellendene upon his preface. 1788. 4. (1 ſh. 6 d.)

CHAPONE, [....] *Mrs.*

* Letters on the improvement of the mind. Vol. 1. 2. 1773. 12. (6 ſh.) Miſcellanies in proſe and verſe. 1775. 12. (3 ſh.) Letter to a new married lady. 1777. 12. (6 d.)

CHAPPLE, [William] *of Exeter.*

Review of part of *Risdon's* Survey of Devon, containing the general deſcription of that county; with additions —. 1785. 4. (6 ſh.)

CHARFY, [Guiniad] *Esq.*

The fiſherman; or, the art of angling made eaſy. 1784. 8. (: ſh. 6 d.)

CHARLEMONT, [....] Earl of, *Preſident of the Roy. Iriſh Academy.*

Antiquity of the woollen manufacture in Ireland. (Tr. of J. A. 1787. p. 17.)

CHARLES, [R....] *Surgeon at Wincheſter.*

On the treatment of conſumptions. 1787. 8. (1 ſh.)

CHARLESWORTH, [J....] *M. A. late Fellow of Trinity College, Cambridge,*

Practical ſermons, ſelected and abridged from various authors. Vol. 1. 2. 1789. 8. (5 ſh. 6 d.) (ſeveral ſingle ſermons.)

CHARLETON, [Rice] *M. D: F. R. S: Phyſician to the General Hoſpital at Bath, Somerſetſhire.*

born .... died d. 23 Oct. 1788.

CHARSLEY, [W....] *M. D.*

On the cauſes of the general mortality by fevers —. 1783. 8. (1 ſh. 6 d.)

CHARTERS, [Samuel] *Miniſter of Wilton.*

Sermons. 1786. 8. (5 ſh.)

CHATTERTON, [Thomas]

born d. 20 Nov. 1752. died d. 24 Aug. 1770.

CHAVASSE, [Nicholas] *Surgeon at Walſall in Staffordſhire.*

Caſe of chronic dyſentery ſucceſſfully treated by large doſes of the vitrum Antimonii ceratum. (London M. J. Vol. 5. p. 297.) Account of a remarkable diſeaſe of the heart. (Ibid. Vol. 7. p. 407.

überſ. Samml. f. A. Th. XI. S. 692.) Miſcellanous obſervations on the medical and ſurgical uſes of cold water. (Ibid. Vol. 7. P. 2. überſ. Samml. f. A. Th. XII. S. 32.)

CHAVASSE, [William] *Surgeon at Burford, Oxfordſhire.*

History of a caſe of tetanus ſucceſſfully treated by the uſe of large doſes of Opium. *(Duncan's* M. C. Vol. 9. p. 374.)

CHAUNCY, [Charles] *D. D. Miniſter of the firſt church in Boſton, New-England.*

* The myſtery hid from ages and generations made manifeſt by the goſpel revelation — by one who wiſhes well to the whole human race. 1784. 8. (5 ſh.) Five Diſſertations on the ſcripture account of the fall and its conſequences. Boſton 1785. 8. (4 ſh.) The benevolence of the deity - conſidered. 1784. 8. (4 ſh.)

CHELSUM, [James] *D. D. Chaplain to the Lord Biſhop of Wincheſter, Rector of Droxford, Hants.*

* Remarks on the two laſt of Mr. *Gibbon's* Hiſtory of the decline and fall of the roman empire. 1776. 8. (1 ſh 6 d.) Ed. 2. (with the author's name) 1778. 8. (2 ſh. 6 d.) Reply to Mr. *Gibbon's* vindication of ſome paſſages in the XV and XVI Chapters of the hiſtory of the decline — of the roman empire —. 1785. 8. (2 ſh.)

CHESSHER, [Robert]

Account of a caſe of luxation of the os humeri, in which the reduction of the bone was facilitated by inducing ſickneſſ and faitneſſ by means of emetic tartar. (Lond. M. J. Vol. VIII. p. 189. überſ. Samml. f. A. Th. 12. S. 561.)

CHESTERFIELD, [Philip Dormer Stanhope, Earl of] born d. 22 Sept. 1694. died d. 24 March 1773.

CHESTON, [Richard Browne] *F. R. S: Surgeon to the Infirmary at Glouceſter.*

Pathological inquiries and obſervations in ſurgery from the diſſection of morbid bodies. 1766. 4. überſ. von *J. C. F. Scherf.* Gotha 1780. 8. Account of an oſſification of the thoracic duct. (Phil. Transact. 1780. p. 323. p. 546.) The caſe of Mr. *Holder* with ſome remarks on the exiſtence of polypoſe

lypose concretions in the heart. (Lond. M. J. Vol. VI. p. 225. übers. Samml. f. A. Th XI. S. 226.)

CHETWYND, [James] *Esq. Barrister at law.*
Treatise upon fines . . 1773. 4. (5 sh.)

CHILCOT, [Harriet] *Miss.* (now Mrs. *Meziere.*)
Elmar and Ethlinda, a tale. Adalba and Ahmora an indian tale: with other pieces 1783. 8. (3 sh.) Moreton Abbey or the fatal mystery. Vol. 1. 2. 1786. 8. (3 sh.)

CHISHOLM, [C....] *Surgeon at St. George's, Grenada.*
The history of a singular affection of the liver, which prevailed epidemically in some parts of the West-Indies. (*Duncan's* M. C. *Dec.* 2. Vol. 1. p. 353.)

CHRISTIE, [Thomas] *Member of the Med. and Antiq Soc. of Edinb.*
Observations on pemphigus. (Lond. M. J. Vol. X. P. 4.)

CHRISTIAN, [....] *Lieutenant.*
*Relation of the battle of Maxen, with a treatise on profiles —. translated by an Officer. 1785. 4. (12 sh.)

CHRYSEL, [Christopher]
Account of a new invention for constructing and setting boilers in fire engines, saltworks —. 1775. 8.

CHURCH, [J....] *M. A: F. M. S.*
Remarks on the ascaris lumbricoides. (Mem. of the M. S of L. Vol. 2.)

CHURCHMAN. [John] *Landsurveyor for the District of the Counties of Delaware and Chester and for part of Lancaster and Berks, Pensylvania.*
Addreß in support of the principles of the magnetic variation and their application in determining the longitude at sea. fol. 1789. Explanation of the magnetic atlas. 1790. 8. Addreß to the members of the different learned societies in Europe and America. fol. (1790.)

CHURCHYARD, [Thomas]
The worthines of Wales, a poem —. 1776. 8. (7 sh. 6 d.)

CHURTON, [Ralph] *M. A. one of his Majesty's preachers at Whitehall.*
Eight sermons on the prophecies respecting the destruction of Jerusalem. 1785. 8. (4 sh.) Sermon,

The

The will of God the ground and principle of civil as well as religious obedience. 1790. 8.

CLARE, [....] *Lord.*

* Faith a poem. 1774. 4. (1 ſh. 6 d.) Verſes addreſſed to the Queen. 1775. 4. (1 ſh.)

— [Peter] *Surgeon.*

On the cure of abſceſſes by cauſtic and on the treatment of wounds and Ulcers —. 1779. 8. (2 ſh. 6 d.) Ed. 2. 1780. überſ. Samml. f. A. Th. 6. S. 110. S. 626. Samml. f. W. A. St. 1. S. 1. On the Gonorrhoea. 1781. 8. (1 ſh.) Ed. 5. 1789. 8. (1 ſh.)

CLARK, [Alexander] *Gardener at Drumcrief in Scotland.*

View of the glory of the Meſſiah's kingdom —. 1763. 8. (2 ſh. 6 d.) Emblematical repreſentation of the paradiſe of God —. 1779. 8. (3 ſh.)

CLARK, [Ewan]

Miſcellaneous poems. 1779. 8.

— [George]

Vindication of the honour of god and of the rights of Men in a letter to Mr. de *Coetlogon*, occaſioned by the publication of Mr. *Edwards's* ſermon on the eternity of hell torments. 1789. 8. (6 d.) Defence of the unity of god in four letters to M. *Harper* —. 1790. 8. (2 ſh. 6 d.)

— [George] *Esq.*

The penal ſtatutes abridged and alphabetically arranged —. 1777. 8. (3 ſh.) Alphabetical epitome of the common law of England —. 1778. 8. (3 ſh. 6 d.) The game laws from King Henry III. to the preſent period —. 1786. 12. (3 ſh.) A defence of the unity of God in IV letters —. 1789. 8. (2 ſh. 6 d.)

— [Hugh] *Heraldic Engraver.*

H. Clark and *Thomas Wormull's* Introduction to Heraldry. 1775. 12. (2 ſh. Hiſtory of Knighthood containing the religious and military orders which have been inſtituted in Europe —. Vol. 1. 2. 1784. 8. (10 ſh 6 d.)

— [James] *Farrier.*

Obſervations upon the ſhoeing of horſes, with an anatomical deſcription of bones in the foot of a horſe. P. 1. 2. 1772. 8. (1 ſh. 6 d.) Ed. 2. 1776. 8. (3 ſh.) überſ. Leipz. 1777. 8. On the prevention

tion of diſeaſes incidental to horſes from bad management in regard to ſtables, food, water, air and exerciſe with obſervations on ſome of the ſurgical and medical branches of farriery. 1788. 8. (7 ſh. 6 d.) überſ. Wien. 1790. 8.

CLARK, [James] *Surgeon in Dominica.*
Hiſtory of an anevriſm of the crural artery with ſingular circumſtances. (*Duncan's* M. C. Dec. 2. Vol. 3. p. 326.) Hiſtory of caſes of abſceſſes in the liver, with obſervations on the effects of opening them. (Ibid. Dec. 2. Vol. 4. p. 317.) Hiſtory of a caſe of ſchirrous liver. (Ibid. Dec. 2. Vol. 4. p. 355.)

—— [John] *F. A. S. Scot.* (born in Scotland.)
Anſwer to *Will. Shaw* on the authenticity of the poems of Oſſian. 1781. 8. (1 ſh.) * The works of the Caledonian bards, tranſlated from the Galic. Vol. I. 1778. 8. (3 ſh.) Tranſlation of the adventures of Telemachus. 1773. 4. (1 ſh. 6 d.)

—— [John] *M. D. Phyſician at Newcaſtle.*
Obſervations on the diſeaſes in long voyages to hot countries, and particularly — in the Eaſt-Indies. 1773. 8. (6 ſh.) Obſervations on fevers, eſpecially thoſe of the continued type —. 1780. 8. (5 ſh.) Obſervations on the hepatitis. (Med. Com. of Ed. Vol. 5. p. 423.) Caſe of obſtructed ſecretion of urine. (Ibid. Vol. 6. p. .) On the influenza as it appeared at Newcaſtle upon Tyne. 1783. 8.

CLARKE, [Cuthbert] *Lecturer in experimental philoſophy.*
Theory and practice of husbandry — with a compendium of mechanics. 1777. 4. (10 ſh. 6 d.) A new complet ſyſtem of weights and meaſures —. 1789. 4. (1 ſh. 6 d.)

—— [Edward] *A. M. Rector of Pepperharrow in Surrey.* born .... died d. Nov. 1786.

—— [Henry]
Practical perſpective —. Vol. I. 1776. 8. (6 Sh.) The rationale of circulating numbers —. 1777. 8. (3 Sh. 6 d.) *Lorgna* on the ſummation of infinite converging ſeries with algebraic diviſors — tranſlated from the latin. 1780. 4. (10 Sh. 6 d.) Supplement. 1782. 4. (2 Sh. 6 d.)

CLARKE, [James] *Land-Surveyor.*
Survey of the lakes of Cumberland, Weſtmorland and Lancaſhire —. 1787. fol. (2 L. 5 Sh.) Ed. 2. 1790. fol. (1 L. 1 Sh.)

— [John] *Licentiate in Midwifery, of the royal college of phyſicians and Teacher in Midwifery in London.*
Eſſay on the epidemic diſeaſe of lying in women of the Years 1787 and 1788. 1788. 4. (2 Sh. 6 d.) (überſ. Samml. f. A. Th. 13. S. 161.) Two ſucceſſful caſes of delivery by the crotchet, in extreme deformity of the pelvis. (Lond. M. J. Vol. VII. P. 1. überſ. Journal für Geburtsh. St. 1. On the cauſe of the death of children when the umbilical cord is compreſſed during labour. (Ibid. Vol. VIII. P. 2.)

— [John] *Firſt-Lieutenant of Marines*
Narrative of the battle fought on the 17 June 1775. — on Bunker's hill near Charlestown in New-England —. 1775. 8. (1 Sh.)

— [Joſeph] *M. D. Phyſician to the lying in Hoſpital at Dublin. F. J. A.*
Obſervations on ſome cauſes of the exceſſ of the mortality of males above that of females. (Philoſ. Transact. 1786. p. 349. London M. J. Vol. IX. P. 2.) On the properties commonly attributed by medical writers to human milk on the changes it undergoes in digeſtion, and the diſeaſes ſuppoſed to originate from this ſource in infancy. (London M. J. Vol. XI. P. 1. Tr. of J. A. 1788.)

— [M... A...] *M. D. and Profeſſor of Midwifry.*
Directions for the management of Children, from the time of their birth to the age of ſeven Years. 1773. 8. (2 Sh.)

— [Samuel] *Teacher of the Mathematics.*
The laws of chance —. 1758. 8. (4 Sh) The britiſh gauger: or trader and officer's inſtructor in the royal revenue of the exciſe and cuſtoms —. 1761. 12. (5 Sh.) Introduction to the theory and practice of Mechanics —. 1764. 4. (6 Sh.) *Sentiments — for the coining of 40,000 pounds worth of ſilver. 1771. 8. (6 d.) Letter to *Rich. Price* containing a refutation of his treatiſe on reverſionary payments. 1777. 8. (2 Sh.)

CLARKE, [Thomas] *Surgeon at Market Harborough.*
A caſe of epilepſy ſucceſsfully treated. (London M. J. Vol. 1. p. 428. überſ. Samml. f. A. Th. 7. S. 201.)

—— [Thomas] *A. M. at Oxford and Gottingen.*
The Criſis of immediate concernments of the britiſh empire. 1786. 8. The ſecond edition of Junius Alter's letter to Mr. O'Leary with a ſhort examination into the firſt cauſes of the preſent lawleſſ ſpirit of the iriſh peaſantry and a plan of reform. 1787. 8.

—— [William] *M. A: Rector at Chicheſter.*
born at Haghman-Abbey, Shropſhire 1696. died d. 21 Oct. 1771.

CLARKSON, [T....] *M. A.*
° Eſſay on the ſlavery and commerce of the human ſpecies particularly the African. 1786. 8. (4 Sh.) Ed. 2. (with the author's name) 1788. (3 Sh.) On the impolicy of the African ſlave trade. 1788. 8. (2 Sh. 6 d.) On the comparative efficiency of regulation or abolition, as applied to the ſlave trade. 1789. (1 Sh. 6 d.) überſ. von *M. C. Sprengel.* Leipz. 1789. 8.

CLATER, [Francis] *Farrier at Newark.*
Every man his own farrier. 1783. 8. (5 Sh. 6 d.)

CLAVERING, [Robert] *Architect.*
On the conſtruction and building of Chimney's and the cauſes of their ſmoaking. 1779. 8. (2 Sh. 6 d.)

CLAYTON, [William] *Esq. of his Majeſty's Navy.*
An Account of Falkland Islands. (Phil. Transact. 1776. p. 99.)

CLEAVER, [E....] *of Whitwell, near York.*
Compariſon between red and white wheat. (*Hunter's* G. E. Vol. 5. p. 245.) On lime. (Ibid. Vol. 5. p. 246.) On preparing ſeed-wheat with oil. (Ibid. Vol. 5. p. 255.)

CLEGG, [James] *of Redivales, near Bury.*
Experiments on dying black. (Philoſ. Transact. 1774. p. 48.)

CLEGHORN, [George] *M. D: Profeſſor of Anatomy in Trinity College, Dublin.*
born at Grantar, near Edinburgh 1716. died d. Dec. 1789.

CLEGHORN,

CLEGHORN, [James] *M. B.*
Hiftory of an Ovarium, wherein were found teeth, hair and bones. (Tr. of I. A. 1787. p. 73.).

CLELAND, [John] *Esq.*
born 1709. died d. 23 Jan. 1789.

CLERKE, [William] *Sir, Baronet: Rector of Bury, Lancafterfhire.*
Thoughts on the means of preferving the health of the poor by prevention and fuppreffion of epidemical fevers. 1790. 8. (6 d.)

CLIFFORD, [Charles] *Esq.*
Remarks on the fpeech of Lord *Thurlow* on a motion for the houfe to refolve itfelf into a committee on the infolvent debtors bill —. 1788. 8. (1 fh.)

CLINTON, [Henry] *Sir, Knight Baron. Lieutenant-General in the army, Colonel of the 70 Regim. of Dragoons and of the 84 Regim. of Foot, Governor of Limeric in Ireland.*
Narrative, relative to his conduct during part of his command of the King's troops in North-America particularly that which refpects the unfortunate iffue of the campaign in 1781. 1782. 8. (2 fh.) Obfervations on fome parts of the anfwer of Earl Cornwallis to — Narrative —. 1782. 8. (1 fh. 6 d.) Letter to the Commiffioners of public accounts, relative to fome obfervations in their 7 report —. 1784. 8. (1 fh.)

CLIVE, [Catherine] *Actrefs.*
born .... died d. 5 Dec. 1785.

CLOWES, [Thomas] *Surgeon at Wingham, in Kent.*
A cafe of hernia. (London M. J. Vol. X. P. 1.)

CLUBBE, [J...] *Surgeon at Ipswich, Suffolk.*
On the inflammation in the breafts of lying in women. 1779. 8. (2 fh 6 d.) On the nature of the venereal poifon. 1782. 8. (2 fh.) On the virulent gonorrhoea. 1787. 8. (1 fh. 6 d.)

— [John] *Rector of Wheatfield and Vicar of Debenham, Suffolk.*
The hiftory and antiquities of the ancient villa of Wheatfield. 1758. 4. (1 fh. 6 d.) Sermon before the widows and orphans of clergymen. 1752. (6 d.) *Phyfiognomy. 1764. 4. (1 fh. 6 d.) Mifcellaneous tracts. Vol. 1, 2. 1771. 8. (6 fh.)

COBB, [James]

The contract or female captain, a farce. 1779. The wedding night. 1780. Who'd have thought it; a farce. 1781. Kensington garden, or the walking jockey. 1781. *The stranger at home, a comic opera. 1785. 8. The humourist, a farce. 1785. The first floor, a farce. 1787. *Love in the east, or the adventures of XI hours, an opera. 1788. 8. (1 sh. 6 d.)

COBB, [John] *D. D. Fellow of St. John's College.*

Eight sermons. 1783. 8. (3 sh. 6 d.)

COCHRANE, [Thomas] *M. D. Physician in St. Christopher's.*

The use of couhage as an anthelmintic. (Med. Com. of Ed. Vol. 2. p 82.) Observations on the use of cold bathing in the cure of tetanus. (Ibid. Vol. 3. p. 183.) The history of a case in which a large wound of the abdomen, with a remarkable protrusion of the intestines, terminated favourably. (*Duncan's* M. C. Vol. 10. p. 276.)

COCKIN, [William]

Account of an extraordinary appearance of a mist. (Phil. Transact. 1780. p. 157.)

COCKELL, [William] *M D of Pontefract.*

On the retroversion of the uterus —. 1785. 4. (1 sh. 6 d.)

COCKSON, [Thomas] *Surgeon at Campden.*

A peculiar case of a species of maggots being discharged from the uterus during menstruation. (Med. Com. of Ed. Vol 3. p 86.)

COETLOGON, [Charles Edward de] *A. M. Chaplain to the Mayoralty.*

Sermons on the 51 psalm. 8. Vol. 1. 2. 17.. Caution against the abominations of the church of Rome. 1779. 8. (6 d.) (several single sermons.)

COGAN, [E....]

Addreß to the diſſenters on claſſical litterature. 1789. 8. (1 sh.)

COGAN, [Thomas] *M. D. Physician in the states of the United Provinces.*

Diſſert. De pathematum animi vi et modo agendi. Lugd. Bat. 1767. 4. Memoirs of the society instituted at Amsterdam in favour of drowned persons for

for the Y. 1761-1771. 1773. 8. (2 ſh.) Philoſophical ſurvey of the Creation. 17.. Hiſtory of *John Buncle*, junior. 17..

COKE, [Edward] *Sir.*
The firſt part of the inſtitutes of the laws of England, or a commentary upon *Littleton*. Ed. 13. with notes by *Francis Hargrave* and by *Charles Butler.* — fol. 1788. (4 L. 4 ſh.)

COLE, [Charles Nalſon] *Esq.*
The works of *Soame Jenyns*. Esq. with his life. Vol. 1-4. 1790.

— [Mary] *Mrs. Cook to the Earl of Drogheda.*
The lady's complete guide; or cookery and confectionary in all their branches —. 1789. 8. (6 ſh.)

— [William] *F. A. S: Vicar of Burnham in Buckinghamſhire.*
born 1714. died d. 16 Dec. 1782.

— [W....] *A. M: Fellow of King's College, Cambridge.*
Key to the pſalms —. 1788. 8. (2 ſh.) Exalted affection, or, Sophia Pringle. a poem. 1789. 8. (1 ſh.)

— [William]
Obſervations — on the nature and properties of light and on the theory of Comets. 1777. 8. (2 ſh.) Oratio de ridiculo habita Cantabrigiae —. 1780. 4. (1 ſh.)

COLEBROOK, [Joſiah]
born.... died d. 16 Aug. 1775.

COLEBROOKE, [Henrietta] *Miſſ.*
Thoughts of *Jean Jacques Rouſſeau*. Vol. 1. 2. 1788. 8. (7 ſh. 6 d.)

COLEMAN, [Charles] *Esq.*
Satirical peerage of England —. 1784. 4. (2 ſh. 6 d.)

COLEMANN, [William] *Surgeon at Sandwich in Kent.*
Two caſes of ſcurvy attended with ſome uncommon circumſtances. (London M. J. Vol. 2. p. 117. überſ. Samml. f. A. Th. 7. S. 205.) Caſe of worms diſcharged through a wound of the groin. (ibid. Vol. 7. P. 3.)

COLERIDGE, [John] *Vicar and Schoolmaſter at Ottery St. Mary, Devon.*
Miſcellaneous diſſertations ariſing from the XVII & XVIII Chapt. of the book of judges. 1768 8. (5 ſh.

(5 sh. 6 d.) A critical latin grammar. 1772. 12. (3 sh.) Fast-sermon on government not originally proceeding from human agency but divine institution. 1777. 4. (1 sh.)

COLEY, [William] *Surgeon.*
Account of the late epidemic ague, as it appeared in the Neighbourhood of Bridgnorth, in Shropshire in 1784. 1784. 8. (1 sh.)

COLLES, [Richard] *Esq. Barrister at Law.*
Reports of cases, upon appeals and writs of error in the high court of Parliament from the Y. 1697 to the Y. 1709 —. 1790. 8. (9 sh. 6 d.)

COLLET, [John] *M. D. Physician at Newbury, Berkshire.*
born .... died d. 12 May 1780.

COLLIER, [George] *Sir.*
Selima and Azor, a dramatic romance. 1776. 8.

—— [Joel] *Organist.*
Musical travels through England. 1774. 8. (1 sh.)

COLLIGNON, [Charles] *M. D: Professor of Anatomy at Cambridge: F. R. S.*
born in London d. 30 Jan. 1725. died d. 1 Oct. 1785.

COLLINGWOOD, [Thomas] *Surgeon at Alnwick.*
Account of an uncommon discharge, from an opening made into a large tumour in the under part of the belly and back. (*Duncan's* M. C. Vol. 9. p. 344.) Observations on the peruvian bark. (Ibid. Vol. 10. p. 265.)

COLLINS, [Walsingham] *Merchant at London.*
Address — with proposals for the regulation of bankers and brokers. 1778. 8. (1 sh. 6 d.)

—— [William] *D. D: F. R. S Edin. Minister of Inveresk and Chaplain in Ordinary to his Majesty.*
born .... died 17..

COLLINSON, [John]
Beauties of british antiquity —. 1779. 8. (6 sh.)

COLLS, [John]
The poet, a poem. 1785. 4. (1 sh.)

COLLYER, [Joseph]
born .... died d. 20 Febr. 1776.

COLMAN, [George] *Esq. Manager of the Theatres of Coventgarden and the Haymarket.*
born d. 28 Apr. 1733.
The jealous wife; a Comedy. 1761. 8. (1 ſh. 6 d.) The Muſical lady; a farce. 1762. 8. A Midſummer's night dream, altered. 1763. 8. Philaſter, a tragedy; altered from *Beaumont* and *Fletcher*. 1763. 8. The Deuce is in him; a farce 1763. 8. A fairy tale. 1764. 8. The comedies of *Terence*, translated. 1765. 4. (1 L. 1 ſh.) Ed. 2. Vol. 1. 2. 1768. (12 ſh.) The clandeſtine marriage, a Comedy. 1766. 8. (1 ſh. 6 d.) The engliſh merchant, a Comedy. 1767. 8. (1 ſh. 6 d.) The hiſtory of King Lear; altered from *Shakespeare*. 1768. 8. T. Harris diſſected. 1768. 4. (1 ſh. 6 d.) * The Oxonian in Town, a Comedy. 1769. 8. (1 ſh.) Man and wife, or the *Shakespeare* Jubilee; a Comedy. 1769. 8. (1 ſh. 6 d.) The Portrait. 1770. 8. The fairy Prince. 1771. 8. Comus. 1772. 8. Occaſional prelude on opening Covent Garden Theater Sept. 1772. 1776. 8. (6 d.) Achilles in petticoats; an Opera. 1774. 8. The man of buſineſſ, a Comedy. 1774. 8. (1 ſh. 6 d.) Epicaene, or the ſilent woman, altered a Comedy. 1776. 8. (1 ſh.) The ſpleen or Islington Spa; a comic piece. 1776. 8. (1 ſh) New brooms, occaſional prelude. 1776. 8. (1 ſh.) Dramatic Works. Vol. 1-4. 1777. 8. (1 L. 1 ſh) Bonduca, a Tragedy. 1778. The manager in diſtreſſ. Prelude. 1780. Translation of *Horace's* Art of poetry. 1783. 4. (7 ſh. 6 d.) Connoiſſeur, a periodical paper. Vol. 1-4. 17.. Miſcellaneous Works. Vol 1-3. 1787. Proſe on ſeveral occaſions, accompanied with ſome pieces in verſe. Vol. 1-3. 1787. 8. (12 ſh.)

COLMANN, [George] *Jun.* (Son of the preceding.)
Two to one, a Comedy. 1784. Turk and no Turk, a Comedy. 1785. Inkle and Yarico, an Opera 1787. 8. (1 ſh. 6 d.) The manager in diſtreſſ; a prelude. 1780. 8. (1 ſh.) Ways and means; or, a trip to Dover. 1788. 8. (1 ſh. 6 d.)

COLTMAN, [John]
Every Man's monitor; or the univerſal counſellor, in proſe and verſe, being a collection of ſelect ſentences,

tences, choice maxims and divine precepts. 1781. 8. (2 ſh. 6 d.)

COMBE, [Charles] *F. R. S: F. A. S.*

Nummorum veterum populorum et urbium in Muſeo *Guil. Hunteri* Deſcriptio. 1782. 4. (2 L. 15 ſh.) Obſervations on an inedited coin in the collection of D. *Hunter*. (Arch. Vol. 5. p. 280.)

COMBER, [Thomas] *LL. D. Rector of Buckworth and Morborne, Huntingdonſhire and Chaplain to the Counteſſ Dowager of Balcarras.*

Reflections on Dr. *Middleton's* examination of (*Thom. Sherlok's*) Biſhop's of London diſcourſes on prophecy, 1750. 8 (1 ſh. 6 d.) Vindication of the great revolution in England 1688. and of the characters of King *William* and Queen *Mary* — 1758. 8. (1 ſh 6 d.) Correſpondance on the (*Young's*) farmer's letters to the people of England. 1770. 8. (2 ſh.) Real improvements in Agriculture. 1772. 8. (1 ſh. 6 d.) Translation of *Theodoret's* treatiſe of laws 1776. 8. (2 ſh.) *Chriſtopher Wandesforde's* book of inſtruction. 1777. 8. (1 ſh. 6 d.) The *part ſecond* under the title: Memoirs of the life and death of the Lord *Wandesforde*. 1778. 8. (2 ſh. 6 d.)

CONSETT, [Matthew]

Tour through Sweden, Swediſh-Lapland, Finland and Denmark in a ſeries of letters. 1789. 4. (10 ſh. 6 d.) überſ. Leipzig. 1790. 8.

CONWAY, [Henry Seymour] *Governor of the Island of Jerſey and privy Counſellor.* (Brother to the Earl of Hertford.)

The depopulated vale, a poem. 1774. 4. (2 ſh.) Falſe appearances, a Comedy, altered from the french. 1789. 8. (1 ſh 6 d.) Speech — on moving in the houſe of commons May 5. 1780 8. (1 ſh. 6 d.) Deſcription of a druidical monument in the Island of Jerſey. (Arch. Vol. 8. p. 386.)

COOK, [. . . . .] *Taylor.*

A ſure guide againſt waſte in dreſſ; or the woollen Draper's Man Mercer's and taylor's aſſiſtant —. 1787. 8. (5 ſh.)

COOK, [Adam Moſes Emanuel]
The King cannot err, a Comedy. 1762. 8. The heroic converted, or the maid of bath married. 1771. 8.

— [James] *Captain, Commander of the ſhip, the Endeavour F. R. S.*
born at Whitby in Yorkſhire 1728. died at O-Whyhe d. 14 Febr. 1779.

— [John] *M. D. Phyſician at Hamilton, Lanerk.*
On diſeaſes of children. 1769. 8. (1 ſh.) Voyage and travels through the Ruſſian empire, Tartary and part of the kingdom of Perſia. Vol. 1. 2. 1770. 8. (12 ſh.) Treatiſe of poiſons, vegetable, animal and mineral with their cure. 1770. 8. (1 ſh.) Natural hiſtory of Lac, Amber and Myrrh. 1770. 8 (6 d.)

— [R....] *Surgeon at Barking, in Eſſex.*
Account of a — cure of a dropſy of the belly, after the patient had been tapped ſixteen times. (London M. J. Vol. VII. P. 1. überſ. Samml. f. A. Th. XI. S. 720.) Account of a fracture of the ſcull, by a piſtol-ball, that entered the cranium at the right temple and was ſucceſſfully extracted. (London M J. Vol. 3. p 72.)

COOKE, [James] *M. A*
Drill husbandry perfected —. 1784. 12. (1 ſh.)

— [John] *M A. Chaplain of Chriſt church, Oxford, and Rector of Wentnor, Salop.*
The preacher's aſſiſtant — containing a ſeries of the texts of ſermons and diſcourſes publiſhed either ſingles or in volumes, by divines of the church of England and by the diſſenting clergy ſince the reſtoration to the preſent time. — Vol. 1. 2. 1783. 8. (16 ſh.) — and *John Maule's* Account of the royal hoſpital for ſeamen at Greenwich. 1789. 4. (7 ſh. 6 d.)

— [John] *Surgeon at Glouceſter.*
Account of the diſcovery of the corpſe, of one of the abbots of Glouceſter. (Arch. Vol. 9. p. 10.)

— [William] *Greek Profeſſor of King's College, Cambridge, Rector of Hempſted Norfolk*
Ariſtoteles De poetica, cum verſione et notis. 1785. 8. (3 ſh. 6 d.) Praelectio ad actum publicum habita Cantabrigiae. 1787. 4. (1 ſh.) Poetical eſſays

on

on ſeveral occaſions. 1775. 4. (5 ſh.) The Revelations, translated and explained. 1789. 8. (6 ſh.) (ſeveral ſingle ſermons.)

COOKE, [William] *M. A: Rector of Oldbury and Didmarton, Glouceſterſhire, Vicar of Enford, Wiltſhire and Chaplain to the Earl of Suffolk.*
born .... died d. 25 Febr. 1780.

—— [William] *A. B. Fellow of new College, Oxford and Chaplain to the Marquis of Tweedale.*
The conqueſt of Quebec, a poem. 1769. 4. (1 Sh. 6 d.) The Way to the temple of true honour and fame by the paths of heroic virtue —. Vol. 1-4. 1773. 12. (12 ſh.) The capricious lady, a Comedy, altered from *Beaumont* and *Fletcher.* 1783. 8.

—— [William] *Esq. of Lincoln's Inn.*
Compendious ſyſtem of the bankrupt law. 1786. 8. (8 ſh.) Ed. 2. Vol. 1. 2. 1788. 8. (10 ſh.)

—— [William] *Esq. of the Middle temple.*
The Elements of dramatic criticiſm —. 1775. 8. (4 ſh.) überſ. (von J. Andr. *Engelbrecht* u. Alb. *Wittenberg*) Lübeck. 1777. 8.

COOKSON, [James] *Clerk. A. B. Rector of Colemere and Prior's Deane, Hants.*
Thoughts on polygamy —. 1782. 8. (6 Sh.)

—— [John] *M. B.*
born 1700. died at Wakefield, Yorkſhire, d. 4 May 1779.

COOLEY, [William] *Surgeon in Bridgnorth, Shropſhire.*
Account of the late epidemic ague in the Y. 1784. with obſervations on a dyſentery that prevailed at the ſame time. 1785. 8. (1 Sh.)

COOMBE, [Thomas] *D. D.*
The peaſant of Auburn, or the emigrant, a poem. 1783. 4. (1 Sh.) (ſeveral ſingle ſermons.)

—— [Thomas] *Esq.*
Meteorological obſervations made at Philadelphia. (Tr. of A. S. Vol. 1. p. 70.)

COOPER, [Allen] *Esq. Maſter of the Atlas Eaſt-India Men.*
Account of the effects of lightning on board the Atlas. (Phil. Transact. 1779. p. 160.)

—— [Samuel] *D. D. Miniſter of Great-Yarmouth.*
Definitions and axioms relative to charity, charitable

table inſtitutions and the poor's laws. 1764. 8. (2 ſh.) Explanations of ſome difficult textes in the New Teſtament. 1771. (3 Sh.) Addreſſ to perſons after confirmation. 1783. 8. (1 Sh.) Conſolation to the mourner and inſtruction both to Youth and old age, from the early death of the righteous. 1786. 8. (2 Sh. 6 d.) The one great argument for the truth of chriſtianity from a ſingle prophecy, evinced in a new explanation of the 70 Chapt. of Iſaiah. 1786. 8. (3 Sh. 6 d.) (ſeveral ſingle ſermons.)

COOPER, [Thomas] *Esq.*
Letters on the ſlave trade. 1787. 8.

— [William] *D. D: F. R. S: Archdeacon of York.*
born .... died d. 10 Jul. 1786.

— [William] *M. D: Phyſician at London.*
born .... died d. 4 May 1779.

— [William]
Poems. 1782. 4.

COOTE, [Charles] *A. M.*
Elements of the grammar of the engliſh language. 1788. 8. (5 Sh.)

COPE, [J... A...] *M. D.*
Eſſay on the virtues and properties of the Ginſeng-tea. 1786. 8. (1 Sh.)

COPLAND, [Samuel] *D. D. Miniſter of the Goſpel at Fintray.*
Eſſay on the chriſtian character —. 1785. 8. (3 Sh.)

CORBET, [John]
Conciſe ſyſtem of engliſh grammar. 1784. 12.

CORDINER, [Charles] *Miniſter at Bamff in Scotland.*
Antiquities and Scenery of the North of Scotland. 1780. 4. (12 Sh. 6 d.) Remarkable ruins and romantic proſpects in the North of Scotland. Number 1-6. 1786. 4. (1 L. 10 Sh.) überſ. *Ebeling's* Neue Samml. von Reiſebeſchreib. Th. 5. S. 95.

CORDWELL, [J..]
New ſyſtem of phyſic founded on the principles of nature and not on the materia medica. 1768. 8. (1 Sh.) **Second* tract. 1770. 8. (1 Sh. 6 d.) *Remarks on *Warner's* — account of the gout —. 1769. 8. (1 Sh.)

CORNISH, [James] *Surgeon at Totneſſ, Devonſhire.*
Of the torpidity of ſwallows and martins. (Phil. Transact. 1775. p. 343.)

CORNISH, [Joſeph] *Paſtor to the church of Proteſtant Diſſenters at Colyton, Devon.*
The life of Mr *Thom. Firmin*, Citizen of London. 1780. 8. (2 Sh.) On importance of claſſical learning with remarks on *Knox's* liberal education. 1783. 8 (1 Sh. 6 d.)

CORNWALLIS, [Charles] *Earl. Lieutenant-General, Knight of the Garter and privy counſellor.*
Anſwer to *Henry Clinton's* narrative —. 1783. 8. (3 Sh. 6 d)

CORNWELL, [B....] *M. D.*
The domeſtic phyſician or guardian of health. 1784. 8. (7 Sh. 6 d) überſ. Erfurt. 1788. 8.

CORP, [William] *M. D: Phyſician to the pauper charity of Bath.*
Eſſay on the jaundice in which the property of uſing the Bath waters in that diſeaſe — is conſidered. 1785. 8. (1 Sh. 6 d.)

COSENS, [....] *Miniſter of Teddington, Middleſex; Chaplain to the Earl of Denbigh.*
The oeconomy of beauty; in a ſeries of fables. 1777. 4. (10 Sh. 6 d.)

COSTARD, [George] *M. A. Vicar of Twickenham, Middleſex.*
born 1710. died 1782.

COSTIGAN, [Arthur William] *Esq. late Captain of the Iriſh brigade in the ſervice of Spain.*
Sketches of ſociety and manners in Portugal. Vol. 1. 2. 1788. 8. (10 Sh. 6 d.) überſ. Th. 1. 2. Leipz. 1789. 8.

COTTER, [Georg Sackville] *A. M. of Trinity College, Cambridge.*
Poems. Vol. 1. 2. 1788. 8. (7 Sh.)

COTTON, [....] *Captain of his Majeſty's ſhip Pallas.*
Extracts relative to the britiſh forts in Africa — with obſervations of *John Roberts* —. 1778. 8. (1 Sh.)

—— [Charles] *M D.* (Proprietor of a private madhouſe near St. Alban's.)
born ... died d. 2 Aug. 1788.

COVEY, [John] *Apothecary at Baſingſtoke in Hampſhire.*
Obſervations and facts on the inoculation of the ſmallpox. (London M. J Vol 7. P. 2.) Further obſervations on the inoculation of the ſmallpox. (Lon-

(London M. J. Vol. 8. P. 1.) übers. Samml. f. A. Th. 12. S. 57. On the good effects of Mercury in a disease apparently of the lymphatic system attended with nervous symptoms. (London M. J. Vol VIII. P. 2. übers. Samml. f. A. Th. 12. S. 542.)

COURCY, [Richard de] *Vicar of St. Alkmond's, Shrewsbury.*

Two sermons: National troubles a proper ground for national humiliation. 1776. 8. (1 sh.) The rejoinder —. P. 1. 1777. 8. (3 sh.) Two sermons: The Lord's controversy with a guilty nation. 1778. 8. (1 sh) Letter of solemn counsel from a minister of the gospel to a person in a declining state of health. 1778. 8. (6 d.)

COURTENAY, [John] *Member of Parliament.*

Poetical review of the literary and moral character of D. *Sam. Johnson.* 1786. 4. (2 sh.) Philosophical reflections on the late revolution in France and the conduct of the dissenters in England. 1790. 8. (2 sh.) Ed. 3. with additions. 1790. 8. (2 sh.)

COWLEY, [H....] *Mrs.*

The Runaway; a Comedy. 1776. 8. (1 sh. 6 d.) Who's the dupe? a farce. 1779. 8. (1 sh.) Albina, countess Raimond; a Tragedy. 1779. 8. (1 sh. 6 d.) The maid of Aragon; a Tale. 1780. 4. (2 sh. 6 d.) The school for eloquence. 1780. The world as it goes, or a trip to Montpelier, a Comedy. 1781. Second thoughts are best; a Comedy. 1781. The Bell's stratagem; a Comedy. 1782. 8. (1 sh. 6 d.) Which is the man? a Comedy. 1783. 8. (1 sh. 6 d.) A bold stroke for a husband, a Comedy. 1784. 8. (1 sh. 6 d.) More ways than one; a Comedy. 1784. 8. (1 sh. 6 d.) The school for grey beards, or the mourning bride, a Comedy. 1786. 8. (1 sh. 6 d.) Scottish village or pitcairne green, a poem. 1786. 4. (2 sh.) The fate of Sparta, or, the rival kings, a Tragedy. 1788. 8. (1 sh. 6 d.)

COWLING, [Richard] *M. D. Surgeon to the 85 Regiment of footh.*

Diss. De rhevmatismo. Edinb. 1775. 8. Case of hemiplegia, succeeded by mania. (London M. J. Vol. 2. p 198. übers. Samml. f. A. Th. 7. S. 485.

COWPER, [Henry] *Esq. Barrister at law, of the Middle-Temple.*

Reports

Reports of cases adjudged in the King's bench from 1774 – 1778. fol. 1788. (1 L. 16 sh.)

COWPER, [Spencer] *D D. Dean of Durham.*
born.... died d. 25 March. 1774.

—— [William] *of the Inner-Temple.*
Poems. Vol. 1. 1782. Vol 2. the task a poem with an epistle-to Jos. Hill; Tirocinian or a review of schools; and the history of John Gilpin. 1785. 8. (8 Sh.)

COX, [A... M...]
Joseph: a poem. 1783. 12. (3 Sh.)

—— [Joseph Mason] *M. D. at Fishponds, near Bristol.*
History of a case of insanity, cured by the use of the Digitalis purpurea. (*Duncan's* M. C. Dec. II. Vol. 4. p. 261.)

—— [N...] *Esq.*
The fowler, containing the methods of taking land and water fowl. 1788. (1 Sh. 6 d.)

COXE, [Samuel Compton] *of Lincoln's Inn.*
William Peere William's collection of reports of cases argued and determined in the high court of chancery —. Ed. IV. 1787. 8. (1 L. 11 Sh. 6 d.)

—— [William] *M. A; F. R. S; F. A. S; Rector of Bemerton and Chaplain to the Duke of Marlborough.*
Sketches of the natural civil and political state of Swisserland. 1779. 8. (6 Sh.) übers. Zürich. 1781. 8. Travels in Switzerland. Vol. 1 – 3. 1789. 8. (1 L. 4 Sh) Account of the Russian discoveries between Asia and America. 1780. 4. (18 Sh.) übers. Frankf. u. Leipz. 1783. 8 Supplement: Comparative view of the russian discoveries, with those made by Capt. Cook and Clerke. 1787. 4. (1 Sh. 6 d.) Account of the prisons and hospitals in Russia, Sweden and Denmark. 1781. 8. (1 Sh. 6 d.) Travels into Poland, Russia, Sweden and Denmark — with cartes and engravings Vol. 1. 2. 1784. 4. (2 L. 2 Sh.) übers. von *J. Pezzl.* Th. 1. 2. Zürich. 1785. 4. Letter to *Mich. Price* upon his discourse on the love of our country. 1790. 8. (1 Sh.)

COYTE, [William B...] *M. B. Physician at Ipswich, Suffolk.*
The consequences of a crown-piece swallowed by an epileptic man. (Med. Transact. Vol. 3. p. 30.)

COZENS,

COZENS, [Alexander]
Principles of beauty relative to the human mind. 1778. fol. (1 L, 5 Sh.) A new method of aſſiſting the invention in drawing original compoſitions of Landſcape. 1785.

CRABBE, [George] *Chaplain to the late Duke of Rutland.*
* The library, a poem. 1781. 4. (2 Sh.) The village, a poem. 1783. 4. (2 Sh. 6 d) * The ſkull, a tale. 1783. 4. (2 Sh.) The news-paper, a poem. 1785. 4. (2 Sh.) Sermon on the death of the Duke of *Rutland.* 1788. 4. (1 Sh.)

CRADDOCK, [Joſeph] *M. A: F. R. S.*
* Letters from Snowdon deſcriptive of a tour through the northern counties of Wales —. 1770. 8. * Zobeide, a Tragedy. 1771. 8. (1 Sh. 6 d.) * Village memoirs —. 1775. 8. (3 Sh.) * Account of ſome of the romantic parts of North-Wales. 1777. 8. (2 Sh. 6 d.)

CRAIG, [William] *D. D. Miniſter of St. Andrew's church, Glasgow.*
born d. Febr. 1709. died 1783.

CRAKELT, [William] *M. A. Rector of Nurſted and Ifield in Kent.*
John Entick's new ſpelling dictionary —. 1785. 12. (2 Sh.) Ed... 1788. 4. (4 Sh.)

CRAMMOND, [Hercules] *M. D.*
Outlines of human life. 1787. 8. (3 Sh.)

CRANE, [John] *Phyſician at Dorcheſter.*
Account of the nature, properties and medicinal uſes of the mineral water at Nortington, near Weymouth, Dorſet. 1789. 8. (1 Sh.)

— [Thomas] *Miniſter of St. Olave, Cheſter; Chaplain to Earl Verney.*
The common engliſh translation of the 109 pſalm — corrected —. 1772. 4. (6 d.). The common engliſh translation of the 45 pſalm — corrected. 1774. 8. (1 Sh.) The poetic works of *William Smith*, D. D. late Dean of Cheſter, with his life and writings. 1788. 8. (1 Sh. 6 d.)

CRAVEN, [Elizabeth] *Baroneſſ.* (Daughter of the Earl *Aug. Berkeley.* At preſent by the court of Anſpach.)
The ſleep-walker. 1778. 8. The family picture. 17.. Modern anecdote, or the hiſtory of the

Baron

Baron Kinkvervankotsdarsprakengotchderns. 17.. The silver tankard. 1781. *The miniature picture; a Comedy. 1781. 8. (1 Sh. 6 d.) Nuriad, Comedie en 3 Actes. Anspac. 1787. Journey through the Crimea to Constantinople. 1789. 4. (18 Sh.) übers. Leipz. 1789. 8.

CRAVEN, [William] *B. D. Professor of Arabic at Cambridge.*

Sermons on the evidence of a future state of rewards and punishments —. 1776. 8. (1 Sh. 6 d.) Ed. 2. 1783. 8. (2 Sh. 6 d.)

CRAUFURD, [C...] *Captain of the Queen's regiment of Dragoon guards.*

—— [R...] *Capt. of the* 101 *Regt.*

Translation of *J. G. Tielke's* account of events of the war between the Prussians, Austrians and Russians from 1756-1763. Vol. 1. 2. 1788. 8. (1 L. 10 Sh.)

—— [George] *Esq.*

On the actual resources for establishing the finances of Great-Britain. 1785. 8. (2 Sh 6 d.) Enquiry into the situation of the East-India company. 1789. (3 Sh.)

CRAWFORD, [Adair] *M. D: F. R. S. at Edinburgh and London, Member of the philos. Soc. of Dublin and Philadelphia.*

Experiments and observations on animal heath and the inflammation of combustible bodies. 1779. 8. (2 Sh. 6 d.) Ed. 2. 1788. 8. (7 Sh) übers. mit *W. Morgan's* Erinnerungen wider diese Theory. Leipz. 1785. 8. übers. von C. *Crell.* Leipz. 1789. 8. *Lichtenberg's* u. *Forster's* Göttingisches Magazin. Jahrg. 1. St. 5. Experiments on the power that animals, when placed in certain circumstances, possess of producing cold. (Phil. Transact. 1781. p. 479.)

—— [Charles] *Esq. Fellow commoner of Queen's College, Cambridge. M. A.*

Dissertation on the phaedon of Plato; or, dialogue of the immortality of the Soul —. 1773. 8. (4 Sh. 6 d.) Sophronia and Hilario; an Elegy. 1774. 4. (1 Sh 6 d.) The revolution, a poem. Canto I. 1776. 4. (1 Sh. 6 d.) Richmond-Hill; a poem. 1777. 4. (1 Sh.) The Christian: a poem. 1781.

1781. 8. (2 Sh.) Liberty, a pindaric ode. 1789. 4. (1 Sh.)

CRAWFORD, [James] *Esq.*
born .... died at Edinburgh d. 18 Apr. 1783.

— [John] *Surgeon.*
On the nature, cauſe and cure of a diſeaſe incident to the liver —. 1772. 8. (2 Sh.) The human muſcles claſſed as they appear in diſſection —. 1785. 4. (2 Sh.)

— [William] *M. A. one of the Chaplains of the firſt Tyrone regiment.*
Remarks on the Earl of *Cheſterfield's* letters to his ſon. 1776. 12. (2 Sh.) Hiſtory of Ireland; from the earlieſt period to the preſent time. Vol. 1. 2. 1783. 8. (12 Sh.)

CREECH, [....]
* Account of the trial of *William Brodie* and *James Smith* — for breaking into and robbing the general exciſe office of Scotland. 1788. 4. (3 Sh. 6 d.)

CRESWICK, [....] *Teacher of Elocution.*
The female reader; or miſcellaneous pieces in Proſe and verſe; ſelected from the beſt writers — for the improvement of young women with a preface, containing ſome hints on female education. 1790. 12. (3 Sh.

CRIBB, [William] *Surgeon in high Holborn.*
On the uſe of injections in the gonorrhoea. 1773. 8. (1 Sh. 6 d.) Caſe of a luxation of the thigh bone. (London M. J. Vol. 5. p. 412.)

— [William] *Surgeon at Biſhops Stortford in Hertfordſhire.*
Caſe of a ſtrangulated hernia ſucceſſfully treated with remarks on the uſe of cold applications in the reduction of Herniae. (London M. J. Vol. VI. p. 259.)

CRICHTON, [Alexander] *M. D.*
Account of the effects of the Aſtragalus Exſcapus *Linn.* in the cure of the venereal diſeaſe. tranſlated from the German. (London. M. J. Vol. IX. Part. 4.) On the medicinal effects of the lichen Islandicus and Arnica montana. (London M. J. Vol. X. Part. 3.)

CROCKER,

CROCKER, [Abraham] *Schoolmaster at Ilminster.*
Introduction to english grammar and rhetorik. 1772. 12. Instructions for young people in the public worship of god. 1776. 12. (3 d) The catechism of the church of England, with notes. 1780. 12. (2 Sh. 6 d.)

CROFT, [Georg] *D. D Vicar of Arncliff, Master of Brewood school and Chaplain to the Earl of Elgin.*
General observations concerning education. 1776. 8. (6 d.) A plan for education delineated and vindicated —. 1784. 8. (1 Sh 6 d.) Eight sermons preached before the university of Oxford. 1786. 8. (4 Sh.) Sermon; the test laws defended. 1790. (1 Sh.)

—— [Herbert]
* Love and madness; a story. 1780. 8. (3 Sh. 6 d.)
* The will of King Alfred. 1788. 4. (3 Sh, 6 d.)

—— [John] *F. A. S.*
On the wines of Portugal — on the nature and use of wines in general, or pertaining to luxury and diet. 1787. 8. (1 Sh.)

—— [Richard] *Surgeon at Tutbury, in Staffordshire.*
Account of a successful method of reducing the funis in cases in which it comes down before the head of the foetus. (London M. J. Vol. VII. P. 1. übers. Journal für Geburthshelfer. St. 1.)

CROMPTON, [Georg] *Esq. of the Inner Temple.*
Practice common placed; or the rules and cases of practice in the courts of King's bench and common pleas —. Vol. 1. 2. 1780. 8. (16 Sh.) Ed. 2. 1783. 8. (16 Sh.)

CROOKSHANK, [John] *Commander of his Majesty's ship the Lark.*
Conduct and treatment — relating to his attempt to take the glorioso, a Spanish ship of war 1747 — 1759. 8. Reply to Admiral *Knowles* pamphlet. 1759. 8. (6 d.) Letter to *Rob. Kirke.* 1772. 8. (6 d.)

CROSS, [John] *Clerk.*
Cash tables at five pounds and XV per cent, on the duties of excise and malt —. 1779. 8. (1 Sh.)

CROSSE, [Thomas] *Esq.*
The power of friendship, a poetical epistle. 1785. 4. (1 Sh.)

CROWE, [C....] *Esq. of Kipling.*
Method of making excellent butter from the milk of cows fed upon turnips. (*Hunter's G. E.* Vol. 5. p. 209.)

—— [William] *LL. B. of New-College, Oxford.*
Sermon before the University of Oxford. 1781. 4. (1 ſh.) °Lewesdon Hill, a poem. 1788. 4. (2 ſh. (6 d.) Oratio. 1788. 4. (1 ſh.)

CRUDEN, [Alexander] *M. A.* born at Aberdeen 1701. died d. 1 Nov. 1770.

—— [John] *Esq. President of the aſſembly of the united loyaliſts.*
Addreſſ to the loyal part of the britiſh empire and the friends of monarchy. 1784. 8.

CRUIKSHANK, [William]
Anatomy of the abſorbing veſſels of the human body. 1786. 4. (12 ſh.) Ed. 2. 1790. 4. überſ. von *C. F. Ludwig.* Th. 1. 2. Leipz. 1789. 4.

CRUISE, [William] *Esq. of Lincolns-Inn.*
°Eſſay on the nature and operation of fines. 1783. 8. (3 ſh. 6 d.) On the nature and operation of common recoveries. 1783. 8. (2 ſh. 6 d.)

CRUSO, [John] *Apothecary.*
Treaſury of eaſy medicines, translated of latin. 1771. 8. (3 ſh.)

CRUTTWELL, [Clement]
The Holy Bible — with notes by *Thom. Wilſon* and various renderings —. Vol. 1-3. 1785. 4. (4 L. 14 ſh. 6 d.) A concordance of parallels, collected from bibles and commentaries —. 1790. 4.

—— [C....] *Surgeon at Bath.*
Advice to lying in Women, on the cuſtom of drawing the breaſts. Ed. II. 1779. 4. (1 ſh.)

CRUWYS, [H... S...]
Enquiries into the Archetype of the LXX verſion, its authenticity and different editions. 1774. 8. (1 ſh. 6 d.)

CULLEN, [Charles] (Son to D. *Will. Cullen.*)
Translation of *Luyart's* chemical analyſis of Wolfram, with a translation of *Sheele's* analyſis of the Tungſten —. 1785. 8. (1 ſh. 6 d.) *F. S. Clavigero* Hiſtory of Mexico — translated. Vol. 1. 2. 1787. 4. (2 L. 2 Sh.)

CULLEN, [Edmund] *M. D. Fellow of the college of Physicians at Dublin.*
T. Bergmann's physical and chemical essays — translated, with notes. Vol. 1. 2. 1785 8. (13 Sh.)

—— [William] *M. D. Professor of the practice of physic in the University of Edinburg.* born 1709. died d. 5 Febr. 1790.

CULLEY, [George] *Farmer at Fenton, Northumberland.*
Observations on live stock. 1786. 8. (3 Sh.)

CULLUM, [John] *Sir: Baronet: F. R. S: F. A. S.* born 1733. died at London d. 9 Oct. 1785.

—— [Thomas Gery] *Surgeon at St. Edmundsbury.*
An encysted watery tumour, adhering to the posterior part of the bladder and to the whole length of the rectum, which brought on a fatal suppression of urine. (Med. Obs. Vol. 6. p. 91.) Account of an unusual exfoliation of the cranium. (Mem. of M. S. of L. Vol. 1. p. 194.)

CUMBERLAND, [Richard] *Solicitor and Clerk of the reports in the trade and plantation Office.*
The banishment of *Cicero*, a Tragedy, 1761. 4. (2 Sh. 6 d.) The summers tale, a comedy. 1765. 8. (1 Sh. 6 d). *Amelia, a musical entertainment. 1768. 8. (1 Sh.) Ed. 2. 1771. 8. (1 Sh.) *The Brothers, a Comedy. 1769. 8. (1 Sh. 6 d.) Timon of Athens, a Tragedy. 1771. 8. (1 Sh. 6 d.) *The West-Indian, a Comedy. 1771. 8. (1 Sh. 6 d.) übers. (von *Joh. Joach. Bode*) 1772. 8. *The fashionable lover, a Comedy. 1772. 8 (1 Sh. 6 d.) übers. durch *K. C. H. Rost*, unter dem Titel: Miss *Obre*, oder die gerettete Unschuld. Leipz. 1774. 8. *The note of Hand, or a trip to new market. 1774. 8. (1 Sh.) The choleric man; a Comedy. 1775. 8. (1 Sh. 6 d.) übers. Mannheim. 1785. 8. Odes. 1775. 4. (1 Sh.) *The princess of Parma, a Tragedy. 1778. The battle of Hastings; a Tragedy. 1778. 8. (1 Sh. 6 d.) Calypso, a new masque. 1779. 8. (1 Sh. 6 d.) Anecdotes of eminent printers in Spain during the XVI and XVII Centuries. Vol. 1. 2. 1782. 8. (5 Sh.) The mysterious husband, a Tragedy. 1783. 8. (1 Sh. 6 d.) Letter to Richard Lord Bishop of Landaff on the subject of his Lordship's letter to the late Archbishop of Canterbury. 1783. 8. (1 Sh. 6 d.) The carmelite, a Trage-

Tragedy. 1784. 8. (1 Sh. 6 d.) The natural son, a Comedy. 1785. 8. (1 Sh. 6 d.) übers. Leipzig. 1785. 8. Character of the late Lord *Sackville*. 1785. 8. (6 Sh.) * The observer. 1785. 8. (6 Sh.) Ed. 2. Vol. 1 - 5. 1786 - 1790. 8. (17 Sh. 2 d.) Catalogue of the several paintings in the kings of spains palace at Madrid with account of the pictures in the Buen-Retiro. 1787. 12. (2 Sh. 6 d.) * Arundel. Vol. 1. 2. 1789. 8. (5 Sh.) The impostors, a Comedy. 1789. 8. (1 Sh. 6 d.)

CUMYNS, [Eliza] *of Brompton.*
Introduction to geography and astronomy for the use of young ladies. 1787. 4. (5 Sh.)

CUNNINGHAM, [John]. born at Dublin 1729. died at Newcastle d. 18 Sept. 1773.

— [John]
Inquiry into the Copernican system, respecting the motions of the heavenly bodies. 1789. 8. (1 Sh. 6 d.)

— [T...] *Esq. Barrister at law. F. A. S.*
The practice of a justice of peace: containing the statutes which give jurisdiction to that magistrate. Vol. 1. 2. 1762. 8. (14 Sh.) A new and compleat law dictionary, or, general abridgment of the law —. Vol. 1. 2. fol. 1767. (3 L. 12 Sh.) History of the customs, aids, subsidies, national debts and taxes of England from William the conqueror to the Y. 1778. Ed. III. 1778. 8. (6 Sh.) Historical account of the rights of election of the several counties, cities and boroughs of Great Britain —. P. 1. 2. 1783. 8. (5 Sh.) The law of Simony —. 1784. 8. (3 Sh. 6 d.) Supplement to *Bacon's* abridgment containing a table of the names of the cases; a table of the statutes, or acts of parliament cited; a table of the reporters and other writers —. fol. 1786. (6 Sh.)

CURREY, [Mary] *Mrs.* (maiden name *Elliot.*) born 1745. died d. 1 Oct. 1788.

CURRIE, [James] *M. D.*
Memoirs of the late Dr. *George Bell.* (Mem. of M. Vol. 2. p. 381.)

CURRY, [John] *M. D. Physician at Dublin.* born ... died d. 24 March. 1780.

CURTIN, [Samuel] *Physician at Rio Bueno, in Jamaica.*

Observations on the Yellow fever of the West-Indies. (*Duncan's* M. C. Vol. 9. p. 286.)

CURTIS, [Anne] (Sister to Mrs. *Siddons.*)

Poems on miscellaneous subjects. 1783. 12. (5 Sh.)

—— [Roger] *Lieutenant of his Majesty's sloop the Otter.*

Particulars of the country of Labradore. (Philos. Transact. 1774. p. 372.)

—— [William] *Demonstrator of Botany to the Company of Apothecaries.*

Experiments and observations on bulbous roots, plants and seeds growing in water. (Phil. Transact. 1748. p. 267.) On the structure and formation of the teeth. 1769. 8. (1 sh. 6 d.) Catalogue of the 50 plants from Chelsea garden. (Phil. Transact. 1774. p. 302.) Fundamenta entomologiae. 1772. 4. (2 sh. 6 d.) History of the brown tail moth. 1782. 4. (1 sh. 6 d.) Flora Londinensis. Numb. 1-63. 1777-1780. fol. (15 L. 15 sh.) Catalogue of the british-plants in the London botanical garden. 1783. 8. (3 sh. 6 d.) The botanical magazine; or, flower-garden displayed. N. 1-24. 1788. (1 L. 4 sh)

CUTHBERTSON, [John] *Mathematical Instrument-maker at Amsterdam.*

Description on an improved air pump. 1787. 8. übers. Samml. z. P. u. N. G. Th. 4. S. 83. Allgemeene Eigenschappen van de Electriciteit. Deel. 1. 2. Amstel. 1782. übers. Leipz. 1786. 8. Beschreibung einer Electrisir-Maschine, übers. a. d. Holländ. Leipz. 1790. 8.

CUTLER, [Manasseh] *F. A. A: F. S. Philad.*

Observations of the transit of Mercury over the Sun Nov. 12. 1782. (Mem. of B. A, Vol. 1. p. 128.) Observations of an eclipse of the Moon March 29, 1782. and of Eclipse of the Sun on the 12 April at Ipswich. (Ibid. p. 162.) Meteorological observations at Ipswich in 1781, 1782, and 1783. (Ibid. p. 336. Account of some of the vegetable productions, naturally growing in this part of America botanically arranged. (Ibid. p. 396.)

DADE,

DADE, [William] *F. A. S; Rector at Barmston, Yorkshire.* born.... died d. 2 Aug. 1790.

DALE, [....]

°Supplement to calculations of the value of annuities —. 1777. 8. (2 ſh. 6 d.)

DALGLIESH, [William] *Miniſter of the goſpel at Peebles.*

The ſum of chriſtianity —. Vol. 1. 2. 1786. 8. (10 ſh. 6 d.)

DALLAS, [George] *Esq. Member of the committee — in Bengal.*

Speech - praying redreſſ againſt an act of parliament —. 1786. 8. (1 ſh. 6 d.)

DALLAWAY, [James] *M. A. of Trinity - College, Oxford.*

Letters of the late *Thomas Rundle*, L. L. D. Lord-Biſhop of Derry in Ireland to Mrs. *Barbara Sandys*, of Miſerden — with introductory memoirs. Vol. 1. 2. 1789. 8. (6 ſh.)

DALRYMPLE, [Alexander] *Esq. F. R. S.*

Diſcoveries made in South pacific Ocean. 1767. 8. Two letters to the court of Directors for affairs of the united company of merchants of England, trading to the Eaſt-Indies. 1768. 4. (1 ſh. 6 d.) On the formation of Islands. (Phil. Transact. 1767. p. 394.) Plan for extending the commerce of this kingdom and of the Eaſt-India company. 1769. 8. (1 ſh. 6 d.) Hiſtorical collection of the ſeveral voyages and diſcoveries in the ſouth pacific Ocean — a litterary translation from the ſpaniſh writers. Vol. 1. 2. 1770. 4. (1 L. 11 ſh.) überſ. *Ebelings* N. Samml. v. Reiſebeſchr. Th. 8. S. 175. Letter to D. *Hawkesworth* occaſioned by ſome groundleſſ and illiberal imputations in his account of the late voyages to the South. 1773. 4. (1 ſh.) Proof that the Spaniards can have no claim to Balambangan. 1774. 8. (1 ſh.) Collection of voyages, chiefly in the ſouthern Atlantic Ocean, publiſhed from original Mſſ. 1775. 4. (5 ſh.) Journal of a voyage to the Eaſt-Indies in the ſhip *Grenville*, Capt. *Burnet Abercrombie* in the Y. 1775. (Phil. Transact. 1778. p. 389.) Account of the loſſ of the Grosvenor Indiaman. 1783. 8. (1 ſh.) °Account of the Gentoo made of collecting the revenues on the coaſt of Coromanromandel. 1783. 8. (1 ſh.) *Retroſpective view of the ancient ſyſtem of the Eaſt-India company —. 1784. 8. (1 ſh. 6 d.) Account of a curious Pagoda near Bombay, drawn up by Capt. *Pyke*, who was afterwards Governor of St. Helena. (Arch. Vol. 7. p. 323.) The ſpaniſh pretenſions fairly diſcuſſed, 1790. 8. (1 ſh.) The ſpaniſh memorial of the 4th of June, conſidered: 1790. 8. (1 ſh.)

DALRYMPLE, [David] *Sir*, Lord *New-Hales*.
*Memorials and letters relating to the hiſtory of Britain in the reign of James I. 1762. 8. (2 ſh. 6 d.) *The ſecret correſpondence of Sir Rob. Cecil with James VI. King of Scotland. 1765. 8. (3 ſh.) *Memorials and letters relating to the hiſtory of Britain in the reign of Charles I. 1766. 8. (3 ſh.) Hiſtorical memorials. 1769. 4. Remarks on the hiſtory of Scotland. 1773. 8. (4 ſh. 6 d.) Annals of Scotland, from the acceſſion of Malcolm III. — to the acceſſion of the houſe of Stewart. Vol. 1. 2. 1775. 1779. 4. (1 L. 7 ſh. 6 d.) Inquiry into the ſecondary cauſes which Mr. Gibbon has aſſigned for the rapid growth of chriſtianity. 1786. 4. (7 ſh. 6 d.)

—— [George] *Cook by Sir John Whitefoord*.
The practice of modern Cookery —. 1781. 8. (6 ſh.)

—— [John] *Sir*, *Earl of Stair*: born ... died 1790.

—— [John] *Sir*, *Baronet of the Kingdom of Scotland*.
Memoirs of Great-Britain and Ireland from the diſſolution of the laſt parliament of Charles II. until the Sea battle of la Hogue. Vol. 1. 2. 1773. 4. (2 L. 3 ſh.) Three letters to Viſcount *Barrington*, late Secretary at War. 1778. 8. (2 ſh.) On the exportation of wool. 1781. (1 ſh.) Letter to the landed gentlemen and Graziers of Lincolnſhire. 1782. 8. (1 ſh.) Memoirs of Great-Britain and Ireland from the battle of la Hogue till the capture of the french and ſpaniſh fleets at Vigo. Vol. 1. 2. 1771. 1788. 4. (12 ſh.) Addreſſ — upon the intereſt which they have in the ſtate of the diſtillery laws. 1786. 8. (2 ſh.) Queries concerning the conduct which England ſhould follow in foreign politics in the preſent ſtate of Europe. 1789. 8. (2 ſh. 6 d.)

—— [William] *Major*.
Travels through Spain and Portugal in 1774 with an account of the ſpaniſh expedition againſt Algiers

giers in 1775. 1777. 4. (7 Sh. 6 d.) übers. Leipz. 1778. 8. Tactics. 1781. 8. (5 Sh.)

DALRYMPLE, [William] *D. D. Minister at Ayr.*
History of Christ for the use of the unlearned —. 1787. 8. (6 Sh.) Family worship explained in four sermons. 1787. 8. (2 Sh.)

DALTON. [Maria Regina]
The vicar of Landsdowne. Vol. 1. 2. 1789. 8. (6 Sh.)

— [Richard] *Esq. Antiquarian to the King.*
Remarks on XII historical designs of Raphael and the Musaeum Graecum et Aegyptiacum or antiquities of Greece and Egypt. 1751. 8. (6 d.) Every one his own physician, or, the present practice of physic. 1780. 8. (2 Sh. 6 d.) Remarks on prints intended to be published, relative to the manners, customs — of the present inhabitants of Egypt —. 1781. 8. (1 Sh.)

DALZEL, [Andrew] *M. A. Professor of greek in the University of Edinburgh.*
* Collectanea graeca, minora, cum notis philologicis atque lexico. 1787. 8. (5 Sh.)

DANCER, [Thomas] *M. D. Physician to the troops.*
History of the expedition against Fort San Juan, so far as it relates to the diseases of the troops —. 1782. 4. (2 Sh. 6 d.)

DANIEL, [Samuel] *M. D. Physician at Crewkherne in Somersetshire.*
Diss. De Ictero. Edinb. 1776. 8. A case of ptyalism, apparently occasioned by a diminished secretion of urine. (M. C. Vol. 1. p. 155.) A case of painful menstruation, attended with vomiting. (London M. J. Vol. 5. p. 183.)

DANNET, [Henry] *M. A. Minister of St. John's, Liverpool.*
Examination of Mr. Harris's scriptural researches on the Licitness of the slave trade. 1788. 8. (2 Sh.)

DARBEY, [....] *Apothecary to the Infirmary at Manchester.*
Account of good effects from the vapour-bath in an hydropic case. (*Duncan's* M. C. Vol. 9. p. 305.)

DARBY, [John] *Jun. Surgeon at Diss, in Norfolk.*
Case of emphysema. (London M. J. Vol. VIII. P. 4.)

DARWALL, [John] Political lamentations —. 1777. 4. (2 Sh.)

DARWIN, [....] The botanic garden — a poem. 1789. 4. (12 Sh.)

—— [Charles] born at Lichtfield d. 3 Sept. 1758. died at Edinburgh, (where he was ſtudying phyſic,) d. 15 May. 1778.

—— [Eraſmus] *M. D. F. R. S.* Remarks on the opinion of *Henry Eeles* concerning the aſcent of vapours. (Phil Transact. 1760. p. 240.) An uncommon caſe of an haemoptyſis. (Ibid. 1761. p. 526.) Experiments on animal fluids in the exhauſted receiver. (Ibid. 1774. p. 344.) A new caſe in ſquinting. (Ibid 1778. p. 86.) Account of the ſucceſſull uſe of foxglove in ſome dropſies and in the pulmonary conſumption. (Med. Transact. Vol. 3. p. 255.) Account of an artificial ſpring of water. (Phil. Transact. 1785. p. 1.) Frigorific experiments on the mechanical expanſion of air, explaining the cauſe of the great degree of cold on the ſummits of high mountains: the ſudden condenſation of aerial vapour and of the perpetual mutability of atmoſpheric heat. (Ibid. 1788. p. 43. überſ. *Gren* J. d. Ph. Th. I. S. 73.)

—— [Robert Waring] *M. D.* New experiments on the ocular ſpectra of light and colours. (Phil. Transact. 1786 p. 313.)

DAVIDSON, [David] Thoughts on the ſeaſons — partly in the ſcottiſh dialect. 1789. 8. (3 Sh.)

—— [George] Account of a new ſpecies of the barktree found in the island of St. Lucia. (Phil. Transact. 1784. p. 452.)

—— [Thomas] *Surgeon in Carriacou.* Facts relative to the ſmall-pox. (Lond. M. J. Vol. X. P. 4.)

—— [William] *Architect and Landſurveyor.* Arithmetic and meaſurement, improved by examples and plain demonſtrations —. 1779. 8. (2 Sh. 6 d.)

DAVIES, [Arabella] *Mrs.* Letters from a parent to her children. 1788. 12. (2 Sh. 6 d.)

—— [David] *Esq. of the Middle-Temple.* The juryman's guide; or the engliſhman's right —. 1779. 8. (1 Sh. 6 d.)

—— [Edward] *Lecturer of Sodbury.* Vacunalia: conſiſting

fting of essays in verse; on various subjects; with some translations. 1788. 8. (4 Sh.)

DAVIES, [Thomas] *Captain Lieutenant of Artillery.* Method of preparing birds for preservation. (Philos. Transact. 1770. p. 184.)

— [Thomas] *Bookseller at London.* born .... died d. 5 May. 1785.

— [William]. Plays. 1786. 8. (6 Sh.)

DAVIS. [Henry Edward] *B. A. of Balliol College, Oxford.* born d. 11 July 1756. died d. 19 Febr. 1784.

DAVISON, [J....] A system of Algebra. 1789. 8. (4 Sh.)

DAVY, [C....]

— [F....] Translation of *Bourrit's* journey to the glacieres. 1775. 8. (6 Sh.)

— [Charles] *M. A. Rector of Onehouse in Suffolk.* Letters — upon subjects of litterature; including a translation of *Euclid's* section of the canon and his treatise on harmony with an explanation of the greek musical modes, according to the doctrine of Ptolemy. Vol. 1. 2. 1787. 8. (14 sh.)

— [William] *A. B.* System of divinity in a course of sermons —. Vol. 1–6. 1786. 12. (1 L. 1 sh.)

DAWES, [Matthew] *Esq.* Two sermons. 1763. 8. (1 sh.) Philosophical considerations, or a free enquiry into the merits of a controversy between Dr. *Priestley* and Dr. *Price* on matter and spirit and philosophical necessity —. 1780. 8. (1 sh. 6 d.) On Intellectual liberty and toleration. 1780. 8. (2 sh. 6 d.) Letter to *John Horne Tooke.* 1782. 8. (1 sh.) On crimes and punishments. 1782. 8. (5 sh.) The nature and extent of supreme power. 1783. 8. (1 sh.) England's Alarm! on the prevailing doctrine of libels —. 1785. 8. (1 sh. 6 d.) The deformity of the doctrine of libels. 1785. 8. (1 Sh.) Vindication of the proceedings of the Lords and Commons upon the regency —. 1789. 8. (1 Sh.) Commentaries on the laws of arrests in civil cases —. 1789. 8. (1 Sh.)

DAWSON, [Abraham] *M. A. Rector of Ringsfield, Suffolk.* English translation of the Chapt. 1. 2. 3. of Genesis with illustrations and notes. 1763. 4. (2 Sh. 6 d.) English translation of the Chapt. 4. 5. of Genesis —. 1772. 4. (3 Sh.) The VI and XI following

wing Chapters of Genesis translated with Illustrations and notes 1786. 4. (3 Sh. 6 d.)

DAWSON, [Ambrose] *M. D. fellow of the college of Physicians.* On human calculi; shewing them to be of very different kinds. (Med. Transact. Vol. 2. p. 105.) Thoughts on the hydrocephalus internus (Letters and Essays by different practitioners. Artic. IX.) Observations on the hydatides in the heads of cattle. (ibid. Art. X.)

—— [Benjamin] *LL. D. Rector of Burgh in the County of Suffolk.* Sermons VIII. on logos. 1765. 8. (4 Sh.) Addreß to the writer of a second letter to the author of the confessional. 1767. 8. (1 Sh. 6 d.) Examination of an essay on establishments in religion, with remarks upon it, considered as an answer to the confessional. 1767. A short and safe expedient for terminating the present debates about subscriptions occasioned by — the confessional. 1769. 8. Letter in vindication of the petition for the removal of subscription to human formularies of religious faith and doctrine. 1773. 8. (1 Sh. 6 d.) The necessitarian; or, the question concerning liberty and necessity stated. 1783. 8. (2 Sh. 6 d.) Published: free thoughts on the subjects of a farther reformation of the church of England, with remarks of the editor by the author of a — expedient for terminating the present debates about subscription. 1771. 8. (2 Sh. 6 d.) (several single sermons.)

—— [John] *Surgeon at Sedbergh in Yorkshire.* Account of a singular fact in the practice of inoculation of the small-pox. (Med. Transact. Vol. 3. p. 385. London M. J. Vol. 7. P. 1.)

—— [Thomas] *M. D.* born .... died at Hackney, near London d. 29 Apr. 1782.

DAY, [Thomas] born 1748. died d. 28 Sept. 1789.

—— [Thomas] *Surgeon.* On the different ways of removing confined and infectious air —. 1784. 8. (1 Sh. 6 d.) übers. Altenb. 1788. 8.

DEACON, [....] *Jun.* Poems. 1790. 4. (4 Sh.)

—— [H....] On the venereal disease, gleets —. 1789. 8. (3 Sh. 6 d.)

DEANE, [Samuel] *F. A. A.* Account of yellow and red pigment, found at Norton, with the proceß for

for preparing the yellow for use. (Mem. of B. A. Vol. 1. p. 378.)

DEANE, [Silas] *Ambassadour of the XIII united provinces at Paris.* born at Groton, Connecticut 1736. died d. 23 Sept. 1789.

DEARBORN, [Benjamin] Description of a pump-engine, or, an apparatus to be added to a common pump. (Mem. of B. A. Vol. 1. p. 520.) Description of a fire-engine of a new construction. (Ibid. p. 523.)

DEASE, [William] *Surgeon to the united hospitals of St. Nicholas and St. Catharine, Dublin.* Observations on wounds of the head —. 1776. 8. (2 Sh. 6 d.) Introduction to the theory and practice of Surgery. Vol. 1. 1780. 8. (3 Sh.) Observations in midwifery particularly on the different methods of assisting women in tedious and difficult labours —. 1783. 8. (3 Sh.) übers. von C. F. *Michaelis.* Zittau u. Leipz. 1788. 8. Observations on venereal warts. (Med. Com. of Ed. Vol. 4. p. 335.) Observations on the extirpation of a cancerous ulcer in the lower lip. (Ibid. Vol. 5. p. 299.) Observations on the different methods of treating the venereal disease. 1781. 8. übers. von C. F. *Michaelis.* Zittau 1790. 8. Account of the fatal effects produced by attempting to remove a ganglion by seton. (London M. J. Vol. 5. p. 172. übers. Samml. f. A. Th. 10. S. 157.

DEBRAW, [John] *Apothecary to Addenbrook's hospital at Cambridge.* Discovery on the sex of bees, explaining the manner in which their species is propagated —. (Phil. Transact. 1777. p. 15.)

DELAP, [John] *D. D.* Hecuba, a Tragedy. 1762. 8. * The royal suppliants: a Tragedy. 1781. 8. (1 Sh. 6 d.) The captives, a Tragedy. 1786. 8. (1 Sh. 6 d.) Elegy on the death of the Duke of Rutland. 1788. 4. (1 Sh.)

DELAVAL, [Edward Hussey] *F. R. S. of London and of Gottingen.* Several electrical experiments. (Phil. Transact. 1761. p. 83.) Several experiments in electricity. (Ibid. 1762. p. 353.) Account of the effects of lightning on St. Bride's church, fleet-street June 18. 1764. (Ibid. 1764. p. 227.) Experiments and observations on the agreement between the specific gravities of the several metals and their colours

lours when united to glass, as well as those of their other proportions. (Ibid. 1765. p. 10.) Experimental inquiry into the cause of the changes of colours in opake and coloured bodies. 1777. 4. (5 Sh.) Inquiry into the cause of the permanent colour of opake bodies. (Mem. of M. Vol. 2. p. 131.) übers. (von *Meyneke*) 1788. 8.

DELL, [John] Poetical effusions of the heart. 1783. 8.

DEMPSTER, [George] *Esq.* Discourse, containing a summary of the proceedings of the directors of the society for extending the fisheries of Great-Britain. 1789.

DENHAM, [James Stevart] *Sir; Baronet*, of Coltness and Westshield. born ... died d. 25 Dec. 1780.

DENMANN, [Thomas] *M. D. Physician - man - midwife to the Middlesex Hospital and Teacher of Midwifery in London.* On the puerperal fever and on puerperal convulsions. 1768. 8. (1 Sh. 6 d.) Ed. 3. 1785. 8. übers. Altenb. 1777. 8. On the construction and method of using vapor baths. 1769. 8. (1 Sh.) Observations to prove that in cases where the upper extremities present, at the time of birth, the delivery may be effected by the spontaneous evolution of the child. (London M. J. Vol. 5. p. 64. p. 301.) On uterine haemorrhages depending on pregnancy and parturition. 1786. 8. (2 Sh.) On natural labours. 1786. 8. (2 Sh.) On preternatural labours. 1786. 8. (2 Sh.) Observations on the use of the globe pessary. (London M. J. Vol. 7. P. 1.) übers. Journ. f. Geburtsh. St. 1. Aphorisms on the application and use of the forceps on preternatural labours and on labours attended with hemorrhage. 1786. 8. (2 Sh.) übers. Journal f. Geburtsh St. 2. Collection of engravings, tending to illustrate the generation and parturition of animals, with two plates of a ruptured and inverted uterus. 1786. fol. (13 Sh.) Introduction to the practice of midwifery. P. 1. 1787. 8. (6 Sh.) On difficult labours. P. 1. 1787. 8.

DENNE, [Samuel] *F. A. S.* Observations on Rochester Castle. (Arch. Vol. 6. p. 381.) Memoir on Hokeday. (Ibid. Vol. 7. p. 244.) Doubts and conjectures concerning the reason commonly assigned for inserting or omitting the words ecclesia and pres-

presbyter in Domesday Book. (Ibid. Vol. 8. p. 218.) Observations on the persons called Waldenses who where formerly tenants of the manor of Darenth in the county of Kent. (Ibid. Vol. 9. p. 292.) On the time when *William of Newburgh* wrote his history. (Ibid. p. 310.)

DENNETT, [....] Examination of *Harris's* researches on the licitness of the slave trade. 1788. 8. (2 Sh.)

DENT, [John] The candidate; a farce. 1782. 8. (1 Sh.) Too civil by half; a farce. 1783. 8. (1 Sh.) The receipt tax; a farce. 1783. The lawyers panic; or Westminster-Hall in an Uproar; a Prelude. 1785. 8. (1 Sh.) The force of love; in a series of letters. Vol. 1. 2. 1785. 8. (5 Sh.)

DERBY, [John] *A. M: Chaplain of Lord Bishop of Rochester and Rector of Southfleet and Longfield.* born .... died d. 6 Oct. 1778.

DEVERELL, [Mary] *Mrs.* Gloucestershire. Sermons, on friendship, on gratitude to god, on mercy, on pride, on sinful anger, on the advantages of early piety, on the unsearchableness of god's ways and the benefits of afflictive providence. 1774 8. (5 Sh.) Miscellanies in prose and verse —. Vol. 1. 2. 1782. 12. (7 Sh.) Theodora and Didymus or the exemplification of pure love and vital religion; an heroic poem. 1785. 8. (5 Sh.)

DEVIS, [Ellen] *The accidence or first rudiments of english grammar. 1774. 8. (1 Sh. 6 d.) Ed. 3. 1778. 8. (1 Sh. 6 d.) Miscellaneous lessons. 1784. 12. (2 Sh. 6 d.)

DEWELL, [T....] *M. D. Malmesbury, Wilts.* The philosophy of physic or phlogistic system —. 1784. 8. (1 Sh. 6 d.) Ed. 2. 1785. 8. (3 sh. 6 d.)

DEXTER, [Samuel] *Esq.* Letter on the retreat of house-swallows in Winter. (Mem. of B. A. Vol. 1. p 494.)

DIBDEN, [Charles] The Shepherd's artifice; a dramatic pastoral. 1765. 8. (1 Sh.) Damon and Phillida, altered from Cibber. 1768. 8. *The wedding ring, a comic opera. 1773. 8. (1 Sh.) The deserter. 1773. 8. *The waterman or the first of August, an Opera. 1774. 8. (1 Sh.) *The two miseres; a musical farce. 1775. 8. (1 Sh.) The cobler; or, a wife of ten thousand, a Ballad Opera. 1774.

1774. 8. The Metamorphosis, a comic Opera. 1775. 8. The Seraglio. 1776. 8. The Quaker, a comic Opera. 1776. 8. Poor Vulcan, a Burletta. 1778. 8. The gipsies, a comic Opera. 1778. 8. Rose and Collin, a comic Opera. 1778. 8. The wives revenged, a comic Opera. 1778. 8. Annette and Lubin, a comic Opera. 1778. 8. The chelsea pensioner, a comic Opera. 1779. 8. The Mirror; or Harlequin every where. 1779. 8. The shepherdess of the alps, a comic Opera. 1780. 8. The islanders, a comic Opera. 1780. 8. Jupiter and Alcmena. 1781. 8. The marriage act. 1781. 8. Liberty Hall, or the test of good fellow ship. 1785. 8. Harvest home, a comic Opera. 1786. 8. (1 sh.)

DICK, [John] *Gardener.* The new gardiner's dictionary, or the whole art of gardening. 1769. fol. übers. von *J. E. Zeiher.* Th. 1. 2. Leipz. 1774. 8.

—— [William] *Surgeon of Artillery, Bengal Establishment.* Observations on dropsies prevailing among the troops in the East-Indies. (*Duncan's* M. C. Vol. 10. p. 207.)

DICKINSON, [....] Speech in the assembly of Pennsylvania —. 1764. 8. (6 d.) Reply to a piece, called the speech of *Joseph Galloway.* 1765. 8. New essay on the constitutional power of Great-Britain over the colonies in America —. 1774. 8. (2 sh.)

—— [Caleb] *M. D.* Inquiry into the nature and causes of fever —. 1785. 8. (3 sh.) übers. von *J. Chr. Fahner.* Göttingen. 1787. 8.

DICKSON, [Adam] *A. M: Minister at Whittingham.* born... died d. 25 March. 1776.

—— [James] *Fellow of the Linnaean society.* Plantae cryptogamicae. Fascic. 1. 2. 1785. 1790. 4. (8 sh.) Collection of dried plants named on the authority of the Linnaean herbarium and other original collections. Fasc. 1. 1789. fol. (12 sh. 6 d.) Fasc. 2. 1790. fol. (12 sh.)

—— [Michael] *M. D: Physician at Taunton, Somersetshire.* born.... died d. 28 Dec. 1778.

—— [Stephen] *M. D: Professor of Physic in the city of Dublin. F. R. J. A.* Observations on pamphigus. (Tr. of I. A. 1787. p. 47. London M. J. Vol. IX. P. 3. übers. Samml. f. A. Th. 13. S. 133.)

—— [Thomas] *M. D: F. R. S: Physician to the London Hospital.* born.... died d. 1 June 1784.

DICKSON, [William] *Formerly private secretary to the late Governor of Barbadoes Ed. Hay.* Letters on slavery. 1789. 8. (3 Sh. 6 d.)

DILLON, [John Talbot] *Count of the Roman empire.* born in Ireland. Travels through Spain. 1780. 4. (1 L. 1 sh.) übers. (durch *J. Andr. Engelbrecht*) Th. 1. 2. Leipz. 1782. 8. *Letters from an english traveller in Spain in 1778. 8. 1781. (6 sh.) Survey of the sacred roman empire. 1782. 8. (4 sh.) Translation of *Mengs's* Sketches of the art of painting. 1782. 8. (2 sh.) History of the reign of Peter the cruel, King of Castile and Leon. Vol. 1. 2. 1788. 8. (10 sh.) Historical and critical memoirs of the general Revolution in France in the Y. 1789. 1789. 4. (1 L. 1 sh.)

— [P...] *Surgeon of the* 105 *Regt. of foot.* Case of a fistula in Ano, cured by means of a caustic. (London M. J. Vol. 5. p. 392.) Case of an extrauterine foetus. (Ibid. P. 4.)

DIMSDALE, [Thomas] *M. D: F. R. S. Body Physician and actuel Counsellor of state, to her imperial Majesty of all the Russies.* born.... died 1784.

DINE, [William] *Clerk of the parish of Chiddingly in Sussex.* Poems on several occasions —. 1771. 8. (1 sh.)

DINGLEY, [Somerville] Appendix to the XIV edition of *Burn's* justice. 1785. 8. (3 sh.) The parish officer's companion; or a new library of parish law. 1786. 8. (2 Sh. 6 d.)

DISNEY, [John] *D. D: F. A. S.* Four sermons on Christmas day. 1771. 8. *Thoughts on the great circumspection necessary in licensing public alehouses. 1776. 8. Reasons for resigning the Rectory of Panton and Vicarage of Swinderby — and quitting the church of England. 1783. 8. Memoir of the life and writing of *Arthur Ashley Sykes.* 1785. 8. (5 Sh.) *Dialogue between a common unitarian christian and an Athanasian. 1784. 8. Ed. 2. 1785. Published, the works, theological, medical, political and miscellanious of *John Jebb* M. D. 1787. 8. Vol. 1–3. (1 L. 1 Sh.) Published, *Sam. Disney's* (late Vicar of Halstead, Essex) Discourses on various subjects, with a preface. 1788. 8. (6 Sh.) (several single sermons.)

DISON,

DYSON, [John] born.... died 1776.

DIXON, [George] *Captain.* Voyage round the world; but more particularly to the North-West-Coast of America, by *Portlock* and *Dixon*. 1789. 4. (1 L. 1 Sh.) übers. von *J. R. Forster*. 1790. 4. Voyage round the world. 1789. 8. (Ein Auszug) übers. Berlin. 1789. 8.

—— [Joseph] *M. D. Physician in Whitehaven.* History of a case of Angina polyposa. (*Duncan's* M. C. Vol. 9. p. 254.) übers. Samml. f. A. Th. XI. S. 403. Account of appearances on the dissection of a child dying of hydrocephalus. (Ibid. Vol. 10. p. 312. übers. Samml. f. A. Th. XI. S. 685.)

DOBBS, [Francis] *Esq. Barrister at law.* born in Ireland. The patriot king; or, irish chief; a Tragedy. 1774. 8. (1 Sh. 6 d.) Letter to Lord North, on his propositions in favour of Ireland. 1778. 8. (6 d.) Thoughts on the present mode of taxation in Great-Britain —. 1783. 8. (1 Sh.) Letter to Lord North and Mr. Fox. 1784. 8. Universal-history —. Vol. 1. 1787. 12. (3 Sh.)

DOBSON, [Mary] *Mrs.* (Wife to *Matthew Dobson's*). Translation of the life of Petrarch. Vol. 1. 2. 1775. 8. (12 Sh.) Ed. 2. Vol. 1. 2. 1776. 8. (12 Sh.) * Dialogue on friendship and society. 1776. 8. (2 Sh. 6 d.) * Translation of *St. Paley's* litterary history of Troubadours. 1779. 8. (6 Sh.) * Translation of *St. Paley's* memoirs of ancient Chivalry. 1784. 8. (5 Sh.)

—— [Matthew] *M. D. Physician at Liverpool.* *F. R. S.* born.... died at Bath d. 25 July 1784.

—— [Robert] *M. D. Physician at Kirkham.* Diss. de Amenorrhoea. Edinb. 1771. 8. A case of a very obstinate ophthalmia, successfully treated by an emetic and the consequent use of the Peruvian bark. (Med. Com. of Ed. Vol. 3. p. 411.)

DODD, [A... Charles] The contrast or strictures on select parts of Dr. *Price's* additional observations on civil liberty —. 1777. 8. (1 Sh.)

—— [James Solas] *Surgeon and Manmidwife.* Natural history of the herring. 1752. 8. (3 Sh.) Physical account of the case of *Elizab. Canning*. 1753. 8. (1 Sh.) * A satyrical lecture on hearts. 1767. 8. (1 Sh.) All the prescriptions contained in the new practi-

practice of Physic of *Thom. Marryat* — translated. 1774. 8. (2 sh. 6 d.) The antient and modern history of Gibraltar — translated from the Spanish: 1781. 8. (2 sh. 6 d.)

DODD, [William] *Doctor of Laws, Prebendary of Brecon and Chaplain in Ordinary to his Majesty.* born at Bourne, Lincolnshire d. 29 March 1729. executed at Tyburn d. 27 June 1777.

DODDRIDGE, [....] *Mrs.* born:... died at Tewkesbury, Gloucestershire d. 20 Apr. 1790.

DOGERTY, [Thomas] Crown circuit assistant; being a collection of precedents of indictments, informations, convictions by justices, inquisitions, pleas —. 1787. 8. (9 sh.)

DOLLOND, [Peter] *Optician.* Account of an improvement in his new telescopes. (Phil. Transact. 1765. p. 54.) Additions and alterations made to *Hadley's* quadrant, to render it more serviceable at sea. (Ibid. 1772. p. 95.) Account of an apparatus applied to the equatorial instrument for correcting the errors arising from the refraction in altitude. (Ibid. 1779. p. 332.) Some accounts of the discovery made by the late Mr. *John Dollond.* F. R. S. — 1789. 4. (1 sh.)

DONALDSON, [J....] at Edinburgh. Elements of beauty. 1780. 12. (2 sh.) übers. N. Bibl. der schönen Wiss. Th. 27. S. 5-38. Ed. 2. with an analysis of the human mind. 1787. 8. (3 sh.) Poems. 1786. 4. (2 sh. 6 d.)

— [John] Miscellaneous proposals for increasing our national wealth, 12 Millions a Year, and also for augmenting the revenue without a new tax —. 1790. 8. (1 sh. 6 d.)

— [William] *late Secretary to the government of Jamaica.* Agriculture considered as a moral and political duty. — 1777. 8. (3 sh. 6 d.)

DONAVAN, [John] *Surgeon.* Remarks upon the treatment and cure of venereal and scorbutic disorders —. 1788. 8. (1 sh. 6 d.)

DONE, [William Stafford] *D. D. Prebendary of Lincoln and Arch-Deacon of Bedford.* born:... died d. 1 June 1783.

DONN, [Benjamin] *Master of the Academy at Kingston near Taunton.* Mathematical essays on vulgar and deci-

decimal arithmetic —. 1758. 8. (6 ſh.) The accountant and geometrician; containing the doctrine of circulating decimals, logarithms, book-keeping and plane geometry —. 1766. 8. (6 ſh.) Epitome of natural and experimental philoſophy including geography, with the uſe of the globe. 1770. 8. (2 ſh 9 d.) The britiſh mariner's aſſiſtant; containing 40 tables adapted to the ſeveral purpoſes of trigonometry and navigation —. 1774. 8. (6 ſh.) The uſe of the Geoorganon and improved analemma or ſubſtitutes for the terreſtrial and celeſtial globe. 1788. 8. (1 ſh.)

DORNFORD, [Joſiah] *of Lincoln's Inn: LL. D. of the Univerſity of Gottingen.* Translation of *Putter's* hiſtorical developement of the preſent political conſtitution of the germanic empire &c. with notes. Vol. 1-3. 1790. 8. (1 L. 1 ſh.)

— [Joſiah] Two memorials to the committee appointed by the court of common-council —. 1784. 8. (1 ſh.) Addreſſ to the livery and citizens of London on the proceedings of the court of common council-reſpecting Mr. Alderman *Clarke* and Mr. *Dornford.* 1785. 8. (6 d.) Seven letters-pointing out the cauſes of the depravity of the lower orders of the people, the corrupt ſtate of our goals. 1785. 8. (1 ſh.)

DOSSIE, [Robert] *Chymiſt.* born:... died d. 20 Febr. 1777.

DOUGALL, [William] *Surgeon at Keith.* Hiſtory of a caſe of Ileus, in which a conſiderable portion of the inteſtine was voided by ſtool. (*Duncan's* M. C. Vol. 9. p. 278.)

DOUGLAS, [....] Edwin, the baniſhed prince. 1784. 8.

— [Andrew] *M. D: at London.* Diſſ. De variolae inſitione. Edinb. 1775. 8. Account of the efficacy of Hemlock in ſchirrous caſe and ulcers. (Med. Obſ. Vol. 5. p. 113.) Obſervations on an extraordinary caſe of ruptured uterus. 1785. 8. (1 ſh. 6 d.) überſ. Journal für Geburtshelfer. St. 2. Obſervations on that ſpecies of haemorrhage which is occaſioned by an attachment of the placenta to the cervix uteri. (M. C. Vol. 1. p. 107.) Obſervations

vations on the rupture of the gravid uterus. 1789. 8. (3 ſh.)

DOUGLAS, [Archibald] *M. D. of London.* Caſe of a ſingular cough. (Med. Obſ. Vol. 6. p. 163.)

— [Charles] *F. R. S. Captain of his Majeſty's ſhip the Emerald.* Experiments and obſervations upon a blue ſubſtance, found in the Peat Moſſ in Scotland. (Phil. Transact. 1768. p. 181.) Account of the reſult of ſome attempts made to aſcertain the temperature of the ſea in great depths near the coaſts of Lapland and Norway. (Ibid. 1770. p 39.)

— [Francis] General deſcription of the eaſt coaſt of Scotland from Edinburgh to Cullen —. 1782. 8. (2 ſh. 6 d.)

— [George] *Teacher of Mathematics in the Academy, at Ayr.* The elements of Euclid —. 1776. 8. (6 Sh.)

— [James] *F. A. S.* *Travelling anecdotes through various parts of Europe. Vol. 1. 2. 1782. (12 ſh.) Ed. 2. (with the Author's name) (6 ſh.) On the antiquity of the earth. 1785. 4, (10 ſh. 6 d.) Nenia Britannica; or, an account of ſome 1000 ſepulchres of the ancient inhabitants of Britain 1786. fol. Numb. 1-5. (1 L. 5 ſh.) Letter to *Melvil's* obſervations on the Sword. (Arch. Vol. 7. p. 376.)

— [John] *D. D: F. R. S: Biſhop of Carlisle.* Milton vindicated from the charge of Plagiariſm brought againſt him by Mr. *Lauder.* 1750. (1 ſh. 6 d.) *The Criterion, or, miracles examined —. 1753. 8. (5 ſh.) *The Detection of *Archib. Bower.* 1757. 8. (2 ſh.)

— [Robert] The variation of the compaſſ; containing 1719 obſervations to, in, and from the Eaſt-Indies, Guinea, Weſt-Indies and Mediterranean, with the latitudes and longitudes at the time of obſervation —. (Phil. Transact. 1776. p. 18.)

— [Robert] *Miniſter of Galaſhiels* Obſervations on the nature of oaths, and the danger of multiplying them. 1783. 8. (2 ſh.)

— [....] *Lieutenant of the North Lincolnſhire Militia.* **Guibert's* general eſſay on tactics translated. Vol. 1. 2. 1781. 8. (12 ſh.)

— [Sylveſter] *of Lincoln's Inn.* Account of the Tokay and other wines of Hungary. (Phil. Transact.

1773.

1773. p. 292.) Hiſtory of the caſes of controverted elections which were tried and determined during the firſt ſeſſion of the XIV parliament of Great-Britain —. Vol. 1-4. 1777. 8. (1 L.) Reports of caſes — determined in the Court of King's bench in the 19, 20, 21 Years of — George III. 1783. fol. (1 L. 16 ſh.)

DOW, [Alexander] *Lieutenant Colonel in the Eaſt-India company's Service.* born in Scotland... died in Eaſt-India 1779.

DOWNES, [Henry] *Miniſter at Sheffield.* Sermons on various ſubjects. Vol. 1. 2. 1784. 8. (10 ſh)

DOWNING, [George] *Actor.* born.... died 1780.

DOWNMANN, [Hugh] *M. D. Phyſician at Exeter.* The land of the muſes, a poem. 1767. 4. (2 ſh. 6 d.) Infancy, a poem. Book 1. 2. 3. 1775. 4. (4 ſh.) 1776. 8. (2 ſh.) 1788. 8. (2 ſh. 6 d.) *Lucius Junius Brutus*: or the expulſion of the Tarquins, an hiſtorical play. 1779. 8. (3 ſh.) The death ſong of *Ragnar Lodbroch*, King of Denmark translated from the latin of *Wormius*. 1781. 4. (1 ſh.) Editha, a Comedy. 1783. 8. (1 ſh. 6 d.)

DRAKE, [William] *A. M: F. A. S: Rector at Islaworth, Middleſex.* On the origin of the word romance. (Arch. Vol. 4. p. 142.) On two roman ſtations in Eſſex. (Ibid. Vol. 5. p. 137.) On the origin of the engliſh language. (Ibid. p. 306. p. 379.) Account of ſome diſcoveries in the church of Brotherton in Yorkſhire. (Ibid. Vol. 9. p. 253.) On the derivation of the engliſh language. (Ibid. p. 332.)

DRAPER, [William] *Sir. Knight, Baron, Lieutenant-General.* born.... died d. 8 Jan. 1787.

DRAY, [Thomas] *Surgeon.* Reflections on *Cadogan's* diſſertation on the gout and all chronic diſeaſes. 1772. 8. (6 d.)

DREW, [William] Translation of *Fontanieu's* art of making coloured cryſtals to imitate precious ſtones. 1788. 8. (2 ſh.)

DREWE, [Edward] *Major.* Military ſketches. 1784. 8. (2 ſh. 6 d.)

DRINKWATER, [John] *Captain of the late 72 regiment, or, royal Manchester Voluntairs.* History of the late siege of Gibraltar —. 4. 1786. (1 L. 7 sh.)

DRUMMOND, [T...] *Surgeon at Bombay.* Account of the successful employment of Laudanum in the confluent small-pox. (*Duncan's* M. C. Dec. 2. Vol. 4. p. 300.)

DRURY, [Obrien] *Captain: of the royal Navy.* Observations on the magnetic fluid. (Tr. of I. A. 1788.)

—— [R....] Illustrations of natural history. Vol. 1-3. 1770-1782. 4. (7 L. 18 sh.) übers. durch *G. W. Fr. Panzer.* Nürnb. 1785. 4.

DRYDEN, [John] *Jun.* born.... died 17..

—— [John] *Surgeon in Jamaica.* Account of a rupture of the oesophagus from the action of vomiting. (*Duncan's* M. C. Dec. II. Vol. 3. p. 308.)

DRYSDALE, [W...] *Teacher of languages.* Popery dissected: or, a speech against the popish toleration bill —. 1779. 8. (1 sh.)

DUBOIS, [Dorothea] *Mrs.* (Daughter to the Earl *Anglesea.*) born.... died 1774.

DUCAREL, [Andrew Coltee] *LL. D: F. R. S: F. A. S: Commissary of the city and Diocese of Canterbury.* born at Greenwich 1714. died d. 29 May 1785.

DUCHE, [Jacob] *Preacher at Bow church in Cheapside.* Discourses on various subjects. Vol. 1. 2. 1779. 8. (10 sh. 6 d.) * *Caspipina's* letters: containing observations on a variety of subjects literary, moral and religious — with the life and character of *Will. Penn.* Vol. 1. 2. 1777. 8. (5 sh.) (several single sermons.)

DUDLEY, [Henry Bate] *Clerk, Justice of the peace for the county of Essex.* Henry and Emma. 1774. 8. Rival candidates, a comic Opera. 1775. 8. (1 sh.) The blackamoor wash'd white, a comic Opera. 1776. 8. Flitch of Bacon, a comic Opera. 1779. 8. (1 sh.) The dramatic puffers. 1782. 8. The magic picture, a play. 1783. (1 sh. 6 d.) Remarks on *Gilbert's* last bill for the relief of the poor. 1788. 8. (1 sh.)

DUFF, [William] *A. M.* * Essay on original genius and its various modes of exertion in philosophy and the

the fine arts, particularly in poetry. 1767. 8. (5 Sh.) Critical obſervations on the writings of the moſt celebrated original geniuſes in poetry, a ſequel to the eſſay on original genius. 1770. 8. (5 Sh.)

DUGUD, [Patrik] *Phyſician at Durham.* Hiſtory of a convulſive diſorder treated by the uſe of the flowers of zinc. (Med. Com. of Ed. Vol. 5. p. 84.)

DUIGENAN, [Patrick] *LL. D. Profeſſor of common law in Trinity college, Dublin.* *Theophilus Addreſſ to the nobility and gentry of Ireland. 17..

DULANCEY, [Oliver] *Lieutenant Colonel.* *Conſiderations on the propriety of impoſing taxes in the britiſh colonies. 1765. 8. (1 Sh. 6 d.) Ed. 2. (with the author's name) 17..

DUN, [...] Sermons. Vol. 1. 2. 1790. 8. (10 Sh.)

DUNBAR, [James] *L. L. D. Profeſſor of Philoſophy, King's College, Aberdeen.* De primordiis civitatum oratio, in qua agitur de bello civili inter M. Britanniam et Colonias nunc flagranti. 1779. 4. (1 Sh. 6 d.) On the hiſtory of mankind —. 1780. 8. (5 Sh.) Ed. 2. 1782. 8. (6 Sh.) überſ. Leipz. 1781. 8.

DUNCAN, [....] *Moral hints to the riſing generation, an epiſtle of *Horace* —. 1783. 8. (1 Sh.)

—— [Andrew] *M. D. Phyſician to his Royal Highneſſ the Prince of Wales and Profeſſor of the Univerſity of Edinburgh. F. R. S: F. A. S.* Diſſ. De alvi purgantium natura et vſu. Edinb. 1770. 8. Elements of Therapeutics. 1770. 8. (4 Sh.) Obſervations on the operation and uſe of Mercury in the venereal diſeaſe. 1772. 8. (3 Sh.) überſ. Frankf. u. Leipz. 1773. 8. Medical caſes. 1778. 8. (5 Sh.) überſ. Leipz. 1779. 8. Oratio de laudibus *Guil. Harvei.* 1778. 8. Account of the life and writings of *Alex. Monro* 1780. 8. (1 Sh.) Medical commentaries for the Year 1780. (6 Sh.) 1781. 1782. (6 Sh.) 1783. 1784. (6 Sh.) 1785. (6 Sh.) 1786. (6 Sh.) 1787. (6 Sh.) 1788. (6 Sh.) 1789. (6 Sh.) Heads of lectures on the theory and practice of Medecine. 17.. Ed. 2. 1781. 8. (3 Sh.) Ed. 4. 1788. 8. Letter to *Rob. Jones* — on the caſe of Mr. *J. B. Iſaacſon.* 1782. 8. (1 Sh.) *Will. Lewis's* translation of *Hoffmann's* ſyſtem of the practice of medecine reviſed and completed. Vol. 1. 2. 1783. 8. (12 Sh.) Account of the late Dr. *John Parſons.* 1786. 8. (1 Sh.)

(1 Sh.) Account of good effects obtained from the uſe of the vitriolic acid in the cure of obſtinate ſingultus. (*Duncan's* M. C. Dec. 2. Vol. 4. p. 371.)

DUNCAN, [John] *D. D. Rector of Southwarmborough, Hants.* Eſſay on happineſſ. 1762. 4. (2 Sh. 6 d.) Ed. 2. (with the author's name) 1773. 8. (5 Sh.) (Several ſingle ſermons.)

DUNCOMBE, [John] *M. A. Rector of St. Andrew's and St. Mary Bredman's and one of the VI preachers in Chriſt church, Canterbury.* born 1730. died d. 19 Jan. 1786.

DUNDAS, [David] *Colonel.* Principles of Military movements, chiefly applied to infantry —. 1788. 4. (1 L. 1 Sh.)

—— [David] *Surgeon at Richmond, in Surry.* On hydrophobia. (London M. J. Vol. VIII. P. 2.)

DUNDONALD, [...,.] Earl of. The preſent ſtate of the manufacture of ſalt explained: — 1785. 8. (2 Sh.) überſ. Leipz. 1787. 8. On the qualities and uſes of Coal tar and Coal Varniſh —. 1785. 8. (1 Sh.]

DUNN, [Samuel] *Teacher of the mathematical and philoſophical ſciences, London.* Lecture on the aſtronomy and philoſophy of comets. 1759. 8. Some obſervations of the planet Venus, on the diſk of the Sun, June 6. 1761. with a preceding account of the method taken for verifying the time of that phaenomenon and certain reaſons for an atmoſphere about Venus. (Philoſ. Transact. 1762. p. 184.) Attempt to aſſign the cauſe why the Sun and Moon appear to the nacked eye larger when they are near the horizon: with an account of ſeveral natural phaenomena relative to this ſubject. (Ibid. 1762. p. 462.) Reaſons for a lunar atmoſphere. (Ibid. 1762. p. 578.) Account of the eclipſe of the Sun, Oct. 16. 1762. (Ibid. 1762. p. 644.) Account of an appulſe of the Moon to the planet Jupiter, obſerved at Chelſea. (Ibid. 1763. p. 31.) Remarks on the cenſure of Mercator's chart, in a poſthumous work of Mr. Weſt of Exeter. (Ibid. 1763. p. 66.) Account of a remarkable meteor, Oct. 6. 1763. (Ibid. 1763. p. 351.) Obſervations on the eclipſe of the Sun, April 1. 1764. at Bromp-

Brompton Park. (Philos. Transact. 1764. p. 114.) Improvements of the doctrine of the sphere, astronomy, geography, navigation. 1765. 4. (2 sh. 6 d.) Determination of the exacts moments of time, when the planet Venus was at external and internal contact with the Sun's limb in the transits of June 6th 1761. and 3 June 1769. (Phil. Transact. 1770. p. 65.) A new and general introduction to practical astronomy. 1775. 8. (12 sh.) The navigator's guide to the oriental or indian seas. 1776. 8. (15 sh) A new epitome of practical navigation or guide to the indian seas. 1778. 8. (9 sh.)

DUNSTER, [C....] *A. M.* The frogs, a Comedy translated from the greek of *Aristophanes.* 1785. 4. (3 sh. 6 d.)

DUPRE', [Edward] *M. A. Fellow of Pembroke College.* Sermons on various subjects. 1782. 8. (6 sh.) (Several single sermons.)

—— [John] *M. A. Fellow of Exeter College. Oxford.* Sermons on various subjects. Vol. 1. 2. 1787. 8. (12 sh.)

DURELL, [David] *D. D. Principal of Hertford College, Oxford, Prebendary of Canterbury and Vice-Chancellor of Oxford.* born .... died d. 16 Oct. 1775.

DURNFORD, [Charles] *Barrister at law.* — and *Edw. Hyde East's* reports of cases argued and determined in the court of Kinch's bench from Michaelmas term 26 Georg III. to Michaelmas term 28 Georg III. Vol. 1. 2. 1788. (4 L. 9 sh.)

DWIGHT, [Timothy] * The conquest of Canaan, a poem. 1788. 12. (3 sh. 6 d.)

DYMOND, [Joseph] see *Will. Wales.*

EASON, [Alexander] *M. D. Physician in Dublin.* A case of an imperforate hymen. (Med. Com. of Ed. Vol. 2. p. 187.) Account of the effects of lightning, in discussing a tumour of the breast. (Ibid. Vol. 4. p. 82.) Account of the effects of electricity in removing a fixed contraction of the fingers. (Ibid. Vol. 5. p. 83.) History of a case of hydrocephalus successfully treated by the use of mercury. (*Duncan's* M. C. Vol. 8. p. 325.) On crystallisation. (Mem. of M. Vol. 1. p. 29.) On the

On the uſe of acids in bleaching of linen. (Mem. of M. Vol. I. p. 240.) On the aſcent of vapour. (Ibid. Vol. I. p. 395.)

EAST, [Edward Hyde] *Barriſter at law.* See *Charles Durnford.*

EDEN, [William] *LL. D. Member of Parliament.* *Principles of penal laws. 1771. 8. (5 ſh.) Four letters to the Earl of Carliſle. 1779. 8. (2 ſh. 6 d.) Ed. 3. with a 5 letter. 1780. 8. (4 ſh.) Letter to the Earl of Carliſle on the ſubject of the late arrangement. 1786. 8. (1 ſh.) Letter on the political arrangement. 1786. 8. (1 ſh.) View of the treaty of commerce with France, ſigned at Verſailles 20 Sept. 1786. 1787. 8. (2 ſh.)

EDGEWORTH, [Richard Lovell] *Esq. F. R. S: F. J. A.* Account of diſcoveries in the turf bogs of Ireland. (Arch. Vol. 7. p. 111.) Experiments upon the reſiſtance of the air. (Phil. Transact. 1783. p. 136.) Account of the meteor of the 18 Aug. 1783. (Ibid. 1784. p. 118.) Account of ſome experiments on wheel carriages. (Tr. of I. A. 1788.)

EDIE, [Georg] On engliſh ſhooting —. 1772. 8. (1 ſh.)

EDMONSON, [Joſeph] *F. A. S.* born.... died d. 17 Febr. 1786.

EDMONSTONE, [William] *Surgeon.* On the prevention of an evil highly injurious to health. 1784. 8. (2 ſh.) The reviewers corrected; or falſe criticiſm analyſed —. 1785. 8. (6 d.)

EDWARDS, [....] *Miſſ.* Otho and Rutha, a dramatic tale. 1781. 8.

— [Bryan] Thoughts on the late proceedings of government reſpecting the trade of the Weſt-India Islands with the united ſtates of North-America. 1784. 8. (1 ſh.) Speech delivered at a free conference between the council and aſſembly of Jamaica held d. 25 Nov. 1789. — concerning the ſlave trade. 1790. 8. (2 ſh.)

— [Georg] *F. R. S: F. A. S.* born at Stratford, Eſſex d. 3 Apr. 1694. died d. 23 July. 1773.

— [Georg] *Esq. M. D.* The aggrandiſſement and national perfection of Great-Britain —. Vol. I. 2. 1787. 4. (1 L. 5 ſh.) The royal and conſtitutional regeneration of Great-Britain —. Vol. I. 2. 1790. 4. (15 ſh.)

(15 ſh.) The practical means of effectually exonerating the public burthens; of paying the national debts, and of raiſing the ſupplies of war without new taxes —. 1790. 4. (7 ſh. 6 d.)

EDWARDS, [John] *B. A.* Aſtronomical problems. (N. A. 1781.) Additions to the logarithmic ſolar tables annexed to the nautical Almanac of 1771. (N. A. 1781.) Directions for making the beſt compoſition for the metals of reflecting teleſcopes; and the method of caſting, grinding, poliſhing and giving them the true parabolic figure. (N. A. 1787.) Account of ſeveral compoſition of metals and ſemi - metals, on which trials were made to find out the moſt proper mixture for the ſpecula of reflecting teleſcopes. (N. A. 1787.) Account of cauſe and cure of the tremors particularly affecting reflecting teleſcopes more than refracting ones. (N. A. 1787.)

—— [John] *F. S. A.* On the plant called gooſe - graſſ. 1784. 8. (1 ſh.)

—— [John] *Major of Light Dragoons in the volunteer Army of Ireland.* The patriot ſoldier, a poem. 1784. 4. (2 ſh.)

—— [Jonathan] *A. M: Preſident of the College of New-Jerſey, New - England.* born.... died 17..

—— [Richard] *Clerk, Vicar of Mamble in the county of Worceſter and Curate of Pont - y - pool.* Letter to John Hanbury Esq. 1772 4. (1 ſh.) Letter to Shute Barrington, Lordbiſhop of Landaff. 1773. 4. (1 ſh.)

—— [Thomas] *D. D.* A new engliſh translation of the pſalms from the original hebrew — with notes —. 1755. 8. (6 ſh.) The doctrine of irreſiſtible grace proved to have no foundation in the writings of the new teſtament. 1759. 8. (5 ſh.) Prolegomena in libros V. T. poeticos; ſive Diſſertatio, in qua *Franc. Harii* — de antiqua hebraeorum hypotheſin ratione et veritate niti, oſtenditur —. 1762. 8. (3 ſh. 6 d.) Epiſtola ad *Rob. Lowth* in qua nonnulla, quae ad nuperae ſuae de ſacra hebraeorum poeſi praelectionum editionis calcem habet, expenduntur. 1765. 8. (1 ſh) Two diſſertations; on the abſurdity and injuſtice of religious bigotry and perſecution — and on the principal qualifications and canons, neceſſary for the right interpretation of of the New Teſtament. 1767. 8. (1 ſh. 6 d.) Duae diſſertationes: in quarum priore probatur, variantes lectiones et menda — non labefactare ejus auctoritatem in rebus, quae ad fidem et mores pertinent; in poſteriore vero, praedeſtinationem Paulinam ad gentilium vocationem totam ſpectare. 1768. 8. (2 ſh.) Selecta quaedam *Theocriti* idyllia — cum notis. 1779. 8 (5 ſh.) (Several ſingle ſermons.)

EELES, [Henry] On the cauſe of thunder. (Phil. Transact. 1757. p. 524.) On the cauſe of the aſcent of vapour and exhalation and thoſe of winds; and of the general phaenomena of the weather and barometer. (Ibid. 1759. p. 124.) Philoſophical eſſays — containing a diſcovery of the cauſe of thunder. 1773. 8. (4 ſh.)

EGAN, [Robert] The general exchanger: comprehending the principal direct and croſſ-exchanges of Europe —. 1781. 4. (14 ſh.)

EATON, [Samuel] *D. D.* born... died 17..

EGELSHAM, [Wells] *Printer.* born.... died d. 4 Apr. 1786.

EGERTON, [....] Theatrical remembrancer, containing a complete liſt of all the dramatic performances in the engliſh language —. 1788. 8. (3 ſh. 6 d.)

— [Charles] New hiſtory of England in verſe —. 1780. 12. (3 ſh.)

EKINS, [John] *M. A: Rector of Quainton, Bucks.* The loves of Medea and Jaſon, a poem, translated from the greek of *Apollonius Rhodius's* Argonautics. 1770. 4. (3 ſh. 6 d.)

ELIBANK, [....] *Lord.* *Conſiderations on the preſent ſtate of the peerage of Scotland — by a peer of Scotland. 1771. 8.

ELLERAY, [....] On transplanting Potatoe tops. (*Hunter's* G. E. Vol. 5. p. 241.)

ELLIOT, [John] *M. D.* Obſervations on the affinities of ſubſtances in ſpirit of wine. (Phil. Transact. 1786. p. 155.) Experiments and obſervations on light and colours; and the analogy between heat and motion. 1787. 8. (3 ſh.)

— [John] *Apothecary at London.* born.... died in Newgate 1788.

ELLIOT, [R....] *A. B. formerly of Bennet College, Cambridge.* Dipping not baptizing: or, the author's opinion of the subject, mode and importance of water-baptism, according to scriptures. 1787. 8. (2 Sh. 6 d.)

—— [Robert] *Clergyman and Methodist.* born .... died d. 28 Dec. 1788.

—— [Thomas] *Minister of the Gospel at Cavers.* Improvement of the method of correcting the observed distance of the Moon from the Sun or a fixed star. (T. of E. S. Vol. 1. p. 191.)

—— [Thomas] *Fourcroy's* elementary lectures on chemistry and natural history — translated, with additions. Vol. 1. 2. 1785 8. (12 Sh.)

ELLIS, [G:...] * Memoir of a map of the countries comprehended between the black sea and the Caspian, with account of the Caucasian nations and vocabularies of their languages. 1788. 4. (9 Sh.)

—— [John] *F. R. S: Agent for the Province of Westflorida and for the Island of Dominica* born.... died d. 5 Oct 1776.

—— [Thomas] *Gardner at Lincoln.* Gardener's pocket Calendar. 1776. 12. (3 Sh.)

—— [William] *A. M. Master of the Grammarschool at Alford in Lincolnshire.* *Aristotle* on Government, translated. 1778. 4. (13 Sh.) Collection of English exercises; translated from *Cicero* —. 1782. 8. (2 Sh. 6 d.)

—— [William] *Assistant-Surgeon to both vessels.* Narrative of a voyage performed by Capt. *Cook* and *Clerke* — during the Years 1776-1780. in search of a North-West passage between the continents of Asia and America. Vol. 1. 2. 1782. 8. (12 Sh.) Übers. Frankf. 1783. 8.

—— [William] *Apothecary in London.* On the cure of the venereal gonorrhoea. 1771. 8. (2 Sh. 6 d.)

ELPHINSTONE, [James] Analysis of the french and english language. Vol. 1. 2. 1755. 8. (5 Sh.) Education, a poem. 1762. 8. (3 Sh.) * Apology for the monthly review. 1762. 8. (2 Sh.) Collection of poems from the best authors. 1763. 8. (3 Sh. 6 d.) The principles of the english language digested; or english grammar reduced to analogy. 1764. 8. Vol. 1. 2. (8 Sh.) The principles

ciples of the english language digested for the use of schools 1765. 8. (3 Sh.) Verses, english, french, and latin. 1767. fol. (1 Sh.) Animadversions upon elements of Criticism 1771. 8. (2 Sh. 6 d.) A finishing plan of education. 1776. (6 d.) Translation of *Martial's* epigramm with a comment. 1782. 4. (1 L. 1 Sh.) *Martialis* epigrammata. 1783. 8. (5 Sh.) °The hypercritic. 1783. 8. (1 Sh.) Propriety ascertained in her picture, or english speech and spelling reduced mutual guides. Vol. 1. 2. 1787. 4.

ELSE, [Joseph] *Surgeon to St. Thomas's Hospital.* born .... died d. 10 March 1780.

ELSTOB, [....] °Trip to Kilkenny, from Durham by way of Whitehaven and Dublin in the Year 1776. 8. 1778. (2 Sh.)

ELVING, [Alexander] *Teacher of Mathematics in Edinburgh.* Synopsis of practical mathematics —. 1772. 12. (4 Sh)

EMERSON, [William] born d. 14 May. 1701. died at Hurworth near Darlington d. 20 May 1782.

EMLYN, [Henry] of *Windsor.* Proposition for a new order in architecture, with rules for drawing the several parts. 1782. fol. (1 L. 1 Sh.)

EMMERICH. [A....] *Lieutenant Colonel.* The culture of forests with an appendix, in which the state of the royal forests is considered and a system proposed for their improvement. 1789. 8. (2 Sh. 6 d.) The partisan in war; or the use of a corps of light troops to an army. 1789. 8. (3 Sh.)

ENFIELD, [William] *LL. D. Lecturer on the belles letters in the dissenting Academy at Warrington, Lancashire.* Sermons for the use of families. Vol. 1. 2. 1768. 1771. 8. (3 Sh.) übers. (von *J. C. F. Schulz*) Halle 1774. Prayers for the use of families. 1770. 8. (3 Sh.) Ed. 2. 1777. 8. (4 Sh.) übers. von *F. E. Wilmsen.* Halle 1773. 8. °The preacher's directory; or a series of subjects proper for public discourses. 1771. 4. (6 Sh.) °The english preacher: or sermons on the principal subjects of religion and morality, selected and abridged from various authors. Vol. 1-9. 1773. 8. (1 L. 11 Sh. 6 d.) übers. Bremen. 8. Th. 1. 17.. Biographical sermons: or, a series of discourses on the

the principal characters in ſcripture. 1777. 8. (3 Sh.) überſ. Leipz. 1777. Eſſay towards the hiſtory of Leverpool, drawn from papers left by the late M. *George Perry* and from other materials ſince collected. 1774. fol. (12 Sh.) Obſervations on litterary property. 1774. 4. (2 Sh.) The ſpeaker, or miscellaneous pieces ſelected from the beſt engliſh writers with an eſſay on elocution. 1775. 8. (6 Sh.) Exerciſes in elocution. 1780. 8. (the *ſecond* Part of the ſpeaker) (3 Sh. 6 d.) Inſtitutes of natural philoſophy, theoretical and experimental. 1785. 4. (12 Sh.) (Several ſingle ſermons.)

ENGLEFIELD, [Henry] *Sir. Baronet. F. R. S: F. A. S.* Account of the appearance of the ſoil at opening a Well at Hanby in Lincolnſhire. (Phil. Transact. 1781. p. 345.) Obſervations on reading Abbey. (Arch. Vol. 6. p. 61.) Obſervations on the antient buildings at York. (Ibid. Vol. 6. p. 104.) Additions to Mr. *King's* account of Lincoln caſtle. (Ibid. Vol. 6. p. 376.) Obſervation on the variation of light in the ſtar Algol. (Phil. Transact 1784. p. 1. & p. 5.) Tables of the apparent places of the comet of 1661. whoſe return is expected in 1789. with a new method of uſing the reticule rhomboid. 1788. 4. (2 Sh. 6 d.) Letter to the author of the review of the caſe of the proteſtant diſſenters — with an abſtract of, and ſome general obſervations upon the laws now in force againſt the engliſh Proteſting catholic diſſenter. 1790. 8. (1 Sh. 6 d.)

ENGLISH, [Robert] *formerly Chaplain by the navy George.* Naval review, a poem. 1773. 4. (1 Sh.) Ed. 2. 1774. 4. (1 Sh. 6 d.) Elegy on the death of Sir *Charles Saunders.* 1777. 4. (1 Sh.)

ENTICK, [John] *M A. Rector at Stapney.* born 1713. died d. 22 May 1773.

ERSKINE, [Andrew] Town eclogues — 1773. 4. (1 Sh. 6 d.)

—— [Charles] *Surgeon.* The inſtitutions of medicinal pathology of *H. D. Gaubius* translated. 1778. 8. (4 Sh.)

—— [David] *Earl of Buchan in Scotland.* Speech of the Earl of Buchan. 1780. 4. (2 Sh. 6 d.)

—— [John] *D. D. Miniſter of Edinburgh.* Theological Diſſertations: containing 1) the nature of the Sinai cove-

covenant. 2) The character and privileges of the apostolic churches with an examination of Dr. *Taylor's* key to the epistles. 3) The nature of saving faith. 4) the law of nature sufficiently promulgated to the heathens. 5) Attempt to promote the frequent dispensing the Lord's supper. 1766. 12. (3 Sh.) Shall i go to war with my American brethern? 1769. 8. (1 Sh.) Ed. 2. 1776. 8. Considerations on the spirit of popery. 1779. 8. *The equity and wisdom of administration. 1776. 8. *Reflections on the rise, progress and probable consequences of the contentions with the colonies. by a freeholder. 1776.

ERSKINE, [Robert] *Engineer.* The facts and accusations set forth in a late pamphlet the conduct and treatment of *John Crookshanks* proved to be false and groundless. 1759. 8. (6 d.) Dissertation on rivers and tides —. 1770. 8. (6 d.) Ed. 2. 1780. 8. (1 Sh.)

ESSEX, [James] of Cambridge: *F. A. S.* Remarks on the antiquity and the different modes of brick and stone buildings in England. (Arch. Vol 4. p. 73.) Some observations on Lincoln cathedral. (Ibid. p. 149.) On the origin and antiquity of round churches; and of the round church at Cambridge in particular. (Ibid. Vol. 6. p. 163.) Description and plan of the ancient timber bridge at Rochester. (Ibid. Vol. 7. p. 395.) On Croyland abbey and bridge. (Biblioth. Topogr. Brit. Numb. 22. p. 525.)

ESTE, [Charles] *a Clergyman.* My own life. 1787. 8. (1 Sh. 6 d.) (Principal Director of the newspaper, the World.)

— [Charles] *Member of the company of Apothecaries in London.* Tracts on medical subjects. 1776. 4. (1 Sh. 6 d.)

ESTWICK, [Samuel] *L. L. D.* Letter to Dr. *Tucker*, in answer to his humble address —. 1776. 8. (1 Sh. 6 d.) *Considerations on the Negroe cause. by a West-Indian. 1772. 8. (1 Sh.) Ed. 3. (with the author's name). 1788. 8. (2 Sh.)

EVANS, [Caleb] *M. A. Anabaptist Clergyman in Bristol.* Two sermons on the deity of the son and holy spirit. 1765. 8. Reply to the letter to him on his two sermons. 1765. 8. Letter to *John Wesley*, occa-

occasioned by his calm addreſſ to the American colonies. 1775. 8. Reply to *Fletcher's* vindication of *Wesley's* calm addreſſ to our American colonies. 1775. 8. Political ſophiſtry detected; or — remarks on — *Fletcher's* — American patriotiſm. 1776. 8. (5 d.) Publiſhed: Miſcellaneous pieces in verſe and proſe by *Theodoſia* (Mrs. *Anne Steel's*) Vol. 1–3. 1781. 8. (3 Sh.) Chriſt crucified; or the ſcripture doctrine of the atonement — illuſtrated in 13 Diſcourſes. 1789. 8. (2 Sh.)

EVANS, [Evan] born .... died d. 4 Sept. 1788.

—— [John] *M. D. Phyſician in Liverpool.* Hiſtory of a caſe of retroverted uterus. (Med. Com. of Ed. Vol. 6. p. 215.) Hiſtory of an obſtinate affection of the bowels, cured by the injection of a decoction of tobacco. (Ibid. p. 332.) Hiſtory of a caſe of hydrocephalus, terminating ſucceſſfully. (*Duncan's* M. C. Vol. 10. p. 299.) überſ. Samml. f. A. Th. XI. S. 676. Hiſtory of an uncommon ſwelling of the lower extremities in a pregnant woman, terminating favourably immediately after an abortion. (Ibid. p. 302.) Caſe of Ganglion of the tendons, opened and ſucceſſfully treated. (London M. J. Vol. VIII. P. 2.)

—— [Thomas] *Solicitor in Chancery and one of the Attorneys of the court of King's bench in England.* Refutation of *Linguet's* memoirs of the baſtile —. 1783. 8. (1 Sh. 6 d.)

EVANSON, [Edward] *M. A. Clergyman.* Three Diſcourſes. 1) upon the man after God's own heart. 2) the faith of Abraham. 2) The ſeal of the foundation of God. 1773. 8. (1 Sh. 6 d.) Letter to the biſhop of Lichtfield (*Hurd*) on the prophecies of the New Teſtament —. 1777. 8. (2 Sh.)

EWEN, [James] *Ovid's* Heroid; or epiſtles from the heroines of Antiquity translated into engliſh verſe. 1787. 8. (6 Sh.)

EWER, [J....] *M. D. Phyſician in Trinidad.* Account of the medicinal properties of a bark — from South-America. (London M. J. Vol. X. P. 2.) überſ. Samml. f. A. Th. 13. S. 321.

EWING, [Alexander] *Teacher of Mathematics in Edinburgh.* Synopſis of practical mathematics. 1771. 8. 4 Sh.) Inſtitutes of Arithmetic. 1773. 12. (2 Sh.)

EWING, [John] D. *Provost of the University of Pennsylvania.* Calculation of the Transit of Venus over the Sun as it is to happen June 3. 1769. for the city of Philadelphia. (Tr. of A. S. Vol. 1. p. 5.) Account of the observations on the transit of Venus over the Sun on the 3. of June 1769. and of the transit of Mercury Nov. 9. both as observed in the state-house square, Philadelphia. (Ibid. p. 42.) Improvement in the construction of *Godfrey's* (commonly called *Hadley's*) Quadrant. (Ibid. App. p. 21.)

EYRE, [Joseph] Observations on the prophecies relating to the restoration of the jews —. 1771. 8. (2 sh. 6 d.)

FADEN, [William] *Geographer to his Majesty.* Geographical exercises —. 1778. fol. (15 sh.)

FAIRMAN, [William] *Teacher of Mathematics.* A new method for obtaining the longitude at sea. 1783. 4. (1 sh.) On geography, the uses of the globes and astronomy —. 1788. 8. (4 sh.)

FALCK, [N.... D....] *M. D. at London.* The ready observator for determining the latitude. 1771. 4. (3 sh.) Dissertation on the diving vessel projected by Mr. *Day*, and sunk in Plymouth sound —. 1775. 4. (2 sh. 6 d.) Description of an improved steam engine. 1776. 8. (2 sh.) On the venereal disease. 1772. 8. (7 sh. 6 d.) übers. (von *J. W. Müller*) Hamburg. 1775. 8. The seaman's medical instructor —. 1774. 8. (4 sh. 6 d.) On the medical qualities of mercury. 1776. 12. (3 sh. 6 d.) übers. Leipz. 1777. 8. Published: *Rich. Wilkes's* historical essay on the dropsy. 1777. 8. (7 sh.) Guardian of health. Vol. 1. 1778. 12. (3 sh.)

FALCONAR, [Harriet] (born 1774.) and
—— [Maria] (born 1772.) Poems. 1788. 12. (3 sh. 6 d.) Poems on Slavery. 1788. 8. (1 Sh. 6 d.)

FALCONBRIDGE, [Alexander] *late Surgeon in the African trade.* Account of the slave trade on the coast of Africa. 1788. 8. (9 d.) übers. von *M. C. Sprengel.* Leipzig. 1789. 8.

FALCONER; [Magnus] *Surgeon and Prof. of Anatomy.* see *Will. Hewson.* Synopsis of a course of lectures on anatomy and surgery. 1778. 8. (6 sh.)

FALCONER, [Thomas] *Esq. of the city of Chester.* Sketch of the materials for a new history of Cheshire —. 1772. 4. (2 ſh. 6 d.)

—— [William] *M. D: F. R. S: Phyſician to the Bath Hoſpital.* ° The Shipwreck, a poem, by a ſailor. 1762. 4. (5 ſh.) Ed. 2. 1764. 8. (2 Sh. 6 d.) Diſſ. De nephritide vera. Edinb. 1766. The univerſal dictionary of the marine. 1769. 4. (1 L. 1 ſh.) On the Bath waters. 1770. 8. (3 ſh.) Ed. 2. Vol. 1. 2. 1774. 8. (10 ſh.) Obſervations on Dr. *Cadogan's* Diſſertation on the gout and all chronic diſeaſes. Ed. 2. 1772. 8. (1 ſh. 6 d.) überſ. (von *C. G. Selle*) Berlin. 1773. 8. Obſervations and experiments on the poiſon of copper. 1774. 8. (2 ſh.) On the water commonly uſed at Bath. 1775. 8. (3 ſh.) überſ. von *C. F. Sam. Hahnemann.* Leipz. 1777. 8. Experiments and obſervations. P. 1–3. 1777. 8. (2 ſh.) Obſervations on ſome of the articles of diet and regimen uſually recommended to valetudinarians. 1778. 8. (1 ſh.) Remarks on the influence of climate, ſituation, nature of country, population, nature of food and way of life. 1781. 4. (18 ſh.) überſ. (von *E. B. G. Hebenſtreit*) Leipz. 1782. 8. Account of the epidemic catharrhal fever, called the influenza. 1782. 8. (1 Sh.) *Matth. Dobſon* on fixed air with an appendix on the uſe of the ſolution of fixed alkaline ſalts — in the ſtone and gravel. 1785. 8. (4 Sh.) Remarks on the knowledge of the ancients. (Mem. of M. Vol. 1. p. 261.) On the influence of the ſcenery of a country on the manners of its inhabitants. (Ibid. p. 271.) Thoughts on the ſtyle and taſte of gardening among the ancients. (Ibid. p. 297.) Remarks on the knowledge of the ancients reſpecting glaſſ. (Ibid. Vol. 2. p. 95.) On the influence of the paſſions upon the diſorders of the body. 1788. 8. (3 Sh.) überſ. von *C. F. Michaelis.* 1789. 8. On the efficacy of the application of cold water to the extremities in a caſe of obſtinate conſtipation of the bowels. (Mem. of M. S. of L. Vol. 2.) Remarks on the palſy. (Ibid.) On the preſervation of the health of perſons employed in agriculture, and on the cure of the diſeaſe incident to that way of life. 1789. 8. (1 Sh. 6 d.) Practical Diſſertation on the

medi-

medicinal effects of the Bath-waters. 1790. 8. (4 Sh.)

FALKENER, [....] *Surgeon at Southwell, in Nottinghamshire.* A case of the hydrophobia. (Med. Transact. Vol. 2. p. 222.)

FALKNER, [Thomas] Description of Patagonia and the adjoining parts of South-America —. 1774. 4. (7 Sh. 6 d.) übers. (von *S. H. Ewald*) Gotha. 1775. 8. übers. in *Hirschfeld's* Geschichte der Menschheit, Bändgen 3.

FALL, [Robert] Observations on the report of the committee of the house of Commons appointed to inquire into the state of the british fishery. 1786. 8. (2 Sh.)

FARLEY, [Edward] *Esq.* Imprisonment for debt unconstitutional and oppressive; proved from the fundamental principles of the constitution and the rights of nature. 1789. 8. (3 Sh.)

FARMER, [A... W...] ° Free thoughts on the proceedings of the continental congress, held at Philadelphia Sept. 5. 1774. by a Farmer. 1775. 8. (1 Sh.) The congress canvassed; or, an examination into the conduct of the delegates at their grand convention held in Philadelphia Sept. 1. 1774 —. 1775. 8. (1 Sh.) View of the controversy between Great-Britain and her colonies —. 1775. 8. (1 Sh. 6 d.)

— [Hugh] *Pastor of Protestant Dissenters at Walthamston near London.* born 1714. died d. 26 Febr. 1787.

— [Richard] *D. D. Principal Librarian to the University of Cambridge.* On the learning of Shakespeare. 1766. 8. (1 Sh.)

FARQUHARSON, [William] *of Edinburgh. M. D.* Case of a scirrhous oesophagus. (Mem. of M. S. of L. Vol. 2.) Account of a singular case in midwifery. (*Duncan's* M. C. Dec. II. Vol. 3. p. 344.)

FARR, [Samuel] *M. D. F. R. S.* Diss. De Animo ut causa morborum. Lugd. Bat. 1765. 4. Extract of a meteorological journal for the Year 1767. kept at Plymouth. (Phil. Transact. 1768. p. 136.) — for the Year 1768. (Ibid. 1769. p. 81.) On the medical virtues of acids. 1769. 8. (2 Sh.) Philosophical enquiry into the nature, origin and extent of of animal motion. 1771. 8. (6 Sh.) Aphorismi de Marasmo, ex ſummis medicis collecti. 1772. 4. (1 Sh. 6 d.) Extract of a meteorological journal for the Y. 1774. kept at Briſtol. (Phil. Transact. 1775. p. 194.) — for the Y. 1775. (Ibid. 1776. p. 367.) — for the Y. 1776. (Ibid. 1777. p. 353.) — for the Y. 1777. (Ibid. 1778. p. 567.) — for the Y. 1778. (Ibid. 1779. p. 551.) On blood letting in conſumptions. 1775. 8. (1 Sh.) überſ. Samml. f. A. Th. 3. St. 1. S. 124.) Obſervations on the character and conduct of a phyſician. 17.. Translation of *Hippocrates's* hiſtory of epidemics. 1780. 4. (1 L. 1 Sh.) On the uſe of cantharides in dropſical complaints. (Mem of M. S. of L. Vol. 2.) * Elements of medical jurisprudence. 1788. 8. (2 Sh. 6 d.)

FARRELL, [John] *A. M.* Translation of *Francis d'Ivernois's* view of the conſtitution and revolutions of Geneva in XVIII Century. 1784. 8. (5 Sh.)

FARRER, [....] *Mrs.* (Wife of Capt. *Farrer.*) The appeal of an injured wife againſt a cruel husband. 1788. 8. (2 Sh.)

—— [J....] *Maſter of the grammar-ſchool at Witton le Wear in Durham.* *M. Corderii* colloquiorum centuria ſelecta —. 1785. 12. (1 Sh 3 d.)

—— [John] *of Queen's College, Oxford.* The reign of death, a poem. 1780. 8. (1 Sh.) Selection of hebrew poems, translated. 1780. 4. (3 Sh. 6 d.) America, a poem. 1780. 4. (2 Sh.)

—— [W...] *M. D.* * Obſervations on ſpecific medicines —. 1767. 8. (2 Sh. 6 d.) Account of the rickets in children and remarks on its analogy to the king's evil. 1773. 12. (1 Sh.)

FARROE, [....] *M. D.* The royal golden inſtructor for Youth throughout the britiſh dominions — being an abridgment of the royal univerſal britiſh grammar and vocabulary. 1776. 12. (1 Sh. 6 d.)

FAULKNER, [B...] *of Little Chelſea.* Obſervations on the general and improper treatment of inſanity with a plan for the more ſpeedy and effectual recovery of inſane perſons. 1789. 8. (1 Sh.)

—— [George] *Esq. and Alderman.* Epiſtle to *Gorges Edm. Howard*, with notes. Ed. VI. 1772. 8. (1 Sh.)

FAW-

FAWCETT, [Benjamin] *M. A.* Candid reflections on the doctrine of the Trinity. 1777. 8. Ed. 2. 1778. with appendix. 1780. 8. (2 Sh.) Observations on religious melancholy. 1780. 8. (1 Sh.) übers. von *J. F. Lehzen*. Leipz. 1785. 8. (Several single sermons.)

FAWCETT, [John] *Master of a Boarding school at Brearley-Hall near Halifax.* Critical exposition of the 9 chapter of the epistle to the Romans —. 1752. 8. (1 Sh.) The sick Man's employ or views of death and eternity realized. 1775. 12. (6 d.) Advice to Youth; or, the advantages of early piety —. 1778. 12. (1 Sh. 6 d.) Ed. III. 1786. 12. (1 Sh. 6 d.) Hymns —. 1782. 8. (2 Sh.) Death of Eumenio; a Poem. 1780. 8. (6 d.) The reign of death. a Poem. 1780. 8. (1 Sh.) Essay on anger. 1787. 12. (1 Sh. 6 d.)

FAWKES, [Francis] *M. A: Vicar of Hayes, Kent.* born in *Yorkshire.* died d. 26 Aug. 1777.

FAYERMAN, [Richard] *M. A.* Contemplation, a poetical essay, on the works of creation. 1776. 4. (2 Sh.)

FEARNE, [Charles] *Barrister of law; of the Inner temple, Conveyancer.* Impartial answer to the doctrine delivered in a letter, which appeard in the public advertiser on the 10th of Dec. 1769. under the signature of Junius. 1770. 8. (1 Sh.) ° Lexigraphical chart of landed property in England. 17.. Essay on the learning of contingent remainders and executory devises. 1772. 8. (1 Sh. 6 d.) Copies of opinions ascribed to eminent counsel on the will which was the subject of the case of Perrin v. Blake before the court —. 1781. 8. (1 Sh.)

FEARON, [Henry] *Surgeon to the Surry Dispensary.* On cancers. 1784. 8. (1 Sh. 6 d.) Ed. 2. 1786. 8. (2 Sh. 6 d.) Ed. 3. 1790. 8. (3 Sh. 6 d.) übers. Duisburg. 1790. 8. Account of a tumour, supposed to have been a diseased kidney. (M. C. Vol. 1. p. 416.) Observations on cancers. (Mem. of M. S. of L. Vol. 2.) An improved method of amputating a cancerous breast. (London M. J. Vol. 4. p. 406.)

FELL, [Elizabeth] *of Newcastle.* Fables, odes and miscellaneous poems. 1771. 8. (3 Sh.) Poem on the

the times. 1774. 4. (1 ſh.) Poems. 1777. 4. (4 ſh.)

FELL, [John] *a Diſſenting Clergyman.* Genuine proteſtantiſm; or the unalienable rights of conſcience defended. 1773. 8. (1 ſh. 6 d.) A fourth letter to Mr. *Pickard* on genuine proteſtantiſm; 1775. 8. (1 ſh.) Daemoniacs. Inquiry into the heathen and the ſcripture doctrine of Daemons, in which the hypotheſis of Mr. *Farmer* and others are conſidered. 1779. 8. (5 ſh.) The idolatry of Greece and Rome diſtinguiſhed from that of other heathen nations. 1785. 8. (2 ſh. 6 d.)

FELLOWS, [John] *Grace triumphant, a ſacred poem — by Philantropos. 1770. 8. (2 ſh.) Elegy on the death of *John Gill*, D. D. 1771. 8. (6 d.) Hymn's on believers baptiſm. 1773. 12. (1 ſh.) Elegiac poem on the death of *Aug. Montagu Toplady*. 1778. 8. (6 d.) The Hiſtory of the holy bible in verſe —. Vol. 1-4. 1778. 12. (8 ſh.) The proteſtant alarm; or, popiſh cruelty fully diſplayed —. 1780. 12. (3 ſh.)

FENN, [John] *M. A; F. A. S.* Original letters, written during the reigns of Henry VI. Edward IV and Richard III. by various perſons of rank or conſequence. Vol. 1-4. 1787. 1789. 4. (4 L. 4 ſh.)

FENNEL, [James] Statement of facts, occaſional of, and relative to the late diſturbances at the theatre royal, Edinburgh. 1788. 8. (1 ſh.)

FENTON, [....] The Earl of Warwick, a Tragedy. 1767. 8. Poems. 1774. 4. (6 ſh.)

FERGUSON, [Adam] *LL. D. Emeritus Profeſſor of Philoſophy in the Univerſity of Edinburgh.* Hiſtory of civil ſociety. 1766. 4. (15 ſh.) überſ. (von C. F. *Jünger*) Leipz. 1768. 8. Inſtitutes of moral philoſophy. 1769. 8. (3 ſh.) nachgedr. Mentz and Francfort. 1786. 8. überſ. von *Garve*. 1772. Hiſtory of the progreſſ and termination of the roman republic. Vol. 1-3. 1783. 4. (2 L. 12 ſh. 6 d.) überſ. von *C. D. Beck*. Th. 1-3. Leipz. 1784. 8.

—— [Andrew] *Gardener at Brentford.* The Gardener's univerſal guide. 1787. 8. (5 ſh.)

—— [James] *F. R. S: Lecturer in Natural Philoſophy and Aſtronomy.* born at Keit in Bampfſhire 1710. died d. 16 Nov. 1776.

FERGU-

FERGUSON, [John] *A. M. Captain in the service of the East-India Company.* Dictionary of the hindostan language — with a grammar. 1773. 4. (2 L. 2 sh.)

—— [Robert] Poems. 1774. 12. (2 sh. 6 d.)

FERNYHOUGH, [William] *A. B.* Trentham park, a poem. 1789. 4. (1 sh.).

FERON, [J....] *late Surgeon-Major of the english squadron under M. de Ternay's command in North-America and of the Marine hospitals at Boston and in Rhode-Island.* Experiments on the waters of Boston. (Mem. of B. A. Vol. 1. p. 556.)

FERRAR, [J....] *Citizen of Limerick.* History of Limerick, ecclesiastical, civil and military from the earliest records to the Y. 1786. 1787. 8. (6 sh.)

FERRIS, [Samuel] *M. D. Extraordin. Member of the Roy. Soc. at Edinburgh.* Diss. De sanguinis per corpus vivum circulantis putredine. Edinb. 1784. Dissertation on Milk. 1785. 8. (3 Sh.) übers. von *C. F. Michaelis.* Leipz. 1787. 8.

FIELDING, [Charles John] The brothers, an eclogue. 1781. 4. (1 sh.)

FIGGES, [James] *Excise officer.* Excise Officer's vade mecum or ready assistant. 1783. 8. (2 sh. 6 d.)

FILSON, [John] The discovery, settlement and present state of Kentuke and an essay towards the topography and natural history of that important country. 1784. 8. (10 sh.) übers. Leipz. 1790. 8.

FINCH, [Thomas] Precedents in Chancery: being a collection of cases in Chancery from 1689 to 1722. Ed. II. 1786. 8. (10 sh. 6 d.)

FINDLAY, [Robert] *D. D. Professor of Divinity in the University of Glasgow.* Vindication of the sacred books and of *Josephus* — from various misrepresentations and cavils of *Voltaire.* 1770. 8. (5 sh. 6 d.)

FINGLASS, [Esther] *Miss.* The recluse, or history of Lady Gertrude Lesby. Vol. 1. 2. 1788. 8. (5 sh.)

FISHER, [Joseph] *of Drax, in Yorkshire. M. D.* Remarks upon the remarker on *Lindsey's* scripture confutation —. 1775. 8. (1 sh. 6 d.) Review of Dr. *Priestley's* doctrine of philosophical necessity —. 1779. 8. (1 sh. 6 d.) The practice of medicine made easy —. 1785. 8. (2 sh. 6 d.)

FISHER, [Joſhua] *F. A. S.* Caſe of a remarkable large tumour found in the cavity of the abdomen. (Mem. of B. A. Vol. 1. p. 537. Lond. M. J. Vol. 7. P. 3.)

FISKE, [Jonathan] *Bookſeller.* The caſe of *J. Fiſke* — tried and — acquitted at the ſeſſions in the Old Bailey — upon the infamous proſecution of *Patrik Roche Farrill.* 17 11. 8. (1 Sh.) The life and tranſactions of *Margaret Nicholſon* —. 1785. 8. (1 Sh. 6 d.)

FITZGERALD, [George Robert] *Esq.* born .... executed for the murder of M'Donnel in Ireland 17..

—— [Gerald] *Fellow of Trinity-College, Dublin.* The academic ſportsman; or, a Winter's day; a poem. 1773. 4. (1 Sh.)

—— [Keane] *F. R. S.* Experiments on applying the Rever. D. *Hale's* method of diſtilling ſalt water to the ſteam engine. (Phil. Tranſact. 1760 p. 53. p. 370.) Attempt to improve the manner of working the ventilators by the help of the fire engine. (Ibid. 1760. p. 727.) Deſcription of a metalline thermometer. (Ibid. 1761. p. 823.) Experiments on checking the too luxuriant growth of fruit trees, tending to diſpoſe them to produce fruit. (Ibid. 1762. p. 71.) Deſcription of a new thermometer and barometer. (Ibid. 1762. p. 146.) Method of leſſening the quantity of friction in engines. (Ibid. 1763. p. 139.) Account of ſome improvements made on a new wheel barometer, invented by him. (Ibid. 1770. p. 74.) *Eſſay on the Eaſt-India trade, and its importance to this Kingdom —. 1770. 8. (1 Sh.) Letter to the directors of the Eaſt-India Company. 1777. 8. (1 Sh.) *Conſiderations on the important benefits to be derived from the Eaſt-India Company's building and navigating their own ſhips. 1778. 8. (1 Sh.) Experiments with Chineſe hemp ſeed. (Phil. Tranſact. 1782. p. 44.)

—— [Samuel] *Phyſician at Mullingar.* Hiſtories of two caſes: The diſcharge of a large calcareous concretion and the extraction of the bones of a foetus by the rectum. (*Duncan's* M. C. Vol. 8. p. 329.)

—— [William] *of Gray's Inn.* Ode to the memory of Capt. *James Cook.* 1780. 4. (1 Sh.)

FITZPATRICK, [J...] *of Dublin.* Account of extraordinary effects from the application of cold water after delivery. (*Duncan's* M. C. Vol. 9. p. 227.) History of a case of catalepsis successfully treated. (Ibid. Vol. 10. p. 242.)

FLAGG, [Henry Collins] *of South-Carolina.* Observations on the Numb-Fish or torporific eel. (Tr. of A. S. Vol. 2. p. 170.)

FLEET, [Edward] Junior; *B. A. of Oriel College, Oxford.* Examination of *Maclaine's* answer to *Soame Jenyns* on his view of the internal evidence of the christian religion —. 1777. 8. (2 Sh.) Address and reply relative to his examination of *Maclaine's* answer to *Soame Jenyns* —. 1777. 8. (6 d.)

FLEMING, [Caleb] *D. D. Pastor of a Protestant dissenting church.* born 1698. died d. 21 July 1779.

—— [Thomas] *Minister of the Gospel at Kenmore.* Account of a remarkable agitation of the waters of *Lock Tay.* (Tr. of E. S. Vol. 1. p. 200.)

FLETCHER, [Charles] *M. D.* Maritime state considered as to the health of seamen —. 1786. 8. (5 Sh.) The Cock-pit, a poem. 1787. 4. (2 Sh.)

—— [John] *Vicar of Madeley, Salop and Chaplain by the Earl of Buchan.* born .... died d. 14 Aug. 1785.

FLOOD, [Henry] Speech on the commercial treaty with France. 1787. 8. (1 Sh.)

FLOWER, [Henry] (born in America.) Observations on the gout and rhevmatism —. 1766. 8. (6 d.) Proofs of curing the gout, and other disorders —. Ed. 2. 1771. 8. (6 d.)

—— [Robert] The radix: a new way of making logarithms. 1771. 4. (3 Sh.)

FOGERTY, [....] *Mrs.* Memoirs of Col. *Digby* and Miss *Stanley.* Vol. 1. 2. 1773. 12. (5 Sh.) The fatal connexion. Vol. 1. 2. 1773. 12.

FOOT, [James] Penseroso; or, the pensive philosopher in his solitudes. a poem. 1771. 8. (4 Sh.)

—— [Jesse] *Surgeon at London.* On the diseases of the urethra. 1774. 8. (1 Sh. 6 d.) Ed. 2. 1781. Ed. 3. 1785. 8. übers. Altenb. 1777. 8. Observations on the new opinions of *J. Hunter* in his treatise on the venereal disease. P. 1-3. 1787. 8. (5 Sh. 6 d.) Ed. 2. 1787. 8. (8 Sh. 6 d.) On the bite of a mad doge —. 1788. 8. (2 Sh.) A new discovered fact, of a relative nature, in the venereal poison. 1790. 8. (1 Sh. 6 d.)

FOOTE, [Samuel] *Actor.* born at *Truro*, *Cornwall.* 1717. died d 20 Oct. 1777.

FORBES, [Daniel] *Surgeon at Dornock.* History of a case of Ileus, in which great benefit was derived from the application of a blister. (*Duncan's* M. C. Vol. 9. p. 266.)

—— [Eli] Account of the effects of lightning on a large rock in Gloucester. (Mem. of B. A. Vol. 1. p. 253.)

—— [Francis] The extensive practice of the new husbandry —. 1778. 8. (5 Sh.) The improvement of waste lands, viz, wet, moory land, land near rivers and running waters, peat land —. 1778. 8. (3 Sh. 6 d.)

FORD, [Edward] *Surgeon of the Westminster General Dispensary.* An extraneous body cut out from the joint of the knee. (Med. Obs. Vol. 5. p. 329. übers. Samml. f. A. St. 5. S. 96.) A case of proptosis. (M. C. Vol. 1. p. 95.) Account of a method of curing the hydrophthalmia by means of a seton. (Ibid. p. 409.) Account of a hairy excrescence in the facies of a new-born infant. (Ibid p. 444.) A case of hydrophthalmia successfully treated. (London M. J. Vol. 1. p. 346.) Account of a remarkable operation on a broken arm. (Ibid. Vol. 2. p. 46.) Case of a fatal ulceration of the bladder, occasioned by a caries of the os pubis. (Ibid. Vol. 3. p. 80. übers. Samml. f. A. Th. 8. S. 45.) Case of strangulated hernia. (Ibid. Vol. 6. p. 118.) Two cases of fracture of the scull. (Ibid. Vol. 8. P. 4.) Case of the spontaneous cure of anevrism, with remarks. (Ibid. Vol. 9. P. 2.) Remarks on hydrocephalus internus. (Ibid. Vol. 11. P. 1. übers. Samml. f. A. Th. 13. S. 369.)

FORD, [William] born 1736. died d. 26 Jan. 1783.

FORDE, [Brownlow] The miraculous cure, or the citizen outwitted, a farce. 1771. 8.

FORDYCE, [George] *M. D. F. R. S.* Dissert. De Catarrho. Edinb. 1758 (see *Smellie's* Thesaur.: Diss. Edin. Vol. 2. p. 501.) Elements of the practice of physic P. 1. 2. 1768. 8. (4 Sh. 6. d.) Ed. 2. 1771. 8. Ed. 3. 1784. übers. Kopenh. 1769. 8.

Ele-

Elements of Agriculture and vegetation. 1771. 8. (2 Sh. 6. d.) übers. *Fr. Schwediauer.* Wien. 1778. 8. New Inquiry into the causes symptoms and cure of putrid and inflammable fevers. 1773. 8. Of the light produced by inflammation. (Phil. Transact. 1776. p. 504.) Examination of various ores in the museum of Dr. *Will. Hunter.* (Ibid. 1779. p. 527.) A new method of essaying copper ore. (Ibid. 1780. p. 30.) Account of some experiments on the loss of weight in bodies on being melted or heated. (Ibid. 1785. p. 361.) Account of an experiment on heat. (Ibid. 1787. p. 310.) The Croonian lecture on muscular motion. (Ibid. 1788. p. 23.)

FORDYCE, [James] *D. D. Minister at Brechin.* (Brother to Sir *Will. Fordyce.*) The temple of Virtue; a dream. 1756. 8. (1 Sh. 6. d.) * Letters on the eloquence of the pulpit. 1764. 8. (1 Sh. 6. d.) Letters between Theodosius and Constantia. 17 . . * Sermons to young women. Vol. 1. 2. 1765. 8. (6 Sh.) übers. Th. 1. 2. Leipzig. 1767. 8. The character and conduct of the female sex. 1776. 8. (1 Sh. 6. d.) übers. Leipzig. 1776. 8. Address to young men. Vol. 1. 2. 1777. 8. (7 Sh.) übers. Th. 1. 2. Leipz. 1778. 8. Addresses to the deity 1785. 8 (2 Sh. 6. d.) Ed. 2. 1787. (3 Sh.) Poems. 1787. 8. (3 Sh.)

— [William] *Sir, Baronet. M. D. Physician at London.* Review of the venereal disease and its remedies. 1768. 8. (2 Sh.) Ed. 2. 1777. 8. Ed. 5. 1785. 8. übers. Altenburg. 1769. 8. Inquiry into the causes, symptoms and cure, of putrid and inflammatory fevers —. 1773. 8. (3 Sh.) übers.: mit einem Anhang von dem Hectischen Fieber und der — Bräune. Leipz. 1774. 8. Fragmenta chirurgica et medica. 1784. 8. (3 Sh.) Attempt to discover the virtues of the sarsaparilla root in the venereal disease. (Med. Obs. Vol. 1. p. 149.) On the virtues of the muriatic acid or spirit of Sea-salt in the cure of putrid diseases. 1789. 8. (1 Sh.)

FOREST, [Theophilus] born: . . . . died d. 5 Nov. 1784.

FORREST, [Thomas] *Captain.* Voyage to new Guinea and the Moluccas, from Balambangan — during the Years 1774. 1775. 1776. with a vocabulary ry of the Magindano tongue. 1779. 4. (1 L. 11 Sh. 6. d.) überſ. im Auszug. Hamb. 1782. 8. *Ebeling's* neue Sammlung von Reiſebeſchreib. Th. 3. S. 1. On the monſoons in India. 1783. 8. (2 Sh.)

FORSTER, [Nathaniel] *D D. Rector of all ſaints, Colcheſter and Tolleskunt knight's, Eſſex; Chaplain to the Counteſſ Dowager of Northington.* born: .... died d. 12 Apr. 1790.

FOSTER, [Anne Emelinda] *Mrs.* (maid-name *Maſtermann*) born 1747. died at Margate d. 24 March 1789.

—— [Edward] *M. D: Teacher of Midwifery in Dublin.* born: .... died 17..

—— [John] born at Windſor 1731. died 1773.

—— [William] *Farrier.* The Gentleman's experienced farrier; containing the methods of diet, exerciſe, bleeding, purging — of horſes —. 1787. 8. (6 Sh.)

FOTHERGILL, [Anthony] *M. D: F. R. S. Northampton.* Diſſ. De febre remittente. Edinb. 1763. 8. Two caſes of an incontinency of urine cured by a bliſter to the region of the os ſacrum. (Med. Obſ. Vol. 3. p. ...) The caſe of a man affected with a difficulty in paſſing urine, occaſioned by a diſcharge of wind from the urethra. (Med. Com. of Ed. Vol. 2. p. 194.) Obſervations made during the laſt froſt at Northampton. (Phil. Transact. 1776. p. 587.) Account of the cure of the St. Vitus's dance by electricity. (Ibid. 1779. p. 1.) Account of an improved method of treating the puerperal fever. (London M. J. Vol. 3. p. 411.) On the nature and qualities of the Cheltenham water. 1785. 8. (1 Sh. 6. d.) Ed. 2. 1788. 8. (2 Sh.) Obſervations on longevity. (Mem. of M. Vol. 1. p. 355.) A fatal caſe of morbid enlargement of the proſtate gland, with a ſingular appearance in the bladder. (Mem. of M. S. of L. Vol. 1. p. 202.) On the efficacy of the hyoscyamus or Henbane in certain caſes of inſanity. (Ibid. p. 310.) On the efficacy of the gummi rubrum Aſtringens Gambienſe. (Ibid. Vol. 2.)

—— [John] *M. D: F. R. S: F. A. S.* (Quacker) born d. 8 March. 1712. in Wensley Dale, Yorkſhire. died d. 26. Dec. 1780.

FOWKE, [Francis] *Esq.* On the vina or indian lyre. (Asiat. Res. Vol. I. p. 295.)

FOWLER, [......] General account of the calamities occasioned by the late tremendous hurricanes and earthquakes in the West-India islands —. 1781. 8. (1 Sh. 6. d.)

— [John] *Surgeon at Ayton, Berwickshire.* Some hints relative to the recovery of persons drowned and apparently dead —. 1784. 8.

— [Thomas] *M. D: Physician to the General Infirmary of the County of Hertford.* Diss. De methodo medendi variolas auxilio Mercurii. 1777. History of two cases from the poisonous effects of the seeds of the thorn apple. (Med. Com. of Ed. Vol. 5. p. 161.) A remarkable case of the morbid effects of lightning, successfully treated. (Ibid. Vol. 6. p. 194.) History of a case of rhevmatism, cured by the volatile elixir of guajacum. (*Duncan's* M. C. 1780. p. 94. übers. Samml. f. A. Th. 6. S. 99.) Observations on the effects of different anthelmintics applied to earth-worms —. (*Duncan's* M. C. Vol. 8. p. 336.) Medical reports of the effect of tobacco principally — in the cure of dropsies and dysuries with observations on the use of clysters of tobacco in the treatment of colic. 1785. 8. (2 sh.) übers. Samml. f. A. Th. XI. S. 335.) Medical reports of the effect of arsenic in the cure of agues, remitting fevers and periodic head-aches. 1786. 8. (3 sh.) (London M. J. Vol, 7. P. 2.)

FOWNES, [Joseph] *Dissenting Minister at Shrewsbury.* born 1714. died d. 14 Nov. 1789.

FOX, [Charles James] *Member of Parliament* (born 1749.) Epistle from him, partridge shooting, to J. Townshend cruising. 1779. 4. (1 sh.) Invocation to poetry, a poem. 17.. Lines addressed to Mrs. *Crewe* of Cheshire. 17.. Speech to the Electors of Westminster. 1782. 8. (1 sh.) Speech on the East-India Bill. 1783. 8. (1 sh.) *Fox* and *Pitt's* speeches in the house of commons. 1784. 8. (2 sh. 6. d.) Speech on the Irish resolutions 1785. 8. (2 sh.) Speech on the 4th Irish proposition. 1785. 8. (1 sh.) Reply to Mr. *Pitt* upon re-

reporting the 4th proposition of the Irish system. 1785. 8. (6. d.)

FOX, [Edward] *Apothecary by the Princess Amalia.* Formulae medicamentorum selectae. 1778. 8. (7 sh.)

—— [Henry] French and English Dictionary —. 1769. 8. (4. sh.) View of universal modern history of Chev. *Mehegan.* Vol. 1-3. 1779. (18 sh.)

—— [Joseph] The parish Clerk's vademecum being a collection of singing psalms —. 1752. (6 d.) The Parish Clerk's pocket companion —. 1778. 8. (2 Sh.)

FRANCIS, [Anne] *Miss.* Poetical translation of the song of Solomon, from the original hebrew. 1781. 4. (7 Sh. 6. d.) The obsequies of Demetrius Poliorcetes. a Poem. 1785. 4. (1 Sh. 6. d.) Charlotte to Werter, a poetical epistle. 1787. 4. (1 Sh. 6. d.) Miscellaneous poems. 1790. 8. (3 Sh.)

—— [Benjamin] The conflagration: a poem. Ed. 2. 1786. 8. (1 Sh.)

—— [Philip] *Rector of Barrow in Suffolk.* born: .... died at *Bath*: d. 5 March. 1773.

—— [Philip] *Member of Parliament.* Original minutes — on the settlement and collection of the Bengal revenues —. 1782. Speech in the house of Commons. 1784. 8. (1 Sh. 6. d.) Two speeches in the house of Commons on the East-India Bill. 1784. 8. (1 Sh. 6. d.) Speech in the house of Commons. 1786. 8. (2 Sh.) Answer to the charges exhibited against him Gen. *Clavering* and Colonel *Manson* by Sir *Elijah Impey* — on his defence of the Nunducomar charge. 1788. 8. (1 Sh.)

FRANKLIN, [Benjamin] *LL. D.* born at *Boston, North-America*, d. 17 Jan. 1706. died d. 17 Apr. 1790. (*D' Alembert* bewillkommte ihn bey seiner Aufnahme in die Französische Akademie mit diesen Worten: Eripuit fulmen coelo, mox sceptra tyrannis.)

—— [J.....] Account of a luminous arch. (Phil. Transact. 1790. p. 46.)

—— [Thomas] *D. D. Chaplain in Ordinary to his Majesty, and Rector of Brasted, Kent.* born: ..... died d. 15 March 1784.

FRANK-

FRANKLIN, [William] *Enſign on the Company's Bengal Eſtabliſhment.* Obſervations made on a tour from Bengal to Perſia in the Years 1786. 87. with a ſhort account of the remains of the celebrated palace of Perſepolis and other intereſting events. London. 1790. 8. (6 Sh.) überſ. von *Joh. Reinh. Forſter.* Berlin. 1790. 8.

FRANKLYN, *[G.....]* Obſervations, occaſioned by the attempts made in England to effectuate the abolition of the ſlavetrade —. 1789. 8. (2 Sh. 6. d.) Anſwer to *Clarkſon's* eſſay on the ſlavery and commerce of the human ſpecies. 1789. 8. (5 Sh.)

FRANKS, [John] Obſervations on animal life and apparent death, from accidental ſuſpenſion of the functions of the lungs, with remarks on the *Brunonian* ſyſtem of Medicine. 1790. 8. (3 Sh.)

FRASER, [A......] Certain arrangements in civil policy neceſſary for the farther improvement of husbandry, mines, fiſheries and manufactures in this kingdom —. 1785. 8. (1 Sh.)

— [John] Hiſtory of the agreſtis Cornu copiae; or the new American graſſ; and a new botanical deſcription of the plant —. 1789. fol. (2 Sh. 6. d.)

FREE, *[B... D...] M. A.* Tyrocinium in hoſpitiis curiae: or, exerciſes for the firſt Year in the inns of court, preparatory to the ſtudy of the law. Vol. I. 2. 1784. 8. (6 Sh. 6 d.)

FRENCH, *[G...]* Fifteen minutes inſtructions on the venereal diſeaſe. 1776. 12. (1 Sh)

— [William] *Surgeon.* A caſe of hydrops ovarii and aſcites. (Mem. of M. S. of L. Vol. I. p. 234.)

FREND, *[W...] M. A. of Jeſus College, Cambridge.* ° Addreſſ to the member of the church of England and to proteſtant trinitarians in general, exhorting them to turn from the worſhip of three perſons, to the worſhip of the one true god. 1788. 8. (2. d.) Thoughts on ſubſcription to religious teſts —. 1788. with Appendix. 1789. 8. (2 Sh.)

FRESTON, *[A...] A. M. Curate of Farley, Hants.* Elegy. 1787. 4. (6 d.) Poems on ſeveral ſubjects. 1787. 8. (2 Sh. 6 d.)

FREWEN, *[Thomas] M. D. of Lewes in Suſſex.* Account of the condition of the town of Haſtings after it had been viſited by the ſmall-pox. (Phil. Trans-

Transact. 1747. p. 108.) Letter in answer to Dr. *Watts*. 1756. 8. (6 d.) On the cure of the small-pox by antidote. 1759. 8. (1 Sh.) Case of a patient, who voided a large stone through the perinaeum from the urethra. (Ibid. 1762. p. 258.) Case of a young man stupified by the smoke of sea coal. (Ibid. 1762. p. 254.) Physiologia. 1780. 8. (6 Sh.)

FREWIN, [Richard] — — and *Will. Sims*; the rates of merchandise. 1782. 8. (7 Sh.)

FRY, [William] *Teacher of languages and mathematical sciences.* A new vocabulary of the most difficult words in the english language. 1785. 12. (2 Sh. 6 d.)

FRYER, [Edward] *M. D.* Ode to health: inscribed to his Royal Highness, Prince Augustus. Gottingen. 1788. 8. Ode to the genius of patriotism. Gottingen. 1789. 4.

FULLARTON, [William] *Member of Parliament. F. R. S. of London and Edinburgh; late Commander of the southern army on the Coast of Coromandel.* View of the english interests in India and an account of the military operations in the southern parts of the Peninsula during the campaigns of 1782-1784 —. 1787. 8. (5 Sh.) Ed. 2. 1788. 8. (5 Sh.)

FULLER, [....] *Miss.* Alan Fitz-Osborne, an historical tale. Vol. 1. 2. 1787. 12. (5 Sh.) ° The son of Ethelwolf: an historical tale by the author of Alan Fitz-Osborne. Vol. 1. 2. 1789. 8. (6 Sh.)

FULLER, [John] *Surgeon at Ayton, Berwickshire.* New hints relative to the recovery of persons drowned and apparently dead. 1784. 8. (1 Sh.)

— — [Stephen] *Agent for Jamaica.* The act of assembly of the island of Jamaica, for the better order and government of slaves - commonly called the consolidated act —. 1788. 4. (2 Sh.) The new act of assembly of the island of Jamaica — being the present code noir of that island —. 1789. 4. (1 Sh.) Two reports from the committee of the house of assembly of Jamaica — on the subject of the slave trade and the treatment of the Negroes. 1789. 4. (1 Sh.) The code of laws for the government of the Negro-slaves in the Island of Jamaica. 1789. 4. (1 Sh.)

FULLMER. [Samuel] *Gardener.* Young gardener's best companion —. 1781. 12. (2 Sh. 6 d.)

FURNEAUX, [Philipp] *D. D.* born at *Totness, Devonshire.* 1726. died d. 23 Nov. 1783.

FYFE, [Andrew] *Assistant to Dr. Monro, Prof. of Anatomy at Edinburgh.* *System of Anatomy and physiology. Vol. 1. 2. 1786. 8. (15 Sh.) Ed. 2. (with the Author's name) Vol. 1-3. 1787. 8. (18 Sh.)

FYNNEY, [Fielding Best] *Surgeon at Leek in Staffordshire.* The history of a case of imperforate hymen (Med. Com. of Ed. Vol. 3. p. 194.) Account of the extirpation of a polypous excrescence from the os uteri. (Ibid. Vol. 4. p. 228.) A uncommon case in midwifery, accompanied with a luxation of the maxilla inferior, occasioned by convulsions. (*Duncan's* M. C. Vol. 9. p. 380.) Case of *Ann Davenport.* (Phil. Tr. 1777. p. 458.)

GABRIEL, [R. . . . . B. . . . .] *D. D. late fellow of Worcester College, Oxford.* Facts relating to Dr. *White's* Bampton lectures. 1789. 8. (1 sh. 6. d.)

GADESBY, [R. . . .] Introduction to geography. 1776. (2 sh. 6. d.)

GAHAGAN, [Mathias] *Physician in Grenada.* History of a curious case of the translation of inflammation from the lungs to the brain ending fatally in hydrocephalus. (*Duncan's* M. C. Vol. 3. Dec. 2. p. 353.) History of two cases, in which, after suppuration at the Perinaeum, the urine was discharged at preternatural openings. (Ibid. Dec. 2. Vol. 4. p. 271.) History of a case, in which singular tumours from indurated and enlarged glands produced a fatal termination. (Ibid. p. 281.)

GALE, [......] *Essay on the nature and principles of public credit. Ess. 1. 2. 3. 4. 1784-1787. 8. (11 sh.)

— [Benjamin] *F. A. A: F. S. Philad. and F. R. S.* Observations on the culture of Smyrna wheat. (Mem. of B. A. Vol. I. p. 381.) Historical memoirs, relating to the practice of inoculation for the small pox in the british American provinces, particularly in New England. (Phil. Transact. 1766. p. 193.) Account of the successfull application of salt to wounds made by the bite of rattle ſnakes. (Ibid. p. 244.)

GALE, [Roger] On the horologia of the antients. (Arch. Vol. 6. p. 133.)

GALLIARD, [Bradſhaw] Odes. 1774. 4. (2 ſh. 6 d.)

GALLOWAY, [Joſeph] *Member of the American Congreſſ.* Speech — in anſwer to the ſpeech of *John Dickinſon.* 1764. 8. (2 ſh.) * Candid examination of the mutual claims of Great Britain and the colonies —. 1775. 8. (1 ſh.) überſ. Hamburg. 1780. 8. The examination of *Joſ. Galloway.* 1779. 8. (2 ſh.)

GAMBOLD, [John] *A. M. Biſhop of Herrnhutian church at Nevils Court, Fetter Lane.* born: .... died d. 13 Sept. 1771.

GANDER, [Gregory] Poetical tales. 1779. 4. (1 ſh.)

GANNETT, [Caleb] *A. M: F. A. A.* Obſervations of a ſolar eclipſe made at the Univerſity in Cambridge Oct. 27. 1780. (Mem. of B. A. Vol. I. p. 146.) Hiſtorical regiſter of the aurora borealis from Auguſt 8. 1781. to Aug. 19. 1783. (Ibid. p. 327.)

GARDEN, [Alexander] *M. D: F. R. S.* Account of the gymnotus electricus, or electrical eel. (Phil. Transact. 1775. p. 102.)

—— [James] * The hiſtory of Henry III. King of France. 1783. 8. (6 ſh.)

GARDINER, [John] *M. D. Preſident of the Royal College of Phyſicians and F. R S. of Edinburgh.* Diſſ. De Vino. 17.. A particular method of giving the ſolution of corroſive ſublimate mercury in ſmale doſes. (Eſſ. and Obſerv. Edinb. Vol. 3. p. 380.) Obſervations on the animal oeconomy and on the cauſes and cure of diſeaſes. 1784. überſ. von *E. B. G. Hebenſtreit.* Leipz. 1786. 8.

—— [Richard] *Captain of Marines on board his Majeſty's ſhips Rippon.* born: .... died ....

GARDNER, [Edward] Liberty, a poem. 1776. (2 ſh.)

—— [John] *Surgeon at Betley, Staffordſhire.* Hiſtory of a caſe in which there occurred a very uncommon preſentation of a child, to whoſe neck there was attached a tumour nearly about the ſize of the child's head. (Med. Com. of Ed. Vol. 5. p. 306.)

GARLICK, [William] *Surgeon at Marlborough.* Caſe of an enlargement of the ſpleen; with an account of of ſome remarkable appearances obſerved on opening the body of a gentleman whoſe death was occaſioned by a perforation in his bladder. (London M. J. Vol. 5. p. 186.)

GARNET, [John] *Lord-Biſhop of Clogher.* born..... died d. 1 March. 1782.

— [Thomas] *M. D.* Experiments and obſervations on the horley-green ſpaw near Halifax, with an account of two other mineral waters in Yorkſhire. 1789. 8. (2 ſh.) Account of a ſuppuration of the liver —. (*Duncan's* M. C. Dec. 2. Vol. 3. p. 303)

GARRICK, [David] *Actor.* born at Hereford. d. 20 Febr. 1716. died d. 20 Jan. 1779.

GARTSHORE, [Maxwell] *M. D: F. R. S: F. A. S. Phyſician to the britiſh Lying in Hoſpital, St. Martins-Lane, Weſtminſter.* Diſſ. De papaveris uſu — in parturientibus ac puerperis. Edinb. 1764. 8. Caſe of a fatal ileus. (Med. Obſ. Vol. 4. p....) Two caſes of the retroverted uterus. (Ibid. Vol. 5. p. 381.) A caſe of difficult deglutition, occaſioned by an ulcer in the oeſophagus, with an account of the appearances on diſſection. (M. C. Vol. I. p. 242.) A remarkable caſe of numerous births, with obſervations. (Phil. Transact. 1787. p. 344. London M. J. Vol. X. P. I.) Obſervations on extra-uterine caſes and on ruptures of the uterus. (London M. J. Vol. VIII. P. 4.)

GAST, [John] *Deacon at Glandelagh.* The Rudiments of Grecian hiſtory —. 1754. 8. (6 ſh.) The hiſtory of Greece —. 1782. 4. (1 L. 1 ſh.)

GEACH, [Francis] *F. R. S. Surgeon at Plymouth.* Caſe of a man who had ſix ſtones taken out of the gall bladder. (Phil. Transact. 1763. p. 231.) Caſe of a man wounded in the left eye with a ſmall ſword. (Ibid. 1763. p. 234.) Medical and chirurgical obſervations on inflammations of the eyes, on the venereal diſeaſe, on ulcers and gunſhotwounds. 1766. 8. (1 ſh.) überſ. Zittau und Görliz. 1768. 8. Obſervations on Dr. *Baker's* eſſay on the endemial colic of Devonſhire. 1768. 8. (1 ſh.) Reply to Dr. *Saunders's* pamphlet, relative to the diſpute concerning the Devonſhire cyder, 1769. 8. (1 ſh.)

Observations on the present epidemic dysentery. 1781. 8. (1 sh.) übers. Samml. f. A. Th. 7. S. 544.

GEDDES, [Alexander] *D. D. a Roman catholic Clergyman.* Select satires of *Horace*, translated into english verse. 1779. 4. (5 sh.) Prospectus of a new translation of the holy bible — compared with the ancient versions, with various readings, explanatory notes and critical observations. 1786. 4. (7 sh. 6 d.) Queries, doubts and difficulties relative to a vernacular version of the holy scriptures; being an appendix to a prospectus. 1787. 4. (3 sh. 6 d.) Letter to *Priestley*, in which he attempt to prove that the divinity of Jesus Christ was a primitive tenet of christianity. 1787. 8. (1 sh.) Letter to the Lord Bishop of London. 1787. 4. (5 sh.) Proposals for printing by subscription a new translation of the holy bible. 1788. 4. (1 Sh. 6 d.) General answer to the queries, counsils and criticisms, that have been communicated to him since the publication of his proposals for printing a new translation of the bible. London 1790. 4.

GENT, [Thomas] *Printer.* born: .... died 1778.

GENTLEMAN, [Francis] *Actor.* born in Ireland d. 23 Oct. 1728. died d. 21 Dec. 1784.

GERARD, [Alexander] *D. D. Prof. of Divinity, King's College, Aberdeen.* Plan of education in Mareshal's College. 1755. übers. (von *Gottl. Schlegel*) Riga. 1770. 8. (4 Sh.) übers. nebst *Voltaire's* und *Alembert's* Abhandl. über den Geschmack: Breslau und Leipz. 1766. 8. Dissertations on subjects relating to the genius and the evidences of christianity. 1765. 8. (6 Sh.) On the Genius. 1784. 8. übers. von *C. Garve.* Leipzig. 1776. 8. Sermons. Vol. 1. 2. 1782. 8. (10 Sh.)

GERARD, [James] *M. D. Physician in Liverpool.* The History of a speedy recovery after the operation of the trepan. (*Duncan's* M. C. Vol. 9. p. 272.) The history of a case of ileus, terminating fatally with an account of the appearances on dissection. (Ibid. Vol. 10. p. 293.)

GIBBES, [P....] *Mrs.* Louisa Stroud. 17. The niece, or the history, of Miss Sukey Thornbey, a novel Vol. 1-3. 1787. 8. (9 Sh.)

GIBBON, [Edward] Essai sur l'etude de la litterature. 1760. 8. (2 Sh. 6 d.) translated into english 1763. 8. (2 sh.) History of the decline and fall of the roman empire Vol. 1-6. 1775-1788. 4. (6 L. 6 Sh.) nachgedruckt Basil. 1787. 8. Vol. 1-13. übers. von *F. A. W. Weck* und *Schreiter*. Th. 1-4. Leipz. 1789. 8. übers. von *C. W. v. R.* Th. 1-7. Magdeb. 1789. 8. übers. u. abgekürzt (von *G. K. F. Seidel*) Berlin. 1790. 8. Historische Uebersicht des römischen Rechts oder des 44sten Cap. übers. von *Hugo*. Göttingen. 1789. 8. Das Leben des Attila, Königs der Hunnen. Lüneb. 1787. 8. Die Bekehrung des Kaisers Constantins des Grossen — übers. (von *A. H. W. v. Walterstern*) Altona 1784. 8. Vindication of some passages in the XV. XVI. Chapters of the history of the decline. 1779. 8. (2 Sh. 6 d.)

GIBBONS, [Thomas] *D. D. Pastor of Protestant Dissenters in London.* born 1721. died d. 22 Febr. 1785.

— [William] *Iron Manufacturer at Bristol.* Reply to Sir *Lucius O' Brien* — on the present state of the iron trade between England and Ireland. 1785. 8. (1 Sh. 6 d.)

GIBBS, [....] *Mathematician and Musician.* born: ... died at *Rhotherhite* d. ... Dec. 1779.

GIBSON, [John] *M. D.* On continual, intermitting, eruptive and inflammatory fevers. 1769. 8. (6 Sh.) The principles, elements, or primary particles of bodies —. 1772. 8. (2 Sh. 6 d.)

— [John] *Surgeon and Man-midwife in Harwich.* Hints and admonitions — on the practice of midwifery. 1772. 12. (1 sh.)

— [Joseph] *Merchant at Glasgow.* History of Glasgow. 1777. 8. (5 sh.)

— [William] M. A. Conscience; a poetical essay. 1772. 4. (1 sh.) Religion; a poetical essay. 1775. 4. (2 sh.) Jerusalem destroyed: a poem. 1781. 4. (2 sh.)

GIDDIES, [Alexander] Select satires of Horace. 1779. (5 sh.)

GIFFORD, [Andrew] *D. D. F. A. S. Assistant to Joseph Planta, Under-Librarian to the British Museum.* born d. 17 Aug. 1701. died d. 19 June 1784.

GIFFORD, [J. . . . .] *Reflections on the unity of God —. by *J. G.* 1782. 8. (1 sh.) Ed. 2. 1784. 8. (1 sh.) Ed. 4. 1786. 8. (3 sh.) *Letter to *John* Lord Archbishop of Canterbury. 1785. 8. (1 sh.)

— [Richard] *B. A. Rector of North Okendon, Essex.* Outlines of an answer to Dr. *Priestley's* disquisitions relating to matter and spirit. 1781. 8. (2 sh. 6 d.)

GILBANK, [William] *A. M: Rector of St. Ethelburga, London, Chaplain to the Duke of Gloucester.* The scripture history of Abraham. 1773. 8. (4 sh.) The day of Pentecost, or man restored. a poem. 1789. 8. (5 sh)

GILBERT, [Thomas] *Esq. Commander of the Charlotte.* Voyage from new South Wales to Canton in the Year 1788. with views of the islands discovered. 1789. 4. (8 sh.)

— [Thomas] *Member of Parliament and Chairman of the committee of supply and ways and means in the house of Commons.* Plan for the better relief and employment of the poor —. with a supplement. 1781. 8. (2 sh. 6 d.) Observations on the bills for amending and rendering more effectual the laws relative to houses of correction for the better relief — of the poor. 1782. 8. (6 d.) Considerations on the bills for the better relief and employment of the poor. 1787. 8. (1 sh.) Heads of a bill for the better relief and employment of the poor and for the improvement of the police of this country —. 1787. 8. (1 sh.)

— [W. . . . .] *Opinion on the power of courts martial to punish for contempts; occasioned by the case of Major *John Browne* of the 76 Regiment. 1788 8. (1 sh. 6 d.)

GILDING, [Elizabeth] The breathings of genius, being a collection of poems. 1776. 8. (2 sh. 6 d.)

GILES, [William] On marriage. 12. 1771. (1 sh. 6 d.) Collection of poems on divine and moral subjects. 1775. 8. (3 sh.)

GILL, [Jeremiah] Thoughts on a reform in the british representation on government — and the affairs of Ireland —. 1785. 8. (6 d.)

— [John] *D. D.* born: . . . . died d. 14 Oct. 1777.

GILL, [Thomas] *Surgeon, Prescot, Lancashire.* Two cases of ulcer in the cheek, with which the salivary duct communicated, cured. (*Duncan's* M. C. Dec. 2. Vol. 2. p. 322.)

GILLESPIE, [Leonard] *Surgeon of the Navy and late Assistant Surgeon to his Majesty's Naval Hospital at St. Lucia.* Observations on the putrid ulcer. (London M. J. Vol. 6. p. 373. übers. Samml. F. A. Th. 12. S. 156.)

GILLIES, [John] *LL. D: F. R. S: F. A. S.* The Orations of *Lysias* and *Isocrates*, translated from the greek. 1778 4. (18 sh.) Die Einleitung hat *J. C. Macher* übersezt unter dem Titel: Betrachtungen über die Geschichte, Sitten und den Charakter der Griechen vom Schluss des Peloponnesischen Kriegs an bis zur Schlacht bey Chäronea. Gött. und Bremen. 1781. 8. History of ancient Greece, its colonies and conquests from the earliest accounts till the division of the Macedonian empire in the East. Vol. 1. 2. 1786. 4. (2 L. 2 Sh.) übers. Leipz. Th. 1. 2. 1786. 8. View of the reign of Frederik II. of Prussia with a parallel between that Prince and Philipp II. of Macedon 1789. 8. (6 sh.)

— [John] *D. D. Minister in Glasgow.* (born in Scotland.) Milton's paradise lost, illustrated with texts of scripture 8. 1788. 3 Sh. 6 d.) Memoirs of the life of *George Whitefield* M. A. Chaplain to the Countess of Huntingdon. 1772. 8. (4 Sh.)

GILLINGWATER, [Edmund] *Overseer of the poor at Harleston, Norfolk.* On parish work-houses. 1786. 8. (1 Sh.)

GILLUM, [W.....] Miscellaneous poems — with a farce called, what will the world say? 1787. 8. (3 Sh.)

GILPIN, [J......] *Vicar of Wrockardine, Salop.* *J. Fletcher's* essay upon the peace of 1783. translated from the french. 1785. 4. (2 Sh. 6 d.)

— [John] Observations on the annual passage of herrings (Tr. of A. S. Vol. 2. p. 236.)

— [Thomas] Account of a horizontal wind — mill. (Tr. of A. S. Vol. 1. p. 339.)

— [William] *M. A. Vicar of Boldre in Newforest, near Lymington.* The life of *Bernard Gilpin.* 1751. 8. (5 Sh.) The life of *Hugh Latimer.* 1754. 8.

 (2 sh)

(2 Sh.) The lives of *John Wicliff* and of the most eminent of his disciple Lord *Cobham*, *John Huss*, *Jerome* of Prague and *Zisca* 1764. 8. (5 Sh.) übers. von *C. F. Duttenhofer* Frankf. und Leipz. 1769. 8. Lectures on the catechism of the church of England. Vol. 1. 2. 1779. 8. (6 Sh.) Observations on the river Wye and several parts of south Wales. 1782. 8. (12 Sh.) Ed. 2. 1789. 8. (17 Sh.) The life of *Thom. Cranmer*, Archbishop of Canterbury. 1784. 8. (3 Sh. 6 d.) Observations relative to picturesque beauty made in the Year 1772. on several parts of England, particularly the mountains and lakes of Cumberland and Westmoreland. 1787. 8. Ed. 2. Vol. 1. 2. 1788. 8. (1 L. 11 Sh. 6 d.) Two sermons. 1788. 8. (1 Sh. 6 d.) Observations relative to picturesque beauty made in the Year 1776. on several parts of Great Britain particularly the highlands of Scotland. Vol. 1. 2. 1789. 8. (1 L. 16 Sh.) Exposition of the new testament; intended as an introduction to the study of the scriptures, by pointing out the leading sense and connexion of the sacred writers. 1790. 4.

GILSON, [David] *M. A. Curate of St. Saviour's, Southwark.* Sermons on practical subjects. 1788. 8. (6 Sh.)

GIRDLESTONE, [Thomas] *M. D.* Essays on the hepatitis and spasmodic affections in India —. 1788. 8. (2 Sh.)

GIRTON, [Daniel] The complete pigeon — fancier or a new treatise on domestic pigeons —. 1779. 8. (1 Sh. 6 d.)

GISBORNE, [Thomas] *M. A.* The principles of moral philosophy investigated and applied to the constitution of civil society —. 1789. 8. (3 Sh. 6 d.)

GLADWIN, [Francis] *Esq.* ° The Ayin Akbary, or the institutes of the emperor Akbar: translated from the original Persian. 1777. 4. (5 Sh.) Ayeen Akbery, or the institutes of the emperor Akber. translated from the original Persian: Vol. 1-3 1783 - 1786. 4. History of Hindostan, during the reigns of Jehangir, Shah Jehan and Aurungzebe. Vol. 1. 1788. 4. The memoirs of Khojeh Abdulkurreem, a Cashmerian of distinction, who

who accompanied Nadir Shah on his return from Hindostan to Persia — translated from the Persian. Calcutta. 1788. 8. (5 Sh.) Narrative of the transactions in Bengal during the Soobahdaries of Azeem us Shan — Jaffer Khan —. translated from the Persian. 1788. Calcutta. 8. (5 Sh.) Pundnameh, a compendium of Ethics, translated from the Persian. Calcutta. 1788. 8. (—)

GLASS, [Thomas] *M. D: of Exeter.* born: ..... died 17. .

GLASSE, [George Henry] *M. A. Rector of Hanwell, Middlesex.* On the affinity of certain words in the language of the Sandwich and Friendly Isles in the pacific Ocean with the hebrew. (Arch. Vol. 8. p. 81.) (Several single sermons.)

— [George Henry] *A. B. Aedis Christi Alumnus.* Translation of *Mason's* Caractacus into greek. 1781. 8. (5 sh.) *Joh. Miltoni Samson* Agonistes, graeco carmine redditus cum versione latina. 1788. 8. (5 sh.)

— [Samuel] *D. D: F. R. S: Chaplain in Ordinary to his Majesty.* Advice from a Lady of Quality to her children, translated from the french. Vol. 1. 2. 1779. 8. (5 sh.) (Several single sermons.)

GLENIE, [James] *A. M. Lieutenant in the royal regiment of Artillery.* History of gunnery —. 1776. 8. (4 sh. 6 d.) On the division of right lines, surfaces and solids. (Phil. Transact. 1776. p. 73.) The general mathematical laws, which regulate and extend proportion universally —. (Ibid. 1777. p. 450)

GLOSTER, [Archibald] *of Antigua.* Remarkable case of a tetanos and locked jaw cured by amazing quantities of opium. (Tr. of A. S. Vol. 1. p. 315.)

GLOVER, [Richard] *Merchant.* born 1711. died d. 25 Nov. 1785.

GOADBY, [Robert] *Printer and Bookseller at Sherborne, Dorsetshire.* born 1721. died 1778.

GODBOLD, [N.......] On consumptions, and their cure. 1786. 8. (1 sh.)

GODDARD, [Peter Stephen] *D. D. Master of Clare-Hall.* born: .... died d. 8 Nov. 1781.

GODMAN, [Thomas] *Surgeon to the Charterhouse at London.* born: .... died d. 30 Aug. 1784.

GODSCHALL, [William Man] *Esq. of Weston House in Surry, one of his Majesty's justices of the Peace for that County.* General plan of parochial and provincial police. 1787. 8. (2 sh.)

GODWIN, [William] *Dissenting Clergyman.* Sketches of history: in VI sermons. 8. 1784. (2 sh. 6 d.)

GOLDSMITH, [Oliver] born at *Fernes in Ireland* d. 29 Nov. 1731. died d. 4 Apr. 1774.

GOLDSON, [William] *Member of the corporation of Surgeons.* An extraordinary case of lacerated vagina, at the full period of gestation. 1787. 8. (1 sh. 6 d.)

GOLLEDGE, [John] Free thoughts on the death threatened against Adam, in case of disobedienee. 1789. 12. (6 d.)

GOMERSALL, [ ] *Mrs.* of Leeds. *Eleonora, in a series of letters. Vol. 1. 2. 1789. 8. (6 sh.) The citizen. Vol. 1. 2. 1790. 8. (6 sh.)

GOOCH, [Benjamin] *Surgeon at Shottisham in Norfolk.* Cases and remarks in Surgery. 1758. 8. (4 sh.) Ed. 2. Vol. 1. 2. 1769. On wounds and other chirurgical subjects - with an account of the rise and progress of surgery and anatomy. 1768. 8. Vol. 1. 2. (14 sh.) (Der zweyte Theil enthält: the cases and remarks in Surgery.) Medical and chirurgical observations, as an appendix. 1773. 8. (5 sh. 6 d.) Account of the cuticular glove. (Phil. Transact. 1769. p. 281. übers Samml. F. A. Th. 1. St. 2. S. 1.) Remarks and considerations relative to the performance of amputation above the knee by the single circular incision. (Phil. Transact. 1775. p. 273.) Remarks concerning anevrysms in the thigh. (Ibid. p. 378.)

—— [.....] *Mrs.* (Wife of *Will. Gooch*, Esq.) An appeal to the public, on the conduct of Mrs. *Gooch*, written by herself. 1788. 4. (2 sh. 6 d.)

GOODENOUGH, [.....] born: ...., died d. 27 Dec. 1781.

GOODHALL, [James] Florazene, or the fatal conquest 1754. 8. King Richard 2. altered and imitated from *Shakspeare.* 1772. 8.

GOODRIDGE, [John] *Formerly Commander of one of his Majesty's packet-boats stationed at Falmouth.* The phoenix; — or that the comet — is real phoenix

nix of the ancients. 1781. 8. (3 sh.) Series of observations on and a discovery of the period of the variation of the light in the bright star called Algol. (Phil. Transact. 1783. P. 2.) On the period of the changes of light in the star Algol. (Ibid. 1784. p. 287.) A series of observations on and a discovery of the period of the variation of the star marked δ by *Bayer* near the head of Cepheus. (Ibid. 1786. p. 48.)

GOODWIN, [T.....] The loyal shepherd: or, the rustic heroine, a dramatic pastoral poem —. 1779. 8. (1 sh.)

— [W.....] *Surgeon at Earl Soham in Suffolk.* Case of fragility of the bones. (London M. J. Vol. VI. p. 288.) Case of an encysted tumour of the Eyelid which was found to contain hair. (Ibid. Vol. VI. p. 292.) Account of a case of mollities ossium (Ibid Vol. VIII. P. 1.)

GOODWYN, [Edmund] *M. D.* Diss. de morte submersorum. Edinb. 1786. The connexion of life with respiration; or, an experimental inquiry into the effects of submersion, strangulation, and several kinds of noxious airs, on living animals: —. 1788. 8. (3 sh.) übersezt von *C. F. Michaelis.* 1790. 8.

GORDON, [Duncan] *M. D.* Letter to *John Hunter.* 1786. 4. (1 sh. 6 d.)

— [George] *Lord.* Letter to the Attorney General of England in which the motives of his Lordship's public conduct, from the beginning of 1780 to the present time, are vindicated. 1787. 8. (1 Sh. 6 d.)

— [Georg Alexander] *M. D.* Complete english physician. 1779. 8. (2 Sh.)

— [Robert] *Surgeon to the* 54th *Regiment.* A remarkable case of deafness cured by salivation. (Med. Com. of Ed. Vol. 3. p. 80.)

— [Thomas] *Esq.* Principles of naval architecture —. 1784. 8. (5 Sh.)

— [William] *D. D.* History of the rise, progress and establishment of the independence of the united states of America; including an account of the late war; and of the XIII colonies from their origin to that period. Vol. 1-4. 1788. 8. (1 L. 4 Sh.)

GOR-

GORDON, [William] *Master of the Mercantile Academy, Edinburgh.* Institutes of Arithmetic, elementary and practical: the mensuration of surfaces and solids and the use of logarithms in all the parts of Arithmetic: to which are added tables of annuities, lives —. 1789. 8. (5 sh.)

GORSUCH, [William] *Minister of Holy-Cross in Salop.* Extract from the register of the parish of Holy-Cross in Salop, from 1760-1770. (Philos. Transact. 1771. p. 57.) Extract of the Register of the parish of Holy-Cross, Salop, from 1770-1780. (Ibid. 1782. p. 53.)

GOSLING, [—]. *Mrs.* Moral essays and reflections. 1789. 8. (3 Sh.)

GOSTLING. [William] *M. A. Vicar of Stone in the Isle of Oxney.* born 1705. died d. 9 March 1777.

GOUGH, [J.....] *A. B. Rector of Kirk Ireton, Derbyshire.* *Discourse concerning the resurrection of bodies by Philalethes. 1789. 8. Ed. 2. (with the Author's name.) 1790. 8.

— [Richard] *Esq. F. A. and R. S.* *Anecdotes of British Topography. 1768. 4. (1 L. 1 Sh.) Ed. 2. Vol. 1. 2. 1780. 4. (2 L. 12 Sh. 6 d.) *Comparative view of the ancient monuments of India. 1785. 4. (5 Sh.) *Bibliotheca Topographica Britannica. Numb. I-XIII. 1781. 4. *Sepulchral monuments in Great Britain —. 1786. fol. (6 L. 6 Sh.) Observations on the round tower at Brechin, in Scotland. (Arch. Vol. 2. p. 83.) Conjectures on an antient tomb in Salisbury cathedral. (Ibid. p. 188.) On the deae matres. (Ibid. Vol. 3. p. 105.) Observations on some roman altars found 1771 near Graham's Dyke. (Ibid. p. 118.) Observations on the invention of cards and their introduction into England. (Ibid. Vol. 8. p. 152.) Observations in vindication of the authenticity of the Parian chronicle (Ibid. Vol. 9. p. 157.) Observations on certain stamps or seals used antiently by the oculists. (Ibid p. 227.) *W. Camden's* Britannia: or chorographical description of the flourishing kingdoms of England, Scotland and Ireland, translated and enlarged. Vol. 1-3. 1789. fol. (10 L.)

GOUR-

GOURLAY, [William] *M. D. Physician in the Island of Madeira and Member of the Med. Soc. of Edinb.* A case of encysted sarcocele. (*Duncan's* M. C. Vol. 9. p. 330.)

GOWER, [Foote] *M. D: F. A. S:* born: .... died d. 27 May. 1780.

GRAEME, [James] born at *Carnwath. Lanarkshire* 1749. died 1771.

GRAHAM, [......] *Physician in Stirling.* On the external application of deadly nightshade. (Med. Com. of Ed. Vol. 1. p. 419.) Account of violent pains from a particular species of worm under the skin. (*Duncan's* M. C. Dec. 2. Vol. 2. p. 366.)

— [Catherine Macaulay] *Mrs.* (Maden Name *Sawbridge;* Her first Husband was *Kenneth Macaulay.* DD. and Clergyman in Scotland: Her second *Graham.)* History of England from the accession of James I. to the Revolution. Vol. 1 - 8. 1763 1782. 4. (6 L.) *Loose remarks on *Hobbes's* rudiments of government and society. 1767. 8. (1 sh) Ed. 2. 1769. 4. (1 sh. 6 d.) Observations on *Edm. Burke's* thoughts on the cause of the present discontents. 1770. 8. (1 sh.) A modest plea for the property of Copy-Right. 1773. 8. (1 sh. 6 d.) Address to the people of England, Scotland and Ireland on the present important crisis of affairs. 1774. 8. (6 d.) History of England, from the revolution to the present time. Vol. 1. 1778. 4. (15 sh.) On the immutability of moral truth. 1783. 8. (5 sh.) Letters on education: with observations on religious and metaphysical subjects. 1790. 8.

— [Robert] *Esq. President of the Delegates from the Burgesses.* Letter to *Will. Pitt* — on the reform of the internal government of the royal boroughs of Scottland. 1788. 8. (1 sh. 6 d)

— [William] *Rector of Stapleton.* The eclogues of *Virgil*, translated into english verse. 1786. 8.

GRANGER, [Edmond] *Rector of Sowden and Vicar of Honiton Clift, Somersetshire.* born: .... died d. Sept. 1777.

— [James] *Vicar of Shiplake, Oxfordshire.* born: ... died d. 5 Apr. 1776.

GRANT,

GRANT, [......] *Minister of the Gospel at Newcastle.* Sermons, doctrinal and practical, on several subjects. 1786. 12. (2 sh. 6 d.)

—— [Alexander] *Surgeon of his Majesty's Military Hospitals during the late war in North-America.* Observations on the use of opium in removing symptoms supposed to be owing to morbid irritability. (London M. J. Vol. VI. p. 1. p. 131. übers. Samml. f. A. Th. XI. S. 68.)

—— [D.....] *M. A. Vicar of Hutton-Rudby, Yorkshire.* Two Dissertations on popish persecution and breach of faith —. 1771. 8. (2 sh. 6 d.)

—— [George] *Surgeon.* Case of an abscess in the lower part of the belly which communicated with the intestine —. (London M. J. Vol. XI. P. 2.)

—— [James] *Advocate at the Scotish Bar.* Origin of society, language, property, government, jurisdiction, contracts and marriage —. 1785. 4. (7 Sh. 6 d.)

—— [P.....] *Surgeon at Stonehaven.* Account of singular effects from the external application of a strong infusion of tobacco employed for the cure of Psora. (*Duncan's* M. C. Dec. 2. Vol. 1. p. 327. übers. Samml. f. A. Th. 13. S. 37.)

—— [William] *M. D. Physician to the Misericordia Hospital in London.* born: .... died d. 30 Nov. 1786.

GRATTAN, [Henry] Speech on tithes. 1788. 8. (1 Sh. 6 d.)

GRAVES, [Richard] *Rector of Claverton and Vicar of Kilmersden in the county of Somerset.* (born at *Mickleton* in the County of *Gloucester* d. 4 May 1715.) * The spiritual Quixote; or, the summer's ramble of Mr. Geoffry Wildgoose, a comic romance. Vol. 1-3. 1773. 8. (7 Sh. 6 d.) * The love of order; a poetical essay. 1773. 4. (1 Sh. 6 d.) Peter of Pomfret. 17.. The distressed Anchoret. 17.. Poems. Vol. 1. 2. 17.. Columella. 1778. * Euphrosine, or amusements on the road of life. Vol. 1. 2. 1780. (6 Sh.) Echo and Narcissus. 1780. 8. * Recollection of some particulars in the life of the late *Will. Shenstone.* 1788. 8. (3 Sh.)

GRAY, [Alexander] *M. D. Surgeon to the 3d Reg. of Seapoys in the service of the East-India Company in Bengal.* History of a case of rabies canina attended with singular circumstances, and terminating

ting fatally, after a falivation had been induced by mercury. (*Duncan's* M. C. Dec. 2. Vol. 2. p. 304.)

GRAY, [Andrew] *D. D Minifter of Abernethy.* Delineation of the parables of our bleffed faviour. 1777. überf. (von *Joh. Fried. Roos*). Hannover 1783. 8. (6 Sh.)

— [Edward] *M. D. F. R. S.* Account of the epidemic catarrh of the Year 1782. (M. C. Vol. 1. p. 1.)

— [Edward Whitaker] *M D: F. R. S.* Obfervations on the manner in which glafs is charged with the electric fluid and difcharged. (Phil. Transact. 1788. p. 121.) überf. *Gren* J D. P. Th. 1. S. 83. Obfervations on the clafs of animals called, by *Linnaeus* Amphibia; particularly on the means of diftinguifhing thofe ferpents which are venomous from thofe which are not fo. (Ibid. 1789. p. 21.)

— [John] Translations of fome odes and epiftles of *Horace.* 1778. 8. (1 Sh. 6 d.)

— [Robert] Key to the old teftament and apocrypha: in which is given an account of their feveral books, their contents and authors and of the times in which they were refpectively written. 1790. 8.

— [Thomas] *Profeffor of modern hiftory at Cambridge.* born at *Cornhill* d. 26 Dec. 1716. died d. 30 July 1772.

GREATHEAD, [Bertie] The regent, a Tragedy. 1788. 8. (1 Sh. 6 d.) überf. unter dem Titel: der Statthalter. Berlin 1790. 8. Mannheim 1790. 8.

GREEN, [Charles] *Formerly Affiftant at the royal Obfervatory at Greenwich and* Lieut. *James Cook, of his Majefty's fhip the Endeavour.* born: ... died at fea in the paffage home from *Batavia* 17..

— [John] *D. D. Bifhop of Lincoln.* born in *Yorkfhire* 1706. died d. 25 Apr. 1779.

— [John] *M. D. Phyfician at Greenwich.* born: .... died d. 2 Jan. 1778.

— [J.... L.....] *Surgeon at Peckham in Surry.* Defcription of a curious lufus naturae. (London M. J. Vol. 4. p. 403.)

— [Thomas] *Efq.* Account of an ancient urn found in the parifh of Kilranelagh, in the county of Wicklow. (Tr. of J. A. 1787. p. 161.)

GREEN, [Rupert] The secret plot. a tragedy. 1777. 8.

—— [Valentine] *F. A. S. Mezzotinto Engraver to his Majesty and to the Elector Palatine.* Survey of the city of Worcester. 1764. 8. (5 Sh.) Review of the polite arts in France — under Louis the XIVth compared with their present state in England 1783. 4. (3 Sh.)

—— [William] *M. D.* born: .... died d. 30 Aug. 1788.

—— [William] *M. A. Rector of Hardingham, Norfolk.* The song of Deborah, reduced to metre; with a new translation and commentary —. 1753. 4. New translation of the prayer of Habakuk the prayer of Moses and the 139 psalm, with a commentary —. 1755. 4. (1 Sh. 6 d.) New translation of the psalms — with notes critical and explanatory — with a dissertation on the last prophetic words of Noah. 1763. 8. (3 Sh. 6 d.) Moral and religious essays upon various important subjects. by *W. Green* and *John Penn.* 1766. 12. Vol. 1. 2. (6 Sh.) New translation of Isaiah VII, 13. to the end of LIII. — with notes. 1776. 4. (1 Sh.) Poetical parts of the old testament — translated — with notes. 1781. 4. (6 Sh.) übers. (von *J. F. Roos*) Giessen. 1783. 8.

GREENAWAY, [.....] *A new translation of some parts of Ecclesiastes. P. 1-3. 1787. 8. (5 Sh. 4 d.)

GREENE, [Edward Burnaby] born: .... died d. 12 March. 1788.

—— [Thomas] *of Ware, Herfordshire.* born: ..... died 17..

GREENFIELD, [William] *M. A: F. R. S. Edin. Minister at St. Andrew's-church and Professor of Rhetoric in the University of Edinburgh.* On the use of negative quantities in the solution of problems by algebraic equations. (Tr. of E. S. Vol. 1. p. 131.)

GREENLEAF, [Joseph] Account of an experiment for raising indian corn in poor land. (Mem. of B. A. Vol. 1. p. 383.)

GREENVILLE, [George] see Earl of Temple.

GREENWOOD, [J....] Rhapsody on the Worcester election. 1776. 4. (1 Sh.)

—— [William] *Fellow of St. John's College, Cambridge and Rector of Bignor, Sussex.* A Poem written du-

during a ſhooting excurſion on the moors. 1786. 4. (2 Sh.)

GREGORY, [G.....] *Curate of St. Nicholas's church in Liverpool. F. A. S.* Eſſays hiſtorical and moral. 1785. 8. (5 Sh.) Ed. 2. 1788. 8. (6 Sh.) Sermons, with thoughts on the compoſition and delivery of a ſermon. 1787. 8. (6 Sh.) Translation of *Lowth's* lectures on the ſacred poetry of the hebrews —. Vol. 1. 2. 1787. 8. (12 Sh.) The life of *Thom. Chatterton* with criticisms on his genius and writings and a view of the controverſy concerning *Rowley's* poems. 1789. 8. (5 ſh.) *Hiſtory of the chriſtian church from the earlieſt periods to the preſent time. Vol. 1. 2. 1790. 8. (8 ſh.)

— [James] *M. D, Profeſſor of Medicine in the Univerſity of Edinburgh.* (Son to *John Gregory*). Diſſ. De morbis coeli mutatione medendis. Edinb. 1774. 8. Conſpectus Medicinae Theoreticae. Ed. 2. Vol. 1. 2. 1782. 8. (12 Sh.) Ed. 3. Vol. 1. 2. 1788. 8. (12 Sh.) überſ. Leipzig. Th. 1. 2. 1784. 8. Theory of the moods of verbs (Tr. of E. S. Vol. 2. p 193.)

— [John] *M. D: F. R. S. Profeſſor of Medicine in the Univerſity of Edinburgh.* born at *Aberdeen* 1725. died d. 10 Febr. 1773.

GRENVILLE, [W..... W.....] *Speaker of the houſe of Commons.* Speech 1789. 8. (1 ſh. 6 d.)

GREY, [Richard] *Prebendary at Paul's church, London.* born 1693. died 1771.

GRIEVE, [John] *M. D: F. R. S. Edin. late Phyſician to the Ruſſian army at Nigene Nowgorod, now Phyſician in London.* The hiſtory of a caſe of inveterate dropſy, ſucceſſfully treated with obſervations on the advantages from combining cathartics and diuretics. (*Duncan's* M. C. Vol. 9. p. 286.) Account of the method of making a wine, called by the Tartars, Koumiſſ; with obſervations on its uſe in medicine. (T. of E. S. Vol. 1. p. 178.) (London M. J. Vol. X. P. 2.)

— [William] *Surgeon in Grenada.* On the uſe of the bark of the Angeline tree, as an anthelmintic. (*Duncan's* M. C. Vol. 9. p. 365.)

GRIFFIES, [Thomas] The journey to Brighton; an heroi-comic poem. 1788. 4. (2 ſh. 6 d.)

GRIFFIN, [Gregory] *of the College of Eton.* The microcosm, a periodical work. 1787. 8. (7 sh.)

—— [Robert] Interest tables on an improved plan —. 1775. 8. (6 sh.)

GRIFFITH, [Amyas] *Esq. late Surveyor of Belfast and formerly Inspector general of the province of Munster.* Observations on the Bishop of Cloyne's pamphlet: in which the doctrine of tithes is illustrated and the argument for the insecurity of the protestant religion demonstrated to be groundless and visionary. 1787. 8. (1 sh. 6 d.)

—— [Guyon] *D. D. Rector of St. Mary Hill.* born: .... died d. 1 Jan. 1784.

—— [Moses] *M. D. at Colchester.* Practical observations on the cure of hectic and slow fevers and the pulmonary consumption, with a method of treating several kinds of internal haemorrhages. 1775. 8. (2 Sh.) übers. Samml. f. A. Th. 6. S. 579.

GRIFFITHS, [Frances] *Mrs.* *Letters between Henry and Frances Vol. 1-6. 1756-1770. (17 Sh.) * Memoirs of Ninon de l'Enclos, translated. Vol. 1. 2. 1761. (6 sh.) The platonic wife, a Comedy. 1765. 8. Amana. 1765. 4. The double mistake, a Comedy 1766. 8. *Two novels, in letters. Vol. 1-4. 1768. (10 sh.) *The school for rakes, a Comedy. 1768. 8. (1 sh. 6 d.) *Translation of Mad. de *Caylus's* Memoirs, anecdotes and characters of the court of Lewis XIV. Vol. 1. 2. 1770. 8. The shipwreck and adventures of Monf. *Pierre Viaud*, translated from the French. 1771. 8. (4 sh.) History of Lady *Barton*, in letters. Vol. 1. 2. 3. 1771. (7 sh. 6 d.) A wife in the right, a Comedy. 1772. 8. (5 sh.) The story of Lady *Juliana Hartley*, a Novel, in letters. Vol. 1. 2. 1775. (6 Sh.) The Morality of *Shakespeare's* drama illustrated. 1775. 8. (7 Sh. 6 d.) Letter from. Monf. *Desenfans* to Mrs. *Montague* translated. 1777. 8. (1 sh. 6. d.) The times 1779. 8. Essays addressed to young married women. 1782. 8. (2 Sh. 6 d.) nachgedr. Berlin. 1787. 8.

GRIGG, [John] *Practitioner in Midwifery.* Advice to the female sex in general, particularly those in a state of pregnancy and lying — in woman. 1789. 8. (3 Sh. 6 d.) übers. Leipzig. 1791. 8.

GRIM-

GRIMSTON, [John] *Surgeon at Ripon.* Case of a fractured scull unsuccessfully treated. (London M J. Vol. X. P. 3.)

GROOMBRIDGE, [William] Sonnets. 1789. 8. (1 Sh.)

GROSE, [......] Rules for drawing caricaturas, with an essay on comic painting. 1788. 8. (2 sh.)

— [Francis] *F. R. S: F. A. S: Captain in the Essex militia.* The antiquities of England and Wales. Vol. 1-4. 1773. 4. (9 L. 1 Sh.) Ed. 2. Vol. 1-3. 1784. 8. (4 L. 9 Sh.) Collection of plans of the antiquities of England and Wales. 1775. 4. (10 Sh. 6. d.) Description of an ancient fortification near Christchurch Hampshire. (Arch. Vol 5. p. 237.) On ancient armours and weapons. 1786. 4. (2 L. 2 Sh.) Provincial glossary with a collection of local proverbs and popular superstitions. 1787. 8. (5 Sh.) Ed. 2. 1790. 8. (5 Sh.) Observations on antient spurs. (Arch Vol 8. p. 111.) Military antiquities respecting a history of the english army from the conquest to the present time. Vol. 1. 2. 1788. 4. (4 L. 4 Sh.) The Antiquities of Scotland. Numb. 1-18. fol. 1790. (3 L. 4 Sh.)

— [John] *F. A. S.* Ethics, rational and theological with remarks on the general principles of Deism. 1782. 8. (6 Sh.)

GROVE, [W.....] The faithful shepherd, a Pastoral: translated from *Guarini.* 1782. 8.

GULLET, [Christopher] On the effects of elder in preserving growing plants from insects and flies. (Philos. Transact. 1772. p. 348.)

GURDON, [Philipp] *M. A. Fellow of Magdalen College, Oxford.* Sketch of the distinguishing graces of the christian character —. 1778. 8. (2 Sh. 6 d.)

GUTCH, [John] *M. A. Chaplain of all Soul's College.* * Archbishop *Sancroft's* Collectanea curiosa: or, miscellaneous tracts, relating to the history and antiquities of England and Ireland, the universities of Oxford and Cambridge and a variety of other subjects. Vol. 1. 2. 1781. 8. *Ant. Wood's* History and antiquities of the colleges and halls in the University of Oxford — with a continuation to the present time —. 1786. 4. (1 L. 6 sh.)

GUTHRIE, [Matthew] *M. D. Physician at St. Petersburgh. F. R. S.* Observations on the plague, quarantaines —. (*Duncan's* M. C. Vol. 8. p 345.) Nouvelles experiences pour servir a determiner le vrai point de congelation du mercure et la difference que lè degré de pureté de ce metal pourroit y apporter. a St. Petersburgh. 1785. 8. übers. in Auszug in *Tralles* physikal. Taschenbuch für das J. 1786. On the antiseptic regimen of the natives of Russia. (Phil. Transact. 1778. p. 622.) Account of the manner in which the russians treat persons affected by the fumes of burning Charcoal, and other effluvia of the same nature. (Ibid. 1779. p. 325.) On the effects of a cold climate on the land scurvy. (*Duncan's* M. C. Dec. 2. Vol. 2. p. 328. übers. Samml. f. A. Th. 13. S. 48.) On the climate of Russia (Tr. of E. S. Vol. 2. p. 213.)

GUY, [Melmoth] *Surgeon.* Select number of scirrhous and cancerous cases. 1777. 8. (1 sh.)

GWYNN, [John] London and Westminster improved and illustrated by plans: 1771. 4. (9 sh.)

HADLEY, [George] *Esq. Formerly Captain on the Bengal Establishment.* *Short grammar and vocabulary of the Moors language. 1771. 8. (1 sh. 6 d.) Grammatical remarks on the Indostan language commonly called Moors. —. 1772. 8. (2 sh. 6 d.) Ed. 3. 1784. 8. (4 sh) Grammatical remarks on the persian language —. 1776. 4. (7 sh. 6 d.)

HAFFENDEN, [Richard] *Esq.* Account of the effects of lightning on a house which was furnished with a pointed conductor at Tenterden, in Kent. (Phil. Transact. 1775. p. 336.)

HAIGH, [James] *Silk and Muslin Dyer, Leeds.* The dyer's assistant in the art of dying wool and woollen goods. —. 1778. 12. (5 sh. 6 d.) A Hint to the dyers and Clothmakers —. 1780. 8. (6 d.)

HAIGTON, [J.....] *Surgeon, London.* The history of two cases of the fractured Olecranon, with some remarks. (*Duncan's* M C. Vol. 9. p. 382.) Attempt to ascertain the powers concerned in the act of vomiting —. (Mem. of M. S. of L. Vol. 2.) Case of hydrophobia. (London M. J. Vol. 6. p. 361.)

HAIR, [Lancelot] *Surgeon at Southminster in Essex.* Remarks on Mr. *Lucas's* practical observations on amputation. (Lond. M. J. Vol. 7. P. 4.)

HALE, [.....] *Lieutenant-General.* Speech. 1785. 8. (1 sh.)

— [John] *Surgeon to the New Finsbury Dispensary.* Case of a fracture of the sternum. (London M. J. Vol. VIII. P. 4.)

HALES, [Charles] Salivation not necessary for the cure of the venereal disease in any degree whatever and all gleets curable. London 1764. 8. Letter, thoughts and observations in the cure of the venereal disease —. 1770. 8. (1 sh.)

— [William] *D. D. Rector at Killesandra.* Sonorum doctrina rationalis et experimentalis —. 1778. 4. (6 sh.) De Motibus planetarum —. 1786. 8. (1 sh. 6 d.) Analysis aequationum —. 1786. 4. (10 sh.) Observations on the political influence of the doctrine of the *Pope's* supremacy. 1787. 8. (2 sh.) Survey of the modern state of the church of Rome, with additional observations on the doctrine of the Pope's supremacy. 1789. 8. (3 sh. 6 d.)

HALHED, [Nathaniel Brassey] *Officer of the East-India Company at Hoogly in Bengal.* *A Code of gentoo laws; or ordinations of the pundits, from a persian translation, made from the original, written in the Shancrit language. 1776. 4. Ed. 2. 1777. 8. (7 sh. 6 d.) übers. von *R. E. Raspe.* Hamb. 1778. 8. Grammar of the Bengal language. printed at Hoogly in Bengal. 1778. 4. (1 L. 1 sh.) Narrative of the events which have happened in Bombay and Bengal relative to the Maharatta empire since July 1777. 1779. 8.

HALIDAY, [W.....] On the Siberian or Haliday Barley. (*Hunter's* G. E. Vol. 2. p. 87.)

HALL, [.....] *Captain.* *History of the civil war in America. Vol. 1. 1780. 8. (5 sh.)

— [......] *Mrs.* *Moral tales — by lady ** 1783. 4. (2 sh. 6. d)

— [C.....] *M. D.* The family medical instructor-with an appendix on canine madness. 1785. 8. (2 sh. 6 d.)

— [Charles] *Surgeon to the 14th Regiment of Infantry.* Account of a new species of palsy. (Med. Com. of Ed. Vol. 6. p. 71.)

HALL, [John] *of Broadstreet, Surgeon and Teacher of Anatomy in London.* Case of an anevrism in the aorta and in the left carotid artery, which burst into the trochea. (Med. Obs. Vol. 6. p. 23.) Observations on the contents of medullary cells, dropsy. (London M J. Vol. VII. P. 2.) übers. Samm. f. A. Th 12. S. 17.)

—— [Isaac] *Physician at Petersburgh in Virginia.* An uncommon tumour on the thigh successfully extirpated. (Med. Com. in Ed. Vol 1. p. 89.)

—— [Richard] *Surgeon to the Manchester infirmary.* Account of the successful extirpation of a remarkable schirrus of the scrotum. (Lond. M. J. Vol. VIII. P. 1.)

—— [Samuel] *A. M. Chaplain to the Manchester military association* Sermon before the military association —. 1783. 4. (1 sh) Attempt to shew, that a taste for the beauties of nature and the fine arts, has no influence favourable to morals. (Mem. of M. Vol. 1. p 223.)

HALLIFAX, [Samuel] *D. D. Bishop and Archdeacon at St. Asaph.* born 1730, died in Westminster, d. 5 March 1790.

HALYBURTON, [William] *D. D.* Georgics, in a series of letters to a friend. 1782. 8. (6 sh.)

HAMILTON, [Alexander] *M. D. F. R. S. Professor of Midwifery at Edinburgh.* Elements of the practice of midwifery. 1776. 8. (5 sh.) Treatise of midwifery. 1781. 8. (6 sh.) übers. von *J. P. Ebeling.* Leipz. 1782. 8. Outlines of the theory and practice of midwifery. 1783. 8. (5 sh.) *Will Smellie's* anatomical tables with explanations and an abridgment of the practice of midwifery. 1787. fol (2 L. 5 sh.)

—— [Augustus] *M A.* Account of the transit of Mercury over the sun of Nov. 12. 1782., observed at Cook's Town in Ireland. (Phil. Transact. 1783. P. 2.)

—— [Charles] Esq. *Officer in the Service of the East-India Company, on the Bengal establishment.* Historical relation of the origin, progress and final dissolution, of the government of the Rohilla Afgans, in the northern provinces of Hindostan, compiled from a persian Msct. —. 1787. 8. (5 sh.) Description

ption of the Mahwah (or Maduca) tree. (Asiat. Res. Vol. I. p. 300.)

HAMILTON, [Charles] °The patriot. a Tragedy. 1784. 8. (1 sh. 6 d.)

— [Hugh] *D. D. F. R. S. Dean of Armagh.* De sectionibus conicis. 1758. 4. (10 sh. 6 d.) The properties of the mechanic powers demonstrated, with some observations on the methods that have been commonly used for that purpose. (Phil. Transact. 1763. p. 103.) On the nature of evaporation and seueral phaenomena of air, water and boiling liquors. (Ibid 1765. p. 146.) Geometrical treatise of the conic sections — translated from the latin. 1773. 4. (12 sh.) *Four introductory lectures in natural philosophy. 1773. 8. (2 sh.) Attempt to prove the existence and absolute perfection of the supreme unoriginated being. 1785. 8. (3 sh. 6 d.)

— [James Archibald] *D. D. Member of Roy. Irish Acad.* Account of Parhelia seen at Cookstown Sept. 24. 1783. (Tr. of J. A. 1787. p. 23.)

— [James Edward] 1 and 2 letter to the people of England, upon the present crisis. 1790. 8. (1 Sh.) Attempt to explain the termes Democracy, Aristocracy, Oligarchy, Monarchy and Despotism. 1790. 8. (6 d.)

— [R. . . . .] *LL. D. Professor of Philosophy at Aberdeen.* System of Arithmetic and book keeping. with a supplement containing answers to the arithmetical questions. 1788. 8. (2 Sh. 6 d.)

— [Robert] *D. D. Professor of Divinity in the University of Edinburgh.* born: . . . . died d. 2 Apr. 1787.

— [Robert] *LL. D. Master of the academy at Perth.* Introduction to Merchandize. Vol. 1. 2. 1777. 8. (9 Sh.)

— [Robert] *M. D. Physician at Ipswich.* The duties of a regimental surgeon considered; with observations on his general qualifications. Vol. 1. 2. 1788. (10 Sh.) übers. von Hunczovsky. Wien 1790. 8.

— [Robert] *M. D. F. R. S. and Physician at Lynn-Regis, Norfolk.* Account of a suppression of urine cured by a puncture made in the bladder through the anus. (Phil. Transact. 1776. p. 578.) Thoughts on establishing a fund for sick soldiers and their

 wives.

wives. 1783. 8. (1 Sh.) Description of the influenza. 1782. 8. (1 sh.) übers. Samml. f. A. Th. 8. S. 52.) Account of a successfull method of treating inflammatory diseases, by mercury and opium. (*Duncan's* M. C. Vol. 9. p. 191. übers. Samml. f. A. Th. XI. S. 265.) Case of angina pectoris, from which it would appear that the complaint is sometimes hereditary. (Ibid. Vol. 9. p. 307.) A case of a diseased testicle successfully treated. (London M. J. Vol. 4. p. 172.) Several instances of the good effects of opium in mortifications. (London M. J. Vol. 5. p. 75. p. 190.) Remarks on the means of obviating the fatal effects of the bite of a mad dog, or other rabid animal. 1785. 8. (5 Sh.) übers. von *C. F. Michaelis*. Leipz. 1787. 8. A case of hydrophobia. (London M. J. Vol. 7. P. 1.) Case of worms discharged through an opening in the navel. (London M. J. Vol. 7. P. 4.) History of a case in which an epistaxis occurred vicarious to the menstrual discharge. (*Duncan's* M. C. Dec. 2. Vol. 1. p. 337.) History of a remarkable case of nostalgia affecting a native of Wales and occurring in Britain. (*Duncan's* M. C. Dec. 2. Vol. 1. p. 343.) Remarks on the influenza in spring 1782. (Mem. of M. S. of S. Vol. 2.) The duties of a regimental surgeon considered; with observations on his general qualifications. Vol. 1. 2. 1788. 8. (10 Sh. 6 d.) Account of a distemper by the common people in England vulgery called the mumps. (London M. J. Vol. XI. P. 2. Tr. of E. S. Vol. 2. p. 59.)

HAMILTON, [Thomas] *Student of Medicine at Edinburgh.* On the benefit of cyder in the cure of dropsy and on the induction of artificial emphysema. (*Duncan's* M. C. Dec. 2. Vol. 2. p. 370.) übers. Samml. f. A. Th. 13. S. 76.

— [William] *A. M: F. T. C. D: M. R. J. A.* Letters concerning the northern coast of Antrim, in Ireland — 1786. 8. (4 sh) übers. (von *Kühn*) Leipz. 1787. 8. Account of experiments made to determine the temperature of the earth's surface in the kingdom of Ireland in the Y. 1788. (Tr. of J. A. 1788. p. 143.

— [William] *Sir. Britannic Majesty's Envoy to the Court of Naples. Knight Baron. F. R. S.* Account of the late

late eruption of Mount Vesuvius Nov. 17. 1764. (Phil. Transact. 1767. p. 192.) Account of the eruption of mount Vesuvius in 1767. (Ibid. 1768. p. 1.) Some farther particulars of mount Vesuvius and other Volcanos in that neighbourhood. (Ibid. 1769. p. 18.) Account of a Journey to mount Etna. (Ibid. 1770. p. 1.) Remarks upon the nature of the soil of Naples and its neighbourhood. (Ibid. 1771. p. 1. p. 48.) Observations on mount Vesuvius, mount Etna and other Vulcanos. 1772. 8. (3 sh. 6. d.) Schola Italica picturae — The Italian school of painting. fol. 1773. (4 L. 14 sh.) Account of the effects of a thunder storm on the 15th of March 1773 upon the house of Lord *Fylney* at Naples. (Phil. Transact. 1773. p. 324.) Campi Phlegraei; or observations on the Volcanos of the two Sicilies. Vol. 1. 2. 1776. Supplem. 1779. fol. (15 L. 4 sh.) On the discoveries at Pompeji. (Arch. Vol. 4. p. 160.) übers. von *C. G. Murr.* Nürnb. 1780. 4. Account of certain traces of Volcanos on the banks of the Rhine. (Phil. Transact. 1778. p. 1. übers. Samml. zur P. u. Ng. Th. 2. S. 453.) Account of an eruption of mount Vesuvius in Aug. 1779. (Ibid. 1780. p. 42.) Account of some scoria from iron works, which resemble the vitrified filaments. (Ibid. 1782. p. 50.) Account of the earthquakes which happened in Italy from Febr. to May 1783. (Ibid. 1783. p. 169.) übers. von *L. Wittenberg.* Altona 1783. 8. Some particulars of the present state of mount Vesuvius; with the account of a Journey into the province of Abruzzo and a voyage to the island of Ponza. (Ibid. 1786. p. 365. übers. Dresden 1787. 4.

HAMPE, [John Henry] *M. D. at London.* born 1697. died 1777.

HAMPSON, [John] A blow at the root of pretended Calvinism, or real Antinomianism. 1788. 8. (1 sh.)

— [George] *M. A.* Candid remarks upon *Taylor's* discourse entitled, the scripture doctrine of atonement examined. 1752. 8. (1 sh 6 d.) Answer to *Priestley's* objections to the doctrine of the atonement by the death of Christ in the history of the corruptions of Christianity. 1785. 8. (2 sh.)

HAMPTON, [James] *Rector of Moor-Monkton and Folkton.* born: .... died d. 15 July 1778.

HANBURY, [W....] *A. M. Rector of Church-Langton, Leicestershire.* Essay on planting —. 1758. 8. (1 sh.) History of the rise and progress of the charitable foundations at Church Langton —. 1767. 8. (6 sh.) Complete body of planting and gardening. Vol. 1. 2. 1771. fol. (4 L. 4 sh.)

HANCOCK, [Blith] *Teacher of the Mathematics.* The doctrine of eclipses, both solar and lunar —. 1783. 8. (3 sh.) The astronomy of comets. 1786. 8. (2 sh. 6 d.)

HANDASYD, [Talbot Blayney] Account of antiquities near *Bagshot.* (Arch. Vol. 7. p. 199.)

HANDS, [Elizabeth] *Mrs.* (Wife of a Blacksmith.) The death of Ammon, a poem. 1790.

HANGER, [George] *Major to the Cavalry of the British Legion.* Address to the army on *Tarleton's* history of the campaigns of 1780 et 1781. 1789. 8. (4 sh.)

HANKIN, [Edward] *A. M.* Panegyric on Great Britain —. 1786. 8. (1 sh.) Reflections on the infamy of smuggling —. 1790. 8. (1 sh.)

HANLEY, [P....] *M. D.* Account of an extraordinary steatomatous tumour in the abdomen of a woman. (Phil. Transact. 1770. p. 131.) übers. Samml. f. A. Th. 2. S. 139.)

HANSARD, [Hugh Iosiah] Letters and thoughts which may promote christian knowledge and justice. 1784. 8.

HANWAY, [Jonas] *Commissioner of the victualling office.* born at *Portsmouth, Hampshire* d. 12 Aug. 1712. died at *London* d. 5 Sept. 1786.

HARDHAM, [John] born: .... died d. .. Sept. 1772.

HARDWICK, [Thomas] *F. A. S.* Observations on the remains of the amphitheatre of Flavius Vespasian at Rome as it was in the Year 1777. (Arch. Vol. 7. p. 369.)

HARDWICKE, [....] *Earl of*, born d. 20 Dec. 1720. died d. 16 May. 1790.

HARDY, [Francis] *Esq. M. R. J. A.* Thoughts on some particular passages in the Agamemnon of *Aeschylus.* (Tr. of J. A. 1788. p. 55.)

HARDY, [James] *M. D. of Barnſtaple, Devonſhire.* Examination of what has been advanced on the colic of Poitou and Devonſhire —. 1778. 8. (3 Sh. 6 d.) Anſwer to Dr. *Riollay's* letter on the origin of the gout. 1780. 8. (1 Sh.)

— [.....] *Admiral.* Chronological liſt of the captains of the royal navy from 1673 to 1783. 1788. (7 Sh. 6 d.)

— [Samuel] *Rector of little Blackenham in Suffolk.* The Theory of the moon —. 1752. 8. (1 Sh.) Account of the nature and ends of the holy euchariſt —. 8. 1763. (1 Sh.) Translation of *Scheffer's* treatiſe on the emendation of dioptrical teleſcopes —. 1769. 8. (1 Sh. 6 d.) The principal prophecies of the old and new teſtament - compared and explained. 1770. 8. (6 ſh.) Vindication of the church of England, in requiring ſubſcription to her 39 articles of religion. 1773. 8. (1 Sh.) Translation of St. Paul's epiſtle to the Hebrews. 1783. 8. (1 Sh. 6 d.)

HARGRAVE, [Francis] *Esq. Barriſter at law.* On the caſe of *James Somerſett*, a Negro, lately determined by the court of King's Bench: wherein it is attempted to demonſtrate the preſent unlawfulneſſ of domeſtic ſlavery in England, to which is prefixed, a ſtate of the caſe. 1772. 8. (2 Sh.) Argument in defence of literary property. 1774. 8. (1 ſh. 6 d.) Collection of ſtate trials and proceedings for high treaſon and other crimes and misdemeanours. Vol. I-XI. fol. 1781. (11 Guin.) Collection of tracts relative to the law of England, from Manuſcript. 1787. 4. Vol. I. (1 L. 7 ſh.) *Edw. Coke's* commentary upon Littleton. Ed. XIII. with additions and notes by *Fr. Hargrave* and *Charles Butler* —. 1788. fol. (3 L. 3 Sh.)

HARGROVE, [E.....] Hiſtory of the caſtle, town and foreſt of *Knaresborough* with *Harrogate* and its medicinal waters —. 1782. 8. (1 Sh. 6 d.) Ed. 4. 1789. 8.

HARINGTON, [John Herbert] Deſcription of a Cave with an inſcription near Gyá, (Aſiat. Reſ. Vol. 1. p. 276.)

— [Henry] *A. B. of Queen's College, Oxford.* Nugae antiquae; being a miſcellaneous collection of origi-

original papers in profe and verfe: written in the reigns of Henry VIII. Edward VI. Mary, Elizabeth, James I. felected from authentic remains of *John Harrington* —. 1769. 8. (3 Sh.) Ed. 2. 1775. Vol. 1. 2. (3 Sh.)

HARLEY, [George Davies] *of the Theatre-Royal, Norwich.* Monody on the death of Mr. *John Henderfon* late of Covent-Garden Theatre. 1787. 4. (2 fh.)

HARMER, [Thomas] *Diffenting Minifter at Watesfield, Suffolk.* born: .... died d. 27 Nov. 1788.

HARPER, [Andrew] The oeconomy of health; or, a medical effay: containing new and familiar inftructions for the attainment of health, happineff and longevity —. 1789. 8. (2 Sh.) On the real caufe and cure of infanity —. 1789. 8. (2 Sh.)

HARPLEY, [T......] *T. Harpley* and *W. Sancroft* poems on various fubjects, moral, fentimental, fatyrical and entertaining. 1785. 8. (3 Sh.)

HARRINGTON, [.....] *Mrs.* °New and elegant amufements for the ladies of Great Britain. by a Lady. 1772. 8. (2 Sh. 6 d.)

—— [Robert] *M. D.* Enquiry into the firft and general principles of animal and vegetable life. —. 1781. 8. (5 Sh.) Thoughts on the properties and formations of the different kinds of air —. 1785. 8. (5 Sh.) Letter to *Prieftley, Cavendifh, Lavoifier* and *Kirwan* endeavouring to prove, that their newly adopted opinions of inflammable and dephlogiftical airs forming water; and the acids being compounded of the different kinds of air, are fallacious. 1788. 8. (3 fh.)

—— [Thomas] Science improved; or, the true theory of the univerfe —. 1774. 4. (7 Sh. 6 d.)

HARRIS, [James] *F. R. S. Truftee of the Britifh Mufeum.* born at *Clofe, Salisbury*: 1708. died d. 21 Dec. 1780.

—— [Jofeph] *Secretary.* born 1751. died d. 31 Aug. 1789.

—— [Mofes] The Aurelian, or hiftory of Englifh infects. 17.. The englifh Lepidoptera: or, the Aurelian's pocket companion —. 1775. 8. (2 Sh.)

—— [R....] Scriptural refearches on the licitneff of the flave trade. —. 1788. 8. (1 Sh. 6 d.)

HAR-

HARRIS, [Richard] *M. D. Physician at Clonmel.* Collectanea hibernica medica. Nro. 1. 1783. 8. (2 Sh. 6 d.)

— [William] *D. D. Dissenting Clergyman at Honiton, Devonshire.* born: ..... died d ... Febr. 1770.

— [William] *Prebendary of Landaff and Curate of Cairell.* Observations on the Julia strata and on the roman stations, forts, and camps in the counties of Monmouth, Brecknock, Caermarthen and Glamorgan. (Arch. Vol. 2. p. 1.)

HARRISON, [.....] *Lieutenant.* The travellers, a comedy. 1788. 8. (1 Sh. 6 d.)

— [.....] Memoires of Charles Frederic, King of Prussia by *Sam. Johnson*, LL. D. with notes and a continuation, with translations of select poems written by the King of Prussia. 1786. (6 Sh.)

— [Edward] *Member of the royal medical society at Edinburgh.* Letter to Dr. (*Will.*) *Stevenson*, occasioned by a postscript published in the IId Edition of his medical cases —. 1782. 8. (1 Sh.)

— [Gustavus] Agriculture delineated: or, the farmer's complete guide; — —. 1775. 8. (5 Sh.)

— [John] *Surgeon, of Mountstreet, Berkeleysquare.* The remarkable effects of fixed air in mortifications of the extremities, with a history of some worm cases. 1785. 8. (1 Sh.) On the cure of the dry belly-ach. —. 1786. 8. (1 Sh.) A case of the stone in the urinary bladder, successfully treated; by giving water impregnated with fixed air, by means of salt of tartar and weak spirit of vitriol. (Mem. of M. S. of L. Vol. 1 p. 225.) History of some remarkable cures in worm cases by a mild and efficacious medicine —. 1786. 8.

— [John] *Mechanician.* born at *Fulby* in the parish of *Wragby* 1693. died d. 24 March 1776.

— [Richard] *M. A. Minister of Brompton Chapel and Lecturer of St. Peter's, Cornhill.* Institutes of English grammar. 1780. 8. (Several single sermons)

— [R....] *Musical Professor.* Sacred harmony; or, a collection of psalm tunes, ancient and modern —. 8. 1784. (5 Sh.)

HARROD, [W....] The antiquities of Stamford and St. Martin. Vol. 1. 2. 1780. 8. (7 Sh.)

HARSTON, [Hall] The counteſſ of Salisbury. a Tragedy. 1767. (1 ſh. 6 d.) Youth, a poem. 1773. 4. (2 Sh.)

HART, [Cheney] *M. D. In the Commiſſion of the peace, for the County of Salop and ſenior Phyſician of the Infirmary at Shrewsbury.* born 1726. died d. 21 June 1784.

HARTE, [Walter] *M. A.* born: .... died at Bath. 1773.

HARTLEY, [David] Esq. *Member of Parliament in Yorkſhire.* Speech on the ſtate of the nation and the preſent civil war in America. 1776. 4. (1 Sh.) Letters on the American War —. 1778. 4. (3 Sh.) Two letters — to the committee of the county of York. 1780. 8. (6 d.) Addreſſ to the committee of the county of York. 1781. 8. (1 Sh.) Conſiderations on the propoſed renewal of the bank Charter. 1781. 8. (1 Sh.) Addreſſ to the — Mayor and Corporation — of the Trinity houſe and to the — burgeſſes of the town of Kingſton upon Hull. 1784. 8. (1 Sh.)

—— [James] born ..... died 1780.

—— [Thomas] *M. A. Rector of Winwick, Northamptonſhire.* born: .... died d. 10 Dec. 1784.

—— [Winchcombe Henry] *Member of Parliament.* Addreſſ to the public on the loan. 1781. 8. (6 d.)

HARTSON, [Hall] born in Ireland .... died d. .... March. 1773.

HARVEST, [George] *M. A. Fellow of Magdalen College.* Collection of ſermons — on various ſubjects. 1763. 8. (4 Sh.) Reasonebleneſſ and neceſſity of ſubſcription. 1772. 8. (2 Sh. 6 d.)

HARVEY, [Stanhope] *Esq.* On soot uſed upon graſſ grounds. (*Hunter's* G. E. Vol. 5. p. 267.)

HARWOOD, [Buſick] *F. R S. Profeſſor of Anatomy in the Univerſity of Cambridge.* Synopſis of a courſe of lectures on anatomy and phyſiology. 1787. 8. (2 Sh. 6 d.)

—— [Edward] *D. D.* Letter to *Caleb* Evans occaſioned by his curious confeſſion of faith. 1767. 8. (1 Sh.) New introduction to the ſtudy and knowledge of the new teſtament. Vol. 1. 2. 1767. 1771. (11 Sh.) überſ. von *J. Cph. Fr. Schulz.* Th. 1–3. Halle 1770. Liberal translation of the New Teſtament. Vol.

Vol. 1. 2. 1768. (12 Sh.) The melancholy doctrine of predestination exposed and the delightful truth of universal redemption represented. 1768. 8 (1 Sh. 6 d.) Five Dissertations: 1) on the Athanasian doctrine: 2) on the Socinian sheme. 3) On the person of Christ. 4) On the rise, progreſſ, perfection and end of Christ's kingdom. 5) On the causes which probably conspired to produce our Saviour's agony. 1772. 8. (4 Sh.) überſ (von *Krüger*) Berlin 1774. 8. überſ. Leipzig 1774. 8. The life and character of Jesus Christ. 1773. 8. (4 Sh. 6 d.) On temperance and intemperance. 1774. 8. (2 Sh. 6 d.) überſ. Leipzig 1776. 8. *Abauzit* Miſcellanies on hiſtorical theological and critical ſubject — translated from the french. 1774. 8. (6 Sh.) *Catulli*, *Tibulli*, *Propertii* Opera. 1774. 8. (3 Sh.) New Teſtament — with notes. Vol. 1. 2. 1776. 8. (7 Sh.) *(La Roche,)* Memoirs of Miſſ *Sophie Sternheim* translated. Vol. 1. 2. 1776. (6 Sh.) Sermons on the parable of the sower. 1777. 8. (3 Sh. 6 d.) Biographia claſſica: The lives and characters of the greek and roman claſſics. 1777. Vol. 1. 2. (6 Sh.) View of the various editions of the greek and roman claſſics. 1775. 8. (3 Sh.) überſ. von *F. K. Alter*. Wien 1778. 8. On the ſocinian sheme. Ed. 2. 1784. 8. (1 Sh. 6 d.) überſ. von *J. C. F. Schulz*. Leipz. 1773. 8. The caſe of *Harwood*; an obſtinate palſy relieved by electricity. 1784. 8. (1 Sh.) Letter to the Rev. *S. Badcock*, the Monthly reviewer, in which his uncharitableneſſ, ignorance and abuſe of Dr. *Prieſtley* are exposed. 1784. 8. (1 Sh.)

(Several ſingle ſermons.)

HARWOOD, [Thomas] *of Univerſity College, Oxford.* De death of Dion, a Tragedy. 1787. 8. (1 Sh. 6 d.) Annotations upon geneſis; —. 1789. 8. (5 Sh.)

HASSEL, [J.....] Tour of the Isle of Wight. Vol. 1. 2. 1790. 8. (1 L. 11 ſh. 6 d.)

HASTED, [Edward] *F. R. S: F. A. S.* Letter to Dr. *Ducarel*, concerning Chesnut trees. (Phil. Transact. 1771. p. 160.) Hiſtory and topographical ſurvey of the county of Kent. Vol. 1-3. 1778-1790. fol. (5 L. 5 Sh.)

HASTIN-

HASTINGS, [Thomas] The tears of Britannia; a poem on the death of William Earl of Chatham. 1778. 4. (1 Sh.)

— [Warren] *late Governor General of Bengal.* Narrative of the late transaction at Benares. 1782. 8. (2 Sh. 6 d.) Narrative of the insurrection, which happened in the Zemeedary at Benares. Calcutta 1782. 4. (10 Sh. 6 d.) Letter to the court of directors of East India Company 1783. 8. (1 Sh. 6 d.) Letter - with remarks and authentic documents. 1786. 8. (1 Sh.) The defence at the bar of the house of commons. P. 1. 2. 1786. 8. (5 Sh.) Review of the state of Bengal. 1786. 8. (3 Sh.) auch unter dem Titel: Memoirs relative to the state of India. 1786. 8. (4 Sh.) The present state of the East Indies. 1786. 8. (2 Sh.) Letter to the court of Directors relative to their censure on his conduct at Benares - with a letter - on the subject of money privateley received. 1786. 8. (1 Sh. 6 d.) Answer to the articles exhibited by the knigths, citizens and burgesses in parliament assembled — in maintenance of their impeachment against him for high crimes - supposed to have been by him committed. 1788. 8. (4 Sh.)

HATSELL, [John] *Esq. Clerk to the house of commons.* * Collection of cases of privilege of parliament from the earliest records, to the Year 1628. 4. (6 Sh.) Vol. 1. 1778. Precedents of proceedings in the house of commons, under separate titles; with observations. Vol. 1-3. 1781. 4. (16 Sh.)

HATTON, [Thomas] *Watchmaker.* Introduction to the mechanical part of Clock and watch work —. 1773. 8. (6 Sh. 6 d.) Essay on Goldcoin. 1773. 8. (2 Sh.)

HAVARD, [Neast] *Town Clerk of the Borough of Tewkesbury.* born: .... died d. Jan. 1787.

— [William] *Actor.* born: .... died. d. 20 Febr. 1778.

HAWEIS, [Thomas] *LL. B. Rector of Aldwinkle and Chaplain to the Earl of Peterborough.* Evangelical principles and practice —. 1763. 8. (5 Sh.) Improvement of the church catechism —. 1776. 12. (2 Sh.) Scriptural refutation of the arguments for

for polygamy. —. 1781. 8. (1 Sh. 6 d.) Hints respecting the poor. 1788. 8. (1 Sh.)
(Several single sermons.)

HAWES, [William] *Apothecary. M. D.* Account of the late Dr. *Goldsmith's* illness, so far as relates to the exhibition of Dr. *James's* powders —. 1774. 4. (1 sh.) Examination of *John Wesley's* primitive physic. 1776. 8. (1 sh. 6 d.) Address against to hasty interments. 1777. 8. Address on the recovery of suspended animation —. 1782. 8. (2 sh.) *Editor of Reports of the humane society, instituted in the year 1774. for the recovery of persons apparently drowned, for the years 1781 and 1782. 8. Address on the important subject of preserving the lives of its inhabitants. 1782. Observations on the general bills of mortality. 1783. 8. (3 sh.)

HAWKE, [....] *Mrs.* ° Julia de Gramont, a Novel. Vol. 1. 2. 1788. 12. (7 sh.)

HAWKESBURY, *Lord.* see *Charles Jenkinson.*

HAWKESWORTH, [John] *LL. D. of Brombey in Kent.* born 1719. died d. 17 Nov. 1773.

HAWKINS, [A....] Translation of *Mignot's* history of the Turkish or Ottoman empire from 1300-1740. Vol. 1-4. 1788. 8. (1 L. 4 sh.)

— [George] *Esq.* The Royal letter Writer. 17.. On female education. 1781. 8. (1 sh. 6 d)

— [John Sidney] *Sir, Knight. One of his Majesty's justices of the peace of Midlesex and Chairman of the Court of quarter session.* born: 1718. died d. 21 May. 1789.

— [John] Address to *Priestley;* containing an apology for those who conscientiously subscribe to the articles of the church of England; and in particular, to the doctrines of the trinity —. 1788. 8. (1 sh. 6 d.)

— [Thomas] *M. A. of Magdalen-College, Oxford.* The origin of the english drama. Vol. 1-3. 1773. 8. (9 sh.)

— [William] *M. A.* Discourses on scripture mysteries. 1787. 8. (5 sh.) Poems, chiefly pastoral. 1787. 8. (1 sh.)

HAWTHORN, [John] *Light Dragoon in the Inniskilling regiment.* Poems. 1779. 4. (3 sh.)

HAY, [Charles] *Captain.* Description of a roman hypocaust discovered near Brecknock. (Arch. Vol. 7. p. 205. Vol. 8. p. 441.)

HAYES, [....] Natural history of british birds. 1775. fol. (5 L. 15 sh. 6 d.)

—— [Samuel] *M. A. Fellow of Trinity college. Usher of Westminster school.* Duelling, a poem. 1775. 4. (1 sh.) Prayer, a poem. 1777. 4. (1 sh.) Prophecy, a poem. 1777. 4. (1 sh.) The nativity of our saviour, a poem. 1778. 4. (1 sh.) The Ascension, a poetical essay. 1781. 4. (1 sh.) Hope, a poem. 1783. 4. (1 sh. 6 d.) Creation, a poem. 1784. 4. (1 sh.) The exodus, a poem. 1785. 4. (2 sh.) Published *Sam. Johnson's* sermon for the funeral of his wife. 1788. 8. (1 Sh) Published *John Taylor's* L. L. D. sermons on different subjects. Vol. 1. 2. 1789. (10 Sh.) Verses on his Majesty's recovery. 1789. 4. (1 Sh. 6 d.) Thanksgiving sermon. 1789. 4. (1 Sh).

HAYES, [Thomas] *Surgeon at London.* *Addreſſ to the public on the dangerous consequences of neglecting common coughs and colds. 1784. 8. (1 Sh. 6 d.) Ed. 2. (with the Author's name) 1785. Ed. 3. 1786. 8. (2 Sh. 6 d.) übers. von *C. F. Michaelis.* Leipz. 1787. 8. Remarks on the nature and treatment of intermittents, as they occurred at *Hampstead* in the spring of 1781. (London M. J. Vol. 2. p. 267. übers. Samml. f. A. Th. 7. S. 493.

—— [Thomas] *Surgeon at Hampstead.* born:... died 17..

HAYGARTH, [John] *M. D: F. R. S.* A case of angina pectoris, with an attempt to investigate the cause of the disease by dissection and a hint suggested concerning the method of cure. (Med. Transact Vol. 3. p. 37.) Apparent effects of mercury in cases that were supposed hydrocephalus. (Med. Obs. Vol. 6. p. 58.) Experiments on the cerumen or earwax in order to discover the best method of dissolving it when causing deafneſſ. (Ibid. p. 198.) Bill of Mortality for Chester for the Y. 1772. (Phil. Transact. 1774. p. 67.) Bill of Mortality for Chester for the Y. 1773. (Ibid 1775 p. 85.) Bill of Mortality for Chester for the Y. 1774. (ibid. 1778. p. 131.) Observations on the population and diseases of Chester in the Year 1774. (Ibid.

(Ibid. 1778. p. 131.) Account of a newly invented machine for impregnating water or other fluids with fixed air. (Mem. of M. Vol. 1. p. 41.) Inquiry how to prevent the ſmall pox. 1784. 8. (3 Sh.) überſ. von *J. F. L. Cappel*. Berlin. 1786. 8.

HAYLEY, [William] at *Eartham*. *Poetical epiſtle to an eminent painter. (Mr. *Romney*) 1778. 4. *Elegy on the ancient greek medal. 1779. 4. (1 Sh. 6 d.) *Epiſtle to a friend on the death of *John Thornton*. 1780. 4. (1 Sh.) Eſſay on hiſtory, in 3 Epiſtles to *Edw. Gibbon*. 1780. 4. (7 Sh. 6 d.) *Ode inſcribed to *John Howard*. 1780. 4. (1 Sh. 6 d.) The triumphs of temper; a poem. 1781. 4. (6 Sh.) Eſſay on epic poetry. 1782. 4. (10 Sh. 6 d.) Plays. 1784. 4. (12 Sh.) Poems and plays. Vol. 1-6. 1785. 8. (1 L. 1 Sh) *Philoſophical hiſtorical and moral eſſay on old maids; by a friend to the ſiſterhood. Vol. 1-3. 1785. 8. (10 Sh. 6 d) überſ. Leipz. Th. 1-3. 1786. 8. Occaſional ſtanzas. 1788. 4. (2 Sh.)

HAYSHAM, [John] *M. D.* Account of the jail fever, as it appeared at *Carlisle* in the Year 1781. 1782.

HAYTER, [Thomas] *A. M. Fellow of King's College, Cambridge. Preacher at his Majeſty's Chapel in Whitehall.* Remarks on *Hume's* dialogues concerning natural religion. 1780. 8. (1 Sh. 6 d.) Two ſermons. 1788. 8. (1 Sh.)

HAYWOOD, [...] *Mrs.* A new preſent for a ſervant maid: containing rules for her moral conduct —. 1771. 12. (2 Sh.)

HEADLEY, [Henry] *A. B. at Norwich.* born 1765. died d. 15 Nov. 1788.

HEALDE, [Thomas] *M. D: F. R. S. Lumleyan Lecturer at the college of phyſicians and ſenior phyſician of the London Hoſpital.* On the uſe of oleum asphalti in ulcers of the inteſtines, lungs and other viscers. 1769. 8. (1 Sh.) The new pharmacopoea of the royal college of phyſicians of London, translated into engliſh with notes —. 1788. 8. (5 Sh.)

HEARD, [William] Valentine day; a muſical drama. 1775. 8. The Snuffbox; or a trip to bath, a comedy. 1775. 8. (1 Sh.) A ſentimental journey to

Bath, *Briſtol* and their environs; a poem, with miſcellaneous pieces. 1778. 4. (5 Sh.)

HEARNE, [Gilbert] *of Hertford. Antiquarian.* born: .... died d. 17 Sept. 1771.

HEASEL, [Anthony] The ſervant's book of knowledge, containing tables of wages —. 1773. 8. (1 Sh. 6 d.)

HEATHCOTE, [Ralph] *D. D. Clergyman.* Sketch of Lord *Bolingbroke's* philoſophy. 1754. 8. (1 Sh. 6 d.) The uſe of reaſon aſſerted in matters of religion or natural religion the foundation of revealed. Ed. 2. 1755. 8. (1 Sh. 6 d. Reply to Dr. *Patten* Sermon on St. *Peter's* chriſtian apology. 1756. 8. (2 Sh.) A diſcourſe upon the being of God: againſt Atheiſts in two ſermons. 1763. 4. (1 Sh.) * Letter to the Lord Major — from an old ſervant. 1762. 8. (1 Sh. 6 d.) Sylva or the wood. 17.. The Irenarch: or juſtice of peace's manual. 2) miſcellaneous reflections upon the laws, policy, manners. 3) Aſſize ſermon 1781. 8. (3 Sh.)
(Several ſingle ſermons.)

HEBERDEN, [William] *M. D: F. R. S: F. A. S.* Antithyriaca, eſſay on Mithridaticum and Theriaca. 1755. 8. Remarks on the pumpwater of London and on the methods of procuring the pureſt water. (Med. Transact. Vol. 1. p. 1.) Obſervations on the Ascarides. (Ibid. p. 60.) On the effect of common ſalt in an extraordinary caſe of worms. (Ibid. p. ..) Of the night-blindneſſ or Nyctalopia. (Ibid. p. 60.) On the chicken-pox. (Ibid. p. 427.) The epidemical cold, in June and July 1767. (Ibid. p. 437.) On the hectic fever. (Ibid. Vol. 2. p. 1.) Remarks on the pulſe. (Ibid. p. 18) Account of a diſorder of the breaſt. (Ibid. p. 59.) Account of the diſeaſes of the liver. (Ibid. p. 123.) Account of the nettle raſh. (Ibid. p. 173.) Account of the noxious effects of ſome fungi. (Ibid. p. 216.) Account of the angina pectoris. (Ibid. Vol. 2. p... Vol. 3. p...) Of the meaſles. (Ibid. Vol. 3. p. 389.) The method of preparing Ginseng root in China. (Ibid. Vol. 3. p...) A table of the mean heat of every month for ten Years in London from 1763 to 1772. incluſively. (Phil. Tranſact. 1788. p. 66.)

HECKFORD, [William] *Esq.* Characters, or historical anecdotes of all the kings and queens of England. 1789. 8. (3 Sh.)

HEDLEY, [William] System of practical arithmetic and three forms of book-keeping —. 1779. 8. (2 Sh. 6 d.)

HEELY, [Joseph] *Esq.* Letters on the beauties of Hagley, Envil and the Leasowes, with observations on the modern taste in gardening. Vol. 1. 2. 1777. 12. (5 Sh.) übers. Leipz. 1779. 8.

HELLINS, [John] *Curate of Constantine, in Cornwall.* Theorems for computing logarithms. (Phil. Transact. 1780. p. 388.) A new method of finding the equal roots of an equation by division. (Ibid. 1782. p. 417.) Mathematical essays on several subjects —. 1788. 4. (7 Sh. 6 d.)

HELME, [Elizabeth] *Mrs.* Louisa, or the cottage on the moor. Vol. 1. 2. 1787. 8. (6 Sh.) Clara and Emmelina, or the maternal benediction. Vol. 1. 2. 1788. 8. (5 Sh.) *Vaillant's* travels from the Cape of good Hope into the interior parts of Africa — translated from the french. Vol. 1. 2. 1790. 8. (12. sh)

HELSHAM, [Henry] *Surgeon at Stoke in Norfolk.* Account of different medical cases. (*Duncan's* M. C. Dec. 2. Vol. III. p. 278.)

HEMMING, [John] *M. D: Physician to the Offulston dispensary.* History and chemical analysis of the mineral water lately discovered in the city of Gloucester —. 1789. 8. (1 Sh.)

HENDERSON, [Andrew] *M. A.* Arsinoe: or, the incestuous marriage, a tragedy. 1752. 8. (1 Sh.) *Voltaire's* history of Frederik, King of Sweden, translated. 1752. 8. (1 Sh. 6 d.) Memoirs of Dr. *Archib. Cameron* —. 1753. 8. (1 Sh.) Memoirs of the Field-Mareshal *Leopold* Count *Daun* — translated from a french Manuscript —. 1757. 8. (1 Sh. 6 d.) Memoirs of the life and actions of *James Keith* Field-Mareshal in the Prussian armies —. 1759. 8. (1 Sh.) Considerations whether the act of parliament establishing a militia through England ought to extend to Scotland in time of war? 1760. 8. (1 Sh.) The life of *William* the Conqueror, Duke of Normandy and King of England. 1764. 8. (2 Sh. 6 d.) The life of *William Augu-*

ſtus Duke of Cumberland —. 1766. 8. (5 Sh.) Letter to the Lord Biſhop of Cheſter on his ſermon before the Lords. 1774. 8. Letter 1. 2. to *Sam. Johnſon* on his journey to the Weſtern Isles. 1775. 8. (1 ſh. 6 d.)

HENDERSON, [John] *B. A.* born at *Bellegarance in Ireland* d. 27 March 1757. died d. 2 Nov. 1788.

HENDERSON, [Stewart] *Surgeon of his Majeſty's ſhip Aſtrea, at Jamaica.* Account of the ſucceſsfull treatment of an ulcer of the leg, with remarks on ulcers of the legs in general, in warm climates. (*Duncan's* M. C. Dec. 2. Vol. 3. p. 292.)

HENDERSON, [William] *M. D. Member of the R. Med. Soc. of Edinb.* Obſervations concerning thoſe things which are probable or in ſome meaſure aſcertained relative to the hiſtory and cure of the plague. 1789. 8. (1 ſh. 6 d.)

HENDY, [James] *M. D. Phyſician general to the militia and one of the phyſicians to the general diſpenſary at Barbadoes.* On glandular ſecretion —. 1775. 8. (2 ſh.) On the glandular diſeaſe of Barbadoes. 1784. 8. (2 ſh. 6 d.) überſ. von *A. F. A. Diel.* Frankf. 1788. 8. Vindication of the opinions and facts, contained in a treatiſe of the glandular diſeaſe of Barbadoes. 1789. 8. (3 ſh.)

HENLEY, [Samuel] *F. S. A: Rector of Rendlesham, Suffolk.* Obſervations on the ſubject of the IV eclogue, the allegory in the third georgic and the primary deſign of the aeneid of *Virgil,* with remarks on ſome coins of the jews. 1788. 8. (2 ſh. 6 d.)

—— [Samuel] *Curate of Northall in Middleſex.* Diſſertation on the controverted paſſages in St. Peter and St. Jude concerning the angels that ſinned and who kept not their firſt eſtate. 1778. 8. (2 ſh.)

—— [William] *F. R. S.* Account of the death of a perſon destroyed by lightning in the chapel in Tottenham-Court-road and its effects on the building. (Philoſ. Transact. 1772. p. 131.) Experiment concerning the different efficacy of pointed and blunted rods, in ſecuring buildings againſt the ſtroke of lightning. (Ibid. 1774. p. 133.) Account of ſome new experiments in electricity —. (Ibid. 1774. p. 389.) Remarks on Mr. *Haffenden's* account of the effects of lightning on a houſe furnished with a poin-

pointed conductor at Tenterden in Kent. (Ibid. 1774. p. 336.) Experiments and obſervations on a new apparatus, called, a machine for exhibiting perpetual electricity. (Ibid. 1776. p. 513.) Experiments and obſervations in electricity. (Ibid. 1777. p. 85.) Obſervations and experiments tending to confirm Dr. *Ingenhousz's* theory of the electrophorus; and to ſhew the impermeability of glaſs to electric fluid. (Phil. Transact. 1778. p. 1049.) überſ Samml. zur P. u. N. G. Th. 2. S. 536.

HENRY, [Robert] *D. D. Miniſter of Edinburgh. F. A. S. Edinb.* Hiſtory of Great-Britain from the firſt invaſion of it by the Romans under Julius Ceſar. Vol. 1-5. London. 1771-1785. 4. (5 L. 5 ſh.) Letter to the Authors of the Critical Review. (Crit. Review. Vol. 46. p. 320.)

(Several ſingle ſermons.)

— [Thomas] *Apothecary at Mancheſter F. R. S.* Account of an improved method of preparing magneſia alba. (Med. Transact. Vol. 2. p. 226.) Experiments and obſervations on the preparation, calcination and medicinal uses of magneſia alba. 1773. 8. (2 ſh. 6 d.) Account of the medicinal virtues of magneſia alba — 1773. 8. Letter to Dr. *Glaſſ*, containing a reply to his examination of the ſtrictures on Dr. *Glaſſ's* magneſia. 1774. 8. (6 d.) Experiments on the comparative powers of ſoft and hard water in diſſolving reſinous ſubſtances. (*Percival's* Eſſays. Ed. 3. Vol. 1.) Letter on the ſolution of lead in water impregnated with nitrous air. (*Prieſtley's* Exper. and Obs. on air. Vol. 1. p. 323.) *Lavoiſier* eſſays phyſical and chemical translated. 1776. 8. (7 ſh.) Account of the earthquake which was felt at Mancheſter and other places, on the 14th day of Sept. 1777. (Phil. Transact. 1778. p. 221.) On the effects of fixed air in preserving fruit and its influence on vegetation, milk —. (*Prieſtley's* Exp. and Obs. on air. Vol. 3. p. 369.) On the action of lime and marl as manures; and the making of artificial marl for the purposes of Agriculture (*Hunter's* G. E. Vol. 5. p. 65.) Account of a method of preserving water at ſea from putrefaction. 1781. 8. (2 ſh.) *Lavoiſier's* eſſays on effects produced by various pro-

processes on atmospheric air. 1783. 8. (2 ſh. 6 d.) Memoirs of *Alb. Haller*. 1783. 8. (2 ſh. 6 d.) Inſtances of the medicinal effects of magnetism. (London M. J. Vol. 3. p. 303.) On the advantage of litterature and philosophy in general and especially on the conſiſtency of literary and philosophical with comercial purſuits. (Mem. of. M. Vol. 1. p. 7.) On the preſervation of ſea water from putrefaction by means of quicklime. (Mem. of M. Vol. 1. p. 41.) On the natural hiſtory and origin of magneſian earth, particularly as connected with those of ſeasalt and of nitre, with obſervations on ſome of the chemical properties of that earth, which have been hitherto, either unknown or undetermined. (Ibid. p. 448.) Experiments and obſervations on ferments and fermentation. 1785. 8. (Ibid. Vol. 2. p. 257.) überſ. Samml. zur P. u. Ng. Th. 3. S. 643. Obſervations on the influence of fixed air on vegetation and on the probable cauſe of the difference in the results of various experiments, made on that ſubject. (Ibid. p. 341.) A caſe of a head-ach attended with uncommon ſymptoms. (Mem. of M. S. of L. Vol. 1. p. 294.)

HENRY, [William] *of Lancaſter*. Deſcription of a ſelf-moving or ſentinel regiſter (Tr. of A. S. Vol. 1. p. 286.)

HERBERT, [William] *of Cheshunt, Herts*. *Jos. Ames's* typographical antiquities: or account of the origin and progreſſ of printing in Great-Britain and Ireland — conſiderably augmented. Vol. 1-3. 1785-1790. 4. (1 L. 1 Sh.)

HERIOT, [George] *Deſcriptive poem, written in the Weſt-Indies. 1781. 4. (2 ſh.)

HERON, [Robert] ſee *Pinkerton*.

HERRIES, [John] *M. A.* The elements of ſpeech. 1773. 8. (4 ſh.) Sermon on the frequent and enormous crime of ſuicide. 1774. 4. (1 ſh.)

HERRING, [Thomas] *Archbiſhop of Canterbury*. born: .... died 1774.

HERVEY, [Chr....] *Esq.* Letters from Portugal, Spain, Italy and Germany in the years 1759-1761. Vol. 1-3. 1785. 8. (18 ſh.)

—— [G.... A....] ſee *Payne*.

HEWGILL, [Edwin] *Enſign and Adjutant in the Cold-ſtream*

ſtream Regiment of foot guards. J. G. Tielke's field Engineer; or, inſtructions upon every branch of field fortification translated —. Vol. 1. 2. 1789. 8. (1 L. 8 Sh.)

HEWLETT, [John] *A. M. of Magdalene College, Cambridge, Lecturer of the united parishes of St. Vedaſt, Foſterlane and St. Michael le Querne.* Sermons on different ſubjects. 1786. 8. (6 ſh.) Introduction to reading and ſpelling, written on a new plan —. 1786. 8. (1 ſh.) Vindication of the authenticity of the parian chronicle in answer to a diſſertation on that ſubject. 1789. 8. (4 ſh.) Answer to ſome critical ſtrictures, relative to the controversy on the authenticity of the parian chronicle in a letter to *J. Roberiſon* —. 1789. 8. (1 ſh. 6 d.)

HEWSON, [William] *F. R. S. and Teacher of Anatomy*: born at *Hexham* in *Northumberland*. d. 14 May. 1739. died d. 1 May 1774.

HEY, [Richard] *L. L. D. Fellow of Magdalen College Cambridge and Barriſter at Law of the middle temple.* Diſſertation on the pernicious effects of gaming. 1783. 8. (1 ſh. 6 d.) Diſſertation on duelling. 1784. 8. (1 ſh. 6 d.) Observations on the nature of civil liberty and the principles of government. 1776. 8. (1 ſh.)

— [William] *F. R. S. Surgeon-General to the Infirmary at Leeds.* Account of an extrauterine foetus. (Med. Obs. Vol. 3. p. . .) Account of a rupture of the bladder from a ſuppreſſion of urine in a pregnant woman. (Ibid. Vol. 4. p. 58.) Experiments on fixed air and an account of its utility as a medicine in putrid fevers. (Phil. Transact. 1772. p. . .) On the effects of fixed air, applied by way of clyſter. (*Prieſtley's* Experim. on air: Vol. 1. p. 292.) überſ. Samml. f. A. Th. 3. S. 272. Account of the effects of electricity in the amaurosis. (Med. Obs. Vol. 5. p. 1.) Experiments to prove that there is no oil of vitriol in water impregnated with fixed air. (*Prieſtley's* experiments on air. Vol. 1. p. 288.) On the acidity of fixed air: (Ibid. Vol. 3. p. 383.) Observations on the blood. 1779. 8. (1 ſh.) Account of ſome luminous arches. (Phil. Transact. 1790. p. 32.)

HEYDON, [C.....] *Jun.* The new aftrology 1786. 12. (2 fh. 6 d.)

HEYLYN, [Peter] *D. D. Prebendary of Weftminfter.* A help to englifh hiftory —. 1774. 8. (8 fh.)

HEYSHAM, [John] *M. D. Phyfician at Carlisle in Cumberland.* Diff. De rabie canina. Edinb. 1777. 8. Account of the jail fever, or typhus carcerum —. 1782. 8. (1 fh.) Account of a painful affection of the antrum maxillare, from which three infects were difcharged. (M. C. Vol. 1. p. 430.) A remarkable cafe of epilepsy and dysphagia fpasmodica cured by the use of cuprum ammoniacum. (*Duncan's* M. C. 1780. p. 428. and p. 438.)

HICKS, [George] *M. D. Phyfician to the Weftminfter Hospital.* Diff. De Enteritide. Edinb. 1768. 8. A cafe of peripnevmony, attended with emphysema. (M. C. Vol. 1. p. 173.)

HIFFERNAN, [Paul] born in *Ireland*: .... died d. 12 Jun. 1777.

HIGGINS, [Bryant] *M. D.* Actual fire and detonation produced by the contact of tinfoil, with the falt composed of copper and the nitrous acid. (Phil. Transact. 1773. p. 137.) Philosophical effay concerning light. Vol. 1. 1776. 8. (6 fh.) On the use of an amalgam of zinc, for the purpose of electrical excitation. (Phil. Transact. 1778. p. 861.) Experiments and obfervations made with the view of improving the art of compofing and applying calcareous cements and of preparing quicklime —. 1780. 8. (5 fh.) Experiments and obfervations relating to acetous acid, fixable air, dense inflammable air, oils and fuel —. 1786. 8. (6 fh.)

—— [William] *of Pembr. Coll. Oxford.* Comparative view of the phlogiftic and antiphlogistic theories — with an analyfis of the human calculus and obfervations on its origin —. 1789. 8. (7 fh.)

HIGHMORE, [Anthony] *Jun. Attorney at law.* Doctrine of bail in civil and criminal cases. 1783. 8. (4 fh.) Review of the hiftory of Mortmain —. 1787. 8. (4 fh.)

—— [John] Journal of travels made through the principal cities of Europe, — translated from the French of *M. L. Dutens* —. Ed. 2. 1782. 8. (3 fh. 6 d.)

HIGHMORE, [Joseph] *Painter and Professor by the Academy of Painting, Sculpture, at London.* born in the Parish of St. *James, Garlickhithe, London.* d. 13 Jun. 1692. died d. 3 March. 1780.

HILL, [Brian] *A. M. Chaplain to the Earl of Leven.* Henry and Acasto: a moral tale. 1785. 8. (1 ſh.) (Several ſingle ſermons.)

—— [James] *Surgeon at Dumfries in Scotland.* Account of the discharge of feces mixed with the urine from the urethra of a woman. (Med. Com. of Ed. Vol. 2. p. 192.) Account of ſingular appearances from affections of the liver in two cases. (Ibid. p. 303.) The hiſtory of an anomalous tumour on the eyebrow of a child of 15 months old. (Ibid. Vol. 3. p. 313.) Caſes in Surgery, particularly of cancers and disorders of the head from external violence with observations. 1775. 8. (4 ſh. 6 d.) Hiſtory of a large prolapsus uteri. (Med. Com. of Ed. Vol. 4. p. 88.)

HILL [John] *Sir. Knight of the Polar-Star. Botaniſt to the royal garden at Kew.* born: 1717. died d. 21 Nov. 1775.

—— [John] *M. A: F. R. S. Edin. and Profeſſor of Humanity in the Univerſity of Edinburgh.* Eſſay upon the principles of hiſtorical compoſition, with an application of thoſe principles to the writings of *Tacitus.* (Tr. of E. S. Vol. 1. p. 76. et pag. 181.) überſ. von *J. G. Buhle*: Philoſ. u. Hiſtor. Abhandl. der Wiſſenſch. zu Edinburgh Th. 1 S. 123.

—— [Richard] *Baronet and Member of Parliament.* (a Methodiſt.) * Pietas Oxonienſis: or, an account of the expulſion of VI ſtudents from St. Edmon-Hall —. 1768. 8. (1 ſh.) * Goliath slain being a reply to Dr. *Nowell's* Answer to pietas Oxonienſis —. 1769. 8. (2 ſh. 6 d.) * Review of all the doctrines taught by — *John Wesley* containing an answer to a book: a ſecond check to Antinomianism. 1771. 8. (1 ſh. 6 d.) * Five letters to the Rev. *M. F—r.* relative to his vindication of the minutes of — *John Wesley* — by a friend. 1771. 8. (6 d.) * Some remarks on a pamphlet, entitled, a third check to Antinomianism by the author of pietas Oxonienſis. 1771. 8. (3 d.) Logica Weslejenſis —. 1773. 8. (1 ſh.) The finishing ſtroke;

ke; containing ſome ſtrictures on *Fletcher's* logica Genevenſis. 1773. 8. (1 ſh.) A preſent for your neighbour; or, the right knowlege of god and of ourselves. 1773. 8. (4 d.) Three letters — to — *J. Fletcher* — ſetting forth reaſons for declining any further controversy relative to *Wesley's* principles. 1774. 8. (6 d.) *A groſſ impoſition upon the public detected, or, Archbishop *Cranmer* vindicated from the charge of Pelagianism — by the author of pietas Oxonienſis — 1775. 8. (6 d.) Pietas Redingenſis, or, a vindication of — *John Hallward's* ſermon. 1776. 8. (6 d.) The goſpell ſhop, a Comedy. 1778. 8. (2 Sh) The bleſſings of polygamy displayed in an — addreſſ to *Martin Madan*, occaſioned by his work Thelyphthora. 1781. 8. (3 ſh.) The tables turned a letter to the author of a pamphlet observations on the election of members for the borough of Ludlow. 1781. 8. (6 d.) *The skyrocket: or thoughts during the eaſter receſſ of Parliament, on ſeveral very important ſubjects and on ſeveral recent events. 1781. 8. (1 ſh.) A ſhort catechism, containing the fundamental principles of Chriſtianity. 1788. (6 d.)

HILL, [Robert] *Esq. of Cambridge.* Poems on ſeveral occaſions —. 1775. 8. (5 ſh.)

— [Rowland] *M. A.* Impoſture detected and the dead vindicated —. 1777. 8. (6 d.) Answer to *J. Wesley's* remarks upon the defence of the character of Whitefield and others. 1778. 8. (6 d.)

— [Thom. F.....] *Antient Erſe poems —. 1784. 8. (—)

HILDITCH, [Ann] *Miſſ.* Roſa de Montmorien. Vol. 1. 2. 1787. 12. (5 ſh.)

HINDE, [Robert] *of the ſix Clerks Office.* The modern practice of the high court of Chancery —. 1785. 8. (9 Sh.)

— [......] *Captain of the Royal Regiment of light Dragoons.* born: .... died d. 29 Sept. 1786.

HINGESTON, [James] *M. A. Vicar of Raydon in Suffolk.* Discourses upon the divine covenants: or, an enquiry into the origin and progreſſ of religion, natural and revealed. Part. 1. 1771. 8. (5 ſh.)

HIRD, [William] *M. D. at Leeds in Yorkshire.* (a Quaker) born 1724. died d. 23 Aug. 1782.

HITCH-

HITCHCOCK, [—] The macoroni. a Comedy. 1773. 8. The coquet; or, the miſtakes of the heart. a Comedy. 1777. 8.

HITCHIN, [Edward] *B. D. Diſſenting Miniſter.* born 1726. died d. 11 Jan. 1774.

HOADLEY, [John] *LL. D. Chancellor of the Dioceſe of Wincheſter.* born d. 8 Oct. 1711. died d. 16 March. 1776.

HOBHOUSE, [Thomas] Elegy to the memory of *Sam. Johnſon.* 1784. 4. (6 d.) *Kingsweſton hill, a poem. 1784. 4. (1 Sh. 6 d.) Ed. 2. (with the Author's name.) 1787. 4. (1 ſh. 6 d.)

HOBSON, [John] *Miniſter of a congregation of proteſtant diſſenters at Kingswood Worceſtershire.* Discourſe on prayer. 1787. 8. (6 d.) Remarks upon *George Croft's* ſermon, the teſts laws defended. 1790. 8. (1 Sh.)

HODGE, [....] *Farmer.* The hampſtead conteſt; —. 1776. 4. (6 d.)

HODGES, [William] *R. A.* Select views in Aqua tinta of Antiquities in India, drawn on the ſpot in the Years 1780–1783. Vol. 1. 2. Numb. 1–12. fol. (12 L. 12 ſh.) überſ. von Riem. Heft. 1. Berlin. 1789. fol.

HODGSON, [....] Miscellaneous poems. 1788. 4. (1 ſh. 6 d.)

— [Henry] *Curate of Market Kasen, Lincolnshire.* Letters to Mrs. *Kindersley.* 1778. 8. (6 d.) The duty of universal benevolence enforced; in 3 ſermons. 1778. 8. (1 ſh.) Effuſions of the heart and fancy; in verse and prose. 1779. 8. (3 ſh. 6 d.)

— [Bernard] *L. L. D. Principal of Hertford College Oxford.* Salomon's ſong translated from the hebrew. Oxford. 1786. 4. (5 Sh.) The proverbs of Salomon, translated. 1788. 4. (7 ſh. 6 d.)

— [Henry] *Letter — on the right of fishing in public ſtreams. 1787. 8. (1 Sh.)

— [Thomas] Cursory observations on *Phil. Stern's* medical advice to the consumptive and aſtmatic people of England —. 1784. 8. (1 Sh.)

HODSON, [J....] *M. D.* Jesus Chriſt the true god —. 1787. 12. Vol. 1. 2. (5 Sh.) The Young's chriſtian's introduction to the knowledge of his god and ſaviour Jeſus Chriſt. 1788. 12. (6 d.)

The

The worship of Jesus Chriſt, as the true god of heaven and earth vindicated. 1789. 8. (6 d.)

HODSON, [William] *M A. Fellow of Trinity college.* The dedication of the temple of Solomon: a poetical eſſay. 1770. 4. (1 Sh.) *Arſaces, a tragedy. 1775. 8. (1 Sh. 6 d.) *Zoraida, a Tragedy, with obſervations on Tragedy. 1780. 8. (1 ſh. 6 d.) The adventures of a night, a farce. 1783. 8.

HOGG, [John] Thanksgiving ſermon. 1759. (6 d.) *Nathan. Lardner's* hiſtory of the heretics of the two firſt centuries after Chriſt, with additions. 1780. 4. (18 ſh.)

HOLCROFT, [Thomas] *Actor at Drury-Lane Theater.* (born in the county of *Lancaſter.*) Elegies: on the death of *Sam. Foote*: on age. 1777. 4. (1 ſh.) The Criſis; or, love and fear, a Comedy. 1778. Duplicity, a Comedy. 1780. 8. (1 ſh. 6 d.) Alwyn; a novel. Vol. 1. 2. 1780. Human happineſſ; or, the ſceptic, a poem. 1783. 4. (3 ſh.) The family picture, or domeſtic dialogues on amiable and intereſting ſubjects. Vol. 1. 2. 1783. 8. (6 ſh.) The noble peaſant; a comic opera. 1784. 8. (1 ſh 6 d) The follies of a day, a Comedy. 1784. 8. (*Foucher d'Obſonville's*) Philoſophical eſſays on the manners of various foreign animals, with obſervations on the laws and cuſtoms of ſeveral eaſtern nations translated from the french. 1784. 8. (5 ſh.) *Beaumarchais* follies of a day or the marriage of Figaro, a Comedy, translated. 1785. 8. (1 ſh. 6 d.) Mad. *Genlis's* — Tales of the caſtle — translated. Vol. 1 - 5. 1785. 8. (15 ſh.) The choleric fathers, a comic Opera. 1785. 8. (1 ſh. 6 d.) An amorous tale of the chaste loves of Peter the long and of his — Dame *Blanche Bazu.* 1786. 8. (3 ſh. 6 d.) Mad. *Genlis's* ſacred dramas translated. 1786. 8. (5 Sh.) Caroline of Lichtfield translated from the french. Vol. 1 - 3. 1786. 8. (9 Sh.) Seduction, a Comedy. 1787. 8. (1 Sh. 6 d.) The life of *Frederik* Baron *Trenck*, translated from the german. Vol. 1 - 3. 1788. 8. (12 Sh.) *Lavater's* eſſays on phyſiognomy — translated. Vol. 1 - 3. 1789. 8. (5 L. 5 Sh.) *Frederik's II.* Hiſtory of my own time — translated. Vol. 1. 2. 1789. 8. (7 Sh.)

HOLDEN, [John] Eſſay towards a rational ſyſtem of Muſic. 1770. 4. (7 Sh. 6 d.)

HOLDER, [....] at *Barbadoes.* Syſtem of french accidence and ſyntax —. 1782. 12. (3 Sh. 6 d.) Ed. 2. 1790. 8. (3 Sh. 6 d.) Eſſay on the ſubject of Negroe Slavery, with a particular reference to the Island of *Barbadoes.* 1788. 8. (1 Sh.)

HOLE, [Richard] *LL. B.* *Homer's* hymn to Ceres, translated into engliſh verſe. 1781. 8. (2 Sh.) Arthur; or the northern enchantment, a poetical romance. 1789. 8. (4 Sh.)

HOLLAND, [Samuel] *Esq. Surveyor General of Lands for the Northern diſtrict of America.* Some Eclipſes of Jupiter's ſatellites, obſerved near Quebec. (Phil. Transact. 1774. p. 171.) Aſtronomical obſervations, for aſcertaining the longitude of ſeveral places in North-America. (Ibid. p. 182.)

HOLLIDAY, [F....] Introduction to practical gunnery; or, the art of engineering —. 12. 1757. (3 Sh.) Introduction to fluxions —. 1777. 8. (6 ſh.)

HOLLINGBERY, [Thomas] *D. D. Archdeacon of Chicheſter and Chaplain in Ordinary to his Majeſty, F. R. S. F. A. S.* *Alex. Cunningham's* hiſtory of Great-Britain from the revolution in 1688 to the acceſſion of George I. with *Will. Thomſon's* account of the author and his writings. Vol 1. 2. 1787. 4. (1 L. 16 ſh.) überſ. Breslau. Th. 1. 2. 1789. 4.

HOLLINGSWORTH, [Henry] *of Elk-Ridge.* The method of deſtroying wild garlic. (Tr. of A. S. Vol. 1. p. 241.)

— [S....] *Account of the preſent ſtate of Nova Scotia. 1786. 8. (3 ſh.) On the manners, governments and ſpirit of Africa — with obſervations on the preſent application to Parliament for aboliſhing Negroe ſlavery —. 1788. 4. (2 ſh. 6 d.) überſ. Halle. 1790. 8.

HOLLIS, [Thomas] *F. R. S. F. A. S.* born in London d. 14 Apr. 1720. died d. 1 Jan. 1774.

HOLLOWAY, [John] Letter to Dr. *Price* containing a few ſtrictures upon his ſermon „The love of our country. 1790. 8. (6 d.)

— [Robert] *Gent. of Gray's Inn Attorney at law.* *Letter to the citizens of London on a very interesting

esting subject. 1771. 8. (1 sh.) Letter to *John Wilkes* on the extortion and expression of sheriffs officers —. 1771. 8. (1 Sh.) Letter to Sir *John Fielding*. 1772. 8. (1 Sh. 6 d.) Letter to the jury who convicted Mr. *Shelly* the Silversmith —. 1781. 8. (1 Sh.) The rat-trap —. 1773. 8. (2 Sh. 6 d.)

HOLMANN, [Charles] *Surgeon at Milverton, in Somersetshire.* History of a case in which symptoms of pulmonary consumption were suddenly relieved by the expectoration of a piece of carious bone. (London M. J. Vol. VII. Part 2.)

HOLMES, [Edward] *M. A. Master of Scorton school. Newcastle.* Comment on the Apostle's creed, for the use of unlearned christians. 1788. 12. (6 d.) Attempt to prove the materiality of the soul, by reason and scripture —. 1789. 8. (2 sh.)

—— [Robert] *D. D. Professor of Poetry in the University of Oxford.* Alfred, an ode, with six sonnets. 1778. 4. (1 sh. 6 d.) Eight sermons at *Bampton's* lecture. 1782. 8. (5 sh.) Four tracts. 1) on the principle of religion, 2) on the principle of redemption 3) on the angelical message to the virgin Mary. 4) On the resurrection of the body, with a discourse on humility. 1788. 8. (5 sh.) The *first* annual account of the collation of the MSS. of the LXX version. 1789. 8. The *second* annual account —. 1790. 8.

HOLROYD, [John] see Lord *Sheffield*.

HOLT, [J....] Characters of the kings and Queens of England. Vol. 1-3. 1786-1788. 8. (8 sh. 6 d.)

HOLWELL, [John Zephaniah] *F. R. S.* (Formerly Servant of the East India Company.) Narrative of the deplorable deaths of the english gentlemen and others, who where suffocated in the blackhole, in Fort William at Calcutta in the kingdom of Bengal in the night succeeding the 20 day of June 1756. 8. 1757. (1 sh.) Address to the proprietors of East India stock. 1763. 4. (2 sh.) India tracts containing 1) address to the proprietors of East India stock. 2) Refutation of a letter from certain gentleman of the Council at Bengal. 3) important facts regarding the East India company's affairs in Bengal from the Y. 1752 to 1760. 4) Narrative of the deplorable deaths of the english gentlemen —. 5) defence of Mr. *Vansittart's* conduct. 1763. 4. (6 sh.) Interesting historical events relative to the provinces of Bengal and the empire of Indostan. P. 1-3. 1764-1771. 8. (9 Sh. 6 d.) übers. mit Anmerk. von *J F Kleuker*. Leipz. 1778. 8. Account of the manner of inoculating the smallpox in the East-Indies. 1767. 8. (1 sh.) Account of a new species of oak. (Phil Transact. 1772. p. 128.) New experiment for the prevention of crimes. 1786. 8. (1 sh.) Dissertations on the origin, nature and pursuits of intelligent beings and on divine providence, religion and religious worship —. 1787. 8. (2 sh. 6 d.)

HOLWELL, [William] *B. D: F. A. S: Chaplain in Ordinary to the King.* The beauties of *Homer*, selected from the Iliad. 1775. 8. (4 sh) Extracts from Mr. Pope's translation corresponding with the beauties of *Homer* —. 1776. 8. (4 sh)

HOLYOKE, [Edward Augustus] *M. D: F. A. A: F. M. S.* A Bill of mortality for the town of Salem for the Years 1782 and 1783. (Mem. of B. A. Vol. 1. p. 546.)

HOME, [Everard] *F. R. S: Surgeon.* Description of a new marine animal. (Phil. Transact. 1785. p 333.) Account of Mr. *Hunter's* method of performing the operation for the popliteal anevrism. (London M. J. Vol. 7. P. 4. Vol. 8. P. 2.) Dissertation on the properties of pus. 1788. 4. (übers. Samml. f. A. Th. 12. S. 653.)

— [Francis] *M. D. Professor of Medicine and of Materia medica in the University at Edinburgh.* Diss. De febre remittente. Edinb. 1750 4. On the contents and virtues of Dunse spaw — 1751. 8. (3 sh. 6 d.) Experiments on bleaching. 1756. 8. (4 sh.) übers. Leipz. 1777. 8. Principia medicinae. 1758. 8. (5 sh.) Ed. 2. 1762. übers Frankf. u. Leipz. 1772. übers. von *J. F. Ehrmann* Nürnb. 1778. 8. The principles of agriculture and vegetation. 1758. 8. (3 sh.) Ed. 3. 1776. übers. von *J. Cph. Wöllner.* Berlin. 1779. 8. Medical facts and experiments. 1759. 8. (4 sh.) übers. durch *G. H. Koenigsdörfer.* 1768. 8. Inquiry into the nature cause and cure of the croup. 1765. 8. (1 sh.) Clinical

nical experiments histories and dissections. 1780. 8. (6 sh.) übers. Leipz. 1781. 8.

HOME, [Henry] see Lord *Kaims*.

—— [John] *Clergyman*. (born in *Scotland*.) *Douglas, a Tragedy. 1757. 8. (1 sh. 6 d.) *Agis, a Tragedy. 1758. 8. (1 sh. 6 d.) *The siege of Aquileja; a Tragedy. 1760. 8. (1 sh. 6 d.) *The fatal discovery, a Tragedy, 1769. 8. (1 sh. 6 d.) *Alonzo, a Tragedy. 1773. 8. (1 sh. 6 d.) *Alfred, a Tragedy. 1778. 8.

—— [Robert] *Surgeon to the Savoy*. The efficacy and innocency of solvents —. 1783. 8. (1 sh. 6 d.) übers. Samml. f. W. A. St. 8. S. 61.

HOMER, [Philip Bracebridge] *A. M. Magdalen-College, Oxford*. Anthologia; or, a collection of flowers. In blank verse. 1789. 4. (1 sh.)

HOOD, [Robert] *D. D. Minister of the Chapel in Hanover Square, Newcastle*. Sermon on the nature of Christ's Kingdom. 1780. 8. (6 d.) XIV. sermons on various subjects. 1782. 8. (5 sh.)

HOOK, [James] Hours of love. 17.. The wreath: a collection of Arietts for the voice and Harpsichord. 1788. (5 Sh.)

HOOLE, [....] Critical essays on some of the poems of several english poets by *John Scott*, Esq. with an account of his life and writings. 1785. 8. (5 sh. 3 d.)

—— [Charles] *Clergyman; (Son to John Hoole)* *Modern manners; in a series of familiar epistles. 1781. 8. (2 sh. 6 d.) *Aurelia, or the contest: a poem. 1783. 4. (2 sh. 6 d.)

—— [John] *Auditor to the East-India Company*. Translation of *Tasso's* Jerusalem delivered. Vol. 1. 2. 1762. 8. (12 sh.) Translation of *Metastasio's* works. Vol. 1. 2. 1767. 8. (6 sh.) Translation of *Metastasio's* Artaxerxes, the Olympiad, Hypsipile, Titus, Demetrius, Demophon. Vol. 1. 2. 1767. 8. Cyrus; a Tragedy. 1768. 8. (1 sh. 6 d.) Timanthes; a Tragedy. 1770. 8. (1 sh. 6 d.) Translation of *Ariosto's* Orlando furioso. Vol. 1–5. 1773–1783. 8. (1 L. 11 sh. 6 d.) Cleonice; princess of Bithynia: a Tragedy. 1775. 8. (1 sh. 6 d.)

—— [Samuel] *A. M.* Sermons, 1786. 8. (5 Sh.) Edward:

ward, or the curate; a poem. 1787. 4. (3 ſh.) Poems. Vol. 1. 2. 1790. 8. (6 ſh.)

HOOPER, [John] *Surgeon, Fellow of Medical Society.* Hiſtory of a caſe of cicuta. (Mem. of M. S. of L. Vol. 2.)

—— [Joſeph] *Surgeon. F. M. S.* Caſes of hydrocephalus internus (Mem. of M. S. of L. Vol. 1. p 165.) A caſe of Angina pectoris. (Ibid. p. 238.) The caſe of a retroverted uterus. (Med. Obſ. Vol. 5. p. 104.) A ſecond caſe of a retroverted uterus. (Ibid. p. 378.) Caſe of the uterus lacerated by the force of the labour pains. (Mem. of M. S. of L. Vol. 2.)

HOOPER, [William] *M. D.* Baron *Bielfeld's* letters translated. Vol. 1–4. 1768. 8. (11 ſh.) Baron *Bielfeld's* elements of univerſal erudition translated. Vol. 1–3. 1770. 8. (18 ſh.) Memoirs of the Year 2500 translated. Vol. 1. 2. 1772. 8. (5 ſh.) Rational recreations, in which the principles of members and natural philoſophy are clearly and copiously elucidated —. Vol. 1–4. 1774. 8. (1 L. 1 Sh.) *Geſſner's* new idyls translated. 1775. fol. (16 Sh.) *Helvetius* on man, his intellectual faculties and his education, translated. Vol. 1. 2. 1777. 8. (12 Sh.)

HOPE, [John] *M. D: Profeſſor of Medicine and of Botany at Edinburgh. F. R. S.* born at *Edinburgh* d. 10 May 1725. died d. 10 Nov. 1786.

—— [John] born:... died at *Newcaſtle upon Tyne* d. ... Jun. 1785.

—— [John] *Esq.* Letters on certain proceedings in Parliament, during the ſeſſions of the Years 1769 and 1770. 8. 1772. (1 Sh. 6 d.) Thoughts in proſe and verſe. 1780. 8. (6 Sh.) Letters on credit. 1784. 8. (1 Sh. 6 d.)

HOPKINS, [William] *B. A: Vicar of Bolney and Maſter of the Grammar-ſchool of Cuckſield, Suſſex.* Exodus; a translation with notes. 1784. 4. (7 Sh.)

HOPKINSON, [Francis] *Esq. Judge of the Admiralty in Pennſylvania.* Deſcription of a machine for meaſuring a ſhip's way thro' the ſea. (Tr. of A. S. Vol. 2. p. 159.) Account of a worm in a horſe's eye. (Ibid. p. 183.) An improved method of quilling a harpſichord. (Ibid. p. 185.)

HOPSON, [Charles] *M. D. Phyſician in London.* Diſſ.

De Tribus in uno. Lugd. Bat. 1767. 4. *J. G. Zimmermann* on the dysentery translated. 1771. 8. (4 Sh.) Essay on fire. 1781. 8. (2 Sh. 6 d.) °Translation of *J. G. Zimmermann's* treatise on experience in Physic. Vol. 1. 2. 1782. 8. (12 Sh.) *Wiegleb's* general system of Chemistry, translated from the german. 1789. 4. (1 L. 7 Sh.)

HOPSON, [Edward] *Esq. of Norwich.* °Rational conduct of the human mind, moral and religious —. 1777. 12. (3 Sh.)

HORBERRY, [Matthew] *D. D. Rector of Standlake, Oxfordshire and Canon Residentary of Lichtfield.* born: ... died 17..

HORDE, [Thomas] *Jun. Esq.* °Leander and Hero, a Tragedy, 1769. 8. °Zelida, a Tragedy. 1772. 8. Damon and Phebe, an Opera. 1774. 8. Dramatic love. 17.. Disappointed Villany. 17.. The Empiric. 17.. As the world goes. 17.. Paradise of fools. 17.. Pretended puritain. 17.. It was right at the last. 17.. The whimsical serenade. 17.. The female pedant. 17.. Intrigue in a Cloister; a farce. 1786. 8. (1 sh.)

HORN, [Henry] Essays concerning iron and steel —. 1773. 12. (2 Sh. 6 d.)

—— [John] The description and use of the new invented patent universal sowing machine for broadcasting, or drilling every kind of grain, pulse and seed. 1786. 8. (1 sh. 6 d.)

HORNE, [George] *D. D. Dean of Canterbury and President of Magdalen - College, Oxford.* State of the case between *Js. Newton* and *Hutchinson.* 1752. 8. (1 Sh. 6 d.) View of Mr. *Kennicott's* method of correcting the hebrew text —. 1759. (6 d.) Commentary on the psalms. Vol. 1. 2. 1776. 4. (1 L. 1 Sh.) Discourses on several subjects and occasions. Vol. 1. 2. 1779. 8. (12 Sh.) °Letter to *Adam Smith* — on the life, death and philosophy of *Dav. Hume*, by one of the people called christians. 1777. 8. (1 sh.) °Letters on infidelity by the author of a letter to Dr. *Ad. Smith.* 1784. 8. (3 Sh.) (Several single sermons.)

—— [John] see *Tooke.*

HORNSBY, [Thomas] *M. A: Professor of Astronomy in the University of Oxford. F. R. S. of London and of of Gottingen.* On the parallax of the Sun. (Phil. Transact. 1763. p. 467.) Observations on the solar eclipse April 1, 1764. at Oxford. (Ibid. 1764. p. 145.) Account of the improvements to be made by observations of the transit of Venus in 1769. (Ibid. 1765. p. 326.) Observations on the transit of Venus and eclipse of the Sun, June 3. 1769. (Ibid. 1769. p. 172.) The quantity of the Sun's parallax, as deduced from the observations of the transit of Venus, on June 3. 1769. (Ibid. 1771. p. 574.) Inquiry into the quantity and direction of the proper motion of Arcturus; with some remarks on the diminution of the obliquity of the ecliptic. (Ibid. 1773. p. 93.

HORSLEY, [Samuel] *D. D. F. R. S. Lord Bishop of St. Davids.* Computation of the distance of the sun from the earth. (Phil. Transact. 1767. p. 179.) Attempt to determine the height of the sun's atmosphere from the height of the solar spots above the sun's surface. (Ibid. p. 398.) On the computation of the sun's distance from the earth, by the theory of gravity. (Ibid. 1769. p. 153.) Observations on the transit of Venus and eclipse of the Sun June 3. 1769. (Ibid. 1769. p. 183.) Difficulties in the *Newtonian* theory of light. (Ibid. 1770. p. 417.) Supplement. (Ibid. 1771. p. 547.) *Apollonii Pergaei* Inclinationum libri 2. 1770. (9 sh.) The sieve of *Eratosthenes*, being an account of his method of finding all the prime numbers. (Phil. Transact. 1772. p. 327.) *De Luc's* rules, for the measurement of heights by the barometer, compared with theory reduced to english measures of length and adapted to *Fahrenheit's* scale of the thermometer; with tables and precepts for expediting the practical application of them. (Ibid. 1774. p. 214.) Remarks on the observations of *(Phipp's)* voyage towards the Northpole, for determining the acceleration of the pendulum, in latitude 79° 50'. 1774. 4. (1 sh.) An abridged state of the weather at London in the Year 1774. (Phil. Transact. 1775. p. 167.) De polygonis area vel perimetro maximis et minimis, inscriptis circulo, vel circulum circumscribentibus. (Ibid. p. 301.) An abridged state of the weather at London in the Y.

1775. (Ibid. p. 354.) *Js. Newtoni* Opera, cum commentario. Vol. 1. P. 1. 2. Vol. 2-5. (8 L. 11 ſh.) *Letters from the Archdeacon of St. Alban's, in reply to Dr. *Prieſtley* —. 1784. 8. (3 ſh.)

(Several ſingle ſermons.)

HORSLEY, [William] born 1701. died d. 22 Febr. 1776.

HOSSACK, [Colin] *M. D: Phyſician to his late R. H. Frederik, Prince of Wales.* born 1706. died d. 11 Dec. 1782.

HOTHAM, [Richard] Reflections on Eaſt-India ſhipping. 1773. 8. (1 Sh.) On the Eaſt-India ſhipping for the Year 1773. 1774. 4. (2 Sh.) Appendix 1775. 4. (6 d.)

HOUGH, [John] *of the Inner-Temple.* The paſtor —. 1777. 4. (1 Sh.) Second thought is best, an Opera. 1778. 8. (1 Sh.)

HOULSTON, [Thomas] *M. D: Phyſician to the Liverpool Infirmary* Diſſ. De inflammatione. Lugd. Bat. 1767. 4. A new method of treating the ſmallpox, translated from the latin of *J. F. Cloſſ.* 1767. 8. Il preſente metodo d' innestare il vajuolo del *D. T. Dimsdale.* Napoli. 1768. Lettres ſur les ravages de la petite verole et les inoculations faites a Montpellier. (Journal de Medec. 1771. Fevr et Avril.) Lettre ſur les purgatifs drastiques reſineux. (Journ. de Medec. 1771. Oct. Journal Encyclopedique. 1771. Vol. V.) On the Liverpool Spa-Water. 1773. 8. (1 Sh.) Obſervations on mineral poiſons. (Med. Com. of Ed. Vol. 6. p. 325.) Obſervations on canine madneſſ. (*Duncan's* M. C. Vol. 8. p. 304.) Caſe of a boy poiſoned by the root of hemlock-dropwort. (London M. J. Vol. 2. p. 40.) On poiſons and uſe of mercury in the cure of obſtinate dyſenteries. 1784. 8. (1 Sh.) Ed. 2. 1787. 8. (1 Sh. 6 d.) überſ. Altenb. 1786. 8. überſ. Samml. f. A. Th. 10. S. 373. A remarkable inſtance of a patient's recovery after taking a very large doſe of corroſive ſublimate. (London M. J Vol 6. p. 271.) Experiments on the duration of the infectious power of variolous matter. (Ibid. Vol. VII. P. 1.) Remarks on the hydrophobia and on the efficacy of the Ormskirk medicine for the bite of a mad dog. (*Duncan's* M. C.

C. Dec. 2. Vol. I. p. 330. übers. Samml. f. A. Th. 13. S. 39.)

HOULSTON, [William] *Surgeon.* Case of injury of the brain, occasioned without any blow or external violence upon the head. (London M. J. Vol. 5. p. 292.) *J. O. Justamond's* surgical tracts — with notes. 1790. 4. (1 L. 1 Sh.)

HOUNSFIELD, [George] *Surgeon at Sheffield in Yorkshire.* On the good effects of electricity in four cases of a diseased testicle. (Lond. M. J. Vol. VII. P. 3.)

HOWARD, [Frederic] Earl of *Carlisle.* Poems: 1) Upon the death of Mr. *Gray.* 2) For the monument of a favourite spaniel. 3) Another inscription for the same. 4) Translation from *Dante*, Canto 33. 1773. 4. (1 sh.) The father's revenge; a Tragedy. 1783.

— [George Edmond] *Esq. Attorney in Dublin.* Cases on the laws against the further growth of popery in Ireland. 1775. 8. (6 sh.) Almeyda; or the rival kings: a Tragedy. 1770. 8. (1 sh. 6 d.) The siege of Tamor; a Tragedy. Ed. III. 1773. 8. (1 sh. 6 d.) Miscellaneous works, in verse and prose. Vol. 1. 2. 3. 1782. 8. The female gamaster, a Tragedy. 1778. 12.

— [John] *F. R. S. Sheriff of the county of Bedford.* born at *Lower Clapton.* 1725. died d. 20 Jan. 1790.

— [John] *Surgeon.* On the medical properties of mercury. 1782. 8. (2 sh.) On the method of curing the hydrocele by means of a seton. 1783. 8. (1 sh. 6 d.) On the natural history and cure of the venereal disease. Vol. I. 2. 1787. 8. (10 sh.) übers. von C. F. *Michaelis.* Th. I. 2. 1790. 8.

— [Sarah] Thoughts on female education —. 1783. 12. (1 sh.)

HOWE, [William] *Sir.* Narrative of his conduct during his late command of the King's troops in North-America with some observations on the letters to a nobleman. 1780. 4. (3 sh.)

HOWEL, [James] Description of the people and country of Scotland — a satire. 1788. 12. (6 d.)

— [Thomas] *M. D.* Journal of the passage from India — through Mesopotamia, Armenia and Natolia

tolia or Asia minor —. 1789. 8. (5 sh.) übers. in *Sprengel's* und *Forster's* N. Beitr. zur Völker und Länderk Th. 3. S. 1.

HOWLET, [John] *A. B. Vicar of Great Dunmow, Essex* Examination of Dr. *Price's* essay on the population of England and Wales and the doctrine of an increased population in this kingdom, with remarks on Dr. *Price's* argument of a decreased population — 1781. 8. (2 sh. 6 d.) * Political enquiry into the consequences of inclosing waste lands and the causes of the present high price of butchers meat. 1785. 8. (2 sh. 6 d.) Enquiry into the influence which enclosures have had on the population of this kingdom. 1786. 8. (1 sh.) On the population of Ireland. 1786. 8. (1 sh. Enclosures a cause of improved agriculture, of plenty and cheapness of provisions, of population, and of both private and national wealth, being an examination of two pamphlets — 1787. 8. (2 sh.) The insufficiency of the causes to which the increase of our poor and of the poor's rates have been commonly ascribed with enquiry on the mortality of countryhouses of industry —. 1788. 8. (2 sh. 6 d.) (Several single sermons.)

HOYLAND, [.....] Odes. 1785. 4. (1 sh.)

HUBBARD, [Leverett] *M. D. of Newhaven in Connecticut.* History of a gangrene of the scrotum. (Mem. of M. S. of L. Vol. 1. p. 462.)

HUDDART, [.....] *Captain.* Sketch of the straits of Gaspar, a passage between the islands of Banks and Billiton, with remarks for sailing through the straits. 1788. 8. (5 sh.)

—— [Joseph] Account of persons who could not distinguish colours. (Phil. Transact. 1777. p. 260.)

HUDDESFORD, [William] *B. D. Keeper of the Ashmolean Museum at Oxford.* born: .... died d. 11 Oct. 1772.

HUDSON, [R.....] The Land valuer's assistant. 1781. (3 sh. 6 d.)

—— [Thomas] Miscellaneous poems. 1788. 4. (1 sh.)

—— [William] *F R. S. Horti Chelsean: Praefectus et Praelector botanicus.* Catalogue of the 50 plants from Chelsea garden presented to the royal society by by the — company of Apothecaries for the Year. 1767. (Philos. Transact. 1770. p. 541.) Flora Anglica. 1762. 8. Ed. 2. Vol. 1. 2. 1778. 8. (10 ſh. 6 d.)

HUGHES, [.....] *Mrs.* Poems. 1784. 8. (3 ſh.) Moral dramas intended for private representation. 1790. 8. (3 ſh.)

— [Benjamin] *Curate of Wisbich St. Peter's in the Isle of Ely.* *An Epiſtle to Junius. 1774. 4. (2 ſh. 6 d.) Simon Magus, a poem. 1775. 4. (2 ſh.)

— [Charles] *Profeſſor of Horsemanship.* — The complete Horseman; or, the art of riding made easy. 1772. 8. (1 ſh.)

— [Samuel] *M. A.* Creation, a poem. 1785. 4. (1 ſh.)

— [T....] *Surgeon at Stroud water, in Glouceſtershire.* Case of cancer of the breaſt, with remarks. (London M. J. Vol. X. P. 1.)

— [Thomas] *M. A.* The ascenſion: a poetical eſſay. 1780. 4. (1 ſh.)

— [W......] *M. A.* Sermon on abolition of slavery in the british Weſt Indies. 1788. 4. (1 Sh.) Answer to Mr. *Harris's* ſcriptural researches on the licitneſſ of the slave trade. 1788. 8. (1 Sh.) Ed. 2. 1788. 8. (1 Sh.)

HULKE, [William] *of Deal in Kent.* Account of a remarkable ſpasmodic affection. (London M. J. Vol. 5. p. 389.)

HULL, [Thomas] *Actor at Covent-Garden theatre and Deputy-manager there.* Pharnaces, an Opera. 1765. 8. (1 Sh.) The ſpanish lady, a muſical entertainment. 1765. 8. The perplexities, a Comedy. 1767. 8. The fairy favour. 1767. 8. *The royal merchant; an Opera. 1767. 8. (1 ſh. 6 d.) *Preſton's* genuine lettes from a gentleman to a young lady his pupil — revised and published with notes by *Thom Hull.* Vol. 1. 2. 1772. (6 ſh.) The prodigal ſon, an Oratorio. 1773. 4. (1 ſh.) Henry the ſecond, or, the fall of Rosamond: a Tragedy. 1774. 8. (1 ſh. 6 d.) Richard Plantagenet, a legendary tale. 1774. 4. (2 Sh.) Select letters between late Ducheſſ of Somerset and others on the manners of the republic of Venise and ſome poetical pieces. Vol. 1. 2. 1778. 8. (12 ſh.) Altera-

 tion

tion of *James Thomson's* Edward and Eleonora, a Tragedy. 1775. 8. (1 sh.)

HULME, [Nathan:] *M. D. Physician in Ordinary to the city of London lying in Hospital.* Diss. De scorbuto. Edinb. 1765. 8. De Natura, causa, curationeque scorbuti. 1768. 8. (3 sh.) On the puerperal fever —. 1772. 8. (3 Sh.) übers. Leipzig. 1772. 8. Oratio de re medica cognoscenda et promovenda —. 1777. 4. (1 Sh. 6 d.) A — remedy for the relief of the stone and gravel, the scurvy. — 1778. 4. (2 Sh.) übers. Leipz. 1778. 8. übers. von *J. Lippert.* Wien. 1781. 8.

HUME, [A.....] *M D.* Every woman her own physician —. 1776. 12. (2 Sh.)

—— [David] born at *Edinburgh* d. 26 Apr. 1711. died d. 25. Aug. 1776.

—— [David] *Esq. Advocate, F. R. S. Edin. and Professor of Scots Law in the University of Edinburgh.* Account of Sir *Thom. Miller* of Glenlee, Bart. Lord President of the Court of Session and F. R. S. Edin. (Tr. of E. S. Vol. 2. App. p. 63.)

HUMPAGE, [Benjamin] *Surgeon.* On the rupture called hydrocele: explaining the anatomy of the parts affected; with objections to the incision, seton —. 1788. 8. (1 Sh.)

HUMPHRIES, [David] *Esq. Colonel in the service of the United States.* Poem to the united states of America. 1785. 4. (2 Sh.) Poem on the happiness of America. 1786. 4. (2 Sh.)

HUNT, [John] *Surgeon.* On the circulation of the blood and the effects of bleeding 1787. 8. (2 Sh.)

HUNTER, [Alexander] *M D. F R. S. Physician at York.* Diss. De Cantharidibus. Edinb. 1751. 4. *Georgical essays. Vol. 1-5. 1770-1777. (11 Sh.) On drill-sowing (G. E. Vol. 3. p. 109.) On Top-Dressings. (Ibid. p. 167.) On the preparation of carrots for the use of seamen on long voyages. (Ibid. Vol. 5. p. 1.) On nutritive lime. (Ibid. p. 182.) On carrots for the use of the distiller. (Ibid. p. 263.) *John Evelyn* silva: or discourse of forest trees and the propagation of timber, with notes. 1776. 4. (2 L. 12 Sh. 6 d.) Ed. 2. Vol. 1. 2. 1786. 4. (2 L. 15 Sh.) *J. Evelyn* terra, a philosophical discourse of earth — with notes — 1778. 8.

8. (3 Sh.) Ed. 2. 1787. 4. (5 Sh.) On the Buxton waters. 1776. 8.

HUNTER, [David] D. D. *Minister at St. Andrew's in Scotland.* Observations on the history of Jesus Christ —. Vol. 1. 2. 1770. 8. (7 Sh.)

— [Henry] *D. D.* Sacred Biography or the history of the Patriarchs from Abraham to Isaac. Vol. 1–4. 1784–1788. (1 L. 4 Sh.)

(Several single sermons.)

— [John] *M. D: F. R. S: and Physician to the Army.* (Brother of *Will. Hunter.*) Natural history of the human teeth, explaining their structure, use, formation, growth and diseases. 1771. 4. Supplement. 1778. 4. (1 L. 1 Sh.) übers. Th. 1. 2. Leipz. 1780. Diss. De Hominum varietatibus et harum caussis. Edinb. 1775. 8. On the digestion of the stomach after death. (Phil. Transact. 1772. p 447.) Anatomical observations on the torpedo. (Ibid. 1773. p. 481.) Account of certain receptacles of air in birds, which communicate with the lungs, and are lodged both among the fleshy parts and in the hollow bones of those animals. (Ibid. 1774. p. 205.) Observations on the Gillaroo trout, called in Ireland the Gizzard trout. (Ibid. p. 310.) Account of the Gymnotus electricus. (Ibid. 1775. p. 395.) Experiments on animals and vegetables, with respect to the power of producing heat. (Ibid. p. 446. übers. Samml. z. P. und Ng. Th. 1. S. 420.) Proposals for the recovery of people apparently drowned. (Ibid. 1776. p. 412. übers. Samml. f. A. Th. 4. S. 144.) Of the heat — of animals and vegetables. (Ibid. 1778. p. 7.) Account of the free martin. (Ibid. 1779. p. 279.) Account of a woman who had the smallpox during pregnancy and who seemed to have communicated the same disease to the foetus. (Ibid. 1780. p. 128.) Account of an extraordinary pheasant. (Ibid. p. 527.) Account of the organ of hearing in fish. (Ibid. 1782. p. 379.) Account of the successfull treatment of a supposed hydrocephalus internus. (Med. Obs. Vol. 6. p. 52.) Some experiments made upon rum, in order to ascertain the cause of the colic, frequent among the soldiers in the Island of Jamaica in the Years. 1781. and 1782. (Med. Transact.

Transact. Vol. 3. p 227.) Account of a case of an uncommon disease in the omentum; and of a double kidney on one side of the body with none on the other. (Ibid. p. 250.) Observations on the disease commonly called the jail or hospital fever. (Ibid. p. 345.) Experiment to determine the effect of extirpating one ovarium upon the member of young produced. (Phil. Transact. 1787. p. 233. London M. J. Vol. IX. P. 1.) Observations tending to shew that the wolf, jackal and dog are all of the same species. (Phil. Transact. 1787. p. 253. 1789. p. 160.) Observations on the structure and oeconomy of Whales. (Ibid. p. 371.) On the venereal disease. 1786. 4. (1 L, 1 Sh) übers. Leipzig. 1787. 8. Observations on certain parts of the animal oeconomy. 1787. 4. (16 Sh.) Observations on the case of mollities ossium with remarks on that disease. (London M. J. Vol. VIII. P. 1.) Some observations on the heat of wells and springs in the Island of Jamaica and on the temperature of the earth below the surface in different climates. (Phil. Transact. 1788. p. 53. übers. *Gren* J. d. P. Th. 1. S. 411.) Observations on the diseases of the army in Jamaica and on the best means of preserving the health of Europeans, in that climate. 1788. 8. (5 Sh.)

HUNTER, [John] *M. A: F. R S. Edin. and Professor of Humanity in the University of St. Andrews.* Grammatical essay on the nature, import, and effect of certain conjunctions; particularly the greek Δε. (Transact. of E. S. Vol. 1. p. 113.)

— [Thomas] *M. A. Vicar of Weaverham, Cheshire.* born: .... died d. .. Jul. 1777.

— [William] *Physician extraordinary to the Queen and Professor of Anatomy in the Royal Academy.* born at *Kilbridge* in the county of *Lanerk* d. 23 May 1718. died d 15 March. 1783.

— [William] *M A. Rector of St. Anne, Lincoln.* Letter to Dr. *Priestley* in answer to his letter — on the subject of the repeal of the test act. 1787. 8. (1 Sh.) (Several single sermons.)

— [W......] *A. M. Surgeon.* Concise account of the kingdom of Pegu; its climate, produce, trade-

go,

government and inhabitans —. 1785. 8. (5 Sh.) übers. *Ebelin'gs* Neue Samml. von Reisebeschreib. Th. 9. S. 397 —. Account of some artificial caverns near Bombay, (Arch. Vol. 7. p. 286.)

HUNTINGDON, [William] Letter to Mr. *Caleb Evans* — containing a few remarks on a circular letter drawn up by him —. 1790. 8. (1 Sh. 6 d.)

HUNTINGFORD, [George James] *A. M. Fellow of new College, Oxford.* Introduction to the writing of greek —. Ed. III. P. 1. 2. 1782. (4 sh. 6 d.) Metrica quaedam monostrophica. 1783. 8. (3 sh.) Apology for the monostrophics with a second collection of monostrophics. 1784. 8. (4 sh. 6 d.)

— [J. . . . .] *Secretary to the society for the Increase and Encouragement of good servants.* The laws of masters and servants considered — with an account of a society, formed for the encrease and encouragement of good servants. 1790. 8. (2 sh. 6 d.)

HURD, [Richard] *D. D. Lord Bishop of Worcester F. R. S. of Gottingen.* **Horatii* Ars poetica, Epistola ad Pisones: with an english commentary and notes. 1749. 8. (3 Sh.) The opinion of an eminent lawyer concerning the right of appeal from the Vice-Chancellor of Cambridge to the senate, supposed by a short, historical account of the jurisdiction of the University: by a fellow of a College. 1751. 8. Ed. 3. 17.. Letter tho the author of a further inquiry. 1752. 8. The delicacy of friendship. 1755. 8. Remarks on *Dav. Hume's* essay on the natural history of religion. 1757. 8. Letter to Mr. *Mason* on the marks of imitation. 1757. 8. Dialogues moral and political with letters on Chivalry and romances. 1758. 8. (5 Sh.) Ed. 2. 1762. Ed. 3. Vol. 1-3. with two dialogues on the use and abuse of foreign travel. 1764. (9 Sh.) übers. von *L. H. Hölty.* Th. 1. 2. Leipz. 1775. 8. *Letters on chivalry and romance. 1761. 8. (2 Sh.) Introduction to the study of the prophecies concerning the christian church — in XII sermons. 1772. 8. (5 Sh.) übers Leipzig. 1778. 8. Edition of the select works of *Abrah. Cowley*, with notes. Vol. 1. 2. 1772. (6 Sh.) Sermons. Vol. 1-3. 1781. 8. (15 Sh.) *Discord a satire 4. 17..

**Jerem.*

* *Jerem. Taylor's* moral demonſtration of the truth of the chriſtian religion. 1776. 8.

(Several ſingle ſermons.)

HURDIS, [James] *M. A.* Critical Diſſertation upon the true meaning of the word תנינים, Genes. 1. 21. 1790. 8. (1 Sh.)

HURLY, [James] *B. A. Maſter of the grammar — ſchool and curate of St. James's in Taunton.* Ecliptical aſtronomy reſtored to its natural ſimplicity —. 1771. 8. (3 Sh.)

HURN, [William] Heath hill, a poem. 1777. 4. (2 Sh. 6 d.) The bleſſings of peace and guilt of war, a lyric poem. 1784. 4. (2 Sh.)

HURRY, [Thomas] Tables of intereſt, from one pound to five hundred millions for one day —. 1786. 12. (3 Sh.)

HURTLEY, [Thomas] *of Malham.* Account of ſome natural curioſities in the environs of Malham in Craven, Yorkshire. 1786. 8. (5 Sh.)

HUSSEY, [Garret] *M. D: Phyſician to the Merchants-Quay Hospital, Dublin.* Inquiry into the cauſe and cure of fevers. 1784. 8. (6 Sh.) überſ. Maynz. 1789. 8.

HUSTLER, [....] *Manufacturer.* *Obſervations on the bill - for preventing the exportation of Wool—. 1788. 8. (6 d.)

HUTCHINS, [John] *M. A: Rector of the holy Trinity in Warsham and of Swyre, Dorſetshire.* born 1698. died 1773.

—— [Richard] *Rector of Lincoln College, Oxford.* born at *Eyden, Northamptonshire* 1698. died 1781.

—— [Thomas] *Governor of Albany Fort, in Hudſons-Bay.* Experiments on the dipping needle, made by deſire of the royal ſociety. (Phil. Transact. 1775. p. 127.) Account of the ſucceſſ of ſome attempts to freeze quickſilver, at Albany-Fort, in Hudſon's-Bay in the Y. 1775. with obſervations on the dipping needle. (Ibid. 1776. p. 174.) Topographical deſcription of the river Ohio, Kenhawa, Sioto, Cherokee, Wabash, Illinois, Miſſiſippi. 1778. 8. Experiments for aſcertaining the point of mercurial congelation. (Phil. Transact. 1783. P. 2.) Deſcription of a remarkable rock and

and cascade, near the weftern fide of the Youghiogeny river. (Tr. of A. S. Vol 2. p. 50.)

HUTCHINSON, [....] *Lieut. Governor.* Hiftory of the colony of Maffachufetts-Bay, from the firft fettlement thereof in 1628. Vol. 1. 2. 1775. 8. (12 Sh.)

— [B....] *Vicar at Kimbolton in the county of Huntingdon.* Calendar of the weather for the Year 1781 —. 1782. 8. (1 Sh.) Obfervations on the dryneff of the Year 1788. (Phil. Tr. 1789. p. 37.) überf. *Gren* J. d. P. Th. 2. S. 79.) Account of a luminous arch. (Phil. Transact. 1790. p. 45.)

— [John Hely] *His Majefty's Principal Secretary of ftate for the Kingdom of Ireland, Provoft of Trinity-College, Dublin and Privy Counfellor.* Commercial restraints of Ireland. 1779. Letter to conftituents of the city of Cork in defence of Mr. *Pitt's* Irish propofitions. 1785.

— [William] *F. A. S.* The fpirit of mafonry —. 1776. 8. (3 Sh. 6 d.) Oration at the dedication of free mafon's Hall in Sunderland in the county of Durham. 1778. 4. (1 Sh.) View of Northumberland. Vol. 1. 2. 1778. 4. (1 L. 10 Sh.) Hiftory and antiquities of the county palatine of Durham. Vol. 1. 2. 1787. 4. (1 L. 1 Sh.) Account of antiquities in Lancashire. (Arch. Vol. 9. p. 211.)

— [William] *Mariner and Dockmafter of Liverpool.* On practical feamanship —. 1777. 4. (12 Sh. 6 d.)

HUTCHISSON, [John] *M. D: of Dublin.* Cafe of chronic tetanus, cured — by the ufe of electricity. (Mem. of M. S. of L. Vol. 2. p. 138.)

HUTTON, [Charles] *LL. D. F. R. S. Lond. and Edin. Profeffor of Mathematiks in the Royal Military Academy at Woolwich.* On menfuration both in theory and practice. 1771. 4. (15 Sh.) Ed. 2. 1788. 8. (15 Sh.) The principles of bridges. 1772. 8. (2 Sh. 6 d.) The diarian miscellany, confifting of all the ufeful and entertaining parts, both mathematical and poetical, extracted from the Ladies diary — with many additional folutions and improvements. Vol. 1-5. 1775. 8. (1 L. 9 Sh.) A new and general method of finding fimple and quickly-converging feries; by which the proportion of the

the diameter of a circle to its circumference may easily be computed to a great number of places of figures. (Philoſ. Transact. 1776. p 476.) Demonſtration of two theorems mentioned in article XXV of the Philoſ. Transact. for the Year 1775. (Ibid. p. 600.) The force of fired gun-powder and the initial velocities of cannon balls, determined by experiments. (Ibid. 1778 p. 50.) Account of the calculations made from the ſurvey and meaſures taken at Schehallien, in order, to aſcertain the mean denſity of the earth. (Ibid 1778. p. 689.) Of cubic equations and infinite ſeries. (Ibid. 1780. p. 387.) Calculations to determine at what point in the ſide of a hill its attraction will be the greateſt. (Ibid. 1780. P. 1,) Project of a new diviſion of the Quadrant. (Ibid. 1784. p 21.) Tables of the products and powers of numbers. 1784. fol. (7 Sh. 6 d.) Mathematical tables: containing common, hyperbolic and logiſtic logarithms. 1785. 8. (14 Sh.) Tables of intereſt from one pound to 500 millions for one day —. 1786. 8. (3 Sh.) Key to *Hutton's* Arithmetic —. 1786. 8. (3 Sh.) Tracts mathematical and philoſophical. 1786. 4. (14 Sh.) The compendious meaſurer. 1786. 8. (3 Sh.) Abſtract of experiments made to determine the true reſiſtance of the air to the ſurfaces of bodies, of various figures, and moved through it with different degrees of velocity. (Tr. of I. A. Vol. 2. p. 29.)

—— [James] *M. D: at Edinburgh. F. R. S. Edin.* Conſiderations on the nature, quality and diſtinctions of coal and culm —. 1777. 8. (1 Sh.) The theory of rain. (Tr. of E. S. Vol. 1. p 41) Theory of the earth; or an inveſtigation of the laws obſervable in the compoſition, diſſolution and reſtoration of land upon the globe. (Ibid. p. 209.) Of certain natural appearances of the ground on the Hill of Arthur's ſeat. (Ibid. Vol. 2. p. 3.) Anſwer to the objections of M. *De Luc*, with regard to the Theory of rain. (Ibid. Vol. 2. p. 39.) On written language as a ſign of ſpeech. (Ibid. Vol. 2. p. 5.)

HUTTON, [W.....] *F. A. S. Edin.* Hiſtory of Birmingham. 1782. 8. (7 Sh. 6 d.) Journey from Birming-

Birmingham to London. 1785. 12. (2 ſh. 6 d.) The court of requeſts —. 1787. 8. (6 Sh.) The battle of Bosworth-field between Richard III. and Henry Earl of Richmond 1485 —. 1788. 8. (5 ſh.) Diſſertation on juries: with a deſcription of the hundred court as an appendix to the court of requeſts. 1789. 8. (1 ſh.)

JABET, [William] *B. A. Lecturer of St. Bartholomew's Chapel in Birmingham.* born: .... died 17..

JACKMAN, [Isaac] *a Gentleman of Ireland.* The Mileſian, a Ballad Opera. 1776. 8. All the world's a ſtage, a farce. 1777. 8. The divorce, a farce. 1782. 8. Hero and Leander. 1787. 8. Almirina. 1787.

JACKSON, [Andrew] born 1695. died d. 25 July 1778.

— [.....] Thoughts on the causes of the delay of the Weſtminſter ſcrutiny. 1784. 8. (1 ſh.)

— [Humphrey] *Esq. F. R. S:* of *Pattersea* in *Surrey.* On the invention of engraving and printing in chiaro oscuro — and the application of the making paper-hangings of taſte, duration and elegance. 1754. 4. Account of the discovery of the manner of making iſinglaſſ in Ruſſia; with a particular deſcription of its manufacture in England from the produce of Britiſh fiſheries. (Phil. Transact. 1773. p. 1.)

— [John] of *Clement's — Lane.* Account of the diſcoveries in digging a ſewer in Lombard-ſtreet and Birchinlane. 1786. (Arch. Vol. 8. p. 116. et p. 127.)

— [Lawrence] *B. D: Prebendary of Lincoln.* born: ... died d. 26 Febr. 1772.

— [Robert] *M. D. Phyſician at Stockton in the county of Durham.* Observations on the connexion of the new and full moon with the invaſion and relapse of fevers. (Lond. M. J. Vol. VIII. P. 1. überſ. Samml. f. A. Th. 12. S. 83.) On the ſupposed influence of the moon in fevers. (Lond. M. J. Vol. VIII. P. 3. überſ. Samml. f. A. Th. 12. S. 548.)

— [Seguin Henry] *M. D. Phyſician to the Weſtminſter general dispensary in London.* Diſſ. De phyſiol:

et patholog: dentium eruptione. Edinb. 1778. 8. On ſympathy. P. 1. 2. —. 1781. 8. (4 ſh.) Hiſtory of a ſingular affection of respiration with an account of the appearances on diſſection. (Med. Com. of Ed. Vol. 6. p. 208.) The caſe of a patient whose ſtomach, on diſſection, was found to contain two piſtol bullets. (Ibid Vol. 4. p. . . . .)

JACKSON, [Theodore] *A M.* Addreſſ to the Queen, Prince of Wales and the public relative to his Majeſty's unhappy ſituation. 1788. 4. (1 ſh.)

—— [William] *of Lichtfield Cloſe.* The beauties of nature displayed —. 1769. 8. (5 ſh.) Letter to the monthly reviewers in reply to their critique on his beauties of nature displayed. 1770. 8. (1 ſh.)

—— [William] *B. D. Student of Chriſtchurch and Preacher to the ſociety of Lincoln's Jnn.* The Conſtitution of the ſeveral independent ſtates of America. 1783. 8. (6 ſh.) (Several ſingle ſermons.)

—— [William] *Organiſt and Composer of Exeter.* Lycidas. 1767. 8. The Metamorphoſis, a comie Opera. 1783. * Thirty letters on various ſubjects. Vol. 1. 2. 1783. 8. (4 ſh.) Ed. II. (with the Author's name.) Vol. 1. 2. 1784. (4 ſh.)

—— [William] *Member of the corporation of Surgeons.* Observations on the inefficacious use of irons in caſes of luxations and diſtortion of the ancle joint and children born with deformed and crooked feet. 1787. 8. (1 ſh.)

JACOB, [Edward] *F. A. S.* born 1710. died d. 26 Oct. 1788.

—— [Edward] *Jun. Surgeon at Faversham, in Kent.* Case of an extra - uterine foetus. (London M. J. Vol. VIII. P. 2.)

—— [J. . . . .] Observations on the ſtructure and draught of wheel carriages. 1773. 4. (6 ſh.) Animadverſions on the use of broad wheels and the preservation of the public roads. 1773. 4. (1 ſh. d d.)

JAGO, [Richard] *M. A: Vicar of Sniterfield, Warwickſhire: Rector of Kimcote, Leiceſterſhire.* born: . . . . died d. 8 Apr. 1781.

JAIR, [James] The life of *Servetus*, the Antitrinitarian. 1771. (4 ſh.)

JAMES, [Charles] *Esq. Petrarch to Laura*, a poetical epistle. 1787. 4. Poems. Vol. 1. 2. 1789. 8. (6 Sh.)

—— [Robert] *M. D.* born: .... died d. 23 March. 1776.

—— [Thomas] *Lieutenant-Colonel.* The history of the Herculean straits, now called the straits of Gibraltar —. Vol. 1. 2. 1771. 4. (2 L. 2 sh.)

JAMESON, [Thomas] *Surgeon of his Majesty's Navy.* On diluents and enquiry of the human body —. 1789. 8. (2 sh. 6 d.) übers. Leipz. 1790. 8.

JAMIESON, [J.....] *A. M: F. A. S. Scot.* The sorrows of slavery, a poem. 1789. (2 Sh.)

JANES, [Thomas] *of Bristol.* The beauties of the poets, or, a collection of moral and sacred poetry, from the most eminent authors. 1778. 8. (3 sh.)

JARDINE [......] *Artillerie-Major.* Observations on the transit of Venus June 3. 1769. at Gibraltar. (Phil. Transact. 1769. p. 347.) Observations on the eclipse of the sun June 4. 1769. at Gibraltar. (Ibid.) *Letters from Barbary, France, Spain, Portugal — by an Officer. Vol. 1. 2. 1788. 8. (12 sh.) übers. im Auszug. Leipz. 1790. 8.

JAY, [James] *M. D.* Letter to the governors of the college of New York respecting the collection that was made in 1762 and 1763. for the colleges of Philadelphia and New York. 1771. 8. (1 sh.) Reflections and observations on the gout. 1772. 8. (2 sh.) Letter to the Universities of Oxford and Cambridge — in respect to the collection that was made for the colleges of New York and Philadelphia. 1773. 8. (6 d.)

IBBETSON, [.....] Thoughts on bonds of resignation. 1783. 8. (1 sh.)

—— [James] *D. D. Archdeacon of St. Alban's, Rector of Bushy.* born: .... died d. 9 Aug. 1781.

—— [James] *Esq. Barrister at Law.* On the judicial customs of the Saxon and Norman age. 1780. 4. (1 sh. 6 d.) Dissertation on the national assemblies under the Saxon and Norman governments. 1781. 4. (2 sh.)

JEBB, [John] *M. D: F. R. S.* (formerly *Minister at Homersfield, Suffolk.* born in London d. 16 Febr. 1736. died d. 2 March. 1786.

JEBB, [Samuel] *M. D. Physician at Stratford.* born: ... died at Derby. 1772.

JEFFERSON, [......] Poems. Ed. 2. 1773. 8. (2 ſh. 6 d.)

—— [Thomas] *Summary view of the rights of British America. 1774. 8. (1 ſh. 6 d.) Notes on the ſtate of Virginia; — with a map. 1788. 8. (7 ſh.)

JEFFRIES, [......] Narrative of the two aerial voyages of Dr. *Jeffries* with Monſ. *Blanchard:* with meteorological observations and remarks —. 1785. 4. (7 ſh. 6 d.)

JENKINS, [Joseph] *A. M.* Calm reply to the firſt part of de *Courcy's* rejoinder —. 1778. 8. (1 Sh.) Discourses on ſelect paſſages of the ſcripture hiſtory. Vol. 1. 2. 1779. 8. (6 Sh.) The inconſiſtency of infant ſprinckling with chriſtian baptism — a reply to *Matth. Henry's* treatise on baptism. 1784. 8. (1 Sh.) The beauty of a believer's baptism. — 1778. 12. (2 d.)

JENKINSON, [Charles] Lord *Hawkesbury.* (Son of a Clergyman in Oxfordshire.) *Discourse on the eſtabliſhment of a national and conſtitutional force in England. 1756. 8. (1 Sh.) *Discourse on the conduct of the government of Great Britain in reſpect to neutral nations, during the present war. 1757. 4. (2 ſh. 6 d.) Collection of treaties of peace, commerce and alliance between Great-Britain and other powers from the Y. 1619 to 1734. 1781. (2 ſh. 6 d.) Collection of all the treaties of peace, alliance and commerce, between Great Britain and other powers from the Y. 1648 to 1783. Vol. 1-3. 1785. 8. (18 Sh.)

—— [James] Generic and ſpecific description of British plants translated from the genera et ſpecies plantarum of *Linnaeus.* 1775. 8. (5 ſh. 3 d.)

JENNENS, [Charles] born: .... died 1773.

JENNER, [Charles] *M. A. Rector of Claybrooke in the County of Leiceſter.* born: .... died d. 11 May. 1774.

—— [Edward] Observations on the natural hiſtory of the Cuckoo. (Phil. Transact. 1788. p. 219.)

JENNER, [J..... C.....] *Surgeon at Painswick in Glouceſtershire.* Cases of an excrescence in the ure-

urethra of a female patient successfully treated. (Lond. M. J. Vol. VII. P. 2.) Account of a general inoculation at Painswick. (Ibid. p. 109. übers. Samml. f. A. Th. 12. S. 52.) On the efficacy of arsenic in intermittents. (Ibid. Vol. IX. P. 1.)

JENNINGS, [Jos.] *of Fenchurchstreet.* born: .... died d. 2 Jan. 1782.

JENYNS, [Soame] born in London 1705. died d. 18 Dec. 1787.

JEPHSON, [Robert] *Esq. Officer in the Irish Army. Member of Parliament in Ireland.* * Braganza; a Tragedy. 1775. 8. (1 sh. 6 d.) The law of Lombardy; a Tragedy. 1779. 8. (1 sh. 6 d.) The count of Narbonne; a Tragedy. 1781 8. (1 sh. 6 d.) The hotel, or servant with two masters, a farce. 1784. 12. The campaign or love and war; an Opera. 1785. Julia or the italian lover, a Tragedy. 1787. 8. (1 sh. 6 d.)

JERNINGHAM, [John] *A Roman Catholic and brother to Sir William Jerningham.* Poems on various subjects —. 1766. 8. (2 sh.) Amabella: a poem. 1767. 4. (1 sh.) The Deserter; a poem. 1769. 4. (1 sh.) The funeral of Arabert, Monk of la Trappe: a poem. 1771. 4. (1 sh.) Faldoni and Teresa. 1773. 4. (1 sh.) The swedish curate, a poem. 1773. 4. (1 sh.) Poems. 1774. 8. (2 sh. 6 d.) The fall of Mexico, a poem. 1775. 4. (2 sh. 6 d.) Fugitive poetical pieces. 1778. 8. (1 Sh. 6 d.) The ancient english wake; a poem. 1779. 4. (1 Sh. 6 d.) Honoria or the day of all souls, a poem, with other poetical pieces. 1782. 4. (1 sh. 6 d.) The rise and progress of scandinavian poetry; a poem in two parts. 1784. 4. (2 sh.) Poems. Vol. 1. 2. 1786. 8. (5 sh.) Enthusiasm; a poem. 1789. 4. (2 sh.)

JESSE, [William] *Rector of Dowles and Chaplain to the Earl of Glasgow.* Parochialia; or observations on the discharge of parochial duties —. 1787. 8. (2 Sh. 6 d.) Defence of the established church: or, letters — in which Dr. *Priestley's* arguments against subscription and the peculiar doctrines of christianity, are examined. 1788. 12. (2 sh. 6 d.)

JESSE, [William] *Vicar of Hutton-Cranswick, Yorkshire.* Remonftrance to the proteftant affociation containing obfervations on their conduct —. 1780. 8. (1 Sh.)

JESTON, [H. ....] *M. A. Mafter of the Royal Grammar School at Henley-upon-Thames.* The facred drama of Jofeph fold by his Brethren; and other poems. 1790. 8. (1 fh. 6 d.)

ILLINGWORTH, [James] *D. D.* The figns of the times: or a fyftem of true politics —. 1781. 8. (1 Sh. 6d.) Sermon on the duty to God and the king. 8. (6 d.)

IMISON, [John] *Mechanician at London.* born: .... died d. 16 Aug. 1788.

IMPEY, [John] The new inftructor clericalis —. 1782. 8. (8 Sh.) Office of Sheriff, fhewing its hiftory and antiquity —. 1786. 8. (9 Sh.)

INCHBALD, [Elizabeth] *Mrs. Actrefs at Covent-Garden Theatre.* (Her maiden name *Simpson.* born. 1756.) The mogul tale; a farce. 1784. I'll tell you what, a comedy. 1786. 8. (1 Sh. 6 d.) *Appearance is againft him, a farce. 1786. (1 Sh.) *The widows vow, a farce. 1786. 8. (1 Sh.) Such things are, a play. 1787. 8. (1 Sh. 6 d.) Ed. 2. 1788. 8. (1 Sh. 6 d.) All on a fummers day. 1788. Midnight hour, translated from the French of *Dumaniant.* 1787. The child of nature; a dramatic piece. 1788. 8. (1 Sh. 6 d.) The married man, a comedy. 1789. 8. (1 Sh. 6 d.)

INGLEFIELD, [Ann] *Mrs.* Iuftification, containing the proceedings in the ecclefiaftical court, before the right worfhipful *Peter Calvert.* LL. D. 1788. 8. (2 Sh.)

—— [John] *Captain in the Navy.* Narrative, concerning the loff of his majefty's fhip the Centaur —. 1783. 8. (1 Sh.)

INGRAM, [Dale] *Surgeon to the Chrift's Hospital.* Effay on the gout. 1743. 8. Practical cases and obfervations in furgery, with remarks —. 1751. 8. (4 Sh.) Translation of *Verdier's* Anatomy of the human body —. 1753. 8 (6 Sh.) Account of the feveral plagues in the world fince. 1346 —. 1755. 8. (2 Sh. 6 d.) *Verdier's* Anatomy of the human body, translated. 1756. 8. Origin and

nature

nature of magnesia alba and the properties of Epsom waters —. 1768. 8. (1 Sh.) The blow or inquiry into the causes of the late *Mr. Clarke's* death —. 1769. 8. (1 Sh.) Impartial enquiry into the cause and death of the late *Will. Scawen.* 1777. 8. (3 Sh.)

INGRAM, [Robert] *Vicar of Wormingford and Boxted in Essex.* Explanation of the prophecy of the seven vials or the seven last plagues contained in the revelation of St. John. Chap. 6. 7. 1780. 8. (1 Sh.) Further observations — on the prophecy of the 7 vials —. 1783. 8. (1 Sh.) Exposition of Isaiah's vision Chap. VI. 1784. 8. (6 d.) View of the great events of the 7 plague, or period, when the mystery of God shall be finished. Apoc. X. 7. 1786. 8. (3 d.)

INNES, [George] *of Aberdeen.* Fourteen discourses on practical subjects. 1783. 12. (3 Sh.)

—— [James Dunbar] *A. M. Surgeon at London.* On the venereal disease —. 1783. 8 (2 Sh.)

—— [John] *Prosector at Edinburgh.* Description of the human muscles —. 1776. 8. (3 Sh.) Eight anatomical tables of the human body —. 1776. 4. (6 Sh. 6 d.)

JODREL, [Richard Paul] *Sir, Knight. F. R. S: F. A. S: M. D: Physician to the Nabob of Arcot.* A widow and no widow, a Comedy. 1780. 8. (1 Sh. 6 d.) Illustrations of Euripides, on the Jon and the Bacchae. 1781. 8. (10 Sh.) The Knight and friars; an historic tale. 1785. 4. (2 Sh.) The persian Heroine; a Tragedy. 1786. 4. (6 Sh.) 8. (3 Sh.) *Seeing is believing, a Comedy. 1786. 8. (1 Sh.) Select dramatic pieces —. 1787. 8. (6 Sh.) Illustrations of Euripides, on the Alcestis. 1790. 8.

JOEL, [Thomas] Introduction to English grammar. 1775. 12. (1 Sh.)

JOHNSON, [.....] *Mrs.* Retribution. 17.. The gamesters. 17.. Calista a novel. Vol. 1. 2. 1789. 8. (5 Sh.)

—— [Alexander] *M. D.* Account of a Society at Amsterdam, instituted in the Y. 1767. for the recovery of drowned persons. 1773. 8. (2 Sh.) übers. nach der 12. Ausg. Hamburg. 1788. 8. Collection of authentic cases, proving the practicability of recovering persons visibly dead by drowning, suffocations, stifling, swooning, convulsions and other accidents. 1773. 8. (2 Sh.)

JOHNSON, [Cuthbert] *M. D: of Sherborne, Dorset.* The history of a dropsy of the ovarium, terminating fatally, with an account of the appearances on dissection. *(Duncan's* M. C. 1780. p. 91.)

—— [Henry] Introduction to logography —. 1783. 8. (2 Sh.) (Das Buch selbst ist auf diese Art gedruckt.)

—— [J.....] A complete abridgment of the law respecting gaming and usury —. 1787. 8. (1 Sh. 6 d.)

—— [James] *Surgeon at Lancaster.* Observations on the internal use of the vitriolum album in a case of epilepsy and in diarrhoea. (Med. Com. of Ed. Vol. 5. p. 311.) Case of hydatids discharged by coughing. (London M. J. Vol. VI. p. 293.) Case of pyuria successfully treated. (Ibid. p. 295. übers. Samml. f. A. Th. XI. S. 213.) Case of a fractured scull successfully treated. (Ibid. p. 354.) A Case of plumbstones retained in the intestines. (Ibid. p. 355.)

—— [John] *M. A. Chaplain in Ordinary to his Majesty.* An enigmatical question, relating to things sacred and divine. 1755. 8. (1 Sh.) Evangelical truths vindicated —. 1758. 8. (1 Sh.) Review of the Prebendary of *Litchfield's* sermon and address to Quakers. 1762. 8. (9 d.) Divine truth, being a vindication of the three immutable attributes — of God — 1769. 8. (3 sh) Address to *Sam. Fisher* of Norwich, concerning the errors charged upon him by the fictitious Quaker —. 1773. 8. (6 d.) The riches of gospel grace opened in XII Discourses — Vol. 1. 2. 1776. 8. (8 sh.) A scriptural illustration of the book of the revelation. 1779. 8. (5 sh.) Observations on the military establishment and discipline of his majesty the King of Prussia — translated from the French. 1780. 8. (2 Sh.)

(Several single sermons.)

—— [Robert Wallace] *M. D: Physician at Brentford.* Friendly cautions to the heads of families. 8. 17.. New system of midwifery, in 4 parts founded on practi-

practical observations, the whole illustrated with copper plates. 1769. 4. (1 L. 1 sh.) Ed. 2. 1777. 4. (1 L. 1 sh.) übers. von *J. C. Loder.* Th. 1. 2. Leipz. 1782. (übers. Samml. f. WA. St. 2. S. 92. u. S. 95.)

JOHNSON, [Samuel] *LL. D.* (Son of a Bookseller at *Litchfield*, *Warwickshire.*) born at *Litchfield.* 1709. died d. 14 Dec. 1784.

— [William] *Sir: Baronet.* born: .... died at *Johnson-hall* in the province of *New-York in America.* d. 11 July. 1774.

JOHNSTON, [Alexander] *Surgeon in the Royal Navy.* History of two cases of amputation, in which compression of the artery was successfully made by the finger of an assistant, as there was no room for applying the Tourniquet. *(Duncan's* M. C. Dec. 2. Vol. 3. p. 366.)

JOHNSTONE, [.....] *(*Lessing's)* Disbanded officer: or the baronesss of Bruchsal; (translated.) 1786. 8. (1 sh. 6 d.)

— [Edward] *M. D: F. R. S. of Edinb: Physician to the general hospital at Birmingham.* Diss. De febre puerperali. Edinb. 1779. 8. Case of angina pectoris. (Mem: of M. S. of L. Vol. 1. p. 306.) History of a case of obstinate obstipatio, depending on a stricture of the rectum. (Med. Com. of Ed. Vol. 5. p. 302.) History of a case of puerperal fever; with remarks on the treatment of that affection in general. *(Duncan's* M. C. 1780. p. 98.) übers. Samml. f. A. Th. 6. S. 103.

— [James] *M. D. Physician at Kidderminster, Worcestershire.* born: .... died. d. 2 Aug. 1783.

— [James] *A. M. Rector of Maghera-Cross.* Anecdotes of Olave the black, king of Man and the hebridian princes of the Somerled family — —. 1780. 8. (2 sh.) Lodbrokar — quida; or, the death-song of Lodbroc — with an English translation. 1783. 8. The Norwegian account of *Haco's* expedition against Scotland 1263 —. 1786. 8. (3 sh.) Antiquitates Celto-Normanniae, containing the chronicle of Man and the Isles —. Copenhagen. 1786. 4. (10 sh. 6 d.) Antiquitates Celto Scandicae, s. series rerum gestarum inter nationes Britannitannicarum insularum et gentes septentrionales. 1786. 4. (10 sh. 6 d.)

JONES, [A......] The art of playing at Skittles; or the laws of nine pins. 1773. 12. (1 sh.)

—— [Daniel] *of Hindsdale.* Account of Westriver mountain, and the appearance of there having been a Volcano in it. (Mem. of B. A. Vol. I. p. 312.)

—— [E......] *Teacher of the classics and geography, at Bromley, Kent.* The Young geographer and astronomer's best companion. 1773. 12. (3 sh. 6 d.) *Cicero's* Brutus, or the history of the famous orators — translated. 1776. 8. (6 sh.)

—— [Edward] *of Henblas, Llanddersel, Merionetshire.* Musical and poetical relics of the welsh bards —. 1784. fol. (1 L. 1 sh.)

—— [G.....] *An journeyman Woll-Comber.* Miscellaneous poetic attempts. 1786. 8. (3 sh.)

—— [Henry] born at *Drogheda* in *Ireland*: died d. ... Apr. 1770.

—— [J.....] *President.* Remarks on the english language. 1775. 4. (1 sh.)

—— [John] *at Indian River, Worcester County, Maryland.* Account of a new species of Grape Vines. (Tr. of A. S. Vol. I. p. 340.)

—— [John] *Schoolmaster in Kidderminster.* Elegy on winter and other poems; with a memory of the late Lord *Lyttelton.* 1779. 4. (1 sh.)

—— [Philipp] *Tailor:* On crookedness or distortions of the spine —. 1788. 8. (4 sh.)

—— [R.....] *Lieutenant of Artillery.* On skating. 1772. 8. (2 sh. 6 d.)

—— [Robert] *M. D: F. A. S. at Edinb.* Inquiry into the state of Medicine, on the principles of inductive philosophy. 1782. 8. (5 sh. 3 d.) Inquiry into the nature, causes and termination of nervous fevers —. 1789. 8.

—— [Rowland] *of the Inner temple.* The origin of language and nations —. 1764. 8. (10 sh. 6 d.) Hieroglyfic or a grammatical introduction to an universal hieroglyfic language —. 1768. 8. (2 sh. 6 d.) The philosophy of words —. 1769. 8. (2 Sh.) The circles of Gomer; or an essay towards an investigation and introduction of the english as an universal language —. 1771. 8. (5 sh.)

The Jo triads; or the tenth Muse —. 1773. 8. (2 ſh. 6 d.)

JONES, [Thomas] *of Briſtol.* born: .... died 17..

— [Thomas] *Surgeon at Bingley, near Bradford, Yorkshire, late Surgeon to the Leed's infirmary.* A Caſe of a flap operation united by the firſt intention. (*Duncan's* M. C. Vol. 9. p. 326.)

— [W......] On the art of Muſic —. 1785. fol. (1 L. 1 Sh.)

— [W......] *Clerk, Curate of Shinfield and Swallowfield.* Neceſſity and advantages of education. 1786. 8. (2 Sh.)

— [William] *Sir, Knight, one of the judges of the supreme court of judicature at Calcutta in the Eaſt-Indies. Preſident of the Aſiatik Society. F. R. S.* (Formerly Barriſter at Law, fellow of Univerſity College, Oxford.) Hiſtoire de Nader-Chah, connu sous le nom de Thahmas Kuli Kahn, Empereur de Perse. Vol. 1. 2. 1770. 4. (1 L. 4 ſh.) überſ. Greifswald 1773. 4. The Hiſtory of the life of Nader Schah, King of Perſia. 1773. 8. (6 ſh.) (Ein Auszug aus dem Franzöſiſchen.) *Diſſertation ſur la litterature orientale. 1771. 8. (1 ſh.) Grammar of the Perſian language. 1771. 4. (10 ſh. 6 d.) Lettre a M. *Anquetil* du *Perron* dans laquelle eſt compris l'examen de sa traduction des livres attribuês a Zoroaſtre. 1771. 8. überſ. *Hiſsmann's* Magazin für die Philoſophie Th. 3. S. 9. *Poems, conſiſting chiefly of tranſlations from the Aſiatic languages, with two eſſays, on the poetry of the Eaſtern nations and on the arts, commonly called imitative. 1772. 8. (4 ſh.) Ed. 2. 1777. 8. (6 ſh.) Poeſeos Aſiaticae commentariorum libri VI. 1774. 8. (9 ſh.) recudi curavit *J. G. Eichhorn.* Lipſiae 1777. 8. The ſpeeches of *Isaeus*, in causes concerning the law of ſucceſſion to property at Athens —. 1779. 4. (10 ſh. 6 d.) *Inquiry into the legal mode of ſuppreſſing riots. 1780. 8. (1 ſh.) Eſſay on the law of bailments. 1781. 8. (2 ſh.) Speech to the aſſembled inhabitants of the counties of Middleſex and Surrey —. 1782. 8. (6 d.) The Mahomedan law of ſucceſſion to the property of inteſtates, in arabic with a translation and notes 1782. 4. (5 ſh.)

The

The Moallakat, or seven Arabian poems, which were suspended on the temple at Mecca; with a transtion and arguments. 1783. 4. (10 ſh. 6 d.) On the orthography of Aſiatik words in roman letters. (Aſiat. Res. Vol. 1. p 1.) Discourse on the inſtitution of a society for enquiring into the hiſtory, civil and natural, the antiquities, arts, sciences and litterature of Aſia. 1784. 4. (1 ſh. 6 d.) (Aſiat. Res. Vol. 1. p. 1.) On the Gods of Greece, Italy and India. (Ibid. p. 221.) A converſation with Abram an Abyſſinian, concerning the city of Gwender and the Sources of the Nile. (Ibid. p. 383. überſ. in *Sprengel's* und *Forſter's* Länder- und Völker-Kunde. Th. 3. S. 189. überſ. in *Eichhorn's* Bibliothek Th. 2. S. 1020.) Second Anniversary discourse on the Hindus. (Ibid. p. 405.) The third discourse on the Hindus. (Ibid. p. 415.) *Sacontala; or the fatal ring: an Indian drama by *Calidas* translated from the original Sanscrit and Pancrit. 1790. 4.

JONES, [William] *A M: Rector of Paston in Northamptonshire, Miniſter of Nayland, Suffolk. F. R. S.* *A full answer to the eſſay on spirit —. 1753. 8. (2 ſh. 6 d.) The catholic doctrine of a Trinity — proved from ſcripture. 1757. 8. (2 ſh.) Eſſay on the firſt principles of natural philoſophy. 1762. 4. (9 ſh.) Remarks on the principles and spirit of a work: the Confeſſional. 1770. 8. (2 Sh. 6 d.) Zoologia ethica, a disquiſition concerning the mosaic diſtinction of animals into clean and unclean. 1771. 8. (2 Sh.) Three Diſſertations on life and death. 1771. 8. (1 Sh. 6. d.) Hiſtory of all the religious houſes in the counties of Devon and Cornwall, before the diſſolution. 1779. 8. (2 Sh. 6 d.) Phyſiological disquiſitions, or, discourses on the natural philoſophy of the elements —. 1781. 4. (1 L. 1 Sh.) Courſe of lectures on the figurative language of the holy ſcripture and the interpretation of it from the ſcripture itself. 1787. 8. (6 Sh.) (Several ſingle ſermons.)

—— [William] *F. R. S.* born: .... died 17...

—— [William] *Surgeon in Birmingham.* Account of two cases of insanity, one of which was cured by the

the use of the fox glove: also a case of hemoptysis cured by the same remedy. (*Duncan's* M. C. Dec. II. Vol. 1. p. 302. et 380. übers. Samml. f. A. Th. 13. S. 23.) Account of an expeditious cure of a fractured scull, with remarks on the case by *Rob. Mynors*. (London M. J. Vol. 5. p. 278.

JORTIN, [John] *D. D. Arch-Deacon of London, Rector of St. Dunstan in the East and Vicar of Kensington.* born in *London* d. 23 Oct. 1698. died d. .. Aug. 1770.

IRELAND, [John] The Emigrant. a poem. 1785. 4. (1 Sh.) Letters and poems by *John Henderson* with anecdotes of his life. 1786. 8. (4 Sh)

— [Samuel] A picturesque tour through Holland, Brabant and part of France, made 1789. Vol. 1. 2. 1790. 8. (2 L. 12 Sh. 6 d.)

IRONSIDE, [.....] *Lieutenant-Colonel.* Of the culture and uses of the son or sun — plant of Hindostan with an account of the manner of manufacturing the Hindostan paper. (Philos. Transact. 1774. p. 99.)

IRVING, [Ralph] *M. D.* Experiments on the red and quill peruvian bark with observations on its history, made of operation and uses. 1785. 8. (3 Sh.) übers. Leipz. 1787. 8. Some remarks on the supposed effects of lime and magnesia in promoting the solubility of peruvian bark. (Lond. M. J. Vol. 7. P. 4.) *The Edinburgh new Dispensatory — by Gentlemen of the faculty at Edinburgh. 1786. 8.

— [Thomas] *M. D. Physician at Lisburne.* Account of a singular fracture of the cranium; and of the haemorrhage, from amputation of penis, stopt by slight compression for a few minutes. (*Duncan's* M. C. 1790. Dec. 2. Vol. 5. p. 363.)

IRWIN, [Eyles] *In the service of the East Indian Company.* Bedukah, or the self devoted, an Indian pastoral. 1776. (2 Sh. 6 d.) A series of adventures in the course of a voyage up the red sea, on the coasts of Arabia and Egypt — in the Year 1777. in letters to a lady. 1780. 4. (15 Sh.) Ed. 3. Vol. 1. 2. 1787. 8. (12 Sh.) übers. (durch *Joh. Andr. Engelbrecht.*) Leipzig 1781. 8. *Eastern eclogues —. 1780. 4. (2 Sh. 6 d.) Occasional epi-

epistles, written during a journey from London to Busrah in the Gulph of Persia in the Years 1780 and 1781. —. 1783. 4. (3 Sh.) Ode to *Robert Brooke* — occasioned by the death of Hyder Ally. 1784. 4. (1 Sh. 6 d.)

JUBB, [George] *D. D. Professor of Hebrew in the University of Oxford.* born: .... died d. 13 Nov. 1787.

JUNIPER, [Julius] *Poet Laureat to the Royal College of Physicians.* The Brunoniad: an heroic poem, in VI Cantos, containing a solemn detail of certain commotions which have, of late, divided the kingdom of physic against itself, a critical and truly Homerican catalogue of our present Luminaries of Medicine —. 1789. 4. (3 Sh. 6 d.)

JUSTAMOND, [John Obadiah] *Surgeon to the Westminster hospital. F. R. S.* born: .... died d. 27 March. 1786.

IVERY, [John] *Teacher of Music at Northaw in Hertfordshire.* The Hertfordshire melody; or, psalm-Singer's recreation —. 1773. 8. (2 Sh. 6 d.)

IVES, [Edward] *Surgeon in East-India.* born: .... died d. 25 Sept. 1786.

—— [John] *F. R. S. and F. A. S. Suffolk Herold extraordinary.* born at Yarmouth 1751. died d. 9 June 1776.

KAIMS, [Lord] (HENRY HOME.) *Judge in the courts of Session and Justiciary at Edinburgh.* born: .... died d. 27 Dec. 1782.

KEAN, [T....] A new and easy method of finding the longitude at sea. 1774. 8. (1 Sh. 6 d.)

KEARNEY, [Michael] *D. D. Professor of History at Dublin.* Lectures concerning history. 1776. 4. (2 Sh. 6 d.)

KEARSLEY, [G....] Annual Taxtables, including all the new ones of the Year 1785 —. 1785. 8. Table of trades for — the benefit of young men. 1786. 8. (1 Sh.)

KEATE, [George] *F. R. S. F. A. S.* Account of the ancient history, present government and laws of the republic of Geneva. 1760. 8. (3 Sh.) The alps, a poem: 1763. 4. (1 Sh. 6 d.) The ruins of Netley Abbey, a poem. 1764. 4. (6 d.) *Poem to to the memory of Mrs. *Cibber.* 1766. 4. (6 d.) Ferney; an epistle to Mr. *Voltaire.* 1767. 4. (1 Sh.) The monument in Arcadia, a poem. 1773. 4. (2 Sh). Sketches from nature, taken and coloured in a journey to Margate. Vol. 1. 2. 1779. 8. (5 Sh.) nachgedr. Dresden 1784. 8. Poems. Vol. 1. 2. 1781. 8. The mummy, an epistle to *Angel. Kauffmann.* 1781. 4. (2 Sh.) Observations on the roman earthen ware found in the sea on the kentish coast between whistable and reculver on the borders of the isle of Thanet. (Arch. Vol. 6. p. 125.) A probationary ode for the Laureatship. 1787. 4. (2 Sh.) Distressed poet, poem. 1787. 4. (4 Sh.) Account of the Pelew-Islands — composed from the journals and communications of Capt. *Henr. Wilson* and some of his officers — 1783. - 1788. 4. (1 L. 1 Sh.) nachgedr. Basil. Vol. 1. 2. 1790. 8. übers. von *G. Forster.* 1789. 8. The interesting and affecting history of Prince Lee Boo, a native of the Pelew-Islands, brought to England — with a short account of those islands, and a sketch of the manners and customs of the inhabitants. 1789. 12.

KEATE, [T....:] *Surgeon extraordinary to her Majesty and Surgeon to the Prince of Wales and Duke of York.* Cases of the hydrocele with observations on a peculiar method of treating that disease. 1788. 8. (2 Sh.)

— [William] *M. A. Prebendary of Wells and Rector of Laveston, Somerset.* Examination of Dr. *Price's* and *Priestley's* sermon. 1790. 8. (2 Sh.) The address of *Will. Bull* — to *Will. Poole* —. 1790. 8. (1 Sh.) Quotation against quotation, or cursosy observations on Dr. *Priestley's* letters to the inhabitants of Birmingham —. 1790. 8. (1 Sh. 6 d.)

(Several single sermons.)

KEEBLE, [John] *Organist of St. George's Church at London.* The Theory of harmonics: or an illustration of the Grecian harmonica —. 1784. fol. (1 L. 1 Sh.)

O' KEEFE, [John] *Actor in the Irish Stage.* (born in *Ireland.*) Tony lumpkin in town, a farce. 1780. 8. (1 Sh.)

KEELING, [Bartholom.] *M. A. Rector of Tiffield and Bradden, in Northamptonshire and Chaplain to the Earl*

Earl Temple. Three sermons on St. Paul's wish. 1766. 8. (2 Sh.) Three discourses on Moses's petition and Character. 1767. 8. (1 ſh. 6 d.) Eight discourses of the behaviour of the malefactor's crucified with our bleſſed Lord. 1773. 8. (3 Sh.)

KEIR, [Archibald] Thoughts on the affairs of Bengal. 1772. 8. (1 ſh. 6 d.) Of the method of diſtilling as practiſed by the natives at Chatra in Ramgur, and in the other provinces, perhaps, with but little variation —. (Aſiat. Res. Vol. 1. p. 309.)

—— [James] *Esq. of Stourbridge. F. R. S: F. A. S. Edinb.* **Macquer's* Dictionary of chemiſtry translated. Vol. 1. 2. 1771. 4. (1 L. 8 Sh.) On the cryſtallization observed on glaſſ. (Phil. Transact. 1776. p. 530.) *Treatise on the various kinds of permanently elaſtic fluids or gases 1777. 8. Experiments on the congelation of the vitriolic acid. (Phil. Transact. 1787. p. 267.) Dictionary of Chemiſtry. Part. 1. 1789. 4. (10 ſh.) Experiments and observations on the diſſolution of metals in acids, and their precipitations; with an account of a new compound acid menſtruum, useful in ſome technical operations of parting metals. (Phil. Transact. 1790. p. 359.)

—— [William] *M. D. Phyſician to St. Thomas's Hospital at London and Lecturer on Chemiſtry in London.* born at Perth in Scotland 1753. died d. 6 Jun. 1783.

KEITH, [Alexander] *Esq. F. R. S: F. A. S. Edinb.* Description of a mercurial level. (Tr. of E. S. Vol. 2. p. 14.)

—— [George Skene] *M. A. Miniſter of Keith-Hall, Aberdeenshire.* Sermons and discourses on ſeveral occaſions. 1785. 8. (5 Sh.)

(Several ſingle ſermons.)

—— [Thomas] *Teacher of the Mathematics.* Introduction to the ſcience of geography. 1787. 12. (1 ſh. 6 d.) The complete practical arithmetician. 1788. 8. (3 ſh.)

KELHAM, [Robert] *of Lincolns Inn.* Dictionary of the Norman or old French language —. 1779. 8. (6 ſh.) Domesday book illuſtrated —. 1788. 8. (5 ſh.)

KELLIE, [George] *Surgeon in Leith.* Account of the paracentesis being performed in the thorax, for the cure of an emphysema. (Med. Com. of Ed. Vol. 2. p. 427.)

KELLY, [Hugh] (O'-KELLY.) *Member of the Middle Temple at London.* born on the Banks of *Killarney Lake in Ireland.* 1739. died. d. 3 Febr. 1777.

KELSALL, [R....] *Lieutenant.* Thoughts on the present manner of quartering the troops on the coast —. 1784. 8. (6 d.)

KELSO, [Hamilton] *M. D.* On elementary air. 1786. 8. (1 sh.)

KEMBLE, [John] *Actor.* (Brother to Mrs. *Siddons.* born at *Lancashire.*) The pilgrim a comedy of *Fletcher*, altered. 17.. The palaces of *Mersey.* 17.. Fugitive pieces. 1780. 8. (1 sh. 6 d.) The maid of honour, a comedy, altered from *Massinger.* 1785. Projects, a farce. 1786. Criticism on the performance of Hamlet. 1788. 8. (6 d.) The farmhouse, a Comedy. 1789. 8. (1 sh.) Love in many masks: altered from Mr. *Behn's* Rover. 1790. 8. (1 sh. 6 d.) The tempest; or, the enchanted Island: written by *Shakespeare:* with additions from *Dryden.* 1790. 8. (1 sh. 6 d.)

KEMEYS, [John Gardner] *Esq. of Plantain garden river plantation in Jamaica and of Bartholey in the County of Monmouth.* Reflections by the late additional duties on sugars and on rum —. 1783. 8. (2 sh. 6 d.)

KENNEDY, [James] Description of the pictures, statues, bustos, basso — relievos, and other curiosities at the Earl of *Pembroke's* House at *Wilton* —. 1758. 8. (2 sh. 6 d.) Description of the antiquities and curiosities in Wiltonhouse illustrated with 25 engravings —. 1770. 4. (16 sh.)

— [John] *Rector of Bradley in Derbyshire.* A new method of stating and explaining the scripture chronology —. 1752. 8. (5 sh.) Examination of *Jackson's* chronological antiquities. 1753. 8. (1 sh. 6 d.) The doctrine of a commensurability between the diurnal and annual motions —. 1753. 8. (6 d.) A complete system of astronomical chronology, unsolding the scriptures —. 1763. 4. (1 L. 5 sh.) Discussion of some important and uncertain

certain points in chronology —. 1773. 8. (1 ſh.) Explanation and proof of the complete ſyſtem of aſtronomical chronology —. 1775. 8. (1 ſh. 6 d.)

KENNICOTT, [Benjamin] *D. D. Canon of Chriſtchurch, Keeper of the Radcliſſe Library and Vicar of Culham, Oxfordshire.* born at *Tottneſſ, Devonshire.* 1718. died d. 18 Aug. 1783.

KENRICK, [.....] *Lecture on the perpetual motion. P. 1. 2. 1770. 4. (5 ſh.)

—— [.....] *Millot's* elements of the hiſtory of England, from the invaſions of the romans to the reign of George II. translated: Vol. 1. 2. 1771. 8. (8 ſh.)

—— [William] *LL. D.* born: ..... died d. 9 June. 1779.

KENT, [Nathaniel] *of Fulham.* Hints to gentlemen of landed property. 1775. 8. (5 ſh.)

KENTISH, [Richard] *M. D: F. A. S. Edin.* Experiments and obſervations on a new ſpecies of bark —. 1785. 8. (2 ſh. 6 d.) überſ. Leipz. 1787. 8. Eſſay on ſea-bathing and the internal use of ſea water. 1786. 8. (1 ſh. 6 d.) Oration on the method of ſtudying natural hiſtory —. 1787. 8. (2 ſh.) Advice to gouty persons. 1789. 8. (1 ſh. 6 d.) Hiſtory of a case of universal latent cancer. *(Duncan's* M. C. Dec. 2. Vol. 1. überſ. Samml. f. A. Th. 13. S. 18.)

KENTON, [James] Eſſay on death, a poem. 1777. 4. (2 ſh. 6 d.)

KER, [L. ....] *M. B.* Minor poems, or poetical pieces. 1787. 4. (1 Sh.)

KERR, [James] *Surgeon to the civil hospital at Bengal.* Account of the tree producing the terra japonica. (Med. Obs. Vol. 5. p. 148.) The culture of the white poppy and preparation of opium in the province of Bahar. (Ibid. p. 317.) Natural hiſtory of the inſect which produces the gum laua. (Phil. Transact. 1781. p. 374. überſ. Samml. zur P. u. Ng. Th. 3. S. 479.)

—— [James] *Captain.* *Narrative of the rise and rapid advancement of the Mahratta ſtate: translated from the Perſian into English. 1782. 8. (2 Sh. 6 d.)

—— [Robert] *F. R. S: F. A. S. Edinb.* *Lavoiſier* elements of chemiſtry translated —. 1789. 8. (10 Sh.) *Bertholet's* eſſay on the new method of bleaching, by means of oxygenated muriatic acid; with an ac-

account of the nature, preparation and properties of that acid and its application, translated. 1789. 8.

KEYES, [John] The practical bee-master —. 1781. 8. (4 Sh.)

KIDDELL, [John] Three Dissertations on the inspiration of the holy scriptures. 1779. 8. (2 Sh.) übers. von *J. S. Semler*. Halle. 1783. 8.

(Several single sermons.)

KILGOUR, [Thomas] *Surgeon in Jamaica.* The history of a case, in which worms in the nose, productive of alarming symptoms, were successfully removed by the use of tobacco. *(Duncan's* M. C. Vol. 8. p. 75.)

KIMBER, [E.....] The peerage of England —. 1766. 8. (3 Sh.) The peerage of Scotland —. 1767. 18mo (3 Sh.) The peerage of Ireland. 1768. 12. (3 Sh.) *E. Kimber* and *R. Johnson*, The baronetage of England —. Vol. 1-3. 1771. 8. (1 L. 1 sh.)

KINDAN, [.....] On the construction of a mine augar. 1788. (2 Sh.)

KINDERSLY, [.....] *Mrs.* Letters from the island of Teneriffe, Brazil, the Cape of good hope and the East-Indies. 1777. 8. (3 Sh. 6 d) übers. Leipzig 1777. 8.

KING, [Edward] *F. R. S: F. A. S. and late President of the Society of Antiquaries.* On the English constitution and government. 1766. 8. (2 Sh. 6 d.) Attempt to account for the universal deluge. (Phil. Transact. 1767. p. 44.) Attempt to account for the formation of spars and chrystals. (Ibid. p. 58.) Account of a very remarkable aquatic insect. (Ibid. p. 72.) Observations on *J Lloyd* account of Elden Hole in Derbyshire. (Ibid. 1771. p. 250.) Account of the effects of lightning at Steeple, Ashton and Holt in the county of wilts on the 20 June 1772. (Ibid. 1773. p. 231.) Observations on a singular sparry incrustation found in Somersshire. (Ibid. 1773. p. 241.) Remarks on the Abbey church of Bury St. Edmund's in Suffolk. (Arch. Vol. 3. p. 311.) Account of the great seal of Ranulph Earl of *Chester*, and of two ancient inscriptions found in the ruins of St. Edmund Bury Abbey. (Ibid. Vol. 4. p. 119.) Observations on antient castles. (Ibid. p. 364. Vol. 6. p. 231.)

Observations on antient caſtle. 1777. 4. Account of an old piece of Ordnance. (Ibid. Vol. 5. p. 147.) Account of a petrefaction found on the coaſt of Eaſt-Lothian (Phil. Transact. 1779. p. 35.) *Proposals for eſtabliſhing, at ſea, a marine ſchool, or ſeminary for ſeamen —. 1785. 8. (1 Sh.) *Morſels of criticiſm, tending to illuſtrate ſome few paſſages in the holy ſcripture upon philoſophical principles and an enlarged view of things. 1788. 4. (1 L. 1 Sh.)

KING, [John] Thoughts on the difficulties and diſtreſſes in which the peace of 1783. has involved the people of England. 1783. 8. (1 Sh. 6 d.)

—— [John Glen] *D. D. Rector of Wormley, Preacher at Spring Garden Chapel. F. R. S: F. A. S.* born at Norfolk. 1732. died d. 3 Nov. 1787.

—— [Richard] The frauds of London detected. 1779. 12. (1 Sh.)

—— [Samuel Croker] *Dublin.* Case of a feather or pen, XI inches in length, which was fortunately extracted from the oesophagus of a man, who had put it into his throat to excite vomiting, and had let it slip down. (Med. Obs. Vol. 5. p. 231.)

—— [Thomas] *Actor at Drury-Lane Theater.* (born in *London* 1730.) Love at firſt ſight. 1763. 8. *Neck or nothing, a farce. 1765. 8. (1 Sh.) *A peep behind the curtain; or the new rehearſal, a comedy. 1766. 8. (1 Sh.) Wit's laſt ſtake, a comedy. 1769. 8. (1 Sh.)

KINGLAKE, [Robert] *Surgeon at Chipping-Norton, in Oxfordſhire.* Account of a caſe, in which a part of the femoral artery was dilated in conſequence of its being laid bare by a wound and which was ſucceſſfully treated by obliterating the cavity of the artery, at that part, by compreſſion. (London M. J. Vol. VIII. P. 4.) Account of a remarkable diſeaſe of the heart, lungs and one of the external mammae —. (Ibid. Vol. X. P. 4.)

KINGSFORD, [William] Appeal to the ſcriptures in general, on the univerſality of divine love to man and the univerſal extent of our ſaviour's death. 1788. 8. (5 Sh.) Vindication of the baptiſts from the criminality of a charge exhibited againſt them by Mr. *Wesley.* 1789. 8. (2 d.) Three letters to Mr. *Wesley*, containing remarks on on a piece lately published with his approbation: and three challenges to all the methodists in the kingdom. 1789. 8. (1 Sh.)

KINNAIRD, [William] *Apothecary in Edinburgh.* Experiments and observations on the temperature of the atmosphere and on the viciſſitudes to which it is ſubjected from different causes. (*Duncan's* M. C. Vol. 9. p. 425.)

KINNERSLEY, [Ebenezer] New Experiments in electricity. (Phil. Transact. 1763. p. 84.) On ſome electrical experiments made with Charcoal. (Ibid. 1773. p. 38.)

KIPPIS, [Andrew] *D. D: F. R. S: F. A. S.* Vindication of the proteſtant diſſenting miniſters, with regard to their late application to parliament. 1772. 8. (1 ſh. 6 d.) Ed. 2. 1773. 8. (2 ſh.) überſ. Brittiſches theolog. Magazin. Th. 4. S. 529. u. S. 721. Biographia Brittannica. Vol. 1-4. 1778-1789. fol. (6 L. 7 ſh. 6 d.) Six Discourses delivered by *John Pringle*, with the life of the author. 1783. 8. (6 ſh.) *Conſiderations on the proviſional treaty with America and the preliminary articles of peace with France and Spain. 1783. 8. (2 ſh. 6 d.) Observations on the late conteſts in the royal society. 1784. 8. (2 ſh. 6 d.) The life of Capt. *James Cook*. 1788. 4. (1 L. 1 ſh.) nachgedr. Baſil. Vol. 1. 2. 1788. 8. überſ. Th. 1. 2. Hamb. 1789. 8. The life of *Nath. Lardner*, prefixed to the firſt volume of the works of *N. Lardner*. 1788. 8. *Jos. Fownes's* enquiry into the principles of toleration, with some account of the author. 1789. 8. (2 ſh. 6 d.)

KIRBY, [Thomas] Eſſay on criticism in the course of which the theory of light and the gravity of the earth are conſidered. 1758. 8. (6 d.) Analyſis of the electrical fire —. 1778. 8. (6 d.)

KIRK, [M.....] *of Wilderspool, near Mancheſter.* On the beſt method of raiſing early potatoes. (*Hunter's* G. E. Vol. 5. p. 185.)

KIRKE, [Robert] *Advocate.* Minutes and proceedings of a Court-Martial held on *John Crookshanks* — formerly Captain of his Majeſty ſhip the Lark. 1772. 8. (2 ſh. 6 d.)

KIRKLAND, [Thomas] *M. D. Phyſician at Ashby de la Zouch, Leiceſterſhire.* On Gangrenes. 1754. 8. (1 ſh 6 d.) überſ. von *Huth.* Nürnberg 1761. 8. On the use of ſpunge after amputations. (Med. Obs Vol. 2. p. 278.) On the methods of ſuppreſſing haemorrhages from divided arteries. 1763. 8. (1 ſh) On the cure of thoſe diseases which are the causes of fevers. 1767. 8. (1 ſh. 6 d.) Reply to *Maxwell's* answer to *Kirkland's* eſſay on fevers —. 1769. 8. (2 ſh.) Obſervations upon *Pott's* general remarks on fractures. 1770. Appendix. 1771. 8 (2 ſh. 6 d.) überſ. Altenb. 1771. 8. On child-bed fevers — with two diſſertations on the brain and nerves. 1774. 8. (3 ſh.) überſ. von *J. C. F. Sherf.* Gotha 1778. 8. Animadverſions on Dr. B —'s treatiſe on the King cough, with an eſſay on the hooping cough. 1774. 8. Thoughts on amputation with an eſſay* on the use of opium in mortifications. 1780. 8. (2 ſh.) (* überſ. Samml. f. A. Th. 5. S. 555.) Inquiry into the present ſtate of medical surgery. Vol. 1. 2. 1783. 1786. 8. (12 ſh. 6 d.) überſ. Leipzig 1785. 8. On the use and abuse of mercury in the cure of the syphilis. (London M. J. Vol. VII. p. 1. überſ. Samml. f. A. Th XI S. 714.)

KIRKPATRIK, [H.....] Sermons on various ſubjects —. 1785. 8. (5 ſh.)

—— [J.....] *M. D: at London.* born: .... died 1770.

—— [James] *Esq.. Lieutenant Colonel in the Eaſt-Indies Company service.* * Conſiderations on the expediency of a corps of light troops to be employed on detached service in the Eaſt-Indies. 1769. 8. (1 ſh.) Ed. 2. with the Author's name 1781. 8. (1 ſh.)

KIRSHAW, [Thomas] On the comparative merit of the ancients and moderns, with reſpect to the imitative arts. (Mem. of M. Vol. 1. p. 405.)

KIRWAN, [Richard] *F. R. S: F. I. A.* Experiments and obſervations on the ſpecific gravities and attractive powers of various ſaline ſubſtances. (Phil. Transact. 1781. p. 6. 1782. p. 129. 1783. p. 15.) überſ. von *Lor. Crell.* Berlin u. Stettin. 1785. 8. Remarks on *Cavendish's* experiments on air. (Ibid. 1784. p. 154. — 178.) Elements of Mineralogy. 1784. 8. (5 ſh.) überſ. von *L. Crell.*

L. Crell. 1785. 8. Remarks on specific gravities taken at different degrees of heat and an easy method of reducing them to a common ſtandard. (Phil. Transact. 1785. p. 267.) Experiments on hepatic air. (Ibid. 1786. p. 118.) Eſſay on phlogiſton and on the conſtitution of acids. 1787. 8. (3 ſh. 6. d.) Eſtimate of the temperature of different latitudes. 1787. 8. (3 ſh.) On the variations of the barometer. (Tr. of J. A. 1788. p. 43.) Observations on coral mines. (Ibid. p. 157.) *Lor. Crell.* ſammlete dieſe Schriften zuſammen und gab ſie unter dem Titel heraus: Phyſisch chemiſche Schriften. Th. 1-3. Berlin 1788. 8.

KITCHEN, [Thomas] *Hydrographer to his Majeſty.* born: .... died d. 19 July 1784.

KITE, [Charles] *Surgeon at Gravesend in Kent.* Account of a remarkable nervous affection. (London M. J. Vol. 3. p. 300.) A case of paralyſis of the lower extremities ſucceſſfully treated by an iſſue. (Ibid. p. 405.) Recommendation of electricity for the cure of the cataract. (Ibid. Vol. 7. P. 2. überſ. Samml. f. A. Th. XII. S. 43.) Account of two cases of violent conſtipation of the bowels, the firſt treated by the internal and external application of coldwater; the second by a discharge of matter from the vagina. (Ibid. Vol. VIII. P. 2. überſ. Samml. f. A. Th. 12. S. 551.) On the recovery of the apparently dead. 1788. 8. (5 ſh.) überſ. von *C. F. Michaelis.* Leipzig 1790. 8.

KNIGHT, [D.... M....] Proposal for peace between Great Britain and North America —. 1779. 8. (6 d.)

— [Francis] *Surgeon to the Coldſtream Regim. of Foot-Guards.* Two cases of obſtructed liver, followed by dropsy, succesfully treated by mercurial friction. (Med. Transact. Vol. 3. p. 368.) On the effect of a large dose of saccharum saturni. (London M. J. Vol. 4. p. 286.)

— [J.....] The ears of Cheſterfield and parson Goodmann; translated from the French of *Voltaire.* 1786. 12. (1 ſh 6 d.)

— [Samuel] *A. M. of Trinity College, Cambridge.* *Elegies and sonnets. 1785. 4. (3 ſh.) Ed. 2. with the Author's name. 1786. 4. (3 Sh.)

KNIPE, [Eliza] Six narrative poems. 1787. 4. (3 Sh. 6 d.)
—— [Rest] The new birth —. 1771. 8. (1 Sh. 6. d.)

KNOWLES, [Thomas] *D. D. Prebendary of Ely.* Answer to an essay on spirit —. 1753. 8. (1 Sh. 6 d.) Observations on the divine mission and administration of Moses. 1763. 8. (1 Sh. 6 d.) Letters between Lord *Hervey* and Dr. *Middleton* concerning the roman senate. 1778. 4. (12 Sh.) On the passion. 1780. 8. (3 Sh.) Primitive christianity; or, testimony from the writers of the first four centuries, to prove that Jesus Christ was worshipped as God from the beginning of the christian church. 1789. 8. (2 Sh. 6 d.) (Several single sermons.)

KNOX, [Hugh] *D. D. Minister of the Gospel in St. Croix.* Discourses on the truth of revealed religion and other important subjects. Vol. 1. 2. 1768. (6 Sh.) Letter to *Green* pointing out some difficulties in the calvinistic scheme of divinity —. 1772. 12. (1 Sh. 6 d.) The moral and religious miscellany. 1775. 8.

—— [John] born: .... died at *Dalkeith*, near *Edinburgh*. 1790.

—— [Vicesimus] at *Tunbridge*, *in Kent. M. A.* *Essays moral and litterary. 1777. 8. (4 Sh. 6 d.) with the Author's name. Ed. 2. Vol. 1. 2. 1778. 8. (7 Sh. 6 d.) Ed. 3. Vol. 1. 2. 1782. 8. (7 Sh. 6. d.) Ed. 4. Vol. 1. 2. 1784. 8. (8 Sh.) übers. von *J. P. Bamberger*. Th. 1. 2. Berlin 1781. 8. Liberal education: or, a practical treatise on the methods of acquiring useful and polite learning. 1781. 8. (3 Sh. 6 d.) Ed. 7. Vol. 1. 2. 1785. 8. (6 Sh.) Ed. 10. Vol. 1. 2. 1790. 8. (12 Sh.) **Juvenalis* in usum scholarum. 1784. 8. (5 Sh.) **Horatius* in usum scholarum. 1784. 8. (6 Sh.) Letter to Lord *North*, Chancellor of the University of Oxford. 1789. 8. (6 d.)

—— [William] *late Under-Secretary of the late American Department.* *Observations upon the liturgy —. 1789. 8. (3 Sh.) *Extraofficial state papers — for the preservation of the constitution and promoting the prosperity of the British empire. 1789. 8. (4 Sh.) *Considerations on the present state of the nation —. 1790. 8. (1 Sh. 6. d.)

KNOX,

KNOX, [William] *M. D: of the Northern Regiment of Scots Fencibles.* History of a case in which cataracts in both eyes were removed by electricity. (*Duncan's* M. C. Vol. 9. p. 303.)

KUCKAHN, [T.... S....] On the preservation of dead birds. (Philos. Transact. 1770. p. 302.)

KYLE, [Thomas] *Gardener to the Bar. Steuart of Moredun.* On forcing fruit trees. 1784. 8. (3 Sh.)

KYNASTON, [In....] *M. A.* born at *Chester* d. 5 Dec. 1728. died at *Wigan* in *Lancashire* d... June 1783.

LABILLIERE, [Peter] *Major.* Letters to the majesty of the people and a declaration of those rights of the commonalty of Great Britain and Ireland without which they cannot be free. 1784. 8. (6. d.)

LACY, [John] *The Universal system: or mechanical cause of all the appearances and movements of the visible heavens —. 1779. 8. (1 sh.)

LAMBE, [Robert] *Vicar of Norham upon Tweed.* History of the battle of Floddon in verse, written about the time of Queen Elizabeth —. 1774. 8. (4 sh.) History of Chess —. 1774. 8. (2 Sh. 6 d.)

LAMBERT, [George] Sermons on various subjects. Vol. 1. 2. 1779. 1788. 8. (9 Sh.)

—— [James] *Landscape-Painter at Lewes.* Account of a very extraordinary effect of lightning on a bullock at *Swanborow* in the parish of *Iford* near *Lewes*, in *Sussex.* (Phil. Transact. 1776. p. 493.)

LAMONT, [David] *D. D. Chaplain to his Royal Highness the Prince of Wales.* Sermons. Vol. 1. 2. 1780-1787. (11 Sh.)

LAMPORT, [William] born: .... died at *Honiton, Devonshire* d. 5 March 1788.

LANCASTER, [Nathanael] *Rector of Stanford Rivers Essex.* born: .... died 1775.

LANDELLS, [James] *M. A.* Collection of prose and verse. 1782. 12. (2 Sh. 6. d.)

LANDEN, [John] *F. R. S.* born at *Peakirk* in *Northamptonshire* d. 23 Jan. 1719. died d. 15 Jan. 1790.

LANDMANN, [J....] *Professor of Fortification and Artillery to the Royal Military Academy at Woolwich.* (*Saldern's*) Elements of tactics and introduction to military evolution for the infantry; translated from the German —. 1787. 8. (7 Sh. 6 d.)

LANE, [John] *Secretary to the Commissioners.* The report of the Commissioners — appointed to examine, take and state, the public accounts of the kingdom. Vol. 1-3. 1785. 1787. 4. (3 L. 16 Sh.)

—— [Rachael] *Mrs. Midwife.* Addreſſ to pregnant ladies, and others, pointing out such women as are fit to be inſtructed and particularly to be employed in the practice of midwifery. 1785. 8.

—— [Timothy] *F. R. S.* Account of two persons having a bronchocele, wherein the use of burnt sponge appeared to have a very conſiderable effect. (Mem. of M. S. of L. Vol. 1. p. 217.)

LANGFORD, [Abraham] born 1711. died d. 18 Sept. 1774.

—— [William] *D. D.* born 1704. died d. 23 Apr. 1775.

LANGHORNE, [John] *D. D. Rector of, Blagdon, Somersetshire.* born at *Kirby Stephen, Weſtmoreland*, 17.. died d. 1 Apr. 1779.

—— [William] *M. A: Rector of Hawkinge and Miniſter of Folkſtone in Kent.* Job, a poem. 1760. 4. (2 Sh. 6 d.) Poetical paraphrase on part of the book of Isaiah. 1761. 4. (2 Sh. 6 d.) *Plutarch's* lives. Vol. 1-6. 1770. 8. (1 L. 11 Sh. 6 d.) Sermons. Vol. 1 2. 1773. 8. (7 Sh.)

LANPHIER, [Simon] *Phyſician, Waterford.* Hiſtory of a case of rheumatiſm, cured by electricity. (*Duncan's* M. C. Vol. 8. p. 314.)

LATHAM, [John] Obſervations on the earth quake at Liſbon Nov. 1, 1775. made at Zsusqueira. (Phil. Transact. 1759. p. 411.) Case of a man seized with a fever from the effects of meal-duſt. (Ibid. 1770. p. 451.) Account of an extraordinary dropſical case. (Ibid. 1779. p. 54.) General ſynopſis of birds. Vol. 1-3. and supplem. 1782-1787. 4. (8 L. 13 Sh.)

LATTER, [Mary] *Mrs. a Shopkeeper at Reading in Berkshire.* born: .... died d. 4 March 1777.

LAUDER, [William] *Profeſſor of the Eccleſiaſtical Hiſtory and Mathematik at Dundee.* born: .... died 1771.

LAUGHTON, [George] *D. D. of Richmond in Surry.* The progreſſ and eſtabliſhment of chriſtianity in reply to *Gibbon's* XV Chapt. of the decline and fall of

of the roman empire. 1780. 4. (1 Sh. 6 d.) History of ancient Egypt. 1774. 8. (5 Sh.)
(Several single sermons.)

LAVINGTON, [.....] *M D: at Tavistok in Devonshire.* born: .... died d. 12 Oct. 1782.

— [John] *Jun.* The case of desertion and affliction considered in a course of sermons on the Ps. 77, v. 1-10. 1789. 12. (3 Sh.)

LAURENTS, [Philippe] born 1737. died d. .. Nov. 1787.

LAW, [Edmund] *D. D. Lord Bishop of Carlisle.* born in the parish of *Cartmel* in *Lancashire* 1702. died d. 14 Aug. 1787.

LAWRENCE, [Thomas] *M. D. Physician in London.* born d. 25 May 1711. died at *Canterbury* d. 6 June 1783.

LAWRIE, [John] *A. M.* History of the wars in Scotland, from the battle of the Grampian hills in the Year 85 to the battle of Culloden in the Year 1746. 1785. 12. (3 Sh.)

LAWSON, [John] *B. D: Rector of Swanscombe in Kent.* born: .... died d. 13 Nov. 1779.

— [Robert] *Surgeon at Leith.* Account of the dissection of two singular cases. (*Duncan's* M. C. Dec. II. Vol. 3. p. 299.)

LAYARD, [Charles Peter] *D. D: F. R. S: F. A. S:* Charity, a poetical essay. 1773. Poetical essay, on duelling. 1776. 4. (1 Sh.) (Several single sermons.)

— [Daniel Peter] *M. D: F. R. S: of London and of Gottingen. F. A. S:* Case of a fracture of the os ilium, and its cure. (Phil. Transact. 1753. p. 537.) Account of a young lady, who had an extraordinary impostume formed in her stomach. (Ibid. 1756. p. 406.) Account of the earth quake March 8. 1749-50, at London. (Ibid. 1756. p. 621.) On the usefulness of inoculation of horned cattle to prevent the contagious distemper among them. (Ibid. 1760. p. 528.) Case of a diseased eye. (Ibid. 1760. p. 747.) On the bite of a mad dog. 1763. 8. Ed. 2. 1766. Ed. 3. 1772. Account of the Somersham water in the county of Huntingdon. 1767. 8. and in Phil. Transact. 1766. p. 10.) Directions to prevent the contagion of the jail distemper. 1772. 8.

Phar-

Pharmacopoca in ufum gravidarum puerperarum et infantum recens natorum. 1772. 8. Ed. 2. 1776. On the nature, cause and cure of the diftemper among the horned cattle. 1757. 8. Ed. 2. 1770. and in Phil. Transact. 1780. p. 536.

LEACH, [Edmund] *Surveyor.* Treatise of universal inland navigations and the use of all sorts of mines. 1790. 8. (5 Sh.)

—— [Thomas] *Esq: of the Middle Temple, Barrifter at Law.* Cases in Crown law, determined by the 12 judges, by the court of King's Bench — from the 4th Year of Geo. II. to the 29th Year of Geo. III. 1789. 8. (9 Sh. 6 d.)

LEAKE, [John] *M. D: Phyfician to the Weftminfter Lying in Hospital.* On the Lisbon diet drink. 8. 17.. Observations on the child-bed fever, on uterine haemorrhagies and convulfions and other acute fickneffes in pregnancy. 1773. 8. (5 Sh.) überf. Leipzig 1775. 8. A Lecture introductory to the theory and practice of midwifery. 1773. 4. (2 Sh. 6 d.) aus diefer überfezt: von der Verhütung der erblichen Krankheiten: Samml. f. A. Th. 2. St. 2. S. 67. Medical inftructions towards the prevention and cure of chronic or slow diseases peculiar to women. 1777. 8. (6 Sh.) Syllabus: or generals heads of a course of lectures on the theory and practice of midwifery. 1787. 8. (1 Sh.)

—— [Stephan Martin] born: .... died 1773.

LEDWICH, [Edward] *LL. B: Vicar of Aghaboe, Queen's County Ireland. F. A. S. of London, Dublin and Edinburgh.* On the religion of the Druids. (Arch. Vol. 7. p. 303.) Observations on our antient churches. (Ibid. Vol. 8. p. 165.) *Antiquities of Ireland. Nro. 1. 1789.

LEE, [Arthur] *Esq. F. A. A.* Account of the effects of lightning on two houses in the city of Philadelphia. (Mem. of B. A. Vol. 1. p. 247.)

—— [Francis Bacon] Letter to *Sheridan.* 1757. 8. (6 d.) The debauches, a poem. 1771. 4. (2 Sh.) Translation of *Tiffot's* effay on the disorders of people of fashion. 1771. 8. (3 Sh.)

—— [Harriet] *Mifs: at Bath.* Errors of innocence; a novel. Vol. 1-5. 17.. New peerage; or our eyes may deceive us, a Comedy. 1787. 8. (1 Sh. 6 d.)

LEE,

LEE, [James] *Nurseryman at Hammersmith in Middlesex.* Introduction to botany — extracted from the work of *Linnaeus.* 1760. 8. Ed. III. 1776. 8. (7 Sh. 6 d.)

— [John] *M. D: Physician at Bath: F. R. S.* Narrative of a singular gouty case, with observations. 1782. 8. (1 Sh.) überſ. Samml. f. A. Th. 8. S. 91.

— [John] *Actor at Bath.* born: .... died. d. 19 Febr. 1781.

— [Sophia] *Miſſ.* (Siſter of *Harriet Lee.*) The Chapter of accidents: a Comedy. 1780. 8. (1 Sh. 6 d.) überſ. von *Leonhardi:* neu bearbeitet von *Schroeder.* Berlin. 1782. 8. *The receſſ; or the tale of other times. Vol. 1-3. 1783. (13 Sh. 6 d.) überſ. unter dem Titel *Ruinen.* 17.. *The hermit's tale, a poem. 1787. 4. (2 Sh.)

— [William] *Maſter of an Academy in lower Tooting, Surry.* Elegiac poem, ſacred to the memory of a father. 1788. 8. (2 Sh.)

— [William] *Sir. Baronet.* On the use of water impregnated with fixed air, in preserving flesh meat from putrefaction. (*Prieſtley's* Experiments of Natur. Philoſ. Vol. 1. p. 461.)

LEECHMAN, [William] *D. D: Principal of the college of Glasgow.* born at *Dolphington, Lankershire.* 1706. died d. 3 Dec. 1785.

LEEDES, [John] *Surgeon, Hemingſton, Suffolkshire.* Account of a caſe of ſcorbutus occurring on ſhore, and terminating ſucceſſfully. (*Duncan's* M. C. Dec. 2. Vol. 3. p. 320.)

LEGGE, [Thomas] The law of outlawry and practice in civil actions. 1779. 8. (2 Sh. 6 d.)

LEIGH, [John] *M. D.* Experimental inquiry into the properties of opium and its effects on living ſubjects with observations on its hiſtory, preparations and uses. 1786. 8. (2 Sh. 6 d.)

LEIGHTON, [Francis] *of Shrewsbury.* Memoir concerning the roman baths discovered 1788. at Wroxeter, the ancient Uriconium or Viroconium. (Arch. Vol. 9. p. 323.)

LEITH, [Charles] *M. D: at Johnſtone near Montrose.* Hiſtory of a very uncommon convulſive cough cured

red by the flowers of zinc. (Med. Com. of Ed. Vol. 6. p. 343.)

LELAND, [Thomas] *D. D.* born: .... died. 17..

LEMON, [George William] *Rector of Geytonthorpe and Vicar of East Walton, Norfolk.* Graecae grammaticae rudimenta —. 1774. 12. (2 sh. 6 d.) Two tracts and additional observations on the greek accents by the late *Edw. Spelmann*, and the voyage of *Aeneas* from Troy to Italy —. 1775. 8. (2 sh. 6 d.) English etymology; or a derivative dictionary of the english language —. 1783. 4. (1 L. 6 sh.)

LEMPRIERE, [.....] *of Pembroke College, Oxford.* *Bibliotheca classica, or a classical dictionary; containing a full account of all the proper names mentioned in ancient authors, with tables of coins, weights and measures in use among the greeks and romans. 1788. 8. (8 sh.)

LENOX, [Charlotta] *Mrs.* (Her maiden name *Ramsay*: born at *New York in North America.*) *The female Quixote: or, the adventures of Arabella. Vol. 1. 2. 1751. 8. (6 sh.) **Shakespeare* illustrated or the novels and histories on which the plays of *Shakespeare* are founded —. 1752. 8. (6 Sh.) *The memoirs of the countess of Berci, taken from the French. Vol. 1. 2. 1755. (6 Sh.) *Henrietta, a novel. Vol. 1. 2. 1757. (6 Sh.) *Philander, a dramatic pastoral. 1757. 8. (1 Sh.) *Brumoy's* greek theater, translated. Vol. 1-3. 1759. 4. Sophia, a novel. Vol. 1. 2. 1761. (6 Sh.) Memoirs of *Sully* translated. 17.. The sister, a comedy. 1769. 8. (1 Sh. 6 d.) *De la Valliere* meditations and penitential prayers translated. 1774. 8. (2 Sh. 6 d.) Old city manners; a comedy; altered from the original *Eastward Hoe*, written by *Ben Jonson* —. 1775. 8. (1 Sh.) Euphemia. Vol. 1-4. 1790. 8. (12 Sh.)

LEROUX, [J....] *Esq. Justice of peace for the counties of Herford and Middlesex.* Thoughts on the present state of the prisons of this country. 1781. 8. (1 Sh.)

LESLIE, [Charles] *Surgeon at Cork.* Account of the operation for the anevrism being performed upon the

the femoral artery with ſucceſſ. (Med. Com. of Ed. Vol. 2. p. 176.)

LESLIE, [John] *A. M: Profeſſor of Greek, King's College, Aberdeen.* born: .... died d. 30 Jun. 1790.

—— [Matthew] *Esq.* On the Pangolin of Bahar. (Aſiat. Reſ. Vol. 1. p. 376.)

—— [Patrick Dugud] *M. D: F. R. S: Phyſician at Durham.* born 1751. died at *Lisbonne.* d. 12 March. 1783.

LETCHWORTH, [Thomas] *Miniſter of the Gospel among the Quakers.* born: .... died 17..

LETHIEULLIER, [Smart] Observations on ſepulchral monuments. (Arch. Vol. 2. p. 291.)

LETTICE, [John] *B. D: Vicar of Peasemarch, Suſſex.* The converſion of St. Paul, a poetical eſſay. 1765. 4. (1 Sh.) The antiquities of Herculanum, translated from the Italian by *Thom. Martyn* and *John Lettice.* Vol. 1. 1773. 4. (3 L. 3 Sh.) Two ſermons —. 1788. 4. (1 Sh. 6 d.)

LETTSOM, [John Coakley] *M. D: F. R. S: F. A. S. Physician extraordinary to the London Lying — in Hospital.* Obſervationes ad hiſtoriam theae pertinentes. Lugd. Bat. 1769. 4. The natural hiſtory of the tea - tree with obſervations on the medical qualities of tea and effects of tea - drinking. 1772. 4. (4 ſh.) überſ. Leipz. 1776. 8. The naturaliſts and travellers companion. 1772. 8. * Reflections on the general treatment and cure of fevers. 1772. 8. (2 ſh.) Medical memoirs of the general dispensary in London for part of the Years 1773. 1774. —. 1774. 8. (5 ſh,) überſ. Altenb. 1777. 8. Improvement of medicine in London, on the basis of public good. 1775. 8. (1 ſh. 6 d.) Observations preparatory to the use of Dr. *Meyersbach's* medicines. 1776. 8. (1 ſh.) Letter — upon general inoculation 1778. 4. (6 d.) Hiſtory of the origin of medicine. 1778. 4. (5 ſh.) Obſervations on *Dimsdale's* remarks on the letter — upon general inoculation. 1779. 8. (1 ſh) Answer to *Dimsdale's* review of *Lettsom's* observations on *Dimsdale's* remarks —. 1779. 8. Considerations on the propriety of a plan for inoculating the poor of London at their own habitations. 1779. 8. (6 d.) Observations on the plan for eſtabliſhing a dispensary

sary and medical society. 1779. 8. (1 ſh.) On the danger of fragrant flowers in a close room (Monthly Review Vol. 62 p. 504.) *Letter to the King on the subject of a new proposed inſtitution in the medical department: (a public Profeſſorſhip of Anatomy and Surgery) 1781. 4. (1 ſh. 6 d.) Biographical account of Capt. *J. Carver*. 1781. 8. (2 ſh.) Some account of the late *John Fothergill* M. D. 1783. 8. (3 ſh.) Publiſhed: *J. Fothergill's* Works. *Vol.* 1. 2. 1783. 8. (12 ſh.) Ed. 2. 1784. 4. (1 L. 11 ſh. 6 d.) Vindication of Dr. *Lettsom's* conduct relative to the late election at the Finsbury dispensary —. 1786. 8. (6 d.) Hiſtory and diſſection of an extraordinary intro susception. (Phil. Transact. 1786. p. 305.) Cases of palpitation of the heart. (Mem. of M. S. of L. Vol. 1. p. 77. überſ. Samml. f. A. Th. 12. S. 596.) Some remarks on the effects of lignum Quaſſiae amarae. (Ibid. p. 128) Observations on ſome cases of hydrocephalus internus (Ibid. p. 169.) On a disease, succeeding the transplanting of teeth. (Ibid. p. 330.) Case of a biliary calculus. (Ibid. p. 373.) Memoirs of *Jacques Barbeu Dubourg*, Profeſſor Med. of Paris. (Ibid. p. 476.) *Commerell*, on the culture and use of the Mangel Wurzel, translated. 1787. 8. Hiſtory of two cases of hydatides renales. (Mem. of M. S. of L. Vol. 2. p. 32.) Of the digitalis purpurea in hydropic diseases. (Ibid. p. 145.) Case of a diseased rectum. (Ibid. p. 308.) Hiſtory of some of the effects of hard drinking. 1789. 4. (6 d.)

LEVESON, [G. . . . .] *M. D.* On the blood — 1776. 8. (2 ſh. 6 d.) überſ. Berlin 1782.. 8. On the epidemical ſore throat, with the method of treatment. 1778. 8. (1 ſh. 6 d.) Ed. 2. 17 . . überſ. nach der 2ten Aufl. Berlin 1783. 8.

LEVELYN. [William] Treatise on the Sabbath. 1783. 8. (2 ſh. 6 d.)

LEVI [David] *a Jew.* Account of the rites and ceremonies of the jews. — 1783. 8. (4 ſh. 6 d.) Answer to Dr. *Prieſtley's* letter to the jews. P. 1. 2. 1789. (5 ſh.) Lingua ſacra: or, a grammar and dictionary of the Hebrew, Chaldee and Talmudic dialect. Vol. 1-3. 1789. 8. (2 L. 16 ſh. 6 d.) The

Pentateuch — in Hebrew, with the English translation and notes by *Lion Soesmans*, corrected and translated by *Dav. Levi.* Vol. 1-5. 1789. 8 (1 L. 8 sh.)

LEVISON, [G . . .] *M. D: Physician to the Medical Asylum at London.* On the blood. 1776. 8. (1 sh.) Account of the epidemical sore throat. 1778. 8.

LEWIS [. . . .] *Miss.* Poems, moral and interesting. 1788. 8. (4 sh.)

— [John] Uniting and monopolizing farms — disadvantageous to the land - owners and highly prejudicial to the public — 1767. 8. (6 d.) Remarks on an inquiry into the connexion between the present price of provisions and the size of farms — 1773. 8. (2 sh.)

— [Hardwicke] *Esq.* Excursion to Margate, in June 1786. — with anecdotes of well known characters. 1787. 8. (2 sh. 6 d.)

— [L. . .] *Esq.* Lord Walford. Vol. 1. 2. 1789. 8. (6 sh.)

— [Meyer] *Operator for the teeth, at Oxford.* On the formation, structure and use of the teeth. 1772. 8. (1 Sh.)

— [P . . . .] *Actor.* Miscellaneous pieces in verse — 1775. 4. (2 Sh. 6 d.)

— [P . . . .] *M. D.* Inquiry into the nature and properties of common water, with observations on its medicinal qualities. 1790. 8. (3 Sh. 6 d.)

— [William] *M. D. F. R. S. Physician at Kingston, Surry.* born: . . . . died d. 19. Jan. 1781.

LEY, [Charles] *Land - Surveyor.* The nobleman, gentleman, land - steward and surveyor's complete guide — 1787. 8. (3 Sh. 6 d.)

LEYBOURN, [William] Description of an entertaining and useful instrument called *Gunter's* quadrant. 1772. 8. (1 Sh.)

LIDDEL, [R. . . . .] *Purser in the Royal Navy.* The seaman's new vade mecum; containing a practical essay on naval book keeping — 1787. 8. (5 Sh.)

LIGHTFOOT, [John] *A. M. Rector of Gotham, Nottinghamshire and Chaplain to the Duchess Dowager of Portland; F. R. S.* born: . . . . died d. 20 Febr. 1788.

LIMBIRD, [James] *Surveyor to the corporation.* Account of the strata observed in sinking for water at Boston, Lincolnshire. (Phil. Transact. 1787. p. 50)

little Chelsea. On military education. 1773. 8. (2 ſh.) Syſtem of military mathematics. Vol. 1. 2. 1776. 8 (12 ſh.) On caſtrametation. 1778. 8. (4 ſh.) On encampments. 1779. (4 ſh.) Elements of fortification. 1780. 8. (6 ſh.) Elements of field fortification. 1783. 8. (4 ſh.)

LOCKMAN, [John] *Secretary on the British Herring Fishery.* born: .... died d. 2 Febr. 1771.

LOFT, [Capel] *JC.* The praises of poetry; a poem. 1775. 8. (2 ſh.) Observations on *Wesley's* ſecond calm addreſſ and incidentally on other writings upon the american queſtion. 1777. 8. (1 ſh.) Observations on Mrs. *Macaulay's* hiſtory of England —. 1778. 4. (2 ſh. 6 d.) Principia cum juris univerſalis, tum praecipue anglicani. Vol. 1. 2. 1779. 8. (6 ſh.) *An argument on the nature of party and faction. 1780. 8. (1 ſh.) Eudoſia; or a poem on the universe. 1781. 8. (2 ſh. 6 d.) *Translation of the firſt and ſecond Georgic of *Virgil.* 1784. 8. (2 ſh. 6 d.) °Eſſay on the law of libels —. 1785. 8. (2 ſh. 6 d.) Three letters on the queſtion of regency. 1789. 8. (1 ſh. 6 d.) Observations on the firſt part of Dr. *Knowle's* teſtimonies from the writers of the firſt four centuries. 1789. 8. (2 Sh. 6 d.) Hiſtory of the corporation and teſt acts. 1790. 8. (1 Sh.) Remarks on the letter of *Edm. Burke* concerning the revolution in France and on the proceedings in certain ſocieties in London, relative to that events. 1790. 8. (2 Sh.)

LOFTIE, [William] *Surgeon at Canterbury.* born 1700. died 1778.

LOFTUS, [Smyth] *M. A: Vicar of Coolock.* Reply to the reasonings of Mr. *Gibbon,* in his hiſtory of the decline and fall of the roman empire —. 1778. 8. (1 ſh.)

LOGAN, [......] at *Edinburgh.* °Diſſertation on the government, manners and ſpirit of Aſia. 1787. 4. (1 Sh. 6 d.)

—— [John] *F. R. S: Miniſter of Leith.* born: .... died d. 28 Dec. 1788.

LONG, [Robert] *D. D: F. R. S: Maſter of Pembroke-Hall and Profeſſor of Aſtronomy and Geometry in the Univerſity of Cambridge.* born: .... died d. 16 Dec. 1770.

LONGFIELD, [John] *M. D: at Cork in Ireland.*

Lon-

Longitude of *Cork* deduced from astronomical observations: (Phil. Transact. 1779. p. 163.)

LONGMATE, [B.....] Supplement to the 5 Edit. of *Collins's* peerage of England —. 1784. 8. (7 Sh. 6 d.)

LONNERGAN, [Andrew] *Teacher of the Military Sciences.* The fencer's guide —. 1772. 8. (7 Sh.)

LONSDALE, [.....] *The spanish rivals, a musical farce. 1784. 8. (1 Sh.)

LORIMER, [J.....] Letter, containing some remarks on the climate, vegetable productions — of Westflorida. (Tr. of A. S. Vol. I. p. 250.) Description of a new dipping-needle. (Phil. Transact. 1775. p. 79.)

LORT, [Michael] *D. D: F. R. S: Vice President of A. S. Rector of S. Matthew Friday-street of St. Michael Mile-end, near Colchester, Prebendary of St. Pauls.* born: ..... died d. 5 Nov. 1790.

L'OSTE, [Charles] *A. M: Rector of Langton in Lincolnshire.* The truth of the christian religion, a poem —. 1776. 8. (5 Sh.)

LOTHIAN, [William] *D. D: Minister of Canongate:* born at *Edinburgh* d. 5 Nov. 1740. died d. 17 Dec. 1783.

LOTT, [Yeoman] *Addreff to the people of England: containing an enquiry into the cause of the great scarcity of timber throughout the dominions belonging to his majesty —. 1766. 8. (1 sh. 6 d.) *Important hints towards an amendment of the royal dock-yards. by a man of Kent. 1767. 8. (1 Sh.) The case of the late agent of the royal hospital at Plymouth superceded in July 1774 —. 1776. 8. (1 sh. 6 d.) Proposals for the benefit of the naval service. 1776. 8. (1 sh. 6 d.)

LOVE, [James] *Actor.* (His real name was *Dance.*) born: .... died 1774.

LOVEFUN, [A..... G.....] A new cure for the spleen: being a collection of advertisements humorous, curious, farcical, satirical —. 1778. 8. (1 sh.)

LOVELASS, [Peter] *of the Inner temple.* The will, which the law makes: or, how it disposes of a person's estate, in case he dies without a will —. 17.. (the same book under the title:) On intestacy and wills. 1786. 8. (3 sh. 6 d.) Ed. 3. (with the title:) The laws disposal of person's estate who dies with-

 out

out a will or teſtament. 1786. 8. (3 ſh. 6 d.) Explanation of the law concerning the bills of exchange, promiſſory notes and the evidence on a trial by jury relative thereto: with description of Banknotes and the privilege of attornies. 1789. 8. (3 Sh.)

LOW, [....] Chiropodologia; or a ſcientific enquiry into the causes of corns, warts, onions and other painful or offenſive cutaneous excrescences —. 1786. 8. (3 ſh.)

LOWDELL, [Stephen] *Surgeon: F. M. S.* The case of a burn and another of ſtones in the kidnies. (Mem. of M. S. of L. Vol. 1. p. 315.)

LOWE, [John] Jun. of *Mancheſter.* Liberty or death; by which is vindicated the obvious practicability of trading to the coaſt of Guinea for its natural productions —. 1790. 4. (1 ſh.)

LOWNDES, [Francis] *Medical Electrician.* Observations on medical electricity —. 1787. 8. (1 ſh. 6 d.)

LOWTH, [Robert] *D. D: Lord-Biſhop of London.* born 1711. died d. 3 Nov. 1787.

LUCAS, [Bernard] *of Chesterfield, Derbyshire.* The ſolution of the quadrature. 1788. 4. (1 ſh. 6 d.)

—— [Henry] *A M.* Love in disguise: an Opera. 1767. Tears of Alnwick; a paſtoral elegy in memory of the late Ducheſſ of Northumberland. 1777. 4. (1 ſh.) Viſit from the ſhades; or, Earl *Chatham's* Adieu to his friend Lord *Camden* —. 1778. 4. (2 ſh. 6 d.) Poems to her Majeſty. 1780. 4. (10 ſh. 6 d.) The earl of Somerset: a Tragedy. 1780. 4. The cypreſſ-wreath; or meed of honour, a poem to the memory of Lord *Rob. Manners.* 1782. 4. (1 ſh.) Alnwick's condolence; a paſtoral elegy — in memory of the late Duke of Northumberland. 1786. 4 (1 ſh.)

—— [James] *Surgeon to the Leed's Infirmary.* Account of a ſingular nervous case. (Med. Obs. Vol. 5. p. .) On the amputation of the ankle with a flap. (Ibid. p. 323.) On cataracts. (Ibid. p. 250.) Observations on amputation. (London M. J. Vol. 7. P. 3. Vol. 9. P. 1.) Remarks on elaſtic bandages. (Ibid.) Remarks on febrile contagion. (Ibid. Vol. X. P. 3.) A case of retention of urine —. (Ibid. Vol. XI. P. 2.) Account of the ſingular effects of muſic on a patient. (Ibid.)

(Ibid.) Hints on the management of women in certain cases of pregnancy. (Mem. of M. S. of L. Vol. 2. p. 409.)

LUCAS, [Robert] *B. D: of Trinity College.* Translation of *Homer's* hymn to Ceres. 1781. 4. (3 ſh.) Three ſermons on the ſubject of ſunday ſchools — with few hints on parochial clubs. 1787. 8. (2 ſh.)
(Several ſingle ſermons.)

— [William] *of the Middle temple.* The laws concerning horses: or every horsekeeper his own lawyer. 1786. 8. (1 ſh. 6 d.)

LUCKOMBE, [Philipp] see *Thomas Pride.*

LUDERS, [Alexander] *Barriſter at Law, of the Inner-Temple.* Reports of the proceedings in committees of the house of commons, on controverted elections —. Vol. 1. 2. 1785. 1789. (14 ſh.)

LUDLAM, [William] *M. A: F. R. S: Rector of Cockfield and Vicar of Norton,* born: . . . . . died d. 16 March. 1788.

LUFFMANN, [John] Account of Antigua — written in the Years 1786 – 1788. 8. 1789. (1 Sh.) überſ. von *J. H. Wiedmann.* Leipzig. 1790. 8.

LUKENS, [John] *Surveyor - General of Pennsylvania.* Account of the transit of Venus over the ſun's disc, as observed at Norriton June 3d 1769. (Tr. of A. S. Vol. 1. p. 8.) Observations on the tranſit of Venus June 3. 1769. in Philadelphia. (Phil. Transact. 1769. p. 289.)

LUND, [John] Ducks and peas, or the London rider, a farce. 1776. 8.

LUSIGNAN, [. . . .] History of the revolt of Ali Bey againſt the Ottoman porte, including an account of the form of government of Egypt with a description of grand Cairo and of ſeveral celebrated places in Egypt, Paleſtine and Syria. 1783. 8. (5 ſh.) überſ. Leipzig. 1784. 8. Series of letters containing a voyage and journey from England to Smyrna, from thence to Conſtantinople and to England —. Vol. 1. 2. 1788. 8. (12 Sh.) überſ. *Ebeling's* Neue Samml. von Reiſebeſchr. Th. 10. S. 129.

LUSON, [Hewling] *of the Navy Office.* Inferior politics, or conſiderations on the wretchedneſs and profligacy of the poor, eſpecially in London and its vicinity —. 1786. 8. (2 Sh. 6 d.)

LUTTRELL, [Edward] *Surgeon at Tunbridge.* A case of a gangrene, after castration successfully treated by giving alkalis and acids separately. (Mem. of M. S. of L. Vol. 1. p. 60. übers. Saml. f. A. Th. 12. S. 572.)

—— [Temple] Bill — for the more easy and effectual manning of the royal navy —. 1777. 8. (1 Sh.)

LYNN, [W.....] *Surgeon.* The singular case of a lady, who had the smallpox during pregnancy and who communicated the same disease to the foetus. 1786. 8. (6 d.)

LYON, [John] *Minister of the Gospel at Dover, Kent.* Experiments and observations in electricity. 1780. 4. (12 Sh.) Further proofs that glass is permeable by the electric effluvia —. 1781. 4. (3 Sh.) Description of a Roman bath, discovered at *Dover.* (Arch. Vol. 5. p. 325.) Account of a subsidence of the ground near Folkstone on the coast of Kent. (Phil. Transact. 1786. p. 220.)

LYONS, [Israel] *Astronomer, with Capt. Phipps in his voyage to the Northpole.* born ... died d. 1 May 1775.

LYSONS, [Daniel] *M. D. Physician at Bath and late Fellow of all Souls, College.* Description of the cephus. (Phil. Transact. 1762. p. 135.) Case of the late Rev. *James Bradley.* (Ibid. 1762. p. 635.) Case of a girl who swallowed three pins and discharged them at the shoulder. (Ibid. 1769. p. 9.) On the effects of camphire and calomel in continual fevers —. 1771. 8. (1 Sh. 6 d.) Farther observations upon the effects of camphire and calomel in the dropsy; upon bath waters —. 1771. 8. (1 Sh.) übers. Leipzig. 1774. 8. On Elmbark. (Med. Transact. Vol. 2. p. 203.) Practical essays upon intermitting fevers, dropsies, diseases of the liver, the epilepsy, the colic, dysenteric fluxes and the operation of calomel. 1772. 8. (3 Sh.) Ed. 2. 1783. 8. (5 Sh.)

—— [Samuel] *F. A. S.* Account of some roman antiquities discovered at Comberd-farm, near Cirencester, Gloucestershire. (Arch. Vol. 9. p. 319.)

LYTTELTON, [George] *Lord,* (Baron of Frankley in Worcestershire,) *Privy-Counsellor. F. R. S.* born d. 17 Jan. 1708. died d. 22 Aug. 1773.

MACAULAY, [A.....] *A. M.* Translation of *Nood's* discourses on ſovereign power —. 1781. 8. (5 ſh.)

— [Catharine] ſee *Graham* —.

— [J.....] Unanimity; a poem. 1780. 4. (1 ſh. 6 d.)

— [John] *Esq.* The genius of Ireland, a Masque. 1786. 8. (1 ſh.)

MACBEAN, [Alexander] *M. A.* Dictionary of antient geography —. 1773. 8. (7 ſh.) Dictionary of the bible. 1778. 8. (6 ſh.)

MACBRIDE, [David] *M. D. at Dublin.* born at *Ballymony* in the County of *Antrim* d. 26. Apr. 1726. died d. 13. Dec. 1778.

MACCORMICK, [Joſeph] *D. D: Miniſter at Preſtoupans.* State papers and letters — relating to the public affairs in Great-Britain. 1774. 4. (1 L. 1 ſh.)

— [Samuel] *M. D: Phyſician at Antrim.* A remarkable hiſtory of an imperforate hymen. (Med. Com. of Ed. Vol. 2. p. 188.) Hiſtory of a diabetes ſucceſsfully treated by the use of *Dover's* powder. (*Duncan's* M. C. Vol. 9. p. 349.) überſ. Samml. f. A. Th. XI. S. 413.

MACDONALD, [.....] On the gold of Limong on the island of Sumatra. (Aſiat. Res. Vol. 1. p. 336.) überſ. *Gren* J. d. P. Th. 2. S. 346.

— [Donald] Clergyman in *Scotland.* born 17.. died d. 22. Aug. 1790.

— [John] *Cadet of the family of Keppoch, in Inverneſsſhire.* Travels in various parts of Europe, Aſia and Africa, during a ſeries of thirty years and upwards. 1790. 8. (4 ſh.)

MACFAIT, [Ebenezer] *M. D.* New ſyſtem of general geography —. P. 1. 1780. 8. (5 ſh) Observations on thunder and electricity. (Eſſ. and Observ. Edinb. Vol. 1. p. 189.) Some phaenomena observable in foggy weather. (Ibidem p. 197.)

MACFARLAN, [John] *D. D: F. R. S. Edin: Miniſter of Canongate and Almoner to his Majeſty for Scotland.* born: .... died d. 24. Dec. 1788.

MACGILVRAY, [John] *A. M: Maſter of the Grammar School of Leſtwithiel.* Poems. 1787. 4. (4 ſh.)

MACGOWAN, [John] born 17.. died 17..

MACGREGOR, [Malcolm] *Esq.* (a fictitious name.) *Heroic epiſtle to ſir *W. Chambers*. 1773. 4. (1 ſh.)

*An heroic poſtscript —. 1774. 4. (1 ſh.) Ode to Mr. *Pinchbek* on his newly-invented patent Candle Schnuffers. 1776. 4. (6 d.) Epiſtle to Dr. *Schebbeare.* Ed. 2. 1777. 4. (1 ſh. 6 d.)

MACGREGOR, [Robert] *Reply to the Layman's addreſſ to the baptiſts: 2) Dr. *Gill's* answer to *Addington*, reſpecting the diſturbance in Munſter. 3) The doctrine of baptism. 1774. 8. (6 d.)

MACINTOSH, [.....] Collection of gaelic proverbs and familiar phrases. 1785. 8. (2 Sh.)

MACIVER, [....] Mrs. *Teacher of Cookery and Paſtry in Edinburgh.* Cookery and paſtry. 12. 1787. (2 ſh. 6 d.)

MACKAY, *Supervisor of Excise.* Abridgment of the excise laws. 1781. 8. (7 ſh.)

MACKENZIE, [Alexander] *M. D: Phyſician at New-Tarburt.* A dropſical case. (Med. Obs. Vol. 2. p..) A remarkable ſeparation of part of the thigh bone, (Ibid. p..) Account of a woman in the ſhire of roſſ living without food or drink. (Phil. Transact. 1777. p. 1.)

—— [Henry] *F. R. S. Edin.* (born in *Scotland*) *The man of feeling. 1771. 8. (2 ſh. 6 d.) *The prince of Tunis, a Tragedy. 1773. 8. (1 ſh. 6 d.) *Happineſſ a poem. 1773. 4. (1 ſh.) *The man of the world. Vol. 1. 2. 1773. 8. (5 ſh.) *Fatal curioſity, written by *George Lillo*, with alterations, a Tragedy. 1783. 8. (1 ſh.) Account of the German Theatre. (Tr. of E. S. Vol. 2. p. 154.) (Several treatises in the Mirrour and the Lounger, periodical papers.)

—— [Murdoch] *F. R. S.* born .... died 17..

—— [Roderik] *Lieutenant in the 71ſt. Regiment.* Strictures on *Tarleton's* hiſtory of the campaigns of 1780 and 1781. in the ſouthern provinces of North-America —. 1787. 8. (4 ſh.)

MACKIE, [John] *Surgeon in Huntingdon.* Case of the ſucceſſful treatment of hydrocephalus internus, by mercury. (*Duncan* M. C. 1780. p. 221. überſ. Samml. f. A. Th. XI. S. 159.)

—— [William] Farmer at Ormiſton. 1786, 8. (6 d.)

MACKINTOSH, [.....] Travels in Europe, Aſia and Africa — begun in the Year 1777 and finished 1781. Vol. 1. 2. 1782. 8. (12 ſh.) überſ. (von *C. A. Wichmann*) Th. 1. Leipz. 1785. 8.

MACKLIN, [Charles] *Actor:* born in *Ireland* 1699. King Henry the 7; or, the popish impostor, a tragedy. 1746. 8. Love a la mode, a tragedy. 1760. (1 sh.) The married libertine, a Comedy. 1761. The irish fine lady, a farce. 1767. The man of the world, a comedy. 1787.

MACKNIGHT, [James] *D. D: Minister at Edinburgh.* Harmony of the four gospels. 1756. 4. (15 sh.) The truth of the gospel history. 1764. 4. (17 sh.) Translation of the 1. and 2. epistle of St. Paul to the Thessalonians with a commentary and notes. 1787. 4. (7 sh. 6 d.)

MACLACHLAN, [Alexander] *M. D.* Account of the good effects obtained from the calx of zinc, in a histerical affection. (*Duncan's* M. C. Vol. 10. p. 247.)

MACLAGAN, [Robert] at *Coaltullach.* A fracture of the skull, with the loss of part of the substance of the brain. (Med. Com. of Ed. Vol. 1. p. 97.)

MACLAGGAN, [John] *Surgeon at Coaltullach.* Account of an inflammation of the abdomen terminating in a gangrenous sore, from which a large worm was discharged. (Med. Com. of Ed. Vol. 2. p. 80)

MACLAINE, [Archibald] *D. D: Minister of the English church at the Hague.* born in *Scotland.* *Mosheim's* ecclesiastical history translated. Vol. 1. 2. 1765. 4. Supplement 1768. (2 L. 5 sh.) Series of letters to *Soame Jenyns* on occasion of his view of the internal evidence of christianity. 1777. 8. (3 sh.) Several single sermons.

MACLAURIN, [......] Information for *Mungo Campbell* in a criminal prosecution — for the alledged murder of the late *Alex. Earl. of Eglington.* 1770. 8. (2 sh. 6 d.) Arguments and decisions in remarkable cases before the high court of justiciary and other supreme courts in Scotland. 1774. 4. (1 L. 5 sh.)

— [John] *Esq. Advocate: F. R. S. Edin. Senator of the college of Justice at Edinburgh.* Dissertation to prove that, Troy was not taken by the greeks. (Tr. of E. S. Vol. 1. p. 43.) übers. von *J. G. Buhle.* in den philosoph. und histor. Abhandl. der Gesellsch. zu Edinburgh. Th. 1. S. 215.)

MACLURG, [James] *M. D.* Experiments upon the human bile. 1772. 8. (3 ſh. 6 d.) überſ. Leipz. 1783. 8.

MACMAHON, [Parkins] *Book-keeper to the King's Theater in the Hay Market.* born in *Ireland.* 17.. died d. 14. Jan. 1788.

—— [Thomas O'brien] On the depravity and corruption of human nature. 1774. 8. (3 ſh.) Man's capricious — conduct towards the irrational — part of the creation —. 1775. 8. (2 ſh.) The candour and good — nature of englishmen exemplified —. 1777. 8. (5 ſh.)

MACNAB, [Henry] Plan of reform in the mode of inſtruction, at preſent practised, in engliſh ſchools. 1787. 4. (1 ſh. 6 d.) Synopſis of a courſe of elocution. 1787. 8. (1 ſh.)

MACNALLY, [Leonard] *Esq.* The claims of Ireland and the resolutions of the volnnteers, vindicated. 1782. 8. (1 ſh. 6 d.) Retaliation, a farce. 1782. 8. (1 ſh.) Triſtram ſhandy, a farce. 1783. 8. (1 ſh.) Robin hood, or, ſherwood foreſt: a comic opera. 1784. 8. (1 ſh. 6 d.) Fashionable levities, a comedy. 1785. 8. (1 ſh. 6 d.) Richard Coeur de Lion, a comic opera. 1786. 8 (1 ſh.) Abſtract of all the public acts paſſed in the — parliament from 26. Jan. to Oct. 27. 1786. 12. (2 Sh. 6 d.)

MACNEILL, [Hector] On the treatment of the negroes in Jamaica —. 1788. 8. (1 ſh.) Account of the caves of Cannara, Ambola and Elephanta in the Eaſt-Indies. (Arch. Vol. 8. p. 251.) *The harp; a tale. P. 1. 2. 1789. 4. (1 ſh. 6 d.)

MACNEVEN, [William James] *M. D.* On the conſtruction and use of a mine - auger translated from the German of Mr. *Geiſſ.* 1788. 8. (2 ſh.)

MACONOCHIE, [Allan] *Esq. Advocate: F. R. S. Edin: Profeſſor of Public Law in the Univerſity of Edinburgh.* On the origin and ſtructure of the european legislatures. (Tr. of Ed. S. Vol. 1. p. 3. et pag. 135.) überſ. von *J. G. Buhle* in den philoſ. und hiſtor. Abhandl. der Geſellſch. der Wiſſenſch. zu Edinburgh. Th. 1. S. 1.

MACPACKE, [Jose] *a Bricklayer's labourer.* Oikidia or Nutshells, being ichnographical diſtributions for ſmall villas —. P. I. 1785. 8. (5 ſh.)

MACPHERSON, [James] *Member of Parliament.* (born in *Scotland.*) An ancient epic poem, in ſix books, with ſeveral other poems compoſed by *Oſſian*, the ſon of Fingal; translated from the Galic language. 1762. 4. (10 ſh. 6 d.) The ſongs of Selma. from the original of *Oſſian*, the ſon of Fingal. 1762. 4. (1 ſh.) *Fingal reclaimed. 1763. 8. (6 d.) Temora, an ancient epic poem in 8 books with ſeveral other poems by *Oſſian* —. 1763. 4. (10 ſh. 6 d.) Works of *Oſſian* the ſon of Fingal translated. Ed. 3. 1765. überſ. von *Denis* Th. 1-3. Wien 1768. Fingal a poem by *Oſſian*, translated —. 1772. 8. (4 ſh.) Translation of the Iliad of *Homer*. Vol. I. 2. 1773. 4. (1 L. 11 ſh. 6 d.) Introduction to the hiſtory of Great-Britain and Ireland. 1771. 4. (10 ſh. 6 d.) Remarks on an introduction to the hiſtory of Great-Britain and Ireland. 1772. 8. (1 ſh. 6 d.) Hiſtory of Great-Britain, from the reſtauration. to the acceſſion of the houſe of Hannover. Vol. I. 2. 1775. 4. (2 L. 2 ſh.) Original papers: containing the ſecret hiſtory of Great-Britain from the reſtoration to the acceſſion of the houſe of Hannover. Vol. I. 2. 1775. 4. (2 L. 2 ſh.). *The rights of the engliſh colonies eſtabliſhed in America ſtated and defended —. 1775. 8. (1 ſh. 6 d.)

MACPHERSON, [R.....] On the preſervative from drowning and ſwimmer's aſſiſtant —. 1783. 8. (2 ſh. 6 d.)

MACQUEEN, [Malcolm] *M. D: at Yarmouth.* Some remarks on angina pectoris. (London M. J. Vol. 5. p. 162.) überſ. Samml. f. A. Th. 10. S. 145.

MADAN, [.....] *Mrs.* (Daughter of *Spencer Cowper.* Esq. and mother of *Martin Madan.*) born: ... died. d. 7 Dec. 1781.

— [Martin] *Clergyman of the Methodiſtical Party.* born 1726. died at Epsom 1790.

— [Spencer] *D. D: Rector of St. Philipps.* *Hugo Grotius's* Truth of chriſtianity tranſlated. 1782. 8. (5 ſh.) The call of the gentiles: a poetical eſſay. 1783. 4. (1 ſh.) Letter to *Prieſtley*, in consequence of his familiar letters addreſſed to the inhabitants of the town of Birmingham —. 1790. 8. (1 ſh.) (Several ſingle ſermons.)

MADDOCK, [Abraham] of *Creaton, Northamptonshire.* Letter — on the downfall of Antichriſt —. 1779. 8. (1 ſh.) Popish tyranney and cruelty exemplified and displayed in the hiſtory of the French martyrs at the time of the reformation —. 1780. 12. (3 ſh.)

MADISON, [J....] Meteorological observations made at Virginia. (Tr. of A. S. Vol. 2. p. 141.) Experiments and observations upon what are commonly called the ſweet ſprings. (Ibid. p. 197.)

MAGENISE, [Daniel] *M. D: at London.* The doctrine of inflammation, founded upon reason and experience and entirely cleared from the contradictory ſyſtems of *Boerhaave*, *van Swieten*, and others. 8. 1768. überſ. von *Fr. A. Weber.* 1776. 8. *The reformation of Schoolmaſters, Academy - keepers, ſurgeons, apothecaries, phyſicians, lawyers, divines, farmers —. 1775. 8. (1 ſh.) Ed. 2. (with the Author's name) 1778. 8.

MAGUIRE, [Laurence White] *Surgeon of the Navy.* Case of a lumbar abſceſſ, with an account of the appearances on diſſection. (London M. J. Vol. VII. P. 1.)

MAHON, [Charles] Lord Viscount: ſee *Stanhope.*

—— [Silveſter] *M. D.* *Every lady her own phyſician or the closet companion containing ample inſtruction for the prevention and cure of all disorders incident to the fair ſex. London. 1788. 8. überſ. von *C. F. Michaelis.* Leipz. 1790. 8.

MAINWARING, [John] *B. D: Rector of Church-Stretton Shropshire.* *Life of *Handel.* 1760. Sermons on several occaſions — with a diſſertation on that ſpecies of compoſition. 1780. 8. (5 ſh.) (Several ſingle ſermons.)

MAITLAND, [Robert] *M. D: at Edinburgh.* born 17.. died d... Dec. 1779.

MAKITTRICK, [James] *M. D.* Diſſ. De febre Indiae orientalis maligna flava. Edinb. 1766. 8. Commentaries on the principles and practice of phyſic. 1772. 8. (5 ſh. 6 d.)

MAL-

MALHAM, [John] The ſchool — maſter's complete companion — to arithmetic. 1783. 12. (2 ſh. 6 d.)

MALONE, [Edmund] (born in *Ireland.*) *Supplement to the edition of *Shakeſpeare's* plays publiſhed 1778. by *Sam. Johnſon* and *George Steevens.* Vol. 1. 2. 1780. 8. (18 ſh.) The plays and Poems of *Will. Shakeſpeare* —. 8. Vol. 1-10. 1790. (3 L. 17 Sh.)

MALTON, [Thomas] Royal road to geometry; or, an easy and familiar introduction to the mathematics —. 1775. 8. (10 ſh. 6 d.) On perſpective in theory and practice —. 1776. fol. (2 L. 5 ſh.) Eſſay concerning the publication of works on ſcience and litterature, by ſubſcription. fol. 1777. (1 ſh. 6 d.)

MANLEY, [John] *Esq.* Letter to the proprietors of the undertaking for recovering and preserving the navigation of the river Dee. 1786. 4. (6 d.)

MANN, [Theod. Aug.] On rivers and canals (Phil. Transact. 1779. p. 555.)

MANNERS, [Nicholas] Confutation of *John Fletcher's* appeal to matter of fact and common ſense. 12. 1787. (6 d.)

MANNING, [Henry] *M. D: at London.* On female diseases. 1771. 8. (5 ſh. 3 d.) Ed. 2. 1775. (überſ. Sammlung f. A. Th. 3. S. 734.) Modern improvements in the practice of phyſic. 1780. 8. (5 ſh.) Modern improvements in the practice of Surgery. 1780. 8. (5 ſh.) Ueber die Mutterbeſchwerung: überſ. von *Fr. Sr. Hanke.* Wien. 1790. 8.

— [Owen] *S. Theol. Baccal. Canon Vicarius de Godelming et Rector de Peperharow in Agro Surrienſi: F. R. S.* Dictionarium Saxonico et Gothico — latinum, Auctore *Eduardo Lye* — edidit et auxit. — 1772. Vol. 1. 2. fol. (3 L. 3 ſh.) Discretion in matters pertaining to religion recommended, 1788. 4. (1 ſh.)

MANSELL, [William] Fairy hill, or may day; an Opera. 1784. 8.

MANTE, [Thomas] *Aſſiſtant Engineer during the ſiege of the Havanna and Major of a Brigade in the Campaign of* 1764. *Joly* de *Maizeroy's* use of defenſive arms translated. 1771. 8. (1 ſh. 6 d.) Hiſtory of the late war in North-America and the Islands

lands of the Weſt-Indies, including the campaigns of 1763 and 1764. againſt the Indian enemies. 1773. 4. (1 L. 11 ſh. 6 d.) *Lucinda; or, the ſelf—devoted daughter. 1781. 8. (3 ſh.) Translation of *Joly de Maizeroy's* ſyſtem of Tactics. Vol. 1. 2. 1784. 8. (13 ſh.) Siege of Aubigné, a hiſtorical tale. 17..

MANTELL, [T.....] *Surgeon.* Short directions for the management of infants. 1786. 8. (2 ſh.)

MARAT, [J.... P.....] *M. D.* On gleets. 1776. 4. (1 ſh.) Enquiry into the nature, cauſe and cure of a ſingular diseaſe of the eyes. 1776. 4. (1 ſh.)

MARCH, [R.....] *Hoſier.* On ſilk, wool, worsted, cotton and thread — with remarks on frame — work knitting, knitting with wires —. 1779. 8. (1 ſh.)

MARGETTS, [......] Longitude tables for correcting the effect of parallax and refraction on the obſerv'd diſtance taken between the moon and the ſun or a fixed ſtar —. London 1790. 4.

MARJORIBANKS, [.....] *Major in the army.* (born in *Scotland.*) Trifles in verse. 8. Vol. 1. 2. 17..

MARKHAM, [Robert] *D. D: Rector of St. Mary's Whitechapel and Chaplain in ordinary to his Majeſty.* born: .... died d. 24 Sept. 1786.

MARKHAM, [William] *D. D: Lord-Archbishop of York.* (was Preceptor to the Prince of Wales and the Duke of York from 1771 to 1776.)
(Several ſingle ſermons.)

MARKLAND, [Jeremiah] born 1693. died at *Milton* near *Dorking*, in *Surry* d. 7 Jul. 1776.

MARRIOT, [George] *Rector of Alphamſtone, in Eſſex.* The primate, an ode. 1767. 4. (1 ſh.) The birth of the jeſuit, a poem. 1768. 4. (2 ſh. 6 d.) Three lectures, theological and critical —. 1772. 4. (2 ſh.) The jeſuit, an allegorical poem. 1773. 4. (2 ſh. 6 d.)

MARSDEN, [William] *F. R. S: F. A. S.* Account of a phenomenon obſerved upon the iſland of Sumatra. (Phil. Transact. 1781. p. 383.) Remarks on the Sumatran languages. (Arch. Vol. 6. p. 154.) Hiſtory of Sumatra. 1782. 4. (13 ſh.) überſ. Leipz. 1785.

1785. 8. übers. *Sprengel's* Beytr. zur Völker und Länderk. Th. 3. S. 273. Th. 4. S. 241. Observations on the language of the people commonly called gypsies. (Arch. Vol. 7. p. 382.) On the era of the Mahometans called the Hejera. (Phil. Transact. 1788. p. 414) On the chronology of the Hindoos. (Ibid. 1790. p. 560.)

MARSH, [Charles] On the elegant ornamental Cameos of the Barberini vase, with a view to an explanation of them end their reference to history. (Arch. Vol. 8. p. 316.)

MARSHALL, [Charles] *Master of Aldersgate Ward-School.* Introduction to the english tongue. 17.. Practical introduction to Arithmetic. 1774. 12. (1 sh.)

— [Edmund] *M. A. Vicar of Charing in Kent.* State of the evidence — relating to *Le Fevre's* specific for the gout. 1770. 8. (1 sh. 6 d.) Farther progress of the gout medicine of Dr. *Le Fevre* 1771. 8. (2 sh.)

— [George] *Architect.* Translation of *Anth. Desgodetz's* Ancient buildings of Rome. Vol. 1. 1771. fol. (2 L. 12 sh. 6 d.)

— [Humphry] Sketches of the solar spots. (Phil. Transact. 1774. p. 194.) Minutes of Agriculture, made on a farm of 300 acres of various soils, near Croydon, Surry. 1778. 4. (12 sh.) Experiments and observations concerning agriculture and the weather. 1779. 4. (7 sh. 6 d.) Arbustum Americanum: The american grove or an alphabetical catalogue of forest trees and shrubs, natives of the American united states. 1785. 8. (3 sh.) übers. durch C. *H. Hoffmann.* 1788. 8. Rural oeconomy of the county of Norfolk. Vol. 1. 2. 1787. 8. (12 sh.) Rural oeconomy of Yorkshire. Vol. 1. 2. 1788. 8. (12 sh.) Rural oeconomy of Gloucestershire. Vol. 1. 2. 1789. 8. (10 sh.) Rural oeconomy of the Midland counties; including the management of Live stock in Leicestershire and its environs. Vol. 1. 2. 1790. 8. (14 sh.)

— [Jane] *Mrs.* *History of Miss Clarinda Cathcart and Miss Fanny Renton. Vol. 1. 2. 1765. 8. (5 sh.) *History of Alicia Montagu, a novel. Vol. 1. 2. 1767. 8. (6 sh.) *Sir Harry Gaylove, or, Comedy in Embryo. 1772. 8. (2 sh. 6 d.) * A series of letters. Vol. 1. 2. 1788. 8. (6 sh.)

MARSHALL, [Joseph] born: .... died 17..

—— [William] *Esq.* Account of the black *Canker Caterpillar* which destroys the turnips in Norfolk. (Phil. Transact. 1783. p. 217.)

MARSHAM, [Robert] of *Stratton* in *Norfolk. F. R. S.* On the growth of trees. (Phil. Transact. 1761. p. 7.) On the usefullness of washing and rubbing the stems of trees, to promote their annual increase. (Ibid. 1777. p. 12. 1781. p. 449.) Indications of spring. (Ibid. 1789. p. 154.)

MARTEN, [Thomas] *A. M.* *Matth. Prioris* Almae Lib. III. latino versu donati. 1763. 8. (1 sh.) The marriage or history of four well known characters, translated from the french novel. Vol. 1. 2. 1771. 8. (5 sh.)

M'ARTHUR, [J.......] *of the Royal Navy.* The army and nauy gentleman's companion, or, a new treatise on the theory and practice of fencing —. 1781. 4. (10 sh. 6 d.)

MARTIN, [Benjamin] *Optician.* born 1704. died d. 9 Febr. 1782.

—— [John] Familiar dialogues between Americus and Britannicus in which the right of private judgment — are considered. 1776. 8. (1 sh.) The conquest of Canaan —. 1777. 8. (3 sh.) Thoughts on the duty of man, relative to faith in Jesus Christ —. P. 1. 2. 1789. 8. (3 sh.)

—— [John] *Lincoln's-Inn, London, one of the Solicitor's of the Court of Session — in Scotland.* The marriage law of Scotland stated —. 1787. 8. (1 sh.) Speech on the repeal of such parts of the test and corporation acts as affect conscientious dissenters —. 1790. 8. (6 d.)

—— [Matthew] *Member of the Bath Philosophical Society.* Observations of marine verms, insects —. Fasc. I. 1786. 4. (1 Sh. 6 d.) * The Aurelian's vade mecum, containing an english alphabetical and *Linnaean* systematical catalogue of plants affording nourishment to butterflies, hawk-moths and moths in the state of Caterpillar. 1784. 12. (1 sh.)

MARTINEAU, [Philipp Meadows] *Surgeon to the Norwich and Norfolk Hospital.* History of an uncomcommon enlargement of the abdomen, from an affection of the kidney. (*Duncan's* M. C. Vol. 9. p. 282.) An extraordinary case of a dropsy of the ovarium with some remarks. (Phil. Transact. 1884. p. 471. übers. Samml. f. A. Th. XI. S. 659.)

MARTYN, [Charles] of Lambeth Terrace, *Attorney and Solicitor.* Considerations on the qualifications, clerk ships, admissions, and practice of attornies —. 1790. 8. (1 sh. 6 d.)

MARTYN, [Thomas] *B. D: F. R. S: Professor of Botany in the University of Cambridge.* Sermon for Addenbrook's hospital. 1768. Catalogus horti botanici Cantabrigiensis. 1771. 8. (5 sh. 6 d.) The antiquities of Herculaneum translated from the Italian. Vol. 1. 1773. 4. (3 L. 3 sh.) Elements of natural history. 1775. 8. (1 sh. 6 d.) Addreß to the inhabitants of the parish of St. Anne, Westminster; with supplement: 1777. 8. (1 sh. 6 d.) *Ecclesiastical gallantry; or, the mystery unravelled, a tale. 1778. 4. (2 sh. 6 d.) Letter to — *Will. Wynne* LL. Chancellor of the Diocess of London —. 1780. 8. (1 sh.) *J. J. Rousseau's* letters on the elements of botany — translated: 1785. 8. (7 sh.) XXXVIII. plates drawn and engraved by *F. Nodder* botanical printer to her Majesty with explanations to illustrate *Linnaeus* system of vegetables and particularly adapted to the letters on the elements of botany. 1788. 8. (18 sh.)

— [Thomas] at *London.* The universal conchologist exhibiting the figure of every known shell accurately drawn and painted after nature with a new systematik arrangement. London 1784. fol. (7 L. 17 sh. 6 d.)

— [Thomas] of *Palgrave, Suffolk. F. A. S.* died 17..

— [Thomas] Hints of important uses to be derived from aerostatic globes —. fol. 1784. (2 sh.)

— [Thomas] The soldiers and sailors friend; an appeal to the people of Great-Britain. 1786. 8. (1 sh.)

MARVELL, [Andrew] born: .... died 17..

MARYATT, [Thomas] *M. D: Physician at Bristol, Somersetshire.* Therapevtics, or a new system of physic. 1775. 4. (1 L. 1 sh.)

MASERES, [Frances] *F. R. S: Cursitor Baron of the Court of Exchequer.* Dissertation on the use of the nega-

negative fign in Algebra —. 1759. 4. (14 fh.) Elements of plane trigonometry with a differtation on the nature and use of logarithms. 1760. 8. (7 fh.) View of the ancient conftitution of the english parliament. (Arch. Vol. 2 p. 301.) Account of the proceedings of the british and other proteftant inhabitants of the province of Quebec in North-America —. 1775. 8. (3 fh.) A Method of finding the value of an infinite feries of decreafing quantities of a certain form, when it converges too slowly to be fummed in the common way by the mere computation and addition or fubtraction of fome of its initial terms. (Phil. Transact. 1777. p. 187.) A method of finding, by the help of *Is. Newton's* binomial theorem a near value of the very slowly — converging infinite feries —. Ibid. 1778. p. 895.) A method of extending *Cardan's* rule for refolving one case of a cubik equation — to the other case of the fame equation, which it is not naturally fitted to folve, and which is therefore called the irreducible case. (Ibid. 1778. p. 902.) Appendix. (Ibid. 1780. p. 85.) *The Canadian freeholder. Vol. 1-3. 1779. 8. (15 fh.) Conjecture concerning the method by which *Cardan's* rules for resolving the cubic equation — were probably discovered by *Scipio Ferreus* of Bononia or whoever else was the firft inventor of them. (Phil. Transact. 1780. p. 221.) Principles of the doctrine of life annuities. Vol. 1. 2. 1783. 4. (1 L. 11 fh. 6 d.)

MASKELYNE, [Nevil] *D. D: F. R. S. at London and Gottingen: Aftronomer Royal.* A proposal for discovering the annual parallax of Sirius. (Phil. Transact. 1761. p. 889.) Theorem of the aberration of the rays of light refracted through a lens, on account of the imperfection of the fpherical figure. (Ibid. 1762. p. 17.) Observations to be made on the parallax of the moon at St. Helena, and recommending the fame to be made at Paris and Greenwich to fettle the difference of longitude between Paris and St. Helena. (Ibid. p. 21. p. 26.) Observations on the tranfit of Venus, June 6. 1761. at the island of St. Helena. (Ibid. p. 196.) Observations on Mr. *John Shelton's* clock, made at St.

St. Helena. (Ibid. p. 434.) The results of observations of the distance of the moon from the sun and fixed stars, made in a voyage from England to the island of St. Helena, in order to determine the longitude of the Ship from time to time; together with the whole process of computation, used on this occasion. (Ibid. p. 558.) Observations on the tides at St. Helena. (Ibid. p. 586.) Proposals for determining the difference of longitude between London Paris and Greenwich, by occultations of fixed Stars by the moon. (Ibid. 1762. p. 607.) The british mariner's guide, containing compleat and easy instructions for the discovery of the longitude at sea and land —. 1763. 4. (5 sh) Concise rules for computing the effects of refraction and parallax in varying the apparent distance of the moon from the sun or a star; also an easy rule of approximation for computing the distance of the moon from a star, the longitude and latitude of both being given, with demonstrations of the same. (Phil. Transact. 1764. p. 263.) Remarks upon the equation of time and the true manner of computing it. (Ibid. 1764. p. 336.) Astronomical observations at St. Helena. (Ibid. 1764. p. 348.) Observations on Mr. *Mason's* account of the going of Mr. *Ellicott's* clock at St. Helena. (Ibid. 1764. p. 380.) Astronomical observations at Barbadoes. (Ibid. 1764. p. 389.) Account of the going of *Harrison's* watch at the royal observatory — 1767. (2 sh. 6. d.) Introduction to Mr. *Smeaton's* papers, on the menstrual parallax, arising form the mutual gravitation of the earth and moon, and its influence on the observations of the sun and planets; and on a new method of observing the heavenly bodies out of the meridian. (Phil. Transact. 1768. p. 154.) Introduction to the observations made by *Ch. Mason* and *Jer. Dixon* for determining the length of a degree of latitude, in the provinces of Maryland and Pennsylvania in North-America. (Ibid. 1768. p. 270.) Length of a degree of latitude in the provinces of Maryland and Pennsylvania; deduced form the observations of Mason and Dixon. (Ibid. 1768. p. 323.) On the proportion of english and french measures. (Ibid. 1768.

1768. p. 326.) Observations on the tranſit of Venus over the ſun and on the eclipse of the ſun, June 3. 1769. (Ibid. p. 355.) Observations on the eclipses of Jupiter's firſt ſatellite in 1769. (Ibid. 1769. p. 399.) Observations on the occultations of fixed ſtars in 1769. at Greenwich. (Ibid. 1769. p. 399.) Observations on the eclipse of the moon Dec. 12. 1769. at Greenwich. (Ibid. 1769. p. 399.) Observations of the tranſit of Venus over the ſun, on June 3. 1769. made at the royal observatory Greenwich. (Tr. of A. S. Vol. 1. p. 105.) Letter — giving ſome account of the Hudſon's bay and other northern observations of the tranſit of Venus June 3. 1769. (Tr. of A. S. App. p 1.) Description of a method of measuring differences of right ascenſion and declination with *Dollond's* micrometer —. (Phil. Transact. 1771. p. 536.) Remarks on the *Hadley's* Quadrant —. (Phil. Transact. 1772. p. 99. and Nautical Almanac. 1774.) Method of clearing the apparent diſtance of the moon from a ſtar or the ſun of the effects of refraction and parallax by the help of three tables. (Nautical Almanac. 1772.) *M. de Luc's* rule for measuring hights by the barotér, reduced to the engliſh measure of length and adapted to *Fahrenheit's* thermometer and other ſcales of heat and reduced to a more convenient expreſſion. (Phil. Transact. 1774. p. 158.) Observations of eclipses of Jupiter's firſt ſatellite made at the royal observatory at Greenwich, compared with observations of the ſame made by *Sam. Holland* and others of his party, in ſeveral parts of North-America and the longitudes of the places thence deduced. (Ibid. 1774. p. 184.) Immerſions and emerſions of Jupiter's firſt ſatellite, obſerved at Jupiter's inlet, on the island of Anticoſti, North-America by *Thom. Wright* — and the longitude of the place deduced from compariſon with obſervations, made at Greenwich. (Ibid. 1774. p. 190.) Tables for computing the apparent places of the fixt ſtars and reducing observations of the planets. 1774. fol. (15 ſh) Account of observations made on the mountain Schehallien for finding its attraction. (Phil. Transact. 1775. p. 500.) Proposal for measuring the attraction of ſome hill in this kingdom by by aſtronomical obſervations. (Ibid. 1775. p. 494.) Account of a new inſtrument for meaſuring ſmall angles called the priſmatic micrometer. (Ibid. 1777. p. 799.) Longitude of Cork ſettled from Dr. *Longfield's* obſervations. (Ibid. 1779. p. 179.) Aſtronomical obſervations made at the royal obſervatory at Greenwich from the Y. 1765-1783. Vol. 1. 2. 1776. 1784. fol. (2 L. 8 ſh) Part of Vol. 3. 1788. fol. Advertiſement of the expected return of the comet of 1532 and 1661. in the Y. 1788. (Phil. Tranſact. 1786. p. 426.) The latitude and longitude of the royal obſervatory at Greenwich, with remarks on a memorial of the late M. *Caſſini* de Thury. (Ibid. 1787. p. 151.) Attempt to explain a difficulty in the theory of viſion, depending on the different refrangibility of light (Ibid. 1789. p. 256.) überſ. *Gren* J. d. P. Th. 2. S. 370.

MASON, [Charles] Obſervations for proving the going of *Ellicott's* clock at St. Helena. (Phil. Tranſact. 1762. p. 534.) Obſervations for determining a degree of latitude in Maryland and Pennſylvania. (Ibid. 1768 p. 274.) Aſtronomical obſervations made in the forks of the river Brandivine in Pennſylvania for determining the going of a clock ſent thither by the royal ſociety, in order to find the difference of gravity between the royal obſervatory at Greenwich, and the place where the clock was ſet up in Pennſylvania. (Ibid. 1768. p. 329.) Obſervations on the tranſit of Venus June 3. 1769. at Cavan. (Ibid. 1770. p. 488.) Aſtronomical obſervations made at Cavan near Strabane in the county of Donegal, Ireland. (Ibid. 1770. p. 454.)

—— [John] *Surgeon, at Leiceſter.* Two caſes of dropſy ſucceſſfully treated by moderate doſes of opium. (Med. Obs. Vol. 6. p. 19.)

—— [John Monck] *Commiſſioner of Revenue for the Kingdom of Ireland, privy Counſellor and Member of Parliament. Philipp Maſſinger's* dramatic works — with notes and his life and writings. Vol. 1-4. 1779. 8. (1 L. 1 ſh.) Comments on (*Reed's*) edition of *Shakeſpeare's* plays. 1785. 8. (5 ſh.)

MASON, [Sarah] *Mrs.* °The lady's affiftant for regulating and fupplying her table —. 1773. 8. (6 fh.) Ed. 2. 1775. 8. (6 fh.)

—— [William] *M. A: Prebendary of York.* (born at *Hull Yorkshire.* 1736.) Ode at the inftallation of the Duke of Newcaftle, Chancellor of the Univerfity of Cambridge. 1749. 4. Elfrida; a dramatic poem. Ed. 1. 1751. 4. (2 fh. 6 d.) Ed. 2. 1752. 8. (1 fh. 6 d.) Ed. 3. altered for theatrical representation. 1779. 8. (1 fh. 6 d.) (bearbeitet von *J. J. Bertuch.* 1775. 8. Odes. 1756. 4. (1 fh.) *Caractacus, a dramatic poem. 1759. 4. (2 fh. 6 d.) 1759. 8. (1 fh. 6 d.) Ed. 3. (with the Author's name. 1776. 8. (1 fh. 6 d.) Elegies. 1762. 4. (1 fh.) Poems 1764. 8. (3 fh.) The english garden. Book. 1-4. 1772-1781. 4. (9 fh.) Ed. 2. with commentary and notes by *W. Burgh.* 1785. 8. (4 Sh.) überf. (von C. F. *Weiffe*) Leipz. 1773. 8. überf. Leipz. 1782. °Chorus of the dramatic poem of Elfrida. 1772. 4. (6 d.) *Gray's* poems with memoirs of his life and writings 1775. 4. (15 Sh.) überf. Leipz. 1776. 8. Ode to the naval officers of Great-Britain —. 1779. 4. (6 d.) Ode to the Honourable *Will. Pitt.* 1782. 4. (1 Sh.) *Archaeological epiftle to — *Jerem. Milles* on his edition of *Rowley's* poems. 1782. 4. (1 Sh.) Epiftle to — *Will. Pitt* — petitioning for the vacant Laureatship. 1785. 4. (6 d.) *Ch. Alph. du Fresnoy's* Art of painting, translated with notes by *Josh. Reynolds* 1783. 4. (8 Sh.) *Will. Whitehead's* poems, with his life and writings. Vol. 1-3. 1788. 8. (12 Sh.) Animadverfions on the present government of the York lunatic afylum —. 1788. 8. (1 Sh.) Secular ode in commemoration of the glorious revolution 1688. 4. 1788. (1 Sh.) Sermon on the African slave trade. 1788. 4. (1 Sh.)

MASSEY, [James] *Esq.* On Saltpeter. (Mem. of M. Vol. 1. p. 184.)

MASSON, [Francis] *Gardener.* Account of three journeys from the *Cape Town* into the fouthern parts of *Africa;* undertaken for the discovery of new plants, towards the improvement of the royal botanical gardens at Kew. (Phil. Transact. 1776. p. 268.) Account of the Island of St. Miguel. (Ibid.

(Ibid. 1778. p. 601.) überſ. *Ebeling's* N. Samml. von Reiſen. Th. 2. S. 511.

MASSON, [Georg] An easy, comprehenſive and familiar French grammar —. 1771. 12. (2 ſh.)

MASTERS, [Robert] *B. D: F. A. S: Rector of Landbeach, Cambridgeshire.* Memoirs of the life and writings of the late *Thom. Baker*, B. D. of St. John's College —. 1784. 8. (4 ſh.) Remarks on *Walpole's* hiſtoric doubts on the life and reign of King Richard III. (Arch. Vol. 2. p. 198.) Account of ſome ſtone coffins and ſkeletons. (Ibid. Vol. 8 p. 63.) Account of an ancient painting on glaſſ. (Ibid. p. 321.)

MATHIAS, [Thomas James] Runic odes. 1781. 4. (1 ſh. 6. d.) On the evidence external and internal relating to the poems attributed to *Thom. Rowley* —. 1783. 8. (2 ſh. 6. d.)

MATTHEWS, [John] *Lieutenant in the Royal Navy.* Voyage to the river Sierra Leona on the coaſt of Africa —. 1788. 8. (4 ſh.) überſ. Leipzig. 1789.

— [Stephen] *Surgeon in the Eaſt-India Company's Service.* Observations on hepatic diseases, incidental to Europeans in the Eaſt-Indies. 1783. 8. (5 ſh.)

— [William] Appeal to the ſociety in general and his friends in particular. 1784. 12. (9. d.) The life and character of *Thomas Letchworth.* 1786. 12. (1 ſh. 6. d.) The miſcellaneous companions. Vol. 1-3. 1787. 8. (9 ſh.)

MAUDE, [Thomas] Wensley — dale; or, rural contemplations, a poem. 1772. 8. (2 ſh. 6 d.)

MAUDUIT, [Israel] *F. A. S.* born 1708. died d. 14 Jun. 1787.

MAVE, [Thomas] *Gardener.* ſee *John Abercrombie.*

MAULE, [John] *A. M: Chaplain.* see *John Cooke.*

MAVOR, [William] of *Oxford.* Parnaſſian ſprigs; or, poetic miscellanies. 1777. 8. (2 ſh. 6 d.) Blenheim, a poem. 1787. 4. (3 ſh.) *New description of Blenheim, the ſeat of the Duke of Marlborough with the poem Blenheim. 1789. 8. (3 ſh. 6 d.)

— [William Fordyce] *Maſter of the Academy at Woodſtock.* Univerſal ſtenography; or, a new complete ſyſtem of short-writing —. Ed. 2. 1785. 8. (10 ſh. 6 d.)

6 d.) Elegy to the memory of Capt. *James King*, LL. D: F. R. S. 1785. 4. (1 Sh.)

MAURICE, [Thomas] *A. M: Clergyman of Woodford, Essex.* Netherby; a poem. 1776. 4. (2 ſh. 6 d.) Poems and miscellaneous pieces, with a free translation of the Oedipus Tyrannus of *Sophocles*. 1779. 4. (10 ſh. 6 d.) Jerne rediviva: an Ode. 1782. 4. (1 ſh.) Weſtminſter Abbey: an Elegiac poem. 1784. 4. (3 ſh.) *Letter to the — Court of Directors of the Eaſt-India Company, containing proposals for printing a hiſtory of the revolutions of the Empire of Indoſtan, from the earlieſt ages to the present —. 1790. 8. (1 ſh.)

(Several ſingle ſermons.)

MAWHOOD, [P.....] of *Polandſtreet.* *Appeal to the public, relative to a cause lately determined in the Court of Chancery —. 1774. 4. (1 ſh. 6 d.) *Letter to the Solicitor-general; being an appendix to the appeal to the public —. 1774. fol. (6 d.) *The neceſſity of limiting the power of the practitioners in the ſeveral courts of juſtice and of making effectual the law for taxing the bills of attornies and Solicitors —. 1775. 4. (6 d.) *Petition intended to have been presented to the high court of judicature — relative to a case — published, an appeal to the public —. 1775. 4. (1 ſh.) *Addreſſ to the public, ſetting forth — a case of unlawful imprisonment —. 1775. 4. (1 ſh.) Thoughts on the ſeveral regulations neceſſary to the appointment of an advocate-general —. 1776. 4. (2 ſh.) *A Matter of moment reſpecting the examination of witneſſes in chancery. 1776. 8. (6 d.)

MAXWELL, [Patrick] *Surgeon to the 54th Regiment.* Hiſtory of a ſingular dropſical affection of the ſcrotum, terminating fatally. (*Duncan's* M. C. 1790. Dec. 2. Vol. 5. p. 399.)

MAY, [Edward] Remarkable extracts, ſelected from a work printed in the Year 1687. by *Peter Jurieu*, entitled: the accomplishment of the ſcripture prophecies. 1790. 8. (1 ſh.)

—— [Nicholas] *Surgeon at Plymouth.* born: .... died d. 7 March. 1784.

—— [T....] King Asa, a Poem, in VI books ſounded on 1 Kings XV, 11. 1790. 8. (2 ſh.)

MAY,

MAY, [Vaughan] *Surgeon at Plymouth.* Observations on the influenza, as it appeared at Plymouth in the summer and autumn of the year 1788. (*Duncan's* M. C. Dec. 2. Vol. 4. p. 363.)

— [William] *M. D: Physician at Maidstone.* Account of the successful termination of a case attended with symptoms of phthisis pulmonalis, with remarks on the treatment of that disease. (Lond. Med. Journ. Vol. IX. Part. 3.) übers. Samml. f. A. Th. 13. S. 102. Account of an epidemic fever that prevailed in Cornwall in the Year 1788. (Lond. M. J. Vol. X. P. 2.) Account of an epidemic fever; with remarks on the treatment of fevers in general. 1790. 8.

MAYNE, [.....] *Mrs.* *Abridgment of the sacred history —. 1770. 8. (1 sh.)

MAYO, [Herbert] *D. D: a Dissenting clergyman.* The scripture doctrine of baptism. 1766. *Apology and a shield for protestant dissenters of instability and misrepresentation, four letters to *Newton* — by a dissenting minister. 1784. 8. (2 sh. 6 d.)

MAYWOOD, [Robert] of the *Isle of Wight. M. D.* On the operation of Mercury in the human body —. 1787. 8. (1 sh. 6 d.)

MAZZINGHY, [...] *M. L.* The new guide through the cities of London and Westminster, the borough of Southwark and parts adjacent. 1785. 12. (3 sh. 6 d.)

M'CAUSLAND, [Richard] *Surgeon to the King's* 8 *Regim. of Foot.* Particulars relative to the nature and customs of the Indians of North-America. (Phil. Transact. 1786. p. 229.)

— [Robert] *M. D.* Conjectures on some of the phaenomena of the barometer and on the inversion of objects on the retina. 1788. 8. (1 sh.) Facts and observations on different medical subjects. (*Duncan's* M. C. Vol. 8. p. 247.) übers. Samml. f. A. Th. XI. S. 245.

M'CLUER, [John] Description of the coast of India 1787 and 1788. published at the charge of the East-India Company by *Alex. Dalrymple.* 1789. 4.

M'CULLOCH, [Lewis] Observations on the herring fisheries, on the north and east coasts of Scotland —. 1788. 8. (1 sh. 6 d.)

MEADER, [James] The modern gardener; or universal kalendar —. 1771. 12. (5 sh.) The planter's guide, or, pleasure gardener's companion —. 1779. (3 sh. 6 d.)

MEARES, [John] *Lieutenant of the Royal Navy.* Voyages, made in the Years 1788 and 1789. from China to the North-West coast of America. 1790. 4. Authentic copy of memorial presented to the house of Commons 13 May 1790. containing every particular respecting the capture of the vessels in Nootka Sound. 1790. 8. (1 sh. 6 d.)

MEDALLE, [.....] *Mrs.* (Daughter of *Laur. Sterne*) Published: the letters of *Laur. Sterne* to his most intimate friends with memoirs of his life and family. Vol. 1-3. 1775. 8. (7 sh. 6 d.)

MEDLEY, [Samuel] Intemperate zeal reproved and christian baptism defended, in a letter —. 1776. 8. (1 sh. 6 d.) Sermon: the spiritual merchant described and the gain of true godlineſſ proved. 1777. 8. (6 d.)

MEEK, [John] *M. D: Physician at Tralkirk.* History of a fractured sternum. (Eſſ. and Observ. Edinb. Vol. 3. p. 505.) Account of two people recovered that were apparently drowned. (Reports of the humane society for 1776.)

MEILAN, [Mark Anthony] *Private Teacher of the English Language.* Emilia, a tragedy. 17.. Northumberland, a tragedy. 17.. The friends, a Comedy. 1771. 8. (6 sh.) Dramatic works —. 1771. 8. (6 sh.) Grammar of the English language. 1772. 12. (1 sh. 6 d.) Translation of *Berquin's* children's friend —. 1787. 16. Vol. 1-24. (12 sh.) The friend of youth. Vol. 1-12. 1787. 12. (12 sh.) Sermons for children. Vol. 1-3. 1789. 8. (9 sh.)

MELLISH, [Charles] Observations on *Maseres's* view of the ancient constitution of the English parliament. (Arch. Vol. 2. p. 341.)

MELMOTH, [Courtney] see *Robert Pratt.*

MELMOTH, [William] Letters of *Thom. Fitzosborne.* Ed. 3. 1747. *Ciceronis* epistolae, translated with re-

remarks: Vol. 1-3. 1753. (15 sh.) *Plinii* epistolae translated: 17.. *Ciceronis* Cato; or an essay on old age, with remarks. 1777. 8. (5 sh.) *Ciceronis* Laelius: or an essay on friendship, with remarks. 1777. 8. (5 sh.)

MELMOTH, [William Henry] *Esq.* The new universal story teller. 17... A new, complete and universal roman history. 1781. 12. (3 sh.)

MELVILL, *Lieutenant General: F. A. S.* Observations on an antient sword. (Arch. Vol. 7. p. 374.)

MELVILL, [John] *M. D.* Observations on the nature and properties of fixible air, and on the salutary effects of the aqua salubris, in preserving health, and preventing diseases. 1789. 8. (2 sh.)

MEMIS, [John] *Physician in Aberdeen and a Manager of the Royal Infirmary in that city.* On the prevention and cure of diseases in general. 1786. 8.

MENDHAM, [Thomas] of *Briston, Norfolk.* Dialogue in answer to *Potter* on the poor laws. 1775. 8. (1 sh.) Thoughts on the doctrines of election, reprobation, freewill, the fall of man and his restoration through Christ Jesus. 1780. 12. (1 sh.)

MENNEL, [G....] *Lieutenant of his Majesty's ship, Namur.* Religion; a poem. 1770. 4. (1 sh.)

MEREDITH, [Nicholas] *Optical and mathematical Instrument Maker to his R. H. the Duke of York.* Considerations on the utility of conductors for lightning; —. 1789. 8. (1 sh.)

MERRIMAN, [B....] *Letter to the committee of the court of common council on the effects of the excess of copper money now in circulation —. 1786. 8. (1 sh.)

MERRY, [Robert] *Member of the Florence Academy.* Paulina, or the Russian daughter, a poem. 1787. 4. (3 sh.) (Several poetical pieces in the *Florence Miscellany* and in *the World.*)

— [Walther] Remarks on the coinage of England from the earliest to the present times —. 1789. 8. (2 sh.)

MEYLER, [William] Monody on the death of *Dav. Garrick.* 1779. 4. (1 sh.)

MEYRICK, [William] *Surgeon.* The new family herbal; or domestic physician: enumerating — all the

the known vegetables which are remarkable for medical efficacy —. 1790. 8. (14 Sh.)

M'GOUAN, [John] Extract of meteorological observations made at Hawkhill, near Edinburgh. (Phil. Transact. 1778. p. 562.)

M'GUIRE, [Arthur] Description of a new portable barometer. (Transact. of J. A. 1787. p. 41.)

MICHELL, [Henry] *M. A: Vicar at Brigthelmstone.* born 1714. died d. 31 Oct. 1789.

— [John] *B. D: F. R. S.* On the means of discovering the distance, magnitude of the fixed stairs in consequence of the diminution of the velocity of their light, in case such a diminution should be found to take place in any of them, and such other data should be procured from observations as would be farther necessary for that purpose. (Phil. Transact. 1784. p. 35.)

MICKLE, [Will. Julius] born at *Kelso* in *Cumberland* side of the *Tweed.* 1734. died d. 25 Oct. 1788.

MIDDLETON, [Erasmus] *Lecturer of St. Bennet's and St. Helene's, Chaplain to the Countess of Crawford and Lindsay.* Biographica evangelica: or account of the lives and deaths of the most eminent authors or preachers, both british and foreign in the several denominations of protestant, from the reformation to the present time. Vol. 1-4. 1779-1786. 8. (1 L. 6 sh. 6 d.)

MILES, [Jeremiah] *D. D: Dean of Exeter and President of A. S.* born 1713, died d. 13 febr. 1784.

— [William Augustus] Letter to *John Fielding* on the suppression of the beggar's opera. 1773. 8. (1 sh.) The artifice; a comic opera. 1780. 8. (1 sh.) Remarks on the act 15 Georg III. for the encouragement of the New Foundland fishery —. 1779. 4. (2 sh.) Summer amusements; or, an adventure at Margate, a comic opera. 1779.

MILLAR, [Francis] The husband'mans directory. 1771. 12. (2 sh.)

— [John] *M. D: Physician at Waltham Abbey; Essex.* Diss. De fluxu lochiorum immodico. Edinb. 1757. 8. Observations on the asthma and on the hooping cough. 1769. (3 sh.) übersezt: nebst einem Anhang von der stinkenden Assa. Leipzig. 1769. 8. Obserservations on antimony. 1774. 8. (2 ſh.) *Observations on the practice in the medical department of the Weſtminſter general dispensary — by order of the governors. 1777. 4 (5 ſh.) Observations on the prevailing diseases in Great-Britain —. 1778. 4. (12 ſh.). Observations on the management of diseases in the army and navy, during the American war; with ſome account of the loſſ of Senegal and of the army at York in Virginia in reply to D. *Monro*. 1783. 4. (3 ſh.)

MILLAR, [John] *Profeſſor of Civil and Scottiſh Law in the Univerſity of Glasgow.* Observations concerning the diſtinction of ranks in ſociety 1771. 4. (9 ſh.) Ed. 2. 1773. 8. (5 ſh.) überſ. Leipzig. 1772. 8. Hiſtorical view of the Engliſh government, from the ſettlement of the Saxons in Britain, to the acceſſion of the house of Stewart. 1787. 4. (18 ſh.)

— [John] *Esq. Advocate.* Elements of the law relating to insurances. 1787. 8. (7 ſh.)

— [John] *Surgeon at Stronoway, in the Island of Lewis.* The hiſtory of the case of a girl, who lived for 18 days on a barren moor, and in a cold climate, without any other ſubsiſtence but water. (*Duncan's* M. C. Dec. 2. Vol. 4. p. 360.)

MILLER, [.....] *Mrs.* born: .... died at *Briſtol Hot Wells.* d. 25. June. 1781.

— [Charles] Account of the Island of Sumatra. (Phil. Transact. 1778. p. 160.) überſ. *Ebeling's* N. Samml. von Reiſen. Th. 1. S. 1.

— [Patrick] The elevation, ſection, plan and views of a triple vessel and of wheels. Edinb. 1787. fol.

— [Peter] of *Ephrata in Pennsylvania.* Method of preserving pease from the worms. (Tr. of A. S. Vol. 1. p. 243.) Description of the grotto at Swatara. (Tr. of A. S. Vol. 2. p. 177.)

— [Philipp] *F. R. S: Gardener at Chelsea, Middlesex.* born 1691. died d. 18 Dec. 1771.

— [S.......] On the cause of motion; or a general theory of physics —. 1787. 4. (10 ſh. 6 d.)

MILLINGTON, [L.......] *Esq.* On the cultivation and preparation of aloes in the Island of Barbadoes. (Lond. M. J. Vol. VIII. P. 4.)

MILLS, [Abraham] *Esq* Account of the ſtrata and volcanic appearances in the north of Ireland and weſtern Islands of Scotland. (Phil. Transact. 1790. p. 73.) überſ. Gren. J. d. P. Th. 3. S. 253.

—— [John] *F. R S.* Memoirs of the court of Auguſtus. continued and compleated from the original papers of the late *Thom. Blackwell.* Vol. 3. 1763. 4to (1 L. 1 ſh) *Translation of *Du-Hamel's* practical treatise of husbandry. 1759. 4. (16 ſh.) Syſtem of practical husbandry Vol. 1-5. 1765. 8. (1 L. 4 ſh.) überſezt von *C. F. Jünger.* Th. 1-5. 1767. 8. On the management of bees. 1766. 8. (3 ſh.) On the weather —. 1770. 8. (2 ſh) Translation of *G. A. Gyllenborg's* natural and chemical elements of agriculture. 1770. 8. *Eſſays moral, philosophical and political. 1772. 8. (5 ſh.) Treatise on cattle —. 1776. 8. (6 ſh.)

—— [Samuel Gillam] *Surgeon at Greenwich in Kent.* Account of the dissection of an extraordinary tumour arising from the 5 and 6 ribs. (Med. Com. of Ed. Vol. 5. p. 430) Case of a young lady who ſwallowed a pin. (London M. J. Vol. 6. p. 36.)

—— [William] The georgic of *Virgil*, translated into engliſh verse. 1780. 4. (6 ſh.)

MILMAN, [Francis] *M. D: F. R. S.* Animadversiones de natura hydropis eiusque curatione —. 1779. 8. (3 ſh.) translated by *Schwediaur.* 1786. 8. (3 ſh.) On the ſource of the ſcurvy and putrid fevers —. 1782. 8. (3 ſh.) Account of two inſtances of the true ſcurvy, ſeemingly occasioned by the want of due nourishment. (Med. Transact. Vol. 2. p. 471.)

MILN, [Robert] *A. M.* Course of physico-theological lectures on the ſtate of the world, from the creation to the deluge. 1786. 8. (6 ſh.)

MILNE, [Colin] *D. D: Evening-Preacher to the London Lying — in Hospital.* Botanical dictionary or elements of ſyſtematic and philosophical botany —. 1770. 8. (5 ſh.) *Linnaei* Inſtitutiones botanicae, translated, with a view of the ancient and pre-

present ſtate of botany and a ſynopsis, exhibiting the essential or ſtriking characters which ſerve to discriminate genera of the ſame claſſ and order. P. 1. 2. 1772. Supplement. 1778. 4. (15 ſh.)

MILNER, [Joseph] *M. A: Maſter of the Grammar School of Kingſton upon Hull. Gibbon's* account of chriſtianity considered. 1781. 8. (3 ſh.) Essays on ſeveral religious ſubjects chiefly tending to illuſtrate the ſcripture doctrine of the influence of the holy ſpirit. 1789. 12. (2 Sh.)

—— [Isaac] *B. D: F. R. S. President of Queen's College; Cambridge.* Reflections on the communication of motion by impact and gravity. (Phil. Transact. 1778. p. 344.) Observations on the limits of algebraical equations; and a general demonſtration of *DesCartes* rule for finding their number of affirmative and negative roots. (Ibid. 1778. p. 380.) On the precession of the equinoxes produced by the ſun's attraction. (Ibid. 1779. p. 505.) On the production of nitrous acid and nitrous air. (Ibid. 1789. p. 300.) überſ. *Gren* J. d. P. Th. 3. S. 83.

—— [Thomas] *M. D.* Experiments and observations in electricity. 1783. 8. (2 Sh.)

MILTON, [Marmeduke] *Esq.* St. James ſtreet, a poem. 1790. 4.

MINIFIE, [.....] *Miſſ.* The hiſtories of Lady Frances S — and Lady Caroline S. Vol. 1 - 4. 1763. 8. (12 Sh.) *Family pictures; a novel: —. Vol. 1. 2. 1764. 8. (4 Sh.) The picture: a Novel. Vol. 1. - 3. 1766. 8. (9 Sh.) The cottage; a Novel. 1769. Vol. 1-3. (7 Sh. 6 d.) *Barford Abbey, a Novel; Vol. 1. 2. 1768. 8. The Count de Poland. Vol. 1 - 4. 1780. 8. (10 Sh.)

MINSHULL, [F.....] Ode. 1788. 4. (1 Sh.)

MINTO, [Walter] *L. L. D.* Reſearches into ſome parts of the theory of the planets —. 1783. 8. (2 Sh. 6 d.) — and *Dav. Stewart's* Earl of *Buchan*, account of the life, writings and inventions of *John Napier* of Merchiſton 1788. 4. (7 Sh. 6 d.)

MITCHELL, [Archibald] *Late Major of Engineers; belonging to the Eſtabliſhment of Fort St. George.* Thoughts on the treaty between government and Eaſt India Company —. 1780. 4. (1 Sh. 6 d.)

MITCHELL, [G.....] *Surgeon at Wapping.* Incontinence of urine, cured by the use of the flexible catheter. (Med. Obs. Vol. 6. p. 169.)

MITFORD, [John] *Esq.* On the pleadings in ſuits in the court of chancery by engliſh bill. Ed. 2. 1787. 8. (7 Sh. 6 d.)

—— [William] *Colonel of the Hampſhire Militia, Member of Parliament for Newport in the County of Cornwall F. R. S.* Hiſtory of Greece. Vol. 1. 2. and additions to the Vol. 1. 1784. 1790. 4. (1 L. 19 Sh.)

M'KINNON, [Charles] Eſſays on the following ſubjects; wealth and force of nations: authenticity of *Oſſian;* accompanyment, exiſtence of body, fortification, battle. 1785. 8. (4 Sh.)

M'LACHLAN, [Alexander] *M. D.* Hiſtory of a ſingular caſe of purulent aſcites, cured by tapping. (*Duncan's* M. C. Vol. 9. p. 360.)

M'LAREN, [Archibald] The conjuror, or the ſcotsman in London, a farce. 1781. 8.

M'LEAN, [Archibald] Letter on the ſonship of Chriſt. 1788. 12. (1 Sh.)

M'NAYR, [James] Syſtem of English conveyancing, adopted to Scotland. 1789. 4. (12 ſh. 6 d.) Eſſay to demonſtrate that contingent debts, cannot, by law be ranked on eſtates ſequeſtered in terms of the ſtatute 23. Geo. III. Cap. 18. —. 1790. 8. (2 ſh.)

M'NICOL, [Donald] *A. M: Miniſter of the Highlanders of Scotland.* Remarks on *Sam. Johnson's* Journey to the Hebrides. 1780. 8. (4 ſh.)

MOFFAT, [John] *M. D. Aretaeus*, on the cauſes ſymptoms and cure of acute and chronic diſeaſes. tranſlated from the Greek. 1785. 8. (6 ſh.) The prognoſtics and prorrhetics of *Hippocrates*, tranſlated with an account of the life of *Hippocrates.* 1788. 8. (6 ſh.)

MOFFATH, [John Marks] On the duty and intereſt of private perſons at the preſent juncture. 1778. 8. (2 ſh. 6 d.) Proteſtant's prayer-book —. 1783. 8. (—).

MOFFAT, [Thomas] *M. D: In Connecticut.* born 1700. died. d. 14. March. 1787.

MOIR, [John] *Clergyman.* (born in Scotland.) Diſcourſes on practical ſubjects. 1776. 8. (3 ſh.) Sermons on-

on-interesting subjects in religion and life. 1784. 8. (5 sh.) History of the life and public services of Mr. *Fox*. 17. Transactions in India from 1760 to the present time. 17.

MOIRA, [....] *Countess*. Account of a human skeleton found in *Drumkeragh* in the county of *Down*. (Arch. Vol. 7. p. 90.)

MOLE, [John] Element of Algebra —. 1788. 8. (5 sh.)

—— [Thomas] of *Uxbridge*, *Dissenting Minister*. born: .... died. 17..

MOLINEUX, [Thomas] The Scholar's question-book: or, a practical introduction to arithmetic —. 1781. 12. (2 sh.) Ed. 2. 1787. 12. (1 sh. 6 d.) The key to the second edition of the scholar's question book —. 1787. 12. (6 d.)

MOLLESON, [William] *Secretary to the Commissioners*. Reports of the Commissioners appointed to examine take and state the public accounts of the kingdom —. 1783. 4. Vol. 1. (1 L. 1 sh.) Vol. 2. see *John Lane*.

MOLSEWORTH, [......] Description of the druid temple lately discovered on the top of the hill near St. Hillary in Jersey. (Arch. Vol. 8. p. 384.)

MONBODDO, Lord, see *James Burnet*.

MONKE, [G..... P......] *Lieutenant in the Navy*. The life of *Voltaire* with notes: translated from the French. 1787. 8. (6 sh.)

MONKHOUSE, [Thomas] at *Oxford*. *State papers collected by *Edward* Earl of *Clarendon*. Vol. IIId 1786. fol. (2 L. 2 sh.)

MONRO, [Alexander] *M. D. Professor of Physic, Anatomy and Surgery at Edinburgh*. Diss. De testibus et de semine in variis animalibus. Edinb. 1755. 8. De vasis lymphaticis valvulosis et de earum inprimis origine. Berolini. 1757. 8. Ed. 2. 1770. 8. Observations anatomical and physiological wherein D. *Hunter's* claim to some discoveries is examined. 1758. 8. Answer to the notes on the postscript to observations anatomical and physiological. 1758. 8. A state of the facts concerning the paracentesis of the thorax, on account of air effused from the lungs into the cavities of the pleura; and concerning the discovery of the lymphatics in oviparous

rous animals. 1770. 8. Observations on gravid uteri. (Eſſ. and Observ. Edinb. Vol. 1.) The diſſection of a monſtruous foetus. (Ibid. Vol. 2.) The hiſtory of a genuine valvulus of the inteſtines. (Ibid. Vol. 2.) Experiments to determine how far opium, ardent ſpirits, and eſſential oils affect animals, by acting on the nerves to which they are applied, and bringing the reſt of the ſyſtem into ſufferance, by what is called ſympathy; and how far they affect animals by being absorbed. (Ibid. Vol. 3.) An account of a polypus in the pharynx and oeſophagus. (Ibid. Vol. 3.) A case in proof of the uſefulneſſ of mercury in convulſive disorders. (Ibid. Vol. 3.) Observations on the ſtructure and functions of the nervous ſyſtem. 1783. fol. (2 L. 12 ſh. 6 d.) überſ. (von *Soemmering*) Leipz. 1787. 4. The ſtructure and phyſiology of fiſhes explained and compared with those of man and other animals. 1785. fol. (2 L. 2 ſh.) überſ. von *J. G. Schneider*. Leipz. 1787. 4. Description of all the bursae mucosae of the human body —. 1788. fol. (12 ſh.)

MONRO, [Donald] *M. D: Phyſician to the Army: F. R. S.* The Diſſection of a woman with child. (Eſſ. and Observ. Edinb. Vol. 1. p. 463.) Diſſ. De hydrope. Edinb. 1753. 8. On the dropsy and its different ſpecies. 1755. 8. (1 ſh. 6 d.) Ed. 2. 1756. Ed. 3. 1765. 8. Cases of anevrisms. (Eſſ. and Observ. Edinb. Vol. 3. p. 178.) Account of the Lisbon diet drink. (Ibid. p 402.) Observations on the ſtate of the inteſtines in old dysenteries. (Ibid. p. 516.) On the use of mercury in convulſive disorders. (Ibid. p. 551.) Account of uncommon case of the venereal disorder. (Med. Transact. Vol. 2. p. 337.) Account of a violent ſcurvy of the venereal disorder of an obſtinate intermitting fever, of a tumour on the brain, of a hydrocephalus, of oſſifications in the meſentery. (Ibid. Vol. 2. p. 325.) Account of the diseases in the british military hospitals in Germany from Year 1761-1763. 8. 1764. (5 ſh.) überſ. von *J. E. Wichmann*. Altenb. 1766. Account of ſome neutral ſalts made with vegetable acids and with the ſalt of amber. (Phil. Transact. 1767. p. 479.) On mineral waters. Vol. 1. 2. 1770. 8. (10 ſh. 6 d.) Account of a

puer

pure native cryſtallised natron or foſſile alkaline ſalt, which is found in the country of Tripoli in Barbary. (Phil. Transact. 1771. p. 567.) Account of the ſulphureous mineral waters of Caſtle-Loed and *Fairburn* in the county of Roſſ and of the ſalt purging water of Pitkeathly in the county of *Perth* in Scotland. (Ibid. 1772. p. 15.) Praelectiones medicae ex *Cronii* inſtituto et oratio anniversaria ex *Harveji* inſtituto. 1776. 8. (4 ſh.) (einzelne Stücke überſ. in den Samml. f. A. Th. 5. S. 124-193.) Account of the late influenza. (*Duncan's* M. C. Vol. 9. p. 400.) On the means of preserving the health of ſoldiers and of conducting military hospitals. Vol. 1. 2. 1780. 8. (10 ſh.) überſ. Altenb. Th. 1. 2. 1784. 8. A medical and pharmaceutical chemiſtry and the materia medica. Vol. 1-3. with appendix. 1788-1790. (1 L. 4 ſh.) überſ. Samml. f. A. Th. 13. S. 195.) überſ. von *Sam. Hahnemann.* Th. 1. Leipz. 1791. 8. Account of the method of making the Otter of Roses, as it is prepared in the Eaſt-Indies. (Tr. of E. S. Vol. 2. p. 12.)

MONRO, [Janes] *Captain.* Narrative of the military operations on the Coromandel coaſt, againſt the combined forces of the French, Dutch and Hyder Ally Cawn, from 1780 to the peace in 1784. 4. 1789. (1 L. 1 ſh.)

MONTAGU, [.....] *Mrs.* (Her maiden name *Robinson*, ſiſter to *Matthew Montagu Robinson.*) On the writings and genius of *Shakespeare* chiefly in reply to the animadverſions of *Voltaire* 1769. 8.

—— [Matthew Robinson] ſee *Robinson.*

MONTAGUE, [Edward Worthley] born: ..... died 1776.

MONTRIOU, [J... A... L...] Elements of universal hiſtory of youth —. 1788. 12. (2 ſh. 6 d.)

MOODIE, [James] *Phyſician at Newry in Ireland.* The hiſtory of a case of locked jaw, with uncommon ſymptoms, which terminated favourably. (Med. Com. of Ed. Vol. 3. p. 304.)

MOODY, [James] *Lieutenant.* Narrative of his exertions and ſufferings in the cause of government —. 1783. 8. (1 ſh. 6 d.)

MOORE, [Charles] *M. A: Rector of Cuxton, Vicar of Boughton-bleane.* Inquiry into the ſubjects of suicide

cide — with two treatises on duelling and gaming. Vol. 1. 2. 1790. 4. (1 L. 1 ſh.)

(Several ſingle ſermons)

MOORE, [Francis] Conſiderations on the exorbitant price of proviſions —. 1773. 8. (2 ſh.)

—— [James] *Surgeon at London.* Method of preventing or diminiſhing pain in ſeveral operations of ſurgery. 1784. 8. (2 ſh. 6 d.) On the proceſſ of nature in the filling up of cavities, healing of wounds and reſtoring parts which have been deſtroyed in the human body —. 1789. 4. (3 ſh.)

—— [John] *M. D.* *View of ſociety and manners in France, Switzerland and Germany —. Vol. 1. 2. 1779. (10 ſh.) überſ. Th. 1. 2. Leipzig. 1779. 8. View of ſociety and manners in Italy —. Vol. 1. 2. 1781. 8. (12 ſh.) überſ. Th. 1. 2. Leipz. 8. 1781. Aufl. 2. 1786. Strictures critical and ſentimental on *Thomſon's* ſeaſons, with hints and obſervations on collateral ſubjects. 1777. 8. (4 ſh.) Medical ſketches. P. 1. 2. 1786. 8. (7 ſh.) überſ. Leipz. 1789. 8. *Zeluco; various views of human nature —. Vol. 1. 2. 1789. 8. (12 ſh.) überſ. Th. 1. 1791. 8.

—— [John Hamilton] *Teacher of the Mathematic.* The practical navigator and ſeaman's new daily aſſiſtant. 1772. 8. (5 ſh.) The ſeaman's complete daily aſſiſtant —. 1779. 8. (3 ſh.)

—— [William] *M. D.* Elements of midwifery —. 1777. 8. (4 ſh.)

MORANT, [Philipp] *F. A. S.* born at St. *Saviour* in the Isle *Jerſey.* 1700. died. 1770.

MORE, [Hannah] *Miſſ.* (born at *Briſtol.*) The ſearch after happineſſ, a paſtoral drama. 1773. 8. (1 ſh. 6 d.) The inflexible captive, a tragedy. 1774. 8. (1 ſh. 6 d.) Sir Eldred of the bower and the bleeding rock, two tales. 1776. 4. (2 ſh. 6 d.) * Ode to dragon, Mr. *Garrick's* house dog. 1777. 4. (6 d.) Percy, a tragedy. 1777. 8. (1 ſh. 6 d.) überſ. Hamburg. 1779. 8. Eſſays on various ſubjects, principally deſigned for young ladies 1777. 8. (3 ſh. 6 d.) *The fatal falsehood, a tragedy. 1780. 8. (1 ſh. 6 d.) Sacred dramas — with the poem ſenſibility. 1782. 8. (4 ſh.) *Florio: a tale — and the bas bleu, or converſation: two poems.

poems. 1786. 4. (3 sh.) Slavery, a poem. 1788. 4. (1 sh. 6 d.) *Thoughts on the importance of the manners of the great to general society. 1788. 8. (2 sh.)

MORE, [Jane Elisabeth] of *Bermondsey, in Surry.* Genuine memoirs - written by herself: containing her sentimental journey through Great-Britain, specifying the various manufactures carried on at each town. A comprehensive treatise on the trade, manufactures, navigation, laws and police of this kingdom and the necessity of a country hospital. Vol. 1-3. 1785. 12. (9 sh.)

— [Samuel] *Esq.* Some account of an earthquake felt in the northern part of England. (Phil. Transact. 1787. p. 35.)

MOREL, [John] Letter on the expressing of a fine oil from Beneseed. (Tr. of A. S. Vol. 1. p. 239.)

MORELL, [Thomas] *D. D: Secretary of the Antiquarian Society.* born 1701. died d. 19 Febr. 1784.

MORES, [Edward] *A. M: F. A. S.* Dissertation upon English typographical founders and founderies. 1780. 8. (6 sh.)

— [Edward Rowe] *A. M: F. A. S.* born at *Taunstall, Kent.* 1729. died 1778.

MORETON, [J..... B....] Manners and customs in the West India Islands containing various particulars respecting the soil, cultivation - with the method of establishing and conducting a sugar plantation; also the treatment of slaves and the slave trade. 1790. 8. (3 sh.)

MORFITT, [John] *Esq. Barrister at Law.* Philotoxi Ardenae; the woodmen of Arden; a latin poem, with a translation - and an essay on the superiority of *Dryden's* versification over that of *Pope* and of the moderns by *Joseph Weston.* 1789. 4. (2 sh. 6 d.)

MORGAN, [......] Observations and experiments on the light of bodies in a state of combustion. (Phil. Transact. 1785. p. 190. übers. Samml. z. P. u. N. G. Th. 4. S. 198.)

— [.....] Translation of *Florian's* adventures of Numa Pompilius —. Vol. 1. 2. 1787. 8. (6 sh.)

— [Cesar] *M. A: Chaplain to the Bishop of Ely.* Poems. 1783. 4. (2 sh.) Demonstration, that true phi-

philosophy has no tendency to undermine divine revelation and that a well-grounded philosopher may be a true christian. 1787. 8. (2 sh.) (Several single sermons.)

MORGAN, [John] *M. D: F. R. S: Prof. Theor. et Pract. Physic. at Philadelphiae.* On the expressing of oil, from sun-flower seed (Tr. of A. S. Vol. 1. p. 235.) The art of making anatomical preparations by corrosion (Ibid. Vol. 2. p. 366.) Of a living snake in a living horse's eye and of other unusual productions of animals. (Ibid. p. 383.) Account of a motley coloured or pyed negro girl and mulatto boy —. (Ibid. p. 392.)

—— [John] *of the Inner temple, Barrister at Law.* The attorney's vade mecum and client's instructor —. Vol. 1-3. 1787. 8. (19 sh.) Essays upon. 1) the law of evidence. 2) new trials. 3) special verdicts. 4) trials at Bar. 5) repleaders. Vol. 1-3. 1789. 8. (18 sh.)

—— [N.....] *Master of the Grammar School in the city of Bath.* Grammaticae quaestiones, or a grammatical examination —. 1784. 12. (1 sh. 6 d.)

—— [William] *Actuary to the Society for Equitable Assurances on Lives and Survivorships.* The doctrines of annuities and assurances on lives and survivorships, stated and explained, to which is added Dr. *Price's* essay on the present state of population in England and Wales. 1779. 8. (5 sh.) Examination of Dr. *Crawford's* theory of heat and combustion. 1781. 8. (1 sh. 6 d.) Electrical experiments made in order to ascertain the non conducting power of a perfect vacuum. (Phil. Transact. 1785. p. 272.) On the probability of survivorships between two persons of any given ages and the method of determining the values of reversions depending on those survivorships. (Ibid. 1788. p. 331.) On the method of determining, from the real probabilities of life, the value of a contingent reversion in which three lives are involved in the survivorship. (Ibid. 1789. p. 40.)

MORLEY, [John] *Esq.* On the nature and cure of scrophulous disorders. 1770. (1 sh.)

MORRES, [Harvey] Viscount *Mountmorres* of the Kingdom of *Ireland.* Speech on the appellant jurisdiction of of the house of Lords of Ireland. 1782. 8. (1 ſh.) Reflections upon the queſtion for equalizing the duties upon the trade between Great-Britain and Ireland. 1785. 8. (2 ſh.) The danger of the political balance of Europe translated from the French of the King of Sweden. 1790. 8. (3 ſh.)

MORRIS, [......] *Captain.* Collection of ſongs. 1786. 8. (1 ſh. 6 d.)

—— [Corbyn] *F. R. S: Commiſſioner of the Cuſtoms.* born: ..... died d. 24. Dec. 1779.

—— [Michael] *M. D: F. R. S: Phyſician to the Army and to the Weſtminſter Infirmary.* The proceſſ for making aether, with obſervations on its medical uſe. (Med. Obs. Vol. 2. p. 176.) Account of the effects of caſtor and the peruvian bark in the hooping-cough. (Ibid. Vol. 3. p. 281.) Obſervations and experiments on different extracts of Hemlock. (Phil. Tranſact. 1764. p. 172.) Experiments on Somersham water. (Ibid. 1766. p. 22.) Account of ſome ſpecimens of native lead found in a mine of Monmoutshire. (Ibid. 1773. p. 20.) Experiments on the cortex winteranus or Magellanicus. (Med. Obſ. Vol. 5. p. 56.) Account of a fatal diſease of the ſtomach - with *Henry Watſon's* relation of the appearances on opening the body. (Med. Obſ. Vol. 6. p. 408.)

MORRIS, [Robert] *of Lincoln's Inn, Barriſter at Law and late Secretary to the Supporters of the Bill of Rights.* Letter to *Rich. Aſton* on libels —. 1770. 8. (1 ſh. 6 d.)

—— [Valentine] *late Governor of the Island of St. Vincent.* Narrative of his officiale conduct. 1787. 8. (6 ſh.)

MORRISON, [John] *General and Commander in Chief of the great Mogul's forces; Ambaſſador Extraordinary.* The advantages of an alliance with the great Mogul. Ed. 2. 1774. 8. (1 ſh. 6 d.)

—— [John] *of the Grammar School, Wolverhampton.* The ſecond and fourth books of *Virgil* Aeneid translated into engliſh verse. 1787. (1 ſh. 6 d.)

MORRITT, [J.... S....] *Esq.* On carrots and their uſe in fattening of hogs. (*Hunter's* Georg. Eſſ. Vol. 2. p. 139.)

MORTIMER, [Thomas] British Plutarch or lives of the most illustrious personages of Great-Britain from the reign of Henry VIII. to Georg II. Vol. 1-12. 1762. 8. The universal director; or, the nobleman's and gentleman's true guide to the masters — of the liberal and polite arts and sciences. 1763. 8. (5 sh.) Dictionary of trade and commerce. Vol. 1. 2. 1766. fol. The elements of commerce, politics and finances —. 1772. 4. (1 L. 1 sh.) übers. von *J. A. Engelbrecht*. Leipz. 1781. 8. The student's pocket dictionary, or compendium of universal history, chronology and biography from the earliest accounts to the present time. P. 1. 2. 1777. 8. (3 sh. 6 d.) Every man his own Broker. 1782. 8. *Necker* on the administration of the finances of France. Vol. 1-3. 1786. 8. (1 L. 1 sh.)

MORTON, [David] *Physician at Kingston in Jamaica.* Account of the case of a Negro woman who performed the caesarean operation on herself. (Lond. M. J. Vol. 7. P. 1.)

MORTON, [Joshua] *of Trinity College, Cambridge.* Sermons on various interesting subjects. 1788. 8. (5 sh.)

MOSELEY, [Benjamin] *M. D.* Observations on the dysentery of the West-Indies. 1780. 8. (1 sh.) On the properties and effects of Coffeé. 1785. 8. (1 sh. 6 d.) Ed. 2. 1785. 8. (2 sh. 6 d.) On tropical diseases and on the climate of the West Indies. 1788. 8. (6 sh.) Ed. 2. 1789. 8. übers. Nürnb. und Altd. 1790. 8.

MOSELY, [James] *M. D: Physician at Ludlow.* On the effects of mercury in a case, attended with symptoms of hydrocephalus internus. (Lond. M. J. Vol. 6. p. 113.) übers. Samml. f. A. Th. XI. S. 119.

MOSS, [Thomas] *A. B: Minister of Brierly-Hill.* The imperfection of human enjoyments, a poem. 1783. 4. (2 sh. 6 d.)

—— [William] *Surgeon at Liverpool.* On the management and nursing of children in the earlier periods of infancy —. 1781. 8. (6 sh.) übers. unter dem Titel: der englische Kinder Arzt —. Leipz. 1786. 8. Familiar medical survey of Liverpool —. 1784. 12. (2 sh.)

MOSSMANN, [George] *M. D.* Observations on the *Brunonian* practice of physic, including a reply to an anonymous publication, reprobating the use of ſtimulants in fevers. 1788. 8. (1 Sh. 6 d.)

MOSSOP, [J....] *A.M. Maſter of the boarding ſchool at Brighthelmſtone.* Elegant orations, ancient and modern, for the use of ſchools. —. 1788. 12. (3 ſh. 6 d.)

MOTHERBY, [George] *M. D: Phyſician at Highgate, Middlesex.* A new medical dictionary. 1778. fol. (1 L. 11 Sh. 6 d.) Ed. 2. 1785. fol. (2 L. 2 Sh.)

MOUNTAIN, [James] *A. M.* Poetical reveries. 1777. 4. (1 ſh. 6 d.)

— [William] *F. R. S: Governor of St. Thomas's Hospital and Mathematical Examiner of the Trinity house for the Royal Navy.* born: .... died d. 2 May. 1790.

MOUNTMORRES, Viscount. ſee *Morres.*

MULGRAVE, Lord; ſee *Conſtantine John Phipps.*

MOYLE, [Richard] *Surgeon at Marazion, in Cornwall.* Case of an extrauterine foetus. (Lond. M. J. Vol. 6. p. 52.) Case of a bronchial polypus with remarks on the formation of polypose concretions in the lungs. (Ibid. p. 252.) Account of a remarkable tumour on the head opened and cured. (Ibid. p. 257.)

MUCHALL, [William] Letter to *T. E. Tomlins* — containing ſome observations on his law of wills and codicils —. 1788. 8. (1 Sh.)

MUDGE, [John] *F. R. S: Surgeon at Plymouth.* Several cases of midwifery in Dr. *Smellie's* collection. 1754. Proposal to remedy a defect in the lateral operation for the ſtone. (Phil. Transact. 1756. p. 24.) Two extraordinary dropsical cases with their cure. (Med. Transact. Vol. 2.) On the inoculated ſmall pox. 1776. 8. (2 ſh. 6 d.) überſ. von N. M. Wolff, Danzig. 1778. 8. Directions for making the beſt compoſition for the metals of reflecting telescopes; together with a description of the proceſſ for grinding, polishing and giving the great ſpeculum the true parabolic curve. (Phil. Transact. 1777. p. 296. überſ. Samml. zur P. u. N. G. Th. 1. S. 584.) Cure for a recent catarrhous cough —. 1778. 8. (3 ſh.)

MUGLISTON, [William] *Manufacturer of Hosiery at Alfreton.* Letter on the subject of wool-with remarks on cotton. 1782. 8. (6 d.) A contemplative walk. 1782. 4. (6 d.)

MUIRHEAD, [John] *Minister of the Gospel.* Dissertations on the foederal transactions between god and his church. 1782. 8.

MULLER, [John] *Professor of Artillery and Fortification to the Royal Academy at Woolwich.* born: 1699. died d. Apr. 1784.

MULLIGAN, [Hugh] Poems, chiefly on slavery and oppression, with notes —. 1788. 4. (5 sh.)

MULSO, [Thomas] Callistus, or the man of fashion and Sophronius; or the country Gentleman, in III Dialogues. 1768. 8. (2 sh. 6 d.)

MUNCKLEY, [Nicholas] *M. D: F. R. S.* Case of the efficacy of bark in the delirium of fever. (Phil. Transact. 1760. p. 609. Account of the comet of May 1759. (Ibid. 1761. p. 94.) Observations on the comet of Jan. 1760. at London. (Ibid. 1761. p. 467.) History and cure of a dangerous affection of the oesophagus. (Med. Transact. Vol. 1. p. 165.) A case of the hydrophobia. (Ibid. Vol. 2. p. 46.)

MUNNING, [J....] *Surgeon at London.* Case of a curvature of the spine successfully treated. (London M. J. Vol. 6. p. 358.)

MUNRO, [Jnnes] Narrative of the military operations on the Coromandel coast against the combined forces of the French, Dutch and Hyder Aly Cawn from the year 1780 to 1784. 1789. 4. (1 L. 1 sh.)

MURDIN, [Cornelius] *A. M.* Paraphrase on the general epistle of St. James —. 1774. 8. (1 sh.)
(Several single sermons.)

MURDOCH, [John] *Denina* on the revolutions of litterature, translated. 1770. 8. (3 sh.) *Arnaud's* tears of sensibility, translated. Vol. 1. 2. 1773. 8. (5 sh.) Radical vocabulary of the French language. 1782. 8. (2 sh. 6 d.) Pictures of the heart, Vol. 1. 2. 1783. 8. (5 sh.) The double disguise, a Drama. (see Pictures of the heart) The pronunciation and orthography of the French language. 1788. 8. (1 sh. 6 d.)

MURDOCH, [Patrik] *Mathematician at London.* born ..... died d. 12. Nov. 1774.

MURPHY, [Arthur] *Barrister at law.* Works. Vol. 1-7. 1786. 8. (2 L. 2 ſh.)

— [......] *Captain.* The life of *John Donellan*, Esq. 1781. 8. (1 ſh.)

MURRAY, [.....] Letter to *Will. Mason* on his edition of *Gray's* poems. 1777. 8. (1 ſh.)

— [Anne] *Miſſ.* ſee *Roſſ.*

— [C.....] *Actor.* The new maid of the oaks, a Tragedy. 1778. 8. The experiment, a farce 1779. 8.

— [F.... A.... S....] *Esq.* Thoughts on impriſonment for debts. 1788. (1 ſh. 6 d.)

— [James] of *Newcaſtle.* *Sermons to asses. P. 1. 1768. 8. (3 Sh.) Sermons to Doctors in divinity P. 2. 1771. 8. (3 Sh.). Lectures to Lords ſpiritual —. 1774. 8. (3 Sh.) Ed. 2. 1781. 8. (2 Sh.) (Several ſingle ſermons)

— [Oliver James] The candid inquiſitor; or, mock patriotism displayed; a poem. 1770. 4. (1 Sh. 6 d.)

MUSGRAVE, [Samuel] *M. D: F. R. S: Phyſician at Exeter.* born: ..... died d. 4 July 1780.

MUTLOW, [.....] Account of ſome antiquities found in Glouceſtershire. (Arch. Vol. 7. p. 379.)

MYERS, [J..... H......] *M. D.* Remarks on the Sigualtian operation. (*Duncan's* M. C. Vol. 10. p. 281.)

— [William] *Curate of Tetney, Lincolnshire.* The benefits and advantages of Sunday ſchools conſidered and the eſtablishing of them recommended. 1789. 4. (1 Sh.)

MYNORS, [Robert] *Surgeon at Birmingham.* Practical thoughts on amputations. 1783. 8. (2 Sh. 6 d.) überſ. Jena. 1786. 8. Hiſtory of the practice of trepanning the ſkull and the after-treatment —. 1785. 8. (2 Sh. 6 d.) überſetzt Leipzig. 1787. 8. ſee *Will. Jones.*

NAIRNE, [Edward] *Mathematical Inſtrumentmaker: F. R. S.* Description and use of a new conſtructed equatorial telescope or portable observatory. (Phil. Transact. 1771. p. 107.) Account of a person killed by lightning in Tottenham Court chapel and its

its effects on the building. (Ibid. 1772. p. 131. Experiments on two dipping-needles, which dipping-needles were made agreeable to a plan of Mr *Mitchell* – and executed for the board of longitude (Ibid. 1772. p. 476.) Electrical experiments (Ibid. 1774. p. 79.) Experiments on water obtained from the melted ice of Sea-water, to ascertain whether it be fresh or not; and to determine its specific gravity with respect to other water also experiments to find the degree of cold in which sea-water begins to freeze. (Ibid. 1776. p. 249. Account of some experiments made with an air-pump on Mr. *Smeaton's* principle; together with some experiments with a common air-pump. (Ibid. 1777. p. 614.) Experiments on electricity, being an attempt to shew the advantage of elevated pointed conductors. (Ibid. 1778. p. 823.) übers. Samml. z. P. und N. G. Th. 2. S. 458. Account of the effect of electricity in shortening wires. (Ibid. 1780. p. 334.) Account of wire being shortened by lightning. (Ibid. 1783. p. 223.) Description and use of his patent electrical machine. 1787. 8.

NAPIER, [George] *Member of Roy. Irish Acad.* Observations on gun-powder. (Tr. of J. A. 1788. p. 97.)

—— [William] *Lord.* of Merchiston. born: .... died at Edinburgh d. 2 Jan. 1775.

NARES, [R....] *A. M.* Essay on the demon or divination of *Socrates.* 1782. 8. (1 Sh.) Elements of orthoepy, containing a distinct view of the whole analogy of the English language —. 1784. 8. (5 Sh.) Remarks on the favourite ballad of Cupid and Psyche, with account of the pantomime of the ancients. 1788. 12. (1 Sh. 6 d.)

NASH, [M.....] Stenography —. 1783. 4. (10 Sh. 6 d.)

—— [Treadway] *D. D: Rector of St. Peter's in Droitwich. F. A. S.* Collections for the history of Worcestershire. Vol. 1. 2. fol. 1782. (5 L. 5 Sh.) Observations on the time of the death and place of burial of Queen *Katharine Parr,* (Arch. Vol. 9. p. 1.)

NASMITH, [James] *A. M: F. A. S: Rector of Snailewell in Cambridgeshire.* Itineraria *Symonis Simeonis* et et *Willelmi de Worcestre* —. 1780. 8. (10 Sh. 6 d.) *Thom. Tanner's* notitia monastica - with additions. 1787. fol. (2 L. 2 Sh.)

NEALE, [......] *Surgeon.* Practical observations on venereal complaints —. 1788. 8. (2 Sh.) Practical dissertations on nervous complaints and other diseases incident to the human body. 1788. 8. (1 Sh. 6 d.) übers. Berlin. 1790. 8.

— [Adam] *Gardener.* Catalogue of the plants in the garden of *John Blackburne.* 1779. 8.

— [G. . . . .] Essays on modern manners. 1790. 8. (2 Sh.)

NEEDHAM, [John Tuberville] born at *London* 1713. died at *Brussel.* d. 30 Dec. 1781.

NELME, [L...... D......] Origin and elements of language and letters, that is, sounds and symbols —. 1772. 4. (6 Sh.)

NEVE, [Timothy] *D. D: Professor of Divinity in the University of Oxford.* Animadversions on Mr. *Philipp's* History of the life of Cardinal *Pole.* 1766. 8. (6 Sh.) Eight sermons at Bampton's lecture. 1781. 8. (3 Sh. 6 d.)

NEVILLE, [.....] Plymouth in uproar, a comic opera. 1779. 8.

NEVINSON, [R..... S.....] *Surgeon.* Observations on the use of crude mercury — in obstructions of the bowels — with remarks on the use of castor oil. 1786. 8. (1 sh. 6 d.)

NEWCOME, [William] *D. D. Bishop of Waterford in Ireland.* Harmony of the gospels —. 1778. fol. (1 L. 7 Sh.) Duration of our Lord's ministry particularly considered in reply to a second letter from Dr. *Priestley* on that subject. 1780. 8. (2 Sh.) Observations on our Lord's conduct as a divine instructor, and on the excellence of his moral character. 1782. 4. (16 Sh.) An Attempt towards an improved version, a metrical arrangement and an explanation of the XII minor Prophets. 1785. 4. (10 Sh. 6 d.) Attempt towards an improved version — and explanation of the prophet *Ezekiel.* 4. 1788. (10 Sh. 6 d.)

NEWHAVEN, [William] *Lord.* Address to the public; containing some thoughts how the national debt may be reduced and all home taxes, including land tax, abolished. 1786. 8. (1 Sh.)

NEWLAND, [Charles] *Captain.* Letter – with a new chart of the red fea, with two draughts of the roads of *Mocha* and *Judda* and feveral obfervations made during a voyage on that fea. (Philos. Transact. 1772. p. 77.) Remarks and obfervations made on board the fhip Kelfall, on a voyage to *Judda* and *Mocha*, in 1769. (Ibid. 1772. p. 79.) An eafy method to deftill fresh water from falt water at fea. (Ibid. 1772. p. 90.) Obfervations on the milky appearance of fome fpots of water in the fea. (Ibid. p. 93.)

NEWMAN, [Jere Whitaker] *Surgeon.* On folvents, as neceffary to lithotomy. 1781. 8. (1 Sh. 6 d.) On the principles and manners of the medical profession. 1783. 8. (1 Sh. 6 d.) *Medical effays 1) on the principles and manners of the medical profession 2) inquiry into the merits of folvents for the ftone with additions. 1789. 8. (2 Sh. 6 d.)

NEWTON, [.....] On a method of preventing venereal infection. 1775. 4.

—— [Benjamin] *A. M: Rector of St. Johns in Gloucefter, Vicar of Sandhurft in the county and Diocese of Gloucefter.* born: ..... died d. 29 June. 1787.

—— [James] *Vicar of Old-Cleve, Somerfetshire.* *A new theory of redemption, upon principles equally agreeable to revelation and reason. Vol. 1. 2. 1789. 8. (10 Sh.)

—— [John] a Methodiftical Clergyman. *Rector of St. Mary's Woolnorth.* Six Discourses. 1760. 8. (2 Sh.) Sermons 1767. 8. (5 Sh.) Review of ecclefiaftical hiftory. 1770. 8. (5 Sh.) *Cardiphonia, or the utterance of the heart in the course of a real correspondence. Vol. 1. 2. 1781. 8. (6 Sh.) Omicron's letters. Vol. 1. 2. 1781. 8. (6 Sh.) Olney hymns. Ed. 2. 1781. Authentic narrative relative to the presentation of Mr. *Haweis* the rectory of *Aldwincle.* 17.. *Apologia; four letters to a minifter of an independent church —. 1784. Apologia 2. 1785. 8. (3 Sh.) Meffiah. 50. expofitory discourses, on the feries of fcriptural paffages, which from the fubject of the celebrated oratorio

of

of *Handel.* Vol. 1. 2. 1786. 8. (10 Sh. 6 d.) Thoughts on the African slave trade. 1788. 8. (1 Sh.) (Several single sermons.)

NEWTON, [S.....] of *Norwich.* On the leading sentiments of the Quackers. 1771. Appendix. 1774. 8. (3 Sh. 6 d.)

—— [Thomas] *D. D: Lord Bishop of Bristol and Dean of St. Paul's London.* born at *Lichtfield.* d. 21 Dec. 1703. died d. 14 Febr. 1782.

—— [William] *Architect.* Translation of *Vitruvius's* Architecture. 1771. fol. (1 L. 11 Sh. 6 d.)

NICHOLLS, [Frank] *M. D: Physician in Ordinary to the King.* born in London 1699. died d. 7 Jan. 1778.

—— [F.....] Sable victims: a Barbadoes narration, inscribed to the promoters of the slave-trade. 1789. 4. (2 Sh. 6 d.)

NICHOLS, [John] *Printer: F. A. S.* (Editor of Gentleman's Magazine.) A select collection of poems, with notes, biographical and historical. Vol. 1-8. 1780. 8. (1 L. 6 d.) Biographical memoirs of *Will. Ged* with an account of his progress in the art of block-printing. 1781. 8. Memoirs of *William Lambarde* Esq: 4. 17. Biographical anecdotes of *Will. Hogarth* and a catalogue of his works. 1781. 8. (3 Sh.) Ed. 2. 1782. 8. (6 Sh.) im Ausz. übers. Leipz. 1783. 8. Biographical and litterary anecdotes of *Will. Bowyer,* Printer. 1782. 4. (1 L. 1 Sh.) The epistolary correspondance, visitation, charges, speeches and miscellanies. Vol. 1-4. 1783. 8. (1 L.) Miscellaneous tracts by the late *Will. Bowyer* Printer. 1785. 4. (1 L. 1 Sh.) Bibliotheca Topographica Britannica. 4. Numb. I. - 50. The familiar correspondance of Sir *Rich. Steele.* Vol. 1. 2. 1787. 8. (7 Sh.) History and antiquities of Aston Flamvile and Burbach. 1787. 4. The progresses and public processions of Queen Elizabeth. Vol. 1. 2. 1788. 4. (3 L. 3 Sh.) History and Antiquities of Canonburyhouse at Islington. 1789. 4. *Leonard Welsted's* works, in verse and prose with notes and biographical memoirs of the author. 1789. 8. (6 Sh.)

NICHOLSON, [......] *Teacher of Mathematics in Wakefield.* Account of a ſtorm of lightning obſerved on the 1 March 1774. near Wakefield in Yorkshire. (Phil Tranſact. 1774. p. 350.)

—— [George] Four ſelect evangelical discourses. 1788. 8. (1 Sh.) *Letter to *Joſ. Prieſtley* by a lover of the whole truth as it in Jesus. 1788. 8. (6 d.)

—— [James] *Maſter of languages.* Chambaud improved; or French and English exercises —. 1782. 8. (2 Sh. 6 d.)

—— [Joseph] — and *Rich. Burn's* Hiſtory and antiquities of the counties of Weſtmoreland and Cumberland Vol. 1. 2. 1777. 4. (2 L. 2 Sh.)

—— [William] *F. R. S. Secretary.* Introduction to natural philoſophy. Vol. 1. 2. 1782. (12 Sh.) überſ. von *A. F. Lüdicke.* Th. 1. 2. 1787. 8. The Navigator's aſſiſtant, containing the theory and practice of navigation —. 1784. 8. (6 Sh.) An abſtract of ſuch acts of parliament as are now in force for preventing the exportation of wool —. 1786 (—). The principles and illuſtration of an advantageous method of arranging the differences of logarithms, on lines graduated for the purpose of computation. (Phil. Tr. 1787. p. 246.) Description of an inſtrument which, by the turning of a winch, produces the two ſtates of electricity without friction or communication with the earth. (Ibid. 1788. p. 403.) überſ: *Gren.* J. d. P. Th. 2. S. 61. Experiments and observations on electricity. (Ibid. 1789. p. 265.) überſ. *Gren* J. d. P. Th. 3. S. 49. Description of a new inſtrument for meaſuring the ſpecific gravity of bodies. (Mem. of M. Vol. 2. p. 370.) The firſt principles of Chemiſtry. 1789. 8. (7 Sh.) überſ. von Spöhr. Riga. 1791. Memoirs and travels of *Maur. Aug.* Count de *Benyowsky*, translated from the French. Vol. 1. 2. 1790. 4. (2 L. 2 Sh.) überſ. von J. P. *Ebeling* Th. 1. 2. 1791. 8. überſ. von *G. Forſter.* 1791. 8. überſ. im Ausz. Tübingen 1791. 8.

NICOLA, [Lewis] *of Northampton, Pennsylvania.* An easy method of preserving ſubjects in ſpirits, (Tr. of A. S. Vol. 1. p. 244.)

NIMMO, [William] *Miniſter of Bothkennar.* Hiſtory of Stirlingshire —. 1777. 8. (7 Sh. 6 d.)

NIPCLOSE, [Nicholas] The Theaters; a poetical diſſection. 1771. 4. (3 Sh.)

NISBETT, [.....] *Mrs.* Poems on recent adventures —. 1780. 8. (3 Sh. 6 d.)

— [N.....] *A. M.* Attempt to illuſtrate various important paſſages in the epiſtles of the new teſtament, from our Lord's prophecies of the deſtruction of Jeruſalem and from ſome prophecies of the old teſtament. 1787. 8. (2 ſh. 6 d.) Ed. 2. 1789. 8. (3 ſh. 6 d.) überſ. Nürnb. 1790. 8. Obſervations upon the miraculous conception of our ſaviour — againſt Dr. *Prieſtley.* 1790. 8. (2 ſh.)

NISBET, [Richard] *of the Island of Nevis.* The capacity of Negroes for religious and moral improvement conſidered —. 1789. 8. (3 ſh.)

— [William] *M. D: Fellow of the Royal College of Surgeons at Edinburgh.* Firſt lines of the theory and practice in venereal diſeaſes. 1787. 8. (5 ſh.) überſ. von *C. F. Michaelis.* Leipz. 1789. 8.

NIVEN, [David] *Surgeon.* Hiſtory of a caſe of imperforated hymen cured by inciſion. (*Duncan's* M. C. Vol. 9. p. 330.)

NIXON, [William] *A B: Maſter of the endowed ſchool of Youghal.* Proſody made eaſy. 1781. 8. (2 ſh.)

NOBLE, [Edward] *Journeyman to Mr. T. Payne at the Mewsgate.* born ..... died d. 15 Apr. 1784.

— [Mark] *F. A. S: Rector of Barming in Kent.* Two diſſertations on the mint and coins of the epiſcopal palatines of Durham. 1780. 4. (7 ſh. 6 d.) Genealogical Hiſtory of the preſent royal families of Europe. 1781. 8. (3 ſh.) Memoirs of the protectorat houſe of *Cromwell* —. Vol. 1. 2. 1784. 8. (12 ſh.)

NOLAN, [William] Eſſay on humanity; or a view of abuſes in hospitals, with a plan of correcting them. 1786. 8. (1 ſh.)

NOORTHOUCK, [John] Hiſtory of London —. 1773. 4. (1 L. 11 ſh. 6 d.) Hiſtorical and claſſical dictionary. Vol. 1. 2. 1776. 8. (12 ſh.)

NOOTH, [John Mervin] *M. D: F. R. S.* Diſſ. De Rachitide. Edinb. 1766. 8. Some improvements in the electrical machine. (Phil. Transact. 1773. p. 333.) Deſcriptions of an apparatus for impreg-

impregnating water with fixed air; and of the manner of conducting that processe. (Ibid. 1775. p. 59.)

NORMAN, [H.....] Two letters on subscription to the liturgy and 39 articles of the church of England. 1773. 8. (2 sh. 6 d.)

—— [Elizabeth] *Mrs.* The child of Woe. Vol. 1-3. 1789 12. (7 sh. 6 d.)

—— [Samuel] *Surgeon at Yatton.* Anecdotes of *George Lukins* the Yatton demoniac, with a view of the controversy and a refutation of the imposture —. 1788. 8.

DE NORMANDIE, [John] of *Bristol.* Analysis of the chalybiate waters of *Bristol* in Pennsylvania. (Tr. of Am. Soc. Vol. 1. p. 303.)

NORRIS, [Henry] of *Taunton* Aracyntha; an elegy. 1772. 4. (1 sh.) On the cubical contents of the roman Congius. (Arch. Vol. 6. p. 221.) Observations on *Bernard's* cubic contents of the roman amphora. (Ibid. p. 227.) Inquiry to show, what was the ancient english weight and measure, according to the laws or statutes prior to the reign of Henry VII. (Phil Transact. 1775. p. 48.)

—— [Robert] Memoirs of the reign of Bossa Ahadee, King of Dahomy an inland country of Guiney with his journey to Abomey, the capital, and an account of the African Slave trade. 1789. 8. (4 sh.) übers. Leipz. 1790. 8.

—— [William] *F. M. S: Surgeon to the Charter House and General-Dispensary.* Case of a retention of urine from external violence cured by puncturing the bladder through the rectum. (Mem. of M. S. of L. Vol. 1. p. 117.)

NORTH, [George] *Rector in Codicote, Hertfordshire.* born at *London.* 1707. died 1772.

NORTHCOTE, [S.....] Observations on the natural and civil rights of mankind. 1782.

—— [Thomas] *Chaplain in the royal artillerie.* Corrupt influence removed and the constitution restored: — two letters —. 1780. 8. (1 sh.) Observations on the natural and civil rights of Mankind —. 1781. 8. (1 sh.)

—— [William] *Surgeon.* The marine practice of physic and surgery. Vol. 1. 2. 1770. (12 sh.) Anatomy of the human body. 1772. 8. (6 sh.) Concise hi-

history of Anatomy, from the earliest ages of antiquity. 1772. 8. (3 sh.) Methodus praescribendi exemplificata pharmacopaeis nosocomiorum Londinensium, Edinburgensium. 1772. 8. (3 sh. 6 d.)

NOTT, [John] Translation of select odes from the Persian poet *Hafez*. 1787. 4. (10 sh. 0 d.)

NOURSE, [Charles] *Surgeon at Oxford*. born 1714. died d. 19 Apr. 1789.

NOYES, [Robert] Distress, a poem. 1783. 4. (2 sh. 6 d.) (Several single sermons.)

NUGENT, [.....] *Miss*. — and Miss *Taylor*: The indiscret marriage; or, Henry and Sophia Somerville. Vol. 1-3. 1779. 8. (9 sh.)

—— [Christopher] *M. D: F. R. S.* born: ... died d. 12 Nov. 1775.

—— [Thomas] *LL. D: F. A. S.* born: .... died d. 27 Apr. 1772.

OAKES, [Henry] *Captain*. Narrative of the treatment of the english, who were taken prisoners on the reduction of Bednore by Tippo Saib —. 1785. 8. (2 sh.)

O'BEIRNE, [Thomas Lewis] *Chaplain to Lord Howe*. (born in *Ireland*.) The crucifixion, a poem. 1776. 4. (1 sh. 6 d.) The generous impostor, a Comedy. 1780. 8. (Several single sermons.)

O'BRIEN, [Charles,] *Actor*. Dialogue between the poet and his friend, a Satire. 4. 1755. (6 d.) *Cross purposes, a farce. 1772. 8. (1 sh.) *The duel, a play. 1772. 8. (1 sh. 6 d.) Lusorium, a collection of convival songs, lectures —. 1782. 8. (2 sh. 6 d.)

O'BRIEN, [Dennis] *Barrister at Law*. (born in *Ireland*) Friend in need is a friend indeed. 1783. Defence of the Earl of *Shelburne*. 17.. Lines written at *Twickenham*. 1788. 4. (1 sh.).

—— [Lucius] *Sir, Baronet*. Letters concerning the trade and manufactures of *Ireland* —. 1785. 8. (2 sh.)

O'CONOR, [C....] **John Curry's* Review of the civil wars in *Ireland*. Ed. 2. Vol. 1. 2. 1786. 8. (10 sh. 6. d.)

O'DOGHERTY, [William] Epitome of the history of Europe, from the reign of Charlemagne to the beginning of the reign of George III. 1788. 8. (6 sh.)

O'DON-

O'DONNEL, [John] *Surgeon at Chelmsford, in Essex.* Case of a man, whose body was covered with encysted tumours. (London M. J. Vol. 6. p. 33.)

O'FLAHERTY, [Dennis] *Esq. of Ireland.* Sketch of commotions and disorders in the Austrian Netherlands including transactions from 1 Apr. 1787 —. 1787. 8. (2 sh.)

O'FLANAGAN, [Theophilus] *Student of Trinity College, Dublin.* On an antient inscription in Ogam character on the sepulchral monument of an Irish chief. (Tr. of J. A. 1787. p. 3.)

O'GALLAGHER, [Felix] On the investigation of the first principles of nature —. P. 1. 2. 1786. 8. (11 sh.)

OGDEN, [Samuel] DD: *Rector of Lawford, Essex, Professor at Cambridge.* born..... died d. 23. March. 1778.

OGILVIE, [James] D. D: *Chaplain to Lord Forbes, Curate of Egham: late Rector of Westover parish in Virginia.* Sermons on various subjects. 1787. 8. (6 sh.)

— [John] *D. D: Minister of Midmar.* (born in *Scotland*) The day of judgment: a poem. Ed. 2. 1759. 8. (1 sh.) Ed. 3. to which are added 1) an ode to melancholy. 2) Ode on sleep. 3) Ode on time. 4) to the memory of Mr. *H. M.* an Elegy. 5) to the memory of the late pious and ingenious Mr. *Hervey.* 6) the III Chapt. of *Habakkuk* paraphrased. 1759. 8. (2 sh.) Poems on several subjects with an essay on the lyric poetry of the antients. 1762. 4. (10 sh. 6 d.) Providence; an allegorical poem. 1764. 4. (8 sh.) *Solitude, or the elysium of the poets, a vision with an Elegy. 1766. 4. (2 sh. 6 d.) Sermons on several subjects. 1767. 8. (3 sh.) *Paradise: a Poem. 1769. 4. (1 sh. 6 d.) Poems on several subjects. Vol. 1. 2. 1769. 8. (10 sh. 6 d.) Philosophical and critical observations on the nature, characters and various species of composition. Vol. 1. 2. 1774. (12 sh.) Rona, a poem; illustrated with a map of the Hebrides and engravings. 1777. 4. (12 sh. 6 d.) Enquiry into the causes of the infidelity and scepticism of the times. 1783. 8. (6 sh.)

OGLE, [Thomas] *Surgeon to the Middlesex-dispensary.* Case of a ſingular enlargement of the heart. (Mem. of M. S. of L. Vol. 1. p. 197.)

O'HALLORAN, [Sylveſter] *Surgeon to the County of Limerick Hospital. Memb. of J. A.* On the Glaucoma, or Cataract. 1753. 8. (3 ſh. 6 d.) On gangrena and ſphacelus with a new method of amputation. 1766. 8. (5 ſh.) Introduction to the ſtudy of the hiſtory and antiquities of Ireland. 1772. 4. (12 ſh.) General Hiſtory of Ireland. Vol. 1. 2. 1778. 4. (1 L. 11 ſh. 6 d.) Examination of the parts immediately intereſted in the operation for a cataract; with an attempt to render the operation itſelf, whether by depreſſion or extraction, more certain and ſucceſſful. (Tr. of J. A. 1788. p. 121. London M. J. Vol. 10. P. 4.) A martial ode, ſung at the battle of Cnucha, by *Fergus*, ſon of *Finn* and addreſſed to *Goll*, the ſon of *Morna*, with a literal translation and notes. (Tr. of J. A. 1788. p. 7.)

O'HARA, [Kane] Midas, a farce. 1764. The Golden pippin, a farce. 1773. 8. (1 ſh.) The two miſers. 1775. 8. April day, a Burletta. 1777. 8. Tom Thumb, a Burletta. 1780. 8.

O'KEEFE.. [John] ſee *Keefe.*

OKELY, [Francis] Editio Pſalmorum *John Serrani*—. 1772. 12. (5 ſh.) Translation of *Joh. Eleon. de Merlau*, The nature and neceſſity of the new creature in Chriſt—. 1772. 8. (6 d.) Translation of the viſions of *John Engelbrecht.* Vol. 1. 2. 1781. 8. (3 ſh.) Translation of God's gracious dealings with hiel. 1781. 8. (1 ſh. 6 d.) Translation of God's wonders — in the life of *John Engelbrecht* of Brunswic. 1781. 8. (1 d.) Memoirs of the life, death and wonderful writings of *Jacob Behmen*—. 1780. 8. (2 ſh.) The disjointed watch —. 1783. 12. (2 d.)

O'KELLY, [Hugh] ſee *Kelly.*

O'LEARY, [Arthur] *Roman catholic Clergyman in Ireland.* Remarks on *Wesley's* letters in defence of the proteſtant aſſociations in England. 1780. 8. (1 ſh.) Miſcellaneous tracts. 1781. 8. (5 ſh.) Review of the controverſy between Dr. *Carrol*, *Wharton* and *Hawkins*, 1787. 8. (1 ſh. 6 d.)

OLI-

OLIPHANT, [James] *M. D: Physician at Irvine,* Account of an uncommon case in midwifery, where a preternatural adhesion of twins had taken place. (*Duncan's* M. C. Vol. X. p. 249.)

—— [Isaac] *Surgeon in London.* Two instances of the good effects of blisters in incontinence of urine. (London M. J. Vol. 7. p. 416.) übers. Samml. f. A. Th. XI. S. 701. Case of an abscess of the liver occasioned by a blow. (London M. J. Vol. 7. P. 1.) Account of a suppression of stools and urine occasioned by an accumulation of hardened faeces, in the rectum. (London M. J. Vol. 7. P. 1.)

OLIVER, [Andrew] *Lieutenant Governor of the province of Massachusetts Bay.* born: .... died d. 3 March. 1774.

—— [William] *M. D: Physician Extraordinary to his Roy. Highness the Prince of Wales.* On the effects of camphor in a case of insanity. (Lond. M. J. Vol. 6. p. 120.)

—— [Thomas] Letter to Mr. *Toplady* occasioned by his late letter to Mr. *Wesley.* 1770. 8. (4 d.) A scourge to calumny, in two parts. 1774. 8. (1 sh. 6 d.) A full defence of *John Wesley,* in answer to the several personal reflexions cast on that gentleman by *Caleb Evans* —. 1776. 8. (2 d.)

ORME, [.....] *History of the military transactions of the british nation in Indostan from the Year 1745. with a Dissertation on the establishments made by Mahomedan conquerors in Indostan. 1763. 4. (18 sh.) Ed. 2. Vol. 1. 2. 1778. (3 L.) übers. im Auszug (von *J. W. v. Archenholz*) Leipz. 1786. 8. *Historical fragments of the Mogul empire; of the Morattoes and of the English concerns, in Indostan, from the Year 1759 - 1782. 8. (5 sh.)

ORMEROD, [Richard] *A. B.* Remarks on the XIV section of Dr. *Priestley's* disquisitions on matter and spirit. 1786. 8. (1 sh. 6 d.)

OROURKE, [John] *Count.* On the art of war — 1778. 4. (1 L. 1 sh.)

ORRED, [Daniel] *Surgeon in Chester.* A case in which the head of the os humeri was sawn off and yet the motion of the limb preserved. (Phil. Transact. 1779. p. 6.) A successful method of cure in diseases of the larger joints which have hitherto been thought

to

to require amputation. (*Duncan's* M. C. 1780. p. 325. überf. Samml. f. A. Th. XI. S. 177.)

ORTON, [Job] *S. T. P.* born 1717. died at *Kidderminster* d. 19 Jul. 1783.

OSBORN, [William] *M. D: Physician and Man-Midwife to the General Lying in Hospital and Lecturer on Midwifery in London.* On laborious parturition —. 1783. 8. (4 sh.)

OSWALD, [John] *Lieutenant in the 42 Regiment of Foot.* (born in Scotland.) *Ranae comicae evangelizantes, or the comic frogs turned methodist. 1786. The alarming progress of French politics. 17.. On the commercial treaty. 17.. Euphrosyne, or an ode to beauty 17..

OSWALD, [Thomas] *D. D: Clergyman in Scotland.* *Appeal to common sense in behalf of religion. Vol. 1. 2. 1772. 8. (10 sh.) überf. Th 1. 2. 1774. 8. Two sermons by the death of *Rob. Lawson* A. M. at the Scot church. 1771. 8. (1 sh.)

OTTO, [.....] Account of an oil made from the seeds of the common large sun-flower. (Tr. of A. S. Vol. 1. p. 234.) Memoir on the discovery of America. (Ibid. Vol. 2. p. 263.)

OTWAY, [Sylvester] Euphrosyne, an ode to beauty. 1788. 4. (1 sh.) Poems; to which is added, the humours of *John Bull*, an operatical farce. 1789. 12. (3 sh.)

OULTON, [.....] The busy body, a collection of periodical essays. Vol. 1. 2. 1789. 8. (5 sh.)

OURRY, [J..... A....] *Teacher of Languages, Greenwich.* The French scholar put to trial: or, questions on the French language. 1788. 12. (1 sh. 3 d.)

OUSLEY, [Ralph] *Esq. M. R. J. A.* Account of the moving of a bog and the formation of a lake, in the county of *Galway, Ireland.* (Tr. of J. A. 1788. p. 3.) Account of three metal trumpets found in the county of Limerick. 1787. (Tr. of J. A. 1788. p. 3.)

OWEN, [Edward] *M. A: Rector of Warrington.* *A new latine accidence, or, an introduction to the several parts of latin grammar in english prose.

1770.

1770. 8. (1 sh.) The satires of *Juvenal*, translated into english verse. Vol. 1. 2. 1786. 8. (7 sh.) (Several single sermons.)

OWEN, [Henry] *D. D: F. R. S: Rector of St. Olave, Hart-street, Southwark.* Harmonia trigonometrica. 1748. 8. The intent and propriety of the scripture - miracles considered and explained. 1755. 8. (2 Sh.) Observations on the IV gospels; tending chiefly, to ascertain the times of their publication and to illustrate the form and mannner of their composition. 1764. 8. (2 Sh.) Short directions to young students in divinity and candidates for holy orders. 1766. 8. (1 sh.) Enquiry into the present state of the LXX version of the old testament. 1769. 8. (3 sh.) Sermons on the intent and propriety of the scripture miracles. Vol. 1. 2. 1773. 8. (10 sh.) Critica sacra, or, a short introduction to hebrew criticism. 1774. with supplement. 1775. 8. (2 sh.) Remarks on the time employed in Cesar's two expeditions into Britain. (Arch. Vol. 2. p. 159.) Collatio codicis Cottoniani Geneseos cum editione romana a *J. C. Grabe* jam olim facta, nunc demum edita. 1778. 8. (3 sh.) Critical disquisitions containing some remarks 1) on *Masius's* edition of the book of *Joshua.* 2) on *Origen's* Hexapla. 1784. 8. (1 sh. 6 d.) Account of the LXX version of the old testament with a dissertation on the comparative excellency of the Hebrew and Samaritan Pentateuch. 1787. 8. (2 sh.) The modes of quotation used by the evangelical writers explained and vindicacated. 1789. 4. (10 sh. 6 d.)

OWEN, [N.....] Jun. *A. M.* On the time and duration of *Julius Cesar's* two expeditions in Britannia. (Arch. Vol. 1.) British remains: or a collection of antiquities relating to the Britons — 1777. 8. (3 sh.) Select phrases of *Horace*, translated into english. 1785. 12. (1 sh. 3 d.)

PAGE, [John] Account of an remarkable meteor seen in Virginia. (Tr. of A. S. Vol. 2. p. 173.)

—— [Thomas Hyde] *Knight: F. R. S.* Description of the king's wells at Sheerness, Languard fort and Har-

Harwich. (Phil. Transact. 1784. p. 6.) Considerations on the state of Dover Harbour, with its relative consequence to the navy of Great-Britain —1784. 4.

PAIN, [William] *Architect and Joiner* The practical builder; or workman's general assistant —. 1774. 4. (12 sh.)

PAINE, [John] Junior. The paper-maker's, and stationer's assistant. 1786. 12. (6 d.)

—— [Thomas] *M. A. of the University of Pennsylvania.* Common sense. 1776. 8. (1 Sh. 6 d.) übersezt in *Dohm's* Materialien zur Statistik u. neueren Staaten Geschichte. Lieferung 1. S. 7. Letter to the Earl of *Shelburne* on his speech – respecting the acknowledgment of American independence. 1783. 8. (1 Sh.) Letter to Abbé *Raynal* on the affairs of North-America: in which the mistakes in the Abbe's account of the revolution of America are corrected and cleared up. Ed 3. 1783. 8. (1 Sh. 6 d.) abgedrukt in *Dohm's* Materialien zur Statistik —. Liefer. 5 S. 555. Thoughts on the Rubicon and censuring the measures of the English administration. 17..

PAINTER [W.....] Guide to the lottery; or the laws of chance —. 1787. 8. (2 Sh.)

PALEY, [William] *A. M: Archdeacon of Carlisle.* The principles of moral and political philosophy. Ed. 2. 1786. 4. (1 L. 1 Sh.) übers. von C. *Garve.* Th. 1. 2. Leipzig. 1787. 8. Horae Paulinae; or, the truth of the scripture history of St. Paul evinced, by a comparison of the epistles with the acts of the apostles and with one another. 1790. 8. (6 Sh.)

(Several single sermons.)

PALMER, [G.....] Theory of colours and visions. 1777. 8. (1 Sh.)

—— [John] *Minister to a Society of Protestant Dissenters in New Broad-street.* Prayers for the use of families and persons in private 1773. 8. (3 Sh.) Ed. 2. 1785. 8. (2 Sh.) Letter to Dr. *Balguy* on the subjects of his charge, delivered to the Archdeaconry of Winchester —. 1770. 8. (1 Sh.) A new sheme of short-hand; being an improvement upon Mr. *Byrom's* universal english short-hand. 1774. (10 Sh. 6 d.) Free thoughts on the inconsistency of conforming to any religious test, as a condition

 of

of toleration. 1779. 8. (1 Sh.) Examination of *Mart. Madan's* Thelyphthora on the subject of marriage. 1781. 8. (1 Sh. 6 d.) Observations in defence of the liberty of man, as a moral agent; in answer to Dr. *Priestley's* illustrations of philosophical necessity. 1779. with appendix. 1780. 8. (3 sh. 6 d.) The protestant Dissenter's shorter catechism 1783. (1 sh. 6 d.) A summary view of the grounds of christian baptism —. 1788. 8. (2 sh.) (Several single sermons.)

PALMER, [Samuel] *Pastor of the Independent Congregation at Hackney.* The non-conformist's memorial, or account of the original dissenters of 1662, original written by *Edm. Calamy D. D:* now abridged and corrected. Vol. 1. 2. 1775. 8. (16 sh.) Collection of family prayers. 1783. 8. (3 sh. 6 d.) The Calvinism of the protestant dissenters asserted. 1786. 8. (6 d.) Vindication of the modern dissenters against the aspersions of *Will. Hawkins* and others. 1790. 8. (1 sh.)

PALMERSTONE, Lord Viscount: see *Henry Temple.*

PANDIT, [Ramalochan] An Indian Grant of Land in Y. C. 1018, (found at Tanna) literally translated from the Sanscrit. (Asiat. Res. Vol. 1. p. 357.)

PANTON, [Paul] *Esq.* of *Plasgwyn in Anglesey.* On the increase of population in Anglesey. (Phil. Transact. 1773. p. 180.)

PARISH, [John] Translation of a voyage to the Island of Mauritius, the Isle of Bourbon, the Cape of Good-Hope —. 1775. 8. (4 sh.)

PARK, [H. . . . .] *Surgeon of the Liverpool Infirmary.* New method of treating diseases of the joints of the knee and elbow —. 1783. 8. (1 sh. 6 d.) übers. Samml. f. W. A. St. 9. S. 113. Further account —. (London M. J. Vol. 11. P. 1.)

—— [James Allan] *Esq. of Lincoln's Inn, Barrister at Law.* System of law of marine insurances —. 1787. 8. (10 sh. 6 d.)

PARKER, [Georg] View of society and manners in high and low life. Vol. 1. 2. 1781. 12. (6 sh.) Humourous sketches, satirical strokes and attic observations —. 1782. 8. (4 sh.)

—— [Thomas] *of Lincoln's Inn.* The laws of shipping and insurance —. 1778. 4. (1 L. 1 sh.) Evidence of of our transactions in the East-Indies —. 1782. 4. (10 sh. 6 d.) Thoughts on opening the trade to the East-Indies —. 1784. 4. (6 d.)

PARKHURST, [John] *M. A.* The divinity and preexistence of our Lord and Saviour Jesus Christ —. 1787. 8. (2 sh. 6 d.)

PARKIN, [Miles] *A. B.* Columba, a poetical epistle. 1783. 4. (2 sh. 6 d.)

PARKINSON, [J......] of *Hoxton, Surgeon.* Some account of the effects of lightning. (Mem. of M. S. of L. Vol. 2. p. 493.)

—— [Sidney] *Painter for Sir Jos. Banks.* born: .... died at *Batavia.* 1770.

—— [T......] *M. A: F. R. S:* System of Mechanics: being the substance of lectures upon that branch of natural philosophy. 1787. 4. (16 sh.) System of mechanics and hydrostatics. 1789. 4. (11 sh.)

(Several single sermons.)

PARR, [Bartholomew] *M. D: Physician at Exeter.* Diss. De balneo. Edinb. 1773. 8. Account of the influenza as it appeared in Devonshire in May 1782. (*Duncan's* M. C. Vol. 9. p. 404.)

—— [Samuel] *LL. D: Clergyman.* *Discourse on the late fast by Phileleutherus Norfolciensis. 1781. 4. (1 sh.) On education and on the plans pursued in charity schools. 1786. 4. (2 sh. 6 d.) Preface to the edition of the Works of *Will. Bellenden.* 1787. *Tracts by *Warburton*, not admitted into the collection of their respective works. 1789. 8. (5 sh.)

(Several single sermons.)

PARRY, [Catherine] *Mrs.* Eden vale, a Novel. Vol. 1. 2. 1784. 12. (5 sh.)

—— [John] British harmony; a collection of welsh air. 1781. 8.

—— [Joshua] *Preacher at Cirencester.* born: ..... died 17..

—— [Richard] *D. D: Rector of Witchampton in Dorsetshire and Preacher at Market-Harborough in Leicestershire.* born: .... died d. 9 Apr. 1780.

—— [R......] *Rector of Kemerton, Gloucestershire.* Translation of *Seran de la Tour's* life of *Scipio Africanus* and of *Epaminondas* —. 1787. 8. Vol. 1. 2. (10 sh.)

PARRY, [William] *Remarks on the resolution passed at a meeting of the noblemen, gentlemen and clergy of the county of Warwick. 1790. 8. (1 sh.) Ed 2 (with the Author's name) 1790. 8. (1 sh.)

PARSONS, [.....] *Mrs.* The history of Miss Meridith, a novel. 1790. 8 Vol 1. 2. (6 sh.)

—— [.....] *A poetical tour in the Years 1784-1786. 1787. 8. (4 sh.)

—— [James] *M. D.* born at *Barnstapel, Devonshire.* 1705. died d. 4 Apr. 1770.

—— [John] *Professor of Anatomy at Oxford.* born at *Yorkshire* 1742. died d. 3 Apr. 1785.

—— [John Weddell] *A. B.* Essays on education. 1788. 8. (2 Sh 6 d.) Hints on producing genius. 1790 8. (Sh 6 d) (Several single sermons.)

—— [Philip] *A. M: Minister of Wye in Kent.* Dialogues between the dead and living 17.. Six letters on the establishment of sunday-schools. 1786. 8. (1 Sh 6 d.)

—— [Philip] *B. A: Rector of Eastwell in Kent.* Astronomic doubts: or an enquiry into the nature of that supply of light and heat which the superior planets may be supposed to enjoy. 1774. 8. (1 Sh.)

PARTINGTON, [Miles] A cure of a muscular contraction by electricity. (Phil. Transact. 1778. p. 86.) Account of a case of amaurosis cured by electricity. (Lond. M. J. Vol. 9. Part. IV.)

PASCOE, [James] *Surgeon at Tregony, in Cornwall.* Case of a tumour of the leg, supposed to have been occasioned by a ruptured vein. (London M. J. Vol. 6. p. 141.)

PASMORE, [George] The contest; an english pastoral. 1781. 4. (2 sh.)

PASQUIN, [Anthony] *Esq.* The children of Thespis. P. 1-3. 1788 4. (9 sh.) Poetical epistle from *Gabr d'Estrées* to Henry IV. 1789. 4. (2 sh.) Postscript to the new Bath guide, a poem. 1790. 8. (2 sh 6 d.)

PATERSON, [......] *Speculations upon law and lawyers —. 1788. 8. (2 sh.)

—— [Daniel] *Captain, Assistant to the Quarter-Master General of his Majesty's Forces.* Description of all the direct and cross roads in Great-Britain. 1771. 8. (1 sh. 6 d.) Travelling dictionary; or alpha-

alphabetical tables of the distance of all the principal cities, borough, market and seaport towns in Great-Britain from each other; being the 2d part to the description of roads. 1772. 8. (4 sh.) British itinerary —. Vol. 1. 2. 1785. (2 L. 2 Sh.)

PATERSON, [James] *Clergyman at Aberdeen.* born: .... died 17..

— [Samuel] *Auctioneer.* Ioineriana: or the book of scraps. Vol. 1. 2. 1772. 8. (5 sh.) Coryat junior. Vol. 1-3. 17.. Bibliotheca universalis selecta; a catalogue of books ancient and modern, in various languages and faculties, and upon almost every branch of science and polite litterature —. 1786. 8. (5 sh. 6 d.)

— [William] *Lieutenant.* Account of a new electrical fish. (Phil. Tr. 1786. p. 382.) Account of four journeys into the country of the Hottentots, and Caffraria in the Years 1777-79. 1789. 4. (18 sh.) coloured (1 L. 11 Sh. 6 d.) übers. von *J. R. Forster*. 1790. 8.

PATSALL, [J.....] *A. M. Quintilian's* institutes of the orator. 1774. 8. Vol. 1. 2. (12 sh.)

PATTEN, [....] *D. D:* born: ... died d. 28 Febr. 1790.

— [Samuel] *Surgeon in London.* Account of the good effects of mercury in two cases of impeded deglutition —. (Lond. M. J. Vol. 10. P. 4.)

PATTERSON, [Robert] *Professor of Mathematics in the University of Pennsylvania.* Method of finding a true meridian line, and thence the variation of the compass. (Tr. of A. S. Vol. 2. p. 251.)

PATULLO, [Henry] *Esq.* On the cultivation of the lands and improvements of the revenues of Bengal. 1772. 4. (1 sh. 6 d.)

PAUL, [G.... O.....] *Sir.* Considerations on the defects of prisons —. 1784. 8. (1 sh. 6 d.)

— [John] *Barrister at law.* The parish Officer's complete guide —. 1773. 8. (1 sh. 6 d.) Digest of the laws relating to the game of this kingdom 1775. 8. (2 sh. 6 d.) The law of tythes. 1781. 8. (2 sh. 6 d.) The complete constable. 1785. 12. (1 sh. 6 d.)

PAXTON, [Richard] *Surgeon at Maldon in Essex.* An observation on opening the abdomen and thorax of a young lady, who died after a very short illness. (*Duncan's* M. C. Vol. 8. p. 90.)

PAYNE, [......] (This Gentleman has several names *George Aug. Hervey: Will. Freder. Melmoth.*) *G. A. Hervey* Naval history of Great-Britain. Vol. 1-4.

—— [Thomas] *Surgeon in London.* Case of a wound of the throat successfully treated. (London M. J. Vol. 6. p. 28.)

—— [William] Introduction to Geometry. 1767. 4. (7 sh. 6 d.) Elements of trigonometry, plane and spherical. 1772. 8. (5 sh.)

PAYSON, [Philipps] *F. A. A.* Astronomical observations made at Chelsea. (Mem. of B. A. Vol. 1.)

PEACOCK, [James] Sketches and descriptions of three simple instruments for drawing architecture and machinery in perspective. (Phil. Transact. 1785. p. 366.).

—— [Lucy] *Miss.* *The rambles of fancy: or moral and interesting tales —. Vol. 1. 2. 1786. 8. (5 sh.) *The adventures of the 6 princesses of Babylon in their travels to the temple of virtue, an allegory. 1786. 4. (3 sh. 6 d.)

PEAKE, [John] *Surgeon.* Review of *Jesse Foot's* observations on the new opinions of *John Hunter* in his treatise on the venereal disease. 1788. 8. (2 sh.)

PEARCE, [William] The haunts of *Shakespeare*: a poem. 1778. 4. (1 sh. 6 d.) Songs of the Comic opera the nunnery. 1785. 8.

—— [Zachary] *D. D: Lord Bishop of Rochester, Kent.* born in *High-Holborn* 1690. died d. 29. Jun. 1774.

PEARSE, [Thomas Deane] *Colonel, Commandant of the Artillery and Second in Command of the Bengal Army.* Astronomical observations in Fort William and between Madras and Calcutta. (Asiat. Ref. Vol. 1. p. 57.) Meteorological journal from 1 March. 1785 to 28 Febr. 1786. (Ibid. p. 441.)

PEARSON, [Edward] *M. A: Fellow of Sidney-Sussex College, Cambridge.* (Several single sermons.)

—— [George] *M. D.* Observations and experiments of the tepid springs of Buxton. Vol. 1. 2. 1784. 8. (8 sh.) Directions for impregnating the Buxton water with its own and other gases and for composing artificial Buxton water. 1785. 8. (1 sh.) Account of a singular cure of a dropsy. (Med. Transact. Vol. 3. p. 316.) Account of a division of the liver,

liver, occasioned by a fall. (Ibid. p. 377.) Case of a diseased kidney. (Med. Obs. Vol. 5. p. 236.) Account of the preparation and use of the phosphorated soda. (Lond. M. J. Vol. 9. P. 4. übers. Samml. f. A. Th. 13. S. 148.)

PEARSON, [John] *Surgeon to the Lock Hospital and to the Public Dispensary.* Instance of the good effects of opium, in a dangerous case of retention of urine. (Med. Obs. Vol. 6. p. 246.) Observations and queries on animal heat. (London, M. J. Vol. 7. P. 2.) Principles of surgery. Part. 1. 1788. 8. (5 sh.)

— [S. . . . .] Poems. 1790. 4. (4 sh.)

— [William] Dissertation on the mixed fever, delivered at a public examination for the degree of Bachelor in Medicine, at Cambridge in America. Boston. 1790. 8.

PEART, [E. . . . . .] *M. D.* The generation of animal heat investigated. 1788. 8. (2 sh. 6 d.) On the elementary principles of nature and the simple laws by which they are governed —. 1789. 8. (5 sh.) übers. von *K. G. Kühn.* Leipzig. 1791. 8.

PECKARD, [Peter] *D. D: Master of Magdalen College in the University of Cambridge.* Dissertations on Revelations Chap. XI. 13. 1756. 8. (1 sh.) Observations on the doctrine of an intermediate state between death and the resurrection. 1756. Further observations —. 1757. 8. (2 sh.) Observations on M. *Fleming's* survey of the search after souls —. 1759. 8. (2 sh.) (Several single sermons.)

PECKHAM, [Henry] *King's Counsel and Recorder of the city of Chichester.* born: . . . . died d. 10 Jan. 1787.

PECKWELL, [Henry] *D. D: Chaplain to the Marchioness of Lothian and Rector of Bloxam and Digby, Lincolnshire.* born; . . . . died d. 18. Aug. 1787.

PEDDLE, [. . . . .] *Mrs.* The life of Jacob. 1784. 12. Vol. 1. 2. (5 sh.) °Rudiments of taste. 1789. 12. (2 sh.)

PEGGE, [Samuel] *M. A. Rector of Whittington: F. A. S.* Observations on an antique marble of the Earl of Pembroke. (Archaeol. Vol. 1. p. 155.) Dissertation on an antient jewel of the Anglo-saxons. (Ibid. p. 161.) Of the introduction, progress, state

 and

and condition of the vine in Britain. (Ibid. p.319.) Copy of a deed in latin and saxon, of Odo, Bishop of Bajeux, half brother of William the Conqueror. (Ibid. p. 335.) Of the horn, as a charter or instrument of conveyance; some observations on *Sam. Foxlowe's* horn, as likewise on the nature and kinds of these horns in general. (Ibid. Vol. 3. p. 1.) On shoeing of horses amongst the ancients. (Ibid. p. 39.) Whether England formerly produced any wine from grapes. (Ibid. p. 53.) Remarks on Belatucader. (Ibid. p. 101.) Memoir concerning the sac-friars or fratres de poenitentia Jesu Christi, as settled here in England. (Ibid. p. 125.) Memoir on cock-fighting. (Ibid. p. 132.) On an inscription in honour of Serapis found at York. (Ibid. p. 151.) Remarks on the first noble, coined 18 Edward III. A. D. 1334. (Ibid. p. 316.) Observations on two jewels in the possession of Sir *Charles Mordaunt.* (Ibid. p. 371.) Enquiry into the nature and cause of King *John's* death; wherein is shewn that is wat not effected by poison. (Ib. Vol. 4. p. 29.) Illustration of a gold enamelled ring, supposed to have been the property of Alhstan, Bishop of Sherburne; with some account of the state and condition of the saxon jewelry in the more early ages. (Ibid. p. 47.) Observations on *Kit's Cotty* house, in Kent. (Ibid. p. 110.) Dissertation on a gold coin of *Edmund Crouchback.* (Ibid. p. 190.) Remarks on the bones of fowls found in Christchurch-Twynham, Hampshire. (Ibid. p. 414.) Observations on the mistakes of Mr. *Lisle* and *Hearne*, in respect of King Aelfreds present to the cathedrals. The late use of the stylus, or metalline pen —. (Arch. Vol. 2. p. 68.) The bull-running at Tutbury in Staffordshire. (Ibid. p. 86.) Observations on *Percy's* account of minstrels among the Saxons. (Ibid. p. 100.) Observations on stone hammers. (Ibid. p. 124.) Dissert. on the crane, as a dish served up a great table in England. (Ibid. p. 171.) Narrative of the battle of Chesterfield A. D. 1266. (Ibid. p. 276.) Observations on the history of St. George the patron saint of England. (Ibid. Vol. 5. p. 1.) On the

Rud-

Rudſton pyramidical ſtone. (Ibid. Vol. 5. p. 95.) Remarks on *Pownall's* conjecture, concerning the Croyland boundary ſtone. (Ibid. Vol. 5. p. 101.) Examination of the miſtaken opinion that Ireland and Thanet were void of ſerpents. (Ibid. Vol. 5. p. 160.) On the Twynham ſtone coffins. (Ibid. p. 224.) On an important hiſtorical paſſage of Gildas. (Ibid p. 272.) On the matrices of Conventual seals. (Ibid. p. 346.) Remarks on an antient pig of lead diſcovered in Derbyshire. (Ibid. Vol. 5. p. 369. Vol. 7. p. 170. Vol. 9. p. 45.) The penny with the name of Rodbertus IV —. (Ibid. Vol. 5. p. 390.) On the plague in England. (Ibid. Vol. 6. p. 79.) On the commencement of day amongſt the Saxons and Britains. (Ibid. p. 150.) Illuſtrations of ſome druidical remains in the peak of Derbyshire. (Ibid. Vol. 7. p. 19.) Obſervations on Aldbrough church at Holderneſſ, proving that it was not a Saxon building, as *Somerset* contends. (Ibid. p. 86.) Disquiſition on the lows or barrows in the peak of Derbyshire, particularly that capital British monument called Arbelows. (Ibid. p. 131.) Obſervations on the chariots of the antient Britains. (Ibid. p. 211.) Obſervations on a ſeal of *Thomas*, Suffragan Bishop of Philadelphia. (Ibid. p. 362.) Hiſtory of the asylum or sanctuary from its origin to the final abolition of it in the reign of James. (Ibid. Vol. 8. p. 1.) Obſervations on the Stanton-Moor urns and druidical temple. (Ibid. p. 58.) A circumſtantial detail of the battle of Lincoln, A. D. 1217. (Ibid. p. 195.) Obſervations on ſome braſſ celts and other weapons diſcovered in Ireland. 1780. (Ibid. Vol. 9. p. 84.) Diſcoveries in opening a tumulus in Derbyshire. (Ibid. p. 189.)

[Samuel] *A. M. Prebendary of Bobenhull in the Church of Lichtfield.* *Diſſertation upon Oriuna —. 1751. 4. (2 Sh. 6 d.) Series of diſſertations on ſome elegant and very valuable Anglo-Saxon remains —. 1755. 4. (2 Sh. 6 d.) Memoirs of the life of *Roger de Weſcham*, Dean of Lincoln, Bishop of Coventry and Lichtfield —. 1761. 4. (2 Sh. 6 d.) Aſſemblage of coins, fabricated by authority of the

the Arch-bishop of Canterbury. —. 1772. 4. (7 Sh. 6 d.)

PEGGE, [Samuel] Curialia: or an hiſtorical account of ſome branches of the royal household —. P. 1. 2. 1782. 1784. 4. (8 ſh. 6 d.)

PEIRSON, [R.....] *A. M: F. A. S.* On the connection between botany and agriculture. (*Hunter's* G. E. Vol. 3. p. 7.) On the analogy between plants and animals. (Ibid. Vol. 4. p. 55.) On the ſexes of plants. (Ibid. p. 119.)

PEISLEY, [J.....] A concise compendium of the conſtitutional part of the laws of England. 1783. 12. (1 Sh. 6 d.) Letter to Lord *Thurlow* — on the conduct of parliament towards the insolvent debtors and imprisonment for debt —. 1789. 8. (1 ſh.)

PELHAM, [Henry] A map of the county of Clare in Ireland; in 12 sheets.

PEMBERTON, [Henry] *Profeſſor of Phyſic at Gresham College: F. R. S.* born: .... died d. 9 March. 1771.

PENNANT, [Thomas] *F. R. S.* Account of an earthquake felt in Flintshire Apr. 2. 1750. (Phil. Transact. 1756. p. 687.) Account of ſome fungitae and other curious coralloid fossil bodies. (Ibid. 1759. p. 513.) Account of the different ſpecies of pinguins. (Ibid. 1768. p. 91.) Indian Zoology. P. 1. 1769. fol. (18 ſh.) überſ. von *J. R. Forſter.* Halle 1781. fol. * British Zoology. P. 1-4. fol. 1763-1766. (8 L. 18 ſh. 6 d.) Ed. in 4to Vol. 1-4. 1777. (1 L. 4 Sh.) Ed. in 8o Vol. 1-4. 1768. (1 L. 4 Sh.) überſ. von *C. G. Murr.* Augsb. 1771. fol. Account of two new tortoises. (Phil. Transact, 1771. p. 266.) *Synopsis of Quadrupeds. 1771. 8. (9 Sh.) *Tour in Scotland in the Y. 1769. 1771. 8. (7 Sh. 6 d.) Ed. 2. 1772. 4. Ed. 3. 1774. 4. additions. 1774. 4. überſ. Leipz. 1779. u. in Samml. von Reiſebeſchr. Berlin. Th. 24. S. 260. Genera of birds. 1773. 8. (2 Sh.) *Tour in Scotland and voyage to the Hebrides. P. 1. 2. 1776. 4. (1 L. 11 Sh. 6 d.) überſ. von *J. P. Ebeling.* Th. 1. 2. Leipzig. 1780. 8. *Tour in Wales. 1778. 4. Vol. 1. (1 L. 1 Sh.) überſ. in der Bibliothek der neueſten Reiſebeſchreib. Th. 4. Frankf. u. Leipzig. 8. Vol. 2. P. 1. Journey to Snowdon 1781. Vol. 2. P. 2. 1783. 4. (1 L. 5 Sh.)

Jour-

Journey from Chester to London. 1782. 4. (1 L. 5 Sh.) History of Quadrupeds. Vol. 1. 2. 1781. 4. (1 L. 16 Sh.) Account of the Turkey. (Phil. Transact. 1781. p. 67.) Account of several earthquakes felt in Wales. (Ibid. 1781. p. 193.) Free thoughts on our Militia laws. 1782. 8. (6 d.) Arctic Zoology. Vol. 1. 2. 1786. supplement. 1787. 4. (2 L. 2 Sh.) übers. von *Hoffmann*. Th 1. 2. Leipz. 1787. 4. *Histoire naturelle des oiseaux par Buffon - systematically disposed. 1787. 4. (7 Sh.) Of the Patagonians, formed from the relation of *Falkener*. 1788. 4. *Of London. 1790. 4. (1 L. 1 Sh.) Ed. 2. 1791. 4. (1 L. 5 Sh.) übers. von Joh. Heinr Wiedmann. Nürnberg 1791. 8.

PENNINGTON, [....] *Mrs.* of *Walterhall*, *Yorkshire.* born: .... died d. Oct. 1783.

— [R. . . . .] Description of a sector —. 1780. 8. (1 Sh.)

— [William] Reflections on the various advantages resulting from the draining, enclosing and allotting of large commons and common fields. 1770. 8. (1 Sh. 6 d.) Free enquiry into the origin, progress and present state of pluralities. 1772. 8. (4 Sh.)

PENNY, [......] *Mrs.* Poems. 1771. 4.

PENNYLESS, [Peter] (Pseudonymus) Sentimental lucubrations. 1770. 8. (2 Sh. 6 d.) übers. Leipz. 1770. 8.

PENROSE, [Bernard] *Surgeon's mate.* Account of the last expedition to port Egmont in Falkland's Islands, in the Y. 1772 —. 8. 1775. (1 Sh. 6 d.) übers. von *M. C. Sprengel*: deutsches Museum 1776. St. 4. und Beytr. z. Völker und Länderk. Th. 1. S. 143.

— [F....] *Letters philosophical and astronomical. 1789. 8. (6 sh)

— [Thomas] *Curate of Newbury*, *Berks.* (Several single sermons.)

— [Thomas] *Rector of Beckington and Standerwick*, *Somersetshire.* born 174.. died at Bristol. 1779.

PERCIVAL, [Thomas] *M. D: F. R. S: F. A. S. Physician at Manchester.* Account of a double child. (Phil. Transact. 1758 p. 360.) On the roman colonies and stations in Cheshire and Lancashire. (Ibid. 1758. p. 216.) Diss. De frigore. Lugd. Bat. 1765. 4.

Expe-

Experiments on the Peruvian bark. (Phil. Transact. 1767. p. 221.) Eſſays, medical, philoſophical and experimental. Vol. 1-3. 1768-1776. Ed. 2. 1772. 8. Ed. 4. 1789. 8. (12 ſh.) Einzelne Stücke überſ. in Samml. f. A. Th. 2. On the disadvantages which attend the inoculation of children in early infancy. 1768. 8. (6 d.) Experiments and obſervations on water: particularly on the hara pump water of Mancheſter. 1769. 8. (2 ſh) Account of the courſe of the Ermine-ſtreet through Northamptonshire and of roman burying place by the ſide of it. (Arch. Vol. 1. p. 62.) On the efficacy of external applications in the angina maligna or ulcerous ſore throat. 1770. überſ. Samml. f. A. Th. 2. p. 91. Experiments and obſervations on the waters of Buxton and Matlok in Derbyshire. (Phil. Transact. 1772. p. 455.) Hiſtory and cure of a difficulty in deglutition of long continuance, ariſing from a ſpasmodic affection of the oesophagus. (Med. Transact. Vol. 2. p. 90.) On the different quantities of rain, which fall at different heights over the ſame ſport of ground (*Hunter's* G. E. Vol. 3. p. 177.) On the Orchis root. (Ibid. Vol. 4. p. 163.) On the effects of fixed air on the colours and vegetation of plants. (Ibid Vol. 5. p. 17.) On the action of different manures. (Ibid p. 60.) Obſervations and experiments on the poiſon of lead 1774. 8. (2 ſh) überſ. *Baldinger's* Magazin für Aerzte. St. 3. Neues Magazin Th. 1. S. 97. Account of an extra uterine foetus, voided by ſtool 22 Years after pregnancy. (Med. Com. of Ed. Vol. 3.) The caſe of an angina pectoris, which terminated fatally with the diſſection. (Ibid. p. 180.) On the uſe of flowers of zinc in epileptic caſes. (Ibid. Vol. 2.) On the external uſe of preparations of lead. (Ibid. Vol. 3. p. 199.) Obſervations on the ſtate of population in Mancheſter and other adjacent places. (Phil. Transact. 1774. p. 54. 1775. p. 322. 1776. p. 160.) Obſervations on the medicinal uſes of fixed air. (*Prieſtley's* experim. on different kinds of air. App. p. 300.) überſ. Samml. f. A. Th. 3. S. 281.) On the ſolution of ſtones of the urinary and of the gall bladder by water, impregnated with fixed air. (Ibid.) überſ. Samml. f. A.

Th.

Th. 3. A father's inſtruction to his children; conſiſting of tales, fables and reflections. Vol. 1. 2. 1775. 8. (5 ſh.) überſ. Th. 1. 2. 1778. 8. Philosophical, medical and experimental eſſays. 1776. 8. (5 ſh.) Tables, shewing the number of deaths occaſioned by the ſmallpox in the ſeveral periods of life and different ſeasons of the year, with its comparative fatality to males and females. (Med. Obs. Vol. 5. p. 270.) Tables of the comparative mortality of the measles from 1768 to 1774. (Ibid. p. 282.) Miscellaneous practical observations. (Med. Com. of Ed. Vol. 5. p. 166.) Account of the earthquake at Mancheſter. (Ibid.) Account of a new and cheap method of preparing poth-ash, with observations. (Phil. Transact. 1780. p. 345.) Observations on the medicinal uses of the oleum jecoris aselli, or cod liver oil, in the chronic rheumatiſm and other painfull disorders. (London M. J. Vol. 3. p. 392.) Moral and literary Diſſertations. 1784. 8. (4 ſh.) Miscellaneous facts and observations. (Ibid. Vol. 4. p. 56.) überſ. Samml. f. A. Th. 10. S. 199. Hiſtory of the fatal effects of pikles impregnated with copper; together with observations on that mineral poison. (Med. Transact. Vol. 3. p. 80.) Tribute to the memory of *Charles de Polier*, Esq. (Mem. of M. Vol. 1. p. 287.) On the different quantities of rain which fall, at different heights over the ſame spot of ground, with a letter from *Benj. Franklin*. (Ibid. Vol. 2. p. 106.) Speculations on the perceptive power of vegetables; (Ibid. p. 114.) überſ. Samml. zur P. und N. G. Th. 3. S. 666. On the pursuits of experimental philosophy. (Ibid. p. 326.) Facts and queries relative to attraction and repulſion. (Ibid. p. 429.) Narrative of the ſufferings of a collier, who was confined more than seven days, without ſuſtenance, and exposed to the choke-damp, in a coal-pit not far from Mancheſter, with observations on the effects of famine, on the means of alleviating them, and on the action of foul air, on the human body. (Ibid. p. 467.) Experiments on the ſolvent powers of camphor and other miscellaneous communications. (Mem. of M. S of L. Vol. 2. p. 54.) Medical cautions and remarks particularly relative to pulmonary dis-

or-

orders. (Ibid. p. 288.) — Hints towards the investigation of the nature, cause and cure of the rabies canina. (London M. J. Vol. 10. P. 3.)

PERCY, [Thomas] *D. D: Bishop of Dromore in Ireland.* The ſong of Salomon translated - with a commentary. 1764. 8. Haw Kiou Choean, a Chinese romance. Vol. 1-4. 17.. The little orphan of China, or, the house of Chao, a tragedy. (In Miscellaneous pieces relating to the Chinese 1762.) *Reliques of ancient english poetry. Vol. 1-3. 1765. 8. (10 ſh. 6 d.) Ed. 3. 1775. *The hermit of Warkworth; a Northumberland ballad. 1771. 4. (2 ſh. 6 d.) On ſome large foſſil horns. (Arch. Vol. 7. p. 158.) *Rich. Steele's* tatler, with illuſtrations and notes hiſtorical, biographical and critical. Vol. 1-6. 1786. 8.

PERFECT, [William] of *Weſtmalling* in *Kent. M. D.* Methods of cure in ſome particulars cases of insanity. 1778. 8. (2 ſh. 6 d.) Cases in midwifery. Vol. 1. 2. 1783. 8. (12 ſh.) On the ſubject of insanity. 1784. 4. (1 ſh.) Select cases in the different ſpecies of insanity, lunacy or madneſſ. 1787. 8. (6 ſh.) überſ. von *C. F. Michaelis.* Leipz. 1789. 8.

PERKINS, [John] of *Boſton.* Conjectures concerning wind and water-ſpouts. (Tr. of A. S. Vol. 2. p. 335.)

—— [William Lee] *M. D: Physician at Kingſton upon Thames.* Eſſay for a nosological and comparative view of the cynanche maligna or putrid ſore throat and the ſcarlatina anginosa or ſcarlet fever with angina. 1787. 8. (1 ſh. 6 d.) Ed. 2. 1790. 8. (2 ſh.) Hiſtory of a case of hydrocephalus terminating fatally, after a ſalivation was excited by the use of mercury. (*Duncan's* M. C. Dec. 2. Vol. 1. p. 298.) überſ. Samml. f. A. Th. 13. S. 20.

PERRY, [S.....] *Surgeon.* On the lues venerea, gonorrhoea and tabes dorsalis or gleet. 1786. 8. (2 ſh.)

—— [William] *Maſter of the Academy at Kelso.* The man of buſineſſ and gentleman's aſſiſtant: containing a treatise of practical arithmetic —. 1774. 8. (6 ſh.) The royal ſtandard english dictionary. 1775. 8. (3 ſh.)

PER-

PERRYN, [......] *Baron.* Appendix to "*Thoughts on executive justice*" 1784. 12. (1 sh. 6 d.)

PESHELL, [John] *Sir. Baronet.* The ancient and present state of the city of Oxford, chiefly collected by Mr. *Anthony à Wood*, with additions. 1775. 4.

PETERS, [Charles] *D. D: Rector of Wabyn, Cornwall.* born:.... died d. 17 Febr. 1774.

— [Matthew] The rational farmer, or a treatise on agriculture and tillage. 1771. 8. (2 sh 6 d.) Winter riches; or miscellany of rudiments, directions and observations necessary for the laborious farmer —. 1771. 8. (3 sh. 6 d.) Agricultura: or the good husbandman, being a tract of ancient and modern experimental observations on the green vegetable system —. 1777. 8. (3 sh.)

PETERSON, [Peter] Memorial concerning the woollen manufactory. 1783. 8. (1 sh.)

PETTINGAL, [John] *D. D.* Inquiry into the use and practice of juries among the greeks and romans. 1770. (7 Sh. 6 d.)

PETTMANN, [William] of *Sandwich, in Kent.* Essay concerning the propriety and the manner of cultivating in children and youth a disposition to — any particular office, profession, trade, or employment —. 1781. 12. (2 Sh.)

PEW, [Richard] *M. D.* Account of an astonishing recovery after a wound through the lungs. (Med. Com. of Ed. Vol. 5. p. 188.) Observations on a better mode of providing for the poor —. 1783. 8. (1 Sh.) Medical sketches. P. 1. 1785. 8. (2 Sh. 6 d.) übers. von *C. F. Michaelis.* Leipz. 1787. 8.

PEYTON, [V..... J.....] Les vrais principes de la langue Angloise. 1756. 12. (3 Sh. 6 d.) A new vocabulary or grammar of the true pronunciation of the English in form of a dictionary —. 1759. 12. (3 Sh.) History of the English language —. 1771. 8. (1 Sh.) The French tutor; or, the theory and practice of the French language —. 1773. 12. (4 Sh.)

PHILIPS, [Ambrose] *Esq.* Persian tales for the ladies - designed for pleasure and entertainment. 1790. 8.

PHILIPP, [Arthur] *Governor.* Voyage to Botany Bay with an account of the etablissement of the colonies of Port Jackson and Norfolk Island. 1789. 4. (2 L. 11 Sh. 6 d.) Ed. 2. 1790. 4. (1 L. 11 Sh. 6 d.) Ed. 3. 1790. 8. (10 sh. 6 d.) übers. von C. *Sprengel.* Hamburg. 1790. 8.

PHILIPPS, [John] *Barrister, of the Inner temple.* Election cases, determining during the 1 session of the XV parliament of Great-Britain by committees of the house of commons —. Vol. 1. 1782. 8. (5 sh.)

PHILIPS, [Peregrine] Poetry by *Rich. Crashaw* —. 1785. 12. (3 sh.)

PHILIPPS, [T.....] History and antiquities of Shrewsbury —. 1779. 4. (10 sh. 6 d.)

PHIPPS, [Constantine John] Lord *Mulgrave, of Ireland. M. P: F. R. S.*

— and Capt. *Lutwidge's* Journal of a voyage — toward the North-Pole. 1774. 4. (12 sh. 6 d.) 8. (1 sh. 6 d.) übers. durch *S. Engel.* Bern. 1777. 4. Pieces of fugitive poetry: see *Debrett's* Asylum.

—— [Joseph] The original and present state of man —. 1773. 8. (2 sh.) Reply to Sir *Newton's* appendix — that the quackers are not calvinists. 1774. 8. (1 sh.)

PICARD, [George] The English guide to the French tongue. 1778. 8. (2 sh.)

PICKBOURN, [James] *Master of a boarding-school at Hackney.* Dissertation on the English verb —. 1789. 8. (6 sh.)

PICKERING, [Amelia] *Miss.* The sorrows of Werter: a poem. 1788. 4. (5 sh.)

—— [T.... A.....] Discourse on the doctrine of attachments with a report of proceedings in the court of common pleas, against an attorney —. 1786. 8. (1 sh. 6 d.)

PICKERSGILL, [Richard] *Lieutenant; late Commander of his Majesty's armed Brig Lion.* Track of his Majesty's armed Brig *Lion*, from *England* to *Davis's Streights* and *Labradore*, with observations for determining the longitude by sun and moon and error of common reckoning; also the variation of the compass and dip of the needle, as observed during the said voyage in 1776. (Phil. Transact. 1778. p. 1057.)

PICKETT,

PICKETT, [William] Apology to the public for a continued intrusion on their notice; with an appeal to the free and independent proprietors of bank stock. 1788. 8. (1 sh.) Public improvement; or, a plan for making a convenient and handsome communication between the cities of London and Westminster. 1789. 4. (2 sh. 6 d.)

PIERCY, [Richard] Death improved; an elegiac poem, occasioned by the death of *T. Gibbons*. 1785. 8. (6 d.)

PIERSON, [Thomas] The treacherous son in law, a Tragedy. 1786. 8.

PIESLEY, [J......] Compendium of the constitutional part of the laws of England. 1783. 12. (1 sh. 6 d.)

PIGOTT, [....] Letter —. 1786. 4. (6 d.) *Second* letter to *Will. Pitt*, on the necessity and advantage of a taxation on the public funds. 1787 4. (6 d.)

—— [Edward] *Esq.* Account of a nebula in *Coma Berenices*. (Phil. Transact. 1781. p. 82.) Extract of a letter containing the discovery of a comet: (Ibid. 1784. p. 20.) Observations of a new variable star. (Ibid. 1785. p. 127.) Observations and remarks on those stars which the Astronomers of the last century suspected to be changeable. (Ibid. 1786. p. 189.) Observation of the late transit of mercury over the sun. (Ibid. 1786. p. 389.) The latitude and longitude of York determined from a variety of astronomical observations —. (Ibid. 1786. p. 409.) Account of some luminous arch. (Ibid. 1790. p. 47.) Determination of the longitudes and latitudes of some remarkable places near the severn. (Ibid. 1790. p. 385.)

—— [Nathan] *Esq. F. R. S.* Observations on the eclipse of the sun Aug. 11. 1765. at Caen in Normandy. (Phil. Tr. 1767 p. 402. On the late transit of Venus. Ibid. 1770. p. 257.) Meteorological observations at Caen in Normandy for 1765 - 1769. (Ibid. 1771. P. 1. p. 274.) Astronomical observations made in the Austrian Netherlands in 1772. and 1773. (Ibid. 1776. p. 182) Astronomical observations made in the Austrian Netherlands in the Years 1773, 1774 and 1775. (Ibid. 1778. p. 637.) Double stars discovered in 1779 at Frampton-house, Glamormorganshire. (Ibid. 1781. p. 84.) Aſtronomical observations. (Ibid. 1781. p. 347.) Account of an observation of the meteor of Aug. 18. 1783. made on *Hewit* common near York. (Ibid. 1784. p. 457.) Observations of the comet of 1783. (Ibid. 1784. p. 460.) Observations of the tranſit of mercury over the ſun's disc, made at Louvain, in the Netherlands May. 3. 1786. (Ibid. 1786. p. 384.)

PIGOTT, [Robert] *Esq.* New information and lights, on the late treaty of commerce with France. 1787. 4. (1 Sh.)

PIGUENIT, [C.... D....] On the art of newspaper defamation. 1775. 8. (6 d.)

PIGUENET, [D... J....] Don Quixote, a comedy. 1774. 8.

PIKE, [John Baxter] Forms for public devotion at Lancaſter Chapel. 1784. 12. (2 Sh. 6 d.)

PILGRIM, [Edward Trapp] *Esq.* Poetical trifles. 1785. 12. (1 Sh. 6 d.)

PILKINGTON, [James] Introduction to the knowledge of the eminent painters. 1778. 8. (3 Sh. 6 d.) View of the present ſtate of Derbyshire with an account of its moſt remarkable antiquities. Vol. 1. 2. 1789. 8. (13 Sh.)

PILLING, [William] A caveat addreſſed to the catholics of Worceſter againſt the letter of Mr. *Wharton.* 1785. 8. (1 Sh. 6 d.)

PILLON, [Frederik] *Actor.* born at Corke: ... died d. 11. Jan. 1788.

PINCOT, [Daniel] *Artificial ſtone Manufacturer.* On the origin, nature, uses and properties of artificial stone —. 1770. 8. (1 Sh. 6 d.)

PINDAR, [Paul] The fleajad; an heroic poem, with notes —. 1787. 4. (2 ſh.)

—— [Peter] see *Woolcot.*

PINFOLD, [Peregine] of *Grubb-Hatch, Esq.* Fragment of the hiſtory of *John Bull*, Esq. compiled by *Sir Humphrey Polesworth* — now firſt published —. 1785. 8. (2 ſh. 6 d.)

PINKERTON, [John] (born in *Scotland.*) *Rimes 1781. 8. (2 ſh. 6 d.) Tales in verse. 1782. 4. (3 ſh.) *Two dithyrambic odes 1) on enthuſiasm 2) to laughter. 1782. 4. (6 d.) *Eſſay on medals; or, an introduction to the knowledge of ancient and

and modern coins and medals, especially those of Greece, Rome and Britain. 1784. 8. with the author's name. Vol. 1. 2. 1789. 8. (10 sh. 6 d.) *Letters of litterature, by *Rob. Heron*. 1785. 8. (6 sh.) *Antient Scotish poems - from the Msc. collections of Sir *Rich. Maitland*, with notes, glossary and an essay on the origine of Scotish poetry. Vol. 1. 2. 1786. 8. (6 sh.) Dissertation on the origine and progress of the scythians or goths. 1787. 8. (3 sh. 6 d.) Vitae antiquae sanctorum, qui habitaverunt in ea parte Britanniae nunc vocata Scotia vel in ejus insulis. 1789. 8. Enquiry into the history of *Scotland* preceding the reign of Malcolm III. or the Year 1056. Vol. 1. 2. 1789. 8. (12 sh.) The Bruce, or, the history of Robert I. King of Scotland, written in Scotish verse by *John Barbour* — published from a Msc. — with notes and a glossary. Vol. 1-3. 1789. 8. (12 sh.)

PINNEL, [Peter] *D. D: Prebendary of Rochester, Vicar of that parish and Shorne.* born:.... died d. 16 Aug. 1783.

PIOZZI, [Hester Lynch] *Mrs.* (Her maden name *Salusbury;* Her first husband was *Henry Trale*, Brewer in the borough of Southwark. Her second husband *Piozzi*, Music-master at Bath.) *Florence miscellany. 17.. The three warnings, a tale. 17.. Anecdotes of *Sam. Johnson* LL. D. during the last 20 years of his life. 1786. 8. (4 sh.) Letters to and from *Sam. Johnson*, with some poems. Vol. 1. 2. 1788. 8. (12 sh.) Observations and reflections made in a course of a journey through France, Italy and Germany. Vol. 1. 2. 1789. 8. (12 sh.) übers. von *G. Forster*. Th. 1. 2. 1790. 8.

PIRIE, [Alexander] *Minister of the Gospel at Newburgh.* Dissertation on baptism, intended to illustrate the origin, history, design, mode and subjects of that sacred institution wherein the mistakes of the Quakers and Baptists are pointed out; with an appendix. 1790. 12. (3 sh.)

PITMAN, [Ambrose] *Esq.* The distress of integrity and virtue: a poem. 1783. 4. (1 sh. 6 d.)

PITT, [William] Speech in the house of commons. 1783. 8. (1 sh.) Reply to Mr. *Orde* — on the new

new commercial regulations between the two countries —. 1785. 8. (1 ſh.)

PITTMAN, [Philip] *Captain.* The present ſtate of the European ſettlements on the Miſſiſſippi with a geographical description of that river, illuſtrated by plans and draughts 1770. 4. (6 ſh.)

PLATT, [Joshua] of *Oxford.* born: 1696. died d. 26. Dec. 1776.

PLAYFAIR. [James] *D. D: F. A. S. Edin.* (born in *Scotland.*) Syſtem of chronology. 1784. fol. (2 L. 5 ſh.)

—— [James] *Architect.* Method of conſtructing vapour-bat s —. 1783. 8. (1 ſh.)

—— [John] *A. M: F. R. S. Edin. Profeſſor of Mathematics in the Univerſity of Edinburgh.* On the arithmetic of impoſſible quantities. (Phil. Tr. 1778. p. 318.) Account of the life and writings of *Matth. Stewart,* Profeſſor of Mathematics at Edinburgh. (Tr. of E. S. Vol. 1. App. p. . . .) On the causes which affect the accuracy of barometrical measurements. (Tr of E. S. Vol. 1. p. 87.) Remarks on the aſtronomy of the Brahmins. (Ibid. Vol. 2. p. 135.)

—— [William] (born in *Scotland.*) Regulations for the intereſt of money: 17.. The commercial and political Atlas; representing - the exports, imports and general trade of England, the national debt, and other public accounts —. with *James Carry's* charts of the revenue and trade of Ireland 1786. 4. (1 L. 1 ſh.) On the national debt, with copper-plate charts for comparing annuities with perpetual loans. 1787. 4. (2 ſh. 6 d.)

PLOWDEN, [Francis] *Esq. Conveyancer.* *Inveſtigation of the native rights of British ſubjects 1784. Supplement. 1785. 8. (5 ſh. 6 d.) *Impartial* thoughts upon the beneficial consequences of enrolling all deeds, wills and codicills, affecting lands, throughout England and Wales. 1790. 8 (2 ſh.)

PLUMPTREE, [Robert] *D. D: Profeſſor of Cambridge, Rector of Wimple and Vicar of Whadden.* born:... died d. 29 Oct. 1788.

POLE, [Thomas] *Surgeon.* Of an injury in the hand, ſucceſſfully removed. (Mem. of M. S. of L. Vol. 1. p. 370.) Account of a remarkable ſpasmodic affection

fection from the puncture of a pin, cured by the use of laudanum, with antimonial wine. (Ibid. Vol. 2. p. 373.) Account of ſeveral phaenomena, which occurred upon opening the body of a female infant of premature birth, who died a few hours after delivery. (Ibid. p. 507.)

POLLHILL, [Nathaniel] *M. P.* Letter on Mr. *Debraw's* improvements in the culture of bees. (Phil. Transact. 1778. p. 107.)

POLIER, [Anthony] *Lieutenant Colonel.* The proceſs of making attar, or eſſential oil of roses. (Aſiat. Res. Vol. 1. p. 332.) überſ. *Gren* J. d. P. Th. 2. S. 343.

DE POLIER, [Charles] born: .... died 17..

POLLEN, [Thomas] *A. M.* On the Lord's ſupper. 1770. 8. (2 ſh. 6 d.) The fatal consequences of adultery to monarchies as well as to private families —. 1772. 8. (3 ſh.)

POLOVERI, [John] New geographical tables. 1775. 8. (6 ſh)

POLWHELE, [Richard] *a Clergyman.* *Pictures from nature in 12 ſonnets, to which are added, the lock transformed. 1785. 4. (1ſh. 6 d.) Ed. 2. (with the Author's name.) 1786. 4. (2 ſh.) *The art of eloquence. Book. 1. 1785. 4. (2 ſh. 6 d.) Ed. 2. (with the Author's name; under the title:) The english orator. Book 1-4. 1786-1789. 4. (8 ſh.) The Idyllia, epigrams and fragments of *Theocritus*, *Bion* and *Moschus* with the elegies of *Tyrtaeus*, translated into english verse. 1786. 4. (1 L. 1 ſh) Discourses on different ſubjects. Vol. 1. 2. 1788. 8. (7 ſh.)

POOLE, [T.....] *Butler* to the Lady *Jane* and Sir *Willoughby Aſton.* On ſtrong beer, ale —. fully explaining the art of brewing in the beſt manner —. 1784. 8. (2 ſh 6 d.)

POPE, [Alexander] *Miniſter of Reay.* Description of the Dune of Dornadilla. (Arch. Vol. 5. p. 216.)

—— [Michael] born 1709. died d. 10 Febr. 1788.

POPHAM, [Edward] *D. D: Rector of Chelton Foliat and Vicar of Laycock.* Selecta poemata anglorum latina. Vol. 1-3. 1774. (9 ſh.) Illuſtrium virorum elogia sepulchralia. 1778. 8. (5 ſh.) Two sermons. 1783. 4. (1 ſh.)

PORRETT, [Robert] Clariſſa; or, the fatal seduction; a Tragedy. 1788. 8. (5 ſh.)

PORSON, [R. . . . . .] Letters to Mr. Arch-Deacon *Travis* in answer to his defence of the three heavenly witnesses I John. V. 7. 1790. 8. (6 sh.)

PORTAL, [Abraham] *Bookseller.* Olindo and Sophronia, a Tragedy. 1758. 8. The indiscret lover, a Comedy. 1768. 8. The Lady of Bagdad, a comic opera. 1778. *Elegy on the death of *John Langhorne* D. D: Rector of Blagden, Somersetshire. 1779. 4. (1 sh.) Poems. 1781. 8. (5 sh.)

PORTERFIELD, [W. . . .] *M. D. at Edinburgh.* born: . . . . died 1771.

PORTEUS, [Beilby] *D. D: Lord Bishop of London.* Death, a poetical essay. 1759. 4. (1 sh.) *Thom. Secker's* sermons on several subjects; with his life and character. Vol. 1-7. 1770. 8. übers. Th. 1-6. Lemgo. 1778. Sermons on several subjects. 1783. 8. (5 sh.) (Several single sermons.)

—— [Nathan.] Catechism for children and youth. 1783. 8. (6 d.)

PORTLOCK, [Nathan.] *Captain.* Voyage round the world but more particularly to the North-West coast of America —. 1789. 4. (1 L. 5 sh.)

POSTLETHWAITE, [T. . . . . .] *B. D.* Discourse on Isaiah VII. 14-16. 1781. 4. (1 sh.)

POTE, [Joseph] *Bookseller and Printer.* born: . . . . died d. 3 March 1787.

POTT, [Joseph Holden] *M. A: Prebendary of Lincoln and ArchDeacon of St. Albans.* Poems. 1779. 8. (1 sh. 6 d.) Elegies: with Selmane, a tragedy. 1782. 8. (2 sh. 6 d.) Two sermons for the festivals and fasts of the church of England. 1790. 4. (2 sh.)

—— [Percival] *F. R. S: Surgeon to St. Bartholomews Hospital.* born: 1712. died d. 22 Dec. 1788.

POTTER, [. . . . .] Holkham, a poem. 1758. fol. (1 sh.) Kymber; a monody. 1758. 4. (1 Sh.) Poems. 1774. 8. (3 Sh.) Frederic, or the libertine; including memoirs of the family of Montague. Vol. 1. 2. 1789. 12. (5 Sh.)

—— [. . . . .] The oracle concerning Babylon and the song of exultation from Isaiah Chap. 13. 14. 1785. 4. (1 Sh. 6 d.)

POTTER, [John] *a Clergyman.* The choice of Apollo, a Serenata. 1765. 4. (6 d.) *History and adventures of Arthur O'Bradley. Vol. 1. 2. 1769. 8. (5 Sh.) The curate of coventry: a tale. Vol. 1. 2. 1771. 8. (5 Sh.) *The virtuous villagers. Vol. 1. 2. 1784. 8. (5 Sh.) The favourites of felicity. Vol. 1-3. 1785. 8. (7 Sh. 6 d.)

— [R....] *Observations on the poor laws, on the present ſtate of the poor and on houses of induſtry. 1775. 8. (1 Sh. 6 d.) Ed. 2. with the author's name. 1775. 8. (1 Sh.)

— [R....] *Clergyman of the county of Suffolk.* Translation of the tragedies of *Aeschylus.* 1777. 4. (1 L. 1 Sh.) Notes on the tragedies of *Aeschylus.* 1778. 4. Ed. 2. with notes. Vol. 1. 2. 1779. 8. *The tragedies of *Euripides* translated. Vol. 1. 2. 1781. 1783. (2 L. 2 Sh.) Inquiry into ſome paſſages in *Johnson's* lives of the poets. 1783. 4. (2 Sh. 6 d.) The tragedies of *Sophocles* translated. 1788. 4. (1 L. 1 Sh.)

— [T....] *Surgeon at Northshields near Newcaſtle upon Tyne.* born: .... died. 17..

POULTER, [Edmund] *M. A: Rector of Crawley.* Supplement to the pharsalia of *Lucan*, translated from the latin of *Thomas May.* 1786. 4. (1 Sh. 6 d.)

(Several ſingle ſermons.)

POW, [William] *Chaplain of the Royal Navy.* Reflections on peace and the ſeasons: in which is introduced the character of a patriot King; a poem. 1789. 4. (2 Sh. 6 d.)

POWELL, [J....] *Surgeon at Brecon.* Hiſtory of a case in which hydatids were voided by the mouth and likewise from a large tumour on the back. (London M. J. Vol. 6. p. 139.)

— [John] *B. A: Grammar-Maſter, Monmouth.* Poems on various ſubjects. 1783. 8. (—)

— [John Joseph] *Esq. of the Middle Temple, Barriſter at law.* On the law of mortgages. 1785. (—) Ed. 2. 1787. 8. (6 Sh.) On the learning reſpecting the creation and execution of powers —. 1787. 8. (8 Sh.) Eſſay upon the learning of devises, from their inception by writing, to their consummation by the death of devisor. 1789. 8. (9 Sh.)

POWELL, [William Samuel] *D. D: F. R. S: Vice-Chancellor at Cambridge and Arch-Deacon at Colchester.* born at *Colchester.* 1717. died 1775.

POWER, [John] *Surgeon at Polesworth.* Account of an extraordinary ptyalism, and of its cure. (Med. Transact. Vol. 2. p. 34.) Of the use of fermenting cataplasms in mortifications. (Ibid. Vol. 3. p. 47.)

POWNALL, [John] On a roman tile found at Reculver in Kent. (Arch. Vol. 8. p. 79.)

POWNAL, [Thomas] *F. R. S: F. A. S: Late Governor of Massachusets Bay and South Carolina in North-America.* Principles of polity. P. 1-3. 1752. 4. (4 sh.) *The administration of the British colonies. 1764. 8. (2 sh. 6 d.) Ed. 2: (with the Author's name.) 1765. 8. (4 sh.) Appendix, under the title: Considerations on the points lately brought into question, as to the parliament's right of taxing the colonies and of the measures necessary to be taken at this crisis. 1766. 8. (1 sh.) Ed. 4. P. 1. 2. 1768. 1774. 8. (7 sh. 6 d.) The right interest and duty of the state, as concerned in the affairs of the East-Indies. 1773. 8. (1 sh.) Report from the committee appointed to consider of the method practised, in making flower from wheat, the prices thereof, and how far it is expedient to put the same again under the regulation of the assizes. 1774. fol. A memoir, entitled, "Drainage and navigation, but one united work; and an outfall to deep water, the first and necessary step to it —. 1775. 8. (1 sh.) Topographical description of such parts of North-America as are contained in the annexed map of the middle british colonies. 1776. fol. (10 sh. 6 d.) Letter to *Adam Smith* on his inquiry into the nature and causes of the wealth of nations. 1776. 4. (1 sh. 6 d.) *Memorial to the sovereigns of Europe on the present state of affairs between the old and new world. 1780. 8. (2 sh. 6 d.) Translation of the memorial to the sovereigns of Europe —. 1781. 8. (1 sh.) On the study of antiquities —. 1782. 8. (5 sh.) Two memorials. 1782. 8. (1 sh. 6 d.) Memorial to the sovereigns of America. 1783. 8. (2 sh. 6 d.) Description of the sepulchral monument at New

Grange

Grange near Drogheda in the county of Meath in Ireland. (Arch. Vol. 2. p. 236.) On the boundary ſtone of Croyland Abbey. (Ibid. Vol. 3. p. 96.) Description of the Carn braich y Dinas, on the ſummit of Pen-maen-mavr, in Caernarvonshire. (Ibid. p. 303. p. 350.) Account of ſome Irish antiquities. (Ibid. p. 555. Vol. 7. p. 164.) Memoire on the roman earthen ware fished up within the mouth of the river Thames. (Ibid. Vol. 5. p. 282.) On the vases found on the Mosquito in South-America. (Ibid. Vol. 5. p. 318.) Account of a ſingular ſtone among the rocks at Weſt-Hoadley, Suſſex. (Ibid. Vol. 6. p. 54.) On the roman earthen-ware and the boundary-ſtone of Croyland Abbey. (Ibid. p. 392.) Observations on the Dundalk ship Temple. (Ibid Vol. 7. p. 149.) Observations on a cryſtal vase in the poſſeſſion of the Earl of *Besborough*. (Ibid. p. 179.) Published *S. Ledwich's* letter on the shiptemples in Ireland. (Ibid. p. 269.) Account of ſome roman pottery found at Sandy in Bedfordshire, with a roman speculum. (Ibid. Vol. 8. p. 377.) On the origin and progreſſ of gothic architecture and on the corporation of freemasons supposed to be the eſtablishers of it as a regular order. (Ibid. Vol. 9. p. 110.) Observations on ancient painting in England. (Ibid. p. 141.) Hydraulic and nautical observations on the currents in the atlantic ocean. 1787. 4. (3 ſh. 6 d.) Notices and descriptions of antiquities of the provincia romana of Gaul. 1788. 4. (10 ſh. 6 d.)

PRATT, [Robert] *formerly Bookseller at Bath.* (Schreibt unter dem Nahmen *Courtney Melmoth. Esq.* born at St. *Ives* in *Huntingtonshire.*) The tears of Genius, occaſioned by the death of *Goldſmith* 1774. 4. (1 Sh. 6 d.) *The progreſſ of painting, a poem. 1775. 4. (3 d.) Liberal opinions upon animals, man and providence. Vol. 1-6. 1775. 8. (18 Sh.) überſ. Th. 1-3. Leipz. 1777. 8. Observations on the hight thoughts of Dr. Young —. 1776. 8. (4 Sh.) The ſublime and beautiful of ſcripture; being eſſays on ſelect paſſages of ſacred compoſition. Vol. 1. 2. 1777. (6 Sh.) Apology for the life and writings of Dav. *Hume*. 1777. 8.

8. (2 Sh. 6 d.) The pupil of pleasure; a novel. Vol. 1. 2. 1777. 8. (6 Sh.) übers. von *L. T. Kosegarten.* Th. 1. 2. 1790. 8. Travels for the heart. Vol. 1. 2. 1777. 8. (5 Sh.) übers. Leipz. 1778. 8. Shenstone green or the new paradise lost. Vol. 1-3. 1779. 8. (7 Sh. 6 d.) The shadows of *Shakespeare;* a monody, occasioned by the death of Mr. *Garrick.* 1779. 4. (1 Sh.) *The tutor of truth. Vol. 1. 2. 1779. 8. (6 Sh.) *Emma Corbett; or the miseries of civil war —. Vol. 1-3. 1780. 8. (9 Sh.) *Sympathy: a poem. 1781. 4. (2 Sh. 6 d.) *The fair circassian, a Tragedy. 1781. 8. (1 Sh. 6 d.) School for vanity, a Comedy. 1783. *Landscapes in verse —. 1785. 4. (2 Sh. 6 d.) Miscellanies. Vol. 1-4. 1785. 8. (14 Sh.) *The triumph of benevolence; occasioned by the national design of erecting a monument to *John Howard.* 1786. 4. (1 Sh. 6 d.) *Humanity, or the rights of nature; a poem. 1788. 4. (5 Sh.) *Ode on his Majesty's recovery. 1789. 4. (1 Sh.) The new cosmetic; or, the triumph of beauty, a Comedy. 1790. 8. (2 Sh. 6 d.)

PRENTICE, [S.... W.....] *Ensign of the* 84 *Regiment of Foot.* Narrative of a shipwreck on the Island of Cape Breton in a Voyage from Quebec. 1780. 1782. 12. (1 Sh. 6 d.)

PRESTON, [John] *late an Assistant at Mr. Naudin's Academy, Hackney.* Plain, easy and familiar guide to the knowledge of astronomy —. 1788. 12. (1 Sh. 6 d.)

—— [Robert] *M. A.* Meditations on the seasons; —. 1773. 12. (2 Sh.)

—— [William] *M. J. A.* Thoughts on lyric poetry, with an ode to the moon. (Tr. of J. A. 1787. p. 57.) On ridicule wit and humour. (Ibid. 1788. p. 69.)

PRESTWICH, [John] Dissertation on mineral, animal and vegetable poisons —. 1775. 8. (6 sh.)

PRICE, [James] *M. D. F. R. S.* born: 1752. died d. 3 Aug. 1783.

—— [John] Account of a brass image of roman workmanship found at Cirencester. (Arch. Vol. 7. p. 405.)

PRICE, [Joseph] *Captain in the Army.* Observations and remarks on *Mackintosh's* travels in Europe, Asia and Africa —. 1782. 8. (2 Sh. 6 d.) Letter to *Phil. Francis*, Esq. late a member of the supreme Council of Bengal. 1781. 8. (1 sh.) Commercial and political letter to *Ch. James Fox* — on the subject of his asiatic bills —. 1783. 8. (1 sh. 6 d.) Tracts. Vol. 1. 1783. 8. 1) Five letters conveying some free thoughts on the probable causes of the decline of the export trade of that kingdom; and a rough sketch, or outlines of a plan, for restoring it to its former splendor. 2) Letter to *Philip Francis* —. 3) Letter to the proprietors and directors of East-India stock —. 4) Observations and remarks on (*Mackintosh's* travels in Europe —. Vol. 2. 1783. Letter 1. 2. 3. to *Edm. Burke* on the latter part of the report of the select committee of the house of commons, on the state of justice in Bengal —. Vol. 3. 1783. 1) A series of facts, shewing the present political state of India, as far as concern the powers at war —. 2) Vindication of Gen. *Richard Smith* —. 3) The saddle put on the right horse, or, an enquiry into the reason why certain persons have been denominated Nabobs —. 4) Letter to Sir *Phil. Jen. Clerke* —. 5) Letter to Mr. *Benjam. Lacam* —.

— [Richard] *D. D: LL. D: F. R. S: Fellow of the American Philosophical Societies at Philadelphia and Boston: Dissenting Clergyman at Hackney in Middlesex.* Review of the principles, questions and difficulties in moral, particularly those respecting the origin of our ideas of virtue, its nature, relation to the deity, obligation, subject-matter and sanctions. 1758. 8. (6 sh.) Ed. 3. 1787. 8. Demonstration of the second rule in the essay towards the solution of a problem in the doctrine of chances published in Phil. Transact. Vol. 53. (Phil. Transact. 1764. p. 296.) Observations on the expectations of lives, the increase of mankind, the influence of great towns on population, particularly the state of London with respect to health fulness and number of inhabitants. (Phil. Transact. 1769. p. 89.) Four Dissertations 1) on providence, 2) on prayer, 3) on the reasons for expecting that virtuous men shall meet

meet after death in a state of happineſſ. 4) on the importance of chriſtianity, the nature of hiſtorical evidence and miracles. 1767. 8. (6 ſh.) überſ. von *J. B. R(agler.)* Abth. 1. 2. Leipzig. 1774. 8. Observations on the proper method of calculating the values of reverſions depending on ſurvivor-ships. (Phil. Transact. 1770. p. 268.) On the effect of the aberration of Venus during the laſt tranſit over the ſun. (Ibid. p. 536.) Observations on reverſionary payments, annuities —. 1771. 8. (6 ſh.) Ed. 2. 1773. 8. (6 ſh.) Ed. 4. Vol. 1. 2. 1783. 8. (15 ſh.) überſ. von *J. N. Tetens.* in *Heinze* Samml. zur Geſch. u. Staatswiſſenſchaft. Th. 1. 1789. p. 139. Appeal to the public on the ſubject of the national debt. 1772. 8. (1 ſh. 6 d.) Proofs of the insalubrity of marshy ſituations. (Phil. Transact. 1774. p. 96.) Observations on the difference between the duration of human life in towns and in country pariſhes and villages. (Ibid. 1775. p. 424.) Observations on the nature of civil liberty, the principles of government and the juſtice and policy of the war with America —. 1776. 8. Additional observations. 1777. 8. Supplement. 1778. 8. (5 ſh.) Ed. 2. 1778. 8. (5 ſh.) Theorems for finding in all cases the differences between the values of annuities payable yearly, and of the ſame annuities payable half yearly, quarterly, or momently. (Phil. Tr. 1776. p. 109.) Notions of the nature of civil liberty, shewn to be contradictory to reason and ſcripture. 1777. 8. (2 ſh.) On materialism and philosophical neceſſity in a correspondence with Dr. *Prieſtley* —. 1778. 8. (6 ſh.) Eſſay on the population of England from the revolution to the present time. 1780. 8. (1 ſh. 6 d.) The ſtate of the public debts and finances at ſigning the preliminary articles of peace in January 1783. — 1783. 8. (1 ſh. 6 d.) On the importance of the American revolution and the means of making it a benefit to the world —. 1785. 8. (2 ſh. 6 d.) The evidence for a future period of improvement in the ſtate of mankind —. 1787. 8. (1 ſh.) Sermons on the chriſtian doctrine, as received by the different denominations of chriſtians —. 1787. 8. (5 ſh.) Discourse on the love of our country — with an ap-

appendix containing the report of the committee of the society; an account of the population of France. Ed. I. II. III. 1789. 8. (1 ſh. 6 d.) Preface and additions to the discourse on the love of our country. 1790. 8. (6 d.)

(Several ſingle ſermons.)

E, [Uvedale] *Esq.* Account of the ſtatues, pictures and temples in Greece; translated from the Greek of *Pausanias* 1780. 8. (4 ſh.)

E, [Thomas] — and *Phil. Luckombe*, The traveller's companion; or new itinerary of England and Wales, with a part of Scotland. 1789. 8. (4 ſh.)

STLEY, [Joseph] *LL. D. F. R. S. Diſſenting Clergyman of Birmingham in the County of Warwick.* Rudiments of engliſh grammar. P. 1. 2. 1762. 1768. (3 Sh.) Eſſay on a course of liberal education and active life: with plans of lectures on 1) the ſtudy of hiſtory and general policy 2) the hiſtory of England. 3) The conſtitution and laws of England with remarks on a code of education proposed by Dr. *Brown* in a treatise: thoughts on civil liberty. 1765. 8. (3 Sh. 6 d.) Chart of Biography. 1765. (10 Sh. 6 d.) Hiſtory and preſent ſtate of electricity with original experiments. 1767. 4. Additions. 1770. (1 L. 3 ſh. 6 d.) überſ. von *J. B. Krünitz.* Berlin und Stralſ. 1774. 4. Addreſſ to proteſtant Diſſenters on the ſubject of the Lord's ſupper. 1768. 8. Additions. 1770. 8. (2 ſh.) überſ. Brittiſches Theolog. Magazin. Th. 1. S. 200. Th. 4. S. 112. A catechism for children and young persons. 1768. 8. (6 d.) Account of rings, conſiſting of all the prismatic colours, made by electrical exploſions on the ſurface of pieces of metal. (Phil. Transact. 1768. p. 68.) Experiments on the lateral force of electrical exploſions. (Ibid. 1769. p. 57. pag. 63.) Conſiderations on church authority. 1769. 8. (1 ſh. 6 d.) A serious addreſſ to maſters of families with forms of family prayer. 1769. 8. (9 d.) Conſiderations on differences of opinion among Chriſtians. 1769. 8. (1 ſh. 6 d.) View of the principles and conduct of the proteſtant diſſenters, with reſpect to the civil and eccleſiaſtical conſtitution of England. 1769. 8. (1 ſh. 6 d.) überſ. Brittiſches Theolog. Muſeum. Th. 4. S. 133.

S. 133. On the firſt principles of government and on the nature of political, civil and religious liberty. 1768. 8. (3 ſh.) Introduction to the ſtudy of electricity. 1768. 4. (2 ſh. 6 d.) * Theological repoſitory; conſiſting of original eſſays, hints, queries — calculated to promote religious knowledge. Vol. 1-6. 1770-1788. (1 L. 1 ſh. 6 d.) Letters to the author of remarks on ſeveral late publications relative to the diſſenters. 1770. 8. (1 ſh.) Anſwer to a ſecond letter to Dr. *Prieſtley*. 1770. 8. Inveſtigation of the lateral exploſion and of the electricity communicated to the electrical circuit, in a discharge. (Phil. Transact. 1770. p. 192.) Experiments and obſervations on Charcoal. (Ibid. p. 211.) Introduction to the theory and practice of perſpective. 1771. 8. (5 ſh.) Inſtitutes of natural and revealed religion. Vol. 1-3. 1772-1774. 8. (7 ſh. 6 d.) überſ. (von *J. W. K. Link.*) Th. 1. 2. Frf. und Leipz. 1783. 8. Directions for impregnating water with fixed air; in order to communicate to it the peculiar ſpirit and virtues of Pyrmont water and other mineral water of a ſimilar nature. 1772. 8. (1 ſh.) Hiſtory and preſent ſtate of diſcoveries relating to viſion, light and colours. Vol. 1. 2. 1772. 4. (1 L. 11 ſh. 6 d.) überſ. von *G. S. Klügel.* Th. 1. 2. 1775. 4. Obſervations on different kinds of air. (Phil. Transact. 1772. p. 147. 1775. p. 384.) Account of *Will. Henly's* electrometer. (Ibid. 1772. p. 359.) Addreſſ to proteſtant diſſenters on giving the Lord's ſupper to children. 1773. 8. (1 ſh.) Experiments and obſervations on different kinds of air. Vol. 1-3. 1774-1777. (18 ſh.) überſ. (von *C. Ludewig.*) Wien und Leipzig. Th. 1-3. 1778. 8. Upon the general election in the Y. 1774. *Conſiderations for the uſe of young men. 1775. 8. (2 d.) *Hartley's* Theory of the human mind — by *Joſ. Prieſtley.* 1775. 8. (6 ſh.) überſ. (von *H. A. Piſtorius*) Roſtok. 1772. Examination of Dr. *Reid's* inquiry into the human mind, on the principles of common ſenſe; Dr. *Beattie's* eſſay on the nature and immutability of truth and Dr. *Oswald's* appeal to common ſenſe in behalf of religion. 1775. 8. (6 ſh.) Philoſophical empiriciſm: containing

taining remarks on a charge of plagiarism respecting Dr. H—s, interspersed with various observations relating to different kinds of air. 1775. 8. (1 sh. 6 d.) Addreſſ to proteſtant diſſenters on the ſubject of church discipline. 1776. 8. (2 ſh. 6 d.) *Appeal to the ſerious and candid profeſſors of chriſtianity — by a lover of the gospel. 1776. 8. (1 d.) * A familiar illuſtration of certain paſſages of ſcripture relating to the power of man to do the will of God, original ſin, election and reprobation, the divinity of Chriſt — by a lover of the Gospel. 1776. 8. (4 d.) Observations on respiration and the use of the blood. (Phil. Transact. 1776. p. 226.) Harmony of the evangeliſts in greek; with critical diſſertations in english. 1777. 4. (14 ſh.) Disquiſitions relating to matter and ſpirit with a hiſtory of the philosophical doctrine concerning the origin of the ſoul and the nature of matter, with its influence on chriſtianity especially with reſpect to the doctrine of the pre — exiſtence of Chriſt. 1777. 8. (4 ſh.) The doctrine of philosophical neceſſity illuſtrated; being an appendix to the disquiſitions, relating to matter and ſpirit; with an answer to the letters on materialism and on *Hartley's* theory of the mind. 1777. 8. (4 ſh.) Lectures on oratory and criticism. 1777. 4. (10 ſh. 6 d., überſ. von *J. J. Eſchenburg*. 1779. 8. Free diſcuſſion of the doctrines of materialism and philosophical neceſſity in a correspondance between Dr. *Price* and Dr. *Prieſtley* —. 1778. 8. (6 ſh.) Miscellaneous observations relating to education, more especially as it reſpects the conduct of the mind, with an eſſay on a course of liberal education for civil and active life. 1778. 8. (5 ſh.) Experiments and observations relating to various branches of natural philosophy; with a continuation of the observations on air. Vol. 1-3. 1779-1786. (18 Sh.) überſ. Th. 1-3. Leipzig. 1780. 8. Letter to *John Palmer* in defence of the illuſtrations of philosophical neceſſity. 1779. 8. Second letter — 1780. 8. (2 Sh.) Harmony of the Evangeliſts, in English, with critical Diſſertations, an occaſional paraphrase and notes for the use of the unlearned. 1780. 4. (12 Sh.) Letter to *Jac. Bryant*, in de-

 fence

fence of philosophical neceſſity. 1780. 8. (1 Sh.) Introduction to the theory and practice of perspective, Ed. 2. 1780. 8. Letters to a philosophical unbeliever P. 1. 2. additional letters. 1781-1787. 8. (8 Sh.) überſ. Leipz. 1782. 8. Two letters to Dr. *Newcome*, Bishop of Waterford, on the duration of our Saviour's miniſtry. 1781. 8. (2 Sh. 6 d.) Two discourses 1) on habitual devotion. 2) on the duty of not living to ourselves. 1782. 8. (1 Sh. 6 d.) Hiſtory of the corruptions of chriſtianity. Vol. 1. 2. 1782. (14 Sh.) (auch unter dem Titel:) Doctrine of the three firſt centuries. Vol. 1. 2. 3. 4. 1786. überſ. Th. 1. 2. Hamb. 1785. überſ. Th. 1. 2. Berlin. 1785. Reply to the animadverſions on the hiſtory of the corruptions of chriſtianity in the Monthly Review for June 1783. with observations on the doctrine of the primitive church, concerning the person of Chriſt. 1783. 8. (1 Sh.) Letters to Dr. *Horsley*. (ArchDeacon of St. Alban's) in answer to his animadverſion on the hiſtory of the corruptions of chriſtianity with additional evidence, that the primitive chriſtian church was unitarian. P. 1. 2. 3. 1783-1787. 8. (7 Sh. 6 d.) Forms of prayer for the use of unitarian ſocieties. 1783. 8. (4 Sh.) überſ. Berlin 1786. 8. General view of the arguments for the unity of God and againſt the divinity and preexiſtence of Chriſt —. 1783. 8. (2 d.) Experiments relating to phlogiſton and the ſeeming converſion of water into air. (Phil. Transact. 1783. P. 2.) Remarks on the monthly review of the letters to Dr. *Horsley*. 1784. 8. (6 d.) Observations, relating to air and water. (Phil. Transact. 1785. p. 279.) Observations on the importance of the American revolution and the means of making it a benefit to the world —. 1785. 8. (2 Sh. 6 d.) Experiments and Sermon on the importance and extent of free inquiry in matters of religion: to which are added, reflections on the present ſtate of free inquiry in this country; and animadverſions on ſome paſſages in *White's* ſermons; Mr. *Howes's* discourse on the abuse of the talent of disputation in religion and a pamphlet intitled, primitive candour —. 1786. 8. (1 Sh. 6 d.) Letters to the jews. P. 1. 2. 1787. (2 Sh.) überſ. Frankf.

Frankf. 1787. 8. Letter to Mr. Pitt on the subjects of toleration and church establishment. 1786. 8. (1 sh 6 d.) History of early opinions, concerning Jesus Christ —. Vol. 1-4. 1786. 8. (1 L. 4 sh.) The importance and extent of free inquiry in matters of religion. 1786. 8 (1 sh. 6 d.) Discourses on various subjects. 1787. 8. (6 sh.) Defences of unitarianism for the Year 1787. 8. (2 sh. 6 d.) Letters to Dr. *Horne* — on the subject of the person of Christ. 1787. 8. (3 sh.) On the subjects of toleration and church - etablissements. Ed. 2. 1787. 8 Lectures on history and general policy, with an essay on a course of liberal education for civil and active life. 1788. 4. (1 L. 1 sh.) Letters to the candidates for orders —. 1788. 8. (1 sh.) Sermons on the slave trade. 1788. 8. (1 sh.) History of the sufferings of Mr. *Lewis* de *Marolles* and Mr. *Isaac le Fevre* upon the revocation of the edict of Nantz with a general account of the treatment of the Protestans in the gallics of France, translated from the French. 1788. 8. (3 sh.) Experiments and observations relating to the principle of acidity the composition of water and phlogiston. (Phil. Transact. 1788. p. 147. p 313. übers. *Gren* J. d. P. Th. 1. S. 98. S 404.) Objections to the experiments and observations relating to the principle of acidity, the composition of water and phlogiston, considered; with farther experiments and observations on the same subject (Phil. Transact. 1789. p. 7.) übers. *Gren*. J d. P. Th. 2. S. 66. Experiments on the phlogistication of spirit of nitre. (Phil. Transact. 1789. p. 139. übers. *Gren* J. d. P. Th. 2 S. 94. Th. 3. S. 351.) Experiments on the transmission of the vapour of acids, through an hot earthen tube, and further observations relating to phlogiston. (Ibid. 1789. p. 289.) übers. *Gren* J. d. P. Th. 3. S. 70. The conduct to be observed by dissenters in order to procure the repeal of the corporation and test acts. 1789. (1 sh.) Letters to *Edw Burn* on the infallibility of the apostolic testimony, concerning the person of Christ. 1789. 8. (1 sh.) Defences of Unitarianism for the Years 1788 and 1789 containing letters to Dr. *Horsley*. 1789. 8. (3 sh. 6 d.) General history of the chri-

christian church, to the fall of the western empire. Vol. 1. 2. 1789. 8. (14 sh.) Observations on respiration. (Phil. Transact. 1790. p. 106.) Familiar letters, addressed to the inhabitants of Birmingham in refutation of several charges, advanced against the dissenters — P. 1–5. 1790. 8. (6 sh.)

(Several single sermons.)

PRIMATT, [Humphry] *D. D.* Dissertation on the duty of mercy, to brute animals. 1776. 8. (4 sh.) übers. Halle. 1778. 8.

PRINCE, [John] Account of an air pump on a new construction with observations on the common air-pump and *Smeaton's* improvement. (Mem. of B. A. Vol. 1. p. 497.)

PRINGLE, [John] *Sir. Baronet. M. D: F. R. S:* born at *Stichelhouse* in the County of *Roxburgh, North-Britain* d. 10 Apr. 1709. died at London d. 19 Jan. 1784.

PROBY, [....] Lord *Carysfort.* Letter to the Huntingdonshire committee. 1780. 8. (6 d.) Thoughts on the constitution —. 1783. 8. (1 sh. 6 d.)

PROSSER, [Thomas] Account and method of cure of bronchocele or Derby Neck. 1769. 8. (1 Sh. 6 d.) Ed. 2. 17.. Ed. 3. 1782. 4. (2 Sh. 6 d.) The oeconomy of quackery considered, in a reply to Mr. *Spilsbury's* free thoughts on quacks and their medicines —. 1777. 8. (2 Sh.) On the strangles and fevers of horses —. 1790. 8. (3 sh. 6 d.)

PRYCE, [William] *Surgeon at Redruth, Cornwall.* Mineralogia Cornubiensis —. 1778. fol. (2 L. 2 Sh.)

PUDDICOMBE, [J..... N.....] *M. A: Fellow of Dulwich College, late of Pembroke Hall.* Albion triumphant; or, Admiral *Rodney's* victory over the French fleet, a poem. 1782. 4. (1 Sh. 6 d.) An irregular ode, addressed to *Will. Pitt.* 1784. 4. (1 Sh.) Ed. 2. 1784. 4. (1 Sh.) Sermons. 1786. 8. (5 Sh.) Poem to *Ramsay* and *Clarkson* — and the society of Quakers on their benevolent exertions for the suppression of the slave trade. 1788 4. (1 Sh.) Ode to his majesty, on his happy recovery. 1789. 4. (1 Sh.)

—— [William] of *Topsham.* The mariner's instructor —. 1773. 12. (3 Sh. 6 d.)

PUGH, [Benjamin] *M. D: Physician at Baddow, Essex.* Treatise on midwifery. 1748. 8. Ed. 2. 1754. Account of the succeſſ of the bark in the ſmall pox. (Gentleman's Magazine. 1752. p....) Observations on inoculation. (Gentlem. Magaz. 1753. p....) On the climates of Naples, Rome, Nice –. 1784. 8. (1 ſh. 6 d.) Translation of *Ponzaire's* treatise on the mineral waters of Balaruc in the ſouth of France. 1785. 8. (3 ſh.)

—— [David] Poem on the approaching peace. 1783. 4. (6 d.)

—— [John] Remarkable occurrences in the life of *Jonas Hanway* —. 1787. 8. (4 ſh.) Ed. 2. 1788. 8. (3 ſh. 6 d.)

PULLIN, [Thomas] *A. M.* The fatal consequences of adultery to monarchies as well to private families —. 1772. 8. (3 ſh. 6 d.)

PULTENEY, [Richard] *M. D: F. R. S: Physician at Blandford.* Account of ſome rare plants found in Leiceſtershire. (Phil. Transact. 1759. p. 803.) Observations upon the sleep of plants with an account of that faculty, which *Linnaeus* calls, vigiliae florum; with an enumeration of ſeveral plants which are ſubject to that law. (Ibid. 1760. p. 506.) Case of a man, whose heart was enlarged to a very uncommon ſize. (Ibid. 1762. p. 344.) Diſſ. De cinchona officinali ſive cortice Peruviano. Edinb. 1764. 8. The medicinal effects of a poisonous plant exhibited inſtead of the water parsnep. (Phil. Transact. 1772. p. 469.) Account of baptisms, marriages and burials during 40 Years in the parish of Blandford forum, Dorset. (Ibid. 1778. p. 615.) General view of the writings of *Linnaeus.* 1781. 8. (6 ſh.) Account of the poisonous effects of the Oenanthe Crocata, or Hemlock Dropwort. (London M. J. Vol. 5. p. 192.) Account of an extraordinary conformation of the heart. (Med. Transact. Vol. 3. p. 339. London M. J. Vol. 7. P. 3.) Case of an extraordinary enlargement of the abdomen, owing to a fleshy encyſted tumour. (Mem. of M. S. of L. Vol. 2. p. 261.) Hiſtorical and biographical sketches of the progreſſ of botany in England from its origin to the introduction of the Linnaean ſyſtem. Vol. 1. 2. 1790. 8.

PULTENEY, [William] *Member of Parliament of Shrewsbury.* Thoughts on the present ſtate of affairs with America and the means of conciliation. 1778. 8. (2 ſh.) Conſiderations on the present ſtate of public affairs and the means of raiſing the neceſſary ſupplies. 1779. 8. (1 ſh.) The effects to be expected from the Eaſt-India bill upon the conſtitution of Great-Britain, if paſſed into a law. 1784. 8 (1 ſh. 6 d.) Impreſſ of ſeamen: conſiderations on its legality, policy, and operation. 1786. 8. (1 ſh. 6 d.) Conſiderations on the queſtion - whether the proceedings of commanders in chief of fleets and armies are ſubject to the review of the civil courts of law —. 1787. 8. (1 ſh. 6 d.)

PURCELL, [John] *M. D: Profeſſor of Anatomy in the College of Dublin.* Description of a double uterus and vagina. (Phil. Transact. 1774. p. 472.)

PURKISS, [William] *DD: F. A. S: Chaplain to the King at Whitehall.* On the influence of the present purſuits in learning, as they affect religion. 1786. 4. (1 ſh.; überſ. von *J. G. Burkhard.* Leipz. 1787. 8. The evils, which may arise to the conſtitution of Great-Britain from the influence of a to powerfull nobility. 1790. 4. (1 ſh.)

PURLEWENT, [S.....] *of Lincoln's Inn.* Appeal to the common ſenſe of the nation: containing ſome remarks upon an act for repealing certain duties upon wines imported and for granting new duties —. 1787. 8. (1 ſh.)

PURSHOUSE, [A......] *M. A.* Eſſay on genius. 1782. 4. (3 ſh. 6 d.)

PURVER, [Anthony] (a Quaker), at *Andover, Hampshire* born: .... died d. Aug. 1777.

PURVES, [A.....] *Sir: Baronet.* The method of uſing ſea-weed in Scotland. (Hunter's G. E. Vol. 5. p. 235.)

—— [James] Attempt to inveſtigate and defend the ſcripture doctrine concerning the father, the ſon and the holy ſpirit —. Ed. 2. 1784. 12. (3 ſh.) Observations on prophetic times and ſimilitudes, as they relate to the church and the world from the viſions of the Apoſtle John —. P. 1. 1789. 8. (2 ſh.)

PYE, [Hampden] *Mrs.* born: .... died: 17..

—— [Henry James] *M. P.* The progreſſ of refinement, a poem. P. 1-3. 1783. 4. (3 Sh.) *Shooting, a poem. 1784. 4. (2 Sh. 6 d.) Poems on various ſubjects. Vol. 1. 2. 1787. 8. (12 Sh.) The poetic of *Ariſtotle*, translated — with notes. 1788. 8. (4 Sh.) Amusement, a poetical eſſay. 1790. 4. (2 Sh. 6 d.)

PYLE, [Philipp] *M. A: Rector of Caſtle Riſing and Lynn St. Edmuud in Norfolk.* *Thom. Pyle* Sermons on plain and practical ſubjects, published by his son —. Vol. 1-3. 1773-1784. 8. (17 Sh. 6 d.) One hundred and twenty popular ſermons. Vol. 1-4. 1789. (1 L. 4 Sh.)

QUID, [Oliver] *Tobacco-Merchant.* 1 and 2 letter of advice — on the receipt tax —. 1783. 8. (1 Sh.) Plan for the conduct of all ſorts of money transactions without the use of receipts —. 1783. 12. (4 d.)

QUINCY, [Josiah] *Junior, Counsellor at law in Boſton.* Observations on the act of parliament — called the Boſton Port bill. 1774. 8. (1 Sh. 6 d.)

RACK, [Edmund] *Secretary to the Agriculture Society at Bath.* (a Quacker) born: .... died d. 22 Febr. 1787.

RADCLIFFE, [William] *A. B. of Oriel College, Oxford.* Journey through Sweden - translated from the French. 1789. 8. (5 Sh.) überſ. Leipz. 1790. 8. The natural hiſtory of Eaſt-Tartary - translated from the French. 1790. 8. (4 Sh.)

RAIT, [William] *Surgeon at Dundee.* Account of the good effects of Peruvian bark and Madeira wine, in an obſtinate ulcer of the leg. (*Duncan's* M. C. Vol. 9. p. 354.) On the endemic fever of the coaſt of *Guinea* and on the occurrence of ſmallpox a few days after birth. (Ibid. Dec. 2. Vol. 3. p. 313.)

RALEY, [William] Practical eſſay on the management of potatoes —. 1782. 8. (1 Sh.)

RAMSAY, [Allen] The gentle shepherd, a Scotch paſtoral, attempted in English by *Margaret Turner.* 1790. 8. (5 Sh.)

RAMSAY, [David] *M. D: Member of the American Congreſſ.* (born in America:) Military memoirs of Great-Britain: or, a hiſtory of the war 1755-1763. with copper plates. 1779. 8. Hiſtory of the revolution of South-Carolina. Vol. 1. 2. 1788. 8. (12 Sh.)

—— [James] *M A: Vicar of Teſton, Kent.* born 1734. died d. 20 Jul 1789.

RAMSDEN, [John] *Mathematical, Optical and Philosophical Inſtrumentmaker* (born 1730.) Description of an engine for dividing circles and arches of circles on mathematical inſtruments. 1777. 4. (5 Sh.) The description of two new micrometers. (Phil. Tr. 1779. p. 419.) Description of a new conſtruction of eyeglaſſes for ſuch telescopes as may be applied to mathematical inſtruments. (Ibid. 1783. p. 94.) Description of an engine for dividing ſtrait lines on mathematical inſtruments. 1779. (5 Sh.) Description and method of adjuſting the improved *Hadley's* ſextant. 1790. 4.

RANBY, [J....] *Eſq.* Observations on the petition of the city of London in favour of the tobacconiſts. 1790. 8. (1 Sh.)

—— [J....] *Surgeon to the King.* born 1702. died d. 28 Aug. 1773.

RAND, [Cater] *Writing-maſter and Accomptant, at Lewes in Suſſex.* Tables calculated with great exactneſſ to find the value of any quantity of gold from one grain to 50 ounces. 1773. 8. (1 Sh.)

RANDALL, [Joseph] *Maſter of the Academy at Heath by Wakefield.* born 1709. died d. 8. Aug. 1789.

RANDAL, [......] Excurſion round London —. 1777. 12.

RANDOLPH, [......] *Observations on the present ſtate of Denmark, Ruſſia and Switzerland. 1784. 8. (6 Sh.)

—— [F....] *M. A: Chaplain to his Royal Highneſſ the Duke of York.* Letter to *Will. Pitt* on the proposed abolition of the slave trade. 1788. 8. (1 Sh.)

—— [John] *Profeſſor of Greek language at Oxford.* De graecae linguae ſtudio. 1782. 4. (1 Sh.)
(Several ſingle ſermons)

—— [Thomas] *D. D: Archdeacon of Oxford, Profeſſor of Divinity at Oxford and Preſident of Corpus Chriſti fti College.* born at *Canterbury* d. 30 Aug. 1701. died d. 24 March. 1783.

RANNIE, [John] Poems. 1789. 4. (3 Sh.)

RAPER, [Matthew] *F. R. S: F. A. S*: Enquiry into the measure of the Roman foot. (Phil. Transact. 1761. p. 774.) Remarks on a paſſage of the editor of the connoiſſance des mouvemens celeſtes pour l'année 1762. (Ibid. 1762. p. 366.) Observations on the solar eclipse April. 1. 1764. at Thorley-Hall. (Ibid. 1764. p. 150.) Inquiry into the value of the ancient Greek and Roman money. (Ibid. 1771. p. 462.) *H. M. G. Grellman's* Diſſertation on the gipsies, translated from the German. 1787. 4. (10 ſh. 6 d.)

RASHLEIGH, [Philip] *Esq. F. A. S.* Account of antiquities discovered in Cornwall. 1774. (Arch. Vol. 9. p 187.)

RASTALL, [W.... Dickinson] *A. M. Fellow of Jesus College, Cambridge.* Hiſtory of the antiquities of the town and church of Southwell in the county of Nottingham. 1787. 4. (1 L. 11 ſh. 6 d.)

RAWLINS, [John] *A. M: Rector of Haselton in Glouceſtershire: Chaplain to Lord Archer.* Diſſertation upon heretical opinions. 1772. 8. Second diſſertation —. 1776. 8. (3 ſh. 6 d.)

(Several ſingle ſermons.)

RAYMENT, [Robert] *Esq.* The corn-trade of Great-Britain, for 18 Years, from 1748 to 1765. compared with the 18 Years, from 1771 to 1788; shewing the national loſſ in the latter period to have been above 20 millions of money. 1790. 8. (1 ſh. 6 d.)

RAYNER, [John] *Jun.* *Digeſt of the laws of libels —. 1765. 4. (6 ſh.) Readings on ſtatutes of George II. —. 1775. 4. (9 ſh.) Cases at large, relating to tithes —. Vol. 1-3. 1783. 8. (1 L. 1 ſh.) Observations on the ſtatutes relating to the ſtamp duties —. 1786. 8.

READER, [Thomas] Remarks on the prophetic part of the revelation of St. John. 1778. 8. (4 ſh.) Letter to - *Harry Trelawny*, occaſioned by his ſermon, preached at *Taunton*. 1780. 8 (6 d.) Israel's ſalvation; or, an account from the prophecies of ſcripture, of the grand events which await the

 jews,

jews, to the end of time. 1788. 8. (1 ſh. 6 d.) Remarks on the 3 firſt chapters of the revelation of St. John - with letters on the number of the beaſt and the woman's firſt and ſecond flight. 1785. 8. (1 ſh. 6 d.)

REED, [Joseph] *Rope - maker.* born at *Stockton* in the County of *Durham* 1723. died d. 15 Aug. 1787.

—— [Joseph] *Barriſter of Staple's Inn. Shakespeare's* plays. Vol. 1 - 10. 1785. 8. (3 L. 10 ſh.) *Dodsley's* collection of old plays. Vol. 1 - 11. 17.. Biographia Dramatica. Vol. 1. 2. 17..

REES, [Abraham] *DD: F. R. S: Diſſenting Clergyman and one of the Tutors of a clerical ſeminary of that ſect at Hackney. E. Chambers's* Cyclopaedia: or an universal dictionary of arts and ſciences. Vol. 1 - 4. fol. 1786. (10 L. 9 ſh) The advantages of knowledge, illuſtrated and recommended. 1788. 8. (1 ſh.) (Several ſingle ſermons.)

REEVE, [John] Abridgment of the hiſtory of the old and new teſtament: from the French. 1780. 8. (6 ſh.)

—— [Thomas] *Surgeon, Boterdale in Suffolk.* On the eryſipelatous ſore throat with an account of a case of hemiplegia. 1789. 8. (1 ſh 6 d.) Account of a painful ſwelling of the perinaeum which took place immediately after delivery and terminated in ſphacelus. (London M. J. Vol. IX. P. 2.)

—— [Clara] *Mrs: at Ipswich, Suffolk.* *The Phoenix; or the hiſtory of Polyarchus and Argenis, tranſlated from the Latin. Vol. 1 - 4. 1772. (12 ſh.) *The champion of virtue, a Gothic ſtory. 1777. 8. (3 ſh.) Ed. 2. under the title: The old engliſh Baron, a Gothic ſtory. 1778. 8. (3 ſh.) überſ. von F. St. Nürnberg. 1789. 8. *The two mentors: a modern Story. Vol. 1. 2. 1783. 8. (5 ſh.) *The progreſſ of romance, through times, countries and manners. Vol. 1. 2. 1785. 8. (5 Sh.) The exile, or memoirs of the Count de Cronſtadt. Vol. 1 - 3. 1788. 8. (9 Sh.)

—— [Eliza] Poems on various ſubjects. 1780. 4. (10 Sh. 6 d.)

—— [John] *Esq. Barriſter at law.* Hiſtory of the Engliſh law, from the Saxons to the end of the reign of Edward the firſt. Vol. 1. 2. 1783. 4. (1 L. 4 Sh.)

REID,

REID, [Alexander] *Surgeon to Chelsea Hospital.* On the effects of the Tunquinese medecine. (Phil. Transact. 1753. p. 212.) Case of a person cut for the stone, by the lateral way. (Ibid. 1754. p. 33.) Essay on quantity. (Ibid. 1755. p. 505.) *Mickles's* elements of surgery. Ed. 2. 1764. 8. Translation of le *Dran's* consultations. 1766. 8. Inquiries into the operations in the suppression of urine. 1778. 8. (1 Sh.)

—— [Thomas] *M. D: F. R. S.* On the nature and cure of the phthisis pulmonalis. 1782. 8. (3 Sh. 6 d.) übers. Sammlung f. A. Th. X. S. 515. Ed. 2. with an appendix on the use and effects of frequent vomits. 1785. 8. (5 Sh.) übers. von *A. F. A. Diel.* Offenbach. 1787. 8.

—— [Thomas] *D. D: F. R. S: Emeritus Professor of Moral Philosophy in the University of Glasgow.* Inquiry into the human mind, or the principles of common sense. 1764. 8. (7 Sh.) übers. Leipzig. 1782. 8. On the intellectual powers of man. 1785. 4. (1 L. 5 Sh.) On the active powers of man. 1788. 4. (1 L. 1 Sh.)

RELFE, [Edward] *Saddler at Lewes.* Essay on the seduction of women. 1781. 4. (1 Sh.)

RELHAN, [Anthony] *M. D: Fellow of the Royal College of Physicians in Ireland.* History of Brigthelmstone; with remarks on its air and an analysis of its waters. 1761. 8. (1 Sh.) Refutation of the reflections against inoculation published by Dr. *Rast* of Lyons —. 1765. 4. (1 Sh. 6 d.) *Oratio *Harvejana.* 1771. 4. (1 Sh.)

—— [Richard] *A. M: Capellanus Regalis Collegii: F. R. S.* Flora Cantabrigiensis. 1785. *supplem.* 1. *et* 2. 1786. 1788. 8. (12 Sh.)

REMMETT, [Robert Butler] *M. D: Physician at Plymouth.* A case of hydrocephalus. (Med. Com. of Ed. Vol. 6. p. 422.) Diss. De opii usu in morbis inflammatoriis. Edinb. 1774. 8.

RENNEL, [James] *F. R. S: late Major of Engeneers and Surveyor General in Bengal.* Account of the Ganges and Burrampooter rivers. (Phil. Transact. 1781. p. 78.) Memoir of a map of Hindostan on the Mogul's empire. 1783. 4. (16 Sh.) übers. *Ebelings* Neue Samml. von Reisebeschr. Th. 6. S. 415. Ed.

Ed. 2. with an account of the Ganges and Burrampooter rivers. 1788. 4. (14 Sh.) The map. (1 L. 1 Sh.) Bengal Atlas. fol. 1781. Map of Peninsula of India from the Khrisnah river to cape Comorin. Sheet. 1. 2. 17..

RENNY, [G.....] *Surgeon to the Athol Highlanders.* On the venereal disease. 1782. 8. (3 Sh.)

RENWICK, [William] *Surgeon in the Royal Navy.* *The unfortunate lovers; or the genuine distress of Damon and Celia. Vol. 1. 2. 1771. 12. (6 Sh.) Attempt to restore the primitive natural constitutions of mankind. 1778. 8. (1 Sh.) *Elegiac epistles on the calamities of love and war —. 1780. 8. (2 Sh.) . *Letters on the medical service in the Royal Navy. 1783. 8. (2 Sh.) Addreſſ to parliament, on the situation of the navy surgeons. 1785. 8. (2 Sh.) *Second* addreſſ to parliament, on a subject of the first consequence to the welfare of the state. 1786. 8. (6 d.) *Third* addreſſ, on the preservation of seamen. 1787. 8. (1 Sh. 6 d.) *The solicitudes of absence, a tale. 1788. 12. (3 Sh.)

REPTON, [......] Variety; a collection of essays —. 1788. 8. (3 Sh. 6 d.)

REYNOLDS, [Henry Revell] *M. D: F. R. S: F. A. S,* Letter - on the succesſful use of the preparations of lead in some haemorrhages. (Med. Transact. Vol. 3. p. 217.)

REYNOLDS, [Joshua], *Sir, President of the Royal Academy.* *Discourse at the opening of the Royal Academy. 1769. 4. (1 Sh.) *Discourse to the Royal Academy, on the distribution of the prices. 1769. 4. (1 Sh. 6 d.) *Discourse —. 1770. 4. (1 sh. 6 d.) *Discourse —. 1771. 4. (2 Sh.) *Discourse —. 1772. 4. (2 Sh.) *Discourse —. 1776. 4. (3 Sh.) *Discourse —. 1778. 4. (3 Sh.) *Seven discourses delivered in the Royal Academy. 1778. 8. (5 sh.) *Discourse —. 1782. 4. (3 sh.) Discourse —. 1784. 4. (3 Sh.) *Discourse —. 1786. 4. (3 Sh.) übers. N. Bibl. der Sch. Wiss. Th. 35. S. 1. *Discourse —. 1787. 4. (3 Sh.) *Discourse —. 1788. 4. (3 Sh.) *Discourse —. 1789. 4. (3 Sh.) Akademische Reden über das Studium der Malerey. übers. Dresden. 1781. 8.

RHODES, [T. . . . .] *A journeyman, Ribbon-Weaver.* Dunſtan park, or an evening walk, a poem. 1786. 8. (6 d.)

RICE, [Evan] *A. M.* Two discourses on the virtue and learning, the great ſupports of religion. 1785. 4. (1 Sh. 6 d.)

—— [John] Introduction to the art of reading with energy and propriety. 1765. 8. (4 Sh.) Lecture on rendering the Engliſh language, a branch of female education. 1773. 8. (1 Sh. 6 d.)

—— [Woodford] *Esq.* The Rutland volunteer influenza'd. 1782. 4. (5 Sh.)

RICHARD, [. . . . . .] *Lord Bishop of Landaff. F. R. S.* Obſervation on the ſulphur wells at Harrogate, made in July and Auguſt 1785. (Phil. Transact. 1786. p. 171.)

—— [. . . . . .] *Lord Bishop of Cloyne.* The preſent ſtate of the church of Ireland. 1787. 8. (2 Sh.)

—— [John] Tour from London to Petersburgh, Moscow, Courland, Poland, Germany and Holland. 1780. 12. (2 Sh. 6 d.)

RICHARDS, [William] Obſervations on infant ſprinkling; anſwer to *John Carter.* 1781. 8. (9 d.) The hiſtory of antichriſt or free thoughts on the corruptions of chriſtianity. 1784. 8. (1 Sh. 6 d.) Review of *Mark Noble's* memoirs of the protectoral houſe of Cromwell. —. 1787. 8. (2 Sh. 6 d.)

RICHARDSON, [. . . . . .] Aedes Pembrochianae: or, a critical account of the ſtatues, buſtos, relievos, paintings, medals and other antiquities and curioſities at Wilton Houſe —. 1774. 8. (2 Sh. 6 d.)

—— [Elizabeth] *Miſſ.* (Daughter of a Merchant in London.) born: . . . . . . died d. Oct. 1779.

—— [F. . . . .] *Enſign and Adjutant in the firſt Regiment.* Appeal to the officers of the guards. 1776. 4. (1 Sh.)

—— [J. . . . .] Publiſhed the works of *Jonath. Richardſon* conſiſting of 1) the theory of painting 2) on the art of criticiſm ſo far as it relates to painting 3) the ſcience of a connoiſſeur. 1773. 8. (5 Sh.)

—— [John] Theoretic hints on an improved practice of brewing malt liquors —. 1777. 8. (2 Sh.) Ed. 2. 1781. überſ. (von *J. H. Wittekop*) Berlin und Stet-

Stettin 1788. 8. Statical estimates of the materials of brewing; or on the application and the use of the saccharometer —. 1784. 8. (5 Sh.) Remarks on (*Baverstock's*) hydrometical observations and experiments in the brewery —. 1786. 8. (2 Sh.) The philosophical - principles of the science of brewing. 1788. 8. (6 Sh.)

RICHARDSON, [John] *F. A S: of the Middle Temple and of Wadham College, Oxford.* Specimen of Persian poetry; or, odes of Hafez with an English translation and paraphrase: chiefly from the specimen poeseos Persicae of Bar. *Rewisky.* — 1774. 4. (5 sh. 3 d.) Grammar of the arabic language. 1776. 4. (10 Sh. 6 d.) Dissertations on the language, litterature and manners of eastern nations —. 1777. 8. (7 sh.) übers. von *Fr. Federau.* Leipz. 1779. 8. Ed. 2. 1780. 8. (7 sh) Dictionary Persian, Arabic and English, with a dissertation on the languages, litterature and manners of eastern nations. Vol. 1. 2. fol. 1777. 1780. (10 L. 10 sh.) übers. im Auszug: (von *S. F. G. Wahl.*) Th. 1. 2. 1788. 1790. 8. (Several single sermons.)

— [Robert] *D. D: F. R. S: F. A. S: Prebendary of Lincoln, Rector of St. Ann's, Westminster and Chaplain in Ordinary to his Majesty.* born 1731. died d. 27 Sept. 1781.

— [William] *A. M: F. R. S: Professor of Humanity in the University of Glasgow.* *Analysis and illustration of some of *Shakespeare's* remarkable characters. 1774. 8. (2 sh. 6 d.) Ed. 2. 1780. übers. (von *C. H. Schmid.*) Leipz. 1775. 8. *Poems, chiefly rural. 1774. 8. (2 sh. 6 d.) Ed. 3. 1776. Ed. 4. 17.. Essays on *Shakespeare's* dramatic characters of Richard 3, King Lear and Timon of Athens —. 1783. 8. (3 sh.) *Anecdotes of the Russian empire, in a series of letters. 1784. 8. (5 sh.) *The cacique of Ontario; an Indian tale. 1786. 4. (1 sh. 6 d.) Essays on *Shakespeare's* dramatic character of Sir John Falstaff and on his imitation of female characters with some general observations on the study of *Shakespeare.* 1788. 8. (2 sh.) On the dramatic or ancient form of historical composition. (Tr. of E. S. Vol. 1. p. 99.) übers.

übers. von *J. G. Buhle*: Phil. und Histor. Abhandl. der Gesellsch. zu Edinburgh. Th. 1. S. 195.

RICHARDSON, [William] *M. D: of Ripon, Yorkshire.* born: ..... died d. 23 July 1783.

—— [William] *F. A. S.* born at *Wilshamsted, Bedfordshire* 1698. died. 1775.

RICKMAN, [T.... C....] The fallen cottage, a poem. 1787. 4. (2 sh. 6 d.)

RIDDELL, [Robert] of *Glenriddell.* Esq. Account of the ancient Lordship of Galloway from the earliest period to the Y. 1455. when it was annexed to the crown of Scotland, (Arch. Vol. 9. p. 49.) Remarks on the title of Thane and Abthane. (Ibid. p. 329.)

—— [Thomas] *Esq.* of *Felton Park, Northumberland.* The dimensions of an earthen fence, as made in Northumberland. (*Hunter's* G. E. Vol. 5. p. 196.)

RIDDOCH, [James] *Minister at Aberdeen.* born: ... died 17..

RIDER, [W.....] *B. A. Lecturer of St. Vedast, Curate of St. Faith's and Surmaster of St. Paul's School.* born: .... died d. 30 Nov. 1785.

RIDLEY, [Gloucester] *D. D.* born at the sea, in the navy, the Gloucester East-Indiaman, 1702. died d. 3. Nov. 1774.

RIDPATH, [Philip] *Minister of Hutton, Barwickshire.* born: ...... died d. Jul. 1788.

RIGBY, [Edward] *Surgeon at London.* On the uterine haemorrhage —. 1775. 8. (2 sh. 6 d.) Ed. 3. 1785. (2 sh. 6 d.) übers. Leipzig. 1786. 8. Samml. f. W. A. St. 6. S. 1. Samml. f. A. Th. 3. S. 550. S. 688. On the use of the red Peruvian bark in the cure of intermittents. 1783. 8. (2 sh.) On the theory of the production of animal heat and on its application in the treatment of cutaneous eruptions, inflammations and some other diseases. 1785. 8. (4 sh) übers. von *A. F. A. Diel.* Altenb. 1789. 8. Chemical observations on sugar. 1788. 8. (2 sh.) Reports of the Norwich committee with an account of the savings, which have been produced by the late regulations in the diet of the workhouses —. 1788. 8. (1 sh. 6 d.)

RIGGE, [William] *Deputy Register for the county of Middlesex.* Instruction for registering deeds, conveyveyances, wills and other incumbrances — 1778. 8. (5 ſh.)

RING, [John] *Surgeon at London.* Account of a new method of treating dropsy. (*Duncan's* M. C. Vol. 8. p. 83.)

RINGSTED, [Joſiah] *Esq.* The cattle keeper's aſſiſtant —. 1774. 8. (1 Sh. 6 d.) The farmer. 1781. 8. (2 Sh. 6 d.)

RIOLLAY, [Francis] *M. D: Phyſician at Newbury, Berks.* Letter to *Hardy* — the hints he has given concerning the origin of the gout in his late publication on the Devonshire cholic. 1779. 8. (1 Sh.) Doctrines and practices of *Hippocrates* in ſurgery and phyſic with remarks. 1783. 8. (5 Sh.) Critical introduction to the study of fevers. 1788. 8. (2 Sh.)

—— [Francis] *M. A.* Translation of *Lucian*, on writing hiſtory 1776. 8. (4 Sh. 6 d.)

RIOU, [Stephen] *Captain: Architect.* born .... died d. Jan. 1780.

RITSON, [J....] Select collection of English ſongs. Vol. 1-3. 1784. 8. (12 ſh.). *Homer's* hymn to Venus, translated with notes. 1788. 4. (1 ſh. 6 d.)

RITTENHOUSE, [David] *A. M: of Norriton* in the County of *Philadelphia.* Description of an orrery, executed on a new plan. (Tr. of A. S. Vol. 1. p. 1.) Calculation of the tranſit of Venus over the ſun as it is to happen June 3d 1769. (Ibid. p. 4.) Account of the tranſit of Venus over the ſuns disc, as observed at Norriton in the county of Philadelphia June 3d 1769. (Ibid. p. 8.) Observations on the comet of June and July 1770; with the elements of its motion and the trajectory of its path. (Ibid. App. p. 37.) An easy method of deducing the time of the ſun's paſſing the meridian per clock, without the help of the equation tables, by equal altitudes taken on two succeeding days. (Ibid. App. p. 47.) Explanation of an optical deception. (Ibid. Vol. 2. p. 37.) On a meteor ſeen at Philadelphia. (Ibid. p. 175.) Account of ſome experiments on magnetism. (Ibid. p. 178.) New method of placing a meridian mark. (Ibid. p. 181.) Observations on a comet lately discovered. (Ibid. p. 195.) On optical problem

lem solved, proposed by Mr. *Hopkinson*. (Ibid. p. 201.) Aſtronomical observations (Ibid. p. 260.) Philosophical papers. 1788. 8. (1 ſh.)

RIVET, [William] The uſefulneſſ of decimal arithmetic. 1763. 8. (1 ſh. 6 d.) Ed. 2. 1771. 8. (1 ſh. 6 d.)

ROBERTS, [......] *D. D: Fellow of Eton College and Chaplain in ordinary to his Majeſty.* *Poetical epiſtle to *Chph. Anſtey* on the English poets, chiefly those, who have written in blank verse. 1773. 4. (1 ſh.) Poems. 1774. 8. (4 ſh.) Judah reſtored; a poem. Vol. 1. 2. 1774. 8. (6 ſh.)

-- [.....] Thoughts upon creation. 17.. *Poetical attempts. 1784. 12. (2 ſh. 6 d.)

— [Benjamin] *Surgeon at Salisbury.* Three cases of women inoculated during pregnancy. (London M. J. Vol. 5. p. 399. überſ. Samml. f. A. Th. 10. S. 390.)

— [Eliza] *The beauties of *Rouſſeau*, ſelected by a Lady. Vol. 1. 2. 1788. 12. (5 ſh.)

— [John] *Surgeon.* Observations on fevers —. 1781. 8. (2 ſh. 6 d.)

— [John] *Governor of Cape Coaſt Caſtle, in the ſervice of the late Royal African Company of England* —. ſee *Cotton, Captain.*

— [John] *M. A: Fellow of King's College, Cambridge.* The deluge, a poem. 1789. 4. (1 ſh 6 d.)

— [John Chriſtopher] *Esq. Secretary for the Southern department to the province of Quebec in North-America.* Letter to the preſident and members of the royal ſociety —. 1784. 8. (6 d.)

— [R.......] *Miſſ.* *Selects tales from *Marmontel.* 17.. *Sermons written by a Lady —. 1770. 12. (2 ſh. 6 d.) **Millot's* Element of the hiſtory of France, translated —. 1771. 12. (7 ſh. 6 d.) The peruviam letters, translated from the French. Vol. 1. 2. 1774. 12. (6 ſh.) The triumphs of truth; or, memoirs of Mr. *De la Vilette*, translated from the French. Vol. 1. 2. 1775. 12. (6 ſh.) Malcolm, a tragedy. 1779. 8. Albert, Edward and Laura and the Hermit of Prieſtland, three legendary tales. 1783. 4. (3 ſh.)

— [W.... H....] of *Eton.* Poetical eſſays on the exiſtence of God. P. 1-3. 1771. 4. (3 ſh. 6 d.)

ROBERTSON, [......] *Vicar of Horncastle, Lincolnshire.* *Introduction to the study of polite literature. Vol. 1. 1782. 12. (2 sh.) *Essay on punctuation. 1785. 8. (3 sh.) *The Parian chronicle or the chronicle of the Arundelian marbles with a dissertation concerning its authenticity. 1788. 8. (5 sh.) übers. von *K. F. C. Wagner.* Götting. 1790. 8.

— [David] Poems. 1784. 8. (2 sh. 6 d.)

— [J....] Poems on several occasions. 1773. 12. (3 sh.)

— [James] *Esq: of Edinburgh.* Description of the blunt-headed Cachalot. (Philos. Transact. 1770. p. 321.)

— [John] *Librarian to the Royal society.* born: .... died d. 11. Dec. 1776.

— [Robert] *M. D: Surgeon of King's Navy.* Physical journal on board the Rainbow, in three voyages to the coast of Africa and the West-Indies, in the Years 1772. 1773. 1774. 4to 1778. (12 Sh.) Observations on the jail, hospital or ship-fever. 1783. 8. (5 Sh.)

— [Thomas] *Minister of Dalmeney: F. R. S. Edin.* Inquiry into the fine arts. 4. Vol. 1. 1786. (18 Sh.) Essay on the character of Hamlet in *Shakespeare's* tragedy of Hamlet. (Tr. of E. S. Vol. 2. p. 251.)

— [William] *D. D: Master of the grammar School at Wolverhampton.* born in *Dublin* d. 16 Oct. 1705. died d. 20 May. 1783.

— [William] *D. D. Principal of the University and Minister of the High Church in Edinburgh, Historiographer for the Kingdom of Scotland.* born: 1722. History of Scotland, during the reigns of Queen Mary and of King James VI. till his access into the crown of England. Vol. 1. 2. 1759. 4. (1 L. 1 Sh.) Additions. 1787. 4. (1 Sh.) Ed. XI. 1788. übers. Ulm. Th. 1. 2. 1762. 4. Braunschweig. Th. 1. 2. 1762. 8. History of the reign of emperor Charles V. with a view of the progress of society in Europe, from the subversion of the roman empire, to the beginning of the XVI. century. Vol. 1-3. 1769. 4. (2 L. 12 Sh. 6 d.) nachgedr. Basil. Vol. 1-4. 1788. 8. übers. (von *Mittelstädt*) Th. 1-3. Braunschw. 1771. 8. History of America. Vol. 1. 2. 1777. 4. (1 L. 16 Sh.) Ed... 1783. 8. Additions and

and corrections. 1788. 8. nachgedr. Leipz. Vol. 1–3. 1786. 8. übers. von *J. F. Schiller* Th. 1. 2. Leipz. 1777. 8. (Several single sermons.)

ROBERTSON, [William] *Keeper of the Records of Scotland.* History of ancient Greece, from the earliest times till it became a roman province. Ed. 3. 1787. 8. übers. Leipz. 1779. 8.

ROBINS, [Thomas] Published *Matth. Henry's* treatise on baptism. 1783. 12. (3 Sh.)

ROBINSON, [Maria] *Mrs*: born in *Bristol.* Poems. 1775. 8. (2 Sh. 6 d.) Captivity, a poem and Celadon and Lydia, a tale. 1777. 4. (2 Sh.) The lucky escape, a farce. 1778.

— [.....] *Esq.* The dangerous situation of England —. 1786. 8. (1 Sh. 6 d.)

— [John] The Methodists, an eclogue. 1763. 4. (6 d.) Preferment, a satire. 1765. 4. (1 Sh.) The poet's manual, a satire. 1767. 4. (1 Sh.) Poems of various kinds —. 1768. (2 Sh. 6 d.) *Poems, consisting of tales, fables, epigrams by nobody. 1770. 12. (2 Sh. 6 d.) (with the Author's name.) 1773. 12. (3 Sh. 6 d.) Love fragments, a series of lettres. 1782. 8. (2 Sh. 6 d.) The prize of Venus, or Killarney lake: a poem. 1786. 4. (1 Sh. 6 d.) Jessy, or the forced vow, a poem. 1786. 4. (1 Sh. 6 d.)

— [Lewis] *M. D.* Every patient his own doctor —. 1779. 8. (1 Sh.)

— [Matthew Montagu] *Considerations on measures carrying on, with respect to the british colonies in North-America 1774. 8. (1 Sh. 6 d.) Ed. 2. 1775. 8. (2 Sh.) *A further examination of our American measures and of the reasons on the principles on which they are founded —. 1776. 8. (3 Sh.) Peace the best policy, or reflection on the appearance of a foreign war, the present state of affairs at home and the commission for granting pardons in America. 1777. 8. (1 Sh.) Addreſs to the landed, trading and funded interests of England on the present state of public affairs. 1786.

— [Nich.] *M. D.* born: .... died d. 13 May. 1775.

— [Pollingrove] *A. D.* The beauties of painting, a poem. 1782. 4. (2 Sh) *Handel's* ghost, an ode, on the power of his Messiah. 1784. 4. (1 Sh.)

*The Caſſina, a poem. 1786. 4. (1 ſh.) *A Tou to the Isle of Love. 1788. 12. (2 ſh.) Cometilla or views of nature. Vol. 1. (Introduction to aſtronomy.) 1789. 8. (3 ſh. 3 d.)

ROBINSON, [Robert] *An Anabaptiſt Clergyman* born: .... died at Cambridge d. 10 Jun. 1790.

—— [Thomas] *M. A. Vicar of St. Mary's, Leiceſter.* Scripture characters; or, a practical improvement o the principal hiſtories of the old teſtament, from Adam to Joshua —. 1789. 8. (3 ſh.)

—— [William] *Architect and Surveyor at Hackney.* Supplement to Dr. *Burn's* juſtice of the peace, continuing that work down to the present period. 1774. 8. (3 ſh. 6 d.) The gentleman and builders director. 1774. 8. (1 ſh. 6 d.)

ROBISON, [John] *M. A: F. R. S. Edin: Profeſſor of Natural Philoſophy in the Univerſity of Edinburgh.* The orbit and motion of the Georgium ſidus determined directly from observations, after a very easy and ſimple method. (Tr. of E. S. Vol. 1. p. 305.) Observations of the places of the Georgian Planet, made at Edinburgh with an equatoreal inſtrument. (Ibid. Vol. 2. p. 37.) On the motion of light, as affected by refracting and reflecting ſubſtances, which are also in motion. (Ibid. Vol. 2. p. 83.)

ROBSON, [Francis] *late Captain in the Eaſt-India Company's forces.* The life of *Hyder Aly* with an account of his uſurpation of the kingdom of Mysore. 1786. 8. (4 ſh.)

—— [Horatio] Look before you leap, a Comedy, translated from la bonne mere of *Florian*. 1788. 8. (1 ſh.)

—— [Stephen] The British flora. 1777. 8. (5 ſh.)

RODBARD, [John] *Surgeon at Ipswich.* Case of a rupture of the tendo Achillis. (London M. J. Vol 8. P. 3.)

RODNEY, [George] *Lord.* (before, *George Bridges.*) Letters relative to the capture of St. Euſtathius and its dependencies; ſhewing the ſtate of the war in the Weſt-Indies at that period —. 1789. 4. (5 ſh.)

ROE, [Charles] *Surgeon.* On the natural ſmall-pox. 1780. 8. (2 ſh.) überſ. Lemgo. 1786. 8.

ROE, [Robert] Answer to Earl of *Dundonald*, on his thoughts on the manufacture and trade of salt and of the coal trade of Great-Britain. 1787. 8. (1 sh. 6 d.)

ROEBUCK, [......] *Gardener in York.* On the oil-compost. (*Hunter's* G. E. Vol. 2. p. 225.)

—— [John] *M. D: F. R. S.* Comparison of the heat of London and Edinburgh. (Phil. Transact. 1775. p. 459.) Experiments on ignited bodies. (Ibid. 1776. p. 509.)

ROGERS, [Charles] *F. R. S: F. A. S:* born at *London*: d. 2 Aug. 1711. died d. 2 Jan. 1784.

—— [Samuel] *A. M.* The choice, a poem. 1774. 4. (1 sh.) Poems on various occasions. Vol. 1. 2. 1782. 12. (10 sh. 6 d.)

ROLLO, [John] *M. D: Surgeon at Woolwich.* *Observations on the diseases in the army of St. Lucia in the Y. 1778. 1779. 12. 1781. (2 sh.) *Observations on the means of preserving and restoring health in the West-Indies. 1782. 12. (2 sh.) Remarks on the disease lately described by D. *Hendy* under the appellation of the glandular disease of *Barbados.* 1785. 8. (2 sh) übers. von *A. E. A.* Frankf. 1788. 8. Observations on the acute dysentery —. 1786. 8. (1 sh. 6 d.) übers. von *C. F. Michaelis.* 1787. 8. On the effects of drinking pure spirits in repeated and large quantities. (Lond. M. J. Vol. 7. p. 1.)

ROLT, [.....] History of the Isle of Man. 1773. 8. (3 sh.)

—— [Richard] born: ..... died 1773.

ROMAINE, [William] *M. A: Lecturer of St. Dunstan's church in the West: Rector of St. Andrew Wardrobe and St Ann Black-Friars.* (A Methodistical Clergyman) Twelve Discourses on *Salomon's* song. 1758. 8. (4 Sh. 6 d.) Twelve Discourses upon the law and the gospel. 1760. 8. (3 Sh. 9 d.) On the life of faith. 1764. 8. (2 sh.) On the walk of faith. Vol. 1. 2. 1771. 8. (6 Sh.) Companion for the christian in the field and garden. 1780. 8. (1 Sh. 6 d) (Several single sermons.)

ROMANS, [Bernard] of *Pensacola.* Natural history of East and West Florida. New-York 1776. 8. (16 sh.) On an improved sea compass. (Tr. of A. S. Vol. 2. p. 396.)

RONAYNE, [Thomas] *Esq.* Account of some observations on atmospherical electricity; in regard of fogs, mists —. with some remarks. (Phil. Tr. 1772. p 137.)

ROOKE, [Hayman] *Esq. F. A. S. Major.* Description of two roman camps in Gloucestershire. (Arch. Vol. 5. p. 207.) On druidical remains on Stanton on Hartle Moor in the peak, Derbyshire. (Ibid. Vol. 6. p. 110. Vol. 7, p. 175.) Account of the Brimham rocks in Yorkshire. (Ibid. Vol. 8. p. 209.) Account of the remains of two roman villae discovered near Mansfield Woodhouse. 1786. (Ibid. p. 363.) Observations on the roman road and camps in the neighbourdhood of Mansfield Woodhouse in the county of Nottingham. (Ibid. Vol. 9. p. 193.) Description of some druidical remains on Harborough rocks. — in Derbyshire. (Ibid. p. 206.) Antiquities in Cumberland and Westmoreland. (Ibid. p. 219.)

—— [Henry] *late Major of the 100th Regiment of Foot.* Travels to the coast of Arabica felix. 1783. 8. (2 Sh. 6 d.) Ed. 2. 17.. übers. Leipzig. 1787. 8. Account of a roman building and camp discovered at Buxton in the county of Derby. (Arch. Vol. 9. p. 137.)

—— [Thomas Eldridge] Considerations on the present dearness of provisions and corn in Great-Britain —. 1772. 8. (1 Sh. 6 d.)

ROSE, [George] *Secretary to the treasury, Master of the Pleas office and M. P.* *The proposed system of trade with Ireland explained. 1785.

ROSE, [Hugh] *Apothecary.* Elements of botany, being a translation of the philosophia botanica and other treatises of *Linnaeus* —. 1775. 8. (6 Sh.)

—— [John] *Accomptant.* British farmer's accomptant. 1776. fol. (2 sh.)

—— [William] born: ..... died at *Chywick.* d. 3 Jul. 1786.

ROSENBERG, *Countess*, see *J. Wynne.*

ROSS, [.....] *Miss.* The cottager, a comic opera. 1788. (1 sh. 6 d.)

—— [Anne] *Mrs.* (Her maiden name *Fanny Murray*) born: ..... died d. Apr. 1778.

ROTHERAM, [John] *M. A: Rector of Houghton-le-Spring. Vicar of Seaham and Chaplain to the Lord Bishop of Durham.* On the truth of christianity —. 1752.

1752. 8. (1 ſh. 6 d.) Argument for the truth of chriſtianity. 1754. 8. (1 ſh.) Eſſay on faith and its connection with good works —. 1766. 8. (3 ſh.) Three ſermons on public occaſions —. 1766. 8. (1 ſh. 6 d.) Eſſay on eſtablishments in religion; with remarks on the confeſſional. 1767. 8. (2 ſh.) Eſſay on human liberty. 1782. 8. (1 ſh.) Eſſay on the diſtinction between the ſoul and body of man. 1781. 8. (1 ſh.)

ROTHERAM, [John] *M. D. Fellow of the Linnaean Society, London.* The ſexes of plantes vindicated in a letter to *Will. Smellie*, containing a refutation of his arguments againſt the ſexes of plantes —. 1790. 8. (1 ſh. 6 d.)

ROTHERHAM, [John] *Fellow of Queens College, Oxford.* born: .... died at *Bambrough Caſtle* d. 24. Jul. 1789.

—— [John] *M. D: Phyſician at Newcaſtle upon Tyne.* born: 1719. died d. 18. March. 1787.

ROTHWELL, [J.....] *Maſter of the free-school at Blackrod.* A comprehenſive grammar of the English language. 1787. 12. (2 ſh.)

ROUPE, [Lewis] *M. D.* Observations on diseases incidental to seamen. 1790. (6 ſh.)

ROUS, [Georg] *Letter to the jurors of Great-Britain: occaſioned by an opinion of the court of King's bench — in the case of the King and Woodfall. 1771. 8. (1 ſh. 6 d.) Ed. 2. (with the Author's name.) 1785. 8. (2 ſh.) *Inveſtigation of the present prevailing to pic. 1784. 8. Ed. 3. (with the Author's name.) 1784. 8. (1 ſh.) *Thoughts on government in a letter to a friend. 1790.

—— [Thomas Bates] *Esq.* Observations on the commutation project. 1786. 8. (1 ſh.) Explanation of the miſtaken principle on which the commutation act was founded. 1789. 4. (1 ſh. 6 d.)

ROUTH, [Mart. Joseph] *A. M. Collegii D. Mariae Magdal. Oxon. Socius.* *Platonis* Euthydemus et Gorgias —. 1785. 8. (7 ſh. 6 d.)

ROWE, [John] Introduction to the doctrine of fluxions. 1751. Ed. 2. 1757. 8. (4 ſh. 6 d.) *Letters relative to ſocieties for the benefit of widows and of age —. 1776. 8. (1 ſh.)

ROWLES, [Samuel] Remarks on Dr. *Priestley's* letters to Dr. *Horsley* 1784. 8. (1 sh.) Revealed religion asserted, in a series of letters to *Jos. Priestley*, on eternal punishments, on the doctrine of *Calvin*, on the nature of god and the human soul, and on the atonement of Christ. 1787. 8. (3 sh. 6 d.) Defence of the harmony of satisfaction and free grace in the salvation of sinners; being a reply to *Isaac's* gospel doctrine of free grace maintained. 1788. 8. (1 sh.)

ROWLEY, [.....] *Mrs.* The widow of Kent; or the history of Mrs. *Rowley* —. Vol. 1. 2. 1788. 12. (5 sh.)

—— [William] *M. D. Member of the University of Oxford; of the Royal College of Physicians in London.* On the cure of ulcerated legs, without rest —. 1770. 8. (1 sh. 6 d.) On the cure of the gonorrhoea —. 1771. 8. (1 sh.) On the ophthalmia or inflammation of the eyes. 1771. 8. (1 sh.) On the diseases of the breasts of women. 1773. 8. (1 sh. 6 d.) übers. Gotha. 1781. 8. The new method of curing the venereal disease. 1773. 8. On the principal diseases of the eyes. 1773. 8. (3 sh.) Letter to *Will. Hunter* occasioned by the death of the late Lady *Holland*. 1774. 8. (1 sh.) Second letter to Dr. *Will. Hunter* - being an answer to the illiberal criticisms in the Monthly Review - containing a remarkable cure of a schirrus and cancerous ulcer. 1775. 8. (1 sh.) Medical advice for the use of the army and navy in the American expedition. 1776. 8. (1 sh. 6 d.) Seventy four select cases —. 1779. 8. (1 sh. 6 d.) Answer to the criticism in the Monthly Review 1779 on his 74 select cases. 1780. 8. Gout and rheumatism cured or alleviated. 1779. 8. (2 sh.) On the malignant ulcerated sore-throat —. 1788. 8. (3 Sh.) übers. von C. *Fr. Michaelis*. Breslau. 1789. 8. On female, nervous, hysterical, hypochondriacal, bilious, convulsive diseases; apoplexy and palsy —. 1788. 8. (7 Sh. 6 d.) übers. von *C. F. Michaelis*. Breslau. 1790. 8. Truth vindicated; or, the specific differences of mental diseases ascertained. 1790. 8. (1 Sh. 6 d.)

ROWNING, [John] Description of a barometer wherein the scale of variation may be encreased at plea-

pleasure. (Phil. Transact. 1748. p. 39.) Direction for making a machine for finding the roots of equations universally, with the manner of using it. (Ibid. 1770. p. 240.)

ROWSON, [......] *Mrs.* The inquisitor; or invisible rambler. Vol. 1-3. 1788. 12. (7 Sh. 6 d.) Poems on various subjects. 1788. 8. (3 Sh.)

ROXBURGH, [William] *Assistant Surgeon to the Hospital at Fort St. George.* Meteorological diary kept at Fort *St. George* in the East-Indies from Oct. 1. 1776 to Febr. 28. 1777. (Phil. Transact. 1778. p. 180.) Meteorological diary —— — from March 1777. to May. 1778. (Ibid. 1780. p. 246.)

ROY, [William] *Major-General. F. R. S: F. A. S.* born: .... died at *London* d. 1 Jul. 1790.

ROYERS, [Charles] *Esq.* Collection of prints, in imitation of drawings, to which are annexed lives of their authors with explanatory and critical notes. Vol. 1. 2. 1778. fol.

RUDD, [A.... Blackstone] *M. A: Vicar of Diddleburg in the County of Salop and Reader at Ludlow.* Sermons on religious and practical subjects. 1786. 8.

RUDDER, [Samuel] *New history of Gloucestershire —. 1779. fol. (3 L. 3 Sh.)

RUDSDELL, [Jeremiah] *Pernicious effects of religious contentions and bigotry — by a member of the congregation. 1775. 4. (1 sh.) *Diotrephes reproved: or, remarks on the pernicious effects of religious contentions —. 1776. 4. (1 Sh.) Misguided religious zeal - containing remarks on the diotrephes reproved —. 1776. 4. (1 Sh.)

RUMSEY, [Henry] Jun. *Surgeon at Chesham.* Account of an epidemic sore-throat which appeared at Chesham in Buckinghamshire. 1788. (London M. J. Vol. X. P. 1.)

RUNNINGTON, [Charles] *Barrister at law. Matthew Hale's* History of common law. Ed. IV. with notes and account of the life of the author —. 1779. 8. (10 Sh. 6 d.) On the action of ejectment. 1781. 8. (6 Sh.) *Owen Ruffhead*, the statutes at large, from magna charta to the 25th of George III. with index and an appendix —. Vol. 1-10. 1787. 4. (10 L. 10 Sh.)

RUSH, [Benjamin] *M. D: Profeſſor of Chemiſtry in the Univerſity of Philadelphia.* On the ſpasmodic aſthma of childern. 1770. 8. (1 ſh.) Account of the effects of the ſtrammonium, or thorn apple. (Tr. of A. S. Vol. 1. p. 318.) Account of the uſefulneſſ of wort in ſome ill-conditioned ulcers. (Med. Obs. Vol. 4. p. 367.) Account of an aſthma from an uncommon cause. (Ibid. Vol. 5. p. 96.) Remarks upon bilious fevers and inoculation (Ibid. Vol. 5. p. 32.) Result of ſome observations — of the military hospitals of the united ſtates in the late war. (Mem. of M. Vol. 2. p. 506. überſ. Samml. f. A. Th. XI. S. 722.) Enquiry into the cause of the increase of bilious and intermitting fevers in Pennsylvania, with hints for preventing them. (Tr. of A, S: Vol. 2. p. 206.) Account of the late Dr. *Hugh Martin's* cancer powder, with brief observations on cancers. (Ibid. p. 212. London M. J. Vol. VIII. P. 1. überſ. Samml. f. A. Th. XI. S. 732.) Enquiry into the influence of phyſical causes upon the moral faculty. 1786. 4. überſ. von *A. F. Diel.* Offenbach. 1787. 8. Enquiry into the effects of public punishments upon criminals and upon ſociety. 1787. 8. (1 ſh) Observations upon the cause and cure of the tetanus. (Mem. of M. S. of L. Vol. 1. p. 65. London M. J. Vol. 7. P. 4. überſ. Samml. f. A. Th. XI. S. 703.) Medical inquiries and observations. 1789. 8. (4 ſh.)

RUSSEL, [F. . . .] *Solicitor to the board of Commiſſioners for the affairs of India.* *Collection of ſtatutes concerning the incorporation, trade and commerce of the Eaſt-India Company and the government of the British poſſeſſions in India. 1786. fol. (1 L. 11 ſh. 6 d.)

—— [James] *Apothecary in London.* A case of hydrophobia. (Lond. M. J. Vol. IX. P. 3. überſ. Samml. f. A. Th 13. S. 94.)

—— [John] *Letters from a young painter abroad to his friends in England. Vol. 1. 2. 1750. 8. Elements of painting with crayons. 1772. 4. (5 ſh.)

—— [Patrick] *M. D: F. R. S.* Account of the tabasheer. (Phil. Transact. 1790. p. 273.) Treatise of the plague. 1791. 4.

RUSSEL [Rachel] *Mrs.* Letters —. 1773. 4. (8 sh.) Translation of *Thomas's* essay on the character, manners and genius of women —. Vol. 1. 2. 1773. 12. (6 sh.)

—— [Richard] *F. A. S.* born in the parish of *Bermondsey.* 1723. died d. 30. Sept. 1784.

—— [Thomas] *Fellow of New College, Oxford.* born at *Bridport* in *Dorsetshire* 1762. died at *Bristol* d. 31. Jul. 1788.

—— [William] *Esq.* (born in Scotland.) History of America from its discovery by Columbus to the conclusion of the late war. Vol. 1. 2. 1778. 4. (1 L. 10 sh.) übers. Leipzig. Th. 1-4. 1779. 8. (der *vierte* Theil der Uebersezung hat auch den Titel: Geschichte des Ursprungs und des Fortganges des gegenwärtigen Streites zwischen England und seinen Kolonien. Leipz. 1780.) History of modern Europe; with an account of the decline and fall of the Roman empire and a view of the progress of society from the rise of the modern kingdoms to the peace of Paris 1763. in a series of letters from a Nobleman to his son. Vol. 1-4. 1779. 8. (1 L. 4 sh.) Ed. 2. Vol. 1-5. 1782-1786. 8. übers. von *Zöllner.* Th. 1-8. Berlin. 1785-1790. 8. Ausg. 2. Th. 1. 1790. 8.

RUSTON, [.....] Letter concerning chimney's. (Tr. of A. S. Vol. 2. p. 231.)

RUTHERFORD, [John] *Captain.* Principal orations of *Cicero* translated, with notes. 1778. 4. (1 L. 1 Sh.)

—— [William] *D. D: Master of the Academy at Uxbridge.* Elements of latin grammar —. 1787. 8. (3 sh.) View of ancient history, including the progress of literature and the fine arts. Vol. 1. 1788. 8. (7 Sh.) (Several single sermons.)

RUTTY, [John] *M. D: Physician in Dublin.* born: ... died d. 1. May. 1775.

RYAN, [Dennis] *M. D. late Assistant-Physician to the Military Hospital in Jamaica.* born at *New Park* near *Cashel in Ireland* 1746. died at *Reading* in *Berkshire* d. 16 May. 1782.

—— [Edward] *B. D.* History of the effects of religion on mankind; in countries ancient and modern, barbarous and civilized. 1788. 8. (5 Sh.)

RYAN, [Michael] *M. D: Member of the Antiquarian Society at Edinburgh.* Enquiry into the nature, causes and cure of the consumption of the lungs. 1787. 8. (3 Sh. 6 d.) überſ. Leipz. 1790. 8.

RYLAND, [John] *A. M.* at *Northampton*: (an Anabaptiſt *Clergyman.*) Inſtructions for profitably receiving the word of God. 17.. A ſcriptural preservative of women from ruin. 17.. Playing cards for the inſtruction of youth in the ſcience of hiſtory. 17.. Introduction to mechanics, geometry, plane trigonometry, measuring heights and diſtances, optics, aſtronomy with an eſſay on the advancement of learning by various modes of recreation. 1768. 8. (3 ſh.) The preceptor, or counsellor of human life —. 1776. 8. (3 ſh.)

RYMER, [James] *Surgeon at Ryegate.* Introduction to the ſtudy of pathology — 1775. 8. (3 ſh.) Eſſay on medical education. 1776. 8. (1 ſh. 6 d.) Deſcription of the island of Nevis, with an account of its principal diseases. 1776. 8. (1 ſh.) Practice of navigation. 1778. 4. (5 ſh.) Transplantation; or poor crocus pluckt up by the the root. 1779. 8. (1 ſh.) *Observations and remarks, reſpecting the more effectual means of preservation of wounded seamen and marines —. 1780. 8. (1 Sh.) Letter — on preventing and curing the scurvy. 1782. 8. (6 d.) Analyſis of the ſection of the ſymphyſis of the ossa pubis —. 1783. 8. (1 Sh.) Chemical reflections relating to the nature, causes, prevention and cure of some diseases in particular the sea-scurvy, the ſtone and gravel, the gout —. 1784. 8. (2 Sh. 6 d.) On indigeſtion and the hypochondriac disease —. 1785. 8. (1 Sh.) Ed. 5. 1790. 8. (4 Sh.) On the nature and ſymptoms of the gout —. 1785. 8. (4 d.) Phyſiological conjectures concerning certain functions of the human oeconomy in the foetus and the adult. 1787. 8. (1 Sh. 6 d.) Account of the method of treating scrofula and other glandular affections —. 1790. 8. (1 Sh. 6 d.)

RYVES, [Elizabeth] *Miſs.* The prude, a comic opera. 1777. 8. The triumph of hymen. 1777. 8. Poems on several occaſions. 1777. 8. (5 Sh.) Ode to *Will. Mason.* 1780. 4. (1 Sh.) Epiſtle to Mr. *Fox.* 17..

17.. Epiſtle to Lord *John Cavendish* late chancellor of the exchequer. 1784. 4. (1 Sh.) Dialogue in the elyſian fields, between Caesar and Cato. 1784. 4. (1 Sh. 6 d.)

SAFFORD, [Henry] *Surgeon.* On the causes and effects of ſchirrous tumors and cancers —. 1789. 8. (1 ſh.)

St. ALBYN, [Lancelot] *A. M: Rector of Paracombe, Devon.* Sermons on various ſubjects. 1787. 8. (5 ſh.)

St. JOHN, [James] *M. D.* *Haſſenfratz's* and *Adair's* method of chemical nomenclature - translated from the French. 1788. 8. (5 ſh.)

St. JOHN, [John] (Uncle to the present *Lord Bolingbroke.*) *Observations on the land revenue of the crown. 1787. 4. (10 Sh. 6 d.) Mary Queen of Scots; a Tragedy. 1789. 8. (1 ſh. 6 d.)

St. JOHN, [Paulet] *Sir, Baronet, of Farley, Hants.* Every man his own farrier. 1780. 12. (2 ſh. 6 d.)

SALISBURY, [William] *B. D: Rector of Moreton, Eſſex.* Translation of *Bullet's* Hiſtory of the eſtabliſhment of chriſtianity —. 1776. 8. (5 ſh.)
(Several ſingle ſermons.)

SALOMON, [Nicholas] *Maſter of the Academy - Red-Lion - ſtreet, Clarkenwell.* The French teachers aſſiſtant; or a new and easy method to learn children to ſpell, read and ſpeak French —. 1773. 8. (1 ſh. 6 d.) Rules for the French genders. 1773. 8. (6 d.) The expeditious accountant, or cyphering rendered ſo short that half the trouble attending the common method is ſaved, in moſt occurrences —. P. 1-5. 1774. 8. (3 ſh.) Footſtep to the French language. 1787. 4. (1 Sh. 6 d.) Complete ſyſtem of the French language. 1788. 8. (5 Sh.)

SALTER, [Samuel] *Chaplain by the Earl of Hardwicke.* born: .... died. 1778.

SALTOUN, [Alexander] *Lord, Advocate and F. A. S. Scot.* Thoughts on the disqualification of the eldeſt ſon of the peers of Scotland. 1788. 8. (3 Sh.) Ed. 2. 1789. 8. (3 Sh. 6 d.)

SAMWELL, [David] *Surgeon of the Discovery.* Narrative of the death of Capt. *Jam. Cook* — with obser-

observations respecting the introduction of the venereal disease into the Sandwichs Islands. 1786. 4. (1 Sh. 6 d.)

SANDBY, [......] Collection of 150 select views in England, Scotland and Ireland. Vol. 1. 2. 1771. fol.

SANDEN, [Thomas] *M. D: Physician at Chicester.* Short strictures on Dr. *Dawson's* treatment in the acute rheumatism. 1781. 12. (1 Sh.) Account of some symptoms of fever and of the means of removing them. (London M. J. Vol. 4. p. 289.) Diss. De atmospherae natura et effectibus quibusdam. Edinb. 1774. 8.

SANDERS, [Charlotte Eliz.] *Miss.* Poems on various subjects. 1787. 12. (3 Sh.) The embarrassed attachment. 1788. (—)

— [Robert] born in *Scotland.* 1727. died d. 24 March. 1783.

SANDON, [T.....] *M. D.* On the method of treatment, recommended by *Dawson* in the acute rheumatism. 1782.

SANDYS, [.....] of *Dublin.* The words of Christ, selected from the evangelists, with notes. Vol. 1. 2. 1788. 8. (5 Sh.)

— [Isaac] Table, which reduces deals as imported for the baltic to standard deals —. 1785. 4. (6 Sh.)

SARGENT, [John] *Esq.* The mine: a dramatic poem. 1785. 4. (3 Sh.) Ed. 2. 1789. 8. (5 Sh.)

SARMAN, [Radhacanta] Inscriptions on the Staff of Firuz Shah; translated from the Sanscrit and explained. (Asiat. Res. Vol. 1. p. 379.)

SAVAGE, [.....] *Mrs.* Poems on various subjects and occasions. 1777. 8. Vol. 1. 2. (6 Sh.)

SAUNDERS, [.....] *Miss.* The embarrassed attachment, a novel. 1788. 8. Vol. 1. 2. (6 Sh.)

— [George] On theaters. 1790. 4. (10 Sh. 6 d.)

— [James] *M. D: Physician at Bamff.* born: ..... died d. 28. Nov. 1778.

— [Richard Huck] *M. D: Physician.* born in the County of *Westmoreland.* 1720. died at *London* d. 24. Jul. 1785.

— [Robert] *Physician at Bamff.* Observations on the sore throat and fever that raged in the North of Scotland in the Year 1777. 1778. 8. (1 Sh.)

SAUNDERS, [Robert] *Surgeon at Boglepoor in Bengal.* Account of the vegetable and mineral productions of Boutan and Thibet. (Phil. Transact. 1789. p 79. überſ. *Sprengel's* und *Forſter's* N. Beytr. z. Völker und Länderk. Th. 3. S. 67. überſ. *Gren* J. d. P. Th. 2. S. 88.)

—— [Samuel] Theosophical eſſays: or, the wisdom and goodneſſ of God —. 1789. 8. (1 Sh. 6 d.)

—— [William] *M. D: Phyſician to Guys - Hoſpital. Jos. Jam. Plenck's* method of giving mercury for the venereal disease, translated. 1768. 8. (1 Sh. 6 d.) Ed. 2. 1772. überſ. Samml. f. A. Th. 3. S. 412. Answer to Mr. *Geach's* and Mr. *Alcock's* observations on *Baker's* eſſay on the Devonshire colic. 1768. 8. (1 Sh.) Observationes de antimonio ejusque uſu. 1773. 8. (2 Sh.) überſ. Altenb. 1775. 8. Observations on the mephitic acid in diſſolving ſtones in the bladder. 1777. 8. (1 Sh.) Observations on the efficacy of the red Peruvian bark in the cure of agues and other fevers. 1782. 8. (2 Sh.) Ed. 3. 1783. überſ. von *Ludwig*, nebſt *Bucholz's* Abhandl. über die Mahagony - Rinde. Leipzig. 1783. 8. Account of a new extract of bark prepared in South - America. (Lond. M. J. Vol. XI. P. 1. überſ. Samml. f. A. Th. 13. S. 378.)

SAY, [Benjamin] *Practitioner of Medicine in Philadelphia.* Case of a ſpasmodic affection of the eyes. (Mem. of M. S. of L. Vol. 1. p. 326.)

SAYERS, [F. . . . .] *M. D.* Dramatic sketches of the ancient Northern mythology. 1790. 4. (3 ſh. 6 d.)

SAYER, [Edward] Observations on the police or civil government of Weſtminſter —. 1784. 4. (2 ſh. 6 d.)

—— [Joseph] The law damages. 1771. (4 ſh.)

SCALE, [Bernard] *Land Surveyor, Topographer and Valuer of eſtates.* Tables for the easy valuing of eſtates from 1 Sh. to 5 L. per acre —. 1771. 8. (5 Sh.)

SCHNEBBELIE, [J. . . . C. . . .] (*Quacker*) Travel from Egypt towards the land of Canaan. 1780. 8. (2 Sh.)

SCHOMBERG, [Alexander C.] *M. A. Fellow of Magdalen College, Oxford.* Hiſtorical and chronological

cal view of roman law with notes —. 1785. 8. (3 ſh. 6 d.) On the maritime laws of Rhodes. 1786. 8. (2 Sh.) A ſea manuel recommended to the young officers of the british navy —. 1789. 8. (3 Sh.)

SCOTT, [.....] *Miſſ.* The female advocate, a poem. 1774. 4. (2 Sh.) Meſſiah: a poem. 1788. 4. (2 Sh.)

SCOTT, [A.....] *A. M.* Exercises for turning English into French —. 1774. 12. (1 sh. 6 d.) Rudiments and practical exercises for learning the French language. 1782. 8. (2 Sh. 6 d.) Ed. 2. 1786. 8. (3 Sh. 6 d.) Nouveau recueil; ou melange litteraire, hiſtorique, dramatique et poetique. 1784. 12. (4 Sh. 6 d.)

—— [James] *M. D: Phyſician at London.* Account of a remarkable imperfection of ſight. (Phil. Transact. 1778. p. 611.) On the origin of the gout and a ſafe mode of remedying it. 1780. 8. (3 Sh.) Hiſtories of gouty, bilious and nervous cases. 1780. 8. (6 d.)

—— [John] *Major in the ſervice of the Eaſt-India Company and Member of Parliament.* Short review of the transactions in Bengal during the laſt ten years. 1782. 8. (2 Sh.) Ed. 2. under the title: Narrative of the transactions in Bengal during the adminiſtration of Mr. *Haſtings* 1784. 8. (2 Sh. 6 d.) *Two letters to *Edm. Burke* —. 1783. 8. (1 Sh. 6 d) Letter to Mr. *Fox*, on his bill. 1783. 8. (1 Sh. 6 d.) Reply to Mr. *Burke's* ſpeech on Mr. *Fox's* Eaſt-India bill. 1784. 8. (1 ſh. 6 d.) Speech on a motion, made by *Will. Pitt* for leave to bring in a bill for the relief of the Eaſt-India Company. 1784. 8. (1 ſh.) The conduct of his Majeſty's late Miniſters conſidered, as it affected the Eaſt-India Company and Mr. *Haſtings*. 1784. 8. (2 Sh.) Speech in the house of commons, on the declaratory bill. 1788. 8. (1 Sh.) Obſervations upon Mr. *Sheridan's* comparative ſtatement. 1788. 4. (3 sh.) Charge againſt Mr. *Burke*. 1789. 8. (6 d.) *Seven letters to the people of Great-Britain, by a whig. 1789. 8. (2 Sh.) Letter to *James Fox* on the extraneous matter contained in Mr. *Burke's* ſpeeches in Weſtminſter Hall —. Ed. 2. 1789. 8. (3 Sh.)

A

A ſecond letter to Mr. *Fox*, containing the final deciſion of the Governor general and council of Bengal on the charges brought againſt Rajah *Deby Sing*. 1789. 8. (1 ſh) A third letter to Mr. *Fox*, on the ſtory of *Deby Sing* —. 1789. 8. (1 ſh. 6 d.)

SCOTT, [John] *Esq.* born in London d. 9. Jan. 1730. died d. 12. Dec. 1783. (see *Hoole*.)

— [John] *Esq.* Digeſt of the present act for amendment of the highways —. 1773. 8. (2 ſh.) Digeſt of the general highways and turnpike laws —. 1778. 8. (5 ſh.)

— [Jonathan] *Captain in the Service of the Eaſt-India Company.* Translation of the memoirs of Eradut Khan, a Nobleman of Hindoſtan, containing anecdotes of the emperor Aulumgeer Aurungzebe and of his ſucceſſors, Shaw Aulum and Jehaunder Shaw —. 1786. 4. (4 ſh. 6 d.)

— [Thomas] *M. A: Curate of Weſton Underwood and Ravenſtone, Bucks.* The table of *Cebes* - in English verſes; with notes. 1754. 4. (1 Sh. 6 d.) The books of *Job*, in English verse - with remarks —. 1771. 4. (6 Sh.) Ed. 2. 1773. (6 Sh.) Epigrams of *Martial* - translated with notes. 1773. 8. (3 Sh. 6 d.) Lyric poems, devotional and moral. 1773. 8. (3 Sh. 6 d) The force of truth. 1779. 8. (2 Sh.) (Several ſingle ſermons.)

— [W. . . . .] *Esq: of the Middle temple.* Every farmer his own lawyer: or the country gentleman's complete guide, containing all the acts now in force —. 1787. 8. (3 Sh.)

— [William] *M D: Phyſician at Hawick, Roxburghshire.* Singular effects from a slight wound in the thigh. (Med. Com. of. Ed. Vol. 4. p. 332.) Fatty ſubſtances voided by ſtool. (Ibid. p. 334.) Hiſtory of a case in which obſtinate affections of the inteſtines were radically cured by the discharge of a great number of ſubſtances resembling hydatides, from the use of purgatives. (Ibid Vol. 5. p. 183.) Account of a large quantity of blood evacuated by ſtool. (Ibid. p. 428.) Hiſtory of a case of ascites, remarkable for the quantity of water drawn off by tapping. (Ibid. Vol. 6. p. 440.)

— [William] *M. D. of Stamfordham, Northumberland.* Diſſertation on the scrophula, or King's evil. 1759. 8.

Violent aſthmatic fits, occaſioned by the effluvia of Ipecacuanha. (Med. Com. of Ed. Vol. 4. p. 75. Phil. Transact. 1776. p. 168.) Account of the influenza, as it appeared in Northumberland. 1782. (*Duncan's* M. C. Vol. 9. p. 415.)

SCOTT, [William] New ſyſtem of practical arithmetic. 1771. 8. (3 ſh. 6 d.) Elements of geometry. 1782. 12. (2 ſh. 6 d.)

—— [William] *Teacher in Edinburgh.* Introduction to reading and spelling —. 1776. 8. (1 ſh. 6 d.) Principles of Engliſh grammar. 1777. 12. (1 ſh. 6 d.) Leſſons on elocution; or, miscellaneous pieces in prose and verse —. 1779. 12. (3 ſh.) A new spelling, pronouncing and explanatory dictionary of the Engliſh language —. 1786. 4. (3 ſh.)

—— [William] *M. A: Morning-Preacher at St. Michael's and Afternoon Preacher at St. Catherine by the Tower.* Addreſſ to the Archbiſhops, the biſhops and the clergy on the preſent ſtate of the annual charity for the sons of the clergy. 1769. 4. (1 ſh.) Translation of *Chryſoſtom's* 2 and 3 sermons. 1775. (1 ſh.) Translation of *Chryſoſtom's* 4. 5. 6. panegyric. 1775. 8. (1 ſh. 6 d.)

SCRIVEN, [J..... B.....] *Barriſter at Law.* — and *G. W. Vernon's* reports of caſes determined in the King's courts, Dublin, with ſelect caſes in the houſe of Lords of Ireland. P. 1. 1789. 8. (8 ſh.)

SCROPE, [Richard] *D. D.* Letter on the proſecution of W. C. by the proctors of Oxford. 1773. 4. (1 Sh.)

SEALE, [J..... B.....] *M. A: Fellow of Chriſt College, Cambridge.* Analyſis of the greek metres —. 1784. 8. (1 ſh. 6 d.)

SEALLY, [John] *L. L. D: Maſter of the Academy in Bridgewater ſquare.* The univerſal tutor: or new Engliſh ſpelling-book and expoſitor —. 1767. 12. (1 Sh. 6 d.) The London ſpelling dictionary —. 1771. 4. (2 Sh.) Elements of aſtronomy and geography. 1771. 8. (3 Sh.) Moral tales after the eaſtern manner. Vol. 1. 2. 1773. 8. (6 Sh.) The loves of Caliſto and Emira, or the fatal legacy. 1776. 12. (3 Sh.) The Lady's encyclopedia; or a conciſe

cise analysis of the belles lettres —. Vol. 1-3. 1788. 12. (12 Sh.)

SEARCH, [Edward] *Esq.* The light of nature pursued — the posthumous work of *Abrah. Tucker.* Vol. 1-7. 1768-1778. 8. (1 L. 18 Sh.) übers. von *J. C. P. Erxleben.* Th. 1. 2. 1772. 8.

SEASON, [Henry] *M. D: Physician and Astronomer at Bromham in Wilts.* born: .... died d. 13. Nov. 1775.

SELLERS, [John] *Esq. Representative in Assembly for Chester County.* Account of the transit of Venus over the sun's disc as observed at Norriton June 3d. 1769. (Tr. of A. S. Vol. 1. p. 8. Phil. Transact. 1769. p. 289.)

SELLON, [Baker John] *Esq. of the Inner Temple.* Analysis of the practice of the courts of Kings bench and common pleas with some observations on the mode of passing fines and suffering recoveries. 1789. 8. (3 Sh.)

—— [William] *M. A: Curate of the united parishes of St. James and St. John, Clerkenwell. Preacher at the Magdalen Hospital at London.* born: .... died d. 18 Jul 1790.

SEMPLE, [George] On building in water —. 1778. 4. (15 Sh.)

SERVICE, [John Paterson] Recreation for youth: an — epitome of geography and biography. 1787. 12. (3 Sh. 6 d.)

SEWALL, [Stephen] *F. A. A: Professor of the oriental languages in the University at Cambridge.* Magnetical observations made at Cambridge. (Mem. of B. A. Vol. 1. p. 322.)

SEWARD, [Anna] *Miss.* Elegy on Captain *Cook* with an ode to the son. 1780. 4. (1 Sh. 6 d.) Monody on Major *André*, with letters to her by Major *André* in the Year. 1769. 4. 1781. (2 Sh. 6 d.) Poem to the memory of Lady *Miller* of Bath, Easton villa, near Bath. 1782. 4. (1 Sh. 6 d.) Louisa, a poetical novel in 4 epistles. 1784. 4. (3 Sh. 6 d.) Ode on Gen. *Elliot's* return from Gibraltar. 1787. 4. (1 Sh.) An adjeu to the rocks of Lannow. 1789. (1 Sh.)

—— [Thomas] *A. M: Canon Residentary of Lichtfield.* born: 1708. died d. 4 March. 1790.

SEWARD, [William] *Esq. F. R. S.* The history of a savage girl, caught wild in the woods of Champagne, translated from the French. 17..

—— [....] *Prebendary of Lichtfield Cathedral. (Father of Anna Seward.)* The dramatic works of *Beaumont* and *Fletcher* — with notes critical and explanatory by various commentators and with 54 original engravings. Vol. 1 - 10. 1780. 8. (3 L.)

SEYEN, [Samuel] *M A: Rector of St. Michael's, Bristol.* Serious address to the members of the church of England. 1772. 8. (1 Sh.)

SEYMOUR, [Thomas] Account of the properties and effects of the poudre unique. 1772. 8. (1 Sh.)

SHAPTER, [Thomas] The fugitive; or, happy recess, a dramatic pastoral. 1790. 8. (1 Sh.)

SHARP, [.....] *Archdeacon of Northumberland.* On a roman inscription. (Arch. Vol. 7. p. 82.)

—— [James] Description of some of the utensils in husbandry, rolling-carriages, cart-rollers —. 1778. 4. (2 Sh.)

—— [John] *M. A.* Guide to reading and spelling English for the use of schools. 1781. 12. (1 Sh.)

—— [William] Jun. *Continued corruption, standing armies, and popular discontents considered; and the establishment of the English colonies in America examined. 1768. 4. (3 Sh.) Free address to freemen. 1771. 8. (6 d.) An Englishman's remonstrance. 1771. 8. (1 Sh.) Verses to *John Wilkes* —. 1775. 8. (1 Sh. 6 d.) A ramble from Newport to Cowes, in the isle of Wight. 1784. 4. (2 Sh.) Oration, delivered on the secular anniversary of the revolution —. 1789. 8. (1 Sh.)

SHARPE, [Granville] *President of the Association for the Abolition of the Slave trade.* *Critical Dissertation on *Isaiah.* VII, 13 - 16. 1767. 8. (1 Sh.) Remarks on several very important prophecies, in 5 parts 1) remarks on *Isaiah* VII, 13 - 16. in answer to D *William's* dissertation on the same subject. 2) Diss on the nature and style of prophetical writings. 3) Diss. on *Isaiah* VII, 8. 4) On Genes. XLIX, 10. 5) Answer to some of the principal arguments used by Dr. *William's* in defence of his critical dissertation. 1768.

1768. 8. (2 ſh. 6 d.) Representation of the injuſtice and dangerous tendency of tolerating slavery, or of admitting the leaſt claim of private property in the persons of men, in England; in 4 parts —. 1769. 8. (2 Sh.) Remarks on the diſtinction between manslaughter and murden —. 1773. 8. (1 ſh. 6 d.) Declaration of the people's natural right to a share in the legislature. 1775. 8. On the law of nature and principles of action in man. 1777. 8. (4 ſh.) The legal means of political reformation —. 1780. 8. (1 ſh.) Account of the ancient diviſion of the English nation into hundreds and tithings —. . 1785. 8. *Sketch of temporary regulations for the intended settlement on the grain coaſt of Africa near Sierra Leona. 1788. 8.

SHARPE, [Gregory] *LL. D: F. R. S: F. A. S: Chaplain in Ordinary to his Majeſty.* born: .... died 1770.

SHAW, [Duncan] *D. D: Miniſter of Aberdeen.* View of the several methods of promoting religious inſtruction from the earlieſt down to the present time —. Vol. 1. 2. 1776. 8. (10 ſh.) überſ. Leipz. 1777. 8. Hiſtory and philosophy of judaism —. 1788. 8. (6 ſh.)

— [James] Sketches of the hiſtory of the Auſtrian Netherlands with remarks on the conſtitution, commerce, arts, and general ſtate of these provinces. 1786. 8. (5 ſh.) Review of the affairs of the Auſtrian Netherlands in 1787. 8. 1788. (2 ſh.)

— [John] *A. M: Fellow of Magdalen College at Oxford. Apollonii Rhodii* Argonautica —. Vol. 1. 2. 1777. 4.

— [John] *Headmaſter of the free grammar School at Rochdale in Lancashire.* A methodical English grammar. 1778. 8. (2 ſh.)

— [Joseph] *Surgeon: F. M. S.* An extraordinary case of delivery. (Mem. of M. S. of L. Vol. 1. p. 213.)

— [Lachlan] *Miniſter of the Gospel at Elgin.* Hiſtory of the province of Moray —. 1775. 4. (12 Sh.)

— [Samuel] Alphabetical index of the regiſtered entails in Scotland from the Year 1685-1784. —. 1785. 4. (7 Sh. 6 d.)

SHAW, [Samuel] *M. A: Fellow of Queen's College, Cambridge.* Tour to the weſt of England in the Y. 1788. Lond 1789. 8. (6 Sh.) *Bruce's* travels into Abyſſinia, abridged 1790. 8. (4 Sh.)

—— [William] *A. M: F. A S: Clergyman.* (born in Scotland) Analyſis of the Galic language. 1779. 8. Galic and English dictionary. — Vol. 1. 2. 1780. 4. (2 L. 2 Sh.) Enquiry into the authenticity of the poems aſcribed to *Oſſian* 1781. 8. (1 Sh. 6 d.) Rejoinder to an anſwer from Mr. (John) *Clarke*, on the ſubject of *Oſſian's* poems. 1784. 8. (1 Sh. 6 d.)

SHEBBEARE, [John] *M. D* born 1709. died d. 1. Aug. 1788.

SHEFFIELD, [John] *Lord in Ireland and Member of Parliament* *Obſervations on the commerce of the American ſtates. Ed. 6 1784. 8. (2 Sh. 6 d.) überſ Leipzig. 17.. Obſervations on the manufactures, trade and preſent ſtate of Ireland. Ed. 2. P. 1. 2. 1785. 8 (5 Sh.) *Obſervations on the project for abolishing the slave trade —. 1789. 8. (1 Sh 6 d.)

SHELDON, [Anne] *Miſſ.* ſee Mrs *Archer*.

—— [George] *M. A: Vicar of Edwardſton, Suffolk;* Remarks on the critical parts of a pamphlet "letters to *Benj. Kennicott* by Mr l'Abbe *** —. 1775. 8. (1 Sh 6 d.)

—— [John] *Surgeon; Profeſſor of Anatomy in the Royal Academy of Arts and Lecturer of Anatomy and Surgery. F. R. S. J. N. Lieberkühn* Diſſertationes quatuor now firſt collected. 1782. 4. (6 ſh.) Hiſtory of the abſorbent ſyſtem. P. 1. 1784. 4. (1 L. 1 Sh.) Eſſay on the fracture of the patella or knee-pan. 1789. 8. (2 Sh. 6 d.)

SHELDRAKE, [Timothy] Jun. Remarks on Mr. *Brand's* chirurgical eſſays on the cauſes and ſymptoms of ruptures — with hiſtory of the invention of Mr. *Brand's* patent elaſtic truſſes. 1783. 8. On the various cauſes and effects of the diſtorted ſpine and on the improper methods - to remove the diſtortion; with obſervations on the treatment of ruptures 1783. 8. (2 Sh.)

SHEPHERD, [Richard] *DD: F. R. S: ArchDeacon of Bedford and Chaplain to the Bishop of Durham.*

*Ode

*Ode to the love. 1756. 4. (6 Sh.) The nuptials, a didactic poem. 1762. 4. (2 Sh. 6 d.) Letters to *Soame Jenyns* on his inquiry into the nature and origin of evil with three discourses on conscience, on inſpiration, on a paradisiacal ſtate. 1768. 8. (3 Sh.) Ed. 2. 1772. (3 Sh.) Hector, a dramatic poem. 1770. 4. Bianca, a tragedy. 1772. 8. Miscellanies in prose and verse — Vol. 1. 2. 1776. 8. (7 Sh.) The dying hero, a poem. 1779. 4. (1 Sh.) *Eſſay on education. 1781. 4. (2 Sh.) 1784. (1 Sh.) Free examination of the ſocinian expoſition of the prefatory verses of St. *John's* gospel. 1783. 8. (2 Sh.) *Will. Staff. Done's* D. D: ſermons. 1786. 8. (5 Sh.) The ground and credibility of the chriſtian religion in a course of ſermons —. 1788. 8. (5 Sh. 6 d.)

(Several ſingle ſermons.)

SHEPPARD, [Edward] *A. B: Rector of Bettiscomb, Dorset.* Letter to *Prieſtley* on his corruptions of chriſtianity 1783. 8. (1 Sh.)

SHERIDAN, [....] *Miſſ.* The ambiguous lover, a farce. 1781.

— [Charles Francis] *Under-Secretary of ſtate for the war Department in the Kingdom of Ireland and Member of Parliament.* Hiſtory of the late revolution in Sweden. 1778. 8. (5 Sh.) überſ. (von *K. C. B. Koch.*) Berlin. 1781. 8. *Letters of a Dungannon volunteer respecting the expediency of a parliamentary reform. 17.. *Observations on *W. Blackſtone's* doctrine respecting the extent of the power of the British parliament, particularly with relation to Ireland. 1779. 8. (1 Sh. 6 d.) *Review of the three great national queſtions, relative to a declaration of right, poyning's law, and the mutiny bill. 1781. 8. (2 Sh.)

— [John] *Esq: of the Inner temple.* The present practice of the court of King's bench —. 1785. 8. (7 Sh.)

— [J..... R.....] *Esq.* Account of the revolution in Sweden in the Year. 1772. 1783. 12. (3 ſh.)

— [Richard Brinsley] *M. P:* (born at *Quilca* in *Ireland.* 1752.) *The rivals, a comedy. 1775. 8. (1 ſh. 6 d.) überſ. (von *Joh. Andr. Engelbrecht.*) The Duenna, a comic opera. 1775. The Beggar, an an opera. 17.. St. Patrick's day; or, the sheming Lieutenants. 1776. The ſchool for ſcandal, a comedy. 1777. The critic, or tragedy rehearsed. 1779. 8. (1 ſh.) Ed. 2. 1781. 8. (1 ſh. 6 d.) The critic anticipated; or, the humorous of the green-room; a farce. 1779. 8. (1 ſh.) * Verses to the memory of *Dav. Garrick*. 1779. 4. (1 ſh.) A trip to Scarborough, a comedy. 1781. 8. (1 ſh. 6 d.) Comparative ſtatement of the two bills for the better government of the British poſſeſſions in India —. 1788. 4. (1 ſh. 6 d.)

SHERIDAN, [Thomas] *A. M: Schoolmaſter at Dublin.* born at *Quilca* in *Ireland.* 1720. died at *Murgate* d. 14 Aug. 1788.

SHERLOCK, [Martin] *Chaplain to Frederic Earl of Briſtol and Lord Biſhop of Derry in Ireland.* Lettres d'un voyageur anglois. Geneva. 1779. translated into English. 1780. 4. (3 Sh.) Nouvelles lettres d'un voyageur anglois. London and Paris. 1780. 8. translated into English. 1781. 8. (3 ſh.) überſ. Th. 1. 2 Leipzig. 1782. 8. Conſiglio ad un giovane poeta. Naples. 1779. 8. Letters on several ſubjects. Vol 1. 2. 1781. 8. (5 ſh.) überſ. Th. 1. 2. Leipz. 1782. 8. Fragment on *Shakspeare*, extracted from advice to a young poet, translated from the French. 1786. 8. (1 ſh.)

SHERSON, [Robert] *F. M. S.* Case of rheumatiſm, cured by electricity. (Mem. of M. S. of L. Vol. 1. p. 221.)

SHERWEN, [John] *Surgeon at Enfield, Middleſex.* *Cursory remarks on the nature and cause of the marine scuruy. 1782. 4. (2 ſh. 6 d.) Case of the puncture of a nerve in Phlebotomy. (Med. Com. of Ed. Vol. 4. p. 210.) Hiſtory of the cure of a dangerous obſtruction in the trachea, in which Mr. *Mudge's* inhaler was used with advantage. (*Duncan* M. C. 1780. p. 416.) überſ Samml. f. A. Th. XI. p. 183. Observations on the schirro, - contracted rectum. (Mem. of M. S. of L. Vol. 2. p. 9.) On the effects of emetic tartar by external absorption. (Ibid. p. 386.) On the effects of arsenic, by external absorption. (Ibid. p. 394.)

SHIELD, [William] The farmer, a comic opera. 1788. (6 ſh.)

SHILLITO, [Charles] *The sea fight, an elegiac poem. 1780. 4. (1 ſh. 6 d.)

SHIPLEY, [Jonathan] *D. D: LordBishop of St. Asaph.* born: .... died d. 9 Dec. 1788.

SHIRLEY, [Thomas]. The angler's museum; or, the whole art of float and fly fishing. 1784. 12. (1 ſh. 6 d.)

SHOAFT, [John Thom.] *Student of Medicine at Annapolis.* Account of a case of tetanus ſucceſſfully treated by the use of calomel, bark, wine and the cold bath —. (Mem. of M. S. of L. Vol. 2. p. 108.)

SHRUBSOLE, [W.....] Chriſtian memoirs, or, review of the present ſtate of religion in England. 1777. 8. (5 ſh.) Free-mason sermon: Sheshbazzar and his masons 1787. 8. (9 d.)

SHUCKBURGH, [George] *Sir. Bart. F. R. S.* Obſervations made in Savoy, in order to ascertain the height of mountains by means of the Barometer. (Phil. Transact. 1777. p. 513.) überſ. Samml. z. P. und N. G. Th. 1. S. 731. Comparison between G. *Shukburgh* and Colonel *Roy's* rules, for the measurement of heights with the barometer. (Ibid. 1778. p. 681.) On the variation of the temperature of boiling water. (Ibid. 1779. p. 362.)

SHULDHAM, [Molineux] *Esq.* Account of the sea-cow and the use made of it. (Phil. Transact. 1775. p. 249.)

SHUTE, [.....] *LordBishop of Sarum.* Letter to the clergy of the diocese of Sarum with directions relating to orders, inſtitutions and licences. 1789. 8. (1 Sh.)

SIDDONS, [Henry] *Modern break faſt, or, all asleep at noon. 1790. 8. (1 ſh.)

SILVESTER, [John Baptiſt] *Sir, Knight: M. D: F. R. S: Phyſician to the London Hospital.* born: ... died at *Bath.* d. 8. Nov. 1789.

SIMEON, [John] *Esq. of Lincoln's Inn, Barriſter at Law.* On the law of elections, in all its branches. 1789. 8. (7 ſh. 6 d.)

SIMES, [Thomas]. *Esq. late Captain of the Queen's Royal Regiment of Foot.* The military Guide. :7.. The military medly, containing the moſt neceſſary rules and directions for attaining a competent knowlege of the art; —. 1767. (10 Sh. 6 d.) Military course for the government and conduct of a battalion —. 1777. 8. (10 sh. 6 d.) The military instructor for non-commissioned officers and private men of the infantry. Ed. 2. 1780. 12. (2 Sh. 6 d.) On the military science —. 1780. 4. (13 Sh.)

SIMMONS, [John] *Surgeon at Chatham, Kent.* On the cause of lightening —. 1775. 8. (1 Sh.) On electricity. 1776. 8.

—— [Samuel Foart] *M. D: F. R. S:* The case of patient voiding stones through a fistulous sore in the loins, without any concomitant discharge of urine by the same passage. (Phil. Transact. 1774. p. 108.) Diss. De rubeola. Lugd. Bat. 1776. 4. Elements of anatomy and the animal oeconomy, from the French of Mr. *Person*, corrected and augmented. 1775. 8. (5 Sh.) Ed. 2. 1781. 8. (5 Sh.) Singular effects from the application of blue vitriol. (Med. Com. of Ed. Vol. 4. p. 73.) Some remarks on the treatment of hydrocephalus internus — (Ibid. Vol. 5. p. 415.) Account of the taenia or long tape worm — translated from the French. 1777. 8. (2 Sh.) Anatomy of the human body. 1780. 8. (6 Sh.) übers. Leipz. 1781. 8. Practical observations on the treatment of consumptions —. 1780. 8. (2 Sh.) übers. Samml. f. A. Th. 6. S. 38. Observations on the cure of the gonorrhoea. 1780. 8. (1 Sh. 6 d.) Ed. 2. 1784. übers. Samml. f. A. Th. XI. S. 291. übers. Schweinfurth. 1787. 8. *London Medical Journal. Vol. I-XI. 1781-1790. Account of a caries of the spine and of the appearances on dissection. (London M. J. Vol. 1. p. 271.) Account of the life and writings of *Will. Hunter* —. 1783. 8. (2 Sh.) A singular case of hydatids. (M. C. Vol. 1. p. 101.) Account of an aneurism of the aorta. (Ibid. p. 118.) A case of emphysema, brought on by severe labour pains. (Ibid. p. 176.) Case of an ulceration of the oesophagus and ossification of the heart. (Ibid. p. 228.) On the effects of the digitalis purpurea in dropsy. (London M. J. Vol. 6. p. 55. übers. Samml. f. A. Th. XI. S. 98.) Account of a species of hydrocephalus, which sometimes takes place in cases of mania. London M. J. Vol. 6. p. 159. übers. Samml. f. A. Th.

Th. XI. S. 135.) Of the epidemic catarrh of the Year 1788. (Ibid. Vol IX. Part. 4.)

SIMON, [Stuckey] *Merchant at Dublin.* Two letters concerning the reviviscence of some snails. (Phil. Transact 1774. p. 432.)

SIMPSON, [David] *M. A.* Sacred litterature; shewing the holy scriptures to be ſuperior to the moſt celebrated writings of antiquity —. Vol. 1-4. 1789. 8. (1 L. 1 Sh.)

— [James] *Profeſſor of Medicine in St. Andrews Univerſity*, *Scotland.* born : . . . . died d. 29. Aug. 1770.

— [John] *a Diſſenting Clergyman.* Eſſay to show that chriſtianity is beſt conveyed in the hiſtoric form. 1782. 8. (2 Sh.)

— [Joseph] *Esq.* The patriot, a tragedy. 1785. 8.

— [William] A new and complete intereſt book, exhibiting the intereſt of any ſum of money from 5 Sh. to 1000. L. —. 1780. 8. (2 Sh. 6 d.)

SIMS, [James] *M. D. F. A. S. Preſident of the Medical Society of London.* Diſſ. De temperie foeminea et morbis inde oriundis. Lugd. Bat. 1764. 4. Observations on epidemic disorders. 1773. 8. (5 ſh.) überſ. von *J. W. Möller.* Hamb. 1775. 8. Discourse on the beſt method of prosecuting medical enquiries —. 1774. 8. (2 ſh.) überſ. von *J. W. Möller.* Hamb. 1775. 8. *Edw. Foſter's* principles and practice of midwifery corrected. 1781. 8. (4 ſh. 6 d.) Observations on deafneſſ, from affections of the Euſtachian tube. (Mem. of M. S. of L. Vol. 1. p. 94.) On the ſcarlatina anginosa as it appeared in London in the Year 1786. (Ibid. p. 388.) On the hydrophobia. (Ibid. Vol. 2. p. 1.) On the cure of the jaundice by a particular mode of treatment. (Ibid. Vol. 2. p. 283.)

— [John] *M. D.* Account of a cancerous affection of the ſtomach. (M. C. Vol. 1. p. 421.)

— [Joseph] *M. A: Prebendary of St. Paul's.* Fifteen ſermons on various ſubjects. 1772. 8. (5 ſh.)

— [William] — and *Rich. Frewin*, the rates of merchandise —. 1782. 8. (7 ſh.)

SINCLAIR, [A. . . . . G. . . . .] *M. D.* The critic philosopher, or truth discovered. 1789. 8. (2 ſh. 6 d.)

SIN-

SINCLAIR, [John] *Sir: Baronet: Member of Parliament.* (born in *Scotland.*) *Lucubrations during a short receſſ. 1782. 8. (1 ſh. 6 d.) Observations on the Scottish dialect. 1782. 8. (4 ſh.) Thoughts on the naval ſtrength of the British empire. 1782. 8. (1 ſh.) Hints addreſſed to the public: calculated to dispel the gloomy ideas which have been lately entertained of the ſtate of our finances Ed. 2. 1783. 8. (1 ſh.) Hiſtory of the public revenue of the British empire. 1785. 4. Appendix. 1789. 4. (13 ſh. 6d.) Ed. 2. P. 1. 2. 3. Lond. 1790. 4. (1 L. 1 ſh.) State of alterations which may be proposed in the laws for regulating the election of members of parliament for shires in Scotland. 1787. 8. (1 ſh.) *Sinclair's* and *Anderson's* report of the committee of the highland society of Scotland, to whom the ſubject of Shetland wool was referred —. 1790. 8.

SINGLETON, [.....] Description of the Weſt-Indies, a poem. 1776. 4. (3 ſh.)

SIX, [James] *Esq.* Account of an improved thermometer. (Phil. Transact. 1782. p. 72.) Experiments to inveſtigate the variation of local heat. (Ibid. 1784. p. 428.) Experiments on local heat. (Ibid. 1788. p. 103.) überſ. *Gren.* J. d. P. Th. 1. S. 112.)

SKAIFE, [Thomas] *Carpenter and Joiner.* Key to civil architecture; or the universal British builder —. 1774. 8. (7 ſh. 6 d.)

SKEELER, [Thomas] *Vicar of Lewknor in Oxfordshire and Chaplain to the Earl of Litchfield.* Fourteen ſermons on ſeveral occaſions. 1772. 8. (6 ſh.)

SKEETE, [Thomas] *M. D: Phyſician of Guy's Hospital and New Finsbury Dispensary.* born 1756. died d. 29 June. 1788.

SKINN, [....] *Mrs.* (her maden name *Maſtermann;* of *York.*) The old maid, or hiſtory of Miſſ *Ravensworth.* Vol. 1-3. 1770. 8. (7 ſh. 6 d.)

SKINNER, [.....] *Silk Merchant in London.* The whole proceſſ of the ſilk-worm from the egg to the cocon. (Tr. of A. S. Vol. 2. p. 347.)

—— [James] *Presbyter of the episcopal-church in Scotland at Longſide, Aberdeenshire.* Free thoughts on the extent of the death of Chriſt, the doctrine of reprobation. 1788. 12. (6 d.) Eccleſiaſtical hiſtory of Scotland. Vol. 1. 2. 1789. 8. (14 ſh.)

SKIN-

water and wind, to turn mills and other machines depending on a circular motion. (Ibid. 1761. p. 100.) On the menſtrual parallax ariſing from the mutual gravitation of the earth and moon, its influence on the obſervation of the ſun and planets, with a method of obſerving it. (Ibid. 1768. p. 156.) Deſcription of a new method of obſerving the heavenly bodies out of the meridian. (Ibid. 1768. p. 170.) Obſervations on a ſolar eclipſe June 4. 1760. at Auſthorpe, near Leeds, Yorkshire. (Ibid. 1769. p. 286.) Deſcription of a new hygrometer. (Ibid. 1771. P. I. p. 198.) Experimental examination of the quantity and proportion of mechanic power neceſſary to be employed in giving different degrees of velocity to heavy bodies from a ſtate of reſt. (Ibid. 1776. p. 450.) New fundamental experiments upon the colliſion of bodies. (Ibid. 1782. p. 327.) Obſervations on the graduation of aſtronomical inſtruments, with an explanation of the method invented by the late Mr. *Henry Hindley*, of York, Clockmaker —. (Ibid. 1786. p. 1.) Account of an obſervation of the right aſcenſion and declination of mercury out of the meridian, near his greateſt elongation Sept. 1786. with an equatorial micrometer of his own invention and workmanship; accompanied with an inveſtigation of a method of allowing for refraction in ſuch kinds of obſervations. (Ibid. 1787. p. 318.) Deſcription of an improvement in the application of the quadrant of altitude to a celeſtial globe, for the reſolution of problems dependant on azimuth and altitude. (Ibid. 1789. p. 1.) Narrative of the building and a deſcription of the conſtruction of the Edyſtone lighthouſe with ſtone. 1791. fol. (3 L. 3 ſh.)

SMEETON, [Joseph] The grove of Barzai and his elegy —. 1777. 4. (1 ſh.)

SMELLIE, [William] *M. D: F. R. S: F. A. S. Ed:* Delectus Diſſertationum in Academia Edinenſi. Vol. 1-4. 1778. 8. *Buffon's natural hiſtory tranſlated. Vol. 1-9. 1781-1785. (4 L.) The philoſophy of natural hiſtory. 1789. 4. (1 L. 1 ſh.)

SMELT, [Leonard] Speech at the Yorkſhire meeting. 1780. 8. (2 ſh.) Account of ſome particulars of the meeting at York. 1780. 8. (1 ſh.)

SMETH-

SMETHMAN, [Thomas] *Master of the Academy at Southgate.* The practical grammar. 1774. 12. (1 sh. 6 d.)

SMETHURST, [Gamaliel] *Late member of the Assembly in the Province of Nova Scotia, Comptroller of his Majesty's Customs.* Narrative of an escape out of the hands of the Indians in the gulph of St. Lawrence —. 1774. 4. (1 sh. 6 d.)

SMITH, [Adam] *LL. D: F. R. S: Commissioner of the Customs in Scotland.* born 1723. died at *Edinburgh* d. 17 Jul. 1790.

— [Charlotte] *Mrs.* (her maden name *Turner.*) born: .... died d. 23 Jun. 1786.

— [Daniel] *M. D.* Remarks on *Cadogan's* treatise on the gout. 1772. 8. (1 sh. 6 d.) Observations on *Williams's* treatise on the gout. 1774. 8. (1 sh.) Apology to the public for commencing the practice of physic, particularly in gouty, rheumatic and hysterical cases. 1775. 8. (6 d.) Ed. 2. 1780. On hysterical and nervous disorders. 1778. 8. (1 sh. 6 d.)

— [E.....] Life reviewed; a poem —. 1780. 4. (2 sh. 6 d.)

— [Georg] *Captain: Inspector of the Royal Military Academy at Woolwich.* Universal military dictionary —. 1779. 4. (2 L. 2 sh.) Use and abuse of free masonry —. 1783. 8. (5 sh.)

— [Haddon] *Curate of St. Matthew, Bethnalgreen.* Twelve sermons on the most interest subjects of the christian religion. 1770. 8. (3 sh. 6 d.)
(Several single sermons.)

— [Hugh] *Apothecary, Physician to the Middlesex Hospital at London. M. D.* born ..... died at East-Barnet. d. 26 Jun. 1789.

— [J.....] *Clergyman at Liverpool.* Some remarks on the resolutions which were formed at a meeting of the Archdeaconry of Chester Febr. 15. 1790. 8. (1 sh.)

— [James] *M. A: Chaplain in Ordinary to his Majesty.* Twelve sermons. 1776. 8. (6 sh.)
(Several single sermons.)

— [James] *Vicar of Alkham and Capel, Rector of Eastbridge in Kent.* born ..... died d. 8. Febr. 1784.

SMITH, [J. . . . .] *M. D: Professor of Geometry at Oxford.* Observations on the use and abuse of the Cheltenham waters —. 1786. 8. (1 ſh. 6 d.)

—— [James Edward] *M. D: F. R. S.* °*Linnaeus's* reflections on the ſtudy of nature translated 1785. 8. (1 ſh.) *Linnaeus's* Diſſertation on the sexes of plants, translated. 1786. 8. (2 ſh.) Some observations on the irritability of vegetables. (Philos. Tranſact. 1788. p. 158.) Reliquiae *Rudbeckianae* ſive Camporum Elyſiorum libri primi. 1789. fol. (10 ſh. 6 d.) Plantarum icones haectenus ineditae. Fasc. 1. 2. 1789. fol. (2 L. 2 Sh.)

—— [Jane] Select poems on various ſubjects, with observations on the progreſſ of aſtronomy among the ancients. 1789. 8. (2 ſh. 6 d.)

—— [John] *M. D: Inoculator of the Small Pox.* Choir Gaur, the grand orrery of the ancient Druids commonly called Stonehenge on Salisbury plain —. 1770. 4. (5 ſh.)

—— [John] *A. B: Rector of Nantwich in Cheshire.* Polygamy indefenſible; two sermons, with a letter to Mr. *Madan.* 1780. 8. (1 Sh.)

(Several ſingle ſermons)

—— [John] *Surgeon in Uppingham, Rutlandshire.* Hiſtory of a case in which violent convulſions were induced by surprize and grief (Med. Com. of Ed. Vol. 3. p. 316.) Hiſtory of a case in which the bones of a foetus were discharged by ſtool and from which the patient afterwards recovered. (Ibid. Vol. 5. p. 314.)

—— [John] *D. D: Miniſter of the Gospel at Campbletown.* Galic antiquities conſiſting of a *hiſtory* of the Druids — with a Diſſertation on the authenticity of the poems of *Oſſian* and a collection of ancient poems. 1780. 4. (10 ſh. 6 d.) überſ. Leipz. Th. 1. 2. 1781. 8. View of the laſt judgment. 1783. 8. (5 ſh.) Summary view and explanation of the writings of the prophets 1787. 12. Sean Dana; le Oiſian, Orran, Ulann — ancient poems of *Oſſian*, Orran —. 1787. 8. (6 ſh.)

—— [J. . . . G. . . . .] *Captain.* *J. C. May's* commercial letters according to Profeſſor *Gellert's* rules trans-

translated from the last German edition. 1786. 8.

SMITH [J.... S....] *Captain.* Letter — on the state of negroe slaves. 1786. 8. (6 d.)

— [Michael] *A. B: Vicar of South Mims, in Hertfordshire.* Christianity unmasked; or, unavoidable ignorance preferable to corrupt christianity, a poem. 1771. 8. (4 sh.)

— [Samuel Stanhope] *D. D. and Prof. at New Jersey.* On the causes of the variety of complexion and figure in the human species with strictures on Lord *Kaimes's* discourse on the original diversity of mankind —. 1788. 8. (3 sh. 6 d.) übers. von *F. Theod. Kühn.* Braunschw. 1790. 8.

— [T.....] Original miscellaneous poems. 1790. 8. (3 sh. 6 d.)

— [William] *DD: Prevost of the College and Academy of Philadelphia.* Discourses on several public occasions during the war in America —. 1759. 8. (3 sh. 6 d.) Ed. 2. 1763. 8. (5 sh.) Account of an earthquake Sept. 30. 1750. at Peterborough. (Phil. Transact. 1756. p. 727.) Account of a fire ball July 22. 1750. (Ibid. 1757. p. 1.) Observations on the transit of venus over the sun's disk at Norriton in Pennsylvania June 3. 1769. (Ibid. 1769. p. 289. Tr. of A. S. Vol. 1. p. 8.) Account of the charitable corporation for the widows of clergymen in America. 1769. 4. Observations on the transit of mercury. Nov. 9. 1769. at Norriton. (Phil. Transact. 1770. p. 504.) Account of the terrestrial measurement between the observatories of Norriton and Philadelphia; with the difference of longitude and latitude thence deduced. (Tr. of A. S. Vol. 1. App. p. 5.) Account of the transit of mercury over the sun Nov. 9th as observed at Norriton, in Pennsylvania. (Ib. p. 50.) The sun's parallax deduced from a comparison of the Norriton observations of the transit of venus 1769. with the Greenwich and other European observations of the same. (Ibid. Vol. 1. App. p. 54.)

(Several single sermons.)

— [William] *M. A: Dean of Chester.* born at *Worcester* 1711. died 1787.

SMITH, [William] *M. D: Physician at London.* Dissertation upon the nerves containing an account 1) of the nature of man 2) of the nature of brutes 3) of the nature and connexion of soul and body. 4) of the threefold life of man 5) of the symptoms causes and cure of all nervous diseases. 1768. 8. (6 sh.) New and general system of physic, in theory and practice. 1769. 4. (14 sh.) The student's vademecum, containing an account of knowledge and its general division —. 1770. 8. (4 sh.) The nature and institution of government; containing an account of the feudal and English policy. Vol. 1. 2. 1771. 8. (12 sh.) History of England, from the earliest accounts to the revolution in 1688. Vol. 1. 2. 1771. 8. (12 sh.) Nature studied with a view to preserve and restore health with an account of a most powerful and safe deobstruent medicine —. 1774. 8. (4 sh.) A sure guide in sickness and health, in the choice of food and use of medicine. 1776. 8. (6 sh.) State of the gaols in London, Westminster and borough of Southwark with an account of the present state of the convicts sentenced to hard labour on board the justitia upon the river Thames. 1776. 8. (1 sh. 6 d.) Mild punishments sound policy; or, observations on the laws relative to debtors and felons. 1777. 8. (1 sh. 6 d.)

—— [William More] *Esq.* Poems on several occasions. 1786. 8. (2 sh. 6 d.)

SMITHURST, [Gamaliel] *late Member of the Assembly in the Province of Nova Scotia.* Narrative of an extraordinary escape out of the hands of the Indians in the Gulph of St. Lawrence. 1775. 4. (1 sh. 6 d.)

SMOLLET, [Tobias] *M. D.* born 1720. died at *Leghorn* d. 21 Oct. 1771.

SMYTH, [James Carmichael] *M. D. F. R. S. Physician Extraord. to his Majesty.* Remarks on the influenza of the Year. 1782. (M. C. Vol. 1. p. 71.) On the efficacy of the spiritus vitrioli dulcis in the cure of fevers. (Ibid. p. 135.) Account of the effect of some medicines employed in the cure of cutaneous diseases. (Ibid. p. 191.) A case of cancer of the stomach. (Ibid. p. 427.) Account of the

effects

effects of swinging, employed as a remedy in the pulmonary consumptions and hectic fever. 1787. 8. (2 ſh.) The works of the late *Will. Stark* —. 1788. 4. (10 ſh. 6 d.)

SMYTH, [J... F.... D....] A Tour in the united ſtates of America —. Vol. 1. 2. 1784. 8. (10 ſh. 6 d.)

— [Philip] *L. L. B. Fellow of New-College, Oxford. Henr. Aldrich's* (S. T. P. Dean of Chriſt Church. died 1710.) Elementa architecturae civilis ad *Vitruvii* veterumque disciplinam et recentiorum praesertim *A. Palladii* exempla probatiora concinnata. 1789. 8. (1 L. 5 ſh.)

— [William Auguſtus] The publican's guide; or, key to the diſtill house —. 1779. 8. (2 ſh. 6 d.)

SNELSON, [Jeoffery] *M. A: Vicar of Hanbury, Staffordshire. Matth. Horberry's.* D. D: XVIII ſermons on important ſubjects —. 1774. 8. (5 ſh.)

SNEYD, [Ralph] *LL. B. Rector of Sevington and Vicar of Rye, Suſſex.* Letter to Dr. *Toulmin* M. D. relative to his book on the antiquity of the world. 1783. 8. (1 ſh. 6 d.)

SNOWDEN, [Samuel] *M. D: Phyſician at Stroud, Glouceſtershire.* On the retention of urine removed by electricity. (London M. J. Vol. VII. P. 1. überſ. Samml. f. A. Th. XII. S. 5.)

SOUTHERN, [John] On aeroſtatic machines. 1785. 8. (2 ſh.)

SOWERBY, [James] A botanical drawing book, or, an easy introduction to drawing flowers according to nature. 1789. (4 ſh.)

SPARROW, [Richard] *Surgeon of the charitable infirmary at Dublin.* Account of the extraction and depreſſion of the cataract in the ſame patient; of an encyſted hydrocele of the tunica communis of the ſpermatic chord communicating with the tunica vaginalis teſtis; of an amputation below the knee —. (London M. J. Vol. IX. P. 2.)

SPEECHLEY, [William] *Gardener to the Duke of Portland.* On the culture of the pine apple and the management of the hothouse with a description of the inſects of hothouses and method of deſtroying them. 1779. 8. (1 L. 1 ſh.) A method

of

of raising the pine apple by oak leaves instead of tanners bark. (*Hunter's G. E.* Vol. 5. p. 96.) The method of planting upon the duke of Portland's estates in Nottinghamshire. (Ibid. Vol. 5. p. 109.) On the culture of the vine — with new hints on the formation of vineyards in England. 1790. 4. (1 L. 5 sh.)

SPEER, [William] *M. D: Physician in Dublin.* Account of the advantageous effects derived from the cortex simaroubae, in an obstinate fluor albus. (*Duncan's* M. C. 1780. p. 443.) übers. Samml. f. A. Th. XI. S. 262.

—— [William] *Surgeon of Ardee, County of Lowth, Ireland.* History of an uncommon case in midwifery. (Med. Com. of Ed. Vol. 6. p. 443.)

SPENCE, [David] *M. D: Fellow of the Society of Scottish Antiquaries.* System of midwifery. Vol. 1. 2. 1784. 8. (12 sh.) übers. Schweinfurth. 1787. 8.

—— [George] *Esq: Physician at Hanorca in West-Indies.* The use and abuse of blood-letting. Jamaica. 1777. 8.

—— [George] *Dentist to his Majesty.* Observations on a disease consequent to transplanting teeth. (London M. J. Vol. X. P. 3.

—— [James] *M. D: of Guildford, F. A. S. Edinb.* born: ..., died d. 24 Sept. 1786.

SPENCER, [Sarah Emma] *Mrs.* (Her maiden name *Jackson.*) Poetical trifles. 17.. Memoirs of the Miss *Holmsbys.* Vol. 1. 2. 1788. 12. (5 sh.)

SPILSBURY, [Francis] *Chymist.* The friendly physician. 1773. 8. (1 sh.) *Free thoughts on quacks and their medecines. 1776. 8. (2 sh. 6 d.) Phlebotomy or a reply to the oeconomy of quackery by *Thom. Prosser.* 1777. 8. (1 sh.) Physical dissertations on the scuruy and gout. 1778. 8. (2 sh. 6 d.) Observations on the scuruy, gout, diet and remedy —. 1780. 8. (2 sh. 6 d.). Advice to booksellers, perfumers — not to sell any more stamps with their medicines, nor the public to pay for them; founded on constitutional principles, with strictures on the medicine act. 1784. 8. (1 sh.) Discursory thoughts on the late acts of parliament viz. medicine, horse, window, post, plate —. 1785.

1785. 8. (1 ſh.) The power of gold displayed. 1785. fol. (6 d.)

SPROULE, [George] *Enſign of the 59th Regiment.* Observations of the immerſions and emerſions of the Satellites of Jupiter, taken in the Year 1768. — (Phil. Transact. 1774. p. 177.)

STACK, [John] *F. T. C. D.* and *M. R. J. A.* Eſſay to improve the theory of defective ſight. (Tr. of J. A. 1788.)

— [Richard] *D. D: F. T. C. D: M. R. J. A.* On ſublimity of writing. (Tr. of J. A. 1787. p. 3.) Examination of an eſſay on the dramatic character of Sir *John Falſtaff.* (Ibid. 1788. p. 3.)

— [R..... W.....] of *Bath. M. D.* Medical caſes. 1784. 8. (2 ſh.) überſ. 1788. 8. überſ. Samml. f. A. Th. XI. St. 1.

STAFFORD, [John] *D. D. a Diſſenting Clergyman.* The ſcripture doctrine of ſin and grace conſidered in 25 diſcourſes on the Chapt. 7 of the epiſtle to the Romans. 1772. 8. (6 ſh.)

(Several ſingle ſermons.)

STAINBANK, [R.....] *of Clifford's Inn.* The law directory for the Year. 1784. 8. (1 ſh.)

STAIR, Earl of; ſee *John Dalrymple.*

STALKARTT, [Marmaduke] Naval architecture: or the rudiments and rules of ſhipbuilding —. 1781. fol. (6 L. 6 ſh.)

STANFIELD, [James Field] *late a Mariner in the African ſlave trade.* Obſervations on a Guinea voyage. 1788. 12. (4 d.) The Guinea voyage, a poem. 1789. 4. (2 ſh. 6 d.)

STANHOPE, [Charles] *Earl.* (before *Charles* Viscount *Mahon*, Lord,) *F. R. S.* On the means of preventig fraudulent practices on the gold coin. 1775. 4. Principles of electricity —. 1779. 4. (10 ſh. 6 d.) überſ. von *J. F. Seeger.* Leipzig. 1789. 8. Deſcription of a moſt effectual method of ſecuring buildings againſt fire. (Phil. Transact. 1778. p. 884.) Obſervations on Mr. *Pitt's* plan for the reduction of the national debt 1786. 4. (2 ſh.) Remarks on Mr. *Brydone's* account of a remarkable thunder-ſtorm in Scotland. (Phil. Transact. 1787. p. 130.) Letter to *Edm. Burke.* 1790.

STANHOPE, [Eugenia] *Mrs.* Letters by *Philip Dormer Stanhope*, Earl of *Chesterfield*, to his son – published from the originals –. 1774. 4. Vol. 1. 2. (2 L. 2 sh.)

—— [Philipp Dormer] *Esq. late of the First Regiment of Dragoon Guards.* Genuine memoirs of Asiaticus during five Years residence in different parts of India —. 1784. 12. (3 sh.)

STANLEY, [Edward] *Observations on the city of Tunis and the adjacent country. 1786. 4. (10 sh. 6 d.) übers. im Auszug. Histor. Portefeuille. 1786. Th. 9. S. 233.

—— [J..... Th....] Narrative of a voyage to the Ockney. 1789. 8.

STANTON, [Samuel] *Lieutenant.* The principles of duelling. 1790. 4. (2 sh. 6 d.)

STARK, [James] *Surgeon in Calcutta.* History of a remarkable wound in the trachea and neighbouring parts. (Med. Com. of Ed. Vol. 4. p. 434.)

—— [William] *M. D. at London.* born: .... died. 1770.

STAUB, [J..... R.....] *Notary Public.* Consideration of taxes —. 1782. 8. (1 sh. 6 d.)

STEBBING, [Henry] *D. D: Chaplain to his Majesty; Rector of Gimmingham and Trunch. F. R. S: F. A. S.* born. 1717. died d. 13 Nov. 1787.

STEDMAN, [......] *Laelius and Hortensia; or, thoughts on the nature and objects of taste and genius —. 1782. 8. (5 sh.)

—— [John] *M. D: F. R. S.* Thermometical observations. (Phil. Transact. 1757. p. 4.) The effects of the hyoscyamus albus, or white henbane. (Ibid. p. 194.) Physiological essays and observations. 1769. 8. (2 sh. 6 d.) übers. Leipz. 1777. 8. Of triangles described in circles and about them. (Phil. Transact. 1775. p. 296.) Of the degrees and quantities of winds requisite to move the heavier kinds of wind machines. (Ibid. 1777. p. 493.)

—— [Thomas] *M. A: Vicar of St. Chad's, Shrewsbury.* Letters to and from *Philipp Doddridge* — with notes explanatory and biographical. 1790. 8. (6 sh.)

STEEL, [Anne] *Mrs.* born .... died 17..

—— [David] Junior. Elements of punctuation —. 1786. 8. (3 sh. 6 d.)

STEELE, [Elizabeth] *Mrs.* born: .... died d. 14. Nov. 1787.

—— [Joshua] *F. R. S.* Essay towards establishing the melody and measure of speech to be expressed and perpetuated by peculiar symbols. 1775. 4. (10 sh. 6 d.) Account of a musical instrument, which was brought by Capt. *Fourneaux* from the Isle of Amsterdam in the South Seas to London in the Y. 1774. and given to the Royal Society. (Phil. Tr. 1775. p. 67.) Remarks on a larger system of reed pipes from the Isle of Amsterdam, with some observations on the nose — flute of Otaheite. (Ibid. p. 73.)

STEEVENS, [George Alexander] at *Hampstead.* born in *Holborn:* .... died d. 6 Sept. 1784.

STEFFE, [John] *Vicar of little Baddow, Essex.* Five letters on the intermediate state, on the definitions given of man; on divine worship; on the christian sabbath. 1757. 8. Two letters on the intermediate state —. 1758. 8. (1 sh.) Man naturally inclined to religion —. 1786. 8.

(Several single sermons.)

STENNET, [Samuel] *D D:* (an Anabaptist Clergyman.) Discourses on personal religion. Vol. 1. 2. 1769. 8. (12 sh.) Remarks on the christian minister's reasons for administring baptism by sprinkling or pouring of water. 1772. 8. (1 sh. 6 d.) On the application to parliament of the protestant dissenting ministers. 1772. 8. (6 d.) Discourses no domestic duties. 1783. 8. (8 sh.) Discourses on the parables of the sower. 1787. 8. (3 sh.)

(Several single sermons.)

STEPHEN, [James] *Surgeon in St. Christophers.* Account of the use of the pepper medicine of the West-Indies in the Cynanche maligna. (Duncan's M. C. Dec. 2. Vol. 2. p. 375.)

—— [James] Considerations on imprisonment for debt —. 1770. 8. (1 sh. 6 d.)

STEPHENS, [John] *M. A.* Human nature delineated, or the limits of human knowledge defined. 1760. 8. (4 sh. 6 d.) The principles of the christian religion, compared with those of all the other religions and systems of philosophy. 1777. 8. (4 sh.)

—— [William] *Chief Engineer.* The latitude of Madrass in the East-Indies. (Phil. Transact. 1779. p. 182.)

STERLING, [Joseph] *Clergyman.* History of the Cheval. *Bayard.* 1781. 8. (2 sh.) Poems. 1789. 8. (4 sh.)

STERNHOLD, [Thomas] *Esq.* The daily advertiser, in metre. 1781. 4. (1 sh. 6 d.)

STEVENS, [Thomas] *M. A. Vicar of Bumpsted-Helion, Essex.* *J. F. Osterwald's* lectures on the exercise of the sacred ministry translated. 1781. 8. (5 sh.) (Several single sermons.)

—— [William Bagshaw] Poems consisting of Indian odes and miscellaneous pieces. 1775. 4. (5 sh.) Poems. 1782. 4. (2 sh. 6 d.)

STEVENSON, [.......] *Remarks on *J. Sinclair's* thoughts on the naval strength of the British empire —. 1783. 8. (1 sh.)

—— [James] *Surgeon at Egham in Surry:* Case of a suppression of urine, which terminated fatally, with an account of the appearances on dissection. (London M. J. Vol. IX. Part. IV.)

—— [John] Letter in answer to Dr. *Price's* two pamphlets on civil liberty —. 1778. 8. (1 sh. 6 d.) Addresf to *Brian Edwards*, containing remarks on his pamphlet "thoughts on the late proceedings of government respecting the trade of the West-India islands with the united states of America —. 1784. 8. (1 sh. 6 d.) Abstract of the bill for manning the royal nauy with volunteers —. 1787. 8. (1 sh.) Observations on the coal trade in the port of Newcastle upon-Tyne. 1789. 8. (2 sh.)

—— [William] *M. D.* born: .... died at *Newark upon Trent.* d. 13 Apr. 1783.

—— [William Joseph Hall] *Esq. in Ireland.* born: .... died 1786.

STEWART, [Charles] The cobler of Castlebury, a comic opera. 1779. 8. Ripe fruit, or, the marriage. 1781. Damnation, or hissing hot. 1781.

—— [David] Earl of BUCHAN — and *Walter Minto's* account of the life, writings and inventions of *John Napier*, of Merchiston. 1788. 4. (7 Sh. 6 d.)

—— [David] *Physician in Aberdeen.* The history of a case of the pemphigus major of Mr. *Sauvages.* (Med. Com. of Ed. Vol. 6. p. 79.)

STEWART, [James] a Baronet of Scotland. born .... died 1780.

— [James] The two English gentlemen; or, the sham funeral, a comedy. 1774. 8. (1 ſh. 6 d.) The total-refutation and political overthrow of D. *Price;* or Great-Britain ſucceſsfully vindicated againſt all American rebels and their advocates —. 1776. 8. (1 ſh. 6 d.)

— [John] *Esq. F. R. S.* Account of the kingdom of Thibet. (Phil. Tranſact. 1777. p. 465.)

— [Matthew] *D. D: Profeſſor of Mathematics in the Univerſity of Edinburgh.* born 1717. died d. 23. Jan. 1785.

— [Thomas] Valentia, or the fatal birthday, a tragedy. 1772. 8.

STILLINGFLEET, [Benjamin] born 1701. died 1771.

STINTON, [George] *D. D: Chancellor of Lincoln, Chaplain to the Archbiſhop of Canterbury: F. R. S: F. A. S:* born: .... died d. 30 Apr. 1783.

STIRLING, [William] Earl of

Account of the comet of June and July, 1770. (Tr. of A. S. Vol. 1. App. p. 45.)

STOCKDALE, [.....] The debates and proceedings of the houſe of commons during the V ſeſſion of the XVI Parliament of Great-Britain. Vol. 1-3. 1788. 8.

— [Percival] a *Clergyman.* Churchill defended, a poem. 1765. 4. (2 ſh.) The conſtituents, a poem. 1765. 4. (1 ſh.) Translation of *Taſſo's* Amynta. 1770. 8. (3 ſh. 6 d.) *Edmund Waller's* works, with his life. 1772. 8. (3 ſh. 6 d.) *Lamb. Bos's* Antiquities of Greece, translated. 1772. 8. (6 ſh.) Three discourses: two againſt luxury and diſſipation: one on universal benevolence. 1773. 4. (2 ſh.) *Sabbathier's* inſtitutions, manners and cuſtoms of the ancient nations translated Vol. 1. 2. 1776. 8. (10 ſh. 6 d.) Six discourses: with an introduction containing a view of the genuine ancient philosophy of the natural and effectual tendency of that philosophy and of chriſtian morality to all true prosperity in this world and — observations on a book-view of the internal evidence of the chriſtian-religion. 1777. 8.

 (3 ſh.

(3 sh. 6 d.) Inquiry into the nature and genuine laws of poetry, with a defence of the writings and genius of *Pope*. 1778. 8. (2 Sh. 6 d.) Miscellanies in prose and verse. 1778. 8. (3 sh.) *Poetical excursions in the isle of Wight. 1777. 4. (2 Sh. 6 d.) Letters from Lord *Rivers* to *Charles Cardigan* — translated from the French of Mad. *Riccoboni*. Vol. I. 2. 1778. 8. (6 Sh.) Examination of the question — whether education, at a great school, or by private tuition is remarkable? with remarks on *Knox's* book: liberal education. 1782. 8. (2 Sh.) Essay on misanthropy. 1783. 8. (1 Sh.) Sermons on various subjects. 1784. 8. (6 Sh.) Three poems: 1) Siddons, a poem. 2) a poetical epistle to Sir *Ashton Lever*. 3) an elegy, on the death of a young officer of the army. 1784. 4. (1 Sh. 6 d.) Eight sermons. 1788. 8. (5 Sh.) Ximenes, a tragedy. 1788. 8. (2 sh.)

STOKES, [Anthony] *Barrister at Law: Chief Justice in Georgia*. View of the constitution of the British colonies in North-America and the Westindies at the time the civil war broke out. 1783. 8. (6 Sh.)

STONE, [Edward] *M. A: Rector of Horsenden, Bucks*. *Edw. Stone's* Discourses on some important subjects — published by his Son. 1771. 8. (5 Sh.) Two additional discourses on important subjects. 1777. 8. (1 Sh.)

—— [Francis] *M. A: F. S. A: Chairman of the society of the petitioning clergy. Rector of Cold Norton, Essex*. Method of discharging the national debt —. 1777. 8. (3 Sh.) Political reformation on a large scale: or a plan of an house of commons —. 1789. 8. (2 Sh.)

—— [Thomas] *Land and Tythe Surveyor, Bedford*. Essay on agriculture —. 1785. 8. (6 Sh.) Suggestions for rendering the inclosure of common fields and waste lands a source of population and riches —. 1787. 8. (1 Sh. 6 d.)

STONEHOUSE, [James] *M. D: Rector of Great and Little Cheverel, Wiltshire*. (born at *Bristol*.) *Universal restitution, a scripture doctrine —. 1762. 8. (5 Sh.) *Hints from a minister to his curate for the management of his parish. 1774. 8. (6 d.) Religious instruction of children recommended. 1774. 8.

8. (6 d.) The moſt important truths of chriſtianity ſtated. 1778. 8. (2 d.) The ſick man's friend; or, helps for converſation between the ſick and thoſe who may attend them —. 1788. 8. (3 Sh.) (Several ſingle ſermons.)

STORER, [John] *M. D: Phyſician in Grantham.* Obſervations on the benefit derived from the uſe of the cuprum ammoniacum in a ſpasmodic affection of the abdominal viſcera and in hyſteria. (*Duncan's* M. C. 1780. p. 229. überſ. Samml. f. A. Th. XI. S. 167.)

STORY, [Joshua] Introduction to Engliſh grammar. 1778. 8. (1 Sh. 6 d) Ed. 2. 1781. 12. (1 Sh. 6 d.)

STRACHEY, [Henry] *Secretary to Lord Clive during his laſt expedition to India.* Narrative of the mutiny of the officers of the army in Bengal in the Year. 1766. 1773. 8. (3 ſh. 6 d.)

STRAHAN, [George] *A. M: Vicar of Islington, Middleſex and Rector of little Thurrock, Eſſex.* Prayers and meditations compoſed by *Sam. Johnson* LL. D. and publiſhed from his manuſcripts. 1785. 8. (3 ſh. 6 d.)

STRANGE, [John] *Esq. F. R. S: F. A. S: Engliſh Reſident at Venice.* On the origin of natural paper found near Cortona in Tuſcany. (Phil. Transact. 1769. p. 50.) Account of ſeveral roman ſepulchral inſcriptions and figures in bas relief, diſcovered in 1755. at Bonn in lower Germany. (Ibid. 1769. p. 195.) Account of ſpecimens of ſpongiae from the coaſt of Italy. (Ibid. 1770. p. 179.) Account of two giants cauſeways, or groups of priſmatic baſaltine columns and other curious volcanic concretions in the Venetian ſtate in Italy; with ſome remarks on the characters of theſe and other ſimilar bodies, and on the phyſical geography of the countries in which they are found. (Ibid. 1775. p. 5.) Account of a curious giant's cauſeway or group of angular columns, newly diſcovered in the Euganean Hills, near Padua in Italy. (Ibid. 1775. p. 418.) Account of the tides in the Adriatic. (Ibid. 1777. p. 144.) Account of ſome antient roman inſcriptions, diſcovered in the provinces of Iſtria and Dalmatia, with remarks. (Arch. Vol. 3. p. 337. Vol. 5. p. 169.) Further account of ſome me remains of Roman and other antiquities in or near the county of Brecknock in South-Wales. (Ibid. Vol. 4. p. 1.) Account of some remains of Roman and other antiquities of Monmouthshire. (Ibid. Vol. 5. p. 33.) Remarks on *Will. Harris's* observations on the Roman antiquities in Monmouthshire — with an account of some remains of Antiquity in Glamorganshire. (Ibid. Vol. 6. p. 6.)

STRANGE [Robert] *Sir: Knight: Director of the Royal Society of Artists of Great-Britain: Engraver.* Catalogue of a collection of pictures selected from the Roman, Florentine — schools. 1769. 8. (2 ſh. 6 d.) Rise and eſtabliſhment of the Royal academy of arts with a letter to the Earl of *Bute.* 1775. 8. (2 ſh.)

STRATFORD, [......] *Fontenoy, a poem. *Book* I. with four paſtoral eſſays. 1784. 4. (10 ſh. 6 d.)

—— Earl of *Alborough: an Irish Peer.* *Eſſay on the true intereſts and resources of — Great-Britain and Ireland —. 1783. 8. (6 d.)

STRATHMORE, [......] *Counteſſ of*; The ſiege of Jerusalem, a tragedy. 1774. 8.

STREET, [Tho. Geo.] Aura; or the slave, a poem. 1788. 4. (2 ſh. 6 d.)

STREPHON, [James] Epaphras's letters in the defence of the unity of God. 17.. The spiritual privileges connected with the primitive chriſtian's faith, worship and practice —. 1787. 12. (1 ſh.)

STRICKLAND, [Lucinda] Chriſtmas in a cottage, a poem. 1790. 4. (1 Sh.)

STRUTT, [Joseph] The regal and eccleſiaſtical antiquities of England —. Numb. 1-4. 1773. 4. (2 L. 2 Sh.) Horda Angel-cynnan: or view of the manners, cuſtoms, arms, habits — of the inhabitants of England from the arrival of the Saxons till the reign of Henry VIII. Vol. 1-3. 1774-1776. 4. (4 L. 14 Sh. 6 d.) The chronicle of England from the arrival of Julius Cesar to the end of the Saxon heptarchy. Vol. 1. 2. 1777. (1 L. 10 Sh.) Biographical Dictionary - of all the engravers from the earlieſt period of the art of engraving to the present time —. Vol. 1. 2. 1785. 4. (2 L. 2 Sh.)

STUART, [Andrew] *late Commander in Chief at Fort St. George in the Eaſt-Indies.* (born in *Scotland.*) Four letters to Lord Mansfield. 17..

STU-

STUART, [Charles] The cobler of Castlebury, a musical entertainment 1779. 8. The distressed Baronet; a farce. 1787. 8. (1 Sh.) The stone eater, an interlude. 1788. 8. (6 d.)

—— [Gilbert] *L. L. D: F. A. S. Edinb.* born at *Edinburgh.* 1742. died at *Musselburg,* near *Edinburgh* d. 13 Aug. 1787.

—— [James] *F. R. S: F. A. S:* born at *London.* 1713. died d. 2 Febr. 1788.

—— [James] born 1700. died at *Killin.* d. 30 Jun. 1789.

STUCKEY, [John] *Clergyman in Bristol.* born in *Devonshire.* died 17..

STURCH, [John] *Clergyman.* View of the isle of Wight —. 1778. 8. (1 Sh.) übers. (von *C. A. Wichmann.*) Leipzig 1781. 8.
(Several single sermons.)

STURGES, [John] *D. D: Prebendary of Winchester and Chaplain in Ordinary to his Majesty.* Considerations on the present state of the church establishment in reply to the lectures on non conformity of Mr. *Robert Robinson.* 1779. 8. (3 Sh.)
(Several single sermons.)

SUCKLING, [George] *Esq.* Historical account of the Virgin islands in the West-Indies. 1780. 8. (2 Sh.)

SULIVAN, [Richard Joseph] *Analysis of the political history of India. 1779. 4. (6 Sh.) Ed. 2. (with the Author's name) 1784. 8. (5 Sh.) übers. von *M. C. Sprengel.* Halle. 1787. 8. *Thoughts on martial law and on the proceedings of general courts martial. 1779. 4. (2 Sh. 6 d.) Ed. 2. (with the Author's name) 1785. 8. (2 Sh. 6 d.) *Observations made during a tour through parts of England, Scotland and Wales. 1780. 4. (10 Sh. 6 d.) Ed. 2. (with the Author's name.) Vol. 1. 2. 1785. 8. (10 Sh.) *Philosophical rhapsodies: fragments of Akbur of Betlis; containing reflections on the laws, manners, customs, and religions of certain Asiatic, Afric and European nations. Vol. 1-3. 1785. 8. (15 Sh.)

—— [Stephen] *Esq.* Select fables from Gulistan, or the bed of Roses, translated from the Persian of Sadi. 1774. 12. (2 Sh. 6 d.)

SU-

SUTHERLAND, [.....] *Captain of the 25th. Regiment.* Tour up the ſtraits, from Gibraltar to Conſtantinople. Ed. 2. 1790. 8. (5 Sh. 6 d.) überſ. Lübeck. 1790. 8.

SWAIN, [John Hadley] *Morning Preacher of St. George the Martyr, at London.* Collection of easy sentences from the beſt claſſic writers —. 1786. 8. (2 Sh.) The objections of *Dav. Levi* to the miſsion, conduct and doctrine of the Lord Jesus Chriſt, examined. 1787. 8. (1 Sh. 6 d.)

SWAIN, [Joseph] Redemption, a poem. 1789. 8. (2 Sh. 6 d.)

SWAINE, [John] Memoirs of Osney-Abbey, near Oxford. 1769. 8. (1 Sh.) Every farmer his own cattle Doctor. 1776. 12. (2 Sh.)

SWAINSON, [Isaac] Hints to families on the increaſing prevalence of scrophulas, aſthmas, consumptions and palsies from the present method of treatment in the measles and smallpox. 1787. 8. (6 d.) Account of cures by the vegetable syrup of M. de *Velno's* vegetable syrup in the venereal disease. 1789. 8. (2 Sh.)

SWAINSTON, [Allen] *M. D.* Thoughts physiological and practical; with some cases and anatomico-practical observations. 1790. 8. (7 Sh.)

SWAN, [.....] *Physician at Dumbarton.* Hiſtory of a caſe of retroverted uterus. (Med. Com. of Ed. Vol. 6. p. 217.)

SWAYNE, [G....] *A M. Vicar of Puckle church, Glouceſtershire and of Eaſt Harptry, Somersetshire, Chaplain to the Duke of Gordon.* Gramina pascua, or, a collection of specimens of the common paſture graſſes, arranged in the order of Linnaeus —. 1790. fol. (1 L. 1 Sh.)

SWEDIAUR, [F.....] *M. D. Phyſician in London.* Account of a white swelling, ſucceſsfully treated. (London M. J. Vol. 1. p. 194.) Account of a case in which a cherry ſtone was extracted from an abſceſſ in the abdomen. (Ibid. Vol. 2. p. 337.) A case of tuſſis convulſiva attended with emphysema, that terminated fatally. (Ibid. Vol. 2. p. 408.) A case of calculus, attended with a fungus of the bladder. (Ibid. Vol. 3. p. 194.)

SWIFT,

SWIFT, [Charles] Salivation exploded; or a practical essay on the venereal disease, fully demonstrating the inefficacy of salivation, and recommending an approved succedaneum. 1780. 8.

—— [Deane] *Esq. at Worcester.* born.... died d. 12. July. 1783.

—— [Theophilus] *Esq.* Poetical addreſſ to his Majesty. 1788. 4. (1 Sh.) Letter to the King, in which the conduct of Mr. *Lenox* and the minister in the affair with his Roy. Highneſſ the Duke of York is fully considered. Ed. 2. 1789. 8. (1 Sh. 6 d.) Letter to Sir *Will. Aug. Brown*, Bart. on a late affair of honour with Colonel *Lenox* —. 1789. 8. (1 Sh. 6 d.)

—— [William] Account of some electrical experiments. (Phil. Transact. 1778. p. 155.) Account of some experiments in electricity. (Ibid. 1779. p. 454.)

SWINBURNE, [Henry] *Esq.* Travels through Spain in the Years 1775 and 1776. 1779. 4. (1 L. 1 Sh.) Ed. 2. Vol. 1. 2. 1787. 8. Travels in the two Sicilies in the Year 1777-1780. Vol. 1. 2. 1785. 4. (2 L. 2 Sh.) übers. von *J. R. Forster.* Th. 1. 2. Hamburg. 1785. 8.

SWINDEN, [Henry] History and antiquities of the ancient burgh of Great Yarmouth, in Norfolk. 1774. 4. (1 L. 1 Sh.)

—— [N....] *Gardener and Seedsman at Brentford-End.* The beauties of flora displayed or companion to the flower and kitchen garden. 1778. 12. (2 Sh.)

SWINTON, [John] *D. D. F. R. S. Keeper of the University Archives at Oxford.* born 1698. died d. 4. Apr. 1777.

—— [John] *Esq. Advocate.* Abridgment of the public statutes in force and use relative to Scotland, from the union in the 5 Year of Queen Anne to the 27th Geo. III. inclusive. Vol. 1. 2. 1790. 4. (1 L. 12 Sh.)

SYDENHAM, [.....] *Colonel at St. Thomas Mount, near Madraſſ.* Letter on roman coins discovered in Nellour County. (Arch. Vol. 9. p. 81.)

SYMES, [Richard] *Rector of St. Werburgh, Bristol.* Fire analysed —. 1771. 8. (1 sh. 6 d.)

SYMMONS, [Charles] *B. D. of Clare-Hall, Cambridge and Rector of Narbarth in the county of Pembroke*

broke. Sermons 1787. 8. (5 sh.) Ed. 2. 1789. 8. (6 sh.) (Several single sermons.)

SYMONDS, [John] *LL. D: Professor of Modern History in the University of Cambridge.* *Remarks on the history of colonization of the free states of antiquity —. 1777. 4. (2 sh. 6 d.) Observations upon the expediency of revising the present English version of the IV Gospels and of the acts of Apostles. 4. 1789. (10 Sh. 6 d.)

SYMONS, [J....] *B. D.* *Inquiry into the design of the christian Sabbath. 1779. 8. (1 Sh.) Ed. 2. (with the Author's name.) 1785. 8. (1 Sh. 6 d.)

—— [Jelinger] Index to the excise laws; or an abridgment of all the statutes now in force relating to the excise. 1770. 8. (1 Sh.) Ed. 2. 1775. 8. (4 Sh. 6 d.)

TALBOT, [....] Narrative of the whole of his proceedings relative to *Jonathan Britain.* 1772. 8. (6 d.)

—— [B.....] *Teacher of the Mathematics at Cannock.* The new art of land measuring —. 1780. 8. (6 Sh.)

—— [Catherine] *Miss.* born 1722. died d. 9 Jan. 1770.

—— [Robert] (*Fictitious name.*) Letters on the French nation, considered in different departments, translated from the French Vol. 1. 2. 1771. 12. (6 Sh.)

—— [Thomas] *D. D: Rector of Ullingswick.* born .... died d. 18 Febr. 1788.

TANNER, [Thomas] *DD: Rector of Hadleigh and Monks - Eleigh, Suffolk.* born ...., died d. 11 March. 1786.

TAPLIN, [William] Observations on the present state of the game in England. 1772. 8. (1 Sh.) On matrimony. 1774. 8. (1 Sh.)

—— [William] *Surgeon.* The gentleman's stable directory, or modern system of farriery. Vol. 1. 2. 1790. 8. (10 Sh.) Practical observations upon thorn wounds punctured tendons and ligamentary lameness in horses with instructions for their treatment and cure —. 1790. 8. (1 Sh.)

TAPNER, [John] A new collection of fables in verse. 1787. 8. (2 Sh. 6 d.)

TAPRELL, [Richard] A plain discourse for children. 1789. 12. (4 d.) Meditations for women in pregnant

nant circumstances —. 1789. 8. (1 Sh.) Serious advice to young people —. 1789 8. (1 Sh.) Glory to god and peace to men, the blessed effects of divine grace in the redemption of sinners by Jesus Christ. 1790. 4. (1 Sh.)

TARLETON, [....] *Lieutenant Colonel.* History of the campaigns of 1780 and 1781. in the Southern provinces of North-America. 1787. 4. (1 L. 6 Sh.)

TASKER, [William] *A. B. a Clergyman.* *Ode to the warlike genius of Great-Britain. 1778. 4. (2 Sh.) Ed. 2. with additions. 1778. 4. (2 sh.) Poems 1779. 4. (2 Sh. 6 d.) The carmen seculare of *Horace*, translated into English verse. 1779. 4. (1 sh.) *Congratulatory ode to Admir. Keppel. 1779. 4. (1 sh.) *Elegy on the death of *Dav. Garrick.* 1779. 4. (1 sh.) Ode to speculation 1780 4. (6 d.) Ode to the memory of *Thom. Wilson,* late Lord Bishop of Sodor and Man. 1780. 4. (1 sh.) Select odes of *Pindar* and *Horace* translated, and other original poems with notes critical, historical —. Vol. 1. 1780. 8. Annus mirabilis, or the eventful Year 1782, an historical poem. 1783. 4. (2 sh. 6 d.)

TATHAM, [Edward] *A. M: B. D: Fellow of Lincoln College,* Essay on journal poetry —. 1778. 8. (1 sh.) XII Discourses introductory to the study of divinity —. 1780. 8. (5 sh.) (Several single sermons.)

TAYLOR, [.....] Concise statement of transactions and circumstances respecting the king's theatre in the Haymarket —. 1791. 8. (1 sh.)

—— [.....] *Miss.* of *Twickenham.* see Miss. *Nugent.*

—— [Benjamin] On the atmosphere of London. 1789. 4. (2 sh.)

—— [Daniel] Dissertation on singing in the worship of god —. 1787. 12. (6 d.) Observations on *Andr. Fuller's* reply to Philantrophos, or an attempt to prove, that the universal invitations of the gospel are founded on the universality of divine love and the death of Jesus Christ —. 1788. 12. (1 sh.) On the truth and inspiration of the holy scripture. 1790. 8. (2 sh. 6 d.) The friendly conclusion: occasioned by the letters of Agnostos - respecting the extent of our saviour's death and other subjects connected with that doctrine. 1790. 8. (3 d.)

TAYLOR, [Edward] Memoirs of *Guy Joli* — translated. Vol. 1 - 3. 1775. 8. (9 ſh.)

—— [Henry] *M. A: Rector of Crawley and Vicar of Portsmouth, Hants.* born .... died d. May. 1785.

—— [Henry] *LL. B: Rector of Spridlington in Lincolnshire.* Published: *Henry Taylor's* conſiderations on ancient and modern creeds — with a treatiſe on the exiſtence, immateriality and immortality of the soul by ** 1788. 8. (5 ſh.)

—— [John] of *Norwich.* *Attempt to explain certain paſſages of scripture generally misunderſtand. 1783. 8.

—— [John] *LL. D. Prebendary of Weſtminſter; Rector of Bosworth, Leiceſtershire and Miniſter of St. Margaret's Weſtminſter.* born .... died at *Ashburn, Derbyshire.* d. 29 Febr. 1788. (see *Sam. Hayes.*)

—— [Michael] A sexageſimal table; exhibiting, at ſight, the result of any proportion, where the terms do not exceed 60 minutes. —. 1780. 4. (15 ſh.)

—— [Samuel] *Many Years Profeſſor and Teacher of Stenography at Oxford and the Univerſities of Scotland and Ireland.* Eſſay intended to eſtablish a ſtandard for an universal syſtem of stenography or short hand writing —. 1786. 8. (1 L. 1 Sh.)

—— [Thomas] The elements of a new method of reasoning in geometry. 1780. 4. (2 Sh. 6 d.) Concordance to the holy scripture of the old and new teſtament. 1786. 4. (4 Sh. 6 d.)

—— [Thomas] The myſtical hymns of *Orpheus* translated from the greek with a diſſertation on the life and theology of *Orpheus.* 1787. 8. (5 Sh.) Concerning the Beautiful: or, a paraphrased translation from the Greek of *Plotinus.* Ennead I. Book VI. 1787. 8. (1 Sh. 6 d.) The philosophical and mathematical commentaries of *Proclus* surnamed *Plato's* succeſſor on the 1 book of *Euclid's* elements and his life by *Marinus*, translated with a diſſertation on the *Platonis* doctrine of ideas. Vol. 1. 2. 1788. 4to (1 L. 13 Sh.)

—— [William] *Teacher of the Mathematics and Land Surveyor, Birmingham.* Complete syſtem of practical arithmetic; 1784. 8. (6 Sh.) The arithmetician's guide, or a complete exercise book for the use

use of public schools and private teachers. 1788. 8. (2 Sh. 6 d.)

TEASDALE, [S....] *Minister of the English Chapel, Dundee.* Picturesque poetry: consisting of poems, odes and elegies on various subjects. 1784. 8. (3 Sh.)

TEEDE, [Richard] Corin and Olinda, a legendary tale. 1774. 4. (1 Sh. 6 d.)

TEMPLE, [Anthony] *M. A: Master of the Free-School at Richmond and Vicar of Eastby, Yorkshire.* The written word, the only rule of christian faith and manners — in three discourses. 1772. 8. (1 Sh. 6 d.) Letters to — *Thom. Randolph* — containing a defence of remarks on the layman's scriptural confutation. 1779. 8. (3 Sh. 6 d.) Two discourses on the Lord's supper. 1782. 8. (1 Sh. 6 d.)

—— [George Greenville] *Earl, M. P.* born .... died d. 13. Nov. 1770.

—— [Lancelot] Short ramble through some parts of France and Italy. 1771. 8. (1 Sh. 6 d.) Sketches: or, essays on various subjects. 1758. 8. (1 Sh. 6 d.)

—— [W.... J....] *LL. B: Rector of Mamhead in Devonshire.* Essay on the clergy; their studies, recreations, decline of influence —. 1774. 8. (1 Sh. 6 d.)

TENCH, [Watkin] *Captain: of the Marines.* Narrative of the expedition to Botanybay; with an account of New-South-Wales — and with a list of the civil and military establishment at Port Jackson. 1789. 8. (3 Sh. 6 d.) übers. von *L. T. Spittler.* Göttingisches Histor. Mag. Th. 5. S. 245. übers. Franckf. u. Leipzig. 1789. 8.

THELWALL, [John] Orlando and Almeyda, a legendary tale in the manner of Dr. *Goldsmith.* 1787. 4. (2 Sh.) Poems on various subjects. 1787. 12. Vol. 1. 2. (6 Sh.)

THICKNESS, [Anne] Sketches of the lives and writings of the Ladies of France. Vol. 1 - 3. 1778. (10 Sh. 6 d.)

—— [Philipp] *F. R. S. late Lieutenant Governor of Land Guard Fort.* (Father to *George Thickness Tuchet* Lord *Audley.*) Letter to a young Lady. 1764. 8. (6 d.) Man — midwifery analysed, and the tendency of that practice detected and exposed. 1765. 4. (1 Sh.) Proceedings of a court — martial, on the trial of *Phil. Thicknesse* held 1765. 4. (1 Sh.) Narrative of what passed between General *Harry Erskine* and *Phil. Thicknesse* in consequence of a letter written by the latter, to the Earl of *Bute*, relative to the publication of some original letters and poetry of Lady *Mary Wortley Montague's*. 1766. 8. (1 Sh.) Observations on the customs and manners of the French nation in a series of letters. 1766. 8. (2 Sh.) Hints to those who make the tour of France in a series of letters. 1768. 8. (4 Sh.) *Acount of four persons starved to death at *Datchworth*. 1769. 4. (1 Sh.) On the art of decyphering and of writing in cypher with an harmonic alphabet. 1772. 8. (5 Sh.) A year's journey through France and part of Spain. Vol. 1. 2. 1777. 8. (1 L. 1 Sh.) Ed. 2. with additions Vol. 1. 2. 1778. 8. (10 Sh. 6 d.) übers. Leipz. 1778. 8. *The new prose Bath-guide. 1778. 8. (2 Sh. 6 d.) The valetudinarian's Bath-guide; or the means of obtaining long life and health. 1780. 8. (3 Sh. 6 d.) Epistle to Dr. *Will Falconer* of Bath. 1782. 8. (1 Sh.) Queries to Lord *Audley*. 1782. 8. (1 Sh.) Pere Pascal, a Monk of Montferrat, vindicated —. 1783. 8. (1 Sh. 6 d.) Translation of Abbe *Mann's* extraordinary case and cure of the gout by the use of Hemlock and Wolfsbane 1784. 8. (2 Sh.) Further account —. 1785. 8. (1 Sh. 6 d.) Year's journey through the Paix-Bas and Austrian Netherlands. Vol. 1. 1786. 8. (10 Sh. 6 d.) Letter to *Jam. Makitt. Adair*. 1787. 8. Sketch of life and paintings of *Thom. Gainsborough*. 1788. 8. (1 Sh. 6 d.) Memoirs and anecdotes. Vol. 1. 2. 1788. 8. (10 Sh. 6 d) *Junius discovered by *P. T.* 1789. 8. (2 Sh.)

THISTLETHWAITE, [James] The consultation, a Mock-Heroic. 1775. 8. (1 Sh. 6 d.) The prediction of liberty. 1776. 4. (2 Sh.) Edwald and Ellen, an heroic ballad. 1776. 4. (1 Sh. 6 d.) The chield of misfortune, or the history of Mrs. *Gilbert*. Vol. 1. 2. 1777. 12. (6 Sh.) The man of experience —. 1788. 12. Vol. 1. 2. (6 Sh.)

THOMAS, [Ann] *of Milbrook, Cornwall; an Officer's Widow of the Royal Navy.* Poems on various subjects. 1784. 4. (3 Sh.)

THOMAS, [John] *Curate of Shepton Beauchamp.* Two letters to *Thom. Coke*, LL. D. — on the errors of his clerical conduct. 1777. 12. (6 ſh.)

— [Josiah] *A. B.* Poetic epiſtle to a curate. 1786. 4. (2 ſh. 6 d.)

— [Rowley] Accommodation, a poetical epiſtle to *John Ashby*. 1775. 4. (1 ſh. 6 d.) The frolics of fancy, an epiſtle to a friend. 1776. 4. (1 ſh.)

— [S....] *Merchant.* The britiſh negociator —. 1759. (3 ſh) The commercial palladium; or tradesman's jewel —. 1776. (2 ſh. 6 d.)

— [Thomas] *Surgeon at Tunbridge Wells.* The hiſtory of a case affording a proof of the power of extravasated blood in diſſolving bone. (Med. Com. of Ed. Vol. 6. p. 75.)

— [William] On the gonorrhoea with obſervations on the use of opium in that disease. 1780. 8. (1 ſh. 6 d.)

THOMPSON, [Benjamin] *Colonel; Knight. F. R. S.* New experiments upon gun-powder, with occaſional observations and practical inferences; with an account of a new method of determining the velocities of all kinds of military projectiles and the description of a very accurate eprouvette for gun-powder. (Phil. Transact. 1781. p. 230.) New experiments upon heat. (Ibid. 1786. p. 273.) Experiment on the production of dephlogiſticated air from water with various subſtances. (Ibid. 1787. p. 84.) überſ. Samml. z. P. u. N. G. Th. 4. S. 233. Experiments made to determine the poſitive and relative quantities of moiſture absorbed from the atmosphere by various subſtances under ſimilar circumſtances. (Ibid. 1787. p. 240. London M. J. Vol. IX. P. 2.) On gun-powder; a treatise on fire-arms, and a treatise on the service of artillery in time of war; translated from the Italian of *Aleſſ: Vittorio Papacino d' Antoni* —. 1790. 8. (12 ſh.)

— [Edward] *Commander of the Grampus and Commander in chief of his Majeſty's Squadron in the coaſt of Africa.* born .... died upon the coaſt of *Africa* d. 17 Jan. 1786.

— [Eliza] *Miſſ.* Poems on various subjects. 1787. 4. (2 ſh. 6 d.)

THOMPSON, [Gilbert] *M. D.* Diss. De exercitatione. Edinb. 1753. 8. Memoirs of the life — of *John Fothergill.* 1782. 8. (1 sh. 6 d.)

—, [S....] *Surgeon.* On the intermitting fevers —. 1787. 8. (1 sh.)

— [Thomas] *M. A. Vicar of Reculver in Kent.* (*late Missionary.*) *Letter to a young student lately admitted of the University. 1750. 8. (6 d.) Account of two missionary voyages - for the propagation of the gospel. 1759. 8. (1 sh. 6 d.) Discourse relating to the present time. 1757. 8. (6 d.) The African trade for negro-slaves shewn to be consistent with principles of humanity —. 1772. 8. (6 d.)

— [Thomas] *M. D: Physician to his late R. H. Frederic Prince of Wales.* Origin, nature and cure of the small pox. 1752. 8. (3 sh.) übers. Samml. f. A. Th. 3. S. 1. Medical consultations on various diseases. 1773. 8. (5 sh.) übers. von *H. M. Marcard.* Leipz. 1779. 8.

THOMSON, [Alexander] *M. D.* Nature, cause and method of cure of nervous disorders. Ed. 2. 1782. 8. (1 sh.)

— [Henry] *Surgeon to the London Hospital.* Observations on a dislocated shoulder —. (Med. Obs. Vol. 2. p. 340.) Account of an aneurysm. (Ibid. Vol. 3. p. 57.) Account of the caesarean operation, with remarks. (Ibid. Vol. 4. p. 272.) A case of the softness of the bones. (Ibid. Vol. 5. p. 259.)

— [Henry Frederik] The intrigues of a Nabob —. 1780. 8. (4 sh.)

— [James] *The man in the moon or travels into the lunar regions by the man of the people —. Vol. 1. 2. 1783. 12. (5 sh.) Sir Ralph of Stannerton Green, a poem. 1785. 4. (2 sh.) The denial, or the happy retreat. Vol. 1-3. 1790. 8. (9 sh.)

— [John] *Accomptant in Edinburgh.* The universal calculator, or the merchant's, tradesman's and family's assistant —. 1784. 8. (4 sh.)

— [William] *L. L. D.* The history of the reign of Philipp III. King of Spain; the first four books by *Robert Watson* - the two last by *Will. Thomson.* Ed.

Ed. 2. Vol. 1. 2. 1786. 8. (12 ſh.) Translation of *Alex. Cunningham's* hiſtory of Great-Britain from the revolution to the acceſſion of George I. published by *Thom. Hollingbery*. Vol. 1. 2. 1787. 4. (1 L. 16 ſh.) überſ. Breslau. Th. 1. 2. 1789. 8. Appeal to the people of England and Scotland in behalf of Mr. *Haſtings*. 17.. *Memoirs of the late war in Aſia —. Vol. 1. 2. 1788. 8. (12 ſh.)

THORP, [Robert] *A. M.* *Isaac Newton's* mathematical principles of natural philosophy translated. Vol. 1. 1777. 4. (1 L. 1 ſh.)

—— [John] *M. A: F. A. S.* Letter to Dr. *Ducarel* concerning chesnut trees. (Phil. Transact. 1771. p. 152.) *John de Weſterham* cuſtumale Roffense. 1788. fol. (2 L. 12 ſh. 6 d.)

THRELFAL, [W....] *M. D.* On epilepsy. 1772. 8. (1 ſh.)

THROSBY, [John] Memoirs of the town and county of *Leiceſter* —. 1780. 8. Vol. 1-6. (12 ſh.) Select views in Leiceſtershire — with descriptive and hiſtorical relations. Numb. 1. 1789.

TICKEL, [Richard] *One of the Commiſſioners for the receipt of the Stamp duties.* *Anticipation: containing the ſubſtance of his Majeſty's moſt gracious ſpeech to both houses of parliament on the opening of the approaching ſeſſions; — 1778. 8. (1 ſh. 6 d.) *The project, a poem. 1778. 4. (1 ſh.) *The wreath of fashion, or the art of ſentimental poetry. Ed. II. 1778. 4. (1 ſh.) *An English green box: 1779. 8. (2 ſh.) *Common-place arguments againſt adminiſtration —. 1780. 8. (1 ſh. 6 d.) **Allan Ramsay's* gentle shepherd alterated. 1781. 8. (6 d.) *Songs, Duos, Trios, Choruſſes in the comic opera of the carnival of Venice. 1781. 8. (6 d.)

TICKELL, [William] *Apothecary at Bath.* Account of a new chemical medicine, entitled ſpiritus aethereus anodynus —. 1787. 8. (2 ſh.) Ed. 2. 1788. (5 Sh.) Hiſtory of vitriolic aether, with an account of its peculiar efficacy in gouty affections of the ſtomach. (London M. J. Vol. VI. p. 337. überſ. Samml. f. A. Th. 12. S. 147.)

TIERNEY, [Georg] The real situation of the East-India company considered, with respect to their rights and privileges. 1787. 8. (2 Sh.)

TILLARD, [Richard] *A. M. Vicar of South Leverton, Nottinghamshire.* Letter on *Philipps's* history of the life of *Reginald Pole.* 1765. 8. (1 Sh.) Thoughts concerning the safety and expediency of granting relief, in the matter of subscription —. 1770. 8. (6 d.)

TIMBURY, [Jane] The history of Tobit, a poem; with other poems on various subjects. 1787. 12. (2 Sh. 6 d.) The story of *Le Fevre* from the works of Mr. *Sterne* put into verse. 1787. 8. (1 Sh.) *The power of music, a poem. 1787. 8. (1 Sh.) The male coquet, a novel. Vol. 1. 2. 1788. 12. (5 Sh.) The triumph of friendship, or the history of *Charles Courtney* and Miss *Julia Melville.* Vol. 1. 2. 1789. 8. (5 Sh.)

TINDAL, [Nicholas] *A. M. Chaplain by the Greenwich's Hospital.* born: .... died at Greenwich d. 27 June 1774.

TINWELL, [William] *Teacher of the Mathematic: Newcastle.* On practical arithmetic and book-keeping by single entry. 1785.

TOBIN, [James] *Esq.* *Cursory remarks upon *Ramsay's* essay on the treatment and conversion of African slaves in the sugar colonies —. 1785. 8. (2 Sh. 6 d.) Short rejoinder to *Ramsay's* reply —. 1787. 8. (1 Sh. 6 d.) Farewell address to *James Ramsay* —. 1788. 8. (1 Sh.)

TODD, [Elizabeth] *Miss.* The history of Lady *Caroline Rivers.* Vol. 1. 2. 1788. 12. (5 Sh.)

TOLL, [Michard Newmann] *M. D. Surgeon to the 4th Regiment of Dragoons.* Account of the operation of amputating the thigh at the upper articulation lately performed by Mr. *Will. Kerr,* Surgeon. (Med Com. of Ed. Vol. 6. p. 387.)

TOMKINS, [Thomas] Poems on various subjects. 1780. 8. (2 Sh.)

TOMLINS, [T.... E....] *Barrister at Law of the Inner Temple.* *Explanation of the law of wills and codicils and of the law of executors and administrators —. 1785. 8. (2 Sh. 6 d.) Repertorium juridicum: A general index to the cases and pleadings in law and equity contained in all the reports, yearbooks-hitherto published. 1786. fol. (2 L. 15 Sh. 6 d.)

TOMLINSON, [Thomas] *Surgeon to the General Hospital at Birmingham.* born: .... died 1789.

—— [....] *Lieutenant.* Letters addressed to the Admiralty, on the naval and commercial interests of this kingdom. 1782. 8. (1 Sh.)

TOOKE, [John Horne] *A. M. Elector of Westminster.* (den Nahmen *Tooke* nahm er erst 1782 an, nachdem er von *Andrew Tooke* ein ansehnliches Vermögen erbte.) Letter to Mr. *John Dunning.* 1778. (1 Sh. 6 d.) Letter to Lord *Ashburton* —. 1782. 8. (1 Sh.) Επεα πτεροεντα or the diversions of Purley 1786. 8. (7 Sh.) Letter - on the reported marriage of his Royal Highness the Prince of Wales. 1787. 8. (2 Sh.) Letter in defence of Mrs. *Fitzherbert* 17.. Two pairs of portraits, presented to all the unblessed electors of Great-Britain. 1788. 8. (1 Sh.) *Published: *Bellendenus* de statu, libri tres Ed. 2. 1787. 8. (12 Sh.)

—— [William] *Chaplain to the Factory at Petersburgh. F. R. S.* Translation of *Falconet's* and *Diderot's* pieces on sculpture in general and particularly on the statue of Peter the Great —. 1777. 4. (4 Sh.) Account of the burial-places of the antient Tartars. (Arch. Vol. 7. p. 222.) *Russia; or a complete historical account of all the nations which compose that empire. Vol. 1-4. 1780. 8. (1 L.)

TOOSEY, [G.... P....] Sebastian. 1772. 8.

TOPHAM, [Edmund] *Cornet of his Majesty's Second Troop of Horse Guards.* Address to *Edm. Burke* on his letter relative to the affairs of America. 1777. 4. (1 Sh.)

—— [Edward] *late Captain in the Second Troop of Horse-Guards, Magistrate for the Counties of Essex and York.* Letters from Edinburgh; written in the Years 1774. 1775. containing some observations on the diversions, customs, manners and laws of the Scotch nation —. 1776. 8. (6 Sh.) übers. Leipz. 1777. 8. The fool; a farce. 1786. 8. (1 Sh.) The life of the late *John Elwes* Esq. Member of Parliament for Berkshire. 1790. 8. (3 Sh.)

—— [John] *F. A. S. F. R. S.* Observations on the word Esnecca. (Arch. Vol. 6. p. 116.) On an an-

antient picture in Windsor Castle, representing the embarkation of King Henry VIII. at Dover 1520 —. (Ibid. p. 179.) Subsidy roll of 51. Edward III. (Ibid. Vol. 7. p. 337.) Account of the ancient painting representing the procession of King Edward VI. from the tower of London to Westminster 1547. (Ibid. Vol. 8. p. 406.)

—— [Thomas] A new system on several diseases incident to cattle —. 1788. 8. (6 Sh.)

TOPLADY, [Augustus Montagu] *B. A: late Vicar of Broad Hembury, Devon.* born: .... died d. 26. July. 1778.

TORLESE, [John] *Esq. Chief of Anjingo.* Account of a monstrous birth. (Phil. Transact. 1782. p. 44.)

TOTTIE, [John] *D.D: late Canon of Christ church and ArchDeacon of Worcester.* born: .... died d. 21. Nov. 1774.

TOUCHSTONE, [Timothy] *of St. Peter's College, Westminster.* The trifler, a new periodical miscellany. 1789. 8. (7 sh. 6 d.)

TOULMIN, [George Haggart] *M. D.* Antiquity and duration of the world. 1780. 8. (3 sh.) The eternity of the world. 1785. 8. (3 sh.) The instruments of medicine; or, the philosophical digest and practice of physic. 1789. 8. (5 sh.) The eternity of the universe. 1789. 8. (5 sh.)

—— [H....] View of the life, sentiments and character of Mr. *John Mort*; 1789. 8. (1 sh.)

—— [Joshua] *A. M. Anabaptist Clergyman of the Socinian persuasion.* Sermons addressed to youth with a translation of *Isocrates's* oration Demonius. 1770. 8. (3 sh.) Ed. 2. 1789. 8. (3 sh. 6 d.) Two letters on the address of the dissenting ministers and of a declaration instead of subscription. 1774. 8. (2 sh.) Memoirs of the life, character, sentiments and writings of *Faustus Socinus.* 1777. 8. (6 sh.) Letters to — *John Sturges* in answer to his considerations on the present state of the church establishment. 1782. 8. (1 sh.) Dissertations on the internal evidences and excellence of christianity and on the character of Christ compared with that of some other celebrated founders of religion and philosophy. 1785. 8. (4 sh.) Essay on baptism —. 1786. 8. (1 sh.) *Will. Foot's* account of the ordinadinance of baptism — Ed. 3. 1787. 8. (1 ſh. 6 d.) Review of the life, character and writings of *John Biddle* M. A. who was banished in the isle of Scilly in the protectorate of *Oliver Cromwell.* 1789. 8. (2 ſh.) (Several ſingle ſermons)

TOUP, [Jonathan] *Prebendary of Exeter in Devonshire.* (In ſeinen lezten Shriften nennt er ſich ſelbſt *John.*) born at St. *Ives in Cornwall.* 1713. died d. 19 Jan. 1785.

TOWERS, [John] *Clergyman at Bartholomew Close, West-Smithfield.* Polygamy unscriptural —. 1780. 8. (1 ſh.) (Several ſingle ſermons.)

— [Joseph] *L. L. D. a Diſſenting Clergyman.* Review of the genuine doctrines of chriſtianity —. 1763. 8. (1 ſh. 6 d.) Examination into the nature and evidence of the charges brought againſt *Will. Ruſſel* and *Algernon Sidney* by *John Dalrymple* in his memoirs of Great-Britain. 1773. 8. (1 ſh.) *British Biography —. Vol. I-IX. 17.. Observations on *Hume's* hiſtory of England. 1778. 8. (2 ſh. 6 d.) Vindication of the political principles of Mr. *Loke* in answer to the objections of Dr. *Tucker.* 1782. 8. (2 Sh.) *Letter to the Earl of *Shelburne.* 1782. 8. (1 ſh.) Observations on the rights and duty of juries in trials for libels. 1784. 8. (2 ſh. 6 d.) On the life, character and writings of *Sam. Johnson.* 1786. 8. (2 ſh. 6 d.) Baron de *Herzberg* two discourses — translated. 1786. 8. (2 Sh. 6 d.) Oration on the revolution 1688. 1788. 8. (1 ſh.) Memoirs of the life and reign of *Frederick* III. King of Pruſſia. Vol. 1. 2. 1788. 8. (12 Sh.) Thoughts on the commencement of a new parliament: with an appendix, containing remarks on - *Edm. Burke's* revolution in France. 1790. 8. (2 ſh. 6 d.)

TOWESBY, [.....] New observations on reform in the representative. 1784. 12. (6 d.)

TOWNLEY, [Richard] *Esq.* of *Belfield*, near *Rochdale.* On the culture of potatoes. (*Hunter's* G. E. Vol. 4. p. 23.) Comparative view of Bar. van *Haake's* compoſt, the oil-compoſt and soot mixed with ashes. (Ibid. Vol. 5. p. 163.) On the oil-compoſt. (Ibid. Vol. 5. p. 229.) On Egyptian wheat. (Ibid. Vol. 5. p. 232.)

TOWN-

TOWNSEND, [George] of *Ramsgate.* Teſtimony for truth, in a vindication of the divinity of Chriſt and a trinity in unity denied in Mr. *Frend's* addreſſ to the citizens of Canterbury. 1788. 8. (6 d.) The replication, or a familiar addreſſ to Mr. *Will. Frend* of Jesus College —. 1789. 8. (1 ſh.) The brief rejoinder —. 1789. 8. (6 d.) Word of caution againſt the socinian poison of *Will. Frend* —. 1789. 8. (2 d.)

—— [Joseph] *Rector of Pewsey in Wiltshire.* Observations on various plans offered to the public for the relief of the poor. 1788. 8. (1 Sh. 6 d.) Journey through Spain in the Y. 1786. and 1787. Vol. 1-3. 1790.

TOWNSON, [Thomas] *B. D: Rector of Malpas, Cheshire.* Discourses on the IV gospels —. 1778. 4. (7 Sh. 6 d.) überſ. von *J. S. Semler.* Th. 1. 2. Leipz. 1783. 8. (Several ſingle ſermons.)

TRAPAUD, [.....] The oeconomy of happineſſ 17.. Aglaura, a tale. 1774. 4. (1 Sh.)

—— [Elisha] *Esq. Captain in the Engineer Corps on the Madras Eſtablishment.* Account of the Prince of Wales's Island, or Pulo Peenang in the Eaſt Indies —. 1788. 8. (2 Sh. 6 d.) überſ. *Ebeling's* Neue Samml. von Reiſebeſchr. Th. 10. S. 309. *Letter-given an account of the island of Joanna in the Year 1784. 1789. 8. (1 Sh.)

TRAVIS, [George] *A. M. Prebendary of the Cathedral Church of Cheſter, Vicar of Eaſtham in the county of Cheſter and Chaplain to Lady Dowager Townshend.* Letters to *Edw. Gibbon* in defence of the authenticity of the 7th verse of 5th Chapt. of the firſt epiſtle of St. John. 1784. 4. (5 Sh.)

—— [John] *Surgeon at Scarborough.* The use of copper veſſels in the nauy is one principal cause of the sea scuruy. (Med. Obs. Vol. 2. p. 1.) On a luxation of the thigh bone. (Ibid. p. 99.)

TREBECK, [James] *M. A. Rector of Queenhithe and Holy Trinity, Vicar of Chiswick and Chaplain in Ordinary to his Majeſty.* On the church catechism —. 1787. 12. (1 Sh.)

TRELAWNEY, [Harry] *A. B: Miniſter of the Presbyterian Church at Weſt Looe, Cornwall.* Letter to *Thom. Alcock.* 1780. 8. (6 d.) (Several ſingle ſermons.)

TRIM-

TRIMMER, [Sarah] *Mrs.* of *Brentford.* Easy introduction to the knowledge of nature and reading the holy scripture. Ed. 6. 1789. 8. (3 Sh.) überſ. von H*** Zittau u. Leipzig. 1790. 8. Sacred hiſtory. Vol. 1-6.. 1782-1785. 8. (18 Sh.) Ed. 2. Vol. 1-6. 1788. 8. (1 L. 1 Sh.) The little spelling — book for young children. 1782. 4. (6 d.) Ed. 2. 1786. 4. (6 d.) Easy leſſons for young children. 1786. 4. (6 d.) The servant's friend, a tale. 1786. 8. (9 d.) The two farmers, a tale. 1786. 8. Fabulous hiſtories — for the inſtruction of children —. 1786. 8. (2 Sh. 6 d.) Account of the eſtabliſhment of sunday schools in old *Bremford* extracted from the oeconomy of charity —. 1787. 8. (6 d.) The oeconomy of charity, or, an addreſſ to ladies concerning sunday-schools. 1787. 8. (2 Sh. 6 d.) *Sunday school dialogues —. 1787. 8. (3 d.) The sunday scholar's manual. Part. I. 1788. 8. (1 Sh.) The sunday school catechiſt, conſiſting of familiar lectures. 1788. 8. (2 Sh.) Commentary on Dr. *Watt's* divine songs for children —. 1789. 8. (6 d.) Description of a set of prints of Roman hiſtory contained in a set of easy leſſons. 1789. 4. (1 Sh. 8 d.)

TRINDER, [William Martin] *LL. B. and M. D.* Eſſay on the English grammar. 1781. 8. (1 Sh. 6 d.) Experiments on the Eſſex mineral waters. 1783. 8. (1 Sh.) Practical sermons. 1787. 8. (5 Sh.)

TROTTER, [John] at *Darlington* in the County of *Durham. M. D.* born .... died d. 15 Febr. 1781.

—— [Thomas] *M. D: Surgeon in his Majeſty's Navy.* Observations on the scuruy. 1786. 8. (2 Sh.) überſ. von C. F. *Michaelis.* 1787. 8. Review of the medical department in the British nauy with a method of reform proposed. 1790. 8. (2 Sh.)

TROWARD, [Richard] of *Norfolk Street.* Collection of the ſtatues now in force relative to elections, down to the present time. 1790. 8. (7 Sh. 6 d.)

TRUSLER, [John] *L. L. D. Clergyman.* Chronology, or a concise view of the annals of England. 1769. 8. (1 ſh.) Ed. V. 1772. (1 ſh. 6 d.) Principles of politeneſſ and of knowing the world, extracted from *Cheſterfield's* letters —. P. 1. 2. 1775. 8. (4 ſh.) nachgedr. Berlin. 1784. 8. überſ. von C. P. *Mo-*

Moritz. Berlin. 1784. 8. Account of the Islands lately discovered in the South sea – with account of the country of Chamchatca. 1777. 8. (6 ſh.) Practical husbandry, or the art of farming, with a certainty of gain —. 1780. 8. (3 ſh. 6 d.) The ſublime reader —. 1782. 8. (2 ſh.) View of the common and ſtatute law of England —. 1784. 4. (15 ſh.) Compendium of useful knowledge, containing — explanation of every thing to a young man ought to known —. 1784. 8. (3 ſh. 6 d.) Poetic endings, or a dictionary of rhimes. 1784. 8. (2 ſh. 6 d.) The London adviser and guide —. 1786. 8. (3 ſh.) The country lawyer. 1786. 8. (3 ſh.) The honours of the table, or, rules for behaviour during meals, with the whole art of carving —. 1788. 8. (2 ſh. 6 d.) Eight year almanac from 1788 to 1797 on a sheet. 1788. (7 ſh. 6 d.) Summary view of the conſtitutional laws of England being an abridgment of *Blackſtone's* commentaries. 1788. 8. (3 ſh. 6 d.)

TRYE, [Charles Brandon] *Surgeon to the General Infirmary in Glouceſter.* Remarks on morbid retentions of urine. 1784. 8. (2 ſh. 6 d.) Review of *Jeſſe Foot's* observations on the new opinions of *John Hunter.* 1787. 8. (1 ſh. 6 d.)

TUCKER, [Josiah] *D. D: Dean of Glouceſter and Rector of St. Steven.* Reflections on the expediency of a law for the naturalization of foreign proteſtants. P. 1. 2. 1751. 8. (2 Sh.) 1 and 2 letter concerning the naturalization of jews 1753. 8. (1 Sh.) Reflections on the expediency of opening the trade to Turkey. 1753. 8. (3 d.) Thoughts on freewill, free knowledge and fate, a fragment. 1763. 8. (4 Sh.) Account of a remarkable tide at Briſtol Febr. 11. 1764. (Phil. Transact. 1764. p. 83.) Apology for the present church of England. 1772. 8. (1 Sh. 6 d.) Six ſermons on important ſubjects. 1772. 8. (1 Sh. 6 d.) Letter to Dr. *Kippis* occasioned by his treatise: Vindication of the proteſtant diſſenting miniſters, with regard to their late application to parliament. 1773. 8. (2 Sh. 6 d.) Four tracts, together with two ſermons, on political and commercial ſubjects. 1774. 8. (3 Sh.) View of the difficulties attending the Trinitarian, Arian and

So-

Socinian ſyſtems —. 1774. 8. (3 d.) Religious intolerance no part of the general plan either of the moſaic or chriſtian diſpenſation —. 1774. 8. (1 Sh.) The reſpective pleas and arguments of the mother country and of the colonies diſtinctly ſet forth and the impoſſibility of a compromiſe of differences or a mutual conceſſion of rights plainly demonſtrated. 1775. 8. (1 Sh.) Letter to *Edm. Burke* in anſwer to his ſpeech of March 22. 1775. 8. (1 Sh.) Addreſſ and appeal, whether a connexion with, or a ſeparation from the continental colonies of America be moſt for the national advantage and the laſting benefit of theſe kingdoms. 1775. 8. (1 Sh. 6 d.) Series of anſwers to objections againſt ſeparating from the rebellious colonies and diſcarding them entirely. 1776. 8. (2 Sh.) XVII ſermons on ſome of the moſt important points on natural and revealed religion —. 1776. 8. (5 Sh.) Cui bono? or inquiry what benefits can ariſe either to the Engliſh or the Americans, the French, Spaniards, or Dutch, from the greateſt victories or ſucceſſes, in the preſent war? 1781. 8. (2 Sh.) Ed. 3. 1782. 8. On civil government. P. 1-3. 1781. 8. (5 Sh.) Reflections on the preſent low price of coarſe wools, its immediate cauſes and its probable remedies. 1782. 8. (1 Sh.) Reflections on the preſent matters in diſpute between Great-Britain and Ireland —. 1785. 8. (1 Sh.) On the advantages and diſadvantages which reſpectively attend France and Great-Britain with regard to trade. 1787. 8. (2 Sh.)

TUCKER, [Nathan] The Bermudian, a poem. 1774. 4. (1 Sh. 6 d.)

TUFTS, [Cotton] *M. D: F. A. S: F. M. S.* Account of the horn-diſtemper in cattle with obſervations on that diſeaſe. (Mem. of B. A. Vol. I. p. 529. London M. J. Vol. VII. P. 3.)

TUNSTALL, [James] *D. D.* born: .... died. 1772.

—— [Marmaduke Cuthbert] *Esq: F. R. S: F. A S.* born: .... died at *Wycliffe*, *Yorkshire* d. 11 Oct. 1790.

TURNBULL, [Gordon] Letter to a young planter. 17.. *Apology for negro-ſlavery —. 178‑. 8. (1 Sh. 6 d) Ed. 2. 1786. (2 Sh.) On the ſlavery and commerce of the human ſpecies.

TURNBULL, [William] *Surgeon in his Majesty's Navy.* On the origin and antiquity of the lues venerea with observations on its introduction into the Islands of the South-Sea. 1786. 8. (2 Sh. 6 d.) übers. von *C. F. Michaelis.* Zittau u. Leipz. 1789. 8.

TURNER, [B.... N....] *M. A.* Candid suggestions in VIII letters to *Soame Jenyns* —. 1782. 12. (2 Sh. 6 d.) The true alarm consisting of 1) a descant on the present national propensity 2) a sketch of a refutation of Mr. *Locke* 3) an appendix containing a friendly challenge and thoughts on the ruinous consequences of an equal representation. 1783. 8. (1 Sh.) On the modes of raising money for the improvement of church lands, in cases of enclosure. 1788. 8. (1 Sh. 6 d.)

TURNER, [Daniel] *A. M. a Dissenting Clergyman at Woolwich in Kent.* Compendium of social religion, or the nature and constitution of christian churches —. 1758. 8. (2 Sh.) Letters religious and moral for the entertainment of young persons. 1766. 8. (3 Sh.) The contrast, or the dying profligate and dying christian; in two poetical essays. 1768. 4. (6 d.) Short meditations on select portions of scripture —. 1771. 8. (2 sh. 6 d.) Dissertations moral and philosophical on natural and revealed religion, with expositions on select passages of scripture and other discourses. 1775. 8. (4 Sh.) Discourses on several important subjects of christianity. 1785. 8. (6 Sh.) Essays on important subjects. Vol. 1. 2. 1787. 8. (6 Sh.) The conversion, the practice of St. Paul and the prayer of Jabetz, considered. 1788. 8. (2 Sh. 6 d.)

(Several single sermons.)

— [Edmund] Jun. *Esq.* Description of an ancient Castle at Rouen in Normandy, called le chateau du vieux palais, built by Henry V. King of England. (Arch. Vol. 7. p. 232.)

— [Francis] *Surgeon at Yarmouth.* A case of suppression of urine in which relief was obtained from puncturing the bladder above the pubis, but which afterwards terminated fatally —. (London M. J. Vol. XI. P. 1.)

TURNER, [Margaret] The gentle shepherd, a Scotch paſtoral, by *Allan Ramsay*, attempted in English. 1790. 8. (5 Sh.)

—— [Nicholas] of *Bignor, Suſſex.* Proposal for raising timber and for effectually ſupporting the poor in Great-Britain. 1757. 8. (1 Sh. 6 d.) On draining and improving peat bogs —. 1784. 8. (3 Sh.)

—— [R......] Junior. *L. L. D.* View of the earth, as far as it was known to the ancients —. 1779. 8. (3 Sh.) Easy introduction to the arts and ſciences. 1783. 12. (2 Sh. 6 d.) Epitome of universal hiſtory, ancient and modern; in a ſeries of letters —. 1787. 12. (3 Sh.)

—— [Samuel] *Lieutenant.* Account of an interview with Teeshoo Lama. (Aſiat. Res. Vol. 1. p. 197.) Journey to Tibet. (Ibid. p. 207.) überſ. *Sprengel's* u. *Forſter's* N. Beytr. zur Länder u. Völkerk. Th. 3.

—— [T.....] Jun. *Surgeon at Yarmouth, Norfolk.* Account of an amputation performed with ſucceſſ in the middle of the foot. (London M. J. Vol. IX. P. 1.)

—— [William] Junior. Abſtract of the hiſtory of the bible. 1786. 8. Eſſay on crimes and punishments. (Mem. of M. Vol. 2. p. 293.)

TWADDLE, [Timothy] *Esq.* The anticipation of the review of the horse guards. 1786. 4. (1 ſh.)

TWAMLEY, [J....] Dairying exemplified; or the busineſſ of cheese the moſt approved method of making butter, on apple-trees or the culture of the orchard. 1784. 8. (3 ſh.) überſ. von *C. F. M. Michaelis.* Frankf. 1787. 8.

TWINING, [Richard] Observations on the tea and window act, and on the tea trade. 1784. 8. (1 Sh. 6 d.) Remarks on the report of the Eaſt-India directors reſpecting the sale and prices of tea. 1784. 8. (1 Sh. 6 d.) Answer to the ſecond report of the Eaſt-India directors, reſpecting the ſale and prices of tea, with a letter to *Rob. Preſton.* 1785. 8. (2 ſh.)

—— [Thomas] *M. A: Vicar of White Notly, Eſſex. Ariſtotle's* Treatise on poetry, translated with notes- and two diſſertations on poetical and muſical imitation.. 1789. 4. (1 L. 1 ſh.) A short hiſtory

 of

of the Pharisees, with a parallel between the antient and the modern. 1790. 8. (6 d.)

(Several ſingle ſermons.)

TWISS, [Richard] *F. R. S.* Travels through Portugal and Spain 1775. 4. (1 L. 11 ſh.) überſ. von *Ebeling*. Leipz. 1776. 8. *Tour in Ireland 1776. 8. (5 ſh.) überſ. Leipz. 1777. 8. *Cheſſ. Vol. 1. 2. 1787. 8. (10 ſh.)

TWISTING, [Timothy] *Esq.* The Pittiad: or, poetico-political hiſtory of William II. in five Cantos. 1785. 4. (3 ſh.)

TYER, [Thomas] *Esq. of the Inner Temple.* born 1726. died d. 1 Febr. 1787.

TYRWHITT, [Thomas] *F. R. S: F. A. S.* born: 1730. died at *London*. d. 15 Aug. 1786.

TYSON, [Michael] *B. D: F. A. S: F. R. S.* born: .... died d. 4 May. 1780.

TYTLER, [Alexander Fraser] *Esq: Advocate, F. R. S. Edin: Profeſſor of Civil Hiſtory and of Greek and Roman Antiquities in the Univerſity of Edinburgh.* Plan and outlines of a course of lectures on univerſal hiſtory ancient and modern —. 1783. 8. (5 ſh.) Enquiry into the evidence againſt Mary Queen of Scots. 8. Ed. 4. Vol. 1. 2. 17.. Account of *Robert Dundas* of Arniſton, (Lord Preſident of the Court of ſeſſion in Scotland. F. R. S. Edin.) (Tr. of E. S. Vol. 2. App. p. 37.) Account of ſome extraordinary ſtructures on the tops of hills in the Highlands; with remarks on the progreſſ of the arts among the ancient inhabitants of Scotland. (Tr. of E. S. Vol. 2. p. 3.)

VALLANCEY, [Charles] *Colonel and Ingenieur General of Ireland: LL. D: F. R. S of London, Dublin and Edinburgh: F. A. S.* *Clairac's* field engineer, with remarks on *Saxe's* new ſyſtem of fortification, translated. 1760. 8. (9 ſh.) *Eſſay on the antiquity of the Irish language; being a collation of the Irish with the punic language 1772. 8. Obſervations on the alphabet of the pagan Irish and of the age in which Finn and Oſſian lived. (Arch. Vol. 7. p. 276.) Obſervations on the American inscription. (Ibid. Vol. 8. p. 302.) Eſſay on the ancient hiſtory of the Britannic Isles. Dublin. 1786. 8.

Col-

Collectanea de rebus Hibernicis. Numb. I-XIV. 1786. 8. Memoir of the language, manners and customs of an Anglo-Saxon Colony settled in the baronies of *Forth* and *Bargie* in the county of *Wexford.* (Tr. of J A. 1788. p. 19.) Description on antient monument, discovered 1753 in the church of Lusk in the County of Dublin. (Ibid. p. 57.) On the silver medal lately dug up in the park of *Dungannon,* county of *Tyrone,* the seat of Lord *Welles.* (Ibid. p. 69.)

VALPY, [Richard] *Poetical blossoms, or, a collection of poems, odes and translations —. 1772. 4. (2 sh. 6 d.) *Elements of the latin language —. 1782. 8. (2 sh.) Ed. 5. 1789. 8. (2 sh.)

VANDERSTOP, [Cornelius] The gentle shepherd, a dramatic poem — done into English from the original of *Allan Ramsay.* 1777. 8. (1 sh. 6 d.)

VANE, [Lionel] *Esq.* Letters to a gentleman of fortune relating to his conduct in life. 1753. 8. (3 sh.) History of the life of Tamerlane the Great — translated from Arabian into English, with notes. 1782. 12. (1 sh. 6 d.)

VARLO, [C.....] *Esq.* New system of husbandry. Ed. IV. Vol. 1-3. 1774. (15 sh.) Shemes offered for the perusal and consideration of the legislature, freeholders and public in general —. 1775. 8. (3 sh.)

VAUGHAN, [James] *M. D: Physician to the Leicester Infirmary.* Diss. De Polypo cordis. Edinb. 1762. 8. Two cases of the hydrophobia with observations on that disease —. 1778. 8. (2 sh. 6 d.) Ed. 2. with an account of the caesarian section, with reflections on dividing the symphysis of the ossa pubis. 1779. 8. (3 sh. 6 d.) übers. Samml. prakt. Abhandl. Th. 5. S. 3. Remarkable effects of cantharides in paralytic affections. (Mem. of M. S. of L. Vol. 1. p. 360.) Case of an hernia humoralis. (Med. Obs. and Inq.)

VAUGHAN, [Thomas] The hotel, or the double valet, a farce. 1776. 8. (1 sh.) Love's metamorphosis, a farce. 1776.

— [William] *M. D.* born: 1730. died d. 7. Aug. 1790.

VAUX, [George] *Surgeon.* The works of *Joseph Else,* Surgeon —. 1782. 8. (2 sh. 6 d.)

VENN, [Henry] *A. M: Rector of Yilling, Huntingdonshire.* (a Methodistical Clergyman.) Sermons. 1759. 8. (5 sh.) The compleat duty of man, or, a system of doctrinal and practical christianity —. 1764. 8. (5 sh.) Examination of *Priestley's* addreß on the Lord's supper. 1769. 8. (1 sh. 6 d.) Mistakes in religion exposed in an eßay on the prophecy of Zacharias. 1774. 8. (3 sh.)
(Several single sermons.)

VERE, [James] Physical and moral enquiry into the causes of restleßneß and disorder in man —. 1778. 8. (2 Sh. 6 d.)

VERELST, [Harry] Formerly *Governor at Bengal.* born: .... died at *Bologne.* d. Nov. 1785.

VERNON, [G.... W....] see *J. B. Scriven.*

VESEY, [Francis] *LL. D: Barrister at law.* Cases argued and determined in the high court of Chancery - from the Year 1764 - 1755. Vol. 1. 2. 1771. fol. (3 L. 3 Sh.)

VICTOR, [Benjamin] *Treasurer of Drury - Lane Theater and Poet Laureat of the Kingdom of Ireland.* born: .... died d. 3. Dec. 1778.

VIGOR, [.....] *Mrs.* (Her maiden - name *Goodwin.*) born: 1700. died at *Windsor* d. 12 Sept. 1784.

VINCE, [Samuel] *A. M: F. R. S.* Elements of the conic sections 1781. 8. (2 Sh. 6 d.) Investigation of the principles of progreßive and rotatory motion. (Phil. Transact. 1780. p. 546.) A new method of investigating the sums of infinite series. (Ibid. 1782. p. 389. 1785. p. 32.) On the motion of bodies affected by friction. (Ibid. 1785. p. 165.) On a new method of finding fluents by continuation. (Ibid. 1786. p. 432.) On the preceßion of the equinoxes. (Ibid. 1787. p. 363.) On practical astronomy. 1790. 4. (15 Sh.)

VINCENT, [William] *D. D: Rector of Allhallows the Great and Leß.* Considerations on parochial music. 1787. 8. (1 Sh.)

—— [William] of *Gray's Inn.* Narrative of the late disturbances in the cities of London and Westminster and borough of Southwark. 1780. 8. (1 sh.)

VISPRE', [F.... X....] On the growth of wine in England. 1786. 8. (1 Sh. 6 d.)

VIVIAN, [Thomas] *Vicar of Cornwood, Devon.* Dissertation on the latter part of the XIII Chapt. of the revelation of St. John. 1781. 8. (1 Sh. 6 d.) The book of the revelation of St. John the divine explained, in an hiſtorical view of the paſt and present ſtate of the chriſtian world, compared with the prophetic viſions. 1785. 8. (2 Sh. 6 d.)

UMFREVILLE, [Edward] The present ſtate of Hudsonsbay, containing a full description of that ſettlement, and the adjacent country. 1790. 8. überſ. *Sprengels* u. *Forſters* N. Beytr. zur Völker und-Länderkunde. Th. 6.

UNDERWOOD, [Michael] *M. D: Surgeon to the British - Lying in Hospital.* On ulcers of the legs. 1783. 8. (3 Sh.) überſ. Leipz. 1786. 8. On the diseases of children —. 1784. 8. (3 Sh.) Ed. 2. Vol. 1. 2. 1790. 8. (6 Sh.) überſ. unter dem Titel: der engliſche Kinder-Arzt. 1786. 8. Surgical tracts —. 1788. 8. (4 Sh. 3 d.) Account of a curious fact relative to the effects of crude mercury. (London M J. Vol. VIII. P. 1. überſ. Samml. f. A. Th. XI. S. 729. Caſe of on extra uterine foetus. (Ibid. Vol. VIII. P. 4.)

UNWIN, [Matthew] *Hosier.* born: .... died at *Nottingham* d. 27. Aug. 1786.

UPSDALE, [T.....] *Teacher in the French Language.* A new description of the terreſtrial globe. 1780. 12. (3 Sh.)

UPTON, [......] *Mrs. Governess of the Ladies Academy.* Siege of Gibraltar. 17. Miscellaneous pieces in prose and verse. 1784. 4. (2 ſh.)

— [W......] Poems on ſeveral occaſions. 1788. 8. (5 ſh.)

URQUHART, [.....] *Inſtitutes of hydroſtatics — with an philosophical eſſay on air balloons. 1786. 8. (6 ſh.)

— [George] The experienced ſolicitor in proceedings under the appellant jurisdiction of the house of Lords —. 1773. fol. (10 Sh. 6 d.)

— [.....] *M. A.* The odes of *Anacreon*, translated from the Greek. 1787. 8. (2 ſh.)

USHER, [G.... Neville] The elements of English grammar —. Ed. 2. 1787. 12. (1 ſh. 6 d.)

USSHER, [Henry] *D. D: F. J. A: F. R. S. Professor of Astronomy at Dublin.* born: .... died. d. 7 May. 1790.

VYSE, [Charles] *Teacher of the Mathematics and Master of the Academy in Portland-Street.* A new geographical grammar —. 1774. 8. (4 ſh.) The tutor's guide, being a complete ſyſtem of arithmetic with various branches in the mathematics. 8. 1770. (3 ſh.) The key to the tutor's guide or the arithmetician's repository. 1773. 8. (3 ſh.) The new London ſpelling-book. P. 1-5. 1777. 8. (1 ſh.)

WADDINGTON, [R.....] *Teacher of Mathematics, late Mathematical Maſter of the Roy. Acad. at Portsmouth.* Practical method for finding the longitude and latitude of a ship at sea, by observations of the moon. 1763. 4. Supplement. 1764. 4. (5 ſh.) The sea Officer's companion —. 1770. 4. (2 ſh.) On the longitude 1773. 4. (2 ſh. 6 d.) Epitome of theoretical and practical navigation. 1777. 4. (12 ſh.)

WAGSTAFF, [Walter] The pandemonium ballot — in 3 Cantos. 1773. 8. (2 ſh)

WAKEFIELD, [Gilbert] *B. A. Claſſical Tutor at Warrington, Diſſenting Academy.* Poemata latina cum obſervationibus criticis in *Horatium.* 1776. 4. (3 ſh. 6 d.) Translation of the 1 Epiſtle to the Theſſalonians —. 1781. 8. (6 d.) On inspiration —. 1781. 8. (2 ſh. 6 d.) Account of the nature of baptism, according to the new teſtament, with remark on confirmation and the Lord's supper. 1781. 8. (1 ſh.) Translation of the gospel of St. Matthew, with notes critical, philological and explanatory. 1782. 4. (12 ſh.) Enquiry into the opinions of the chriſtian writers of the three firſt centuries concerning the person of Jesus Chriſt. Vol. 1. 1784. 8. (6 ſh.) The poems of Mr. *Gray,* with notes. 1786. 8. (4 ſh.) Remarks on Dr. *Horsley's* ordination sermon in a letter to the Lord Bishop of Glouceſter. 1788. 8. (4 d.) On the origin of alphabetical characters. (Mem. of M. Vol. 2. p. 278.) *Virgilii Maronis* Georgicon, cum notis. 1788. 8. (3 ſh. 6 d.) Silva critica: ſive in auctores ſacros profanosque commentarius philologicus. 1789.

1789. 8. (3 fh. 6 d.) A new translation of those parts only of the new teſtament, which are wrongly translated in our common version. 1789. 8. (2 ſh. 6 d.) Remarks on the internal evidence of the chriſtian religion. 1789. 8. (2 ſh. 6 d.) Addreſſ to the inhabitants of Nottingham — with an appendix on the subject of the teſt laws. 1789. 8. (1 ſh.) Cursory reflections — on the claims of the diſſenters and the repeal of the corporation and teſt acts. 1790. 8. (6 d.) Addreſſ to D. *Sam. Horsley*, on the subject of an apology for the liturgy and clergy of the church of England. 1790. 8. (1 ſh.) (Several ſingle sermons.)

WAKER, [Joseph] Loue in a cottage, a paſtoral. 1785. 8.

WALBECK; [William] The life of Cervantes, by *Florian*, translated. 1785. 8. (1 ſh.) Socrates and Xantippe, a tale. 1786. 4. (2 ſh.) Tales, apologues, allegories, viſions, epigrams, epitaphs —. in verse. 1788. 8. (2 ſh. 6 d.) Fables, ancient and modern. 1787. 8. (3 ſh. 6 d.)

WALCOTT, [John] *Esq.* Description and figures of petrifactions found in the quarries gravel pits — near Bath. 1779. 8. (2 ſh. 6 d.)

WALDO, [Peter] *Eſſay on the holy sacrement of the Lord's supper. 1771. 12. (2 Sh.) *Commentary — on the liturgy of the church of England —. 1772. 8. (5 Sh.)

WALDRON, [Francis] The maid of Kent, a comedy. 1778. 8.

—— [Thomas] *Actor of Drury Lane Theater.* Ben *Jonson's* sad shepherd, or a tale of Robin hood —. 1783. 8. (3 ſh. 6 d.)

WALES, [Wales] *F. R. S: Maſter of the Roy. Mathematical school in Chriſt's Hospital.* (Formerly *Aſtronomer on Board the Resolution.*) Ode to - *Will. Pitt.* 1762. fol. (1 ſh.) Observations on the transit of Venus, June 3. 1769. at Prince of Wales's fort. (Phil. Transact. 1769. p. 480.) Aſtronomical observations at Prince of Wales's fort, on the North-Weſt coaſt of Hudson's bay. (Ibid. 1769. p. 467.) Journal of a voyage — to Churchill river, on the North-Weſt coaſt of Hudson's Bay - in the Y. 1768. 1769. (Ibid. 1770. p. 100.) *Wales's* and *Joseph*

Dymond's observations on the ſtate of the air, winds, weather — made at Prince of Wales's fort on the North-Weſt coaſt of Hudson's bay in the Y. 1768. 1769. (Ibid. p. 137.) *Wales's* and *Will. Bayly's* original aſtronomical observations made in the courſe of a voyage towards the ſouth pole and round the world —. 1777. 4. (1 L. 1 Sh.) Remarks on *Forſter's* account of Capt. *Cook's* laſt voyage round the world in the Y. 1772-1775. 1778. 8. (1 Sh. 6 d.) Observations on the solar eclipse which happened June 24. 1778. (Phil. Transact. 1778. p. 101.) Hints relating to the use which may be made of the tables of natural ond logarithmic ſines, tangents — in the numerical resolution of adfected equations. (Ibid. 1781. p. 454.) Inquiry into the present ſtate of population in England and Wales —. 1781. 8. (1 Sh. 6 d.)

WALKER, [.....] *Surgeon in Virginia.* Case and remarks relative to diseases of the bones. (Med. Transact. Vol. 3. p. 25.)

—— [Adam] *Lecturer in Natural Philosophy.* Account of the cavern of *Dunmore Park*, near *Kilkenny* in *Ireland.* (Phil. Transact. 1773. p. 16.) On the application of fixed air to an inflamed breaſt. (*Prieſtley* Experim. of Nat. Philosophy. Vol. 1. p. 464.)

—— [George] F. R. S: *Miniſter of a Congregation of Proteſtant Diſſenters in Nottingham.* On the doctrine of the sphere. 1777. 4. (12 ſh.) The diſſenter's plea, or the appeal of the diſſenter's to the juſtice, the honour — againſt the teſt laws. 1790. 8. (1 ſh.) Sermons on various subjects. Vol. 1. 2. 1790. 8. (12 Sh.)

—— [George] *Bookseller at Faversham.* Collection of the minute and rare shells lately discovered — by *Will. Boys.* F. A. S. —. 1784. 4. (5 Sh.)

—— [J....] °Monody on the death of *John Thurlow*, Esq. 1782. 4. (1 Sh.) °Ode addreſſed to the society of universal goodwill. 1785. 4. (1 Sh.)

—— [James] (a Roman Catholic.) General idea of a pronouncing dictionary of the English language — 1774. 4. (1 Sh. 6 d.) Dictionary of the English language —. 1775. 8. (7 Sh.) The child's directory or easy leſſons in 4 parts. 1776. 8. (6 d.)

Exer-

Exercises for improvement in elocution. 1777. 8. (2 Sh.) Elements of elocution —. Vol. 1. 2. 1781. 8. (12 Sh.) Hints for improving in the art of reading. 1782. 8. (2 Sh.) Rhetorical grammar, or course of leſſons in elocution. 1785. 8. (3 Sh. 6 d.) English claſſics abridged: being ſelect works of *Addiſon*, *Pope* and *Milton*. 1786. 8. (3 ſh. 6 d.) The melody of speaking delineated —. 1787. 8. (2 ſh. 6 d.) The academic speaker. —. 1788. 8. (3 ſh. 6 d.)

WALKER, [John] *D. D: M. D: F. R. S: Edinb. Profeſſor of Natural Hiſtory and Keeper of the Museum in the Univerſity of Edinburgh.* Account of a new medicinal well, lately discovered near Moffat in Annandale in the county of Dumfries. (Phil. Transact. 1760. p. 117.) Account of the irruption of Solway Roſſ on Dec. 16. 1772. (Ibid. 1772. p. 123.) Account of the cavern in Dunmore Park, near Kilkenny in Ireland. (Ibid. 1773. p. 16.) Experiments on the motion of the sap in trees. (Tr. of E. S. Vol. 1. p. 3. überſ. Samml. z. P. u. N. G. Th. 4. S. 455.)

— [John] *A. B.* Rhetorical grammar, or course of leſſons in elocution. 1784. 4. (3 ſh.) The academic speaker, or a selection of parliamentary debates, orations, odes, scenes and speeches from the beſt writers. 1788. 8. (3 ſh. 6 d.)
(Several ſingle ſermons.)

— [Joseph C....] *Esq. M. J. A.* (born in Ireland.) Hiſtorical memoirs of the Irish bards, with observations on the muſic of Ireland. 1786. 4. (13 ſh.) Hiſtorical eſſay on the dreſſ of the ancient and modern Irish, with a memoir on the armour and weapons of the Irish. 1788. 4. (18 ſh.) On the Irish ſtage. (Tr. of J. A. 1788. p. 75.)

— [Joshua] *M. D: Phyſician to the Leeds Infirmary.* Diſſ. De aqua ſulfurea Harrowgatenſi. Edinb. 1770. 8. On the waters of Harrogate and Thorp-Arch in Yorkshire —. 1784. 8. (3ſh.) Observations on the use of the cuprum ammoniacum in the cure of the chorea Stl Viti. (*Duncan's* M. C. Vol. 10. p. 288.) überſ. Samml. f. A. Th. XI. S. 672. Some remarks on the prevalence of the atrophia lactantium. (Mem. of M. S. of L. Vol. 2. p. 43.)

WALKER, [Maynard Chamb.] Speech delivered at the Weſtminſter forum —. 1780. 8. (1 ſh.)

— [Mary] *Mrs.* *Obſervations on Mr. *Burke's* bill for the better regulation of the independence of parliament —. 1780. 8. (1 ſh.)

— [Nathan] The devil no fallen angel, proved from ſcripture —. 1772. 8. (1 ſh.) On the ever bleſſed and adorable trinity, and unity in trinity. 1772. 8. (1 ſh. 6 d.) Appeal from the clergy to the laity: with a ſting in the tail, for the benefit of drones that never had a ſting —. 1773. 8. (2 d.) More work for the predeſtination —. 1773. 8. (1 ſh. 6 d.)

— [Richard] *Apothecary to the Radcliffe Infirmary at Oxford.* Experiments on the production of artificial cold. (Phil. Transact. 1788. p. 395.) überſ. *Gren* J. d. P. Th. 1. S. 419. Experiments on the congelation of quick ſilver in England. (Ibid. 1789. p. 199) überſ. *Gren* J. d. P. Th. 2. S. 358.

— [Robert] *Miniſter of the Highchurch of Edinburgh.* born: .... died 1783.

— [Robert] Enquiry into the ſmall pox, medical and political; wherein a ſucceſſful method of treating that diſeaſe is propoſed; the cauſe of pits explained; and the method of their prevention pointed out, with an appendix, repreſenting the preſent ſtate of the ſmallpox. 1790. 8. (6 d.) überſ. von *C. H. Spohr.* Leipz. 1791. 8.

— [Thomas] Anſwer to Mr. Fitzgerald's appeal to the jockey club. 1775. 8. (1 ſh.)

WALL, [John] *M. D: Phyſician at Worcheſter.* born .... died d 28 Jun. 1776.

— [Martin] *M. D: Phyſician and Public Reader of Chemiſtry at Oxford. John Wall's* Medical tracts collected and republiſhed. 1780. 8. (5 ſh.) Diſſertations on ſelect ſubjects in chemiſtry and medicine. 1783. 8. (3 ſh.) Clinical obſervations on the uſe of opium in low fewers. Ed. 2. 1786. (1 Sh. 6 d.) überſ. von Dr. *Diel.* Altenb. 1789. 8. Conjectural remarks on the ſymbols or characters, employed by aſtronomers, to repreſent the ſeveral planets and by the chemiſts, to expreſſ the ſeveral metals —. (Mem. of Mancheſter. Vol. 1. p. 243.) On the origin of the vegetable fixed alkali with ſome collateral obſervations on nitre. (Ibid. Vol. 2. p. 67.) On the phae-

phaenomena between oil and water. (Ibid. p. 419.) On attraction and repulsion. (Ibid. p. 439.)

WALLACE, [.....] *Mrs.* (born in Scotland, Daughter to Sir *Will. Maxwell*, Baronet.) Diamond cut diamond, a comedy, translated from the French of guerre ouverte. 1787. 8. (1 Sh.) *Letter to a friend with the ghost of Werter, a poem. 1787. 4. (1 Sh. 6 d.) The Ton; or follies of fashion, a comedy. 1788. 8. (1 Sh. 6d.) übers. von R. S. Tübingen. 1789. 8.

— [George] *Advocate: F. R. S. Edinb.* System of the principles of the law of Scotland. Vol. 1. fol. (1 L. 5 Sh.) Thoughts on the origin of feudal tenures and the descent of antient peerages in Scotland. 1783. 4. (12 Sh.) The nature and descent of ancient peerages, connected with the state of Scotland, the origin of tenures, the succession of fiefs and the constitution of parliament. 1785. 8. (6 Sh. 6 d.)

— [William] *Sheriff at Ayrshire and Professor of Law at Edinburgh.* born: .... died d. 28. Dec. 1786.

WALLBECK, [William] *Florian's* life of *Cervantes*, translated from the French —. 1785. 8. (1 Sh.) Fables, ancient and modern. 1787. 8. (3 Sh. 6 d.)

WALLER, [Henry] *Major.* A familiar poetical epistle to *Thom. Lamb.* Esq. — — on the manners and characters of the present age —. 1784. 4. (2 Sh. 6d.) A rump and dozen; the conclusion of the letter to *Th. Lamb.* 1784. 4. (2 Sh. 6d.) Avaro and tray, or the difference between reason and brutal instinct, a tale. 1784. 4. (1 Sh.) The dog's monitor, a satirical poem —. 1785. 4. (2 Sh.)

WALLIN, [Benjamin] *M. A.* Lectures on primitive christianity in doctrine, experience, worship, discipline and manners —. 1769. 8. (5 Sh.) Discourses on the parable of the prodigal son. 1775. 8. (3 Sh.) The scripture doctrine of Christ's sonship, being sermons on the divine filiation of Jesus — with three discourses on Psalm 2, 12. 1771. 8. (2 Sh. 6 d.) (Several single sermons.)

WALLIS, [Edward] *M. D. Physician at York.* born. 1704. died d. 13 Oct. 1782.

— [George] *M. D.* On the evil consequences attending injudicious bleeding in pregnancy. 1779. 8. (1 Sh. 6 d.) *Franc. Sauvages* nosologia methodica ea oculorum — translated. 1786. 8. (4 Sh. 6 d.) The works of *Thomas Sydenham*, with notes. Vol. 1. 2. 1788. 8. (12 Sh.)

WALLIS, [George] *The Juvenaliad, a ſatire. 1774. 4. (1 Sh.) Perjury, a ſatire. 1774. 4. (2 Sh.) The mercantile lovers, a dramatic ſatire. 1775. 8. (1 Sh. 6 d.)

—— [Hannah] *Mrs.* The female's meditations; or common occurrences ſpiritualized, in verse. 1787. 4. (3 Sh. 6 d.)

—— [N....] *Architect.* The carpenter's treasure —. 1774. 8. (2 Sh. 6 d.)

WALPOLE, [Horace] *Uſher of his Majeſty's Exchequer, Controller of the pipe and Clerk of the Eſtreats in the Exchequer.* (born 1716.) *Catalogue of the royal and noble authors of England with liſt of their works. Vol. 1. 2. 1758. *Poſtscript to the royal and noble authors. 1786. 8. Anecdotes of painting in England — collected by *George Vertue* and now digeſted from his Mſſ. Vol. 1-4. with hiſtory of modern taſte in gardening. 1762. 4. (4 L.) Additional lives to complete the firſt edition of anecdotes of painting in England. 1767. 4. (3 Sh.) Ed. 2. Vol. 1-4. (3 L. 13 Sh. 6 d.) *The caſtle of Otranto, a Gothic ſtory. 1765. 8. (3 Sh.) Hiſtorical doubts on the life and reign of King Richard III. 1768. 8. (5 Sh.) Myſterious mother, a tragedy. 1768. 8. Miscellaneous antiquities: or, a collection of curious papers. Numb. 1. 2. 1772. 4. (4 Sh.) Memoires du Cte de *Grammont* par. *Ant. Hamilton*, augmenté de notes. 1783. 4.

WALSH, [John] *Esq. F. R. S.* On the electric property of the torpedo. (Phil. Transact. 1773. p. 461.) On torpedos found on the coaſt of England. (Ibid. 1774. p. 464.)

—— [Philipp Pitt] *M. D: Phyſician to the General Lying in and the Brownlow-Street Hospitals.* born at *Kilkenny* .... died d. 25. Dec. 1787.

WALTER, [John] *M. A: Maſter of Ruthin School.* Ode on the immortality of the soul —. 1786. 12. (1 ſh. 6 d.) Letter to *Jos. Prieſtley* on the subject of his letters to *W. Pitt* and to the Dean of Canterbury with a discourse on the natural connection

nection of civil and ecclesiastical establishments. 1787. 12. (2 sh.)

WALTER, [Thomas] Flora Caroliniana, secundum systema vegetabilium *Linnaei* digesta. 1788. 8. (6 sh.)

—— [W.....] Abridgment of the memorial addressed to the King of France by M. de *Calonne*, translated from the French. 1787. 8. (2 sh. 6 d.)

WALTERS, [John] *B. A. Scholar of Jesus College and Sub-Librarian in the Bodlejan Library.* Poems, with notes —. 1780. 8. (5 sh.) Translated specimens of Welsh poetry in English verse, 1782. 8. (1 Sh. 6 d.)

—— [W.....] born 1769. died at *Cowbridge, County Glamorgan.* d. 8. Oct. 1789.

WALTON, [W....] *Land-Surveyor, at West-Lynn, Norfolk.* Essay proving iron far superior to stone of any kind for breaking and grinding of corn, grain and pulse. 1788. 8. (6 d.)

WALWYN, [B.....] Chit-Chat or the penance of polygamy, an interlude. 1781. 8. (6 d.) Essay on comedy, 1782. 8. (1 sh. 6 d.) übers. Neue Bibl. d. Sch. Wiss. Th. 28. S. 1-28. *Errors of nature. Vol. 1-3. 1783. 8. (9 sh.) Love in a cottage. Vol. 1. 2. 1786. 12. (5 sh.)

WANLEY, [Nathaniel] *M. A: late Vicar of Trinity parish, Coventry.* The wonders of the little world. 1774. 4. (18 sh.)

WANOSTROCHT, [N.....] *Teacher of Languages.* Practical grammar of the French language. 1780. 12. (2 sh.) Ed. 2. 1782. 12. (3 sh.) Classical vocabulary, French and English. 1783. 12. (2 sh.) Recueil choisi de traits historiques et de contes moraux. 1785. 12. (3 sh. 6 d.) Petite encyclopaedie des jeunes gens —. 1788. 12. (5 sh.)

WARBOYS, [Thomas] The preceptor, a comedy. 1777. The rival lovers, a comedy. 1777.

WARBURTON, [.....] Letter to the Chancellor of the Exchequer, shewing the necessity of a clerical reform and containing a plan for remedying the grievances of the inferior clergy. 1788. 8. (1 sh. 6 d.)

—— [William] *D. D: LordBishop of Gloucester.* born at *Newark-upon-Trent* d. 24. Dec. 1698. died d. 7. June. 1779.

WARD,

WARD, [Samuel] *Vicar of Cotterſtock and Clapthorne, Northamptonshire.* born.... died d. 31 March. 1790.

—— [W.....] The gentle shepherd, translated from *Allan Ramsay.* 1785. 8. (2 ſh.)

WARE, [James] *Surgeon: Fellow of Med. Society.* On the ophthalmy, psorophthalmy and purulent eye with methods of cure —. 1780. 8 (2 Sh. 6 d.) Ed. 2. 1787. 8. (3 Sh.) überſ. Kleine medizinisch-chirurgiſche Abhandlung aus verſchiedenen Sprachen: Th. 1. Leipzig. 1781. 8. überſ. Samml. f. A. Th. 6. S. 351-445. A case of ſuppreſſion of urine, occaſioned by an enlargement of the proſtrate gland. (Mem. of M. S. of L. Vol. 2. p. 336.)

WARING, [Edward] *M. D: F. R. S of London and of Gottingen, Profeſſor of Mathematics in the Univerſity of Cambridge.* Miſcellanea analytica, de aequationibus algebraicis et curvarum proprietatibus. 1762. 4. Mathematical problems. (Phil. Transact. 1763. p. 294.) New properties in conic ſections. (Ibid. 1764. p. 193.) Two theorems in mathematics. (Ibid. 1765. p. 143.) Meditationes algebraicae. 1770. 4. (10 Sh. 6 d.) Ed. 2. 1782. 4. Proprietates algebraicarum curvarum. 1762. 4. (5 ſh.) Ed. 2. 1772. 4. Meditationes analyticae. 1775. 4. (1 L. 1 ſh.) Ed. 2. 1785. 4. Problems concerning interpolations. (Phil. Transact. 1779. p. 59.) A general resolution of algebraical equations. (Ibid. 1779. p. 86.) On the ſummation of ſeries, whoſe general term is a determinate function of z, the diſtance from the firſt term of the ſeries. (Ibid. 1784. p. 385.) The infinite ſeries. (Ibid. 1786. p. 81.) On finding the values of algebraical quantities by converging ſerieses and demonſtrating and extending propoſitions given by *Pappus* and others. (Ibid. 1787. p. 71.) On centripetal forces. (Ibid. 1788. p. 67.) Some properties of the ſum of the diviſors of numbers. (Ibid. 1788. p. 388.) On the method of correſpondent values. (Ibid. 1789. p. 166.) On the reſolution of attractive powers. (Ibid. 1789. p. 185.)

—— [Richard Hill] *Esq. F. R. S.* On ſome plants found in ſeveral parts of England. (Philos. Transact. 1771. p. 359.)

WARING,

WARING, [William] *J. J. Rousseau's* dictionary of music — translated. 1779. Ed. 2. 17. . 8. (3 Sh.)

WARLTIRE, [John] *Lecturer in Natural Philosophy.* On the refractive power of inflammable air and the decomposition of it by burning. (*Priestley's* Experiments — on air. Vol. 3. p. 365.)

WARNER, [Joseph] *F. R. S: Surgeon to Guy's Hospital in the Borough of Southwark.* Cases in surgery, with remarks. 1754. 8. (2 Sh.) Ed. 4. 1784. 8. (6 Sh.) übers. Leipzig. 1787. 8. Case of an extraordinary tumour growing on the inside of the bladder, successfully extracted. (Phil. Transact. 1756. p. 414.) Case of a successful operation performed on the empyema. (Ibid. 1757. p. 407.) Case of a piece of a bone, together with a stone in the bladder successfully extracted. (Ibid. 1757. p. 475.) Case of the operation for the empyema successfully performed. (Ibid. 1758. p. 270.) On the use of the agaric of the oak in stopping haemorrhages. (Ibid. 1758. p. 588.) On the use of agaric, as a styptic. (Ibid. 1758. p. 813.) Two singular cases of diseased knee joints, successfully treated, the first by topical applications, the second by operation. (Ibid. 1759. p. 452.) Case of an aneurism on the thigh and on the uncertainty of the distinguishing symptoms. (Ibid. 1760. p. 363.) An instance of four rough stones that were discovered in an human urinary bladder, contrary to the received opinion, and successfully extracted by the lateral method of cutting for the stone. (Ibid. 1760. p. 579.) Remarkable case of an empyema: (Ibid. 1761. p. 194.) Account of two stones of remarkable shapes and sizes which, for the space of 6 Years, were firmly lodged in the urethra of a young man and successfully cut out from thence. (Ibid 1761. p. 304.) Account of a very small foetus brought into the world at the same time with a child at its full growth. (Ibid. 1770. p. 451.) Description of human eye and its adjacent parts, with their principal diseases and the method proposed for relieving them. 1773. 8. (2 Sh. 6 d.) Account of the testicles, their common coverings and coats and the diseases, to which they are liable. 1774. 8. (2 Sh.) übers. (von *J. C. F. Scherf.*) Gotha 1775. 8.

WARNER, [Richard] born.... died 1775.

—— [Richard] Jun. of *Sway*, near *Lymington*. Companion in a tour round Lymington, comprehending an account of that place and its environs, the new forest, Isle of Wight and towns of Southampton Christchurch. 1790. 8. (4 Sh.) Hampshire: extracted from Domesday book, with a translation, view of the Anglo-Saxon history and form of governmens from the reign of Alfred. 1789. 4. (1 L. 1 Sh.)

WARREN, [John] *M. D: Physician at Taunton, Somersetshire.* born...., died. d. 12 Nov. 1789.

—— [John] *F. A. S: Professor of Anatomy and Surgery in the University of Cambridge.* History of a large tumour in the region of the abdomen, containing hair. (Mem. of B. A. Vol. I. p. 551. London M. J. Vol. VII. P. 3.)

—— [Richard] *M. D: F. R. S: F. A. S. Physician in Ordinary to the King.* Of the bronchial polypus. (Med. Transact. Vol. I. p. 407.) Of the colica pictonum. (Ibid. Vol. 2. p. 68.)

WARRINGTON, [William] *Chaplain to the Earl of Besborough.* The history of Wales. 1786. 4. (1 L. 1 Sh.)

WARTON, [Joseph] *D. D: F. R. S: Master of Winchestershool.* Ode, occasioned by reading Mr. *West's* translation of *Pindar*. fol. 1749. (6 d.) The works of *Virgil*, in Latin and English —. Vol. 1-4. 1753. 8. (20 Sh.) *On the genius and writings of *Pope*. Vol. 1. 2. 1782. 8. (7 Sh.) The enthusiast or the lover of nature. 17.

—— [Thomas] *D. D. Poet Laureat, Professor of Poetry in the University of Oxford.* born: 1728. died d. 21 May. 1790.

WARWICK, [Thomas] *LL. B: of University College, Oxford.* The rights of sovereignty asserted: an ode. 1777. 4. (1 Sh.) *Edwy, a dramatic poem. 1784. 8. (1 Sh. 6 d.) Abelard to Eloisa, an Epistle, with sonnets and a rhapsody 1784. 4. (2 Sh. 6 d.) Ed. 2. 1785. 8. (1 Sh.)

WASHINGTON, [George] *General and President of the General Congress in America.* Journal to the Ohio, with the governor's letters, a translation of the French officers answer and a new map of the coun-

country, as far as the Miſſiſſippi. 1754. 8. (1 Sh.) Letters to ſeveral of his friends in the Year 1776. 1777. 8. (1 Sh. 6 d.) Letter to General *Green.* 1783. 8. (6 d.)

WASTELL, [Henry] *Surgeon.* Observations on the efficacy of a new mercurial preparation for the cure of the venereal disease. 1779. 8. (2 Sh.)

WATERHOUSE, [B......] *M. D: Prof. of the Theory and Practice of Phyſic in the Univerſity of Cambridge, New-England, and of Natural Hiſtory in the College of Rhode Iſland.* Synopſis of a course of lectures on the theory and practice of medicine. P. 1. Boſton. 1786. 8.

WATHEN, [Jonathan] *Surgeon at London: F. A. S.* A method proposed to reſtore the hearing, when injured from an obſtruction of the tuba Euſtachiana. (Phil. Transact. 1759. p. 213.) *Boerhaave's* academical lectures on the lues venerea, tranſlated. 1763. 8. (4 Sh.) Practical observations on the cure of the venereal disease in mercurials. 1765. 8. (1 Sh. 6 d.) Answer to the letter of Mr. *Keyser*, in which the insufficiency of his medicine for the cure of the venereal disease is further conſidered. 1766. 8. (6 d) Account of a ſingular caries of the skull. (Med. Obs. Vol. 5. p. 187.) A new method of applying a tube for the cure of the fiſtula lachrymalis. 1781. 4. (1 Sh.) überſ. Leipz. 1784. 8. The conductor and containing ſplints; or a description of two inſtruments for the ſafer conveyance and more perfect cure of fractured legs, with an account of two tourniquets —. 1767. (1 ſh.) Ed. 2. 1781. 8. (1 ſh. 6 d.) überſ. Samml. f. W. A. St. 6. S. 228.) On the theory and cure of the cataract —. 1785. 8. (3 ſh.) General remarks and cautions reſpecting ſome cases in ſurgery. (Mem. of M. S. of L. Vol. 1. p. 278.)

WATKINS, [......] *Coucy and Adelaide; a norman ſtory. 1784. 4. (2 ſh.)

WATKINSON, [John] *M. D: Phyſician to St. Thomas's Hoſpital.* born 1743. died d. 28 Aug. 1783.

WATSON, [.....] On the ſuperiority of iron to ſtone, for grinding corn. 1788. 8. (1 ſh. 6 d.)

—— [Henry] *Colonel.* born at *Holbeach.* 1737. died at *Dover* d. 17 Sept. 1786.

WATSON, [Henry] *F. R. S: Surgeon to the Westminster-Hospital.* (see *Mich. Morris.*) Description of the lymphatics of the urethra and neck of the bladder. (Phil. Tr. 1769. p. 392.) Account of the ſtomach of the Gillaroo trout. (Ibid. 1774. p. 121.) Account of Dr. *Maty's* illneſſ and of the appearances in the dead body, which was examined on the 3d of Auguſt 1776. the day after his decease. (Ibid. 1777. p. 608.) Account of a gouty body, diſſected. (M. C. Vol. 1. p. 86.) A caſe of ascites, in which the water was drawn off by tapping the vagina. (Ibid. p. 162.) Account of a large aneurism in the abdominal portion of the aorta; with ſome introductory reflections on the artery in its diseased ſtate. (Ibid. p. 178.) Account of the diſſection of the ſubject of the precedent case, with remarks. (Ibid. p. 234.)

—— [James] *Surgeon to the Roy. North-British Dragoons.* Hiſtory of an uncommon tumour on the breaſt, which was ſucceſſfully cured by means of a ſeton. (*Duncan's* M. C. Dec. 2. Vol. 1. p. 317.) Hiſtory of an uncommon mortification of the inferior extremities, which ſucceeded hard drinking and which terminated fatally. (Ibid. p. 323.) Account of the good effects of calomel in a case of obſtructed menses. (London M. J. Vol. 7. p. 413.) überſ. Samml. f. A. Th. XI. S. 698.

—— [John] *M. A. Rector of Stockport, Cheshire. F. A. S.* born: .... died d. 14 March. 1783.

—— [Richard] *D. D: F. R. S: LordBishop of Landaff; ArchDeacon of Ely and Profeſſor of Divinity in the Univerſity of Cambridge.* (before, Profeſſor of Chemiſtry at Cambridge till the Y. 1771.) Experiments and observations on various phaenomena attending the ſolution of ſalts. (Phil. Transact. 1770. p. 325.) Some remarks on the effects of the late cold in february 1771. (Ibid. 1771. p. 213.) Account of an experiment made with a thermometer, whose bulb was painted black and exposed to the direct rays of the ſun. (Ibid. 1773. p. 40.) Apology for chriſtianity in a ſeries of letters to *Edw. Gibbon.* 1776. 8. (3 ſh. 6 d.) Chemical experiments and observations on lead ore. (Phil. Transact. 1778. p. 863.) Chemical eſſays. Vol. 1-5. 1781-1787. 8.

8. (1 L. 2 sh.) übers. (von *Gallisch*) Th. 1. 2. Leipz. 1782. 8. On Orichalcum. (Mem. of M. Vol. 2. p. 47.) Collection of theological tracts. Vol. 1-6. 1785. 8. (1 L. 11 sh. 6 d.) Sermons on public occasions and tracts on religious subjects 1788. 8. (6 sh.) Addreß to young persons after confirmation. 1789. 8. (1 sh.) (Several single sermons.)

WATSON, [Robert] *D.D. Principal of the University of St. Andrews.* born: .... died d. 7 Apr. 1781.

—— [William] Jun. *M. D: F. R. S.* Account of the blue shark, together with a drawing of the same. (Phil. Transact. 1778. p. 789.) Account of a disease, occasioned by transplanting a tooth (Med. Transact. Vol. 3. p. 325. London M. J. Vol. VII. P. 2.) On time. 1785. 8. (2 sh. 6d.)

—— [William] *Sir. F. R. S. Trustee of the British Museum and Physician to the Foundling Hospital.* born at *London*: .... died d. 10 May. 1787.

WATT, [James] *Engineer.* Thoughts on the constituent parts of water and of dephlogisticated air; with an account of some experiments on that subject. (Phil. Transact. 1784 p 329. and p 354.) On a new method of preparing a test liquor to shew the presence of acids and alkalies in chemical mixtures (Ibid. 1784. p. 419)

WATTS, [Susanna] *Mrs.* The selector: 17.. Chinese maxims, translated from the oeconomy of human life into heroic verse. 1784. 12. (1 sh. 6 d.)

WEALES, [Thomas] *D. D. Vicar.* The christian orator delineated. 1778. 8. (4 sh.)
(Several single sermons.)

WEAVER, [Richard] *Schoolmaster in Chippenham.* Short exposition of the catechism of the church of England with annotations and reflections —. 1789. 8. (2 sh.)

WEBB, [B.....] *Clerk, Master of the Grammar School at Odiham, Hants.* On education. 1783. 8. (1 sh. 6 d.) Some reasons for thinking that the Greek language was borrowed from the Chinese: in notes on the grammatica sinica of *Fourmont.* 1787. 8. (2 sh.)

—— [Daniel] *Esq.* Enquiry into the beauties of painting and into the merits of the most celebrated painters, ancient and modern. 1760. 8. (3 sh. 6 d.) Remarks on the beauties of poetry. 1762. 8. (2 sh.)

*Observations on the correspondence between poetry and music. 1769. 8. (3 ſh.) überſ. von *J. J. Eſchenburg*. Leipz. 1771. 8. Literary amusements in verse and prose. 1787. 8. (2 ſh.)

WEBB, [Francis] *Clergyman*. Sermons. Vol. 1-4. 1766-1772. 8. (11 ſh.) (Several ſingle ſermons.)

—— [Philip Carteret] born: .... died at *Busbridge*. 1770.

—— [T......] New collection of epitaphs. Vol. 1. 2. 1775. 12. (7 Sh.)

WEBSTER, [Charles] *M. D: Phyſician to the Public Dispensary at Edinburgh*. Diſſ. De vasorum ſanguiferorum libramine. Edinb. 1777. 8. Medicinae praxeos ſyſtema ex Academiae Edinburgenae disputationibus. Vol. 1-3. 1780. 8. (13 Sh.) Account of the life and writings of Dr. *Archib. Pitcairne*. 1784. 8. *The Edinburgh new dispensatory — by Gentlemen of the faculty at Edinburgh. 1786. 8.

—— [James] *B. D: Fellow of St. John's College*, in *Cambridge*. Discourses on ſeveral ſubjects —. 1787. 8. (4 Sh.)

—— [J....] The conſtruction of the old wall at Verolam, the Roman bricks compared with the modern. (Arch. Vol. 2. p. 184.)

—— [J..... S.....] *Surgeon at Eaſt Dereham*. Account of a peculiarity of viſion in a girl at Eaſt Dereham in Norfolk. (London M. J. Vol. VIII. P. 3.)

—— [Samuel] Account of an oil-ſtone found at Salisbury. (Mem. of B. A. Vol. 1. p. 380.)

WEDDRED, [John] *Rector of St. John Baptiſt, Peterborough*. On the doctrine of imputed righteouſneſſ. 1782. 8. (6 d.) Apology for the permiſſion of natural and moral evils in a ſtate of trial. Ed. 2. 1786. 8. (1 Sh.) Thoughts on various cauſes of error particularly with regard to modern unitarian writers. 1787. 8. (1 Sh.) Scriptural view of the resurrection and aſcenſion of Jesus Chriſt —. 1787. 4. (1 Sh.)

WEDGWOOD, [Josiah] *F. R. S: F. A. S: Potter to her Majeſty*. Catalogue of cameos, intaglios, medals and bas-reliefs with a general account of vases and other ornaments after the antique —. 1773. 8. (1 Sh.) Ed. 2. 1778. 8. Ed. 3. 1790. 8. Attempt to make a thermometer for measuring the higher de-

degrees of heat, from a red heat up to the ſtrongeſt, that veſſels made of clay can ſupport. (Phil. Tr. 1782. p. 305. 1786. p. 390.) Some experiments upon the ochra friabilis nigro fusca of da *Coſta*, Hiſt. foſſ. p. 102. and called-Black wadd. (Ibid. 1783. P. 2.) Addreſſ to the workman in the pottery —. 1783. 8. Attempt to compare and connect the thermometer for ſtrong fire — with the common mercurial ones. (Phil. Tr. 1784. p. 358.) Letter to-proprietor of the navigation from the Trent to the Mersey, in anſwer, at his requeſt, to the aſſertions in a letter signed *an old proprietor* —. 1785. 4. (1 ſh.) Deſcription abregée du vase Barbarini, maintenant vase de Portland et de la methode que l'on a ſuivie pour en former les bas reliefs; accompagnée de conjectures ſur les ſujets, qui y ſont repreſentés 1790. 8. Description of the Portland vase; the manner of its formation and the various opinions hitherto advanced on the ſubjects of the bas reliefs. 1790 4. On the analysis of a mineral ſubſtance from New-South-Wales. (Phil. Transact. 1790. p. 306.)

WEIR, [John] °Divine truth rescued, or, the doctrine of the adorable trinity vindicated. by *J. W.* 1773. 8. (6d.) °The divinity of Chriſt and his atonement the only foundation of the chriſtian's hope and plea at the throne of grace —. by *J. W.* 1774. 8. (6 d.)

WELCH, [Joseph] A liſt of ſcholars of St. Peter's College, Weſtminſter, as they were elected to Chriſtchurch College, Oxford, and Trinity College, Cambridge, from the foundation by Queen Elizabeth 1561 to the present time —. 1788. 4. (10 ſh. 6 d.)

WELCHMAN, [John] *Surgeon at Kington in Warwickshire.* Caſe of a woman who underwent the ſection of the ſymphysis pubis. (London M. J. Vol. XI. P. 1.)

WELLS, [Chriſtopher] *Curate of St. Olave's, Southwark and Afternoon Preacher at Bermondsey.* Addreſſ to the genius of America. 1776. 4. (1 ſh.) Religion, a poem. 1777. 4. (1 ſh.)

— [David] *F. A. S:* born. d. 1 Aug. 1733. died d. 1 May. 1790.

WELLS, [Richard] Account of a machine for pumping veſſels at ſea without the labour of man. (Tr. of A. S Vol I. p. 229.)

WERNER, [Philipp] *Surgeon of the British Factory at Algiers.* Account of the inoculation of the ſmall pox in Algiers —. (London M J Vol. XI. P. 2.)

WESKETT, [John] *Merchant: Director of the Chamber of Commerce, Cornhill.* born: .... died d. 23. July. 1788.

WESLEY, [John] a *Methodiſt*, born at *Exworth Lincolnshire* 1703. died d. 2 March. 1791.

WEST, [.....] *Mrs* (Wife of a Northamptonshire Farmer.) Miscellaneous poetry. 1786. 4. (2 ſh. 6 d)

—— [Benjamin] *Esq: F. A. A* Account of the tranſit of Venus, as observed at Providence in New-England June 3d 1769 Tr of A. S. Vol. I. p. 97.) Account of the obſervations made in Providence in the ſtate of Rhode-Island, of the eclipse of the ſun d 23 Apr 1781. (Ibid p. 156.) On the extraction of roots. (Ibid p. 165.)

—— [Benjamin] of *Weeden beck, Northamptonshire.* Miscellaneous poems, translations and imitations. 1780. 8. (3 ſh.)

—— [J.....] The humours of Brighthelmſtone. 1788. 4. (1 ſh.) London's glory, on St. George's day 1789. with entertaining observations on the royal excursions —. 1789. 4. (1 ſh.)

—— [John] *Teacher of Mathematics in the Univerſity of St. Andrews.* Elements of mathematics —. 1784. 8. (7 ſh. 6 d)

—— [T....] *Captain.* Naval signals, conſtructed on a new plan 1788. 4 (3 ſh.)

—— [Thomas] born 1716. died d. 10 Jul. 1779.

WESTON, [Joseph] ſee *John Morfitt.*

—— [Richard] * Tracts on practical agriculture and gardening. 1769. 8. (6 ſh) Ed 2. (with the Author's name.) 1773 8. (6 ſh.) The universal botaniſt and nurseryman. Vol 1-3. 1770. 8. (16 ſh. 3 d.) The gardener's and planter's calendar. 1773. 8. (3 ſh. 6 d.)

—— [Stephan] *B D: Rector of Mamhead.* Hermeſianax ſ. conjecturae in *Athenaeum* atque aliorum poetarum loca —. 1784. 8. (3 ſh.) Attempt to translate and ex-

explain the difficult passages in the song of Deborah, with the assistance of *Kennicott's* collations, *Ross's* versions and critical conjecture. 1788. 4. (2 Sh.)

WHALLEY, [Peter Sedgwick] *Clergyman.* *Edwy and Edilda, a tale. 1779. 8. (3 Sh.) *Fatal kiss, a poem: written in a last stage of an atrophy, by a beautiful and unfortunate young Lady. 1781. 4. (2 Sh. 6 d.) Verses addressed to Mrs. *Siddons.* 1782. Mont Blanc, a poem. 1788. 4. (3 Sh.)

WHARTON, [.....] *Chaplain of the Catholic Church.* (born in *America.*) *Letter to the Roman catholics of the city of Worcester stating the motives which induced him to become a member of the Protestant church. 1784. 8. (6 d.)

WHATELY, [Thomas] *Surgeon: Oldjewry.* A large exfoliation of the tibia removed. (Mem. of M. S. of L. Vol. 1. p. 469.) Case of recovery from apparent death, in consequence of taking a large dose of opium. (Med. Obs. Vol. 6. p. 331.)

WHEATLEY, [Thomas] born: .... died 1772.

WHEELDON, [John] *Rector of Wheathamstead, Herts and Prebendary of Lincoln.* Two sermons. 1772. 8. The jewish bard; in 4 odes. 1779. 4. (1 Sh.)

WHEELER, [William] *Apothecary to the Magdalen-Hospital.* Case of a young lady who swallowed a knife, unattended with any disagreeable consequences. (Mem. of M. S. of L. Vol. 1. p. 322.)

WHIRLIGIG, [Christopher] *Esq. Cornet of Horse.* Poetical flights. 1788. 4. (1 Sh. 6 d.)

WHISHAW, [Humphrey] *A. M: Canon Residentiary of the Cathedral Church, Hereford.* Sermons. Vol. 1. 2. 1783. 8. (4 Sh.)

WHITAKER, [E..... W......] *Rector of St. Mildred's and Allsaints, Canterbury.* On the prophecies relating to the final restoration of the jews. 1784. 8. (1 Sh. 6 d.) Sermons on education. 1788. 8. (4 Sh.) Four dialogues on the doctrine of the holy trinity —. 1786. 8. (2 Sh.)

(Several single sermons.)

—— [John] *B. D: Rector of Ruan Lanyhorne, Cornwall: F. A. S.* Survey of the doctrine and argument of St. *Peter's* epistle with a paraphrastical exposition —. 1751. (1 Sh.) The History of Manche-

 ster.

ſter. Vol. 1. 2. 1771. 4. (1 L. 16 Sh.) The principal corrections made on republishing it in octavo 1773. 4. (3 Sh.) Ed. 2. Vol. 1. 2. 1773. 8. The genuine hiſtory of the Britons aſſerted, in a refutation of *Macpherson's* introduction to the hiſtory of Great-Britain and Ireland. 1772. 8. (4 Sh. 6 d.) Sermons upon death, judgment, heaven and hell. 1783. 8. (3 Sh.) *Mary* Queen of Scots vindicated. Vol. 1-3. 1787. 8. (18 Sh.) Ed. 2. Additions and corrections made in the ſecond Edition. 1790. 8. (7 Sh.)

WHITAKER, [L.....] Verses on the approach of peace 1765. Epiſtle to Mr. *Hickington*, to which is added, a ſeſſion of poets. 1770. 4. (1 Sh.)

WHITCHURCH, [J..... Wadham] Eſſay upon education. 1772. 8. (3 Sh.)

—— [S.....] *late of his Majeſty's Navy.* Monody to the memory of Admiral *Hyde Parker* —. 1785. 4. (1 Sh.)

WHITE, [Charles] *F. R. S: Surgeon to the Mancheſter Infirmary. Vice-Preſident of the Literary and Philosophical Society at Mancheſter.* Account of a remarkable operation, on a broken arme. (Phil. Transact. 1761. p. 657.) Account of a complete luxation of a thigh bone, in an adult person, by external violence. (Ibid. 1761. p. 676.) Account of a new method of reducing shoulders — without the use of an ambe. (Med. Obs. Vol. 2. p 373.) Account of the ſucceſſful treatment of a lock'd jaw and other ſpasmodic ſymptoms, ſuppoſed to have been occaſioned by a wound in the 4 finger of the left hand. (Ibid. p. 382.) On the topical application of the ſpunge in the ſtoppage of haemorrhages. 1762. 8. (1 Sh.) On a remarkable operation on a broken arm 1762. 8. (1 Sh.) Cases in which the upper head of the os humeri was ſawed off, a large portion of the bone afterwards, exfoliated and yet the entire motion of the limb was preserved. (Phil. Transact. 1766. p. 39.) Cases in ſurgery, with remarks and with *J. Aikin's* eſſay on the ligature of arteries. P. 1. 1770. (4 Sh. 6 d.) Account of a new method of amputating the leg a little above the encle joint, with a description of a machine particularly adapted to the ſtump. (Med. Obs. Vol. 4. p. 168.) On the management of pregnant and lying in women. 1773. Appendix. 1777. 8. (6 Sh.) Ed.

Ed. 2. 1777. überf. Leipz. 1775. 8. (überf. Von dem Nuzen der rohen Eyer bey der Gelbfucht. Samml. f. A. Th. 2. S. 88.) Account of the late Captain M°° case. (London M. J. Vol. 4. p. 159.) On fwellings in the lower extremities in lying in women. 1784. 8. (2 Sh. 6 d.) überf. Wien. 1785. 8. On the regeneration of animal fubftances. (Mem. of M. Vol. 1. p. 325.) On the natural hiftory of the cow, so far as it relates to its giving milk, particularly for the use of man. (Mem. of M. Vol. 1. p. 442.) Observations on a thigh bone of uncommon length. (Mem. of M. Vol. 2. p. 350.) Observations on gangrenes and mortifications, accompanied with, or occafioned by convulfive fpasms, or arifing from local injury producing irritation. (London M. J. Vol. XI. P. 2.) Observations on gangrenes and mortifications. 1790. 8. (1 fh.)

WHITE, [Gilbert] Account of the house — martin, or martlet. (Philos. Transact. 1774. p. 196.) Of the house-fwallow, fwift and fand-martin. (Ibid. 1775. p. 258.) *The natural Hiftory and antiquities of Selborne in the county of Southampton. 1789. 4. (1 L. 1 fh.)

— [James] *Esq.* The orations of *Cicero* againft *Verres* translated. 1787. 4. (18 fh.) *Hints for a fpecific plan for an abolition of the slave trade and for relief of the negroes in the Weft-Indies. 1788. 8. (1 fh.) Conway caftle; verses to the memory of the late Earl of *Chatham* and the moon, a fimile. 1789. 4. (2 Sh.) The adventures of John of Gaunt, Duke of Lancafter Vol. 1-3. 1790. 8. (9 fh) überf. Helmftädt. 1791. 8. *Earl ftrongbow: or the hiftory of Richard de Clare and the beautiful Geroldа. Vol. 1. 2. 1789. 8. (6 fh.) überf, (von *Georg Friederich Benecke*) Helmftädt 1790. 8.

— [John] *Esq: Surgeon General to his Majefty's forces and to the fettlement in New South-Wales.* Journal of a voyage to New-South-Wales with 65 plates of non descript animals, birds, lizards, ferpents, curious cones of trees and other natural productions. 1790. 4. (2 L.)

— [Joseph] *D. D: Profeffor of Arabic in the Univerfity of Oxford and Prebendary of Gloucefter.* De utilitate linguae Arabicae. 1776. 4. (1 fh. 6 d.)

Sermon on the revisal of the English translation of the old teſtament. 1779. 4. (1 ſh.) Sacrorum evangeliorum verſio Syriaca Philoxeniana —. 1779. 4. (2 L. 2 ſh.) Specimen of the civil and military inſtitutes of Timour or Tamerlane —. 1780. 4. (1 ſh. 6 d.) überſ. von C. F. *Preiſs*. Halle. 1781. 8. *Timour* inſtitutes, political and military, written in the Mogul language, translated into Perſian by *Abu Taulib Alhuſſeini* and there into English by Major *Davy* - published with notes. 1783. 4. (1 L. 11 ſh. 6 d.) Sermons, preached at *Bampton's* lecture in Oxford upon the comparative evidences of Mahometanism and Chriſtianity. 1784. 8. (6 Sh.) Ed. 2. 1785. 8. (7 Sh.) überſ. von *J. G. Burkhard*. Halle. 1786. 8. Fragmentum libri: Narrationes per noctes 1001. (Arabice.) 4. *Abdollatiphi* Hiſtoria Aegypti compendium. s. l. et a. 4. *Abdollatiphi* Compendium memorabilium Aegypti, arabice, praefatus eſt *H. E. G. Paulus*. Tubingae. 1789. 8. überſ. von *Wahl* 1790. 8. A ſtatement of his literary obligations to the late Rev. Mr. *S. Badcock* and the Rev. *S. Parr* LL. D. 1790. 8. (2 Sh. 6 d.)

WHITE, [Joseph] *Rector of Penhurſt, Suſſex.* Eſſay on ſacrifice. 1775. 8. (1 Sh.)

—— [Nathaniel] *Paſtor of the Congregation of Proteſtant Diſſenters at the Old Jewry.* born, 1729. died d. 1 March. 1783.

—— [Robert] *M. D: Practitioner in Surgery and Phyſician at Bury St. Edmunds.* Animadverſions on the increase of fevers and other diseases. 1760. 8. (6 d.) The use and abuse of ſea-water —. 1775. 8. (1 Sh.) Observations on fevers —. 1777. 8. (1 Sh.) The present practice of ſurgery. 1786. 8. (6 Sh.) Account of the ſalutary effect of bliſters in a case attended with ſymptoms of hydrocephalus internus. (London M. J. Vol. 3. p. 402.) On the nature and treatment of cancers. (Ibid. p. 70.)

—— [Thomas] *M. A: Vicar of Dunchurch, Warwikshire.* born: .... died d. 3 May. 1784.

—— [Thomas] *Surgeon in London.* On the ſtruma, or ſcrophula —. 1784. 12. (2 Sh.) überſ. (von *Diel*) Offenbach. 1788. 8. Account of an excurſion through the ſubterraneous cavern at Paris. (Mem. of M. Vol. 2. p. 361.)

WHITE,

WHITE, [William] *F. A. S: M. D: Physician at York.* (Quaker) born. 1744. died d. 25 Oct. 1790.

WHITECHURCH, [.....] The bath lovers; or, mercenary courtship, a tale. 1784. 4. (1 Sh.)

WHITEFIELD, [John] *M. A: Rector of Biddeford.* Conjectures on the Tyndaris of *Horace* and some other of his pieces. 1777. 4. (2 Sh.)

—— [George] (Author of the sect of Methodists at *Newbury in New-England*) born in *Gloucester* d. Dec. 1714. died at *Newbury, New-England.* d. 30 Sept. 1770.

WHITEHEAD, [John] Essay on liberty and necessity. 17.. Materialism philosophically examined —. 1778. 8. (2 Sh. 6 d.)

—— [John] *M. D: Physician to the London Dispensary. Doulce's* report of a new method of treating the child-bed or puerperal fever — translated from the French. 1783. 8. (1 Sh.)

—— [Paul] born at *London* 1710. died d. 30 Dec. 1774.

—— [William] *Poete Laureat; Register and Secretary of the Order of the Bath.* born: .... died d. 14 Apr. 1785.

WHITEHOUSE, [John] of St. *John's College, Cambridge.* Poems. 1787. 8. (3 Sh. 6 d.)

WHITEHURST, [John] *F. R. S.* born at *Congleton, Cheshire.* d. 10 Apr. 1713. died d. 18 Febr. 1788.

WHITELY, [Joseph] *A. M. Curate of Beeston in the Parish of Leeds.* On the necessity of a redeemer —. 1783. 8. (6 d.) Essay on the rewards of eternity. 1785. 4. (1 Sh.) On the advantages of revelation. 1787. 4. (2 Sh.) On the advantages of the knowledge revealed to mankind, concerning the holy spirit. 1788. 4. (1 Sh.) Essay on the following subject: voluntary neglect of any one duty cannot be compensated by strictness of attention to other duties. 1788. 4. (1 Sh.) Essay on the following subject: when the fulness of the time was come, God sent forth his son. 1790. 4. (1 Sh. 6 d.)

WHITING, [Thomas] The London Gentleman's and Schoolmaster's assistant. 1787. 12. (2 Sh.) The mental accountant: containing rules for performing the computations, which usually occur in business, without a pen —. 1788. 12. (1 Sh.)

WHITMORE, [William] Royal tears. 1785. 4. (2 Sh.)

WHITNEY, [Peter] Account of a ſingular apple-tree, producing fruit of oppoſite qualities; a part being frequently ſour and the other ſweet. (Mem. of B. A. Vol. 1. p 386.)

WHITWORTH, [Charles] Sir. *Chairman of the committee of ſupply and ways and means. Member of Parliament.* Obſervations on the new Weſtminſter paving act —. 1771. 8. (1 Sh.) Public accounts of ſervices and grants —. 1771. fol. (5 Sh.) The political and commercial works of *Charles Davenant* L. L. D. relating to the trade and revenue of England collected and reviſed. Vol. 1-5. 1771. 8. (1 L. 5 Sh.) The draught of an intended act for the better regulation of the nightly watch and beadles within the city of Weſtminſter. 1773. (1 Sh.) State of the trade of Great-Britain in its imports and exports, from the Year 1697. P. 1. 2. fol. 1776. (15 Sh.) überſ. *Dohms* Materialien für die Statiſtick —. Lieferung 2. S. 383. Regiſter of the trade of the port of London. Nro. 1. 1776. 8. (2 Sh.) Select orations of *M. T. Cicero:* translated by Prof. *Duncan* — adapted to the English reader. Vol. 1. 2. 1777. 8. (12 Sh.)

WHYTE, [Samuel] *Principal of the English Grammar School* The ſhamrok; or, the hibernian creſſes, a collection of poems, ſongs, epigrams —. 1772. 4. The theatre, a didactic eſſay including an idea of the character of Janeshore —. 1790. 8. (1 Sh.)

WICHE, [J......] Obſervations on the debate now in agitation concerning the divine unity —. 1787. 8. (6 d.)

WICKINS, [James] *Church-Warden of St. Mary's Pariſh.* Addreſſ to the inhabitants of the city of Litchfield on the expediency of uniting the ſeveral pariſhes of St. Mary, St. Michael and St. Chad, into one diſtrict for the better maintenance of their poor —. 1776. 4. (6 d.)

WIER, [Edward]. *Surgeon at Halifax in Nova Scotia.* Account of two caſes of hydrocephalus internus. (London M. J. Vol. 3. p. 78.) Account of ſome extraordinary ſymptoms occaſioned by worms, with farther remarks on hydrocephalus internus. (Ibid. Vol. 5. p. 393.)

WIGGLESWORTH, [Edward] *Professor of Divinity at Cambridge. F. A. S.* View of thermometrical and barometrical observations at Cambridge. (Mem. of B. A. Vol. I. p. 334.) Observations on the longevity of the inhabitants of Ipswich and Hingham and proposals for ascertaining the value of estates held for life, and the reversion of them. (Ibid. p. 565. Mem. of M. S. of L. Vol. VII. P. 3.)

WIGHT, [Alexander] *Advocate: F. A. S. Edinb.* On the laws, concerning the election of the different representatives sent from Scotland to the Parliament of Great-Britain; with a view of the constitution of the parliaments of England and Scotland before the union of the two kingdoms. 1773. 8. (5 sh.) Inquiry into the rise and progress of Parliament, chiefly in Scotland —. 1784. 4. (1 L. 1 sh.)

—— [Andrew] of *Ormiston in East-Lothian.* *Present state of husbandry in Scotland —. Vol. 1-6. 1778-1784. (1 L. 11 sh. 6 d.)

WIGNELL, [J.....] *Actor at Covent-Garden.* born: .... died d. 25 Jan. 1774.

WILBERFORCE, [William] *Esq.* Speeches in the house of Commons on the abolition of the slave trade. 1789. 8. (1 sh.)

WILDBORE, [Charles] On spherical motion. (Phil. Transact. 1790. p. 496.)

WILFORD, [Francis] *Lieutenant.* Remarks on the city of Tagara. (Asiat. Res. Vol. 1. p. 369.

WILKES, [John] *M. P: F. R. S: Lord Mayor of the city of London.* *The North Briton. Vol. 1. 2. 1763. (10 sh. 6 d.) *Essay on woman. 1763. 4. (1 sh.) Letter to a noble member of the club in Albemarle-Street. 1764. 4. (1 sh.) Letter to the electors of Aylesbury in the Y. 1764. 1768. 8. (6 d.) Letter to the Duke of *Grafton*, first Commissioner of his Majesty's Treasury. 1767. 8. (1 sh.) History of England from the revolution to the accession of the Brunswick line. 1768. 4. (2 sh. 6 d.) Letters between the Duke of *Grafton*, the Earls of *Halifax*, *Egremont*, *Chatham*, *Temple* and *Talbot*, Bar. *Botetourt*, *Henry Bilson Legge*, *John Cust*, *Charl. Churchill*, *Voltaire*, *Winckelmann* and *John Wilkes*. with notes Vol. 1. 1769. 8. Controversial letters. 1772. 8. (4 sh.) Speech on *North's* American taxation

tion bills. 1775. fol. (3 d.) Speech on his expulſion. 1775. fol. (6 d.) Speech on the motion for an addreſſ to his Majeſty againſt the Americans. 1775. (3 d.) Speeches — with notes. Vol. 1 - 3. 1777. 8. (8 ſh. 6 d.) Speeches in the house of commons. 1786. 8. (6 ſh.) Speech in the house of commons on Haſtings's impeachment. 1787. 8. (1 ſh.) Theophraſti charaĉteres ethici; graece. 1790. 4.

— [Richard] of *Willenhall* in the County of *Stafford. M. D.* born: .... died 17..

WILKIE, [William] *Profeſſor of Natural Philosophy in the Univerſity of St. Andrew in Scotland.* born: .,.. died d. 9 Oct. 1778.

WILKINS, [Charles] *Senior Merchant in the Service of the Eaſt - India Company on their Bengal Eſtabliſhment. F. R. S.* The Bhaguat - Geeta, or dialogues of Kreeshna and Arjoon in XVIII lectures, with notes. 1785. 4. (7 ſh. 6 d.) A royal Indian grant found at Mongueer - translated from the original Sanscrit. (Aſiat. Res. Vol. 1. p. 123.) An inscription on a pillar near Buddal: translated from the Sanscrit. (ibid. Vol. 1. p. 131.) Translation of a Sanscrit inscription copied from a ſtone at Booddha-Gaya. (Ibid. Vol. 1. p. 284.) Observations on the ſecks and their college. (Ibid. Vol. 1. p. 288.) überſ. *Sprengel's* u. *Forſter's* N. Beytr. zur Länder u. Völkerk. Th. 3. S. 143. The Heetopades of Veeshnoo - Sarma, in a ſeries of connected fables translated from an ancient manuscript in the Sanskreet language with notes. 1787. 8. (6 ſh.)

— [Thomas] Poems, divine and moral on ſeveral occaſions. 1780. 4. (3 ſh.)

WILKINSON, [George] *Surgeon at Sunderland.* Account of the ſucceſſful employment of catgut in a case of fiſtula in perinaeo. (London M. J. Vol. IX. Part. IV.) Case of hepatitis, with remarks. (Ibid. Vol. X. p. 142.) überſ. Samml. f. A. Th. 13. S. 363. Case of fractured ribs which terminated fatally; with the appearances on diſſection and remarks. (Ibid. Vol. XI. P. 2.)

— [T.....] An appeal to England, on behalf of the abused Africans, a poem. 1790. 4. (1 ſh.)

WILLAN, [Robert] *M. D: Physician to the Fensbury and Public Dispensaries in London.* Observations on the ſulphur water at Croſt near Darlington. 1782. 8. (1 ſh. 6 d.) The hiſtory of the miniſtry of Jesus Chriſt. 1782. 8. (4 ſh.) Ed. 2. 1786. 8. (3 ſh. 6 d.) Hiſtory of a case of hydrocephalus, with an account of the appearances on diſſection. (*Duncan's* M. C. 1780. p. 233.) Case of chorea Sti Viti, cured by cuprum ammoniacum. (London M. J. Vol. VII. P. 2.) überſ. Samml. f. A. Th. 12. S. 62. Singular termination of dropsy. (Ibid.) überſ. Samml. f. A. Th. XII. S. 23. On the use of arsenic in intermittent fevers. (Ibid. Vol. VIII. P. 2.) Case of obſtruction of the bowels; with remarks. (Ibid. Vol. 5. p. 401.)

WILLET, [Edward] Letters to Mrs. *Bellamy*, occaſioned by her apology. 1785. 8. (1 ſh. 6 d.)

WILLETT, [Ralph] *Esq: F. A. S.* *Description of the library at Marles in the country of Dorset. 1785. fol. Observations on the origin of printing. (Arch. Vol. 8. p. 239.)

WILLETS, [W.....] *Ebenez. Latham's* ſermons on various ſubjects - transcribed from the Author's own notes. Vol. I. 1774. 8. (5 ſh.) Sketch of the oeconomy of divine providence —. 1776. 8. (6 d.)

WILLIAM, [.....] *Captain.* Narrative, in which is contained particulars relative to the execution of Muſtapha Cawn and observations on the ſpeeches of *Bourgoyne*, *Fox*, *Fullarton*, *Burke* and *Francis*. 1790. 8. (1 ſh. 6 d.)

WILLIAMS, [Alexander] *M. D: Physician at Trinidad.* Account of the medicinal properties of a bark from South America. (London M. J. Vol. X. P. 2. überſ. Samml. f. A. Th. 13. S. 324.)

—— [Anna] *Mrs.* born: 1705. died d. 6 Sept. 1783.

—— [Anthony] *Rector of St. Keverne, in Cornwall.* Account of a remarkable thunder ſtorm. (Philos. Transact. 1771. P. 1. p. 71.)

—— [Benjamin] Discourses on various ſubjects and occations. 1770. 8. (5 ſh.) Diſſertation on ſcripture imprecations. 1780. 12. (1 Sh. 6 d.) The book of Psalms, translated, paraphrased or imitated by ſome of the moſt eminent English poets - with a diſſertation on ſcripture imprecations. 1781. 8. (4 Sh.)

WIL-

WILLIAMS, [Charles Hanbury] *Sir.* Odes. 1775. 8. (2 Sh. 6 d.)

—— [David] *Clergyman.* *Eſſays on public worship, patriotism and projects of reformation. 1773. 8. (1 Sh.) Appendix. 1774. (1 Sh.) *Sermons upon religious hypocrisy. Vol. 1. 2. 1774. 8. (6 Sh.) On education —. 1774. 8. (3 Sh. 6 d.) überſ. von *E. C. Trapp.* Berlin. 1781. 8. Letter to Mr. *Garrick.* 17.. * Liturgy on the universal principles of religion and morality. 1776. 8. (2 Sh.) überſ. von *F. L. Schoenemann.* Leipz. 1785. 8. Letter to proteſtant diſſenters upon the impropriety of the political conduct of their body. 17.. The nature and extent of intellectual liberty in a letter to *George Savile* —. 1779. 8. (1 Sh.) Lectures on the univerſal principles and duties of religion and morality. Vol. 1. 2. 1779. 4. (1 L. 1 Sh.) überſ. von *J. A. Eberhard.* Th. 1. 2. Halle. 1785. Letters concerning education. 1785. 8. (4 Sh.) Lectures on political principles —. 1789. 8. (5 Sh. 3 d.) Lectures on education. Vol. 1 - 3. 1789. 8. (15 Sh.)

(Several ſingle ſermons.)

—— [Edward] Published: *Marth. Morris's* ſocial religion exemplified in an account of the firſt ſettlements of chriſtianity in the city of *Cocrludd.* Ed. 4. 1787. 8. (3 Sh.) Antipaedobaptism examined: or, inquiry into the deſign and mode of baptism —. Vol. 1. 2. 1789. 8. (7 Sh. 6 d.)

—— [Edward] *Major of the Royal Artillery, at Quebec in Canada.* Experiments on the expanſive force of freezing water. (Tr. of E. S. Vol. 2. p. 23.)

—— [Helen Maria] *Miſſ.* *Edwin and Eltruda, a tale. 1782. 4. (2 Sh.) *Ode on the peace. 1783. 4. (1 Sh.) Peru, a poem. 1784. 4. (4 Sh.) Poems. Vol. 1. 2. 1786. 8. (6 Sh.) Poem on the bill for regulating the slave trade. 1788. 4. (1 Sh. 6 d.) Julia, a Novel. Vol. 1. 2. 1790. 8. (6 Sh.) Letters written in France, in the Summer 1790. to a friend in England, containing various anecdotes relative to the French Revolution and memoirs of Mons. and Madame Du F.... 1790. 8. (3 Sh.)

WILLIAMS, [John] *Esq.* The children of Thespis. 17.. The tears of Jerne, a poem; on the death of the late Duke of *Rutland.* 1787. 4. (1 Sh.)

WILLIAMS, [John] *Esq.* *The crisis of the colonies considered, with observations on the necessity of properly connecting their commercial interest with Great-Britain and America. 1785. 8. (1 Sh. 6 d.) Ed. 3. (with the Author's name.) 1787. 8. (1 Sh. 6 d.) An union of England and Ireland proved to be practicable and equally beneficial to each kingdom. 1787. 8. (1 Sh. 6 d.). The rise, progress and present state of the northern governments. Vol. 1. 2. 1777. 4. (1 L. 16 Sh.) übers. von *J. Ch. Adelung*. Th. 1. 2. 1779. Leipzig. 8.

— [John] *L. L. D. a Dissenting Clergyman.* Concordance to the Greek testament with the English version to each word —. 1767. 4. (12 Sh.) *Free enquiry into the authenticity of the 1 and 2 Chapt. of St. *Matthews* gospel - with a dissertation on the original language of that gospel. 1771. 8. (2 Sh. 6 d.) Ed. 2. 1790. 8. Address to the opposers of the protestant dissenting ministers, application for relief in the matter of subscription. 1772. 8. (1 Sh.) Thoughts on the origin and on the most rational and natural method of teaching the languages. 1784. 8. (2 Sh.)

— [John] *M. D.* Some histories of wounds of the head — with remarks on the convulsive cough of the Year 1764. in Cornwall. 1766. 8. (1 sh) On the medicinal virtues of the waters of Aix la Chapelle and Borset —. 1772. 8. (4 sh.) Advice to people afflicted with gout. 1774. 8. (1 sh. 6 d.) Select cases in physic. 1774. 8. (2 sh. 6 d.). On the medicinal virtues of the mineral waters of the German Spa. 1773. 8. (3 sh.)

— [John] *Mineral Engineer.* Account of some remarkable ancient ruins — in the Highlands. 1777. 8. (2 sh.)

— [Joseph] *Esq.* Considerations on the American war —. 1782. 4. (2 sh.) The criterion or disquisitions on the present administration —. 1782. 4. (1 sh.) *Letters on political liberty —. 1782. 8. (1 sh. 6 d.) Parliamentary reformation —. 1783. 4. (2 sh. 6 d.) Loose thoughts on the very important situation of Ireland —. 1785. 8. (1 sh. 6 d.)

— [J...... W......] Compendious digest of the statute law —. 1788. 8. (12 sh. 6 d.)

WILLIAMS, [Peter] *Chaplain of Christ-church.* Letters concerning education. 1785. 8. (4 sh.) (Several single sermons.)

—— [Samuel] *L. L. D: Prof. of Mathematics and Philosophy in the University at Cambridge. F. A. S.* Experiments on evaporation, and meteorological observations made at Bradfield in New-England. (Tr. of A S. Vol. 2. p. 118.) Account of the transit of venus over the sun June 1769. as observed at Newbury in Massachusetts. (Ibid. p. 246.) Memoir on the latitude of the university at Cambridge with observations on the variation and dip of the magnetic needle. (Mem. of B. A. Vol. 1. p. 62.) Astronomical observations, made in the state of Massachusetts. (Ibid. p. 81.) Account of a very uncommon darkness in the states of New-England, May 19. 1780. (Ibid. p. 234.) Observations on the earthquakes of New-England. (Ibid. p. 260.)

—— [Thomas] Method of proceeding to discover the variation of the earth's diameters —. 1786. 4. (4 sh.) Ed. 2. 1788. 8. (5 sh.)

—— [Thomas Walter] *Barrister at Law.* Compendious digest of the statute law comprising the substance and effect of all the public acts of parliament in force from magna charta to the 27 Year of George III. Ed. 2. 1788. 8. Supplement 1789. 8. (12 sh.)

—— [William] *Curate of St. Mary's at Reading and Rector in Pembrokeshire.* born: .... died d. 9 Nov. 1786.

—— [William] *Esq. late of St. John's College, Cambridge.* The christian history — with ten dissertations. 1776. 8. (3 sh.)

WILLIAMSON, [......] The lawyer, a comedy. 1783.

—— [.....] *Captain in the Essex militia.* *Advice to the officers of the British army. 1783. 8. (2 sh.)

—— [Hugh] *M D. at Philadelphia.* On the use of comets and on account of their luminous appearance, with some conjectures concerning the origin of heat. (Tr of A. S. Vol. 1. App. p. 27.) Attempt to account for the change of climate, which has been observed in the middle colonies in North-America. (Ibid. p. 272.) Experiments and observations on the gymnotus electricus or electrical eel. (Phil. Transact. 1775. p. 94.)

WILLIAMSON, [James] D. D: *Professor of Mathematics in the University of Glasgow.* Argument for natural and revealed religion. 1777. 8. (1 sh.) Argument for the christian religion — in XXIV sermons. 1783. 8. (3 sh. 6 d.) The elements of *Euclid*, with dissertations —. Vol. 1. 2. 1789. 4. (1 L. 5 sh.) A defence of the doctrines, establishment and conduct of the church of England, from the charges of *Joseph Berington* and *John Milner*. 1790. 8. (1 sh.)
(Several single sermons.)

—— [W. . . . .] *Teacher of the Stenography in London.* Stenography: or, a concise and practical system of short-hand writing —. 1775. 8. (10 sh. 6 d.)

WILLIARD, [Joseph] D. D: *President of the University and Vice-President of the American Academy at Boston.* Method of finding the altitude and longitude of the nonagesimal degree of the ecliptic; with an appendix, containing calculations from corresponding astronomical observations, for determining the difference of meridians between Harvard-Hall in the University of Cambridge, in the Commonwealth of Massachusetts and the royal observatories at Greenwich and Paris. (Mem. of B. A. Vol. 1. p. 1.) Table of the equations to equal altitudes, for the latitude of the University of Cambridge 42° 23′ 28″ with an account of its construction and use. (Ibid. p. 70.) Observations of a solar eclipse Oct. 27. 1780. made at Beverley; of a lunar eclipse March. 29. 1782. — of a solar eclipse April 12 and of the transit of mercury over the sun's disc, Nov. 12. 1782. (Ibid. p. 129) Observations made at Beverly - to determine the variation of the magnetical needle. (Ibid. p. 318.) Letter, concerning the longitude of Cambridge in New-England. (Phil. Transact. 1781. p. 502.)

WILLIS, [Cecil] D. D: *Vicar of Holbeach and Prebendary of Lincoln.* born: .... died d. 22 Oct. 1786.

—— [John] *B. D: Vicar of Ridge, Herts.* Actions of the apostles, translated. 1789. 8. (10 sh. 6 d.)

—— [Richard] Account of the ancient and modern state of Crim-Tartary and of the imports and exports at the different maritime towns on the coast of the black sea. 1787. 8. (2 sh. 6 d.) Essay on the

Ikineld - ſtreet. (Arch. Vol. 8. p. 85.) On the Roman portway. (Ibid. p. 100.) Account of the battles between Edmund Ironſide and Canute. (Ibid. p. 106.)

WILLIS, [William Auguſtus] *M. D.* The ſacrifice, a ſacred ode. 1779. 4. (1 ſh.)

WILLISON, [Andrew] *Phyſician in Dundee.* Hiſtory of two caſes of compound fractures, demonſtrating the benefit to be derived from the excluſion of air. (*Duncan's* M. C. Dec. 2. Vol. 4. p. 310.) Hiſtory of a caſe, in which remarkable adheſions of the inteſtinal canal terminated fatally. (Ibid. 1790. Dec. 2. Vol. 5. p. 355.)

WILLS, [Thomas] *A. B: Chaplain to the Counteſs of Huntingdon.* Remarks on polygamy — in anſwer to *Madan's* Thelyphthora. 1781. 8. (2 ſh. 6 d.)

WILMER, [B.....] *Surgeon in Coventry, Warwickſhire.* Account of the good effects of dividing the aponevroſis of the biceps muſcle in a painful lacerated wound. (Med. Obs. Vol. 4. p. 338.) Account of a woman accidentally burnt to death in Coventry. (Phil. Tranſact. 1774. p. 340.) Caſes and remarks in ſurgery with the method of curing the bronchocele. 1780. 8. (5 ſh.) Obſervations on the poiſonous vegetables which are either indigenous in Great-Briſain, or cultivated for ornament 1780. 8. (2 ſh.) Practical obſervations on herniae, illuſtrated with caſes 1788. 8. (1 ſh. 6 d.) Account of a large maſſ of hydatids diſcharged from the uterus. (London M. J. Vol. VIII. P. 4.) Hiſtory of a remarkable affection of the legs, terminating fatally. (*Duncan's* M. C. Dec. 2. Vol. 4. p. 302.)

WILSON, [.....] *M. D.* Aphoriſms compoſed for a text to practical lectures on the conſtitution and diſeaſes of children. 1783. 8. (1 ſh.)

— [Alexander] *Profeſſor of Aſtronomy at Glasgow.* born: .... died d. 18 Oct. 1786.

— [Alexander] *M. D.* Obſervations on the influence of climate on vegetable and animal bodies. 1780. 8. (5 ſh.) überſ. Leipzig. 1781. 8.

— [Andrew] *M. D: Fellow of the Roy. College of Phyſicians at Edinburgh.* Diſſertatio de luce. Edinb. 1749. 4. *Eſſay on the autumnal dyſentery, by a phyſician. 1760. 8. (1 ſh. 6 d.) Remarks upon au-

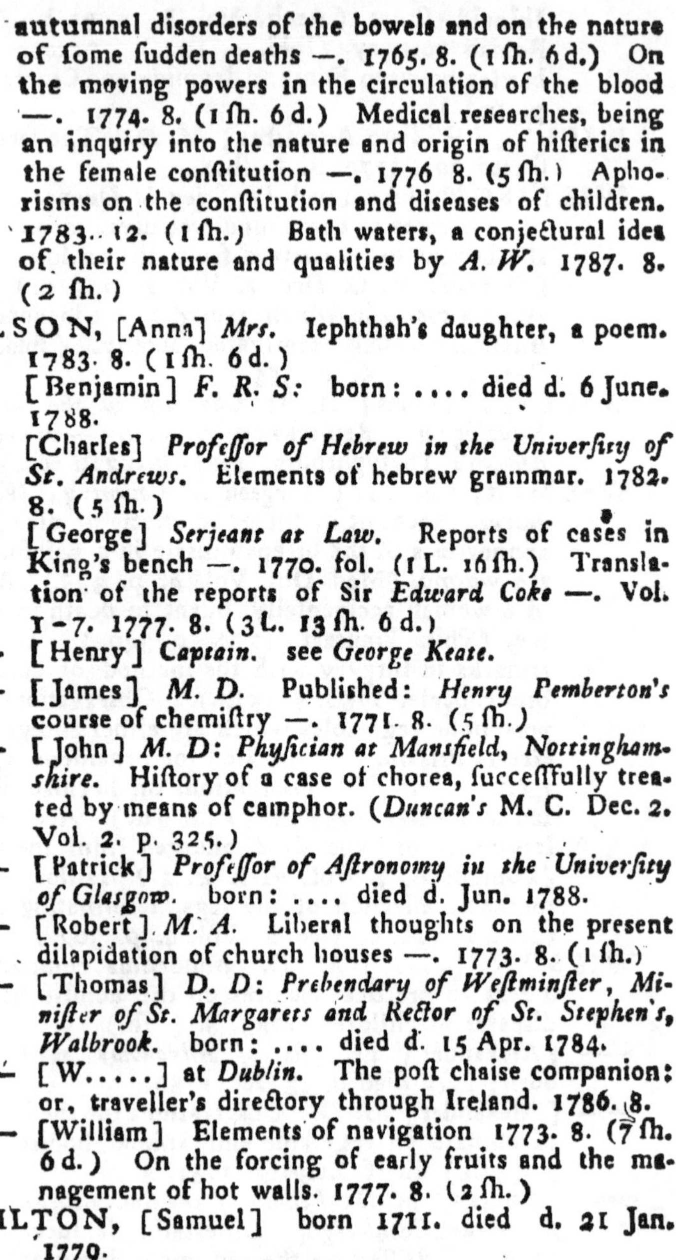

autumnal disorders of the bowels and on the nature of ſome ſudden deaths —. 1765. 8. (1 ſh. 6 d.) On the moving powers in the circulation of the blood —. 1774. 8. (1 ſh. 6 d.) Medical reſearches, being an inquiry into the nature and origin of hiſterics in the female conſtitution —. 1776 8. (5 ſh.) Aphoriſms on the conſtitution and diſeaſes of children. 1783. 12. (1 ſh.) Bath waters, a conjectural idea of their nature and qualities by *A. W.* 1787. 8. (2 ſh.)

WILSON, [Anna] *Mrs.* Iephthah's daughter, a poem. 1783. 8. (1 ſh. 6 d.)

—— [Benjamin] *F. R. S:* born: .... died d. 6 June. 1788.

—— [Charles] *Profeſſor of Hebrew in the Univerſity of St. Andrews.* Elements of hebrew grammar. 1782. 8. (5 ſh.)

—— [George] *Serjeant at Law.* Reports of caſes in King's bench —. 1770. fol. (1 L. 16 ſh.) Tranſlation of the reports of Sir *Edward Coke* —. Vol. 1-7. 1777. 8. (3 L. 13 ſh. 6 d.)

—— [Henry] *Captain.* see *George Keate.*

—— [James] *M. D.* Publiſhed: *Henry Pemberton's* courſe of chemiſtry —. 1771. 8. (5 ſh.)

—— [John] *M. D: Phyſician at Mansfield, Nottinghamſhire.* Hiſtory of a caſe of chorea, ſucceſſfully treated by means of camphor. (*Duncan's* M. C. Dec. 2. Vol. 2. p. 325.)

—— [Patrick] *Profeſſor of Aſtronomy in the Univerſity of Glasgow.* born: .... died d. Jun. 1788.

—— [Robert] *M. A.* Liberal thoughts on the preſent dilapidation of church houſes —. 1773. 8. (1 ſh.)

—— [Thomas] *D. D: Prebendary of Weſtminſter, Miniſter of St. Margarets and Rector of St. Stephen's, Walbrook.* born: .... died d. 15 Apr. 1784.

—— [W.....] at *Dublin.* The poſt chaiſe companion: or, traveller's directory through Ireland. 1786. 8.

—— [William] Elements of navigation 1773. 8. (7 ſh. 6 d.) On the forcing of early fruits and the management of hot walls. 1777. 8. (2 ſh.)

WILTON, [Samuel] born 1711. died d. 21 Jan. 1779.

—— [Samuel] *D. D.* born. 1744. died d. 3 Apr. 1778.

WILTON, [Thomas] born 1745. died d. 5 Aug. 1776.

WIMPEY, [Joseph] Thoughts on exportation of corn on the high price of provisions, on manufactures, commerce. 1770. 8. (1 sh.) Letter to the authors of the monthly review by their remarks on two pamphlets published —. 1771 8. (6 d.) The challenge; or, patriotism put to the test, in a letter to Dr. *Price* —. 1772. 8. (1 sh. 6 d.) On the present high price of provisions. 1772. 8. (1 sh. 6 d.) Defense of thoughts upon several interesting subjects. 1772. 8. (1 sh.) Rural improvements: or essays on the most rational methods of improving estates —. 1777. 8. (5 sh.) Letters occasioned by three dialogues concerning liberty —. 1777. 8. (1 sh. 6 d.) On oeconomical registers. (Mem. of M. Vol 1. p. 134.) On the impropriety of allowing a bounty to encourage the exportation of corn. (Ibid. p 413.)

WINDHAM, [Joseph] *Esq.* Observations upon a passage in *Pliny's* natural history, relative to the temple of Diana at Ephesus. (Arch. Vol. 6. p. 67.)

WINN, [J.... L....] *Captain.* Account of the appearance of lightning on a conductor fixed from the summit of the mainmast of a ship, down to the water. (Phil. Transact. 1770. p. 188.)

— [J.... S.....] Remarks on the aurora borealis. (Phil. Transact. 1774. p. 128.)

WINSHIP, [Amos] of *Boston*, *Massachusetts.* *M. D.* History of a case of incisted dropsy, with a dissection. (Mem. of M. S. of L. Vol. 2. p. 368.)

WINSTANLEY, [T......] *A. M.* *Aristoteles* de poetica, cum observationibus. 1780. 8. (6 sh.)

WINTER, [George] *Member of the Society of Arts in London, of the Bath Agricultural Society, of the Odiham Agriculture Society and of the Society for the Participation of Useful Knowledge at Norwich.* A new compendious system of husbandry —. 1787. 8. (6 sh.)

WINTERSTED, [......] *Wieland's* Socrates out of his senses, or dialogues of Diogenes of Sinope, translated. Vol. 1. 2. 1772. 8. (4 sh.)

WINTHORP, [John] *L. L. D: Professor of Mathematics at Cambridge.* born: .... died 17..

WINTHROP, [James] *Esq. F. A. A.* Account of the tranſit of mercury obſerved at Cambridge Nov. 12. 1782. (Mem. of B. A. Vol. 1, p. 159.)

WINTRINGHAM, [Clifton] *M. D: F. R. S: Phyſician to the King.* Experimental inquiry on ſome parts of the animal ſtructure. 1740. 8. Ed. 2. 1777. 8. Enquiry into the exility of the veſſels of the human body. 1743. 8. The works of the late *Clifton Wintringham* — publiſhed by his ſon —. Vol. 1. 2. 1752. 8. überſ von *Joh. Ephr. Lietzau.* Th. 1. 2. Berlin. 1791. 8. De morbis quibusdam commentarii. 1782. 8. (4 ſh.) überſ. Samml. f. A. Th 8. S. 197. S. 402.

WISE, [Joseph] *Rector of Penhurſt, Suſſex.* The coronation of David. 1766. 8. Providence, a poem. 1766. (1 ſh.) Ed. 2. 1769. 8. (1 ſh 6 d.) Miscellany of poems. 1775. 8. (3 ſh.) Eſſay on ſacrifice. 1775. 8. (1 ſh.) Nadir, a poem. 1779. The ſyſtem, a poem. 1781. 8. (5 ſh. 6 d.)

WISHAW, [Humphrey] *A. M.* Sermons. Vol. 1. 2. 1782. 8. (8 ſh.)

WITHERING, [William] *M. D. Phyſician to the General Hoſpital at Birmingham, Warwikshire: F. R. S.* Experiments on the different kinds of marle found in Staffordſhire. (Phil. Transact. 1773. p. 161.) Diſſ. De Angina gangraenosa. Edinb. 1776. 8. Botanical arrangement of all the vegetables growing in Great-Britain. Vol. 1. 2. 1776. 8. (14 ſh.) Ed. 2. Vol. 1-3. 1789. (17 ſh. 6 d.) Account of the ſcarlet fever and ſore throat. 1779. 8. (1 ſh. 6 d.) überſ. von *J. A. J. Saur.* Frankf. 1781. 8. überſ. Samml. f. A. Th. 5. S. 251. Account of a new method of impregnating water with fixed air. (*Prieſtley's* Experim. in Nat. Philoſophy. Vol. 2. p. 389.) Analysis of two mineral ſubſtances; viz: the *Rowley* ragſtone and the toadſtone. (Phil. Transact. 1782. p. 327.) *Torb. Bergman's* Outlines of mineralogy translated. 1783. 8. (2 ſh. 6 d.) Experiments and obſervations on the terra ponderosa —. (Phil. Transact. 1784. p. 293.) überſ Samml. z. P. u. Ng. Th. 3. S. 737. Account of the foxglove and ſome of its medical uses. 1785. 8. (5 ſh.) überſ. von *C. F Michaelis.* Leipz. 1786. 8. überſ. Samml. f. A. Th. XI S. 155. Account of ſome ex-

extraordinary effects of lightning. (Phil. Transact. 1790. p. 293.)

WITHERS, [......] born: .... died in *Newgate* d. 24 July 1790.

—— [Philipp] *D. D: Chaplain to Lady Dowager Hereford.* Letter to *Sam. Dennis* D. D. in reply to a letter, signed Vindex in the St. James's Chronicle of the 16 Oct. 1783. 8. (6 d.) Philanthropos, or, a letter to *Andr. Fuller* in reply to his treatise on damnation —. 1785. 12. (2 ſh. 6 d.)

—— [Thomas] *M. D: Phyſician to the York County-Hospital.* Diſſ. De febribus continuis medendis. Edinb. 1772. 8. Observations on the abuse of medicine. 1776. 8. (4 ſh.) überſ. Leipz. 1776. 8. Observations on chronik weakneſſ. 1777. 8. (2 ſh. 6 d.) On the aſthma. 1786. 8. (5 ſh.) überſ. von C. F. *Michaelis.* Leipz. 1787. 8.

WITHERSPOON, [John] *DD: Preſident of a College at Prince Town in New-Jersey.* Eſſays on important ſubjects — to which are added eccleſiaſtical characteriſtics, or the arcana of church policy, with an apology. Vol. 1-3. 1764. 8. (9 ſh.) Practical discourses on the leading truths of the gospel. 1768. 8. (3 ſh.) Sermons on practical ſubjects —. 1768. 8. (3 ſh.) Addreſſ to the natives of Scotland residing in America. 1778. 8. (6 d.)

(Several ſingle ſermons.)

WODHUL, [Michael] Ode to the muses. 1760. 4. (1 ſh.) Epiſtle to ***. 1761. 4. (1 Sh.) Two odes, to *Sally Fowler* and to the *Dryads.* 1764. 4. The equality of mankind, a poem. 1766. 4. (1 Sh. 6 d.) The nineteen tragedies and fragments of *Euripides* translated. Vol. 1-4. 1782. 8. (1 L. 1 Sh.)

WODROW, [James] *D. D. Will. Leechman's* D. D. ſermons, with an account of the Author's life and of his lectures. Vol. 1. 2. 1790. 8. (12 Sh.)

WOLLASTON, [Francis] *LL. D: F. R. S: Precentor of the Dioceſs of St. David's and Rector of the Pariſh of St. Mary's, Aldermary, London.* Addreſſ to the clergy of the church of England in particular, and to all chriſtians in general. 1772. 8. (6 d.) Queries relating to the book of common prayer. 1774. 8. (1 Sh.)

WOLLASTON, [Francis] *L. L. D: F. R. S:* Observations of the eclipse of the ſun June 4. 1769. in the morning. (Phil. Transact. 1769. p. 407.) Observations of the tranſit of venus over the ſun June 3. 1769. made at Eaſt Dereham in Suffolk. (Ibid. 1769. p. 407.) Account of the going of an aſtronomical clock. (Ibid. 1771. p. 559.) Aſtronomical obſervations made at Chiſlehurſt in Kent in the Y. 1773. (Ibid. 1773. p. 67. 1774. p. 329. 1775. p. 290.) On a method of deſcribing the relative poſitions and magnitudes of the fixed ſtars; together with ſome aſtronomical obſervations. (Ibid. 1784. p. 181.) Deſcription of a new ſyſtem of wires in the focus of a teleſcope, for obſerving the comparative right aſcenſions and declinations of celeſtial objects; together with a method of inveſtigating the ſame, when obſerved by the rhombus, though it happen not to be truly in an equatorial poſition. (Ibid. 1785. p. 346.) Account of Miſſ *Herſchel's* comet, in Auguſt and September 1786. (Ibid. 1787. p. 55.) The preface to a ſpecimen of a general aſtronomical catalogue arranged in zones of North-Polar diſtance and adapted to Jan. 1. 1790. — 1789. 8. (1 ſh. 6 d.) Specimen of a general aſtronomical catalogue arranged in zones of North-Polar diſtance —. 1789. fol. (3 L. 3 ſh.)

WOLLASTON, [F. J. H.] *M. A: F. R. S.* Obſervations of a luminous arch. (Phil. Transact. 1790. p. 43.)

WOLLSTONECRAFT, [Mary] *Miſſ.* Thoughts on the education of daughters, with reflections on female conduct in the more important duties of life. 1787. 8. (2 ſh.) The rights of men. 17..

WOLSTENHOLME, [Henry] *M. A. Rector of Liverpool.* born: .... died 1771.

WOOD, [James] Grammatical inſtitution, or a practical Engliſh grammar. 1779. 8. (1 ſh. 6 d.)

—— [John] *Architect.* The deſcription of the hot bath at Bath, together with plans, elevations and ſections of the ſame —. 1778. fol. (5 ſh.).

—— [John] *B. D: Rector of Cadleigh in Devonſhire.* Inſtitutes of eccleſiaſtical and civil polity. 1773. 8. (2 ſh.) On the fundamental or moſt important doctri-

doctrines of natural and revealed religion. 1774. 8. (2 ſh.) Conſiderations of the great Mr. *Locke*, on raiſing the value of money —. 1775. 8. (1 ſh. 6 d.)

WOOD, [John] The duke of Rothsay, a tragedy. 1780. 8.

—— [Loftus] *M. D: Phyſician to the Miſericordia General Diſpenſary at London.* Caſes, medical, chirurgical and anatomical, with obſervations ſelected and tranſlated – from the Hiſtory and Memoirs of the R. Acad. of Sciences at Paris from the Y. 1666. to the preſent time. 1776. Vol. 1. N. 1. 2. 3. 8° (3 ſh.) Obſervations on a new and eaſy method of curing diſorders by factitious air without the uſe of drugs. 1780. 8. (1 ſh.) The valetudinarian's companion; or, obſervations on air, exerciſe and regimen, with the medical properties of the ſea and mineral waters of Brighthelmſtone. 1782. 8. (1 ſh 6 d.)

—— [Robert] born: .... died at London. 1772.

—— [Samuel] Strictures on the gout. 1776. 8. (1 ſh. 6 d.)

—— [Thomas] *Miller at Billericay, Eſſex.* The miller's and farmer's guide, containing plain and eaſy tables —. 1777. 8. (2 ſh. 6 d.)

—— [William] *Diſſenting clergyman.* Sermons on ſocial life. 1775. 8. (3 ſh.) Two ſermons on the celebration of the 100 anniverſary of the happy revolution. 1788. 8. (1 ſh. 6 d.)

(Several ſingle ſermons.)

—— [William] Book-keeping familiariſed: or, the young's clerk's manufacturer's and ſhop-keeper's directory. 1778. 8. (4 ſh.)

WOODESON, [Richard] *LL. D. Profeſſor of Law at Oxford.* Elements of juriſprudence. 1783. 4. (5 ſh.)

WOODFALL, [William] *Printer.* *Editor of the morning chronicle. Sketch of the debate in the houſe of commons in Ireland upon the rejection of the twenty commercial propoſitions —. 1785. 8. (3 ſh. 6 d.)

WOODHOUSE, [James] *Iourneyman Schoemaker.* Poems on ſeveral occaſions. Ed. 2. 1766. 8. (5 ſh.) Poems on ſeveral occaſions never before publiſhed. 1787. 4. (3 Sh.)

WOODWARD, [Henry] *Actor.* born in London 1717. died d. 17 Apr. 1777.

WOODWARD, [Richard] *D. D: Bishop of Cloyne in Ireland.* Addreſſ on the expediency of a regular plan for the maintenance and government of the poor. 1776. 8. (3 Sh.) Present ſtate of the church of Ireland conſidered. 1778.

—— [T.....] *Middle Temple.* The law of diſtreſſes for rent. 1789. 8. (1 Sh.)

—— [Thomas] *Esq* Account of a new plant, of the order of fungi (Phil. Transact. 1784. p. 423.)

WOOFFENDALE, [R.....] *Surgeon-Dentiſt at Liverpool.* Practical observations on the human teeth. 1783. 8. (3 Sh. 6 d.)

WOOLCOMB, [Thomas] *Surgeon.* Case of a locked jaw. (Phil. Transact. 1765. p. 85.) Case of a boy, who died of a gun-shot wound. (Ibid. 1770. p. 94.)

WOOLCOT, [John] *M. D: Practitioner of Phyſic in the Island of Iamaica; now in London.* (born at Cornwall.) Lyric odes to the Academicians. 1782. 4. (6 d.) More lyric odes to the Royal Academicians. 1783. 4. (1 Sh.) Lyric odes for the Year 1785. 4. (2 Sh. 6 d.) The Louſiad: an heroic comic poem. Canto. 1. 2. 3. 1785. 1791. 4. (6 Sh.) Farewell odes. 1786. (3 Sh.) A poetical and congratulatory epiſtle to *James Boswell*, on his journal of a tour to the Hebrides. 1786. 4. (2 Sh.) *Bozzy* and *Piozzi* or the british biographers. 1786. 4. (2 Sh. 6 d.) Ode upon ode, or a peep at St. James. 1787. 4. (3 Sh.) An apologetic poſtscript to ode upon ode. 1787. 4. (2 Sh.) Inſtructions to a celebrated Laureat —. 1787. 4. (2 Sh. 6 d.) Brother *Peter*, to brother Tom. 1788. 4. (3 Sh.) *Peter's* pension, a ſolemn epiſtle. 1788. 4. (3 Sh.) Sir *J. Banks* and the Emperor of Marocco. 1788. 4. (1 Sh. 6 d.) Epiſtle to his pretended cousin *Peter* —. 1788. 4. (2 Sh. 6 d) A ſupplicating epiſtle to the reviewers. 17.. (1 ſh.) *Peter's* prophecy; or, the preſident and poet; or, an important epiſtle to Sir *J. Banks* on the approaching election of a preſident of the Royal Society —. 1788. 4. (3 Sh.) Subjects for painters. 1789. 4. (3 Sh. 6 d.) A poetical epiſtle to a falling miniſter; also an imitation of the 12th Ode of *Horace.* 1789. 4. (2 Sh. 6 d.) Expoſtulary odes to a great Duke and a little Lord. 1789. 4. (2 Sh. 6 d.) A benevolent epiſtle to *Sylvanus Urban.* 1790.

1790. 4. (2 Sh. 6 d.) Advice to the future Laureat; an ode. 1790. 4. (1 Sh. 6 d.) Letter to the most insolent man alive. 1790. 4. A complimentary epistle to *James Bruce* Esq. the Abyssinian traveller. 1790. 4. (2 Sh. 6 d.)

WOOLLEY, [William] *Chaplain to the Marshalsea.* Vox clamantis; or, an alarm to the British youth. 1787. 12. (6 d.)

WORMULL, [Thomas] *Engraver.* see *Hugh Clark.*

WORSLEY, [John] of *Hertford.* Grammar for the Latin tongue. 1770. 8. (2 sh.) The new testament translated with notes —. 1770. 8. (6 sh.)

—— [Richard] *F. R. S: late Comptroller of the Household to his Majesty.* *History of the Isle of Wight. 1781. 4 (1 L. 7 sh) Trial with *G. M. Bisset* for criminal conversation with the plaintiff's wife —. 1782. 4. (1 sh.) *The whim; or the maidstone bath, a kentish poetic. 1782. 4. (1 sh. 6 d.) *Genuine anecdotes of Sir Richard Easy and Lady Wagtail. 1782. 8. (2 sh. 6 d.)

WORTHINGTON, [Hugh] Jun. *M. A: Dissenting Clergyman at Leicester.* On the resolution of plain triangles by common arithmetic. 1780. 8. (1 sh.) Discourses on various subjects evangelical and practical. 1786. 8. (5 sh.)

(Several single sermons.)

—— [James] *M. D: Physician at Liverpool, Lancashire.* Experiments on the Spa at Mount Sion, near Liverpool. 1773. 8. (1 sh.)

—— [Joseph] *LL. D.* New universal prayer-book —. 1779. 8. (3 sh.) Preparation for the sacrament of the Lord's supper. 1780. 8. (1 sh.)

—— [Richard] *M. D.* *Letter to the jews - by a layman. 1787. 8. Disquisitions on several subjects, 1) on the nature of time, 2) on the imperfection of human knowledge, 3) on the heavenly bodies. 4) on reason and instinct. 5) on education. 1787. 12. (3 sh.)

—— [William] *D. D: Vicar at Rhaider.* born 1703. in the County *Merioneth:* died 1778.

WOTY, [William] The muse's advice. 1761. 4. (1 sh.) The blossoms of Helicon. 1763. 8. (3 sh.) The poetical calendar, containing a collection of scarce and valuable pieces of poetry — written and se-

ſelected by *Franc. Fawkes* and *W. Wory.* Vol. 1-12. 1763. (18 ſh.) Poetical works. 1770. 12. (6 ſh.) The female advocate, a poem. 1770. 4. (2 ſh.) Church langton, a poem. 1773. 4. (1 ſh. 6 d.) * The eſtate orators, an eclogue. 1774. 4. (1 ſh.) Particular providence, a poetical eſſay. 1775. 4. (1 ſh.) The country gentleman, or the choice ſpirits, a drama. 1786. 8.

WOULFE, [Peter] *F. R. S.* Experiments on the diſtillation of acids, volatile alkalies, — ſhewing how they may be condensed without loſſ and how thereby we may avoid disagreeable and noxious fumes. (Phil. Transact. 1767. p. 517.) Experiments to shew the nature of aurum mosaicum. (Ibid. 1771. p. 114.) Experiments on a new colouring ſubſtance from the Island of Amſterdam in the South Sea. (Ibid. 1775. p. 91.) Experiments made in order to ascertain the nature of ſome mineral ſubſtances; and in particular, to see how far the acids of ſea ſalt and of vitriol contribute to mineralize metallic and other ſubſtances. (Ibid. 1776. p. 605.) Experiments on ſome mineral ſubſtances. (Ibid 1779. p. 11.)

WRAGG, [F.....] *Maſter of the Boarding ſchool, Church-Street, Stoke Newington, Middlesex.* Dialogue betwixt a maſter and his ſcholar —. 1788. 12. (1 ſh. 6 d.)

WRAXALL, [Nath. William] *M. P.* Remarks made in a tour through ſome of the northern parts of Europe, particularly Copenhagen, Stockholm and Petersburgh. 1775. 8. (5 ſh.) überſ. Leipz. 1775. 8. Memoirs of the Kings of France of the race of Valois — with a tour through the weſtern, ſouthern and interior provinces of France. Vol. 1. 2. 1777. 8. (10 Sh. 6 d.) Ed. 2. Vol. 1. 2. 1785. 8. (12 Sh.) Tour through the weſtern, ſouthern and interior provinces in France. 1784. 8. (2 Sh. 6 d.) *Short review of the political ſtate of Great-Britain. 1787.

WRAY, [Daniel] *M. A: F. R. S: F. A. S: Truſtee of the British Museum.* born 1701. died d. 29 Dec. 1783.

WRIGHT, [.....] of *Craike.* On Siberian barley. (*Hunter's* Georg. Eſſ. Vol. 5. p. 262.)

WRIGHT,

WRIGHT, [A..... J.....] Elegia, scripta in sepulchreto rustico, latine reddita —. 1786. 4. (2 Sh.)

— [George] *a Methodistical Dissenter.* *The rural christian; or the pleasures of religion, an allegorical poem with Sylvan letters, or the benefits of retirement by a young gentleman. 1772. 8. (3 Sh.) Young moralist. 17.. Country squire. 17.. The gracious warning; or, a monody on the death of *Joseph Nicoll Scott.* M. D. 1774. 4. (6 d.) Thoughts in younger life on interesting subjects or poems, letters and essays, moral elegiac and descriptive with memoirs of the author. 1779. 8. (3 Sh.) Dear variety. 1782. 8. (2 Sh.) The grave; by *Rob. Blair* with *Gray's* elegy in a country church yard with notes by *G. Wright.* 1786. 8. (1 Sh.) The art of conversing on moral, religious and entertaining subjects. 1785. (1 Sh. 6 d.) *Pleasing reflections on life and manners —. 1788. 8. (3 Sh.)

— [J.....] Epistola Eloisae Abelardo, latine reddita. 1787. 4. (1 Sh. 6 d.)

— [James] *A. M: Minister at Maybole.* Recommendation of brotherly love, on the principles of christianity with an enquiry on the institution of masonry. 1787. 8. (4 Sh.)

(Several single sermons.)

— [Jen....] *Surgeon.* History of an extravasation of blood into the pericardium. (Med. Obs. Vol. 6. p. 1.)

— [John] *M. D.* Addreſſ to the members of both houses of Parliament on the late tax, laid on fustian and other cotton goods —. 1785. 8. (1 Sh)

— [John] Elements of trigonometry plain and spherical —. 1772. 8. (5 Sh.)

— [Paul] *D. D: F. A. S: Vicar of Oakley, Rector of Snoreham.* A help to English history; containing a succession of all the kings of England the kings and princes of Wales by *Peter Heylyn* – continued with great additions. 1773. 8. (8 Sh.) Complete British family bible. 1781.

(Several single sermons.)

— [T.....] Account of the advantages and method of watering meadows by art, as practised in the county of Gloucester. 1789. 8. (1 Sh. 6 d.)

— [William] *M. D: F. R. S. of London and of Edinburgh.* History of an obstruction of the rectum at birth,

birth, fucceffully cured by operation. (Med. Com. of Ed. Vol. 3. p 419.) Description of the Jesuits bark tree of Jamaica and the Caribbees. (Phil. Transact. 1777. p. 504.) Description and use of the cabbage-bark tree of Jamaica. (Ibid. 1777. p. 507.) Account of a child who had the fmallpox in the womb. (Ibid. 1781. p. 372.) Account of a dropsy cured by blue vitriol. (London M. J. Vol. 1. p. 266. Vol. X. P. 2.) überf. Samml. f. A. Th. 6. S. 188. The use of cold bathing in the locked jaw. (Med. Obs. Vol. 6. p. 143.) The antiseptic virtues of vegetable acid and marine falt combined, in various disordres, accompanied with putridity. (Tr. of A. S Vol. 2. p. 284. London M. J. Vol. VIII. P. 1.) überf. Samml. f. A. Th. 12. S. 104.) Account of a remarkable fait relative to the fmallpox. (London M. J. Vol. VII. P. 1. überf. Samml. f. A. Th. XII. S. 17.) Remarks on malignant fevers and their cure by cold water and fresh air. (London M. J. Vol. VII. P. 2. überf. Samml. f. A. Th. 12. S. 25.) Account of the medicinal plants growing in Jamaica. (London M. J. Vol. VIII. P. 3.) Botanical and medical account of the quaffia simaruba or tree, which produces the cortex simaruba. (Ibid. Vol. XI. P. 1. Tr. of E. S. V. 2. p. 72.)

—— [William] The complete tradesman, or, a guide in the feveral parts and progreffions of trade. 1789. 8. (2 fh. 6 d.)

WRIGHTE, [T.... W....] *A. M: Clerk.* Explanation of the two firft chapters of the book of Genesis. 1788. 8. (3 fh. 6 d.) Observations on the 3, 4. 5 Chapters of the book of Genesis. 1790. 8. (3 Sh.)

WRIGHTSON, [W......] *Surgeon in Sedgfield, Durham.* Canine madneff, fucceffully treated. (Med. Transact. Vol. 2. p. 192.)

WYCLIFFE, [Thomas] of *Liverpool.* *On government. 1776. 8. (2 fh.) Ed 2. (with the Author's name.) 1779. 8. (4 fh.) Ed. 3. 1780. 8. (5 fh.)

WYNDHAM, [Henry Penruddock] *A Gentleman's tour through Monmoutshire and Wales. 1775. 8. (2 fh. 6 d.) Ed. 2. (with the Author's name.) 1781. 4. (1 L. 1 fh.) On an ancient building at Warm-

Warmford in the county of Southampton. (Arch. Vol. 5. p. 357.) On a roman pavement found at Caerwent. 1778. (Ibid. Vol. 7. p. 410.) Diary of *George Bubb Doddington*, Baron of Melcombe Regis from 1749-1761. 1784. 8. (6 ſh.) Wiltshire, extracted from Domesday-book: with an English translation. 1788. 8. (6 ſh. 6 d.)

WYNNE, [Catherine] *Richard Wynne's* Introduction to geography, translated. 1787. 8. (4 ſh.)

— [Edward] *Barriſter at Law.* born: .... died at *Chelsea* d. 27 Dec. 1784.

— [J....] (wife of the Count of *Urſini and Roſenberg at Venice.*) *Moral and ſentimental eſſays on miſcellaneous ſubjects. Vol. 1. 2. 1785. 8. (5 ſh.) *Altichiero. a Padoue. 1787. 4. Les Morlaques. Modena. 1790. überſ. von *S. G. Bürde.* Th. 1. 1790. 8.

— [John Huddleſton] General hiſtory of the British empire in America. Vol. 1. 2. 1770. 8. (16 Sh.) The proſtitute, a poem. 1771. 4. (2 Sh.) General hiſtory of Ireland, from the earlieſt account to the preſent time. Vol. 1. 2. 1772. 8. (10 Sh. 6 d.) *Choice emblems, natural, hiſtorical, fabulous, moral and divine for the improvement of youth, in proſe and verſe —. 1772. 8. (2 Sh. 6 d.) Fables of flowers, for the female ſex. 1773. 8. (3 Sh.) Evelina, a poem. 1773. 4. (2 Sh. 6 d.) The four ſeaſons, a poem. 1773. 4. (2 Sh. 6 d.) *The child of Chance; or, the adventures of Harry Hazard. Vol. 1. 2. 1786. 8. (5 Sh.)

— [Richard] *A. M: Rector of St. Alphage, London; Chaplain to the Earl of Dunmore.* Eſſays on education —. 1761. 8. (4 Sh.) The new teſtament, — collated with the Greek —. Vol. 1. 2. 1764. (12 Sh.) Universal English grammar —. 1775. 8. (2 Sh. 6 d.) *A. F. Buſching* Introduction to the ſtudy of geography — translated. 1778. 8. (2 Sh.) Introduction to geography translated into French and Italian by *Cather. Wynne.* 1787. 8. (4 Sh.)

WYVIL, [Chriſtopher] *L. L. B: Rector of Black Notley, Eſſex.* *Thoughts on the articles of our religion with reſpect to their ſuppoſed utility to the ſtate. 1771. 4. (6 d.) Ed. III. (with the Author's name.) 1774. 8. (1 Sh.) Letters to the committee of Belfaſt

fast on the proposed reformation of the parliament of Ireland —. 1783. 4. (1 Sh.) Summary explanation of the principles of Mr. *Pitt's* intended bill for amending the representation of the people in parliament. 1785. 8. (1 Sh.)

(Several single sermons.)

YAIR, [James] *Minister of the Scot's Church in Campocre.* Translation of the life of *Servetus.* 1771. 8. (4 Sh.)

YEARSLEY, [Ann] *A Milkwoman of Clifton, near Bristol.* Poems on several occasions. 1785. 4. (6 Sh.) Poems on various subjects. 1787. 4. (5 Sh.) Poem on the inhumanity of the slave trade. 1788. 4. (2 Sh.)

YEATS, [Thomas Pattinson] Institutions of entomology, being a translation of *Linnaeus's* ordines et genera insectorum. 1773. 8. (5 Sh.)

YONGE, [Georg] *Baronet, Secretary at war. F. A. S.* Letter on *H. Rooke* observations on the Roman road. (Arch. Vol. IX. p. 193.)

—— [J.....] Practical and explanatory commentary on the holy bible —. 1787. 4. (10 Sh. 6 d.)

YORKE, [.......] *Earl of Hardwicke.* born. d. 20. Dec. 1720. died d. 16 May. 1790.

YOUDE, [John] *M. A.* The adventures of Telemachus — translated in English blank verse. 1775. 8. (2 Sh. 6 d.)

YOUNG, [Arthur] *F. R. S.* *The farmer's letters to the people of England —. 1767. 8. (4 Sh.) Ed. 2. 1768. Vol. 2. under the title: The Farmer's letters to the Landlords of Great-Britain. 1771. 8. (12 Sh.) *A six weeks tour through the southern counties of England and Wales —. 1768. 8. (5 sh.) Ed. 2. 1769. 8. (6 sh.) *On the management of hogs. 1769. 8. (1 sh. 6 d.) *A six months tour through the north of England — Vol. 1-4. 1770. 8. (1 L. 4 sh.) übers. Th. 1. 2. Leipz. 1772. 8. *The farmer's guide in hiring and stocking farms. Vol. 1. 2. 1770. 8. (10 sh. 6 d.) *Rural oeconomy, or essays on the practical parts of husbandry —. 1770. 8. (6 sh.) *The expediency of free exportation of corn at this time. 1770. 8. übers. Samml. von Aufsätzen zur Staatswissenschaft. Liegniz u. Leipzig. Th. 2. 1778. 8. A course of

 ex-

experimental agriculture. Vol. 1. 2. 1770. 4. (2 L. 10 ſh.) *The farmer's tour through the Eaſt of England —. Vol. 1 - 4. 1771. (1 L. 1 ſh.) überſ. Leipzig. Th. 1. 2. 1775. 8. *Proposals to the legislature for numbering the people. 1771. 8. (1 ſh.) *Observations on the present ſtate of the waſte lands in Great - Britain —. 1772. 8. (2 ſh.) A comparative view of top - dreſſings (*Hunter's* G. E. Vol. 5. p. 152.) A comparative view of manures. (*Hunter's* G. E. Vol. 5. p. 238.) Political arithmetic. P. 1. 2. 1774. (7 ſh. 6 d.) überſ. (von *C. J. Krauſe*) Königsberg. 1777. 8. Conſiderations on the means of raiſing the ſupplies with in the year. 1779. (1 ſh. 6 d.) Tour in Ireland with general obſervations on the present ſtate of that kingdom: made in the Y. 1776 - 1779. 1780. 4 (1 L. 1 ſh.) überſ. (von *J. A. Engelbrecht.*) Th. 1. 2. Leipzig. 1780. 8. Correspondence with Mr. *Lofft* on building county ships. 1783. 8. (1 ſh. 6 d.) Annals of agriculture and other useful arts. Vol. 1 - 5. 1786. (6 ſh.) überſ. von *S. Hahnemann* u. *J. Riem.* Th. 1. Leipz. 1790.

YOUNG, [David] National improvement upon agriculture. 1785. 8. (5 ſh.) Agriculture the primary intereſt of Britain. 1788. 8. (6 ſh.)

—— [Hercules] *Critical diſſertations on the new teſtament —. Diſſ. 1. 2. 1770. 8. (1 ſh.)

—— [Mary] *Miſſ.* Innocence, an allegorical poem. 1790. 4. (1 Sh. 6 d.)

—— [Matthew] *D. D: F. T. C. D: M. R. J. A.* Enquiry into the principal phaenomena of ſounds and muſical ſtrings. 1784. 8. (4 Sh.) Synthetical demonſtration of the rule for the quadrature of ſimple curves in the analysis per equationes terminorum numero infinitas. (Tr. of J. A. 1787. p. 31.) Antient gaelic poems reſpecting the race of the fians —. (Ibid p. 43.) Enquiry into the different modes of demonſtration by which the velocity of ſpouting fluids has been inveſtigated a priori. (Ibid. 1788. p. 81.)

—— [Robert] Examination of the 3d and 4th definitions of the firſt book of Sir *Iſaac Newton's* principia; and of the three axioms or laws of motion. 1787. 8. (1 Sh. 6 d.) Eſſay on the powers and mechanism of nature —. 1788. 8. (6 ſh.)

YOUNG, [Walter] *M. A: F. R. S. Edin: Minister of the Gospel at Erskine.* Essay on rythmical measures. (Tr. of E. S. Vol. 2. p. 55.)

—— [William] *M. P: F. R. S.* The spirit of Athens —. 1777. 8. (4 Sh.) übers. Leipzig. 1777. 8. History of Athens politically and philosophically considered —. 1786. 4. (15 Sh.) Observations preliminary to a proposed amendment of the poor laws. 1788. 8. (1 Sh. 6 d.)

ZABLY, [John] *D. D.* The law of liberty - at the opening the provincial congress of Georgia. 1776. 8. (1 Sh. 6 d.)

ZINZAM, [Peter] *M. D.* born: .... died d. 9 Nov. 1781.

ZOUCH, [Henry] *Clerk and Justice of Peace.* Remarks on the proposed changes of the poor laws. 1776. 8. (1 Sh.) Observations on a bill - to punish by imprisonment and hard labour, certain offenders —. 1779. 8. (6 d.) A few words in behalf of the poor —. 1782. 4. (6 d.) Account of the practices of night hunters and poachers —. 1783. 8. (1 Sh.) Facts fully established — on the cruelty and oppression of the game laws —. 1784. 8. (1 Sh. 6 d.) Hints respecting the public police. 1786. 8. (1 Sh.)

www.ingramcontent.com/pod-product-compliance
Lightning Source LLC
Chambersburg PA
CBHW031819270326
41932CB00008B/473

* 9 7 8 3 7 4 2 8 8 6 4 5 3 *